THE PHILOSOPHY OF SPINOZA

THE PHILOSOPHY
OF SPINOZA

UNFOLDING THE LATENT PROCESSES
OF HIS REASONING

BY

HARRY AUSTRYN WOLFSON

TWO VOLUMES IN ONE

HARVARD UNIVERSITY PRESS

CAMBRIDGE · MASSACHUSETTS
LONDON · ENGLAND

Library of Congress Cataloging in Publication Data

Wolfson, Harry Austryn, 1887–1974.
　The philosophy of Spinoza.

　Bibliography: p.
　Includes indexes.
　1. Spinoza, Benedictus de, 1632–1677. 2. Spinoza,
Benedictus de, 1632–1677. Ethica. 3. Ethics—History.
—17th century. I. Title.
B3998.W65   1983　　199'.492　　82–23290
ISBN 0–674–66595–3 (pbk.)

PREFACE

To the trained observer the simplest thing in nature has a structure and a history; to the naïve mind the most complicated product of human device appears simple and spontaneous. Imagine a primitive man, brought up in natural surroundings and without ever having witnessed human art in its making. Placed suddenly in one of the canyon-like streets of a modern metropolis, such a primitive man would undoubtedly think of the flanking sky-soaring structures of intricate design and workmanship as something which grew out of the soil like trees and grass. Similarly, imagine a student of philosophy, trained in some miraculous manner in the usages of philosophic concepts and vocabulary of the present day, without any inkling of their past history. Confronted suddenly with the *Ethics* of Spinoza, such a trained student would undoubtedly think of it as something which sprang forth full-grown and completely armored, like Minerva, from the brain of its author, and he would quite naturally try to interpret it in the light of whatever associations it evoked in his mind. Of course, there is no such preposterously trained student of philosophy, any more than there is such a naïve-minded primitive man as he to whom we have compared him. But, still, many a student of Spinoza comes very near treating his *Ethics* in the fantastic fashion which we have described. Like the Bible, the *Ethics* of Spinoza has often been the subject of homiletical interpretations. It has been treated like an amorphous mass of floating clouds in which one's fancy may cut whatever figures it pleases.

Now, I will not deny that we must allow for philosophic license as we allow for poetic license, and that the cutting of imaginary figures in Spinoza's *Ethics* is not without its uses. When Goethe confesses that he cannot tell what he got out of the *Ethics* and what he may himself have put into it, we can only say that we are grateful to Spinoza for having served as a stimulus to the thought of Goethe. In the same way, many a worthy thought of men less distinguished — and perhaps also less frank — than Goethe has had its birth in a misinterpretation of Spinoza or else has received due attention by its having been mounted, gratuitously, on Spinoza's writings. But it would be carrying the analogy of the license too far if we should say that the philosopher in his interpretation is to be as little bound by the truth of scholarship as the poet in his imagery is by the truth of science. It is certainly no compliment to a philosopher of the past who is prominent enough for us to study him to say that only by being misunderstood does he become philosophically important. Indeed, the entire field of the history of philosophy would be placed outside the bounds of exact disciplined study if we should maintain that its study is of philosophical importance only when we superciliously disregard its objective meaning as established by research, or indolently make no effort to acquaint ourselves with it, or blissfully keep ourselves in ignorance of it. The fact is, what is often called subjective interpretation in philosophy is nothing but the explanation of a text in terms of the haphazard knowledge that one happens to possess, just as what is called popularization means nothing but the explanation of a text in terms of the ignorance supposed to be possessed by the readers for whom it is intended. In either of these cases, whatever merit the particular form of presentation possesses is derived from the fact that it helps to give currency to the results of historical scholarship, which in its proper sense means the interpretation of a text in terms of everything that can be known about it, for which a systematic search must be made. The first step, the basic step, in the understanding of any philosopher, one upon which any subjective form of interpretation or any literary form of presentation must rest, is the determination by the method of historical criticism of what the philosopher meant by what he said, how he came to say what he said, and why he said it in the manner in which he happened to say it.

It is this threefold task that we have set ourselves in the present study of Spinoza. Now, the historico-critical method really means the presupposition that in any text treated by it there is a sort of dual authorship — an explicit author, who expresses himself in certain conventional symbols and patterns, and an implicit author, whose unuttered thoughts furnish us with the material for grasping the full significance of those symbols and patterns. In the case of the *Ethics* of Spinoza, there is, on the one hand, an explicit Spinoza, whom we shall call Benedictus. It is he who speaks in definitions, axioms, and propositions; it is he, too, who reasons according to the rigid method of the geometer. Then there is, on the other hand, the implicit Spinoza, who lurks behind these definitions, axioms, and propositions, only occasionally revealing himself in the scholia; his mind is crammed with traditional philosophic lore and his thought turns along the beaten logical paths of mediaeval reasoning. Him we shall call Baruch. Benedictus is the first of the moderns; Baruch is the last of the mediaevals. It is our contention that we cannot get the full meaning of what Benedictus says unless we know what has passed through the mind of Baruch. Starting with the assumption that the *Ethics* is primarily a criticism of fundamental problems of philosophy as they presented themselves to Spinoza, we proceed to analyze these problems, to set forth their salient features, to construct hypothetically the arguments which constitute the criticism, and to show how these arguments and criticism underlie the statements which we have before us in the *Ethics*. As a result of this procedure, the *Ethics* emerges as a logically constructed work throughout which there is order and sequence and continuity: propositions, apparently disconnected, group themselves into unified and coherent chapters; words, phrases, and passages, apparently meaningless or commonplace, assume meaning and significance; and the philosophy of Spinoza, as a systematic whole and in all its fulness of detail, appears in a new light and in a new setting and perspective. Into the fabric of this work, which in form follows the order of the *Ethics*, we have also woven relevant passages from the other writings of Spinoza, so that the study of his philosophy herein presented is based upon his *Ethics* as well as upon all his other writings in so far as they are related to the *Ethics*.

This work can be read as a self-explanatory systematic presentation of the philosophy of Spinoza. It can be read with greater profit as a companion volume to the *Ethics* and a running commentary on it. It can be read with still greater profit together with some standard works or special studies on Spinoza, for, with the exception of general references to the literature on Spinoza whenever they were necessary either for the bibliographical guidance of the reader or as an acknowledgment of indebtedness on certain points, and with the further exception of an occasional expression of disagreement, we have refrained from entering upon an examination and comparison or criticism of the various extant interpretations of Spinoza — a subject which, if dealt with at all, is deserving of a study by itself. Independently of

Spinoza, this work can be read as a study of the development of certain fundamental problems in the history of philosophy, or of the understanding of certain points in the teachings of the authors brought into the discussion and of certain significant texts in their writings. Students who are interested in the relation of Spinoza to other philosophers will find in this work an abundance of undreamed-of new material, culled from the writings of various philosophers ranging from Aristotle to Descartes, though we do not say that every author whom we have found it useful or necessary to quote is to be considered a forerunner of Spinoza or as having had a dominant influence upon his philosophy. The principles on which the selection of this material was made, the manner in which it was used in the interpretation of Spinoza, and the method by which its direct literary relationship to Spinoza and its influence upon him can be determined, are discussed in the opening chapter. The analytical table of contents at the beginning of each volume and the several Indexes at the end of the second volume will serve as guides to the reader in these various uses to which the book may be put.

Chapters III, IV, V, and VIII were published in *Chronicon Spinozanum*, Vols. I (1921), pp. 101–112, II (1922), pp. 92–117, III (1923), pp. 142–178, and IV (1924–1926), pp. 79–103, respectively. Chapter VI appeared in Italian translation in *Ricerche Religiose*, Vol. IX (1933), pp. 193–236. All these chapters are reprinted here with some revisions. The original title and description of this work were announced in the *Chronicon Spinozanum* as "Spinoza the Last of the Mediaevals: a Study of the *Ethica Ordine Geometrico Demonstrata* in the light of a hypothetically constructed *Ethica More Scholastico Rabbinicoque Demonstrata*." This title had to be abandoned, as it did not seem advisable to have the title begin with the word "Spinoza."

The protracted delay in the completion of the work was amply made up for by the promptness with which its publication was undertaken when the manuscript was finished. This was made possible by the Fund for the Support of the Humanities at Harvard University provided by the General Education Board. For this I am profoundly grateful. I am also deeply indebted to Miss Christabel Garner, of the Harvard University Press, for her searching reading of the proofs and for valuable suggestions.

HARRY AUSTRYN WOLFSON

CAMBRIDGE, MASSACHUSETTS
May, 1933

CONTENTS

VOLUME I

CHAPTER I

CHAPTER II

(ETHICS, I)

CHAPTER III

CHAPTER IV

CHAPTER V

CHAPTER VI

Transition from "substance" to "God" (Prop. XI), 158. — Meaning of *necessario existit*, 160. — What the proofs of the existence of God are meant to prove, 161. — Being: *real, fictitious, verbal,* and *of reason*, 161. — Classification of the traditional methods of proving the existence of God, 163. — If God is known immediately, what need is there for proof? 165. — Meaning of the ontological proof, and the stock objection against it, 167. — Meaning of St. Anselm's answer to Gaunilon, 170. — Meaning of the syllogism employed in ontological proofs, 174. — The logical form of the syllogism underlying the ontological proofs, 176.

Evaluation of the ontological proof, 176. — Analysis of the proofs of Descartes and Spinoza and their relation to each other, 178. — Spinoza's *first proof*: its three types, and how the type used in the *Ethics* is a modification of one of the two forms of the proof as given by Descartes, 179. — Spinoza's *second proof*: its composite origin, 184. — Distinction between internal, external, and impedimental causes, 186. — Mediaeval proof for eternity of God, 186. — Distinction between necessary, impossible, possible, and contingent, 187. — Analysis of the cosmological proof of the existence of God: its three stages, 192. — Transformation of the third stage of the cosmological proof into an ontological proof in Spinoza's *second proof*, 197. — Spinoza's *third* and *fourth proofs*: how related to Descartes' second cosmological proof in Meditation III, 200. — Analysis of Descartes' second cosmological proof: a modified form of the traditional proof from creation or conservation, 201. — Why Spinoza calls it a proof from power, 204. — Explanation of Spinoza's *third proof*, 205. — Explanation of Spinoza's *fourth proof*, 207. — Explanation of Scholium to Proposition XI, 208. — Concluding remarks on Spinoza's proofs, 212.

CHAPTER VII

Recapitulation of Spinoza's arguments leading up to his conclusion that extension and thought are attributes of God (Prop. XIV), 214. — The framework of Spinoza's universe and how he came by it, 216.

CHAPTER VIII

CHAPTER IX

Traditional conception of omnipresence of God brought to its logical conclusion by Spinoza (Prop. XV), 296. — Variety of characterizations of Spinoza's conception of God: Deism, Atheism, Acosmism, Pantheism, 298. — Immateriality and causality two fundamental characteristics of the traditional God, 301. — Threefold causality of the traditional God reduced by Spinoza to efficient causality, 302. — Conventional classification of God's efficient causality adopted by Spinoza and applied to his God, 303. — God a *universal* cause (Prop. XVI), 304. — God an *efficient* cause not in the restricted sense of *emanative* cause, 306. — God an *essential* cause, 307. — God a *first* cause, 307.

God a *principal* and *free* cause (Prop. XVII), 308. — Spinoza's definition of freedom, 309. — Mediaeval conception of will and intelligence in divine causality and Spinoza's refutation thereof, 312. — Spinoza's refutation of the view that God omitted to create things which He could create, 314. — Spinoza's contention that the mediaeval conception of the homonymy of divine intelligence and will amounts to an assertion of necessary causality, 316. — Denial of chance and causelessness, 318.

Distinction between external and internal causes, 319. — Two kinds of internal or immanent causes, 321. — Meaning of "transcendent," 322. — Meaning of Spinoza's conception of God as *immanent* cause (Prop. XVIII), 323. — Immanent as whole or universal, 324. — The two kinds of "whole," 325. — Two differences mentioned by Spinoza between the "whole" and the conceptual universal; how they are traceable to Aristotle, 326. — Conjectural addition of a third difference: the concrete and the abstract universal, 327.

God as a conscious but non-volitional cause, 328.

CHAPTER X

CHAPTER XI

CHAPTER XII

VOLUME II

(ETHICS, II)

CHAPTER XIII

CHAPTER XIV

CHAPTER XV

CHAPTER XVI

CHAPTER XVII

(ETHICS, III)

CHAPTER XVIII

(ETHICS, IV)

CHAPTER XIX

(ETHICS, V)

CHAPTER XX

physical basis of Spinoza's remedies for the ailments of the soul (Prop. I), 265. — The six remedies for those ailments (Props. II–X), 266. — The love for God as the sovereign remedy (Props. XI–XV), 272. — Same old Rock of Salvation: purpose of Spinoza's new conception of God, 273.

CHAPTER XXI

THE PHILOSOPHY OF SPINOZA
VOLUME I

CHAPTER I

BEHIND THE GEOMETRICAL METHOD

IN DISCUSSING once with a group of friends the importance of philology and of bookish learning in general for the study of the history of philosophy, I happened to remark that philosophers, after all, see the universe which they try to explain as already interpreted to them in books, with the only possible exception, perhaps, of the first recorded philosopher, and all he could see was water. "How about Spinoza?" challenged one of the listeners. "Was he also a bookish philosopher?" Without stopping to think, I took up the challenge. "As for Spinoza," I said, "if we could cut up all the philosophic literature available to him into slips of paper, toss them up into the air, and let them fall back to the ground, then out of these scattered slips of paper we could reconstruct his *Ethics*."

Not long after that I found myself reconstructing the *Ethics* out of scattered slips of paper figuratively cut out of the philosophic literature available to Spinoza. The problem before us, as I discovered, was like that of a jig-saw puzzle. Suppose we have a box of pieces out of which we are to construct a certain picture. But the pieces contained in the box are more than can be used, and from among them we have to select those which are needed for our purpose. Furthermore, the pieces do not fit together, and they have to be reshaped. Finally, many necessary pieces are missing, and we have to supply them ourselves. But to offset all these difficulties, we have an outline of the picture which we are to construct.

The picture which we have to construct in our own jig-saw puzzle is the *Ethics* as it was originally formed in the mind of

Spinoza, of which the present *Ethics* in its geometrical form is only a bare outline.[1] Since, however, we do not know nor can we ascertain exactly what books Spinoza had actually read, what quotations he had come across in the course of his readings, or what casual information he had gathered from conversations with friends, we must take as our box of pieces the entire philosophic literature available at the time of Spinoza and out of this make our necessary selections. Furthermore, since philosophic texts and ideas are the most plastic of material, capable of assuming a variety of meanings with different philosophers, we must reshape our pieces in the form which we have reason to believe they assumed in the mind of Spinoza. Finally, since the *Ethics* before us is not the result of a syncretism of traditional philosophy but rather the result of criticism, and since this criticism, though implied, is not explicitly expressed, we shall have to supply it ourselves.

In our study of the *Ethics* we must try to follow the same method that Spinoza followed in writing it. Spinoza did not start out with classified lists of bibliographies, outlines, abstracts, quotations, and all the elaborate equipment with which methodical scholarship of today prepares itself for the writing of an informative work of reference. He started out with a certain fund of knowledge acquired through miscellaneous reading which in his mind formed itself into a composite picture of the salient features of traditional philosophy. In this composite mental picture, we may assume, the problems of philosophy presented themselves in a certain order, each problem modelled after a certain pattern and expressed in a certain terminology. Tagged on to this picture, underneath its surface, and deep down into the recesses of Spinoza's consciousness, we may further assume, there was an

[1] Cf. below, p. 59.

aggregation of notes swarming with references to sources of texts, to parentages of ideas, to conflicts of opinions, and to diversities of interpretations, all of them ready to come up to the surface, whenever the occasion arose, and take their place in the picture. In our endeavor to retrace the steps of Spinoza's reasoning, we must, therefore, first of all, equip ourselves with a similar fund of knowledge, or philosophical mass of apperception, as it may be called.

With such an apperceptive mass as our equipment we begin to read the *Ethics*. Without forcing ourselves to understand the book, we let its propositions penetrate into our amassed fund of knowledge and by the natural process of association and attraction become encrusted with terms, phrases, and ideas out of the storehouse of our memory. At first these encrustations are indistinguishable and shapeless clumps, clinging to the propositions as bits of scrap-iron cling to a magnet. But then we let our mind play upon them — to scrutinize them and to study them. By the catalytic action of the mind these indistinguishable and shapeless clumps begin to dissolve; they begin to group themselves, to solidify themselves into larger units, to become differentiated from each other, to assume form, and ultimately to crystallize themselves into distinct topics of recognizable historical problems of philosophy. Thus at the very outset of the *Ethics*, Proposition I, together with Definitions III and V and Axioms I and II upon which it is based, emerges as a distinct topic by itself, which we label the definition of substance and mode. The next five propositions, II–VI, crystallize themselves into a discussion of the unity of substance, made up of two historical problems, the unity of God and creation. Propositions VII–X and XII–XIII shape themselves into a discussion of three closely related topics under the general heading of the Simplicity of Substance, and wedged in between them is Proposition XI, where the term "substance" gives way to the term "God"; this is easily recognized as a discussion of the traditional proofs of the existence of God. Next follow two propositions, XIV and XV, which deal with the attributes of extension and thought, and a Scholium, which deals with the infinity of extension. The remaining propositions of the First Part of the *Ethics* readily group themselves into discussions of the various meanings of the causality of God, among which Spinoza dwells especially upon the immanence, freedom, necessity, and purposelessness of God's causality. In the Second Part of the *Ethics* the propositions fall into the traditional outline of the discussion of the soul, dealing in the conventional order and manner with the definition of the soul, its relation to the body, and the classification of its faculties. The last three parts of the *Ethics* deal with what is traditionally known as practical philosophy as contrasted with the theoretical philosophy of the first two parts, dealing successively with the problems of the emotions, virtues, and the final happiness of man. As our mind scrutinizes still further these groups of propositions it discovers that they follow one upon the other according to a certain order of sequence, which is at once intrinsically logical and extrinsically in conformity with historical patterns. With this, the first stage in our study of the *Ethics* comes to an end.

Then the next stage in our investigation is to find a certain coherence within each group of propositions. The data upon which we have to work are twofold. On the one hand, there are the problems of philosophy as they unfold themselves before us in all their variety of forms in the vast literature that was available to Spinoza. On the other hand, there are the utterances of Spinoza in the *Ethics*, elliptical, fragmentary, disjointed, and oftentimes, if we are to admit the truth to ourselves, enigmatic and unintelligible. Between these two extremes we expect to find the problems as they must have formulated themselves in the mind of Spinoza, the doubts which he must have raised against accepted views, and his own solutions of these doubts which he must have meant to express in his uttered statements in the *Ethics*. The task before us, then, is to reconstruct the process of Spinoza's reasoning in all its dialectical niceties and in all its fulness of detail so that it will lead us to a thorough understanding of the statements which confront us in the *Ethics*. By the method of trial and error we experiment with one conjecture after another, until we finally arrive at a result which seems to us satisfactory. Thus, for instance, at the very outset of the *Ethics*, in Proposition I and its underlying Definitions III and V and Axioms I and II, which we have already set apart as a topic by itself, dealing with definition of substance and mode, we reconstruct out of the material scattered in the literature of philosophy the problem as we assume it presented itself to the mind of Spinoza — the division of being, the definition of substance and accident, the classification of substances, and so on. Again, out of direct internal discussions of these problems which occur in the philosophic literature of the past, or indirectly out of certain suggestions and hints, and sometimes even without these direct or indirect aids, we reconstruct a criticism of these traditional definitions as we assume it formulated itself in the mind of Spinoza. As a result we are enabled to integrate these Axioms, Definitions, and Proposition I into a coherent chapter, containing a logically formed argument.[1] We follow the same method in our study of the next group of propositions, Propositions II–VI, which we have found to reflect two historical problems, the unity of God and creation, and which we have subsumed

[1] Cf. below, pp. 61 ff.

under the heading of the Unity of Substance. Here our task is somewhat more difficult, for we have to deal here not with one single proposition, as is the case in Proposition I, but with five propositions, each of which is followed by a demonstration, and between which there seems to be no unity and transition. Again, by the method of trial and error we ultimately succeed in reconstructing the thought of Spinoza so that in the light of it these five propositions form a connected logical syllogism.[1] And so we go through the entire *Ethics*, and by the use of different devices we succeed in bringing unity, coherence, and harmony within each group of propositions. With this, the second stage of our investigation comes to an end.

Then we take up the third and last stage of our investigation, that of documenting our findings so that we may convince others of the truth of our statements and reasoning. Here, too, we must follow the same method that Spinoza would have followed, had he documented his *Ethics*. We feel that it would not be enough to quote from books which we happen to know, or which happen to be generally known. We must ask ourselves what works Spinoza himself would have used if he had chosen to document his writings. To answer this question we must determine, even though only in a general way, the extent and variety of the philosophic literature available to Spinoza.

Two philosophic literatures were open to Spinoza, the Hebrew and the Latin. His knowledge of Hebrew he had acquired in a school where he had studied it systematically under the guidance of competent teachers probably from the age of seven to the age of eighteen (1639–1650).[2] Latin he

---

[1] Cf. Below, pp. 65 ff.

[2] As for the years of Spinoza's entering and leaving the Hebrew School '*Eẓ Hayyim*, see Dunin-Borkowski, *Der junge De Spinoza* (1910), p. 103, and Freudenthal, *Spinoza Leben und Lehre* (ed. Gebhardt, 1927), I, p. 31.

began to study later, at first not in a school but privately. His systematic study of that language under the tutorage of Francis van den Enden did not begin until 1652, when he was already twenty years old. Though he had also a knowledge of several modern languages, Spanish, Portuguese, Dutch, French, and possibly also Italian, German, and Flemish,[1] the philosophic material in these languages was negligible. Hebrew made accessible to him not only the works of Jewish philosophers but also the works of Arabic philosophers, the works of Aristotle, mostly as incorporated in the commentaries of Averroes, the works of some of the Greek commentators on Aristotle, and also the works of some of the Latin scholastic philosophers. Latin similarly opened to him not only the original Latin writings of the philosophers of the Roman period, of mediaeval scholasticism, and of the Renaissance, but also translations from the Greek, Arabic, and Hebrew. In Hebrew the most important works of Jewish philosophers, whether those translated from the Arabic or those written originally in Hebrew, were already accessible to him in printed form, some of them in several editions; but the translations from non-Jewish authors, with but a few slight exceptions, were accessible to him only in manuscript form. Manuscripts, however, at that time were not yet gathered up and stored away in a few closely guarded central libraries; they were still widely scattered among individual owners and freely circulated, especially in Amsterdam, where Hebrew scholarship and Hebrew printing presses flourished and where privately owned collections of Hebrew manuscripts must have existed. Furthermore, the student of Hebrew philosophic texts could gain a thorough knowledge

---

[1] As for Spinoza's knowledge of languages, see Epistola 19 (*Opera*, IV, p. 95, ll. 12–15); Epistola 26 (p. 159, l. 16); Lucas' *La Vie de feu Monsieur de Spinoza* in A. Wolf, *The Oldest Biography of Spinoza*, pp. 51–52 and 104.

of the contents of the unpublished Hebrew translations of Arabic and Greek authors through the numerous and extensive quotations from their works as well as through the elaborate discussions of their views which were to be found in Hebrew works already published. In Latin the proportion of printed works in philosophy was greater than in Hebrew, even of works which were translated into Latin from the Hebrew. Thus, for instance, the bulk of Averroes' commentaries on Aristotle, which were translated into Latin from the Hebrew, existed in many printed editions in Latin, whereas in Hebrew they existed only in manuscript form.

To Spinoza these three literatures, Hebrew, Latin, and Arabic, represented a common tradition. Whatever differences he noticed between them, they concerned only problems of a purely theological and dogmatic nature; the philosophic basis of all such problems, and especially the discussion of problems of a purely philosophic nature, he could not fail to see, were all of a common origin. They were all based upon Greek philosophy, at the centre of which stood Aristotle. The same Greek terminology lay behind the Arabic, Hebrew, and Latin terminology, and the same scientific and philosophic conceptions formed the intellectual background of all those who philosophized in Arabic, Hebrew, or Latin. The three philosophic literatures were in fact one philosophy expressed in different languages, translatable almost literally into one another. And within each of these philosophic literatures numerous works existed which were encyclopaedic in nature, covering as they did the entire range of philosophy, containing the same roster of problems, the same analyses of those problems, the same definitions of terms, the same metaphysical brocards, the same clash of contrasting views, the same arguments in support or in refutation of each view, and, barring certain individual differences of emphasis or of interpretation, arriving also at the same conclusions. A reader who had mastered any of these books in one of these three languages found himself treading upon familiar ground when he came to read any book in the other languages.

We do not know exactly in what language Spinoza would have written his books had the choice of language been determined by him on the basis of the ease with which he could express himself in it rather than on the basis of the linguistic equipment of the readers whom he wished to reach. Had Spinoza lived in the land of his forefathers, Spain or Portugal, before the expulsion, or in any other European country where Jewish philosophy was cultivated, such as Southern France or Italy, he would have undoubtedly written in Hebrew, for Hebrew had been the exclusive medium of expression of Jewish philosophers and scientists throughout Europe ever since the disappearance of Jewish life in Southern Spain under Moslem rule with the coming of the Almohades in the twelfth century. The particular attitude of an author toward the problems of religion was no deterrent to his use of Hebrew, for every shade of opinion, from extreme adherence to tradition to the most daring adventures into freedom of thought, found expression in Hebrew literature. In the intellectual autonomy which the Jews enjoyed during the Middle Ages, with the systematic pursuit of the study of philosophy and the sciences in Jewish schools out of Hebrew books, Jewish thinkers were always assured of appreciative as well as critical readers among their own people of whatever views they chose to express in Hebrew. But toward the end of the fifteenth century there appeared Jewish philosophers who, though brought up on Hebrew philosophic literature and themselves writing in Hebrew, wrote books in non-Jewish languages for non-Jewish readers. Elijah Delmedigo, better known as Helias Hebraeus Cretensis (1460–1497), wrote his

Quaestiones Tres and his *Adnotationes in Dictis Averrois super Libros Physicorum* [1] in Latin, and Judah Abrabanel, better known as Leo Hebraeus (d. 1535), wrote his *Dialoghi d'Amore* in Italian.[2] In Spinoza's own time and in the community in which he was born, Hebrew was still used extensively by his own teachers and schoolmates in their literary works, but use was also made by some of them of Spanish and Latin. His teacher Manasseh ben Israel wrote on theological problems in Hebrew, Latin, Spanish, and Portuguese. Under these circumstances, what language Spinoza would have used if he had chosen that in which self-expression was the easiest for him can be only conjectured. That it would not have been Latin or Dutch, in which his books happen to be written, is quite evident by his own confession. At the time of the publication of his *Principia Philosophiae Cartesianae* and *Cogitata Metaphysica* (1663) he still felt the deficiency of his Latin, and before allowing his friends to publish these works he stipulated that one of them should, in his presence, "clothe them in more elegant style." [3] In 1665, in one of his letters to Blyenbergh,[4] he intimates that he could express his thoughts in Spanish, "the language in which I was brought up," better than in Dutch. Whether Hebrew was with him, as it was with many Jewish authors of his time and place, a more natural vehicle of literary expression is uncertain.

But it is quite certain that Hebrew literature was the primary source of his knowledge of philosophy and the main stock upon which all the other philosophic knowledge which

---

[1] These two works are printed together with Joannes de Janduno's *Quaestiones in Libros Physicorum*, 1501, and other editions.

[2] It is quite possible, however, that the *Dialoghi d'Amore* was written originally in Hebrew. Cf. I. Sonne, *Lishe'elat ha-Lashon ha-Meḳorit shel Wikkuḥe ha-Ahahab li-Yehudah Abarbanel*, in *Ziyyunim* (Berlin, 1929), pp. 142–148. For new evidence that it was originally written in Hebrew, see below, vol. II, p. 14.

[3] *Epistola* 13 (*Opera*, IV, p. 63, ll. 20–22).　　[4] *Epistola* 19 (p. 95, ll. 12–15).

he later acquired was grafted. He had become familiar with Hebrew philosophic literature before he began to read philosophy in Latin. His nascent philosophic doubt arose as a reaction against the philosophy which he read in Hebrew. With the exception of the new sciences, his readings in Latin supplied him merely with a new vocabulary for old ideas. Throughout his discussions of philosophical problems, especially those bordering upon theology, Hebrew sources appear as the matrix in which the general outline of ideas was formed. Other sources appear as insets. It is Hebrew sources, too, upon which he draws for his casual illustrations. An outstanding example of this is to be found in his discussion in Chapter XV of the *Tractatus Theologico-Politicus* of the two contrasting attitudes shown by philosophers towards the problem of the relation of faith to philosophy or of theology to reason. The problem was an old one, and it had been discussed in Mohammedanism, Christianity, and Judaism alike. In each of these three religions, the two contrasting attitudes had their exponents. In Mohammedanism, such exponents, to mention but two, were Algazali and Averroes. In Christianity, two typical exponents of these attitudes could be found in Bernard of Clairvaux and Abelard. Spinoza, however, mentions none of these. He takes Alpakhar and Maimonides as his examples of typical representatives of these two contrasting views, and he does so simply because these were the two men through whose works he first became acquainted with the nature of the problem. He did not even feel the need, writing as he did in Latin for non-Jewish readers, to substitute two corresponding Christian authors for these two Jewish authors, for in Spinoza's time Jewish philosophy had not yet been eliminated from European philosophy and relegated to the esoteric field of oriental wisdom. From the thirteenth century down through the seventeenth century it was quite fashionable for theologians and philosophers to quote Hebrew authorities by the side of Greek authorities, and those who followed the habit of quoting Greek sources in the original Greek also quoted Hebrew sources in the original Hebrew. The only concession that Spinoza seems to have made to his non-Jewish readers is that he referred to his Hebrew authorities with the aloofness of an outsider.

Following this principle, we go first to Hebrew philosophic literature for our documents. It is not any particular author that we go to, but the field of literature as a whole. If one particular author, Maimonides for instance, happens to be resorted to more often than others, it is not because he has been especially selected for our purpose, but because Spinoza himself would have selected him, for his work is the most excellent depository of mediaeval philosophic lore, where one can find the most incisive analyses of philosophic problems, the most complete summaries of philosophic opinions, the clearest definitions of terms, and all these couched in happy and quotable phrases. But we always try to give sufficient parallels from other Hebrew authors so as not to create the erroneous impression that we are trying to draw parallels between one single Hebrew author and Spinoza. In like manner, in order not to create the erroneous impression that the material drawn upon is unique in Hebrew philosophic literature, we quote, or refer to, similar passages in the works of Arabic or scholastic authors. When the occasion demands, scholastic sources are resorted to in preference to the Hebrew. Furthermore, in order not to create the erroneous impression that there is something peculiarly "mediaeval" about the views we quote from the various mediaeval sources, we trace their origin to Aristotle's works. Frequently we string together a list of names from the various linguistic groups of philosophy in order to indicate that the views under discussion are a common philosophic heritage. Before quoting a passage from a certain book we do not stop to ask ourselves whether that book was known to Spinoza. In several instances we rather suspect that the book in question was unknown to him. But that makes no difference to us. Provided the idea expressed in the passage under consideration is not uncommon, we assume that it was known to Spinoza, even though for the time being we do not know exactly the immediate literary source of his knowledge. In such instances, only one who would arrogate to himself divine omniscience could assert with certainty that the idea could not be found in any source available to Spinoza. The burden of proof is always upon the negative.

But very often certain passages are identified as being the direct and immediate sources of Spinoza. As a rule Spinoza does not quote sources literally, even when he mentions them. In a letter to Meyer, for instance, he introduces his reproduction of Crescas' proof of the existence of God by the words "it reads as follows" (*sic sonat*),[1] and yet the passage which follows is not an exact quotation. But in many instances the evidence points to certain passages as directly underlying the utterances of Spinoza. In determining these direct sources it is not the similarity of single terms or even of single phrases that guides us, for in the history of philosophy terms and phrases, no less than the ideas which they express, have a certain persistency about them and they survive intact throughout their winding transmigrations. It is always a term or a phrase as imbedded in a certain context, and that context by its internal structure and by a combination of enveloping circumstances, that help us to determine direct literary relationships. When we feel that we are in a position,

---

[1] Epistola 12 (*Opera*, IV, p. 61, l. 18).

for instance, to affirm with reasonable certainty that it is Thomas Aquinas from whom Spinoza has taken over in the Scholium to Proposition XXIX of *Ethics*, I, the distinction of *natura naturans* and *natura naturata* it is not because these phrases happen to occur in his works, for as phrases they happen to occur also in the works of other authors; it is only because Spinoza's description of these two phrases seems to be a modification of the description given by Thomas Aquinas, and also because the reason for the modification of the description by Spinoza can be adequately accounted for.[1] When, again, we are in a position to affirm with reasonable certainty that it is Crescas from whom Spinoza has taken over in the Scholium to Proposition XV of *Ethics*, I, the three "examples" by which his "opponents" prove the impossibility of an infinite extension and in refutation of them the three "distinctions" which he mentions in Epistola XII to Meyer, it is not because these "examples" and "distinctions" are to be found in Crescas, for as individual "examples" and "distinctions" they are to be found also in other authors; it is only because these three "distinctions" are used by Crescas as refutations of three arguments which correspond respectively to the three "examples" of Spinoza.[2] Finally, to take but one more example, when we are in a position to affirm with reasonable certainty that Spinoza's discussion of the highest good, of human society, and of the virtues in Propositions XIX–LXXIII of *Ethics*, IV, is based upon Aristotle's *Nicomachean Ethics* it is not because we discover in them certain similarities in individual terms or phrases; it is only because we discover in them definite literary similarities in the construction of the arguments.[3] It is by such methods that direct literary relationship has been

---

[1] Cf. below, pp. 254 f.   [2] Cf. below, pp. 264 ff.
[3] Cf. below, Vol. II, pp. 233 ff.

established between Spinoza and many of the authors quoted in this work.

A list of passages quoted or referred to in this work from various authors will be found in the Index of References, and an analysis of topics of each of these authors will be found in the Index of Subjects and Names. The works quoted or referred to, it will be noticed, are drawn indiscriminately from the various linguistic groups of philosophic literature — Greek, Latin, Hebrew, and Arabic. Conspicuously absent among them, with the exception of a few references, mostly of ancillary importance, to Meir ibn Gabbai, Moses Cordovero, and Abraham Herrera,[1] is the Cabalistic literature, which from earliest time has been considered a source of Spinoza's philosophy. This exclusion was unintentional; it merely happened that in our search for documentation we had no occasion to resort to the Cabalistic literature for source material. Not that the Cabalistic literature could not have furnished us with apt illustrative material, but there is nothing in the Cabalistic literature which could be used for our purpose the like of which we did not find in philosophic literature, for, as has been said by one of the leading Cabalists, Moses Cordovero: "Know that in matters metaphysical oftentimes the true masters of Cabala will be found to agree with the philosophers."[2] "To follow" would perhaps have been a more accurate term than "to agree."

The list of passages is by no means exhaustive. Had we thought it necessary, we could have added innumerable parallels to every passage quoted; but our purpose was not to compile a complete catena of parallel passages. A complete Index of mediaeval philosophy, Latin, Hebrew, and

---

[1] Two of the references to Herrera, however, seem to point to a direct literary connection and are of special significance. Cf. below, pp. 245 and 314.

[2] *Elimah Rabbati*, I, 16.

Arabic, is indeed one of the desiderata of scholarship, but that will have to be done independently of any study of Spinoza. Nor are the passages quoted or referred to by us irreplaceable by similar passages from other works, though we have always tried to select passages which are most suitable for our purpose. It would be quite possible to rewrite considerable portions of this work by substituting other quotations for those used by us, without necessarily changing our present analysis and interpretation of the *Ethics*, for the passages quoted are only representative of common views which were current in the philosophic literature of the past. Had we thought it desirable, then instead of writing one single book on the *Ethics*, we could have written a series of papers bearing such titles as "Aristotle and Spinoza," "Seneca and Spinoza," "Averroes and Spinoza," "Maimonides and Spinoza," "Thomas Aquinas and Spinoza," "Leo Hebraeus and Spinoza," "Descartes and Spinoza," and many other correlations of Spinoza with names of authors who are quoted in this work or who could have been quoted. But our purpose was only to draw upon these authors for material in building up our interpretation of Spinoza and not to establish analogies, and we were especially careful to avoid the extension of analogies beyond the limits of what the actual facts warranted, and also to avoid the suggestion of influences when no direct literary relationship could be established. Had we thought it advisable we could have eliminated all the quotations from our texts, either by omitting them altogether or by giving them in paraphrase form. But the interpretation of texts is an essential part of our work, and since texts had to be used, no paraphrase, however felicitous, could take the place of an exact quotation. Probably the most logical literary form for this work would have been that of a commentary upon the *Ethics* preceded by a few general chapters of introduction. But we chose our present method because our purpose was not to comment upon single and isolated passages of the *Ethics*, but to show the unity, continuity, and logical order that runs throughout the work, and withal to present the philosophy of Spinoza as a systematic whole. Of all the authors quoted or referred to in this work, it is only Maimonides and Descartes, and indirectly through them, and quite as often directly through his own works, also Aristotle,[1] that can be said to have had a dominant influence upon the philosophic training of Spinoza and to have guided him in the formation of his own philosophy. It would indeed have been possible, within certain limits, to depict the philosophy of Spinoza against the simple background of any one of these three philosophers, except for the fact that that would not have been a true presentation of the genesis of his thought, for it had a more complex origin. All the other authors quoted in this work, however helpful they may have been in our reconstruction of the *Ethics*, can be said to have had a direct influence only upon single passages in the *Ethics*, or upon single propositions, or at most upon certain groups of propositions. To go beyond that and to attempt to build up an extended analogy between the philosophic systems of any of these authors and Spinoza, on the mere basis of such isolated parallels of expressions or passages, even when a direct literary relationship between them could be established, would only mean the inflation of footnotes into essays or monographs.

---

[1] For lists of authors in relation to whom Spinoza has been studied, see Ueberweg-Frischeisen-Köhler–Moog, *Die Philosophie der Neuzeit bis zum Ende des XVIII. Jahrhunderts* (12th ed., 1924), pp. 668 ff.; R. McKeon, *The Philosophy of Spinoza* (1928), pp. 322 ff. Among all the studies listed, no less than five on Spinoza and Maimonides and no less than sixteen on Spinoza and Descartes, there is only the following one which deals with Spinoza's relation to Aristotle: Julius Guttmann, "Spinozas Zusammenhang mit dem Aristotelismus," in *Judaica, Festschrift zu Hermann Cohens siebzigstem Geburtstage* (Berlin, 1912), pp. 515–534.

But whether direct or indirect, the sources of Spinoza are more important for us as a means of establishing the meaning of his text and philosophy than as a means of establishing an analogy or priority of doctrine. The text of his *Ethics* is not a mosaic of quoted or paraphrased passages. Nor has his philosophy developed as a rash out of the infection of certain heretical or mystical phrases. It has grown out of the very philosophy which he discards, and this by his relentless driving of its own internal criticism of itself to its ultimate logical conclusion. In our endeavor to reconstruct the processes of Spinoza's reasoning, therefore, it is not phrases that we are to deal with but the thought and the history that lie behind them and the use that he makes of them. When he says, for instance, that God is the immanent cause of all things, it is not enough for us to find some one who had called God an immanent cause. We have to study the meaning of the term "immanent" in its complicated historical development and the particular use made of it by Spinoza throughout his writings. We shall then discover that he means by it something quite different from what we should ordinarily take it to mean.[1] Not that we are to assume that Spinoza had actually gone through all the steps of the investigation which we are to trudge through in discovering the meaning of such terms — for that was not necessary for him. He lived in an age when the traditions of philosophy were still alive, and what we nowadays have to discover by the painstaking methods of research came to him naturally as the heritage of a living tradition.

Studied against the rich background of tradition, even the most colorless of terms and expressions may become invested with technical significance of the utmost importance. A case in point is the special significance which may be discovered in

[1] Cf. below, pp. 323 ff.

Spinoza's choice of the terms "attribute," "created things," and "actuality" in his definition of duration,[1] and of the terms "first thing," "actual," "human mind," "idea," "individual thing," and "actually existing" in his definition of mind.[2] Even when Spinoza is obviously merely restating well-known sources our task is not completed by merely supplying the perfunctory references. We must again study the meaning of the sources quoted and their implications and all the possible uses he could have made of them. We shall often find that what at first sight appears merely as a repetition of what others have said is in reality a criticism of what they have said. For despite Spinoza's expressed aversion toward openly criticizing his opponents,[3] and perhaps because of it, his *Ethics* is primarily an implied criticism of his opponents. Thus, for instance, when he enumerates the various meanings of cause and asserts that God is a universal, efficient, essential, and first cause, it is not enough merely to identify the immediate source of his statement. We must study the implications of these terms, and we shall then find that instead of merely repeating what his predecessors have said, Spinoza is really challenging their right of saying what they have said and of applying to their God the term "cause" in all these senses.[4] And so throughout the *Ethics*, from his opening definition of substance to his concluding description of the religion of reason, we shall find that behind every positive statement there is lurking a negative criticism. With every one of his positive assertions we seem to hear Spinoza's challenge to his opponents: I accept your own definitions of terms, but I use them with greater consistency than you. I am not unwilling to use your own descriptions of God, but

---

[1] Cf. below, pp. 347 ff.   [2] Cf. below, Vol. II, pp. 42 ff.
[3] Cf. below, p. 58.
[4] Cf. below, pp. 304 ff.

they are logically more applicable to my God than to yours.
I see no reason why I should not use your own formulae, but
I must give them an interpretation of my own. It is quite
possible for me to adopt with some reservation one of your
views, but I must reject all the others which you consider of
equal probability.

That the *Ethics* in its literary form is a peculiar piece of
writing is quite apparent. But its peculiarity does not consist in the obvious fact that it is divided into propositions and
demonstrations instead of chapters and sections. It consists
in the fact, which becomes obvious only after a careful study
of the work, that the manner in which it makes use of language
is rather peculiar. It uses language not as a means of expression but as a system of mnemonic symbols. Words do not stand
for simple ideas but for complicated trains of thought. Arguments are not fully unfolded but are merely hinted at by suggestion. Statements are not significant for what they actually affirm but for the denials which they imply. Now, the
mere use of the geometrical method cannot explain that, for
even within the geometrical method Spinoza could have been
clearer and more expatiative. To some extent it may be explained, perhaps, by the cloistered atmosphere in which the
Ethics was conceived and written. No challenging questions
of inquiring students or friends guided Spinoza in the manner
of its exposition or goaded him into a fuller expansion of its
statements. Despite the fact that he allowed himself to enter
into the discussion of problems which troubled the minds of
his correspondents, he never communicated to them the fulness of his own thought or discussed with them the philosophic problems which troubled his own mind. The con-
genial group of merchants, booksellers, medical students, and
holders of public office which formed the immediate circle of
Spinoza's friends had a layman's interest in the general prob-

lems of philosophy, but they could hardly serve as effective sounding-boards for his views during the experimental stages of his thinking. They seem to have had a more vigorous grasp of the problems of theology, in which they were the liberals of their day, but with all the adventuresomeness of their spirit they were just beginning to approach the liberalism of the mediaeval writings of Jewish rationalists read by Spinoza in his early youth, which he had long outgrown. Spinoza was welcomed by them as an exotic genius to whose occasional expression of shocking views they could listen indulgently because they could dismiss them from their minds as a sort of outlandish heresy. In this strange environment, to which externally he seems to have fully adjusted himself, Spinoza never felt himself quite free to speak his mind; and he who among his own people never hesitated to speak out with boldness became cautious, hesitant, and reserved. It was a caution which sprang not from fear but from an inner sense of decorum which inevitably enforces itself on one in the presence of strangers, especially strangers who are kind. Quite early in his new career among his newly found friends he showed evidence of this cautious and guarded attitude, and when on one occasion he became conscious of it, in the case of Casearius, he deluded himself into the belief that it was due to the faults of the latter arising from his youth and immaturity.[1] Little did he understand the real cause of his own behavior, and little did he know to what extent it stamped his general attitude towards all the others who had not the faults of youth and immaturity. So long had the thoughts of this book been simmering in his uncommunicative mind that it was boiled down to a concentrated essence, and it is this concentrated essence that we are served in the form of propositions. The *Ethics* is not a

[1] Epistola 9 (*Opera*, IV, p. 42, ll. 19–26).

communication to the world; it is Spinoza's communication with himself.

In its concentrated form of exposition and in the baffling allusiveness and ellipticalness of its style, the *Ethics* may be compared to the Talmudic and rabbinic writings upon which Spinoza was brought up, and it is in that spirit in which the old rabbinic scholars approach the study of their standard texts that we must approach the study of the *Ethics*. We must assume that the *Ethics* is a carefully written book, in which there is order and sequence and continuity, and in which every term and expression is chosen with care and used with precision. We must try to find out not only what is within it, but also what is behind it. We must try to understand not only what the author says, but also what he omits to say, and why he omits it. We must constantly ask ourselves, with regard to every statement he makes, what is the reason? What does he intend to let us hear? What is his authority? Does he reproduce his authority correctly or not? If not, why does he depart from it? What are the differences between certain statements, and can such differences be reduced to other differences, so as to discover in them a common underlying principle? In order to understand Spinoza in full and to understand him well, we must familiarize ourselves with his entire literary background. We must place ourselves in the position of students, who, having done the reading assigned in advance, come to sit at his feet and listen to his comments thereon. Every nod and wink and allusion of his will then become intelligible. Words previously quite unimportant will become charged with meaning. Abrupt transitions will receive an adequate explanation; repetitions will be accounted for. We shall know more of Spinoza's thought than what is merely expressed in his utterances. We shall know what he wished to say and what he would have said had we been able to question him and elicit further information.

But a question may now naturally come up. How do we know that our interpretation is correct? After all, what we have done is to construct an imaginary setting to fit the *Ethics*. How do we know, then, that the setting is not a mere figment of the imagination? Even if it is admitted that the setting is constructed out of historical material and that the *Ethics* seems to fit snugly in it, still it may be argued that the plot of a historical novel may be similarly constructed out of historical material, the individual incidents may be all historically authenticated, and the personages of the novel may all act in their true historical character, and yet the work as a whole be nothing but an artificial and fictitious production.

In answer to this question we may say, in the first place, that the validity of our interpretation of the *Ethics* rests upon its workability and universal applicability. If there is anything arbitrary in our interpretation it is the initial assumption that Spinoza thought out his philosophy in a logical, orderly, and coherent manner, and that he wrote it down in a work which is logical, orderly, and coherent, and in a language which is self-explanatory. But having started out with this assumption and finding that the *Ethics* is far from being a book which is logical, orderly, and coherent, and that the language in which it is written is far from being self-explanatory, we have a right to believe that any interpretation, historically substantiated, that will help to explain the entire *Ethics* as a logically, orderly, coherently, and intelligibly written book is not fictitious like the plot of a historical novel. It is more like the plot of a work of true historical research in which a meagre and sketchy account of certain historical events preserved in a single fragmentary document is presented in a new reconstructed form by the filling in of gaps, by the supplying of details, and by the explaining of causes and motives, all on the basis of other authentic records. Historical research in philosophy, no less than in literature or politics, is justified in claiming the same test of certainty as the hypotheses of the natural scientists, namely, the test of workability and of universal applicability as a description of all the phenomena that come under observation.

The analogy of our study of the *Ethics* to the scientific method of research holds true in still another respect — in the employment of a method which may be considered as a modified form of what is called in science control-experiment. Invariably in the writings of Spinoza several texts are to be found in which the same problems are dealt with. In our study of Spinoza we have always treated these parallel texts as the scientific experimenter would treat his guinea-pigs, performing our experimental interpretation on some of them and using the others as a control. Thus in working on any problem, instead of collecting at once all the parallel texts and ancillary material in the writings of Spinoza and working on all of them at the same time, we confined our investigations to some particular texts, and then tested our conclusions by the other texts. Thus, for instance, in the problem of the unity of substance,[1] for which Propositions II–VI of *Ethics*, I, Chapter II of *Short Treatise*, I, and Appendix I of the *Short Treatise* are parallel texts, or in the problem of the relation of mind and body,[2] for which Proposition X of *Ethics*, II, Preface to *Short Treatise*, II, and Appendix II of the *Short Treatise* are parallel texts, the problem was fully worked out first in connection with one of these sets of texts and then tested and checked up by the others.

---

[1] Cf. below, pp. 79 ff.
[2] Cf. below, Vol. II, pp. 33 ff.

Then also, again in analogy to the method of research in
the sciences, our investigation was not merely a matter of
classifying data; it consisted mainly in discovering problems,
stating them, and solving them; and the solution, as a rule,
started with a conjecture which was afterwards verified by a
method which in scholarship may be said to correspond to the
method of experiment and prediction in science. One problem with which to start our investigation always presented
itself to us, and that was the problem of linking together apparently disconnected propositions into a coherent argument.
To solve this problem it was required to find the missing links
which in the original form in which the *Ethics* was conceived
in the mind of Spinoza and before it was broken up into geometric propositions supplied a logical transition between the
disconnected statements which we now have before us. Now
sometimes these missing links could be forged out of material
which we happened already to have at our disposal, but most
often they had to be invented imaginatively out of material
which we only assumed to exist and the corroborative evidence
was to be discovered afterwards. And, as a rule, it was discovered. But problems of still greater difficulty presented
themselves to us on frequent occasions, such, for instance, as
apparent misuse of terms on the part of Spinoza, or apparent
contradictions in his own statements, or apparent misrepre-
sentations of the views of others. Invariably in the solution
of such problems we set up some distinction in the use of the
term which Spinoza seemed to misuse, or we discerned some
new aspect in the statement of the idea in which Spinoza
seemed to contradict himself, or we assumed the possibility
of some new interpretation of the view in which Spinoza
seemed to misrepresent others. Here, again, most often
these new distinctions, aspects, and interpretations were invented *ad hoc*, merely for the purpose of solving a certain

difficulty, and the evidence corroborating them was discovered afterwards. This is the method which we have followed
throughout our investigation, though it is not the method
which we have adopted in the presentation of the results. In
the final form which this work has assumed, for the sake of
clearness and brevity, the order of exposition has had to be
the reverse of the order of discovery, and sources, which in
the actual process of investigation were evidence by which
a priori conjectures were corroborated, have had to be presented as data from which conclusions were drawn. The material dealt with in this work did not seem to us to possess
sufficient elements of human interest to justify our attempting to intrigue the reader by presenting each problem in the
form of a mystery story.

A typical illustration of this kind of proof by experiment
or prediction may be found in Spinoza's discussion of the
problem of infinite extension. This is one of the discussions
in which Spinoza makes reference to his opponents, restating
their views and criticizing them. He finds that one of the
reasons why his opponents denied the existence of an infinite
extension was their belief in the divisibility of extension, and
therefore concludes that inasmuch as matter is not divisible
an infinite extension does exist. From the context of his discussion it appears that by divisibility he means divisibility
into indivisible parts or atoms and that by indivisibility he
means indivisibility in the same sense as a point is said to be
indivisible. Having identified his opponents, we found that
that kind of divisibility of extension which he seems to
ascribe to them is explicitly denied by them. Furthermore,
we found that Spinoza, in maintaining the existence of an infinite extension which is indivisible, uses the term "infinite"
in a sense which is explicitly rejected by his opponents. Spi-

noza thus seems to misrepresent his opponents and to commit the fallacy of equivocation. This was the difficulty which confronted us. Now, of course, we could have dismissed this difficulty by assuming either that Spinoza purposely misrepresented his opponents in order to be able to refute them, or that out of sheer ignorance he attributed to them views of which they did not approve. But we preferred to believe that Spinoza was both intellectually honest and accurately informed. We therefore tried to find whether it would not be possible for us to interpret his utterances in such a way as would remove our difficulty. We made several vain attempts, until we finally hit upon a possible distinction in the use of the term "indivisible" and correspondingly in that of the term "divisible." By assuming that Spinoza had used these terms according to this new distinction which we invented *ad hoc*, we were able to explain his statements about his opponents in a fully satisfactory manner. We therefore adopted this as a tentative hypothesis, for the truth of which we had no evidence except the internal criterion of its workability. But then, after we had satisfied ourselves as to the workability of our hypothesis, we began to ask ourselves whether it would not be possible to find some external corroboration of it in the form of a statement by some author, mediaeval or ancient, where that distinction in the use of the terms "indivisible" and "divisible" was made. After some search, we found that this distinction in the use of the term "indivisible" is made by Aristotle and Thomas Aquinas.[1]

Or, to take another illustration. In Spinoza's classification of the stages of knowledge, we traced the history of the classification itself as well as of the terms used in it to Aristotle. Then when Spinoza evaluates these orders of knowledge and

[1] Cf. below, pp. 270, 282 ff.

says that "knowledge of the first kind alone is the cause of falsity; knowledge of the second and third orders is necessarily true" (*Ethics*, II, Prop. XLI), we likewise traced this evaluation to Aristotle. But here we were faced with a difficulty. Aristotle makes use of four terms, naturally in Greek. Two of these terms correspond exactly to the two terms which Spinoza describes elsewhere as the second and third kinds of knowledge, but the other two terms used by Aristotle usually mean in Greek just the opposite of the two Latin terms which are used by Spinoza in his first kind of knowledge. But inasmuch as all the evidence pointed to this Aristotelian origin of Spinoza's evaluation of knowledge, we assumed that somewhere in the history of the transmission of Aristotle's writings from the Greek into Latin the two terms in question were somehow translated or interpreted in a sense corresponding to the two terms used by Spinoza. Then, after we had completed the chapter on the Stages of Knowledge, we began to ask ourselves whether it would not be possible for us to find some work accessible to Spinoza where that unusual translation or interpretation of the two Aristotelian terms in question actually occurred. After some search, we found that in two Latin translations made from the Hebrew of Averroes' Arabic Long Commentary on Aristotle's *Analytica Posteriora* these two Aristotelian terms are translated exactly as they are found in Spinoza.[1]

And so in innumerable instances external corroborative evidence was found for previously conceived conjectures. This gave us a sense of assurance that it was not merely an artificial structure that we were setting up for the *Ethics*, but that to some extent we had succeeded in penetrating into the mind of Spinoza and were able to see its workings, to sense its

[1] Cf. below, Vol. II, pp. 146, 151.

direction, to anticipate its movements, and to be guided to its goal. In order to understand another we must completely identify ourselves with that other, living through imaginatively his experience and thinking through rationally his thoughts. There must be a union of minds, like the union of our mind with the Active Intellect which the mediaevals discuss as a possibility and of which Spinoza speaks as a certainty.

CHAPTER II

THE GEOMETRICAL METHOD

Of the eleven works which bear the name of Spinoza as author, two, the *Ethics* and the *Tractatus Theologico-Politicus*, present his entire philosophy in its definitive form. The *Ethics* treats of the philosophy of nature — of God as the whole of nature, and of man as a part of nature. The *Tractatus Theologico-Politicus* treats of human society — of organized religion with its beliefs and traditions as embodied in Scripture, and of organized government with its powers and authority as embodied in established institutions. All his other works, to the student of Spinoza's philosophy as distinguished from the student of Spinoza's writings, are only ancillary material, not to be studied by themselves but in connection with his two major works. The *Short Treatise on God, Man, and His Well-Being* (*Korte Verhandeling van God, de Mensch en des zelfs Welstand*) is nothing but a tentative draft of that phase of Spinoza's philosophy which was later completed and perfected in the *Ethics*. The *Cogitata Metaphysica* is a summary of certain philosophic views of scholastic origin, just as his *Principia Philosophiae Cartesianae* is, as described by Lodewijk Meyer and by Spinoza himself, a summary of "the first and second parts of Descartes' *Principia Philosophiae*, together with a fragment of the third," [1] and if these two works are not to be altogether disregarded by the student of the *Ethics*, they may be considered only as introductory to it. The *Tractatus de Intellec-*

---

[1] *Principia Philosophiae Cartesianae*, Praef. (*Opera*, I, p. 131, l. 24). Cf. Epistola 13 (*Opera*, IV, ll. 13–17). In his letter Spinoza does not mention the fragment of the third part.

tus Emendatione in its present unfinished form may be considered as supplementary to the discussion of the problems of knowledge and truth which occurs in Part II of the *Ethics*, though from the outline of its plan which appears at the beginning of this treatise it may be assumed that it was originally intended to deal also with the problem of the highest good which is discussed at length in Parts IV and V of the *Ethics*. The *Compendium Grammatices Linguae Hebraeae* was probably intended for the use of those who would undertake the study of the Hebrew Bible along the lines suggested by Spinoza in his *Tractatus Theologico-Politicus*, and the *Tractatus Politicus* is nothing but an extension of the latter part of the *Tractatus Theologico-Politicus*. His *Epistolae*, of course, do not constitute an independent work; and as for his treatises on the Rainbow (*Stelkonstige Reeckening van den Regenboog*) and the calculation of chances (*Reeckening van Kanssen*), they have as much or as little to do with his main philosophy as the woolens, linen, furniture, and silver which were left by him at his death.[1]

All these works of Spinoza, the writing of which, from the first dated letter to the end of his life, cover a period of over sixteen years,[2] are in pursuit of one purpose — to bring to its logical conclusion the reasoning of philosophers throughout history in their effort to reduce the universe to a unified and uniform whole governed by universal and unchangeable laws.[3] That philosophers before him had fallen short of the attainment of this purpose — that they had broken up the universe into discontinuous parts by positing a spiritual

---

[1] For a list of these, see "Inventaire des biens et des meubles délaissés par feu le Seigneur Bénédict de Spinoza," in A. J. Servaas van Rooijen, *Inventaire des Livres formant la Bibliothèque de Bénédict Spinoza* (La Haye, 1889), pp. 111–116.

[2] $\frac{18}{26}$ August, 1661–21 February, 1677. His *Short Treatise*, however, may have been written before that.

[3] Cf. below, Vol. II, Chapter XXI.

God as distinct from a material world, and correspondingly in man a spiritual soul as distinct from a material body, with the resulting beliefs of design in nature and free will in man — was in his opinion due to a logical inconsistency in their thinking. Already in his youth, when he first came out in opposition to traditional belief, he had revealed the main trends of his philosophic thinking. The heresies of which he was accused are said to have been three — that God is corporeal, that angels do not exist, that the soul is identical with life.[1] Interpreted, these heresies meant a denial of the existence of an immaterial God as distinct from the material world, of purely spiritual beings as distinct from material beings, and of a soul as distinct from body, which in maturer years gave expression to the principles that extension and thought are attributes of God, that infinite modes — which in his philosophy were the successors of the Intelligences or angels in mediaeval philosophy [2] — are both of extension and of thought, and that the soul is inseparable from the body. As corollaries to these views he denied also design in nature and freedom of will in man. These are the central ideas which run through all his works and to establish which he fights against his opponents with their own weapons, using their own arguments and their own terminology and confronting them with conclusions drawn from their own premises. Whatever differences may be found between his various works, they are only in the use of terminology, or in the restatement of the views of others, or in the arguments employed against those views. In his essential doctrines no change or even development is to be noticed in all these works.

---

[1] Cf. A. Wolf, *The Oldest Biography of Spinoza* (Lucas' *La Vie de feu Monsieur de Spinoza*), pp. 45–46 and 97–98.

[2] Cf. below, pp. 218 ff.

The titles which Spinoza gives his works are all descriptive of their contents, and some of them are borrowed from, or modelled after, the titles of well-known books. Such terms as *Opusculum*, by which Spinoza refers to what we call the *Short Treatise*,[1] and *Tractatus*, by which he refers to two of his other books, and such a combination as *Theologico-Politicus*, were in common use. Thus, for instance, the short treatises of Thomas Aquinas are each described as *Opusculum*, and the younger Buxtorf calls two of his works *Tractatus de Punctorum . . . Origine . . .* and *Dissertationes Philologico-Theologicae*. His *Principia Philosophiae Cartesianae*[2] retains, of course, the title of Descartes' work upon which it is based. The *Cogitata Metaphysica* is modelled after such titles as the *Disputationes Metaphysicae* of Suarez and the *Institutiones Metaphysicae* of Burgersdijck. The word "compendium" in his *Compendium Grammatices Linguae Hebraeae* may have been suggested by the word "epitome" in the elder Buxtorf's *Epitome Grammaticae Hebraeae*, though in the latter case there was an obvious justification for the use of the term "epitome," for the book was an abridgement of his larger work entitled *Thesaurus Grammaticus Linguae Sanctae Hebraeae*. The title of the *Tractatus de Intellectus Emendatione* is evidently a paraphrase of Ibn Gabirol's ethical work which translated into Latin would read *Tractatus de Animae Virtutum Emendatione*.[3] The title *Ethics* naturally goes back to Aristotle's *Nicomachean Ethics*. Still, its use by Spinoza as the title of his chief work needs some explanation.

According to its contents the *Ethics* may be divided into three parts, corresponding to the three parts into which the

---

[1] Epistola 6 (*Opera*, IV, p. 36, l. 13).

[2] Or, more accurately, *Renati Des Cartes Principiorum Philosophiae Pars I, et II*.

[3] *Sefer Tikkun Middot ha-Nefesh.*

Short Treatise is divided and which, according to a statement by Meyer, must have been described by Spinoza himself as *De Deo, Anima rationali, summa hominis felicitate*.[1] In fact the original division of the *Ethics* into three parts, in which the present Parts III, IV, and V are combined into one, corresponded to this threefold division of the *Short Treatise*. Now, in this original division of the *Ethics*, the term "ethics" in its historical usage describes only the Third Part, or rather the present last three parts, dealing as they do with the emotions of the soul (Part III), virtue and vice (Part IV), and human happiness (Part V). These are exactly the topics which are dealt with in the Aristotelian work called the *Nicomachean Ethics*. The Second Part of Spinoza's *Ethics*, dealing with mind or the rational soul, is historically to be described as psychology, and the First Part, dealing with God, is historically to be described as theology, metaphysics, or first philosophy. Furthermore, these three disciplines — metaphysics, psychology, and ethics — which form the subject-matter of Spinoza's *Ethics* fall, in the traditional classification of the sciences, under different headings. Ethics is contrasted with both psychology and metaphysics as practical science with theoretical science. Again, psychology and metaphysics, though belonging to the same type of science called theoretical, are contrasted with each other in that psychology is a subdivision of physics which differs from metaphysics in its subject-matter.[2] The term "ethics," therefore, would seem not to be used quite accurately by Spinoza as a description of the contents of his work called by that name.

Spinoza, however, had ample justification for the use of

----

[1] Cf. quotation from the *Epilogus* to his *Philosophia S. Scripturae Interpres: Exercitatio Paradoxa*, in *Spinoza Opera*, I, *Textgestaltung*, p. 408.

[2] Cf. *Metaphysics*, VI, 1, 1026a, 6–16. See below, Vol. II, p. 3.

the term "ethics" as the title of a book of which the greater part consisted of metaphysics and psychology. The inclusion of psychology under ethics was recommended by Aristotle himself in his statement that the student of politics — and for that matter, we may say, also the student of ethics — must be a psychologist.[1] Furthermore, in mediaeval philosophy, psychology, or at least the treatment of the higher functions of the soul, was removed from physics and placed under metaphysics. Thus the Iḥwan al-Ṣafa,[2] Baḥya Ibn Pakuda,[3] Judah ha-Levi,[4] Abraham Ibn Ezra,[5] and Shem-Ṭob Falaquera,[6] in their enumeration of the topics of metaphysics, include under it the science of the soul and the intellect. Thus psychology, which originally was a branch of physics, could very well be treated either under ethics or under metaphysics.

But then metaphysics, too, during the Middle Ages, had changed its position in the classification of the sciences. As the first and the highest of the three branches of theoretical science, it stood, in the original Aristotelian classification, contrasted with ethics, which was the first of the three practical sciences, and, in accordance with the Aristotelian conception of the superiority of the contemplative life to the active life, it was superior to ethics. In the Middle Ages, however, when the ethical writings of the pagan authors were supplemented, and sometimes supplanted, by the revealed

[1] Cf. *Nicomachean Ethics*, I, 13, 1102a, 18–19. See below, Vol. II, pp. 181–182.

[2] Cf. Fr. Dieterici, *Die Logik und Psychologie der Araber*, p. 15; Arabic text: *Die Abhandlungen der Ichwân Es-Safâ*, p. 251.

[3] Cf. *Ḥobot ha-Lebabot*, Introduction.

[4] Cf. *Cuzari*, V, 12.

[5] Cf. *Yesod Mora*, I.

[6] Cf. M. Steinschneider, *Die hebraeischen Uebersetzungen des Mittelalters*, § 2, quoting from *De'ot ha-Pilosofim*.

Cf. my "The Classification of Sciences in Mediaeval Jewish Philosophy," in *Hebrew Union College Jubilee Volume* (1925), pp. 290 ff.

writings of religion, ethics sometimes becomes a part of theology or metaphysics. Ethics is thus treated as a part of theology by the Iḥwan al-Ṣafa,[1] al-Mukammas,[2] and Baḥya Ibn Paḳuda.[3] Furthermore, the relative importance of ethics and metaphysics is sometimes also changed. Instead of ethics being a prelude to metaphysics, metaphysics becomes a prelude to ethics. Baḥya Ibn Paḳuda is especially explicit on this point: "All the divisions of philosophy as determined by the difference of their subject-matter are gates which God has opened to rational beings through which they may attain a knowledge of the Law and the world. . . . The science which is more particularly necessary for the Law is that which is regarded as the highest science, namely, theology." [4] In his own ethical work, "The Duties of the Heart" (*Ḥobot ha-Lebabot*), Baḥya gives a concrete example of this view by placing his treatment of theological problems at the beginning of his book as a sort of preamble to his subsequent treatment of ethical problems.

It is thus not without precedent that Spinoza gives the book in which he treats of metaphysics, psychology, and ethics the general title of *Ethics*. By precedent he was quite justified in subsuming psychology either under ethics or under metaphysics, and to treat of metaphysics as merely a prelude to ethics. That that was his purpose is quite evident from the structure of the *Ethics*, the last part of which, he says, "concerns the method or way which leads to liberty" [5] — "liberty" being one of the terms which Spinoza uses as synonymous with "blessedness." [6]

[1] Cf. Fr. Dieterici, *op. cit.*, pp. 16–17; Arabic text, *op. cit.*, pp. 252-253.
[2] *Perush Sefer Yeẓirah le-Rabbi Judah ben Barzilai* (Berlin, 1885), p. 65.
[3] *Ḥobot ha-Lebabot*, Introduction.
[4] *Ibid.*
[5] *Ethics*, V, Praef. (*Opera*, II, p. 277, ll. 7–8).
[6] Cf. below, Vol. II, p. 311.

As in the titles of his works, so also in the form in which they are written Spinoza follows traditional patterns. With the notable exception of the poetical form, in which such philosophers as Parmenides, Cleanthes, Lucretius, Solomon Ibn Gabirol, Dante, and Bruno expounded their philosophy, Spinoza experimented with every literary form in which philosophy throughout its history had been written. The gnomic saying with which the philosophy of the Greeks and the wisdom of Israel had made their beginning is represented in many of Spinoza's propositions, especially those which deal with human conduct, some of which read like verses from the Book of Proverbs or like sayings from the Seven Wise Men. The dialogue form used by Plato and the author of the Book of Job and favored by such authors as Erigena, Abelard, Solomon Ibn Gabirol, Judah ha-Levi, Leo Hebraeus, Galileo, and Bruno is represented in the two Dialogues which are inserted between the second and third chapters of Part I of the *Short Treatise*. Philosophy in the form of exegeses of Scriptural passages which appears alike in the Agadic Midrashim of the rabbis and in the writings of Philo, from whom it passed on to the Christian Church Fathers, and was used by Jews as well as by Christians throughout the Middle Ages, and even up to the very time of Spinoza, is the characteristic literary form of the theological part of the *Tractatus Theologico-Politicus*. The autobiographical method of philosophic writing such as we find in Descartes' *Discours de la Méthode* and in some of the works of other philosophers before him is attempted by Spinoza at the beginning of his *Tractatus de Intellectus Emendatione*. The discussion of problems of philosophy in letters to correspondents such as we find, for instance, in the writings of Cicero, Seneca, Maimonides, and Descartes is represented in his *Epistolae*. In addition to all these forms, Spinoza makes use of the geometrical method in the *Principia Philosophiae Cartesianae*, in the Appendix to the *Short Treatise*, and in the *Ethics*. This method, too, had its precedents.

What the external form of this literary method is may be ascertained by a study of the form of Euclid's *Elements*, which served as a model to all those who used the geometrical method of demonstration in philosophy. The geometrical method may be said to consist of the following parts: First, the primary truths which form the premises in the demonstrations are grouped together and placed apart from the demonstrations as the first principles upon which the demonstrations rest, and are divided into definitions, postulates, and axioms or common notions. Second, that which is sought to be demonstrated, that is, the conclusion which is to be established by the demonstration, is summarized apart from the demonstration in the form of a proposition. Third, the demonstration itself reasons from the known, that is, the first principles, to the unknown, that is, the conclusion. Fourth, supplementary deductions, explanations, and propositions are given in the form of corollaries, scholia, and lemmas.

Now this method of demonstration, which is called geometrical, because it is employed by Euclid in his work on geometry, was also used in part or in whole in philosophy.

An example of one kind of partial application of the geometrical method to philosophy is the reduction of philosophic views to the form of propositions, which may be either followed or not followed by demonstrations. This is to be found in Porphyry's *Sententiae ad Intelligibilia Ducentes* ('Αφορμαὶ πρὸς τὰ νοητὰ) and in Proclus' *Institutio Theologica* (Στοιχείωσις θεολογική). It is also to be found in almost every mediaeval compendium of philosophy. Duns Scotus in his *Theoremata* and Burgersdijck in his *Institutiones Logicae* even designate these propositions by the Euclidian term "theorem." An imitation of this partial form of the geometrical method is also to be discerned in Bruno, when he summarizes the conclusions of his doctrine of the unity and simplicity of God's being in a series of propositions.[1] In Jewish philosophy, the twenty-six propositions at the beginning of Part II of Maimonides' *Moreh Nebukim*, which summarize some of Aristotle's physical and metaphysical principles and to which commentators later added demonstrations, belong to the same type of literary composition. Outside of the field of philosophy and quite independently of Euclid's *Elements*, propositions which may be described as geometrical are to be found in various literatures. In Hebrew literature, this form of proposition is characteristic of the Mishnah, which contains a digest of the teachings of the Tannaim, legal as well as ethical. So impressed was an anonymous early Hebrew author with the similarity between the Mishnaic form and the form of geometrical propositions, with which he must have become acquainted through Euclid, that his geometric work written not later than the tenth century and perhaps as early as the second century, consisting of a series of definitions, constructions, and propositions without demonstrations, is called by him the Mishnah of Geometry (*Mishnat ha-Middot*).

An example of another kind of partial application of the geometrical method to philosophy may be found in the identification of the syllogistic form of demonstration with the Euclidian geometrical form or the transformation of one into the other. Thus Aristotle's first argument against the existence of a vacuum,[2] which is syllogistic in nature and is restated by Crescas in the form of a hypothetico-disjunctive

---

[1] *De Immenso*, I, Ch. 11 (*Opera Latina*, Vol. I, Pars I, Neapoli, 1879, pp. 242 ff.). Cf. J. L. McIntyre, *Giordano Bruno*, pp. 192 f.

[2] *Physics*, IV, 8, 214b, 28–215a, 24.

syllogism,[1] is concluded by both Averroes and Crescas [2] with the equivalent of the phrase *quod erat demonstrandum* with which Euclid concludes his geometrical demonstrations. The same Euclidian phrase is also used by Avicenna at the conclusion of some of his own syllogistic arguments.[3] Conversely, too, Aristotle's arguments against the existence of a circularly moving infinite body in *De Caelo*, I, 5–7, which are obviously written in the form of geometrical demonstrations and are restated by Averroes in the form of geometrical demonstrations, are reduced by Crescas to the syllogistic form.[4] The identification of the syllogistic method of reasoning with the geometrical method is clearly indicated by Saadia, who in his plea for the validity of logical inference as a source of knowledge and for its application to matters religious describes the conclusion arrived at by demonstrative reasoning as that which is "geometrically demonstrated." [5]

Finally, in evident imitation of Euclid, we sometimes find in philosophic demonstrations that the first principles upon which the demonstration hinges are grouped together and put apart from the demonstration itself in the form of a series of propositions sometimes even called by the Euclidian terms, definitions, postulates, and axioms or common notions. Thus Maimonides introduces his restatement of the Aristotelian proofs of the existence of God by a series of twenty-six propositions upon which the proofs rest. Though

[1] Cf. my *Crescas' Critique of Aristotle*, pp. 141–143.

[2] Cf. *ibid.*, p. 339, n. 24.

[3] Cf. Avicenna's treatise on the soul published by S. Landauer under the title of "Die Psychologie des Ibn Sinâ" in *Zeitschrift der Deutschen Morgenländischen Gesellschaft*, 29 (1875), at the end of Chs. 1, 2, 3, and 9.

[4] Cf. my *Crescas' Critique of Aristotle*, pp. 175 ff.

[5] *Emunot we-De'ot*, Introduction: علی ما تتهندس (p. 20), כפי מה שיתברר השעור הכתוב. Cf. H. Neumark, "Saadya's Philosophy," in *Essays in Jewish Philosophy*, p. 183, where the phrase used by Saadia is aptly translated by "in so far as they are deduced *more geometrico*."

these twenty-six propositions, unlike Euclid's "first principles," are themselves subject to demonstration, still they are used in these proofs of the existence of God as the "first principles" are used by Euclid. Prior to Maimonides, Baḥya Ibn Paḳuda, in his un-Aristotelian proof for the existence of God, similarly lays down three propositions, which are again subject to proof but are used by him as first principles, and then says: "And when these three propositions have been established, the conclusion will follow, to him who knows how to use them and to join them together, that the world has a creator." [1] To "join them together" [2] may be taken here as a technical term meaning "to syllogize" (συλλογίζεσθαι). A contemporary of Maimonides, Alanus de Insulis or Nicolaus of Amiens, follows the same method and gives still clearer indication that he is consciously following the geometrical method. In his *De Arte seu Articulis Catholicae Fidei*, before starting upon his main work, which consists of a series of propositions, each followed by a demonstration in syllogistic form, he lays down in the prologue a number of definitions (*descriptiones*),[3] postulates (*petitiones*), and axioms (*communes animi conceptiones*),[4] so that the whole book assumes the geometrical form in its completeness. A complete geometrical form is also used in *Liber de Trinitate*, which is falsely ascribed to Alanus.[5] Boethius in the preface to his *Liber de Hebdomadibus* definitely recommends the mathematical method as the method to be followed also in other branches of learning.[6]

---

[1] *Ḥobot ha-Lebabot*, I, 5.   [2] و تاليفها (p. 43), ‏ולחברן‎.

[3] Cf. below, p. 160, n. 1.

[4] Cf. Migne, *Patrologia Latina*, Vol. 210, Col. 597.

[5] Cf. Cl. Baeumker, "Handschriften zu den Werken des Alanus," in *Philosophisches Jahrbuch*, VI (1893), pp. 428–429.

[6] Cf. M. Baumgartner, *Die Philosophie des Alanus de Insulis* (Münster, 1896), pp. 27–32; Ueberweg-Baumgartner, *Grundriss der Geschichte der Philosophie der*

It was not without precedent, therefore, that one of Descartes' objectors suggested to him to present his *Meditationes* in the geometrical form, that Descartes himself made an attempt at it, and that Spinoza attempted it in the Appendix to the *Short Treatise*, carried it out in full in his *Principia Philosophiae Cartesianae* and *Ethics*, and wanted to use it in his Hebrew Grammar.[1]

Still, the geometrical method which with all his predecessors was only a casual attempt, and which Descartes himself, who attempted it, explicitly characterized as a method which "cannot so conveniently be applied to these metaphysical matters,"[2] is adopted by Spinoza and used consistently in his discussions of metaphysical matters throughout his chief philosophic work. Mere imitation of his predecessors cannot therefore explain his use of the geometrical method. Some other explanation will have to be found for it.

Many students of Spinoza regard his use of the geometrical method as a logical consequence of his mathematical way of looking at things. One of his early biographers declares that Spinoza had a "geometrical mind" (*l'esprit geometre*).[3] Erdmann says: "For no other reason than because it is a necessary consequence of the mathematical way of looking at things, the geometrical form of proof is of great significance, even where the proofs themselves are insipid and marred by inaccuracies."[4] Freudenthal maintains that "it was not

patristischen und scholastischen Zeit (10th ed., 1915), pp. 326–327. For other examples of attempts at the application of the geometrical method to philosophy, mostly of the type described by us here as partial geometrical method, see S. Hahn, *Thomas Bradwardinus* (Münster, 1905), pp. 13–14.

[1] Cf. Preface to *Opera Posthuma* quoted in *Spinoza Opera*, I, *Textgestaltung*, p. 623.

[2] *Secundae Responsiones* (*Oeuvres*, VII, p. 156, ll. 25–26).

[3] Pierre Bayle, *Dictionnaire Historique et Critique* (1st ed., 1695–1697), under "Spinoza (Benoit de)"; A. Wolf, *The Oldest Biography of Spinoza*, p. 160.

[4] *Grundriss der Geschichte der Philosophie*, II, § 272.2 (English translation, II, p. 58).

therefore a capricious notion, which might as well have been dispensed with, that made Spinoza style his system *Ethica Ordine Geometrico Demonstrata*; on the contrary, the method called for in the title follows from the inner necessity of his thought." [1] And Joachim concludes that "the form of Spinoza's exposition is essential to its matter. He casts his system in a geometrical mould, because the subject-matter, as he conceives it, demands such treatment." [2]

But let us consider all the facts in the case and see whether there really is any ground for the assumption that the nature of Spinoza's philosophy demanded that it should be written in the geometrical form. The points which we shall try to establish are as follows: (1) Both Descartes and Lodewijk Meyer make a distinction between the geometrical method of demonstration, which may be either synthetic or analytic, and the geometrical form of literary exposition, which, whether synthetic or analytic, is to be modelled after the literary form of Euclid's *Elements*. (2) The geometrical method of demonstration of the synthetic type is nothing but valid syllogistic reasoning as practised throughout the history of philosophy. (3) The geometrical method of demonstration, whether synthetic or analytic, need not necessarily be written in the geometrical literary form, and, conversely, the use of the geometrical literary form is not determined by the subject-matter of which it treats. (4) Spinoza's mathematical way of looking at things means only the denial of design in nature and freedom in man, and this need not necessarily be written in the geometrical literary form.

The fullest discussion of the geometrical method is to be found in Descartes *Regulae ad Directionem Ingenii*. Though the phrase "geometrical method" in either two of its forms

---

[1] *Spinoza Leben und Lehre* (ed. Gebhardt, 1927), II, pp. 110–111.
[2] *A Study of the Ethics of Spinoza*, p. 13.

ordine geometrico and *more geometrico* — does not occur there, Descartes openly advocates that "in our search for the direct road towards truth we should busy ourselves with no object about which we cannot attain a certitude equal to that of the demonstrations of arithmetic and geometry."[1] This method, which by implication may be called the geometrical method, is contrasted by him with "that method of philosophizing which others have already discovered and those weapons of the schoolmen, probable syllogisms, which are so well suited for dialectical combats."[2] The contrast between the old syllogistic method of the schoolmen and the new geometrical method which he proposes is described as follows: The former deals with "probable knowledge"[3] or "probable opinion";[4] its object is "dialectics"[5] and not the attainment of truth; it had no utility save the solution of empty problems.[6] The geometrical method, on the other hand, he says, deals with "true and evident cognition,"[7] its object is the discovery of truth, and it is to be employed to solve useful problems. This new geometrical method, he then continues, is based on intuition and deduction. It starts with premises which must be self-evidently true, and it arrives at conclusions by the method of inference, proceeding logically from the known to the unknown.[8]

In analyzing these statements of Descartes about the geometrical method, we find that it is nothing but what Aristotle would call a scientific demonstration. Descartes' insistence that truth can be attained only by premises which are self-evidently true and by deduction is nothing but a repetition of Aristotle's theory that demonstrative reasoning as ex-

---

[1] *Regulae ad Directionem Ingenii*, II (*Oeuvres*, X, p. 366, ll. 6–9).
[2] *Ibid.*, II (p. 363, ll. 21–24).
[3] *Ibid.*, II (p. 362, ll. 14–15).
[4] *Ibid.*, II (p. 363, ll. 14–15).
[5] *Ibid.*, II (p. 363, l. 13).
[6] *Ibid.*, IV (p. 373, ll. 26 ff.).
[7] *Ibid.*, II (p. 362, l. 5).
[8] *Ibid.*, IX and XI.

pressed in any syllogism must start with premises which are "true, primary, immediate, more known than, prior to, and the cause of, the conclusion." [1] Furthermore, if we study carefully Descartes' language we shall notice that he does not really contrast his own method with syllogisms in general but with what he calls "probable syllogisms" or what Aristotle would call a "dialectical (διαλεκτικός) syllogism" and a "contentious (ἐριστικός) syllogism," [2] for Descartes' "probable syllogisms" are syllogisms which consist of what Aristotle calls probabilities (τὰ ἔνδοξα), and "probabilities," according to Aristotle, yield a "dialectical syllogism" and a "contentious syllogism." [3] This is exactly what Descartes means when, speaking of "probable syllogisms," he says that they are so well suited for "contentions" (bellis) [4] or, as the French version translates it, "dialectical combats" (combats de la dialectique). [5] His geometrical method, as described by him so far, is thus not contrasted by him with the syllogistic method as such, but rather with the abuse of the syllogistic method.

But as Descartes goes on he adds a new point to his conception of the geometrical method. Ancient geometricians were acquainted with two methods of proof, one by analysis and the other by synthesis, though the proofs in Euclid's *Elements* are of the synthetic type. Descartes refers to the antiquity of the analytic method when he says: "Indeed I seem to recognize certain traces of this true mathematics in Pappus and Diophantus. . . . But my opinion is that these writers then with a sort of low cunning, deplorable in-

---

[1] *Analytica Posteriora*, I, 2, 71b, 21–22.
[2] *Topics*, I, 1, 100a, 29–30, and 100b, 23–24.
[3] *Ibid.*, 100a, 29–100b, 24.
[4] *Regulae ad Directionem Ingenii*, II (*Oeuvres*, X, p. 363, l. 23).
[5] *Régles pour la Direction de l'Esprit*, II (*Oeuvres de Descartes*, ed. Cousin, XI, p. 206).

dced, suppressed this knowledge." [1] These ancients, however, performed their analyses of geometrical problems by means of construction; Descartes performs them by means of algebraic calculations, the process of which is known as analytical geometry. By this change he extends the method of analysis to everything within the realm of mathematics, or, as he expresses himself, to any object in which "the question of measurement arises." [2] This he calls "universal mathematics." [3] But going still further, he applies the method of analysis to the other sciences, thus making the knowledge of all things mathematical. [4]

From this analysis of Descartes' own conception of the geometrical or mathematical method, it is quite clear that he means by it only the method of demonstration itself and not at all the literary form in which Euclid happens to couch the demonstration. Whichever kind of demonstration of the geometrical method is used, the synthetic or analytic, there is no indication in anything Descartes says that it has to be written in the form which Euclid employs in his *Elements*.

That the application of the geometrical method of demonstration to philosophic problems does not necessarily require the use of the external literary form of the Euclidian geometric propositions is still more evident from Descartes' *Secundae Responsiones*.

In a reply to one of his objectors who counselled him to propound the arguments of meditations in the geometrical method (*more geometrico*), [5] he distinguishes in the "geometrical mode of writing" (*modo scribendi geometrico*) two things, namely, the order of proof and the method of proof

[1] *Regulae ad Directionem Ingenii*, IV (*Oeuvres*, X, p. 376, ll. 21–26).

[2] *Ibid.*, IV (p. 378, ll. 3–4).

[3] *Ibid.*, IV (p. 378, ll. 8–9).

[4] *Ibid.*, IV (p. 379, ll. 5 ff.).

[5] *Secundae Objectiones* (*Oeuvres*, VII, p. 128, ll. 13–17).

(ordinem scilicet, & rationem demonstrandi).[1] As for the "order of proof," Descartes explains it, as he does in his *Regulae*, as consisting "merely in putting forward those things first that should be known without the aid of what comes subsequently, and arranging all other matters so that their proof depends solely on what precedes them."[2] This, as we have shown, is nothing but a repetition of what is generally considered to be true of any good syllogistic argument. The "method of proof" is described by Descartes, again as in his *Regulae*, as being twofold. One is analytic; the other is synthetic. The former reasons as it were *a priori*, from cause to effect; the latter reasons as it were *a posteriori*, from effect to cause,[3] the latter being, however, the only method employed by ancient geometers in their writings. Now, in his *Meditationes*, says Descartes, in so far as he tried to put forward those things first that should be known without the aid of what comes subsequently, he did certainly follow the geometrical order of proof. But he admits that, unlike the ancient geometers who had employed only the synthetic method of proof, he employed in his *Meditationes* the analytic method, and he did so for the very good reason that he did not believe that the synthetic method is applicable to the discussion of metaphysical matters. For the synthetic method of proof, he says, must start with certain presuppositions or "primary notions" (*primae notiones*) which are granted by all. Now, in geometry there are certain primary notions which "harmonize with the use of our senses, and are readily granted by all"; in metaphysics, however, "nothing causes more trouble than the making

---

[1] *Secundae Responsiones* (*Oeuvres*, VII, p. 155, ll. 8–10).

[2] *Ibid.* (p. 155, ll. 11–14).

[3] *Ibid.* (p. 155, ll. 23–24; p. 156, ll. 6–7). Cf. French version (*Oeuvres*, ed. Adam and Tannery, IX, pp. 121–122).

the perception of its primary notions clear and distinct . . .
though in their own nature they are as intelligible as, or even
more intelligible than, those the geometricians study." [1]
"This is the reason," concludes Descartes, "why I used the
form of Meditations rather than that of Disputations [and
Questions], as do philosophers, or that of Theorems and
Problems, as do geometers." [2] Still, despite his explanation
of his preference for the analytic method over the synthetic
method, he appends at the end of his reply to the second objections "something in the synthetic style," [3] as he describes it. This "something in the synthetic style" consists of his "arguments demonstrating the existence of God
and the distinction between soul and body drawn up in geometrical fashion," [4] in which he begins like Euclid with a
series of Definitions, Postulates, and Axioms or Common
Notions, and then follows with Propositions each of which
is proved by a demonstration. [5]

Here, then, as in his *Regulae ad Directionem Ingenii*,
Descartes makes it quite clear that by the geometrical
method in its primary and general sense he means nothing
but what Aristotle would call a scientific demonstration consisting of premises which are self-evidently true and of a
conclusion deduced from those premises by logical inference.
Again as in his *Regulae*, the geometrical method is divided
by him into two types, the analytic and the synthetic. Now,
the analytic type of the geometrical method, we know, is as-

[1] *Ibid.* (p. 156, l. 2–p. 157, l. 10).

[2] *Ibid.* (p. 157, ll. 17–19). Cf. French version (*Oeuvres*, ed. Adam and Tannery,
IX, p. 123).

[3] *Ibid.* (p. 159, ll. 13–14).

[4] *Ibid.* (p. 160, ll. 1 ff.).

[5] It is to be noted that, unlike Descartes, Spinoza includes no Postulates among
the first principles which precede his propositions. Postulates are used by him,
however, between Props. 13 and 14 of *Ethics*, II (repeated in *Ethics*, III) and at
the beginning of Part III of *Principia Philosophiae Cartesianae*.

sociated historically with a certain external literary form, though Descartes makes no reference to it here. It is the form in which the few relics of the analytic demonstrations of the ancient geometricians and Descartes' own analytical geometry are written. But this external literary form was not essential, according to Descartes' own admission, to the geometrical method of the analytic type. In Descartes' application of this method to philosophical problems it took the form, as he himself says, of meditations. The external literary form of the synthetic type of the geometrical method is likewise associated historically with certain external literary forms which are alluded to by Descartes himself. In the past, he seems to say, it had taken two literary forms: first, that of "Disputations [and Questions]," by which he means the method used in the scholastic writings, and, second, that of "Theorems and Problems," by which he means the method used in Euclid's *Elements*. The inference to be drawn from this statement, again, is that the Euclidian literary form is not essential to the synthetic geometrical method when applied to philosophical problems, inasmuch as the scholastic "Disputations and Questions" is another type of literary form mentioned by Descartes as one which can be used in the synthetic geometrical method of demonstration, though he himself, as a concession to his correspondent, attempts to reduce a few of his philosophical arguments to the Euclidian literary form.

The same distinction within geometrical method between a method of demonstration and a method of literary exposition is to be found in Meyer's Preface to Spinoza's *Principia Philosophiae Cartesianae*. He speaks there of the "wretched plight of philosophy" (*miserimam Philosophiae fortem*)[1] which finds itself without a proper method. The method in

[1] *Opera*, I, p. 128, ll. 17–18.

vogue in the scholastic literature, which Descartes refers to
as "Disputations and Questions," is described by him as "a
method where the end is attained through definitions and
logical divisions which are indirectly connected with each
other and interspersed with numerous questions and explanations." [1] As against this he describes the new method
which was developed by those who were desirous to "leave
to posterity some studies besides mathematics established
with absolute certainty." He refers to this method as the
"mathematical method" (*methodo . . . mathematica*).[2] At first
it would seem that Meyer refers here to the Euclidian literary form. But as he proceeds and restates Descartes' words
in the *Secundae Responsiones* it becomes clear that he deals
here not with the geometrical literary form but rather with
the geometrical method of demonstration, which, following
Descartes, he divides into analytic and synthetic. Later,
speaking of the Euclidian literary form of demonstration, he
refers to it as "*more Geometris.*" [3] But in the entire discussion there is nothing to indicate that the application of the
geometrical literary form by Spinoza to Descartes' *Principia
Philosophiae* was the outgrowth of the mathematical method
of demonstration employed by Descartes. On the contrary,
the indications are that it was considered to be something
imposed upon it externally.

In Spinoza, beyond the mention of the fact that he has
reduced parts of Descartes' *Principia Philosophiae* to the
geometrical literary form [4] and references to its use in the
work which later came to be known as the *Ethics*,[5] there is no
discussion of its nature as a method of demonstration. He

[1] *Ibid.*, p. 127, ll. 24 ff.
[2] *Ibid.*, p. 128, l. 21.
[3] *Ibid.*, p. 129, l. 27.
[4] Epistola 13 (*Oeuvres*, IV, p. 63, l. 13).
[5] Epistola 2 (p. 8, l. 15); cf. Epistola 3 (p. 10, l. 7).

makes use, however, of certain mathematical analogies, such indeed as are also to be found in the works of Descartes. But in these mathematical analogies Spinoza goes much further than Descartes. In Descartes the mathematical analogies are used only as illustrations in his discussions of the method of demonstration. In no way do these analogies imply that Descartes conceived the universe as a whole to be governed by laws of necessity like those which prevail in mathematics. In his universe, according to his own statements, there was still room for final causes, for a divine will, and for human freedom. In Spinoza, on the other hand, the mathematical analogies are used as illustrations of the existence of inexorable laws of necessity throughout nature. Spinoza gives expression to this view when on several occasions he declares that all things follow from the infinite nature of God according to that same necessity by which it follows from the essence of a triangle that its three angles are equal to two right angles,[1] and when he declares that the human race would have been kept in darkness to all eternity with regard to final ends "if mathematics, which does not deal with ends, but with the essence and properties of forms, had not placed before us another rule of truth,"[2] or, finally, when in denying human freedom he declares, "I shall consider human actions and appetites just as if I were considering lines, planes, or bodies."[3]

It is these two principles — the denial of final causes in the universe and of freedom in human actions — that Spinoza wishes to illustrate by his use of mathematical analogies. It is only this, and nothing more, that his mathematical way of looking at things means. Beyond this, there

[1] *Ethics*, I, Prop. 17, Schol.; II, Prop. 49, Schol.; IV, Prop. 57, Schol.; *Cogitata Metaphysica*, II, 9.
[2] *Ethics*, I, Appendix (*Opera*, II, p. 79, ll. 32–34).
[3] *Ibid.*, III, Praef. (end).

io nowhere any indication that he in any way connected his use of the geometrical litcrary form with this his mathematical way of looking at things, nor can there be any such connection logically established on independent grounds. On the contrary, the fact that his *Short Treatise*, where his mathematical way of looking at things is already fully developed, is not written in the geometrical literary form would seem to indicate that the geometrical literary form was not a logical consequence of his mathematical way of looking at things. Furthermore, the fact that he had applied the geometrical literary form to the philosophy of Descartes, which does not look at things mathematically in Spinoza's sense, would also seem to indicate that there is no logical connection between the contents of a philosophy and the particular literary form in which it is written. Finally, the fact that Spinoza had intended to apply it to the grammar of the Hebrew language would similarly seem to indicate that there is no logical connection btween the geometrical literary form and the subject-matter to which it is applied. The thought that may occur to one that the planned application of the geometrical form to the Hebrew grammar may somehow be connected with a metaphysical conception of language which students of Spinoza maintain to have detected in his theory of the priority of nouns to adjectives and verbs in the Hebrew language [1] may be dismissed as a passing fancy. Spinoza himself does not explicitly link his grammatical view as to the relation of adjectives and verbs to nouns with his metaphysical view as to the relation of modes to substance, and if he did ever link them at all in his mind,

---

[1] Cf. *Compendium Grammatices Linguae Hebraeae*, Chs. V and VIII; J. Bernays in "Anhang" to C. Schaarschmidt, *Des Cartes und Spinoza* (Bonn, 1850), p. 197; J. Freudenthal, *Spinoza Leben und Lehre* (ed. Gebhardt, 1927), I, p. 291; N. Porges, "Spinozas Compendium der hebräischen Grammatik," in *Chronicon Spinozanum*, IV (1924–1926), p. 146.

it must have been in the nature of a literary analogy. All those who have attached a metaphysical significance to this view of Spinoza have failed to notice the fact that an explicit analogy between the relation of adjectives and verbs to nouns and the relation of accidents to substance occurs also in the philosophical grammar of Profiat Duran,[1] and yet no implication of any metaphysical conception of language is to be discerned there.

If, as we have been trying to show, there is no logical connection between the substance of Spinoza's philosophy and the form in which it is written, his choice of the Euclidian geometrical form is to be explained on other grounds. Primarily, we may say, the reason for its choice was pedagogical, the clearness and distinctness with which the geometrical form was believed to delineate the main features of an argument and to bring them into high relief. It was used for the same reason that one uses outlines and diagrams. This pedagogical reason for the application of the geometrical form to philosophy is clearly stated by Descartes' objector, when he suggested to Descartes the use of this form. He says: "This is why it would be well worth the doing if, hard upon your solution of the difficulties, you advanced as premises certain definitions, postulates, and axioms, and thence drew conclusions, conducting the whole proof by the geometrical method, in the use of which you are so highly expert. Thus would you cause each reader to have everything in his mind, as it were, at a single glance, and to be penetrated throughout with a sense of the Divine being." [2] Equally pedagogical is the reason given by Meyer for the reduction of Descartes' philosophy to the Euclidian geometrical form by Spinoza. Conceiving the two types of geometrical method, the Euclid-

[1] *Ma'aseh Efod*, Ch. 9.
[2] *Secundae Objectiones* (*Oeuvres*, VII, p. 128, ll. 13–19).

ian synthetic and the Cartesian analytic, as mutually complementary, the former as the method by which mathematical truths are "written down" (*conscriptae*)[1] and the latter as the method by which they are "discovered" (*inventae*),[2] Meyer recommends the rewriting of Descartes' philosophy, which was discovered by the analytic method, in the Euclidian synthetic method, for the benefit of those who, having read Descartes' philosophy in the non-geometrical form in which it is written, "are not able to follow it for themselves, nor can they teach it to others," [3] and also for the benefit of the many who have made Descartes' opinions and dogmas only a matter of memory and are unable to demonstrate them and defend them against attacks.[4] It is thus always for the benefit of the reader, and because of the clearness with which it is supposed to state an argument, and not because the philosophic system itself demands it, that the geometrical form is made use of.

But there may have been another reason which had prompted philosophers at the time of Descartes and Spinoza to turn to the use of the geometrical form. It may have been as a reaction against the new literary forms which since the Renaissance, under the influence of the works of ancient writers, had been imported into philosophic writings, where it had taken the place of the syllogistic style. The Renaissance philosophers had an aversion toward the syllogistic method of the mediaevals, not so much on intellectual grounds as on purely aesthetic grounds; not so much because the method itself could not be properly used in the discovery of truth or because of the ease with which the method could be abused and be made to lend itself to give a semblance of proof to things which were not true as because

---

[1] *Opera*, I, p. 129, l. 16.   [2] *Ibid.*
[3] *Ibid.*, p. 129, l. 8.   [4] *Ibid.*, p. 129, ll. 18 ff.

it was bare and bleak and skeleton-like. They were dissatisfied with syllogisms for the same reason that people are dissatisfied with food that is merely nourishment, with clothes that are merely warm, or with a house that is merely a shelter. The syllogistic method may have been practical and useful, but it lacked form and was not pleasing to the eye and the ear. They therefore began to experiment with new literary forms, more polished, more refined, and more resonant — dialogues after the manner of Plato, poetry after the manner of Lucretius, and rhetorical prose after the manner of Cicero. But all these new literary forms proved a disappointment. Instead of merely garbing the logical nakedness of the syllogism — that logical syllogism which must inevitably be implied in every sound argument — they sometimes served as a cloak to cover up the lack of any kind of logic and reasoning. Philosophy became metaphorical and effusive. What was thus gained in grace was lost in accuracy and precision. A new method in presenting philosophical arguments was needed. To return to the old syllogistic method openly and directly would have meant a return to scholasticism, for which the world was not yet ready. They therefore returned to it indirectly by adopting the geometrical form. To the philosophers of the seventeenth century the blessed word "mathematics" served as a veneer of respectability for the discredited syllogism.

In the case of Spinoza there may have been still another reason for his use of the geometrical form. It was in order to avoid the need of arguing against opponents. The *Ethics*, as we shall show, primarily consists of conclusions of an elaborate criticism of traditional philosophy. Had Spinoza followed the old traditional method, the method used by rabbis and schoolmen alike, the comparatively small volume of the *Ethics* would have run into many bulky tomes. That method required that the various views held by opponents on each problem should be stated, that the pros and cons for each view should be reproduced, that refutations and rebuttals should be marshalled, and that only then the author's own view should be given and its superiority to those of others pointed out. Spinoza, for reasons which can only be explained psychologically, did not want to go through all this elaborate formality. In a letter to Oldenburg he says, "It is not my custom to expose the errors of others," [1] and in another place he expresses a reluctance "to seem to be desirous of exposing the errors of others." [2] In still another place he declares himself not to be bound "to discuss what every one may dream." [3] By resorting to the use of the geometrical form he could avoid all this, at least openly. But Spinoza never meant to imply that by his use of the geometrical form his philosophy, like the geometry of Euclid, is the unfoldment of certain *a priori* self-evident truths. For his axioms, properly understood, are not necessarily self-evident truths, any more than his propositions are necessarily new truths discovered by demonstration. Most often they are merely restatements of generally accepted mediaeval brocards. It will be noticed that the "Axioms" mentioned in a letter from Oldenburg [4] and also in the geometric appendix to the *Short Treatise* are called "Propositions" in the *Ethics*, for the terms "definitions," "axioms," "propositions," and their like are used by Spinoza more or less indiscriminately as conventional labels to be pasted on here and there in order to give to his work the external appearance of a work of geometry. What the motives were that prompted Spinoza to depart from the old form of exposition

[1] Epistola 2 (*Oeuvres*, IV, p. 8, ll. 18–19).
[2] *Tractatus de Intellectus Emendatione*, § 95 (*Opera*, II, p. 34, ll. 31–32).
[3] *Ethics*, II, Prop. 49, Schol. (*Opera*, II, p. 133, l. 20).
[4] Epistola 3.

can be only conjectured, but among them there may have been the desire to produce a book which externally would be different from all other books on philosophy. He had something new to say, and he wished to say it in a new way. And perhaps, also, he chose the geometrical form in order to avoid the temptation of citing Scripture.

But still, the form in which the *Ethics* is written, we have reason to believe, is not the form in which it formulated itself in the mind of Spinoza. He must at first have thought out all its problems in their full detail after the manner of the rabbis and scholastics, and only afterwards, when he came to write them down, did he break them up into geometric propositions. There is thus behind our present *Ethics*, demonstrated in geometrical order, an *Ethics* demonstrated in rabbinical and scholastic order, just as behind Descartes' own fragmentary attempt to draw up his proofs of the existence of God and of the distinction between soul and body in geometrical fashion are the corresponding parts of the *Meditationes*, just as behind Spinoza's *Principia Philosophiae Cartesianae* is Descartes' *Principia Philosophiae*, and just as behind the geometric Appendix to Spinoza's own *Short Treatise* is Chapter II of Part I of that book. Now, Descartes himself admits that his geometric fragment does not give the full content of the arguments as they are unfolded in the *Meditationes*. "I should, however, like them kindly to notice," he says, "that I have not cared to include here so much as comes into my Meditations . . . nor shall I explain in such accurate detail that which I do include." [1] Spinoza similarly admits that the geometrical method might not convey easily to all the readers what he had in his mind, for in a Scholium, where he gives an outline of the topics dealt with in a subsequent group of propositions, he says:

[1] *Secundae Responsiones* (*Oeuvres*, VII, p. 159, ll. 15-19).

"Before, however, I begin to demonstrate these things by our full geometrical method, I should like briefly to set forth here these dictates of reason, in order that what I have in my mind about them may be easily comprehended by all." [1] Imagine now that Descartes' *Meditationes* and *Principia Philosophiae* and Chapter II of Spinoza's *Short Treatise*, I, were lost, and only Descartes' own geometric fragment, and Spinoza's *Principia Philosophiae Cartesianae*, and the geometric Appendix to the *Short Treatise* were left. In that case, to understand fully these extant geometrically written works we should have to reconstruct the lost works upon which they are based. Similarly, to understand our present *Ethics* we must construct that hypothetical *Ethics* which lies behind it.

But how are we to go about constructing that hypothetical *Ethics*? The answer to this question has already been given in the preceding chapter where we have discussed the method employed by us in the reconstruction of the reasoning that lies behind the *Ethics*. We may now proceed to the actual task of reconstruction.

[1] *Ethics* IV, Prop. 18, Schol.

CHAPTER III

DEFINITION OF SUBSTANCE AND MODE

THERE are certain types of literature which are inseparably associated in our minds with some sort of formal, conventional beginning. We thus all expect a fairy tale to begin with "Once upon a time," and a Christmas ballad with "'Twas the night before Christmas." A Biblical narrative always suggests to our mind the phrase "And it came to pass," and epic poems, from the Iliad to the latest parody, begin with an invocation to the Muse. I suppose we should all be sorely disappointed if we woke up some fine morning to find that Caesar's *Commentaries on the Gallic Wars* did not begin with the familiar "Gallia est omnis divisa in partes tres." Now, like fairy tales, and Christmas ballads, and Caesar's *Commentaries*, metaphysical treatises in the Middle Ages as a rule set out on their philosophical investigation by a statement which might be reduced to the following formula: All Being is divided, etc.

The term "Being" which I have used here represents the Arabic *maujud*,[1] the Hebrew *nimza*,[2] and the Latin *ens*. All these three terms are meant to reproduce the Greek τὸ ὄν, which is used by Aristotle as the main subject of his tenfold division of categories. But at this point the mediaevals depart from Aristotle's method of procedure. They do not say outright at the very beginning that Being is divided into ten categories, and for the very good reason that they do not seem to take the Aristotelian tenfold classification of cate-

---

[1] موجود.   [2] נמצא.

guius as does John Stuart Mill and others who have criticized or ridiculed it — to be a primary, logical, and accurate classification of Being. In their opinion, it would seem, when Aristotle wanted to be logical and accurate he simply divided Being into substance and accident; its subsequent subdivision into ten categories was meant to be merely tentative and was by no means fixed. It is with the logical division of Being into substance and accident, therefore, that the mediaevals mean to begin their metaphysical investigation. But here, again, they do not exactly say that outright. Instead of beginning directly with the statement that all Being is divided into substance and accident, they begin with a rather broader and more general statement, and by gradual paring, whittling, and edging finally narrow it down to the Aristotelian phraseology. Their opening statement usually reads that all Being is divided into that which dwells within a dwelling and that which does not dwell within a dwelling. The term "dwelling"[1] is then investigated, and a special kind of dwelling, named "subject,"[2] is differentiated from the others. At last the wished-for statement is arrived at, namely, that all Being is divided into that which is in itself and that which is in a subject, and the former is given the name of substance whereas the latter is given the name of accident. Thus the formula that everything which exists is either in itself or in another thing occurs in the writings of such philosophers as Joseph Ibn Ẓaddiḳ,[3] Albo [4]

---

[1] משכן, محَلّ. Cf. my *Crescas' Critique of Aristotle*, p. 577.

[2] נושא, موضوع. ὑποκείμενον. Cf. *ibid.*

[3] *'Olam Ḳaṭan*, I, ii (p. 8): "Every existing thing of the things which exist inevitably falls under one of the following four classes: [*a*] It exists in itself, [*b*] it exists in another thing, [*c*] it exists neither in itself nor in another thing, or [*d*] it exists both in itself and in another thing."

[4] *'Iḳḳarim*, II, 11: "Things which exist are divided first into two classes, those which exist in themselves and those which exist in other things."

and Burgersdijck,[1] and the formula that everything is either a substance or an accident occurs still more widely in the writings of such philosophers as Alfarabi,[2] Algazali,[3] Abraham Ibn Daud,[4] Jacob Anatolio,[5] and Burgersdijck.[6] A combination of these two formulae occurs in Eustachius a Sancto Paulo, who divides *ens* into *ens per se* and *ens per accidens*,[7] though he does not use the expressions *ens per se* and *ens per accidens* in the ordinary sense of substance and accident.[8] All these formulae may be traced to Aristotle's statement that "some things can exist apart and some cannot, and it is the former that are substances."[9]

This is how mediaeval thinkers begin their philosophy; and this is how Spinoza would have begun his *Ethics* had he chosen to write it *more scholastico rabbinicoque*. But as a matter of fact, even in its present artificial, geometrical form the *Ethics* begins with this statement, logically though not spatially. It is contained in Axiom I, which reads: "Everything which is, is either in itself or in another."

When we come, however, to Spinoza's formal definition of that thing which is in itself, labelled by the good old name

---

[1] *Institutiones Metaphysicae*, Lib. I, Cap. II, Thesis VIII: "Praeterea deprehendimus Entia quaedam per se subsistere, alia non per se, sed in iis subsistere, quae per se subsistunt."

[2] *Mehut ha-Nefesh*, in Edelmann's *Ḥemdah Genuzah*, I (p. 46): "Everything which exists must inevitably be either a substance or an accident."

[3] *Maḳaṣid al-Falasifah*, II, i (p. 79): "Existence is divided into substance and accident."

[4] *Emunah Ramah*, I, 1 (p. 4): "Things which exist are divided first into substance and accident."

[5] *Ruaḥ Ḥen*, Ch. 10: "All things which exist must inevitably be either substance or accident."

[6] *Institutiones Metaphysicae*, Lib. II, Cap. I, Thesis III: "Itaque partiemur Ens primo in substantiam et accidens."

[7] *Summa Philosophiae*, IV: *Metaphysica*, Pars I, Posterior Disputatio, Quaestio I: "Prima igitur divisio entis latissime sumti est in ens Rei, et ens Rationis: Secunda, entis rei, in ens Per se et ens Per accidens."

[8] Cf. *ibid.*, Quaestio IV.   [9] *Metaphysics*, XII, 5, 1070b, 36–1071a, 1.

"substance," [1] and compare it with the mediaeval definition, we find that while in part they read alike, Spinoza's defini- tion contains a new additional element. The mediaeval definition simply reads, as has been said, that substance is that which is in itself, i.e., not in a subject. [2] But Spinoza adds to "that which is in itself" the statement "and is con- ceived through itself" (Def. III). Again, the mediaeval defi- nition of accident is that which is in another thing. [3] Here, again, using the term "mode" (*modus*) which he identifies with the affections (*affectiones*) [4] of substance, Spinoza first defines it like the traditional accident as "that which is in another thing," but then adds the clause "through which also it is conceived" (Def. V). Furthermore, why did Spinoza reject the term "accident" (*accidens*) in his definitions at the beginning of the First Part of the *Ethics*, and replace it by the term "mode"? And why, too, did he not mention the term "subject" in his definitions of substance and mode? Shall we say that all these are matters of mere accident or carelessness or indifference? This might pass as an explana- tion if we considered the *Ethics* to be an accidentally, care- lessly, and indifferently written book. But we are now work- ing on the assumption that the *Ethics* is as careful a piece of

[1] In one of his letters he speaks, however, of "substantia sive ens." Epistola 9 (*Opera*, IV, p. 44, l. 17 and l. 35).

[2] *Makaṣid al-Falasifah*, II, i (p. 82): "Substance is a term applied to every ex- isting thing not in a subject"; *Emunah Ramah*, I, 1 (p. 4): "Substance is that existing thing which is not in need of a subject"; Burgersdijck, *Institutiones Meta- physicae*, Lib. II, Cap. I, Thesis IV: "Substantia est Ens per se subsistens. *Per se subsistens* non excludit in hac definitione dependentiam ab omnibus causis (nam hoc sensu nullum Ens dici potest per se subsistere quam solus Deus) sed solum- modo dependentiam a subjecto."

[3] *Emunah Ramah*, I, 1 (p. 4): "An accident is that which exists in [another] thing"; Thomas Aquinas, *Quaestiones Quodlibetales*, Quodlibetum IX, Quaest. 3, Art. 5, Ad Secundum: "Substantia est quod per se est; vel, accidens est quod est in alio."

[4] Cf. below, Vol. II, pp. 193–194.

writing even as the *Elements* of Euclid, where every term and phrase and statement has been carefully thought out and chosen, where every variation from what we may with right consider his literary sources must be accounted for; and it is to prove the accuracy of this assumption that is the main burden of our present study.

The solution that would naturally suggest itself to the reader, and one which is generally assumed by students of the *Ethics*, is that Spinoza is following here not the mediaeval authorities but rather Descartes. It is sometimes argued that all the elements of Spinoza's conception of substance are to be found in Descartes, for Descartes, too, considered substance not only as something existing by itself but also as something conceived by itself.[1] However, the formal definition of substance given by Descartes in *Principia Philosophiae*, I, 51, to which Spinoza makes reference in his *Cogitata Metaphysica*, I, 1, describes substance only in terms of existing by itself, without any mention of its being also conceived by itself, though Erdmann, in his exposition of Descartes' definition of mode and substance, introduces from other sources the distinction between "per aliud concipiuntur" and "per se concipiuntur."[2]

Then also with regard to his use of the term "mode" instead of "accident," it may again be traced to Descartes. In fact Spinoza himself ascribes his division of Being into substance and mode to Descartes.[3] Still, while it is true that the term "mode" does occur in the passage of Descartes[4] referred to by Spinoza, Descartes himself uses the term "accident" as synonymous with "mode" and the opposite of "substance."[5]

[1] Cf. A. Léon, *Les Éléments Cartésiens de la Doctrine Spinoziste*, p. 85.
[2] Cf. *Grundriss der Geschichte der Philosophie*, II, § 267.4.
[3] *Cogitata Metaphysica*, II, 5. Cf. also I, 1.
[4] *Principia Philosophiae*, I, 48 and 49. Cf. also I, 56.
[5] *Meditationes*, III (*Oeuvres*, VII, p. 40, l. 15): "modos, sive accidentia."

Why then did Spinoza restrict himself in the *Ethics* to the use of the term "mode" after having used the term "accident" as the equivalent of "mode" in some of his other writings?[1] That his subsequent rejection of the term "accident" is not unpremeditated may be gathered from the following statement in the *Cogitata Metaphysica*, I, 1: "In regard to this, however, and I say it deliberately, I wish it to be noted that Being is divided into substance and modes and not into substance and accident."[2]

The solution of these difficulties, therefore, seems to lie in an entirely different direction. Spinoza, I think, was forced to introduce this additional element in his definition of substance not so much because he differed from the mediaevals in the definition of that term as because he differed from them in the definition of mode. As far as substance itself is concerned, Spinoza's definition, as we shall presently see, does not essentially differ from the mediaeval; he only restricts its application by firmly insisting upon its rigid logical meaning. It is only in his conception of modes that Spinoza strikes out a line of his own; his modes are entirely different from Aristotelian accidents, and it is mainly for this reason that he discards the use of that term, and completely alters its definition by omitting the term "subject." The thesis which I am going to sustain, therefore, is that Spinoza's definition of substance contains nothing new, that the additional element it contains was not unknown to the mediaevals, and that Spinoza introduced this additional element in order to round up his definition of substance so as to make

---

[1] Epistola 4. In *Short Treatise*, Appendix I, Axiom 1, the reading is either "toevallen" (*accidentia*) or "wijzen" (*modificationes*). See *Opera*, I, p. 114 and p. 603. Cf. G. T. Richter, *Spinozas philosophische Terminologie* (Leipzig, 1913), p. 85, n. 507.

[2] Locke, too, substituted the term "mode" for "accident" (cf. *Essay concerning Human Understanding*, II, 12, § 3; 13, § 19). Leibniz, in his criticism of Locke, however, tries to reinstate the term "accident" (cf. *Nouveaux Essais*, II, 13, § 19).

it read as the diametrical opposite of his entirely new definition of mode.

In mediaeval philosophy the definition of substance is immediately followed by the classification of substances. As to
the method by which the different classes of substances are
deduced, something will be said in another connection. Suffice it for the present that the mediaevals speak invariably
of four or five substances, including matter, form, concrete
object, soul, and the separate Intelligences[1] — a classification
which the reader will recognize as a composite view made
up of several statements made by Aristotle.[2] All these substances belong to a class of being which is termed "the possible of existence,"[3] with which is contrasted a single, unique
Being known as "the Necessary of Existence"[4] or God. The
relation between these two kinds of Being is that of cause
and effect. Now, generally speaking, it is the mediaeval
view that the Necessary of Existence or God cannot be called
substance, even though He is in himself, for God cannot be
subsumed with other things under a general term. Characteristic statements on this point are to be found in Algazali,[5] Asher Crescas,[6] and Moses ha-Lavi.[7] But while this view
is generally admitted, it is still maintained by Augustine,[8]

---

[1] Cf. *Maḳaṣid al-Falasifah*, II, i (p. 82); Shahrastani, ed. Cureton, p. 365; cf. my
Crescas' Critique of Aristotle, p. 575.

[2] Cf. *Metaphysics*, VII, 10, 1035a, 1, and *De Anima*, II, 1, 412a, 19.

[3] ممكن الوجود, אפשר המציאות.

[4] واجب الوجود, מחוייב המציאות. Cf. *Cogitata Metaphysica*, I, 1.

[5] *Maḳaṣid al-Falasifah*, II, ii (p. 144): "Eleventh, that of Him who is necessary
of existence, just as it cannot be said that He is an accident so it cannot be said that
He is a substance."

[6] Commentary on *Moreh Nebukim*, I, 57 (2): "But He is neither a substance nor
an accident."

[7] *Ma'amar Elohi*: "It has already been demonstrated that He who is necessary of existence does not come under the category of substance nor under any
of the other categories."

[8] *De Trinitate*, VI, 5 (Migne, *Patrologia Latina*, Vol. 42, Col. 928).

Gersonides,[1] and Descartes[2] that God can be called substance provided only that He is understood to be a substance unlike any other substance. Burgersdijck says explicitly that substance is divided into God and created being.[3]

In view of this application of the term "substance" to concrete objects, which must necessarily exist in some place, and to form, which must necessarily exist in matter, and to soul, which must reside in a body, a certain question naturally arises in our mind. If at least three of the so-called substances in the Aristotelian classification always exist in something else, what, then, did the mediaevals mean when they distinguished substance from accident as that which is in itself and that which is in something else? Why should the snub-nosedness of Socrates, for instance, be called accident, on account of the existance of the snubness in Socrates' nose, any more than Socrates' soul, which equally exists in his body? Or, why should the "redness" of a "red table" be called an accident, on account of its existence in a table, any more than the table itself, which must exist in some definite place, that is to say, in some other body? For this is the implication of space according to Aristotle's definition of the term.[4]

The mediaevals were not unaware of the first-mentioned difficulty, and they answered it as follows: An accident is said to exist in something else as in a "subject," and to exist in a subject means to exist in something without in any

---

[1] *Milḥamot Adonai*, III, 3 (p. 132): "You must know that there are certain attributes which must inevitably be attributed to God, as, for instance, the predication that God is substance, not that the term 'substance' is predicated of God and other beings as a common genus but it is predicated of them *secundum prius et posterius*." *Ibid.*, V, iii, 12 (p. 280): "It can also be shown that God is more truthfully to be called substance than is any other being."

[2] *Principia Philosophiae*, I, 51.

[3] *Institutiones Metaphysicae*, Lib. II, Cap. 1, Theor II: "Et substantiam divide subdividas in Deum et creaturam." Cf. quotation above p. 64, n. 2.

[4] *Physics*, IV, 4.

sense being the cause of the existence of that something. Incarnate soul, therefore, unlike snub-nosedness, is called substance because, while existing in the body, it is the cause of the body's life, and for this very same reason is form called substance, since it confers upon matter, in which it is, actual existence.[1]

I do not know whether the mediaevals have ever discussed directly the second difficulty we have raised, but we can easily answer it for them from their own point of view and out of their own statements. To say that a concrete object exists in something else, they would argue in the manner of Aristotle, may mean two things, either as a body exists in place or as a part exists in the whole.[2] Neither of these two kinds of existence in something else, however, makes a thing an accident, for in both these cases the thing might also exist without that something else. To exist in place, according to Aristotle's definition of place, means to exist in another body, from which the occupant might be removed, for one of the essential characteristics of place is that it must be external to the occupant.[3] Then, again, in the case of existing in the whole as a part, the part can be removed from the whole, if it is a discrete quantity; and the part will have to be a substance like the whole, if it is a continuous quantity. It is only when a thing exists in something else as in a subject, that is, when it cannot exist by itself without its subject, that it is called accident. The mediaevals could have found support for this distinction in the following passage of Aristotle: "I mean by a thing being in a subject (ὑποκείμενον) that which is in anything, not as a part, but so that it cannot exist separately from that in which it is."[4] The red

---

[1] Cf. my *Crescas' Critique of Aristotle*, p. 573, n. 9.

[2] *Physics*, IV, 3, 210a, 16 and 24; *Metaphysics*, V, 23, 1023a, 14–17.

[3] *Physics*, IV, 4, 211a, 1 ff.   [4] *Categories*, 2, 1a, 24–25.

table, therefore, is a substance, because it can exist without that particular place in which it happens to exist; the redness, however, is an accident, because, as that particular redness, it cannot exist without that particular table.

This is how, it appears to me, the mediaevals would have justified to their own satisfaction their formal distinction between substance and accident and their application of the term "substance" to concrete things. But I can see how Spinoza would have balked at such an explanation, and whoever has tried to approach the problems of philosophy by the same road as Spinoza, and to traverse the ground trod by that ex-pupil of the *Yeshibat 'Ez Ḥayyim* of Amsterdam, cannot help feeling that these were the problems that passed through his mind before he broke ground for the foundation of his new system. He would have argued against them somewhat as follows: It is true that concrete objects may be removed from the particular place in which they happen to be; still they cannot be removed from space in general. Everything in the universe must exist in space, which, as has been said before, means in another body. This is an Aristotelian principle which the mediaevals professed to follow. Aristotle says something to the effect that all things are in heaven (οὐρανῷ),[1] by which he does not mean the theological heaven to which martyrs and saints and others with proper introductions are admitted to enjoy a life of eternal bliss and beatitude. What he means is that the universe, which is finite, is all-surrounded by a sphere, which is the outermost of a series of concentric spheres, within which all things exist as in space. Consequently, if everything within the universe is thus within something else, namely, within the outermost sphere, and if a substance must be in itself, then nothing within the universe can be a substance. Or,

---

[1] Cf. *Physics*, IV, 2, 209a, 33; IV, 4, 211a, 24.

in other words, the red table can no more be a substance than the redness.

It is reasoning like this, if not exactly this very same reasoning, that must have led Spinoza to reject the mediaeval distinction between substance and accident, and the artificial distinction of existing in something else and existing in a subject. Everything that is in something else in any sense or manner, he seems to say, cannot be a substance. "That there is no such thing as a finite substance" is the starting point of his philosophy, and indeed it is the statement with which he begins his investigation of "What God Is," in his *Short Treatise*,[1] which is a kind of *Urethik*. It is a challenge hurled at all the mediaeval philosophers, ulema, rabbis, and schoolmen alike, for they were all nursed by the same mother and fed from the same source. It denies the application of the term "substance" to finite things within the universe. Thus in one of his Dialogues, Reason, addressing Desire, says: "What you say, O Desire, that there are different substances, that, I tell you, is false; for I see clearly that there is but One, which exists through itself, and is a support to all other attributes. And if you will refer to the material and the mental as substances, in relation to the modes which are dependent upon them, why then, you must also call them modes in relation to the substance on which they depend."[2] Note that he does not reject the generally accepted definition of substance; on the contrary, he insists upon its rigid application. Only that which is really and absolutely in itself can be called substance, and so only that which is called the Necessary of Existence or God can be truly called substance. All the other things which belong to the so-called possible of existence are not substances; they are what the mediaevals would have called accidents, but which Spinoza prefers to call by a new

[1] I, 2.   [2] *Short Treatise*, I, First Dialogue, § 9.

name, modes, seeing that they are not exactly what is generally meant by accident. He confines the term "accident" to one of its more specific usages, and distinguishes it from mode as follows: "For accident is nothing but a mode of thought and exists only in regard to this [whereas mode is a real being]. For example, when I say that a triangle is moved, the motion is a mode not of the triangle but of the body moved. Therefore, in respect to the triangle, motion is only an accident, but in respect to the body, it is real being or mode; for motion cannot be conceived without a body, but it may without a triangle." [1]

If our account of the processes of Spinoza's mind thus far is right, we can readily see how at this point, with his rejection of finite substances and with his restricting the term "substance" to God alone, Spinoza was confronted with a perplexing problem. How should he define those discarded substances which he has renamed modes? As for his real substance, he could very well retain the old definition, being in itself, for God indeed is in himself. But could he just as well say of mode that it is that which is in something else? Spinoza could have used that definition if he had retained Aristotle's conception of a finite universe, bounded from without by an all-surrounding sphere, for then indeed all modes would have been within something else. But believing as Spinoza did in an infinite universe he could not naturally speak of modes as existing in something else, by this meaning Aristotle's space. Nor, again, could he say that they existed in a "subject," for the term "subject" to him has no meaning at all. And yet, if substance is to be defined as that which exists in itself, mode will, of course, have to be defined as that which exists in something else. But what might that something else be if it is not space nor subject?

[1] *Cogitata Metaphysica*, I, 1.

If we were justified in penetrating thus far behind the uttered statements of Spinoza in unfolding the hidden arguments that lie beneath them, we may be allowed to proceed a little further with the same method and to go through the slow paces of this imaginary tentative reasoning of his until we arrive at a happy conclusion. We can clearly see how Spinoza, in his groping for a new differentiation between substance and mode, would at first strike upon the other sense in which, according to Aristotle, a thing is said to be in something else, namely, as a part in the whole.[1] Substance is thus the whole which exists in itself, whereas mode is the part which exists in something else. Here at last we have arrived at a term with which we so often meet in works on Spinoza. But to Spinoza's mind, steeped in mediaeval philosophic lore as it undoubtedly was and trained as it also was in its rigorous logical discipline, the term "whole" would need further explanation. For there are several kinds of wholes,[2] and which of these, he would ask himself, should he say is substance? The kind of whole that would probably first suggest itself to him as the most applicable in the case in question would be that of a physical quantitative whole, for if substance is simply the whole of the modes it is nothing but the universe, and the universe to Spinoza as to the mediaevals is something physical and quantitative. But such a conception of substance as merely the aggregate sum of the modes is contrary to all the uttered statements of Spinoza. To Spinoza's mediaeval mode of thinking the difficulty of such a conception of substance would appear in the following manner. A quantitative whole must be either discrete, consisting of heterogeneous parts, or continuous, consisting of homogeneous parts. Substance, however, could be neither

[1] Cf. *Physics*, IV, 3, 210a, 16. See also *Short Treatise*, I, First Dialogue.
[2] *Metaphysics*, V, 25.

of these. It could not be a discrete quantitative whole, because the modes, if their nature is to be judged by the two known modes, are each continuous. Even extension is continuous, for Spinoza was an Aristotelian, believing in the continuity of matter. He was no atomist, and for this we have ample evidence in his discussion of infinity.[1] As for the second alternative, there is nothing contradictory in itself in saying that substance is a continuous quantitative whole, for it is not impossible that Spinoza conceived a continuity between extension and thought. Still Spinoza would reject this conception. For if substance were only the aggregate sum of modes, how could one insist upon the unity and simplicity of substance without thereby declaring the differences between modes a mere illusion? To such a view Spinoza could by no means subscribe, for he was no mystic, no idealist of the kind to whom everything that kicks and knocks and resists is unreal. He was, many views to the contrary notwithstanding, a hard-headed, clear-minded empiricist, like most of the mediaevals and like Aristotle.

Spinoza will thus take a final step and declare that substance is a whole which exists over and above and beyond the sum of the modes, and saying this he will rest his case. This may sound alarming and tantalizing, and it may also appear as wholly inconsistent with what we have been accustomed to understand by Spinoza's repeated assertion that God is an immanent cause and not a transeunt cause. But we shall see in a subsequent chapter that the term "immanence" as used by Spinoza in its application to substance is not contradictory to the term "transcendence" in its original meaning of being more general. Quite the contrary, the immanence of Spinoza's substance is a transcendent immanence.[2] Spinoza's substance is thus a whole transcending

[1] See Epistola 12. Cf. below, Chapter VIII.   [2] Cf. below, pp. 323 ff.

the universe, the latter being the sum of the modes, and the relation of substance to the universe is conceived by him after the manner of the relation of the whole to the part, the whole in this particular case being a universal of a special kind, a real universal, as distinguished from the attributes which are only nominal universals.[1] By the same token, when Spinoza speaks of the modes as existing in another thing (*in alio*) he means that the modes, individually or in their aggregate totality, exist in substance in the same sense as when Aristotle says that "the finger is *in* the hand and generally the part *in* the whole,"[2] and that "man is *in* animal and generally species *in* genus."[3]

The term "universal," however, carries associations which would be only confusing in its use in connection with Spinoza. Aristotle himself would have simply spoken of genus and species.   In Arabic and Hebrew literature philosophers also speak of genus and species rather than of universals, though the latter term is not altogether unknown.[4] It is also significant that the famous passage in Porphyry's *Isagoge*[5] to which legendary history assigns the origin of the problem of universals, just as grammar-school readers assign to the falling apple the origin of Newton's laws of motion — even that passage speaks of genera and species rather than of universals.   Spinoza himself, though he makes use of the term "universal" quite frequently, says in one place: "Hence the fixed and eternal things . . . will be like universals to us, or, so to speak, the *genera* of the definitions of individual mutable things."[6]   We shall therefore use here the term "genus," and describe Spinoza's conception of the relation between

---

[1] Cf. below, pp. 327–328.

[2] *Physics*, IV, 3, 210a, 15–16.

[3] *Ibid.*, 210a, 18.

[4] *Moreh Nebukim*, I, 51.   [5] Ch. I.

[6] *Tractatus de Intellectus Emendatione*, § 101 (*Opera*, I, p. 37, ll. 5–8).

mode and substance as that between the individual essence and its genus.

We now come to the last step in our argument. In Aristotelian logic, universal terms like "genus" and "species" perform certain functions in the formation of concepts. They are the elements, or rather the causes, in the terms of which the individual essence of a thing, the "what" of it, can be conceived. They form its definition. Man is thus conceived through his genus "animal" and his species "rational," and he is thus also defined by the combination of these two terms. And so everything that is in something else, as an individual in its genus, may be thus said to be conceived by that something else. This is what Spinoza means by his definition of mode as "that which is in another thing through which also it is conceived"; that is to say, it is in another thing in the sense that it is conceived through it, namely, as the individual in its genus. Substance, on the contrary, "is in itself" absolutely, and "is conceived through itself," inasmuch as it is a *summum genus*. But to be conceived through itself is really a negation. It does not mean anything positively. All it means is that it cannot be conceived through anything else. This is the significance of Axiom II, which reads: "That which cannot be conceived through another must be conceived through itself." The emphasis is that to be conceived through itself merely means not to be conceived through something else. The implication therefore is that Spinoza's substance is inconceivable, and its essence undefinable and hence unknowable.[1]

Thus the mediaeval definition of the term "substance" has not undergone any change in Spinoza, though its application was restricted only to God. It is still defined as that which is in itself. Even the additional fact of its being a

[1] Cf. below, p. 142.

summum genus, undefinable and unknowable, is not new; it is a mediaeval commonplace. That unique substance, God, was thus conceived throughout the Middle Ages among rational theologians. Says Maimonides, and he by no means stands alone in the views he is about to utter, for passages like these can be gathered at random from many a book: "There is no possibility of obtaining a knowledge of the essence of God." [1] Again he says: "The object is described by its definition, as, for example, man is described as a being that lives and has reason. . . . All agree that this kind of description cannot be given of God; for there are no previous causes to His existence, by which He could be defined: and on that account it is a well-known principle, accepted by all philosophers, who are precise in their statements, that no definition can be given of God." [2]

That the something else in which the modes are is substance and that mode is related to substance as the individual essence to its genus is clearly set forth by Spinoza in Proposition I. The proposition affirms the priority of substance to its affections, i.e. modes,[3] which is a truly Aristotelian principle, for the genus, according to him, is prior to, and better known than, the individual.[4] But of particular interest is the expression "prior in nature" (*prior est natura*) used by Spinoza. In Aristotle, the expression "prior in nature" (πρότερον τῇ φύσει) is used in two senses: first, in the sense of better and more excellent, and second, in the sense of being the cause of something.[5] In the latter sense it is very often used in Arabic and Hebrew as well as in Latin philosophic literature. But we find that the expression has acquired in the Middle Ages an additional meaning, namely, as the more universal

---

[1] *Moreh Nebukim*, I, 59.　　　　[2] *Ibid.*, I, 52.
[3] Cf. below, Vol. II, pp. 193–194.　　[4] *Topics*, VI, 4, 141a, 26 ff.
[5] *Categories*, 12, 14b, 4 ff.

to the less universal, as, for example, animality is prior in nature to humanity.[1] This seems to be nothing but a legitimate extension of its use in the sense of "cause," for the genus is considered by Aristotle as the cause of the individual essence.[2] Or it may also reflect Aristotle's statement that the whole is prior in nature to the parts.[3] Spinoza thus rightly says that "substance is prior in its nature to its affections" (Prop. I).

[1] *Maḳaṣid al-Falasifah*, II, i (p. 119): "With regard to [prior] in nature, as when we say, for instance, animality is prior to humanity."

Millot ha-Higgayon, Ch. 12: "Second, prior in nature, as, for instance, animal is prior to man."

Ruaḥ Ḥen, Ch. 8: "In the same way you say that animals are prior in nature to the human species."

Duns Scotus, *Quaestiones in Quatuor Libros Sententiarum*, Lib. II, Dist. I, Quaest. 2, No. 3: "Hic dicit Doctor quod *prius natura* potest dupliciter accipi. Primo positive . . . sicut est de animali et rationali in homine, quia prius natura positive animal præcedit rationale."

[2] *Analytica Posteriora*, II, 2, 90a, 31.

[3] *Politics*, I, 2, 1253a, 19–20.

CHAPTER IV

UNITY OF SUBSTANCE

I

IN HIS definition of substance we have seen how Spinoza, reasoning from the mediaeval definition of the term, has arrived at the conclusion that conditional being can in no sense whatever be called substance. The term is to be applied only to Necessary Being, or God. With this as a starting point, Spinoza now proceeds, in the First Part of the *Ethics*, to describe the properties of substance, beginning in Propositions II–VI with a discussion of its unity, which in manner of treatment, as we shall endeavor to show, runs along the line of the mediaeval discussions of the unity of God.

It is philosophic dualism of which Spinoza's discussion of the unity of substance is aimed to be a refutation, just as theological dualism was the target of mediaeval discussions of the unity of God. The philosophy against which Spinoza took the field, starting with the Aristotelian distinction of matter and form, passed through a hierarchy of beings until it ultimately arrived, again like Aristotle, at a being, unique and absolute, who is pure form. In this philosophy, it may be said, there is to be discerned a twofold dualism. Not only did it posit in the world itself a duality of matter and form, or, as it was better known in the fashionable philosophy of Spinoza's own time, of extension and thought, but it also maintained the duality of a material, multifarious, changeable world and an immaterial, simple, immutable God, who is pure form, whose essence is thought, and whose activity is thinking. Matter and form, in the traditional terminology.

are two substances, which combined form all concrete beings, which are also called substances; and by the extension of the term "substance," for which he had several precedents,[1] Spinoza speaks of the mediaeval contrast between God and the world again as a contrast between two substances. It is upon this latter phase of dualism, the existence of an immaterial God over against a material world, that Spinoza is warring whenever we find him contending against the existence of two substances, in the *Ethics* as well as in the *Short Treatise*.

The object of Spinoza's criticism of this kind of dualism is not to abolish the materiality of the world, but rather to abolish the immateriality of God. He will endeavor to show that the assumption of an absolutely immaterial God is incompatible with the relation which the mediaevals assumed to obtain between God and the world, namely that of cause and effect. He will thus introduce into his discussion of the unity of substance the problem of creation — the first serious problem, it might be said, which the mediaeval religious thinkers encountered when they attempted to identify the Aristotelian pure form, a mere logical concept, with the personal God of tradition, and to use it as a working hypothesis to explain the origin of a created world as well as its governance. The difficulties of the theory of creation, of which the mediaevals were not unaware, were many and varied, all arising out of the conception of God as an immaterial, simple, and immutable being, combined with the Neoplatonic principle that "a simple element can produce only a simple thing." [2] Spinoza will hardly bring out new difficulties which have not already been thought of and fully discussed and answered by the mediaevals themselves, but he will insist that their answers are a kind of special pleading

---

[1] See above, pp. 67–68.   [2] *Moreh Nebukim*, II, 22.

which really does not solve the problem. Had the *Ethics* been written *more scholastico rabbinicoque*, Spinoza would have prefaced his argument in Propositions II–VI with words to the following effect: We shall now proceed to demonstrate that there is no God distinguished from the world after the manner of two substances, one spiritual and the other material. For to posit such a God would involve us in all the difficulties which you have yourselves noticed in the problem of creation, and from which, despite all your efforts, you have not been able to extricate yourselves completely. We shall see that, even in their present form, these five propositions contain a clear-cut, single, consecutive argument which in its external, logical outline is modelled after the mediaeval reasoning against the hypothesis of two deities and which substantially embodies the principal mediaeval arguments against creation.

To the mind of Spinoza, it would seem, the widely scattered mediaeval discussions of the problem of the unity of God [1] presented themselves in the form of a hypothetico-disjunctive syllogism. If there were two gods, either they would have to be absolutely unrelated to each other or there would have to be some kind of relation between them. He could clearly see why the mediaevals would have rejected both these alternatives as untenable. Two unrelated gods would imply the existence of two independent worlds, for in one world there could be no adequate division of labor between them; and two unrelated gods would contradict the very conception of God as something absolutely unrelated. To

---

[1] Spinoza discusses the problem of the unity of God directly in *Cogitata Metaphysica*, II, 2. He reproduces there two arguments which he characterizes as futile. Both these arguments are taken directly from Burgerdijck's *Institutiones Metaphysicae*, Lib. I, Cap. VI, but are also found in *Emunot we-De'ot*, II, 1 and 2, and in *Ḥobot ha-Lebabot*, I, 7, First and Third Arguments. Cf. Freudenthal, "Spinoza und die Scholastik," in *Philosophische Aufsätze, Eduard Zeller . . . gewidmet*, p. 111.

assume such a formulation of the problem in the mind of Spinoza is nothing but to rearrange the mediaeval discussions and weld them into one composite argument.

God to the mediaevals meant the God of a world. Their conception of God, which was the hybrid product of the joining together of the Aristotelian logical principle of prime mover, or first cause, with the Biblical ethical teaching of a creator and supreme ruler, has derived from both these sources its main characteristic feature as that of cause and creator. A cause and creator, however these terms may have become attenuated, must of necessity be the cause and creator of something. God's thinking, which constitutes His sole activity, must either by necessity or by design objectify itself in a world at a certain stage in the process of emanation. An idle, quiescent, passive God, a God who has no world to operate upon, would be an impotent God and an object of commiseration and pity, as the hero of Chamisso's story who was without a shadow. It therefore follows that, granting two absolutely independent deities, there would have to be two absolutely independent worlds. But the existence of more than one world was generally agreed to be impossible. For this there was the overwhelming authority of Aristotle, who with an impressive array of arguments had shown in the latter part of the First Book of *De Caelo* (Chs. VIII–IX) that the existence of many worlds was impossible. It would thus be necessary first to establish the possibility of many worlds before it could be assumed that there was more than one God; and, in fact, Crescas, in his attempt to expose the flimsiness of the philosophic proofs for the unity of God, attacks the problem from that very angle, showing that the existence of more than one world is not impossible.[1]

---

[1] *Or Adonai*, I, ii, 15 and 19. Cf. my *Crescas' Critique of Aristotle*, p. 217 and pp. 472 ff., n. 127.

Since there must be only one world, within that only world, the argument would proceed, two absolutely independent and absolutely unrelated deities could not be conceived to exist and at the same time be active. "A duality could only be imagined in this way, either that at one time the one deity is active, the other at another time, or that both act simultaneously, nothing being done except by both together." [1] But either of these arrangements would be inconsistent with the absolute independence and omnipotence and self-sufficiency of the deities. To say that the two deities act each independently in their own spheres is likewise impossible, for "the whole existing world is one organic body, all parts of which are connected together. . . . Hence it is impossible to assume that one deity is engaged in forming one part, and another deity in forming another part, of that organic body of which all parts are closely connected together." [2] Here, again, Crescas tries to disprove the philosophic proof for unity by suggesting a possibility, with what success does not concern us here, of an adequate division of labor between two gods within this organic world.[3]

If two absolutely mutually independent deities are impossible, the mediaevals would then consider the case of two deities having something in common. Such deities, however, could not properly be called two unless in addition to their possessing something in common they also possessed something in which they differed. But what would that something be in which they differed? Usually in things which are said to have something in common and something in which they differ the identity implied is that of a common genus and the diversity is that of a specific difference, or the identity is that of a common species and the diversity is that of an individual difference, such as accidental qualities. It is for

---

[1] *Moreh Nebukim*, II, 1.   [2] *Ibid.*
[3] *Or Adonai*, I, ii, 19.

this reason that bodiless spiritual beings, between which there is no generic or specific or individual difference, cannot be counted. "Whatsoever is not a body does not admit of the idea of number except it be a force in a body, for then the individual forces may be numbered together with the matters or subjects in which they exist."[1] If two deities therefore existed, having something in common and something in which they differed, they would have to possess the metaphysical distinction of genus and species, or, still worse, they would have to possess physical qualities. Both these are contrary to the very nature of God, who must be absolutely simple and indivisible. The argument is stated as follows: "We say to him who believes that there is more than one God that the essence of the two gods must inevitably be one or more than one. If he says the essence is one, then the thing is one, and there is not more than one Creator; and if he says that the essence of the one deity is unlike that of the other, then it would be necessary to posit a certain difference between them.[2]

There is only one way, the mediaevals would conclude, in which purely immaterial beings can be counted, and that is when they are related to each other as cause and effect. Such is the case of the Intelligences which preside over the spheres. Though immaterial, still they are numbered, their number corresponding to that of the spheres.[3] The basis for their number, according to the view held by Avicenna, is that in the process of emanation they proceed in succession from one another, thus being the cause of one another. "It follows, therefore, that separate beings, which are neither bodies nor forces in bodies, do not admit of any idea of number except

[1] *Moreh Nebukim*, II, Introduction, Prop. 16.
[2] *Ḥobot ha-Lebabot*, I, 7 (4). Cf. *Emunot we-De'ot*, II, 2, and *Moreh Nebukim*, II, 1, and I, 75 (2).
[3] See *Moreh Nebukim*, II, 4.

when they are related to each other as cause and effect." [1]
Number in this sense, however, could not be applied to two
deities. If two deities were postulated to exist, they could
not bear to each other the relation of cause and effect, one
being produced by the other, for that would run counter to
the very conception of God as an uncaused being. "The
hypothesis that there exist two gods is inadmissible, because absolutely incorporeal beings cannot be counted, except as cause and effect." [2]

This then is the mediaeval argument against a duality of
gods as we assume it was formulated in Spinoza's mind.
It begins with the alternative that two deities either would
have to be absolutely different from each other or would have
to have something in common. Showing the impossibility of
the first alternative, it proceeds to reason against the second
alternative by pointing out that if two gods were not absolutely different from each other they would have to be absolutely the same, inasmuch as their natures could not be
divided by being partly different and partly the same. Nor,
having the same nature, could they be differentiated by
their relation to each other as cause and effect. Within this
framework Spinoza's five propositions arrange themselves
in logical order, forming the following consecutive argument:

There are no two substances, that is to say, an immaterial
God and a material world, for if there were, the following
two alternatives would be inevitable:

A. God would be absolutely different from the world, and
hence have nothing in common with it, for "two substances
having different attributes have nothing in common with
one another" (Prop. II). But then,

(1) There could be no causal relation between God and

---

[1] *Ibid.*, II, Introduction, Prop. 16.
[2] *Ibid.*, II, 1, First Proof.

the world, for "If two things have nothing in common with one another, one cannot be the cause of the other" (Prop. III).

B. Or, God and the world would not be absolutely different, but then, God and the world would have to be absolutely the same, for the following reasons:

(1) Things are said to be two only when they differ in essential or accidental qualities, for "two or more distinct things are distinguished from one another, either by the difference of the attributes of the substances, or by the difference of their affections" (Prop. IV).

(2) Consequently, if God and the world were of the same nature and differed neither in accidental nor in essential qualities, they could not be called two, for "in nature there cannot be two or more substances of the same nature or attribute" (Prop. V).

(3) To say that God and the world would differ in so far as one is the cause of the other is impossible, for "one substance cannot be produced by another substance" (Prop. VI).

The logical order of these propositions and their syllogistic form is thus quite apparent. But we must clothe this bare, skeleton-like outline with a body, in order to give to the propositions meaning and weight. Spinoza does not manipulate his terms according to certain rules of the game, as if they were pawns on the chess-board, for the mere pleasure of the play. There is always some concrete application in his reasoning. His propositions and their proofs, whenever they are not an interpretation of facts of nature, are to be taken as a criticism of the philosophy upon which he was nurtured.

Proposition II contains Spinoza's restatement of the me-

diaeval view concerning the distinction between God and
the world. The essence of God, according to this view, is so
different from the essence of the world that no attribute can
be predicated of them in the same, or in any related, sense.
All terms used in describing the divine nature are to be taken
as homonymous terms, none of them having the meaning
with which it is associated in our mind, and none of them con-
veying to our mind any direct knowledge of the divine nature,
which must always remain unknowable and ineffable. When
the mediaevals speak of a knowing God or a living God they
do not mean to attribute to God a kind of knowledge or
life which he shares in common with other beings, for knowledge and life in their application to God must have an absolutely different and unique meaning. "When they ascribe
to God essential attributes, these so-called essential attributes should not have any similarity to the attributes of
other things, and should according to their own opinion not
be included in one and the same definition, just as there is
no similarity between the essence of God and that of other
beings."[1] Again, "this is a decisive proof that there is, in
no way or sense, anything common to the attributes predicated of God, and those used in reference to ourselves; they
have only the same names, and nothing else is common to
them."[2] Referring to this view, Spinoza says: "Two substances having different attributes have nothing in common
with one another" (Prop. II) — that is to say, when the
same attributes, predicated of two substances, are homonymous terms, used in absolutely different and unrelated senses,
the predication of these attributes does not imply any real
relationship in the essence of the two substances. The term
attributa in this proposition should be taken simply in the
sense of predicates, which, as will be shown in another

---

[1] *Moreh Nebukim*, I, 56.   [2] *Ibid.*

chapter, is one of the senses in which the term is used by Spinoza.[1]

The refutation of this view is given in Proposition III. Spinoza seems to be challenging the mediaevals in the following words: If you say that the divine nature is absolutely different from the nature of the world, how then can you interpret your traditional creation, as most of you do, in terms of emanation and call your creative God an emanative cause?

The theory of emanation maintains that the entire universe with all its manifold finite beings is the unfolding of the infinite divine nature, the product of its thinking. There is nothing in the universe which is not involved in the nature of God, and nothing happens in the universe which does not emanate from Him. "Inasmuch as it has been demonstrated that God is incorporeal and has also been established that the universe is His work and that He is its efficient cause. . . . We say that the universe has been created by divine emanation and that God is the emanative cause of everything that comes into being within it."[2] It is for this reason that God is said to know particulars by virtue of His knowledge of himself;[3] it is also for this reason that it is said that by our contemplation upon the nature of the universe we may arrive at the knowledge of the nature of God.[4] This kind of relation which God is said to bear to the world is a causal relation of a particular kind, unlike the causal relation of corporeal agents to the objects upon which they operate. It is called emanative causation. "Inasmuch as the actions of the purely incorporeal Intelligence are clearly manifest in the world, and they are especially manifest in every case of

[1] Cf. below, p. 228.

[2] *Moreh Nebukim*, II, 12

[3] See *Milḥamot Adonai*, III, 4 (p. 138), and *Or Adonai*, II, 1, 4 (p. 32b). Cf. below, Vol. II, p. 14.

[4] See *Ḥobot ha-Lebabot*, II, 1 ff.

change that does not originate in the mere combination of elements, we cannot escape the conclusion that this agent, not being corporeal, does not act by impact nor at a certain definite distance. The action of the incorporeal Intelligence is always termed emanation, on account of its similarity to a water-spring." [1]

This principle of emanation, which was primarily introduced to obviate the difficulty of how an incorporeal agent could act upon a corporeal object, was found to be insufficient even in the eyes of the mediaevals, whose strictures upon this point will be quoted later. Even after interposing a series of immaterial intermediaries between God and the world, they were still harassed by the question how could matter ultimately arise if it were not to be found originally in the nature of God. One of the solutions offered is that God as the emanative cause of the universe does not act by necessity but by volition, and consequently all variety in nature, due to the existence of matter, as well as matter itself, is to be attributed to the design and determination of God. [2]

The principal points in this mediaeval view, so far as we are here concerned, are three. God is the emanative cause of the world, with all that it implies. But God is immaterial, and how could a material world emanate from Him? The answer is that God acts by volition and design.

In opposition to this, Spinoza denies the immateriality of God as well as will and design in His action. He does not hesitate to speak of God as the cause of the world, but he insists that the causality must be mechanical and not intentional. As against those "who think that God is a free cause," and that He creates "by a certain absolute will," he argues that "I think that I have shown with sufficient clearness

[1] *Moreh Nebukim,* II, 12.
[2] *Ibid.,* II, 22.

(Prop. XVI) that from the supreme power of God, or from His infinite nature, infinite things in infinite ways, that is to say all things, have necessarily flowed, or continually follow by the same necessity, in the same way as it follows from the nature of a triangle, from eternity and to eternity, that its three angles are equal to two right angles." [1] This conception of God as a necessary cause is laid down by Spinoza in Axioms III, IV, and V, at the beginning of *Ethics*, I. The term "cause" which occurs in these axioms is to be taken as referring specifically to God, or substance, in its relation to the world. In Axiom III, he affirms that God acts by necessity: "From a given determinate cause an effect necessarily follows." Since God acts by necessity and not by volition, there is nothing in the nature of the world that is not in the nature of God; the two must be mutually implicative. "The knowledge of an effect depends upon and involves the knowledge of the cause" (Axiom IV), for "those things which have nothing mutually in common with one another cannot through one another be mutually understood, that is to say, the conception of the one does not involve the conception of the other" (Axiom V). Starting, therefore, with his own premise that God acts by necessity, he argues against the mediaevals that if God's nature be essentially different from the nature of the world, He could not be the cause of the world, for "if two things have nothing in common with one another, one cannot be the cause of the other" (Prop. III). In an earlier version of the same Proposition, the argument is stated more directly: "That which has not in itself something of another thing, can also not be a cause of the existence of such another thing" [2] — that is to say, if God is immaterial, He cannot be the cause of a material world.

[1] *Ethics*, I, Prop. 17, Schol.
[2] *Short Treatise*, Appendix I, Axiom 5.

Spinoza, however, knew that by this he had not yet fully succeeded in reducing his opponents to silence. To tell them that God could not be the cause of the material world, if He were assumed to be immaterial, would only evoke the reply that it was just to meet this difficulty that emanation was introduced to take the place of direct creation. God as the direct cause of matter would indeed be impossible. But emanation claims only that God is the cause of a single Intelligence, a purely spiritual being, as devoid of matter as God himself. It is this pure spirit of which God is the cause; and matter proceeds not directly from God but from the Intelligences. "In accordance with this axiom, Aristotle holds that the direct emanation from God must be one simple Intelligence, and nothing else." [1] Again, "from the Necessary Existent only one thing can proceed without an intermediary, but many things can proceed from Him by order of succession and through intermediaries." [2] Reduced to Spinoza's terminology, it may be said that there are two substances, namely, God and the first Intelligence, who are related to each other as cause and effect. Why should that be impossible?

The answer to this is to be found in Propositions IV, V, and VI, in which Spinoza will endeavor to show that the interposition of incorporeal intermediaries was merely a makeshift and did not really solve the problem how a purely spiritual God could produce a material world.

To begin with, Spinoza repeats the question raised with respect to the hypothesis of two deities, namely, by virtue of what could God and the first Intelligence be called two? In order to be susceptive of number, things must be distinguished either as separate substances or as separate modes;

---

[1] *Moreh Nebukim*, II, 22.
[2] *Maḳaṣid al-Falasifah*, II, ii, 10 (p. 143).

or, to put it in the words used by Spinoza elsewhere, the distinction between them must be either *realis* or *modalis*,[1] for extramental being, that is, real being (*ens reale*), as distinguished from fictitious being (*ens fictum*) and being of reason (*ens rationis*),[2] must be either substance or mode. Hence Proposition IV: "Two or more distinct things are distinguished from one another, either by the difference of the attributes of the substances, or by the difference of their affections."

Continuing this line of reasoning, he endeavors to prove that the first Intelligence, in the mediaeval theory, could not be distinguished from God and still have something in common with Him, but that the two would have to be either absolutely different or absolutely identical.

God and the first Intelligence, he argues, could not be said to be distinguished from each other *realiter* by differing only in part of their nature, that is to say, by their having something in common and something in which they differed. For since God is the highest genus, He could not share anything in common with any other being, as that would constitute His genus. If God is therefore to be distinguished from the first Intelligence *realiter*, He will have to differ from the latter in His entire nature, having no attribute in common with it. Spinoza thus says: "If they are distinguished only by difference of attributes, it will be granted that there is but one substance of the same attribute (Prop. V, Demonst.). God and the first Intelligence would therefore have to be absolutely different from each other.

Still less could it be said that God and the first Intelligence differed in accidental qualities. Spinoza does not attempt to refute this on the ground that the mediaeval immaterial God

---

[1] *Short Treatise*, Appendix I, Prop. 1, Demonst.
[2] Cf. *Cogitata Metaphysica*, I, 1. Cf. below, p. 161.

and pure Intelligences could not possess qualities which are
accidental to matter. He knew quite well that for the mediaevals that would form no obstacle. They could interpret
these qualities attributed to God and the Intelligences in
the same way as they interpreted the divine attributes,
namely, either as external relations,[1] or as actions and negations.[2] He attacks it, however, from another angle. He seems
to say to his imaginary opponents: However you would take
these qualities, as relations, actions, or negations, you would
have to admit that they are something external; that they
are distinctions existing only in relation to our own mind, and
in no way affecting the nature of God and the Intelligence. In
their own nature and essence, therefore, God and the Intelligence would be identical and hence one. To quote him:
"But if they are distinguished by difference of affections,
since substance is prior by nature to its affections (Prop. I),
the affections therefore being placed on one side, and the
substance being considered in itself, or, in other words (Def. 3
and Ax. 6), truly considered, it cannot be conceived as distinguished from another substance" (Prop. V, Demonst.).

The upshot of this is that God and the first Intelligence
would have to be either absolutely different or absolutely
identical, inasmuch as "in nature there cannot be two or
more substances of the same nature or attribute" (Prop. V).

Spinoza would have been quite satisfied, on mere logical
grounds, in assuming that God and the first Intelligence are
of absolutely the same nature and are to be distinguished
only in so far as the former is related to the latter as cause
to effect. But he would insist that this identity would mean
that both God and the Intelligence must be material; that
is to say, they must have extension as one of their attributes.

---

[1] Cf. *Cuzari*, II, 1, and *Emunah Ramah*, II, iii.
[2] Cf. *Moreh Nebukim*, I, 52 and 58. Cf. below, pp. 143–144.

His own view, as we shall see,[1] is only a modified form of such a doctrine. But the mediaeval thinkers were far from acknowledging such an identity. They were all agreed on the absolute immateriality of God, though there was some difference of opinion as to the immateriality of the Intelligences. Matter makes its first appearance in the Intelligences themselves, according to those who like Ibn Gabirol held the Intelligences to be material, or it arises from the particular nature of the Intelligences, according to those who believed that while the Intelligences are immaterial they possess in their nature a certain possibility which ultimately gives rise to matter. In either case, they all consider God to be different from the Intelligences; and still they all agree that God is the cause of the Intelligences. The difficulty raised by Spinoza in Proposition III thus occurs again, and is restated by him in Proposition VI: "One substance cannot be produced by another."

Proposition VI, as will have been noticed, is a repetition of Proposition III, and in fact its demonstration is based upon the latter proposition. Likewise the second demonstration of the Corollary of Proposition VI is a reproduction of the demonstration of Proposition III. Furthermore, in a letter from Oldenburg (Epistola III), as well as in Appendix I to the *Short Treatise*, the equivalents of Proposition III are given as axioms upon which the equivalents of Proposition VI are based as propositions. That both these should occur in the *Ethics* as propositions would seem to need some explanation. However, in the light of the logical outline in which we have shown these propositions to be connected, there is ample justification for this seemingly useless repetition.

Our discussion of these five propositions may be brought

[1] Cf. below, pp. 218 ff.

to a conclusion by the following remark on the Corollary in Proposition VI. The Corollary begins with the statement, "Hence it follows that there is nothing by which substance can be produced" ("Hinc sequitur substantiam ab alio produci non posse"), and ends with a similar statement, "Therefore absolutely there is nothing by which substance can be produced" ("Ergo substantia absolute ab alio produci non potest"). In *Short Treatise*, I, 2, the proof of the third proposition, "that one substance cannot produce another," which is the same as Proposition VI in *Ethics*, I, is given as follows: "Should any one again maintain the opposite, we ask whether the cause, which is supposed to produce this substance, has or has not the same attributes as the produced [substance]. The latter is impossible, because something cannot come from nothing." Similarly in the proof of the first proposition given in the foot-note in the same chapter of the *Short Treatise* it is said that, if there were a finite substance, "it would necessarily have something which it would have from nothing." Likewise in Epistola IV to Oldenburg Spinoza produces Proposition III, which he proves as follows: "Nam quum nihil sit in effectu commune cum causa, totum, quod haberet, haberet a nihilo." In the light of all these passages, the conclusion of the Corollary here may be interpreted to mean as follows: Therefore, if substance could be absolutely produced, it would have to be produced from nothing (Ergo, si substantia absolute produci posset, a nihilo deberet produci). The main point of the Corollary would thus be to show that if the material world were produced by an immaterial God, something would be produced from nothing. The force of this argument as well as its historical background will be dealt with in the second part of this chapter, in the discussion of the *Short Treatise*, to which we now turn.

II

The second chapter of the First Part of the *Short Treatise*, which bears the title "What God Is," is again, like Propositions II–VI of the *Ethics*, I, a criticism of mediaeval dualism. Our comments upon this chapter will therefore occasionally have to dwell upon matters which have already been dealt with in our discussion of the *Ethics*. Whenever such a repetition occurs, it is to be excused on the ground that it could not be avoided, unless we preferred to be economical at the expense of clearness and completeness.

Mediaeval dualism considers God as something essentially different from the world. God is pure form; the world is material. As a corollary of this, the world is conceived to have all the imperfections of which God as pure spirit is free. The world is furthermore the creation of God; the world is thus called conditional being whereas God is absolute being. Since creation is assumed to be in time, the world is still further contrasted with God as the created substance with the uncreated substance [1] or as the temporal with the eternal. The creation of the world was not by a single act but rather by a process of emanation. Matter did not come directly from God; it has made its appearance at a certain stage in the devolution of the issue of divine thought. God is pure thought, and His only activity is thinking. But as His thinking is a creative power, it becomes objectified in a thought, known as Intelligence, which, while immaterial like God himself, according to one of the prevailing views, [2] is of a less perfect order, inasmuch as by its nature it is only a possible being, having a cause for its existence. The thought of this Intelligence, which is said to possess a dual

[1] Cf. "de substantia increata, sive de Deo" in *Cogitata Metaphysica*, I, 2.
[2] Cf. above, p. 91, and below, p. 223.

nature, objectifies itself in another Intelligence and a sphere. So the process goes on until at a certain stage crass matter appears which is the basis of the sublunar world. The world thus possesses imperfections which are not found in the original thinking essence of God.

In the language of Spinoza these mediaeval contrasts between God and the world are expressed in the phrases "infinite substance" and "finite substance." It is Spinoza's purpose in his discussion of "What God Is" to abolish this dualism between the thinking essence of God and the material, or extended, essence of the world, to identify God with the wholeness of nature, and to conclude "that we posit extension as an attribute of God."[1] He begins in the first proposition by denying the old conception of a hierarchy of substances falling into a general division of spiritual and material substances, or infinite and finite, asserting "that there is no finite substance; but that every substance must be infinitely perfect in its kind."[2] If the mediaevals therefore are pleased to speak of the world as an emanation of the divine thinking essence, that divine thinking essence must contain the material element of which the world is made, "that is to say, that in the infinite understanding no substance can be more perfect than that which already exists in nature."[3]

Spinoza proves this proposition by the method employed by him elsewhere,[4] *ex absurdo contradictorio*, for "should any one want to maintain the opposite, we would ask the following question." Suppose, he says, God is a purely immaterial being and beside Him there is a material created substance. The question would then be raised: how did this material

[1] *Short Treatise*, I, 2, § 18 (*Opera*, I, p. 24, l. 11).
[2] *Ibid.*, § 2 (p. 19, ll. 9 ff.).   [3] *Ibid.* (p. 20, ll. 6–7).
[4] Cf. below, pp. 183, 378.

world come into being? You would have to resort to the various theories of creation offered by the mediaevals. But none of these is free from insurmountable difficulties. And hereupon Spinoza proceeds to discuss some of the difficulties of creation and their attempted solutions by the mediaevals.

In the classic writings of Jewish philosophers the discussion of the problem of creation opens with a consideration of the Epicurean theory of a world having a beginning in time but without necessarily having come into existence through a God. Says Saadia: "After it had become perfectly clear to me that all things are created, I began to inquire whether they could have been produced by themselves or whether they could not have been produced except by some agent not themselves." [1] Says also Baḥya: "The propositions by which may be proved that the world has a creator by whom it has been created from nothing are three: First, a thing cannot produce itself. . . . For anything coming into existence after it has been without existence must inevitably satisfy either one of these conditions — either it has come into existence through itself or it has come into existence through a cause not itself." [2] Similar allusions to a theory of creation through itself, or what is better known as creation by chance,[3] abound also in the writings of Maimonides,[4] Gersonides,[5] and Crescas.[6] Descartes, too, formulates the problem of creation in the form of a disjunctive proposition: "But it seems to me to be self-evident that everything that exists springs from a cause or from itself considered as a cause." [7]

Following his masters, Spinoza similarly begins his in-

---

[1] *Emunot we-De'ot*, I, 2.   [2] *Ḥobot ha-Lebabot*, I, 5.
[3] Cf. below, p. 318.
[4] *Moreh Nebukim*, II, 13 and 20.
[5] *Milḥamot Adonai*, VI, i, 6.
[6] *Or Adonai*, III, i, 3 (p. 63b).
[7] *Primae Responsiones* (*Oeuvres*, VII, p. 112, ll. 3–5).

quiry by asking "whether this substance is finite through itself . . . or whether it is thus finite through its cause." [1]

Spinoza's refutation of this first alternative is found in two versions, one given in the text and the other in the footnote. The latter is not much unlike the refutation given by Saadia. It reads as follows: "It could not have done so itself, because having been infinite it would have had to change its whole essence." [2] The following is Saadia's answer: "If we take any of the existent things and assume it to have made itself, we know that after its coming into existence it must possess a still greater power and ability to create something like itself. If it could therefore produce itself when it was weak and in a state of non-existence, it should be able to produce something like itself after it has become powerful and attained a state of existence. Seeing, however, that it cannot produce something like itself when it is powerful, certainly it could not have produced itself when it was weak." [3] The underlying assumption in both these refutations is that the substance, having made itself, could not so change its nature as to become less powerful or less infinite than before it has made itself. It is somewhat like the following argument quoted from Suarez by those who objected against Descartes: "If anything is self-derived and does not issue from a cause, it is necessarily unlimited and infinite." [4]

Thus disposing of creation through itself, Spinoza takes up the second alternative suggested by the mediaevals, namely, that "it is made finite by its cause, which is necessarily God." [5] Against this alternative Spinoza raises three objections, one of which is found both in the text and in the

[1] *Short Treatise*, I, 2, § 3 (*Opera*, I, p. 20, ll. 11–13).
[2] *Ibid.*, § 2, note 2 (p. 19, ll. 20–21).
[3] *Emunot we-De'ot*, I, 2.
[4] *Primae Objectiones* (*Oeuvres*, VII, p. 95, ll. 16–18).
[5] *Short Treatise*, I, 2, § 4 (*Opera*, I, p. 20, ll. 17–18).

foot-notes; the other two are given only in the foot-notes. It is my purpose to show that these arguments are directed against mediaeval attempts to remove two great difficulties with regard to the theory of creation, and furthermore to show that Spinoza's arguments themselves are taken from the mediaeval discussions.

One of the difficulties about creation in time which the mediaevals grappled with is its obvious inconsistency with the omnipotence and immutability of God, or, as Maimonides puts it, with the belief "that all wants, changes, and obstacles are absent from the essence of God." [1] An omnipotent and immutable God could not be conceived as being active at one time and inactive at another. And then, too, why did God choose one time rather than another for creation? To quote the argument from Maimonides: "An agent is active at one time and inactive at another, according as favorable or unfavorable circumstances arise. . . . As, however, God is not subject to accidents which could bring about a change in His will, and is not affected by obstacles and hindrances that might appear or disappear, it is impossible, they argue, to imagine that God is active at one time and inactive at another." [2]

In answer to this difficulty, Maimonides draws a distinction between the actions of God and the actions of created beings. Human action is an exercise of power, or free will, which is dependent upon external conditions; God's action is an exercise of pure or absolute will and is entirely self-sufficient. "Every being that is endowed with free will and performs certain acts in reference to another being, necessarily interrupts those acts at one time or another, in con-

---

[1] *Moreh Nebukim*, II, 18.

[2] *Ibid.*, II, 14, Sixth Method. Cf. *Milḥamot Adonai*, VI, i, 3 (p. 299), and *Or Adonai*, III, i, 1.

sequence of some obstacles or changes. . . . Thus changed circumstances change his will, and the will, when it meets with obstacles, is not carried into effect. This, however, is only the case when the causes of the actions are external; but when the action has no other purpose whatever but to fulfil the will, then the will does not depend on the existence of favorable circumstances. The being endowed with this will need not act continually even in the absence of all obstacles, because there does not exist anything for the sake of which it acts, and which, the absence of all obstacles, would necessitate the action: the act simply follows the will." [1]

A somewhat different turn to this same argument is given by Gersonides. Creation, he says, is an exercise not only of the divine absolute will but of the divine disinterested goodwill. "If God created the world for His own benefit, there would be some ground for this difficulty. But since it has been made clear that God derives no benefit from His creation and that creation is only an act of goodness and kindness, the time and manner of creation must be attributed to His will." [2]

The argument that any sort of finitude in the world, whether that of creation in time or that of magnitude, implies either a lack of power or a lack of good-will on the part of God is repeated by many other philosophers. Thus Leo Hebraeus asks: "Furthermore, the purpose of the Creator in creating the world was nothing but His will to do good. Since it is so, why should not the good have been made from eternity, seeing that no obstacle could have hindered the powerful God who is most perfect?" [3] Bruno similarly argues that if the world were finite God would have to be

[1] *Moreh Nebukim*, II, 18, Second Method.
[2] *Milḥamot Adonai*, VI, i, 18, Ninth Doubt.
[3] *Dialoghi d'Amore*, III, pp. 238–239 (Bari, 1929).

considered either as unable or as unwilling to make it infinite; in either case God would be evil, for "not to be able is privatively evil, to be able and to be unwilling would be positively and affirmatively evil." [1] Suarez, too, is quoted by those who objected against Descartes as saying that "all limitations proceed from a cause, and the reason why anything is finite and limited is, either that its cause could not, or that it would not, give it more being and perfection." [2] Finally, Abraham Herrera, in his tentative argument against the finite number of emanations, says that if their number were finite, it would have to be "either because God was unwilling to make them infinite . . . and thus His goodness is not perfect, or because He was unable, and thus He is lacking in power." [3]

Drawing upon these passages, without necessarily following them, Spinoza similarly argues that the creation of a finite world by an infinite God would be incompatible with divine power and with divine will or good-will. "Further, if it is finite through its cause, this must be so either because its cause *could* not give more, or because it *would* not give more. That He should not have been able to give more would contradict His omnipotence; that He should not have been willing to give more, when He could well do so, savors of *ill-will*, which is nowise in God, who is all *goodness* and perfection." [4]

Both Maimonides and Gersonides, however, felt the weakness of their solution. To attribute creation in time to divine will, or good-will, would indeed save divine omnipotence and immutability, but it would still allow for change in divine

[1] *De Immenso et Innumerabilibus*, I, 10 (*Opera Latina*, I, 1, Neapoli, 1879, p. 238). Cf. J. L. McIntyre, *Giordano Bruno*, p. 191.

[2] *Primae Objectiones* (*Oeuvres*, VII, p. 95, ll. 14-16).

[3] *Sha'ar ha-Shamayim*, II, 4.

[4] *Short Treatise*, I, 2, § 5 (*Opera*, I, p. 20, ll. 18 ff.).

will. "But, some might ask, even if we admit the correctness of all this, is not change imputed in the fact that the will of the being exists at one time and not at another?"[1] While in one place Maimonides attempts to answer it by drawing a rather arbitrary line of distinction between human will and divine will, the latter of which he declares to be a homonymous term,[2] in another place he answers it in the following words: "The question remains, Why has this thing been produced now and not long before, since the cause has always been in existence? The answer is that a certain relation between cause and product has been absent, if the cause be corporeal; or, that the substance has not been sufficiently prepared, if the cause be incorporeal."[3]

In a like manner Gersonides applies the same answer to his own theory of creation. Unlike Maimonides he does not believe in absolute *ex nihilo*. The world according to him was created from a primordial, formless matter which co-existed with God from eternity, the act of creation being nothing but the investiture of the formless matter with form. The choice of a particular time for creation was determined not by a change in the will of God but by the nature of the matter out of which the world was created. This, according to him, would militate neither against the immutability of the divine will nor against divine omnipotence: "One might say that inasmuch as God exists always in the same manner, His will must also remain always the same; by assuming therefore that God wills to do a thing at one time and does not will to do it at another, there must inevitably be a change in the divine nature. To him we answer that the nature of the material, primordial element is such that it requires that

---

[1] *Moreh Nebukim*, II, 18, Second Method, and cf. *Milḥamot Adonai*, VI, i, 18, Ninth Doubt.　　　　[2] *Moreh Nebukim, loc. cit.*

[3] *Moreh Nebukim*, II, 12.

the existence of the good in it should have a beginning in time, inasmuch as that good must come to it from something without itself, as has been shown before, whence it has also been proved that the world must be created. This being the case, it is clear that the existence of the good in this material, primordial element is due to God, whereas the fact that that good did not exist in it from eternity is due to the imperfect nature of that primordial element, which imperfection has served us as a proof that the good in it must be created, for were it not for this, we have shown, the good in it would have come into being without an efficient cause, which would be absurd, as has already been pointed out. This being the case, the coming of the world into existence necessarily had to be at a certain time. There is no reason therefore for the question, why God did not create the world at an earlier time, because whatever time God created it before this time, the same question could still be asked. And just as God cannot be described as possessing the power to create in a thing two opposites at the same time, inasmuch as He is prevented from doing so by the nature of the object receiving the action, so also cannot God be described as having the power of making the good exist from eternity in the material element out of which the world was created, for the imperfection in the nature of that element requires that the good in it should be created in time." [1]

Against both these passages Crescas argues that absolute nothingness and formless matter cannot be said to possess any nature which would require that its creation should take place at a certain particular time. His argument against Maimonides reads as follows: "The question still remains, What has made God create at one time rather than at another? For it would seem that it could not be explained by

---

[1] *Milḥamot Adonai*, VI, i, 18, Ninth Doubt.

any other reason except that it was the will of God. For if it were for some other reason, that reason would inevitably have to be found either in the Agent who performed the action, or in the object upon which the action was performed, or in something outside both the Agent and the object, as, e.g., the organs through which the action was performed. It could not be in the Agent, for His relation to all times is the same; nor could it be in the object, for it is nothing but non-existence; nor *a fortiori* could it be in something external, for there is nothing external."[1] Against Gersonides he argues in this wise: "That the change would have taken place without a cause can be easily shown by what has already been said. For if the change of God's will had a cause, that cause would have to be found either in God or in the eternal, formless matter, inasmuch as there is nothing else besides these two. But the relation of God is the same to all times, and so also is the relation of that eternal, formless matter, and of all that arises from it, the same to all times. Thus there could be no cause for the change of will implied in choosing a particular time for creation."[2]

This tilt of Crescas against Maimonides and Gersonides is unquestionably the source of Spinoza's argument given in the foot-note: "To say to this that the nature of the thing required such [limitation] and that it could not therefore be otherwise, that is no reply: for the nature of a thing can require nothing while it does not exist."[3]

The second great difficulty of creation which the mediaevals grappled with is the explanation as to how this material, multifarious world could have arisen from the simple, immaterial divine thinking essence. "Ex nihilo nihil fit." This

[1] *Or Adonai*, III, i, 4 (p. 66b).
[2] *Ibid.* (p. 68b).
[3] *Short Treatise*, I, 2, § 5, note 3 (*Opera*, I, p. 20, ll. 23–25).

Aristotelian principle is repeated in Jewish philosophic literature from the earliest time.[1] Matter could not have originated in God, for it is excluded from His nature. Whence
did it come then? The problem is stated by Jewish philosophers in the Neoplatonic formula that "a simple element can
only produce a simple thing."[2] Crescas expresses the impossibility of matter arising directly from God in the following words: "Inasmuch as this matter [in Gersonides' theory]
is extremely imperfect, it could not have come by necessity
from God who is infinitely perfect."[3]

The theory of emanation which purported to be a solution
of this difficulty was found to be unsatisfactory by both
Maimonides and Gersonides. If everything must emanate
from God and if in God there is nothing material, how could
matter appear at all at any stage of emanation unless you
say it sprang up out of nothing and is in no way traceable to
God? It was this reasoning that forced Maimonides to make
emanation a volitional process and Gersonides to accept the
Platonic theory of the pre-existence of an eternal, formless
matter. Their solutions, however, do not interest us now.
We are interested only in their statement of the problem.
Says Maimonides: "I ask the following question: Aristotle
holds that the first Intelligence is the cause of the second,
the second of the third, and so on, till the thousandth, if we
assume a series of that number. Now the first Intelligence
is undoubtedly simple. How then can the compound form
of existing things come from such an Intelligence by fixed
laws of nature, as Aristotle assumes? . . . By what law of
nature did the spheres emanate from the Intelligences? What
relation is there between material and immaterial beings?"[4]
Says Gersonides: "This analogy, when closely examined,

[1] Cf. *Emunot we-De'ot*, I, 2, and *Ḥobot ha-Lebabot*, I, 5
[2] *Moreh Nebukim*, II, 22.   [3] *Or Adonai*, III, i, 4 (p. 68a).
[4] *Moreh Nebukim*, II, 22.

will be found to fall short of proving that matter can be created from absolute nothing. Only forms can arise in this manner, but not matter. In general, form can produce something of its own kind; hence it produces forms, for all forms are things of reason; but how could it produce materiality?"[1]

These discussions as to the rise of matter are reflected in the following argument of Spinoza, also given in a foot-note. "That there can be no finite substance is clear from this, namely, that, if so, it would necessarily have something which it would have from nothing, which is impossible. For whence can it derive that wherein it differs from God? Certainly not from God, for He has nothing imperfect or finite, etc. So, whence then but from nothing?"[2] We have already called attention to other passages where the same argument is advanced by Spinoza.

This first proposition of *Short Treatise*, I, 2, as will have been noticed, corresponds to Propositions II and III of *Ethics*, I. The second proposition, "that there are not two like substances,"[3] corresponds to Propositions IV and V of the *Ethics*. The argument that "if there were two alike they would necessarily limit one another"[4] is reminiscent of the argument after which it is modelled, namely, that if there were two deities they would limit each other by having a common genus and a specific difference.[5] The third proposition of the *Short Treatise*, I, 2, namely, "that one substance cannot produce another,"[6] corresponds to Proposition VI of the *Ethics*, and is proved by three arguments. The first[7] is the argument based upon the impossibility of something arising from nothing which we have already discussed. The

---

[1] *Milḥamot Adonai*, VI, i, 17 (p. 364). A parallel statement in *Ethics*, I, Prop. 15, Schol., is cited by Joël in *Lewi ben Gerson als Religionsphilosoph*, p. 78, n. 1.

[2] *Short Treatise*, I, 2, § 2, note 2 (*Opera*, I, p. 19, ll. 26–30).

[3] *Ibid.*, § 2 (p. 20, l. 4).   [4] *Short Treatise*, I, 2, § 6.

[5] Cf. above, p. 83.

[6] *Short Treatise*, I, 2, § 2 and § 7.   [7] *Ibid.*, § 8.

second,[1] however, is new and somewhat puzzling. It is my purpose to show that it can be rendered clear and intelligible by interpreting it as a criticism of Gersonides' theory that the world was created from an eternal formless element.

In *Cogitata Metaphysica*, II, 10, in a passage which is an undoubted allusion to Gersonides' theory of creation,[2] Spinoza says as follows: "We will not pause to refute the opinion of those who think that the world as chaos, or as matter devoid of form, is co-eternal with God, and so far independent of Him." Here, however, Spinoza does pause to refute Gersonides, and with an argument raised by Gersonides himself. Gersonides begins to argue against his own theory by saying that "it is inevitable that either some part of this formless element remained after the world had been created from it or no part of it remained." He then proceeds to prove that neither of these alternatives is possible, adding that "it is also past comprehension that the size of this primordial element should exactly agree with the size of which the world must be, for it is evident that the size of the world can be neither more nor less than what it is."[3] This is exactly what Spinoza means by the following argument: "Further, that which is created is by no means produced from nothing, but must necessarily have been produced from that which is existent (*die wezentlyk is*).[4] But that something should come forth from that which is existent and that this latter should not have that something less even after it had been produced from it — that we cannot grasp with our understanding."[5] If we take the last part of the passage to mean that the thing "which is created," i.e., the world, after it was produced "from that which is existent," i.e., the eternal formless matter,

[1] *Ibid.*, § 9.   [2] Cf. Joël, *Zur Genesis der Lehre Spinoza's*, p. 48.
[3] *Milḥamot Adonai*, VI, i, 18, First Doubt.
[4] On the meaning of *wezentlyk*, cf. below, p. 141, n. 4, and p. 382, n. 7.
[5] *Short Treatise*, I, 2, § 9 (*Opera*, I, p. 21, ll. 21–26).

could not be less than the latter had been before the world was
produced from it, the meaning of the entire passage may be
restated, in the light of Gersonides' argument, in the following manner: Further, since creation *ex nihilo* has been shown
to be impossible, let us now consider creation from an eternal
pre-existent formless element. This is, however, likewise
inconceivable, for we cannot grasp with our understanding
how the created world, the size of which must be determined
by its own nature, should happen to agree exactly with the
size of the eternal pre-existent element, and not be of a lesser
size, so that no part of that element would remain unused
after the world had been created from it. This unaccounted
for agreement in size is characterized by Spinoza as something which "we cannot grasp with our understanding."
Gersonides similarly characterizes it as something which is
"past comprehension"[1] and as something which "I cannot
comprehend" or "conceive of."[2]

If our interpretation of the last passage quoted from
Spinoza is correct, then the argument contained therein as
well as the argument contained in the parallel passage
quoted from Gersonides is based upon an assumption which
is found in Plato and repeated by Philo, namely, the assumption that the matter out of which the world was created was
completely used up in the creation of the world so that nothing was left of it. Plato states it in the following passage:
"Now the creation took up the whole of each of the four
elements; for the Creator compounded the world out of all
the fire and all the water and all the air and all the earth,
leaving no part of any of them nor any power of them outside.
He intended, in the first place, that the whole animal should
be perfect, as far as possible, and that the parts of which he
was formed should be perfect; and that he should be one,

[1] רחוק.   [2] לא אשער.

leaving no remnants out of which another such world might
be created."[1] Philo restates this view in the following passage: "It is unlikely that any material body has been left
over and was moving about at random outside, seeing that
God had wrought up and placed in orderly position all
matter wherever found."[2] Eusebius quotes another passage
from Philo's lost *De Providentia* as follows: "With a view to
the creation of the world God estimated an exactly sufficient
quantity of matter, so that there might be neither deficiency
nor excess. . . . I shall therefore confidently assert that the
world needed neither less nor more material substance for
its furnishing."[3] This passage from Eusebius is reproduced
in Hebrew by Azariah dei Rossi.[4]

The third argument reads as follows: "Lastly, if we would
seek the cause of the substance which is the origin of the
things which issue from its attributes, then it behoves us to
seek also the cause of that cause, and then again the cause
of that cause, *et sic in infinitum;* so that if we must necessarily stop and halt somewhere, as indeed we must, it is
necessary to stop at this only substance."[5] In this passage
Spinoza would seem to admit the impossibility of an infinite
causal regression, and he would therefore contradict himself,[6]
for elsewhere he denies this impossibility.[7] It seems to me,
however, that the argument contained in this passage has
an entirely different meaning.

It must be borne in mind that Spinoza advances it as a
proof "that one substance cannot produce another," by

---

[1] *Timaeus*, 32C–33A. Translation by Jowett.
[2] *De Palantatione Noe*, II, 5. Translation by G. H. Whitaker.
[3] *Praeparatio Evangelica*, VII, 21. Translation by E. H. Gifford.
[4] *Me'or 'Enayim, Imre Binah*, Ch. 6 (ed. Cassel, p. 125).
[5] *Short Treatise*, I, 2, § 10 (*Opera*, I, p. 21, ll. 26–32).
[6] Cf. A. Wolf, *Spinoza's Short Treatise*, p. 174.
[7] Epistola 12. Cf. below, pp. 195 ff.

which he means to refute the theory that a material world was created by an immaterial God who in so far as He is immaterial is a transeunt cause. Like most of his other arguments it reasons against his opponents from their own premises. The passage therefore is to be divided into two parts, in the first of which he reproduces the premise of his opponents and in the latter of which he draws his own conclusions from the self-same premise. Spinoza seems to say to them as follows: Why do you assume the existence of two substances, God and the world, considering God as the prime cause and rejecting the existence of any other cause prior to Him? It is because you believe with Aristotle that things in change must have a cause and that the series of causes cannot be infinite, and so you argue that "if we would seek the cause of the substance [i.e., God] which is the origin of the things which issue from its attribute, then it behoves us to seek also the cause of that cause, and then again the cause of that cause, and so on *in infinitum*." Your postulating of a prime cause outside the world is therefore dictated by nothing but the alleged need of arbitrarily terminating the series of cause and effect. This being the case, why not stop the series with the world as a whole and postulate the prime cause as something immanent in the world, "so that if we must necessarily stop and halt somewhere, as indeed we must, it is necessary to stop at this only substance [i.e., the world]." The full force of this reasoning will be discussed in our comments on Proposition XVIII of *Ethics*, I.

The fourth and last proposition in this chapter of the *Short Treatise*, though containing in its proof many elements taken from the proofs of the preceding propositions, does not properly belong in our present discussion of the unity of substance. It will be treated subsequently in our discussion of the simplicity of substance.

CHAPTER V

SIMPLICITY OF SUBSTANCE

I. Simplicity and Attributes

In the Appendix at the end of the First Part of the *Ethics*, Spinoza furnishes us with the unused titles for the unmarked chapters into which the book would have undoubtedly been divided had he chosen to write it after the manner of the scholastics and the rabbis. Using the terms "nature" and "properties" advisedly in their technical sense, he says: "In these chapters I have explained the nature of God and His properties." He then proceeds to enumerate these properties: (1) "That He necessarily exists; (2) that He is one; (3) that from the necessity alone of His own nature He is and acts; (4) that He is, and in what way He is, the free cause of all things; (5) that all things are in Him, and so depend upon Him that without Him they can neither be nor be conceived; and, finally, (6) that all things have been predetermined by Him, not indeed from freedom of will or from absolute good pleasure, but from His absolute nature or infinite power." The "nature of God," as we have already seen,[1] is treated in Proposition I, which supplements the definition of substance. Of the six "properties" enumerated by Spinoza the last four will be found to cover Propositions XIV–XXXVI, while the first may serve as a heading for Proposition XI. There remains therefore only the second property, "that He is one," which is to describe the contents of Propositions II–X and Propositions XII and XIII. We have already shown in the preceding chapter[2] that Proposi-

---

[1] Cf. above, pp. 61 ff.   [2] Cf. above, pp. 79 ff.

tions II–VI deal with the traditional problem of the unity of God. We shall now endeavor to show that in Propositions VII–X and XII–XIII Spinoza similarly deals with another traditional aspect of the same problem.

The expression "unity of God" was used by mediaeval philosophers in two senses. In the first place, it was used in the sense of numerical unity, as an assertion of monotheism and a denial of the existence of more than one God. In the second place, it was used in the sense of essential unity, or simplicity, as a denial of any kind of inner plurality in the divine nature.[1] This distinction in the use of the term "unity" may be traced to Aristotle's discussion of the various meanings of the term "one,"[2] which is repeatedly reproduced with the usual modifications and elaborations in mediaeval literature.[3] Unity in the first sense is the subject of the mediaeval proofs of the unity of God; unity in the second sense is the principle underlying the mediaeval discussions of the nature of the divine essence, or what is generally known as the problem of divine attributes.[4] Spinoza follows the traditional method of treatment. Having discussed the numerical unity of God in Propositions II–VI, he now enters upon the discussion of the essential unity, or simplicity, of God in Propositions VII–X and XII–XIII.

The simplicity of God upon which the mediaevals so strongly insisted was meant to emphasize the impropriety of the assertion, or even of the implication, of any kind of inner plurality in the divine essence. They especially mention three of such inner pluralities which the idea of absolute simplicity was meant to deny. First of all, it denies the ex-

---

[1] *Or Adonai*, I, iii, 4.

[2] *Metaphysics*, V, 6.

[3] *Maḳaṣid al-Falasifah*, II, i (p. 114); *Ḥobot ha-Lebabot*, I, 8; *Cuzari*, II, 2; *Emunah Ramah*, II, ii, 1; *'Iḳḳarim*, II, 10.

[4] Cf. *'Iḳḳarim*, II, 7.

istance in God of accidental qualities. These had to be rejected on account of the belief in the absolute incorporeality of God which tradition, if not the actual asseverations of the Bible, had taken for granted — which belief was further intensified when the traditional God was identified with the Aristotelian pure form. "He is not a magnitude that any quality resulting from quantity as such could be possessed by Him; He is not affected by external influences, and therefore does not possess any quality resulting from emotion; He is not subject to physical conditions, and therefore does not possess strength or similar qualities; He is not an animate being, that He should have a certain disposition of the soul, or acquire certain properties, as meekness, modesty, etc., or be in a state to which animate beings as such are subject, as, e.g., in that of health or of illness. Hence it follows that no attribute coming under the category of quality can be predicated of God." [1]

But the simplicity of God denies more than that. It also denies the metaphysical or logical distinction of genus and species in the divine nature, or what are known as essential attributes as distinguished from accidental attributes. Arabic as well as Jewish philosophers are explicit in their denial of the distinction of genus and species in God. [2] It is this principle that underlies the following passage of Maimonides: "The object is described by its definition, as, e.g., man is described as a being that lives and has reason. . . . All agree that this kind of description cannot be given of God; for there is no previous cause to His essence, by which He could be defined. . . . An object is described by part of its definition, as when, e.g., man is described as a living being or as a rational being. . . . All agree that this kind of descrip-

---

[1] *Moreh Nebukim*, I, 52.
[2] *Makaṣid al-Falasifah*, II, ii, 11 (p. 145); *'Iḳḳarim*, II, 6 and 7.

tion is inappropriate in reference to God; for if we were to speak of a portion of His essence, we should consider His essence to be a compound." [1]

There is a third possible kind of distinction in the divine nature which is specifically rejected by the mediaevals in their discussion of the simplicity of God, namely, the distinction of essence and existence. There are certain historical reasons, to be dealt with subsequently, which induced the mediaevals to single out the predicate of existence for special discussion. Suffice it to say for the present that both Arabic and Jewish philosophers deal with this problem specifically in their general discussion of the nature of the divine essence. We may quote here the following typical passage from Maimonides, which occurs in the course of his discussion of attributes: "It is known that existence is an accident appertaining to all things, and therefore an element superadded to their essence. This must evidently be the case as regards everything the existence of which is due to some cause; its existence is an element superadded to its essence. But as regards a being whose existence is not due to any cause — God alone is that being, for His existence, as we have said, is absolute — existence and essence are perfectly identical. He is not a substance to which existence is joined as an accident, as an additional element." [2]

Simplicity in this sense, as a denial of any kind of internal plurality, physical as well as metaphysical and logical, is maintained by Spinoza with regard to substance. Of the three kinds of internal plurality especially rejected by the mediaevals, — the plurality of subject and accidental quality, of genus and species, and of essence and existence, — Spinoza mentions the last one specifically in Proposition VII. As for the second kind of internal plurality, he quotes

---

[1] *Moreh Nebukim*, I, 52.   [2] *Moreh Nebukim*, I, 57.

the mediaevals to the effect that "God is not a species of any genus,"[1] which means the same as to say that in God there is no distinction of genus and species. This, as we have already seen,[2] is the implication of his definition of substance and of Proposition I, which is based upon it. It is this, too, which is meant when he says in one of his letters to Jellis that "of His [i.e., God's] essence we can form no general idea (universalem . . . ideam)."[3] Finally, as for the first kind of internal plurality, in Scholium 2 to Proposition VIII, which really belongs to Proposition VII, he dismisses, in unmistakable terms, the inherence in substance of accidental qualities, and almost in the words of Maimonides he says that those who attribute accidental qualities to substance do so because "they do not distinguish between the modifications of substances and substances themselves," and also because they "confound human nature with divine" and "readily attribute to God human affects." Substance is thus to Spinoza, like God to the mediaevals, absolutely simple, free from accidental as well as from essential attributes, and likewise impervious to the distinction of essence and existence.

The mediaeval insistence upon the absolute simplicity of God did not, however, mean to divest Him of all traits of personality. A God who has been conceived as creator and governor of the world, as lawgiver to man, and judge of human actions, could not possibly be conceived as impassive as a mathematical point and as indifferent as a metaphysical absolute. This belief in the personality of God is summed up by the mediaevals in the statement that "God, blessed be He, must be free of imperfections,"[4] by which is meant that

---

[1] *Short Treatise*, I, 7, § 3.   [2] Cf. above, p. 77.
[3] Epistola 50 (*Opera*, IV, p. 240, ll. 2–3).
[4] *'Ikkarim*, I, 15; cf. II, 7.

"He must possess power and will and the other attributes without which He could not be thought of as perfect."[1] Spinoza restates this view in a letter addressed to Hudde in the following words: "That everything, which includes necessary existence, can have in itself no imperfection, but must express pure perfection."[2] Thus while on the one hand God must be absolutely simple and unqualifiable, on the other hand He must possess all those qualities which make for personality. How these two can be reconciled is the problem of attributes, which does not concern us for the present. The following brief statement from Albo will suffice as an indication of the mediaeval point of view: "All the attributes of perfection that are predicated of God or are conceived to exist in Him are predicated of Him and are conceived to exist in Him only in the sense in which they imply perfection but in none of the senses in which they would imply imperfection."[3] Of particular importance for us here is the use made by the mediaevals of the term "infinite" with regard to these attributes of perfection. In the first place, these attributes of God are to be infinite in number: "It must be understood that the perfections which exist in God are infinite in number."[4] In the second place, each of these attributes must be infinite in two senses: infinite in time, that is, eternal, and infinite in the degree of importance, that is, in its essential nature. "When we ascribe to God any of the attributes by which He may be described, whether negative or positive, that attribute must be taken to be infinite in two respects, infinite in time[5] and infinite in perfection or importance."[6] The term "infinite" applied to God thus means

---

[1] *Ibid.*, I, 15. [2] Epistola 35.
[3] '*Ikkarim*, II, 21. [4] *Ibid.*, II, 25.
[5] The term "time" has two meanings according to Albo, and infinite time in this passage is the equivalent of eternity. Cf. below, pp. 339, 363.
[6] '*Ikkarim*, II, 25.

to designate that He possesses an infinite number of attributes each of which is eternal and absolutely perfect. To quote: "It is with reference to this that the Cabalists designated God by the term Infinite (*En Sof*), to indicate that the perfections which are to be found in Him are infinite in the three senses which we have mentioned "[1] — that is to say, infinite in the number of attributes and each attribute infinite in time and in perfection.

Similarly to Spinoza, while God is absolutely simple and unqualifiable, He may still be described as possessing attributes, infinite in number, and each of them infinite in what the mediaevals called time and perfection. His definition of God at the beginning of the First Part of the *Ethics* is nothing but a restatement of the passages we have reproduced from Albo in the preceding paragraph. "By God, I understand Being absolutely infinite, that is to say, substance consisting of infinite attributes, each one of which expresses eternal and infinite essence." [2] Note the expression "eternal and infinite essence." By "eternal" [3] he means here what Albo calls "infinite in time," and by "infinite" he means again what Albo calls "infinite in perfection or importance." In his definition of God given in a letter to Oldenburg,[4] where incidentally the term "eternal" does not occur, Spinoza himself explains the term "infinite," by which each of the infinite attributes of God is described, as meaning "in the highest degree perfect of its kind." And what he has laid down of God in his definitions, he now tries to prove of substance in his propositions. First he shows that "every substance is necessarily infinite" (Prop. VIII), just as God is "absolutely infinite." Then, just as God is "substance con-

[1] *Ibid.* [2] *Ethics*, I, Def. 6.

[3] For Spinoza's various uses of the term "eternal," see below, pp. 366 ff. and 375 ff.

[4] Epistola 2 (*Opera*, IV, p. 7, ll. 25–26).

sisting of infinite attributes," so substance possesses infinite attributes, for "the more reality or being a thing possesses, the more attributes belong to it" (Prop. IX), and inasmuch as substance has infinite reality or being, it must have infinite attributes. Finally, each attribute of substance must "express eternal and infinite essence," just as the attributes of God, for "each attribute of a substance must be conceived through itself" (Prop. X), and must therefore be identical with substance, and inasmuch as substance is infinite, each of its attributes must be infinite. In Jewish philosophy, too, the infinite nature of each attribute is deduced from the infinite nature of God. "For just as God, blessed be He, is infinite both in time and in importance, so is each of His attributes infinite both in time and in importance."[1]

The attempt of the mediaevals to preserve God's personality by endowing Him with infinite attributes while at the same time insisting upon His absolute simplicity has landed them, as we have already pointed out, in a self-contradiction. Attributes are either accidental or essential; they must be related to the subject either as color and size and weight and suchlike, or as genera and species, as, e.g., life and rationality are related to man. In either case they must imply a distinction of essence and attribute in the subject, though in the latter instance the distinction is only metaphysical or logical. Furthermore, attributes differ among themselves from each other, and therefore the assertion of an infinite number of attributes must imply a corresponding infinite number of differences in the nature of the subject. If the divine nature is to be free from any kind of plurality, how then can it have attributes? This difficulty constitutes the problem of divine attributes in mediaeval philosophy. The solutions offered will be touched upon in the sequel. In a

[1] 'Ikkarim, II, 25.

general way, it may be said that in the attempted solutions two facts are sought to be established: first, all the attributes of God are in reality one attribute, and, whatever differences there may appear to exist between them, they do not affect the nature of God; second, whatever may be the relation between essence and attribute, the assertion of divine attributes does not contravene the simplicity of God's essence.

Similarly Spinoza, after having stated in Propositions VIII, IX, and X that substance has an infinite number of attributes, proceeds to show that though assuming an infinite number of attributes of which two "may be conceived as really distinct, — that is to say, one without the assistance of the other, — we cannot nevertheless thence conclude that they constitute two beings or two different substances" (Prop. X, Schol.), and that "no attribute of substance can be truly conceived from which it follows that substance can be divided" (Prop. XII), concluding that "substance absolutely infinite is indivisible" (Prop. XIII).

This then is the logical argument underlying Propositions VII–X and XII–XIII. Had the *Ethics* been written *more scholastico rabbinicoque* Spinoza would have prefaced these propositions with the following words: We shall now proceed to show that just as substance is like God in its numerical unity (Props. II–VI), so it is also like God in its absolute simplicity. That it has no distinction of genus and species has already been stated (Def. III and Prop. I); that it should have accidental qualities must be dismissed as something incomprehensible to a philosopher (Prop. VIII, Schol. 2). What is therefore left us to show is that like the philosophic God of the mediaevals substance has no distinction of essence and existence (Prop. VII). Furthermore, though like God "every substance is necessarily infinite" (Prop. VIII), that is to say, consisting of infinite attributes (Prop. IX), each one of which expresses eternal and infinite essence (Prop. X), still this infinity of attributes does not imply that substance is in any sense divisible (Prop. X, Schol.; Props. XII–XIII).

With these general remarks we are now ready to discuss more fully the following three topics and the propositions in which they are treated: (1) the problem of essence and existence (Prop. VIII; Def. I); (2) the definition of the term "infinite" (Def. II; Def. VI; Props. VIII–X); (3) the relation of attribute to substance (Def. IV; Prop. X, Schol.; Props. XII–XIII).

II. Essence and Existence

The problem of essence and existence which is dwelt upon by Spinoza not only in his *Ethics* but also in his other writings, the terms in which the problem is couched, and the manner in which it is treated, are all part of the great philosophic heritage which had fallen to him from his predecessors. Two distinct traditions served him as sources of supply. One was the philosophic writings in Hebrew which have preserved the traditions of Arabic philosophy; the other was Descartes, who has preserved the traditions of the Latin scholastics. It can be shown that the two traditions had crossed at one time, and that the scholastic tradition of a later period was greatly indebted to the Arabico-Hebrew influence. But in Descartes, in whom the scholastic tradition reached its culminating point, owing to the influence of Anselm's ontological proof of the existence of God, the assertion of the identity of essence and existence in God assumed a meaning which was entirely different from that which it had in Jewish philosophy. In Jewish philosophy the assertion that in God essence and existence are identical, or however else it is phrased,[1] was merely another way of saying that God is necessary existence out of which arises the eternity, unity, simplicity, immutability, and unknowability of God, and in fact all those negations which tend to make God an absolute and infinite being. It does not however mean that thereby God becomes a "real" being (*ens reale*) as opposed to a being of reason and a fictitious being (*ens rationis, ens fictum*). Or, in other words, the fact that in the idea of God essence involved existence was not used to prove the actual existence of God, for in Jewish as well as in Arabic philosophy that mode of reasoning was not followed.[2] In Descartes the identity of essence and existence means all that, to be sure, but it also means something else in addition. It means also that this very idea of the identity of essence and existence in God proves that He is a "real" being. In Spinoza, as we shall endeavor to show, these two trends of thought meet, and upon the groundwork of philosophic lore inherited from the Hebrew books of his youth he raised the superstructure of Descartes' ontological proofs of the existence of God.

However complicated and important the problem of essence and existence may have become in the course of its development, and however great the significance it has assumed in its later history, the problem seems to me to have had a simple and humble origin. To my mind, it originated in the question as to the meaning of propositions in which the term "existent" forms the predicate, as, for instance, "A is existent." In order to appreciate the significance of this

[1] The other way of phrasing it is that God is existence without essence added thereto. See my "Crescas on the Problem of Divine Attributes," *Jewish Quarterly Review*, n.s., Vol. VII, p. 189, n. 85.

[2] Cf. my "Notes on the proofs of the Existence of God," *Hebrew Union College Annual*, I (1924), pp. 583 f.

question, we must bear in mind that Aristotle, and following him Arabic and Jewish logicians, held that every logical judgment must be synthetic, so that in every proposition the predicate must be a universal term belonging to one of the four or five predicables enumerated by Aristotle and Porphyry. It must be the genus of the subject, its species, a specific difference, a property or an accident. In mediaeval terminology the first three predicables are known as "essential attributes," the last two as "accidental attributes." The common characteristic of all these predicables is that they are all universal terms and are not identical with the essence of the subject. Essential attributes state the elements of which the essence of the subject is constituted or to which it belongs, and though not different from the essence of the subject they are either more extensive or less extensive than it, as, for instance, when the combination of animality and rationality, or either one of these, is predicated of man. Accidental attributes are something different from, and external to, the essence of the subject, adding some adventitious quality to it, as, for instance, when color and size and age are predicated of man. Nothing that is perfectly identical with the subject and co-extensive with it and is a mere verbal repetition of its essence can be affirmed in the predicate, for identity is not a logical relation. Aristotle laid it down as a rule when he stated that "individuals, and whatever is one in number, are predicated of no subject," [1] and the mediaevals condemned as tautological any proposition like "A is A." In view of this the question may be justly raised as to what kind of predicate is the term "existent" in the proposition "A is existent." It cannot be identical with the essence of the subject, for then the proposition would be tantamount to saying that A is A. It is there-

[1] *Categories*, 2, 1b, 6–7.

fore concluded that existence is always an accident superadded to the essence of a thing.[1]

That existence is an element adventitious to the essence
of things would seem to be on the whole in accord with what
we know of Aristotle's views on the subject. According to
him the existence of things is not implied in the knowledge
of their essence which we may attain from their definition,
and thus while we may have an idea of man and knowledge
of his essence, and while we are even capable of defining him,
none of these can prove the actual existence of man. For all
definitions are answers to the question what a thing is but
not to the question whether a thing is. "But 'what man is'
and 'that man exists' are two different questions."[2] Again:
'Evidently those who define according to the present methods of definition do not demonstrate that a thing exists."[3]
To form conceptions of certain essences, to define them, to
describe them in formal propositions, does not imply that
they exist, for definitions and propositions may be purely
nominal in which words rather than things are the subject of
discourse. If a thing does actually exist, it only happens to
exist, just as it only happens to be white or black, large or
small. To assert therefore of such a thing that it is existent
is simply to attribute to it an accidental quality, just as to
say of a black or white thing that it is black or white. This
interpretation of Aristotle, to be sure, might be doubted.
It might be argued that while indeed there are nominal definitions in which existence is not implied, it may be still possible
that in real definitions existence is implied, and that to attribute existence to things that do actually exist is not to
attribute an accidental quality but rather to affirm some-

    [1] This argument is reproduced by Crescas in the name of Avicenna in his *Or
Adonai*, I, iii, 1.
    [2] *Analytica Posteriora*, II, 7, 92b, 10–11.
    [3] *Ibid.*, 92b, 19–20.

thing that is involved in their essence. This indeed would seem to be Averroes' interpretation of Aristotle, for he maintains that existence is always involved in the essence of an actually existent subject.[1] Avicenna, however, and his Jewish followers, as Maimonides, for instance, by maintaining that existence is an accident superadded to the essence would seem to have understood Aristotle as explained above.

But even according to Avicenna and his school, God is an exception. In Him existence cannot be assumed to be added to His essence any more than any of the other attributes could be considered as accidental qualities. This is impossible by reason of the simplicity of the divine nature. It is because of this general principle that existence is accidental to the essence of created beings that the theologians of the Avicennian school have included in their discussion of the divine attributes the statement that God has no essence superadded to His existence, or that in God essence and existence are identical.[2]

It would seem that it was this traditional method of including the problem of essence and existence in the discussion of attributes or the simplicity of God that led Spinoza to lay down his seventh proposition. All of Spinoza's statements with regard to the nature of existence in relation to essence reflect the Avicennian and Maimonidean point of view. Repeating almost verbatim the words of Aristotle, he says that "the true definition of any one thing neither involves nor expresses anything except the nature of the thing involved."[3] Again, corresponding to the Avicennian formula that in created beings existence is an accident superadded to their essence, Spinoza says: "The essence of things produced

[1] Cf. quotation in Munk, *Guide des Égarés*, Vol. I, p. 231, n. 1.
[2] Cf. above, p. 122, n. 1.
[3] *Ethics*, I, Prop. 8, Schol. 2; cf. Epistola 34.

by God does not involve existence." [1] God is however different, for "I define God as a being to whose essence belongs existence." [2] And what is true of God is true also of substance: "It pertains to the nature of substance to exist." [3] The contrast between God and created beings is clearly brought out in the following passage: "Essence in God is not different from existence; indeed the one cannot be conceived without the other. In other things essence differs from existence, for the one may be conceived without the other." [4]

In his proof of Proposition VII, no less than in the proposition itself, Spinoza follows his predecessors. In Jewish philosophy, the negation of the distinction of essence and existence in God, as well as that of any other distinction, is based upon the view that any form of composition requires a cause to bring about that composition and that God can have no cause. "Everything that is composed of two elements has necessarily their composition as the cause of its existence as a composite being, and consequently in respect to its own essence it is not necessary of existence, for its existence depends upon the existence of its component parts and their combination." [5] Again: "Everything which is necessary of existence in respect to its own essence has no cause for its existence in any manner whatsoever or under any conditions whatsoever." [6] With this in mind Maimonides argues for the identity of essence and existence in God as follows: "It is known that existence is an accident appertaining to all things, and therefore an element superadded to their essence. This must evidently be the case as regards everything the existence of which is due to some cause; its

---

[1] *Ibid.*, I, Prop. 24.
[2] Epistola 83 (*Opera*, I, p. 335, l. 5).   [3] *Ethics*, I, Prop. 7.
[4] *Cogitata Metaphysica*, I, 2. Cf. *Ethics*, I, Axiom 7.
[5] *Moreh Nebukim*, II, Introduction, Prop. 21.
[6] *Ibid.*, Prop. 20.

existence is an element superadded to its essence. But as regards a being whose existence is not due to any cause — God alone is that being, for His existence, as we have said, is absolute — existence and essence are perfectly identical; He is not a substance to which existence is joined as an accident, so as to constitute an additional element." [1]

The short proof of Proposition VII given by Spinoza follows the same line of reasoning. The essence of substance must involve existence, he argues, because substance has no cause, for "there is nothing by which substance can be produced." Were existence superadded to its essence, substance would require a cause to produce it. This state of being causeless, which the mediaevals as well as Spinoza himself usually designate by the expression "necessary existence," Spinoza also designates by the expression "cause of itself" (*causa sui*), a phrase which had already been in current use in philosophic literature.[2] *Causa sui*, like the mediaeval "necessary existence," is primarily nothing but a negation, meaning causelessness, and to Spinoza it is only a shorter way of saying that the essence of substance involves existence. He thus says in his first part of the definition of *causa sui*, "By cause of itself, I understand that, whose essence involves existence," [3] though the latter part of the definition, as we shall presently show, introduces a new idea into the phrase.

We thus have in Spinoza the following equation: necessary existence = *causa sui* = that whose essence involves existence. All of these expressions, as we have seen, mean primarily nothing but causelessness. An explicit statement to this effect is to be found in the following passage of Spinoza:

[1] *Ibid.*, I, 57.

[2] Cf. J. Freudenthal, "Spinoza und die Scholastik" in *Philosophische Aufsätze. Eduard Zeller . . . gewidmet*, p. 119; Martineau, *A Study of Spinoza*, p. 118, n. 1.

[3] *Ethics*, I, Def. 1.

"A thing must be conceived either through its essence alone or through its proximate cause. Namely, if a thing be in itself, or, as it is commonly termed, its own cause (*causa sui*), then it must be understood through its essence alone; but if a thing be not in itself, but requires a cause to exist, then it must be understood through its proximate cause."[1] Now, in Arabic and Jewish philosophy the concept of necessary existence as applied to God is the main principle out of which arise all the negations and affirmations about the divine nature. It is from this that it is deduced that God is immaterial, that He is not an accident existing in a subject or a form existing in matter, that His essence and existence are identical, that He is not conditioned by any other cause nor in any other way dependent upon another being, that He is one, that He has no accidental qualities, that He is immutable, that He is the emanative cause of everything, that He is indefinable, and that He is the source of the existence of everything else.[2] By the same token Spinoza undertakes to deduce from the concept of necessary existence, or its equivalents, a similar list of negations and affirmations about God. Says he in one of his letters to Hudde: "I will briefly show . . . what properties must be possessed by a Being that includes necessary existence. To wit: I. It must be eternal. . . . II. It must be simple, not made up of parts. . . . III. It cannot be conceived as determinate, but only as infinite. . . . IV. It must be indivisible. . . . V. [It] can have in itself no imperfection, but must express pure perfection. . . . Lastly . . . there can only be a single Being, of which existence belongs to its nature."[3] Again: "From the fact alone, that I define God as a Being to whose essence belongs exist-

---

[1] *Tractatus de Intellectus Emendatione*, § 92 (*Opera*, II, p. 34, ll. 9–13).
[2] *Makaṣid al-Falasifah*, II, ii (pp. 137 ff.).
[3] Epistola 35.

ence, I infer several of His properties; namely, that He necessarily exists, that He is one, unchangeable, infinite, etc." [1]

Not only from the mediaevals but also from Descartes has Spinoza derived the method of deducing the properties of God from the concept of necessary existence. "Indeed upon this truth alone, namely, that existence belongs to the nature of God, or that the concept of God involves a necessary existence as that of a triangle that the sum of its angles is equal to two right angles, or again that His existence and His essence are eternal truth, depends almost all our knowledge of God's attributes by which we are led to a love of God (or to the highest blessedness)." [2]

But from Descartes Spinoza has borrowed also the ontological proof. A being whose conception involves existence, according to this reasoning, must necessarily exist, and this sort of reasoning forms the basis of Spinoza's proofs of the existence of God in Proposition XI, to be discussed in a subsequent chapter. Now, according to Descartes, the term *a se*, which he applies to God in the same sense as *sui causa*,[3] has both a negative sense and a positive sense. In its negative sense it means that God has no cause; [4] in its positive sense it means that God stands to himself in the same way as an efficient cause does to its effect.[5] The term *causa sui* similarly in Spinoza is not a mere negation, meaning causelessness; it means also something positive: it is an assertion of self-sufficency and hence actual existence. He thus says in the second part of his definition of *causa sui*: "or that, whose nature cannot be conceived unless exist-

---

[1] Epistola 83.

[2] *Principia Philosophiae Cartesianae*, I, Prop. 5, Schol.

[3] *Primae Responsiones* (*Oeuvres*, VII, p. 109, ll. 16 and 21).

[4] *Ibid.* (p. 110, l. 24).

[5] *Ibid.* (p. 111, ll. 6-7).

ing."¹ Likewise Proposition VII of the First Part of the *Ethics*, while on the whole it is a reproduction of mediaeval Jewish discussions, contains also the additional Cartesian element, as is indicated in its phrasing. Spinoza does not say there as he says in *Cogitata Metaphysica*, I, 2, that essence in substance is not different from existence, but he says, "It pertains to the nature of substance to exist."

The identity of essence and existence is also the burden of the fourth proposition in the second chapter of the First Part of the *Short Treatise*. The wording of the proposition somewhat obscures its meaning. It reads as follows: "That in the infinite understanding of God there is no other substance than that which is formaliter in nature." ² The purpose of this proposition, however, becomes clear when it is compared with its restatement at the end of the *Short Treatise*, Appendix I, Proposition IV: "To such an extent does existence pertain by nature to the essence of every substance, that it is impossible to posit in an infinite understanding the idea of the essence of a substance that does not exist in nature." It is clear that this fourth proposition, both in the main text and in the Appendix of the *Short Treatise*, is parallel to Proposition VII in *Ethics*, I, namely, that existence pertains to the nature of substance. In the *Short Treatise*, however, Spinoza utilizes the principle of the identity of essence and existence in substance as an argument for what is the main contention of Chapter 2 of the *Short Treatise*, I. The main contention of that chapter, as we have already shown, is to refute the mediaeval view that there are two substances, God and the world, the latter of which has no existence involved in its essence, inasmuch as it must acquire existence

---

¹ *Ethics*, I, Def. 1.

² *Short Treatise*, I, 2, § 2 (*Opera*, I, p. 20, ll. 6–7). But in § 11 (p. 21, ll. 33–34): "there is no substance or attribute" instead of "there is no other substance."

through an act of creation or emanation. Spinoza seems to say to his mediaeval opponents, in Proposition IV of the *Short Treatise*, I, 2, as follows: You maintain that the world [i.e., conditional substance] had existed prior to its creation only as an "idea" in the "infinite understanding [i.e., intellect] of God," and that only through an act of creation has it acquired existence. But any form of creation, however explained, I have already shown to you to be impossible.[1] Existence therefore must pertain to the essence of the world just as you say it pertains to the essence of God, and there is thus no such distinction between God and the world as that of creator and created, or absolute substance and conditional substance. He thus concludes, in the Corollary to Proposition IV in Appendix I at the end of the *Short Treatise*, that: "Nature is known through itself, and not through any other thing. It consists of infinite attributes, every one of them infinite and perfect in its kind; to its essence pertains existence, so that outside it there is no other essence or existence, and it thus coincides exactly with the essence of God, who alone is glorious and blessed." By "nature" here Spinoza means the universe; God is not outside of it, that is to say, pure form as opposed to matter, but the two are essentially the same, for, as he sums up his conclusions at the end of the four propositions in the same chapter of the *Short Treatise*, "we posit extension [i.e., matter] as an attribute of God." [2]

The proofs of the fourth proposition given in Chapter 2 of the *Short Treatise*, I, are not altogether new. They are only restatements of the arguments already used by Spinoza in his discussion of the first three propositions. We have already pointed out the literary origins of these arguments in our discussion of the unity of substance in the preceding chapter.

---

[1] Cf. above, Chapter IV.
[2] *Short Treatise*, I, 2, § 18 (*Opera*, I, p. 24, l. 11). But see below, pp. 299, 319 ff.

The sources quoted there will throw light upon Spinoza's reference here to an argument "from the infinite power of God, since in Him there can be no cause by which He might have been induced to create one sooner or more than another"[1] (First Argument). They will likewise help to elucidate his reference to an argument that God "cannot omit to do what is good"[2] (Third Argument), as well as his argument based upon the principle "that one substance cannot produce another"[3] (Fourth Argument). There is only left for us to account for his allusion to an argument "from the simplicity of His will"[4] (Second Argument). This I believe to reflect a passage in which Crescas attempts to refute Maimonides' solution of the problem of creation. It will be recalled that Maimonides endeavors to answer the question as to why God created the world at one time rather than at another, as well as to explain the other difficulties of creation, by the general statement that creation was an act of divine will. To this Crescas retorts somewhat as follows: If the world was created by divine will, then inasmuch as the world is composite, the will that has created it will have to be composite, for the creative will must be diffused throughout the parts of the object created. But this is impossible, since God's will, not being distinct from His essence, must be as simple as the essence itself.[5] Hence Spinoza's cryptic statement, "from the simplicity of His will."[6]

---

[1] *Short Treatise*, I, 2, § 11 (*Opera*, I, p. 21, l. 35–p. 22, l. 3).

[2] *Ibid.* (p. 22, ll. 3–4).   [3] *Ibid.* (p. 22, ll. 5–7).

[4] *Ibid.* (p. 22, l. 3).

[5] Cf. *Or Adonai*, III, i, 4 (p. 66b, ll. 42–45): "Granted that the proposition leads to the conclusion that there must be the will of an agent, this very same proposition would also have to make that will produce one simple object, for a will producing a composite object would itself have to be composite, inasmuch as the will must be diffused throughout the composite object which it produces."

[6] Cf. also Descartes' statement that "the will consists only of one single element, and is so to speak indivisible" (*Meditationes*, IV, *Oeuvres*, VII, p. 60, ll. 22–23).

III. Definition of the Term "Infinite"

Coming now to Proposition VIII, that "every substance is necessarily infinite," we shall first endeavor to explain in what sense Spinoza uses the term "infinite." Here, too, it is to his predecessors that we must turn for help and information. Spinoza speaks of two kinds of infinite. There is, first, the "absolutely infinite" (*absolute infinitum*) (Def. VI). With this is contrasted, second, the "infinite in its own kind" (*in suo genere infinitum*) (Def. VI, Expl.). Corresponding to the "infinite in its own kind" there is the "finite in its own kind" (*in suo genere finitum*) (Def. II). These phrases are, to be sure, all defined by Spinoza, but his definitions, as will have been gathered, are in most cases brief restatements of generally accepted and well-known mediaeval concepts. What then is the origin and background of these phrases as well as of the ideas behind them?

In mediaeval discussions of infinity the term "infinite" is said to have two meanings. It may be an accident either of magnitude or of number, or it may be an essence, that is to say, a self-existent substance, immaterial like soul and intellect.[1] As an accident of magnitude it means an unlimited distance or length, something that has no end or boundary. As an accident of number, it means something that is endlessly addible or divisible. "Finite" as the antithesis of this kind of infinite means just the opposite, a distance that is bounded and a number that is limited, or, in other words, something comparable with others of its kind and exceeded by them.

But an essentially infinite substance means something

---

[1] See *Or Adonai*, I, i, 1 (p. 4a–b), based upon Averroes' Middle Commentaries on *Physics*, III, 4, 204a, 2–5, 204a, 32, and *Metaphysics*, XI, 10, 1066a, 35–1066b, 21. Cf. my *Crescas' Critique of Aristotle*, p. 137 and notes on pp. 329–335.

entirely different. It means a substance whose essence is
unique and so incomparable that it cannot suffer any form
of limitation and hence cannot have any form of positive
description, for every description necessarily implies a limitation, or as Spinoza puts it: "determination is negation." [1]
To call a substance infinite in this sense is like calling voice
colorless. When voice is described as colorless it does not
mean the negation of a property which we should expect it
to have and which it may have, but rather the absolute exclusion of voice from the universe of color. By the same
token, when substance is described as infinite in this sense,
it means its absolute exclusion from any form of finitude,
limitation, and description. The negation of finitude implied
in this sense of the term "infinite" is what the mediaeval
Jewish logicians would call "absolute negation" as contrasted with "particular negation" — a contrast which is
expressed in the distinction between "A is not-B" and "A
is not B." There is a suggestion of this distinction in Aristotle,[2] and Spinoza himself uses for these two kinds of negation the terms "negation" (*negatio*) and "privation"
(*privatio*). "Thus privation is nothing else than denying of
a thing something which we think belongs to its nature; negation is nothing else than denying of a thing something because
it does not belong to its nature." [3] Of the parallel passages
in Jewish philosophy the following may be quoted: "You
already know from your reading in logic that negation is of
two kinds. One is particular negation,[4] as, e.g., when we
say 'Balaam does not see,' which is negation in the true
sense of the term. The other is absolute negation,[5] that is
to say, the denying of the subject that which does not natu-

---

[1] Epistola 50 (*Opera*, IV, p. 240, ll. 13–14): "determinatio negatio est." Cf.
Ethics, I, Prop. 8, Schol. 1.   [2] *De Interpretatione*, Ch. 10; *Metaphysics*, V, 22.
[3] Epistola 21 (*Opera*, IV, p. 129, ll. 5–7).
[4] השלילה המיוחדת.   [5] השלילה המשולחת.

rally belong to it, as, e.g., 'The wall does not see,' which is negation in a general sense." [1]

This mediaeval distinction between an essential and an accidental infinite is based upon the following passage in Aristotle: "The infinite is either that which is incapable of being traversed because it is not its nature to be traversed — this corresponds to the sense in which the voice is 'invisible' —, or that which admits only of incomplete traverse or scarcely admits of traverse, or that which, though it naturally admits of traverse, is not traversed or limited; further, a thing may be infinite in respect of addition or of subtraction or of both." [2]

The implication of the passage is this. The infinite is that which has no limit. The term is derived from magnitude and number, and must thus primarily apply to them or to any other thing which may be measured either quantitatively or qualitatively. We may therefore speak of infinite beauty as well as of infinite length and number. All such forms of measurement, however, imply a common standard and a comparison of the thing measured with other things of its kind. But the term "infinite" may be used also in a derivative sense as applied to things which are incapable of being measured on account of their uniqueness and incomprehensibility in a class in which they can be compared with others of their kind. "Infinite" in this sense is an absolute negation, the denial of a thing of any kind of determination and description, as something not belonging to its nature.

In view of this discussion, we may now explain the meaning of the different kinds of finite and infinite in Spinoza.

To be finite or limited means to be comparable, and since only like things can be compared, to be finite means to be included within a class of like things. "If between two things

---

[1] Narboni's commentary on *Moreh Nebukim*, I, 58.
[2] *Metaphysics*, XI, 10, 1066a, 35–1066b, 1; cf. *Physics*, III, 4, 204a, 2–7.

no relation can be found, there can be no similarity [and hence no comparison] between them, and there is no relation between two things that have no similarity to each other; as, e.g., we do not say that this heat is similar to that color, or this voice is similar to that sweetness. . . . You must know that two things of the same kind — i.e., whose essential properties are the same, distinguished from each other by greatness and smallness, strength and weakness, etc. — are necessarily similar." [1] Everything that suffers description may therefore be called finite in its own kind, for it cannot be described except in terms that properly belong to it and limit it. A thing finite is thus something that is similar in some respect to something else of its own kind with which it may be compared and be found greater or smaller, longer or shorter, more important or less important. Hence Spinoza's definition: "That thing is called finite in its own kind which can be limited by another thing of the same nature. For example, a body is called finite, because we always conceive another body which is greater. So a thought is limited by another thought; but a body is not limited by a thought, nor a thought by a body" (Def. II).

"Infinite in its own kind" means simply the superlative degree of comparison, its surpassing of all others of the same kind. It does not mean that the thing so described as infinite is unique and incomparable by possessing an infinite number of qualities, nor does it mean that any of its qualities is unique and incomparable. What it means is that certain ones of its qualities upon being compared with others of their kind will be found to surpass them all. Hence Spinoza's statement: "For of whatever is infinite only in its own kind, we can deny infinite attributes" (Def. VI, Expl.).

But "absolutely infinite" means an absolute exclusion

[1] *Moreh Nebukim*, I, 56.

from the universe of finitude, determination, and description. It implies uniqueness and incomparability; there is no kind to which it may be said to belong. It is *sui generis*. It is an individual essence of its own kind. The number of its attributes is infinite, and so is each of its attributes, and for this reason it suffers no description or determination. Spinoza thus says: "But to the essence of that which is absolutely infinite pertains whatever expresses essence and involves no negation" (Def. VI, Expl.).

It is as an "absolutely infinite" of this kind that God is described by the mediaevals, a description which denies the existence of any relation between the essence of God and that of other beings. "Since the existence of a relation between God and man, or between Him and other beings, has been denied, similarity must likewise be denied." [1] Even those who like Crescas contended for the existence of essential attributes likewise denied that there is any similarity between divine and human attributes, "for they widely differ . . . the one being finite and the other infinite," and "there can be no relation and comparison between the infinite and the finite." [2] In almost exactly the same words Spinoza says: "This I know, that between the finite and the infinite there is no comparison (*proportionem*); so that the difference between the greatest and most excellent creature and God is the same as the difference between God and the least creature." [3] The absolute infinity of God in this sense is described by Maimonides as follows: "Even these negative attributes must not be formed and applied to God, except in the way in which, as you know, sometimes an attribute is negatived in reference to a thing, although that attribute can naturally never be applied to it in the same sense, as, e.g., we say,

---

[1] *Ibid.*, I, 56.
[2] *Or Adonai*, I, iii, 3 (pp. 23b–24a).   [3] *Epistola* 54.

'This wall does not see.'" [1] Says also Judah ha-Levi: "As regards the negative attributes, such as Living, Only, First and Last, they are given to Him in order to negative their contrasts, but not to establish them in the sense we understand them. For we cannot understand life except accompanied by sensibility and movement. God, however, is above them. . . . One cannot, for instance, speak of time as being endowed with life, yet it does not follow that it is dead, since its nature has nothing to do with either life or death. In the same way one cannot call a stone ignorant, although we may say that it is not learned. Just as a stone is too low to be brought into connection with learning or ignorance, thus the essence of God is too exalted to have anything to do with life or death." [2] Exactly the same reasoning, though for a different purpose, is employed by Spinoza: "I say then, first, that privation is not the act of depriving, but simply and merely a state of want. . . . We say, for example, that a blind man is deprived of sight, because we readily imagine him as seeing. This imagination comes about either because we compare him with others who see, or because we compare his present condition with his past condition when he did see. . . . But when the decree of God and His nature are considered, we cannot say of that man any more than of a stone, that he is deprived of sight, for at that time sight pertains to that man no less inconsistently than to a stone." [3]

Hence the term "infinite" stands in Spinoza for such terms as "unique," "incomparable," "homonymous," "indeterminate," "incomprehensible," "ineffable," "indefinable," "unknowable," and many other similar terms. "Unknowable" and "indefinable," however, will be found its most

[1] *Moreh Nebukim*, I, 58.   [2] *Cuzari*, II, 2.
[3] *Epistola* 21.

convenient equivalents. It is in accordance with Aristotle's dictum that "the infinite so far as infinite is unknown," [1] which Spinoza himself repeats in connection with his argument that by an infinite number of methods "we can never arrive . . . at any knowledge whatever." [2]

In the three propositions from VIII to X Spinoza is trying to prove, as we have already indicated, that substance is everything that God has been laid down to be in his definition. Proposition VIII begins by showing that like God, who is "absolutely infinite," substance is also "necessarily infinite." Formally the proof of this proposition is based upon the identity of essence and existence in substance, as stated in Proposition VII, and upon the impossibility of two or more substances having the same nature or attributes, as stated in Proposition V. Materially, however, the proposition rests upon the very definition of substance. For Proposition VII, we may recall, is based upon the principle that substance has no prior cause, and Proposition V is likewise based upon the principle that substance can have no higher genus, both of which principles are implied in the definition of substance So this proposition, too, is derived from the very nature and definition of substance as "something which is in itself and is conceived through itself." In fact, Propositions VII, VIII, IX, and X are all unfoldings of the implications of the definition of substance.

The next step in the analogy between substance and God is to show that by infinity in both cases is meant the possession of infinite attributes. This is the purpose of Proposition IX. The proposition as it stands is incomplete. Only the major premise is given. Its full significance, however, can be brought out by supplying the minor premise and conclusion.

[1] *Physics*, I, 4, 187b, 7.
[2] *Tractatus de Intellectus Emendatione*, § 13 (*Opera*, II, p. 13, ll. 17–23).

"The more reality or being a thing possesses, the more attributes belong to it." But substance possesses infinite reality or being. Hence, to substance belong infinite attributes. In one of his letters to de Vries,[1] as well as in the Scholium to Proposition X, in both of which places Proposition IX is reproduced, Spinoza actually adds the needed conclusion.

There is one incidental comment which I should like to make here with regard to the source of Proposition IX. It seems to me that this proposition reflects Aristotle's discussion with regard to the character of a true *proprium* predicated of a subject. If it can be shown, says Aristotle, that A is a *proprium* of B, it can also be shown that what is more A is also a *proprium* of what is more B. To quote him in full: "The confirmer however [must consider], whether what is simply is the property of what is simply; for the more will be the property of the more, the less also of the less, the least of the least, and the most of the most; thus, since it is the property of fire naturally to tend upwards, it would also be the property of what is more fire naturally to tend more upwards, and in the same manner we must direct attention from other things also, to all these." [2] That Aristotle speaks of *proprium* (ἴδιον) whereas Spinoza here speaks of "attributes" is a matter of indifference. In mediaeval Hebrew literature the term *proprium* in a similar passage of Aristotle is translated by the word which usually means "attribute." [3]

---

[1] Epistola 9 (*Opera*, IV, p. 45, ll. 2–4 and 20–22).

[2] *Topics*, V, 8, 137b, 33–138a, 3.

[3] Cf. *Emunah Ramah*, II, iv, 3 (p. 65): "These are some of the propositions which are derived from the more (היותר) and less (והפחות). Aristotle mentions them in the Book on *Dialectic* (נצוח = جدل), the title of which is translated by Alfarabi as the Book on *Topics* (המקומות – الجدل مواضع; cf. Steinschneider, *Al-Farabi*, p. 53, n. 74). The proposition in question is as follows: If a certain thing has a certain attribute (תואר), and if also the more that thing is the more it has of that attribute, then the attribute belongs to the thing truly by necessity." This

Spinoza himself occasionally uses the term "attribute" in the sense of property.[1] Starting therefore with the definition of attribute as "that which the intellect perceives of substance, as if constituting the essence of substance" (Demonst. of Prop. IX) and assuming it to be thus a true *proprium* of substance, Spinoza concludes that "the more reality (*realitas*) or being (*esse*) a thing possesses the more attributes belong to it" (Prop. IX). Incidentally it may be remarked that since here as well as in his correspondence[2] Spinoza uses *realitas* as the equivalent of *esse* or of *entitas*,[3] the term *wezentheid* (or *wezeendhijd*), which in a corresponding passage in *Short Treatise*, I, 2, § 17,[4] is used in place of *realitas*, should be translated by *esse* (i.e., being, *Sein*) rather than *essentia* (i.e., essence, *Wesenheit*). Spinoza further uses *realitas* as the equivalent of *perfectio*,[5] for which use there is a parallel in Descartes.[6]

Proposition X concludes the analogy between substance and God by showing that each attribute of substance is infinite in all the various senses of infinity. "Each attribute of substance must be conceived through itself." To be conceived through itself, it has already been shown, means to be indefinable, and "indefinable" and "infinite," it has also been shown, are interchangeable terms.[7]

passage is based on *Topics*, V, 8, 137b, 14 ff., where the locus of more (μᾶλλον) and less (ἧττον) is discussed. The Greek term underlying the Hebrew term for "attribute" is *proprium* (ἴδιον).

[1] Cf. below, p. 230.
[2] Epistola 9 (*Opera*, IV, p. 45, ll. 2–3 and 20).
[3] *Ethics*, IV, Praef. (*Opera*, II, p. 207, l. 27).
[4] *Opera*, I, p. 23, ll. 22–24; p. 534. Cf. above, p. 108, n. 4, and below, p. 382, n. 7.
[5] *Ethics*, II, Def. 6, *et passim*.
[6] *Meditationes*, III (*Oeuvres*, VII, p. 40, l. 28).
[7] See above, p. 76.

IV. Relation of Attribute to Substance

The God or substance of Spinoza, like the God of mediaeval rationalists, is unknowable in His essence. He may indeed, in Spinoza's view, be immediately perceived by intuition as a clear and distinct idea, but He is not subject to knowledge that defines its object in terms broader and more general. When Spinoza argues against the mediaeval conception of an unknowable God,[1] he simply argues for the view that God can be known, after a manner, even though He cannot be defined in terms of genus and species. "Of His [i.e., God's] essence," says Spinoza, "we can form no general idea."[2] Spinoza indeed will endeavor to prove the existence of God, but in this he will be merely carrying out the mediaeval tradition that while we can have no knowledge of God's essence we can prove His existence. "There is no possibility of obtaining a knowledge of the essence of God . . . the only thing that man can apprehend of Him is the fact that He exists."[3] Or again: "If knowledge is sought concerning a thing whose very existence is in doubt, the first question to be asked is whether it exists or not. When the question of its existence has been answered positively, the thing then to be asked about it is, What is it? How is it? Wherefore is it? Concerning God, however, man has no right to ask except the question as to whether He exists."[4]

But while the real nature of God must remain beyond comprehension, still God as a living and dynamic force in the world, conceived as creator, lawgiver, caretaker, guide, and guardian, makes himself known to mankind through His

---

[1] *Short Treatise*, I, 7, §§ 3 ff.
[2] Epistola 50 (*Opera*, IV, p. 240, ll. 2–3).
[3] *Moreh Nebukim*, I, 59.
[4] *Hobot ha-Lebabot*, I, 4.

actions and works, and assumes in their eyes a certain character and personality. This character and personality of God was determined, in the Middle Ages, by a set of descriptive terms drawn from the literature of religious tradition. In the philosophic terminology of the time, these descriptive terms were known by the name of divine attributes. There were many kinds of attributes which, when taken in their literal sense, would express the various relations that may exist between attribute and subject. Some of these divine attributes would constitute in their ordinary meaning accidental qualities. Others would designate actions. Still others would only express some external relations. It was, however, generally agreed that attributes could not be taken in a sense which would imply plurality in the divine essence or a similarity between God and His creatures.[1] It was therefore commonly recognized that attributes are not to be taken in their literal sense. The Talmudic saying that "the Torah speaks according to the language of men"[2] is quoted in this connection by the mediaeval Jewish philosophers.[3] Spinoza repeats it in his statement that "the Scripture . . . continually speaks after the fashion of men."[4] How these attributes could be interpreted so as not to contravene the absolute simplicity and uniqueness of God constituted the problem of divine attributes with which all the mediaeval Jewish philosophers had to grapple. That attributes could not be taken as accidental qualities was generally admitted. Whether they should be interpreted as external relations would seem to be a question upon which opinions differed,[5]

---

[1] See my "Crescas on the Problem of Divine Attributes," *Jewish Quarterly Review*, n.s., Vol. VII, p. 9, n. 11.

[2] *Berakot* 31b, and parallels.   [3] *Moreh Nebukim*, I, 26.

[4] Epistola 19 (*Opera*, IV, p. 92, ll. 12–13); Epistola 21 (p. 132, ll. 34 f.).

[5] *Cuzari*, II, 2; *Emunah Ramah*, II, iii; *Ḥobot ha-Lebabot*, I, 10; *Moreh Nebukim*, I, 52 and 58.

though, I believe, it can be shown that the difference was merely in the use of terms. It was agreed by all, however, that attributes may be taken in the sense of actions. There was equally a general agreement that no attribute, in its literal and obvious sense, expresses the real essence of God, inasmuch as the essence of God must forever remain unknowable.

The mediaeval discussion about attributes is sometimes summed up in a distinction drawn between the name Jehovah and the other names of God. Says Judah ha-Levi: "All names of God, save the Tetragrammaton, are predicates and attributive descriptions, derived from the way His creatures are affected by His decrees and measures." [1] Says also Maimonides: "It is well known that all the names of God occurring in Scripture are derived from His actions, except one, namely, the Tetragrammaton, which consists of the letters *yod, he, waw, he.* This name is the *nomen proprium* [2] of God and is on that account called *Shem ha-Meforash*, that is to say, the name which indicates the essence of God in a manner which excludes the implication of its having anything in common with the essence of other beings. All the other glorious names are common appellatives, [3] inasmuch as they are derived from actions to which some of our own are similar." [4] In connection with these divine names Judah ha-Levi quotes Exodus 6, 3, where God says to Moses: "And I appeared unto Abraham, unto Isaac, and unto Jacob, by the name of God Almighty (*El Shaddai*), but by my name Jehovah was I not known to them." [5]

In Spinoza we find this view of the mediaevals restated in almost their own words. Quoting the same verse from

[1] *Cuzari*, II, 2.   [2] שם מיוחד.
[3] מורים בשתוף.   [4] *Moreh Nebukim*, I, 61.
[5] *Cuzari*, II, 2.

Exodus 6, 3,[1] he comments upon it as follows: "We must note that in Scripture no other name but Jehovah is ever found which indicates the absolute essence of God, without reference to created things. The Jews maintain, for this reason, that this is the only *nomen proprium* of God; that the other names are mere appellatives (*appellativa*); and, in truth, the other names of God, whether they be substantives or adjectives, are mere attributes, which belong to God in so far as He is conceived of in relation to created things or is manifested through them." He then concludes: "Now, as God tells Moses that He was not known to the patriarchs by the name of Jehovah, it follows that they were not cognizant of any attribute of God which expresses His absolute essence, but only of His deeds and promises — that is, of His power, as manifested in visible things."[2] Now, Spinoza has adopted the traditional term "attribute," and makes use of it as a description of the manner in which substance, unknowable in itself, manifests itself to the human mind. But how would Spinoza characterize his attributes if he were to classify them according to the mediaeval fashion? They are not accidents, nor relations, nor actions. They are, however, what, as we shall presently see, the mediaevals called essential attributes, that is to say, attributes which constitute the essence. He thus says: "By attribute, I under-

---

[1] In his comment on the divine name *El Shaddai* which occurs in this verse, Spinoza remarks that "*El Shaddai*, in Hebrew, signifies the God who suffices, in that He gives to every man that which suffices for him" (*Opera*, III, p. 169, ll. 3–5). Judah ha-Levi, in the corresponding passage quoted in the preceding paragraph, explains *El Shaddai* as meaning "power and dominion." Spinoza's explanation, however, is found in Rashi's commentary on the Bible (cf. Genesis 17, 1; 28, 3; 35, 11). Maimonides, though he like Rashi derives *El Shaddai* from a word meaning "sufficient," explains it to mean that "His existence is self-sufficient" (*Moreh Nebukim*, I, 63). These two etymologies of *El Shaddai* go back to still earlier sources.

[2] *Tractatus Theologico-Politicus*, Ch. 13 (*Opera*, III, p. 169, ll. 7–24).

stand that which the intellect perceives of substance, as if constituting its essence" (*Ethics*, I, Def. IV).

But here we are met with a difficulty, a natural difficulty, too, which has divided Spinoza scholars into two camps.

The definition may have two meanings, depending upon which of its elements is emphasized. If the expression "which the intellect perceives" is laid stress upon, it would seem that attributes are only *in intellectu*. Attributes would thus be only a subjective mode of thinking, expressing a relation to a perceiving subject and having no real existence in the essence. On the other hand, if only the latter part of the definition is taken notice of, namely, "constituting the essence of a substance," it would seem that the attributes are *extra intellectum*, real elements out of which the essence of the substance is composed. According to both interpretations, to be sure, it is the mind which perceives the attributes, but there is the following difference. According to the former interpretation, to be perceived by the mind means to be *invented* by the mind, for of themselves the attributes have no independent existence at all but are identical with the essence of the substance. According to the latter interpretation, to be perceived by the mind means only to be *discovered* by the mind, for even of themselves the attributes have independent existence in the essence of the substance.[1]

In the discussion of the subject two kinds of evidence have been adduced by scholars in support of their respective interpretations: literary and material. It is not my purpose here, however, to assemble and assess what has been said by either side in support of its own view and in objection to the other. On the whole, the abundance of both literary and material evidence is in favor of the subjective interpretation. This interpretation is in harmony both with the variety of

[1] Cf. Erdmann, *Grundriss der Geschichte der Philosophie*, II, § 272.6.

statements made by Spinoza about attributes and with the place which the attributes occupy in his system. Of the latter we shall have occasion to speak in other chapters. The main objection to this interpretation has been summed up in the statement that "no prae-Kantian reader would have put such a construction on Spinoza's language." [1] We shall therefore address ourselves to this particular objection and try to show that this very controversy between the upholders of the subjective and the objective interpretations of Spinoza's attributes is the question upon which mediaeval Jewish philosophers were divided in their theories of divine attributes, and also to point to certain facts which indicate that Spinoza has consciously and advisedly aligned himself with that group of Jewish philosophers who held a subjective theory of attributes.

The gravamen of the mediaeval discussion of divine attributes is what is known as the problem of essential attributes. By essential attributes are meant those elements which constitute the essence of a subject, or which are related to the essence of the subject as the genus and species are related to the essence of the object defined. It appears primarily as a problem in the exegesis of those adjectives which in the Bible or in the other traditional literature are ascribed to God. Admitting, as we have already pointed out, that attributes are not to be taken literally, that they cannot be interpreted as accidental qualities but may be interpreted as actions, the mediaevals raised the question as to whether any of these adjectives may be taken as being related to God in the same sense as the elements of a definition to the object defined, that is to say, as if constituting the divine essence. The problem, it must be remarked, was not whether the divine essence could be conceived as consisting of a genus and species. The

---

[1] Martineau, *A Study of Spinoza*, p. 184. Cf. Erdmann, *loc. cit.*

absolute simplicity of God is a principle established beyond any question, a simplicity which is to exclude metaphysical and logical plurality no less than physical composition. It is thus generally admitted that God is not a species and can have no genus.[1] The question was merely as to whether the assumption of essential attributes contravened that simplicity of essence. To put the question more bluntly: Assuming that the relation of God's attributes to His essence is analogous to that of the parts of a definition, genus and species, to the essence of the object defined, does that mean that the essence is simple or not? Those who reject essential attributes answer it in the negative; those who admit them answer it in the positive.

The basis of the problem, it seems to me, is to be found in the question as to the nature of the reality of genus and species, or, in other words, of universals. If universals have some kind of reality, then genus and species have some kind of real existence, and a subject to which are attributed terms related to it after the analogy of genus and species cannot be said to be absolutely simple. On the other hand, if universals have no reality at all, then genus and species are mere names, and definitions are purely nominal, and the essence of the subject defined is in reality simple. The problem of essential attributes is thus a problem of universals, the controversy between realism and nominalism. It is, however, not a conflict between Platonism and Aristotelianism. Platonic realism had no followers among the classical Jewish philosophers. It is as Aristotelians, and as interpreters of Aristotle's view, that Jewish philosophers latently formulated their respective theories of universals which are hid away in their discussions of divine attributes. For the real problem of universals, it may be said, began with the rejection of Pla-

---

[1] 'Ikkarim, II, 6 and 7. Cf. Short Treatise, I, 7, § 3.

tonic realism, when speculation became rife concerning those universals which were now said to exist only in the mind.

As spokesman of those who reject essential attributes we may take Maimonides.[1] While essential attributes, says Maimonides, denote the essence of the object and do not imply anything extraneous superadded to it, still they are to be rejected, for they imply that the essence itself is composed, as it were, of genus and species, which as universal terms are considered as previous causes to the existence of the individual essence.[2] It is here that the theory of universals comes into play. Like all Arabic and Jewish philosophers, Maimonides rejects Platonic realism, affirming that "species have no existence except in our own mind."[3] Still this assertion makes him neither a nominalist nor a conceptualist. Nominalism must be rejected as inconsistent with the entire trend of his argument, for if universals were mere words, definitions would be purely nominal, and Maimonides could not reject essential attributes on the ground that "there are no previous causes to His existence, by which He could be defined," and quote with approval those who maintain that "no definition can be given of God."[4] Conceptualism, or the theory that universals have ideal without real existence, is explicitly rejected by Maimonides in his repudiation of "the assertion of some thinkers, that ideas, i.e., the universals, are neither existent nor non-existent."[5] What Maimonides, as follower of Avicenna and in common with all his contemporaries, conceived of universals is that they have both ideal and real existence. Universals, to be sure, exist in the mind, but the human mind does not *invent* them

---

[1] The historical survey which follows is based upon my essay "Crescas on the Problem of Divine Attributes," *Jewish Quarterly Review*, n.s., Vol. VII (1916), pp. 1–44, 175–221.

[2] *Moreh Nebukim*, I, 51 and 52.

[3] *Ibid.*, III, 18.   [4] *Ibid.*, I, 52.   [5] *Ibid.*, I, 51.

out of nothing. What the mind does is only to *discover* them in the multifarious individuals. For prior to the rise of individual beings the universals exist in the mind of God as independent entities, and they remain as such even when they enter upon plurality in material form, though their presence in the individuals is not discernible except by mental activity. Consequently essential attributes, which are related to the subject as genus and species are related to the object defined, must necessarily imply some kind of plurality in the essence of the subject. This plurality, to be sure, would be only mentally discernible, but still it would be inconsistent with the conception of absolute simplicity.

As against this view there are those who maintain that essential attributes are admissible. They insist that universals have no reality at all; their existence in the mind means that they are invented by the mind. Genus and species are thus only generalizations, and definitions consisting of genus and species are only nominal. Averroes, whose view is quoted in Hebrew literature, is clearly outspoken on this point. "It is of the nature of essential attributes that they do not introduce any plurality into the subject which supports them actually. If they do import into them some kind of plurality, it is only in the same sense that the parts of a definition may be said to import some kind of plurality into the object defined, and that is what is called by philosophers an intellectual plurality in contradistinction to an actual plurality." [1] No less outspoken is Moses ha-Lavi in his admission of essential attributes. "Some attributes," he says, "are identical with the essence of the object described, as, for instance, when we describe man by the attribute 'animal.' . . . With reference to such attributes as are identical with

[1] Averroes, *Tahafut al-Tahafut*, V (ed. M. Bouyges, p. 300, ll. 12–15); paraphrased also by Narboni on *Moreh Nebukim*, I, 58.

the essence of the object described, it is evident that God can be described by them, inasmuch as they do not imply any addition to the essence at all." [1] The implication here again is that essential attributes, related to God after the analogy of the genus animal to man, are purely subjective terms, in reality being absolutely identical with the essence of God. Likewise Gersonides, in his argument against Maimonides' negative interpretation of attributes, justifies his own positive interpretation by pointing to their subjective character. He draws a distinction between two kinds of propositions, one in which the relation of subject and predicate is that of *discourse*, the other in which it is that of *existence* [2] — a distinction reminiscent of that made by Aristotle between *nominal* and *real* definitions.[3] Divine attributes are thus to him purely subjective and nominal predications of God, related to Him only in *discourse*, and implying no plurality in His essence, and may therefore be taken as positive terms. It can also be shown that Crescas' insistence upon the admissibility of positive essential attributes is based upon the view that attributes are purely subjective terms. The eclectic Albo, vacillating between the positive and negative interpretations of attributes, endeavors to justify the positive form of attributes by calling them "intellectual conceptions" [4] of divine perfection. "When I awaken from my reflections upon the plurality of attributes I begin to realize that all the attributes are nothing but intellectual conceptions of those perfections which must needs exist in Thy essence but which in reality are nothing but Thy essence." [5]

In view of this controversy over essential attributes in the

[1] *Ma'amar Elohi.*
[2] *Milḥamot Adonai*, III, 3: ‏במאמר . . . במציאות‏.
[3] *Analytica Posteriora*, II, 10, 93b, 29 ff.
[4] ‏בחינות שכליות‏.
[5] *'Iḳḳarim*, II, 25.

philosophic literature with which Spinoza had an intimate
acquaintance, and in view of this insistence upon the subjective nature of essential attributes on the part of many of
his Jewish predecessors, it is not unreasonable to assume that
it is not as a mere turn of speech that Spinoza always refers
to attribute in subjective terms, as when he describes
it, for instance, as that which the intellect perceives (*per-
cipit*)[1] concerning the substance, or as that which expresses
(*exprimit*)[2] or explains (*explicat*)[3] the essence of substance,
or as that under which God is considered (*consideratur*)[4] or
every entity is conceived (*concipi*),[5] or as that which is the
same as substance but is called attribute with respect to the
intellect (*respectu intellectus*).[6] There is, furthermore, evidence that Spinoza was acquainted with the moderately
realistic Avicennian and Maimonidean theory of universals
and that he disagreed with it and criticized it. "They have
set up general ideas," he says, . . . "These ideas, they state,
are in the understanding of God, as many of Plato's followers
have said, namely, that these general Ideas (such as rational,
animal, and the like) have been created by God; and although those who follow Aristotle say, indeed, that these
things are not real things, only things of reason, they nevertheless regard them frequently as [real] things."[7] The
reference in this passage to the objective interpretation of
Aristotle's universals is clear. He finds it to differ only little
from Platonic realism. It would seem that Spinoza himself
considered universals, with the exception of only one uni-

---

[1] *Ethics*, I, Def. 4.

[2] *Ibid.*, I, Prop. 10, Schol.; Prop. 32, Demonst.

[3] *Tractatus Theologico-Politicus*, Ch. 13 (*Opera*, III, p. 169, l. 23).

[4] *Ethics*, II, Prop. 6; Prop. 7, Schol.; Epistola 64 (*Opera*, IV, p. 277, ll. 23–24 and 28–29).

[5] *Ethics*, I, Prop. 10, Schol.; cf. Epistola 9 (*Opera*, IV, p. 45, l. 2).

[6] Epistola 9 (*Opera*, IV, p. 46, l. 4).

[7] *Short Treatise*, I, 6, § 7.

versal, namely, substance,[1] as purely subjective concepts; and what is true of universals is also true of attributes. It is thus not in vain that in his formal definition of attribute Spinoza says that he understands by it "that which the intellect [2] perceives of substance, as if constituting its esssence," instead of merely saying, as does Descartes, that attributes constitute the essence of substance.[3] Elsewhere, too, in the *Ethics* as well as in his other writings attributes are always spoken of in terms which suggest their subjective character.[4] In one place he says explicitly that attributes are distinguished only by reason.[5]

This subjective interpretation of attributes disposes of the difficulty which is raised by those who follow the objective interpretation. "How that essence can be one and self-identical, while its constituents are many, heterogeneous and unrelated, is a question which is hopeless of solution." [6]

---

[1] Cf. below, pp. 327–328.

[2] By the term "intellect" in this definition Spinoza means the finite human intellect. When he says in *Ethics*, II, Prop. VII, Schol., that "we have already demonstrated, that everything which can be perceived by the *infinite intellect* as constituting the essence of substance pertains entirely to one substance, and consequently that substance thinking and substance extended are one and the same substance, which is now comprehended under this attribute and now under that," it is not to be inferred that an attribute of substance is that which can be conceived only by the "infinite intellect." What the passage means to say is that "*everything* which can be conceived of by the *infinite intellect* as constituting the essence of substance" — and the infinite intellect can conceive of an infinite number of things as constituting the essence of substance — is only an attribute of substance and not a substance itself, and consequently extension and thought, which alone can be conceived by the finite human intellect as constituting the essence of substance, are only attributes of substance and not substances themselves.

[3] *Principia Philosophiae*, I, 53: "Substantiae praecipua proprietas [= attributum], quae ipsius naturam essetiamque constituit"; *Notae in Programma* (*Œuvres*, VIII, 2, p. 349, ll. 1–2): "Attributum, quod ejus [substantiae] essentiam naturamque constituit." See Erdmann, *Grundriss der Geschichte der Philosophie*, II, § 272,6.

[4] See references above, p. 152. Cf. Busolt, *Die Grundzüge der Erkenntnisztheorie und Metaphysik Spinozas*, pp. 107–111.   [5] *Cogitata Metaphysica*, I, 3.

[6] Martineau, *A Study of Spinoza*, p. 185.

The question had already been raised by Simon de Vries in a letter to Spinoza: "If I may say that each substance has only one attribute and if I had the idea of two attributes, then I could rightly conclude that where there are two different attributes there are also two different substances." [1] Spinoza's answer is like that given in Jewish literature by those who admitted essential attributes, namely, that attributes are merely different words expressing the same essence. "You desire, though there is no need, that I should illustrate by an example, how one and the same thing can be stamped with two names. In order not to seem miserly, I will give you two." [2] That essential attributes, as suggested in this quotation, are only names by which the essence is denoted is the view held by both those who admit the use of positive attributes and those who reject it. Even Maimonides speaks of essential attributes as being merely "the explanation of a name." [3] If he does reject their positive use, it is only because he endows essential attributes with some kind of objective reality. Were they all names only and nothing else, Maimonides would permit their positive use. Albo well restates Maimonides' view in the following passage: "You must know that God cannot be described by two things which would constitute His essence after the analogy of animality and rationality in Man. . . . He can, however, be described by any attribute which is only the explanation of the name by which He is called." [4]

In the mediaeval endeavor to reconcile the apparent contradiction between the plurality of attributes and the simplicity of essence an attempt is often made to reduce all the different attributes to one. It is shown that the variety of

---

[1] Epistola 8 (*Opera*, IV, p. 41, ll. 10–13).
[2] Epistola 9 (*Opera*, IV, p. 46, ll. 7–9).
[3] *Moreh Nebukim*, I, 51 and 52. Cf. below, pp. 229–230.
[4] '*Ikkarim*, II, 9.

attributes, however different they may appear to us, are in reality one, for they are all involved in our conception of God, they are conceived by us simultaneously, and they are always together in God. "These three attributes [life, power, wisdom] are conceived by our mind immediately and simultaneously without the aid of intermediate reasoning, for conceiving God as we do in the nature of a creator we at once think of Him as living, powerful, and wise. . . . But though these three attributes occur to our mind at once, it is impossible for our tongue to utter them at once, for we do not find in human speech a single word comprehending all the three attributes and we are compelled to resort to the use of three words." [1] Again: "We therefore say that the attributes ascribed to God, though different from each other when used with reference to us, are all one in Him. For with reference to ourselves, inasmuch as we conceive them or acquire them one after the other, we consider them as being different from each other; similarly, inasmuch as we acquire them after we have been without them, we naturally consider them as superadded to the essence. With reference to God, however, we must consider them as unified and unacquired in such a manner as not to imply any plurality in His essence." [2] It is the same reasoning that underlies the following passage of Spinoza: "From this it is apparent that although two attributes may be conceived as really distinct — that is to say, one without the assistance of the other — we cannot nevertheless thence conclude that they constitute two things or two different substances; for this is the nature of substance, that each of its attributes is conceived through itself, since all the attributes which substance possesses were always in it together, nor could one be produced by another;

[1] *Emunot we-De'ot*, II, 4.
[2] *'Ikkarim*, II, 21.

but each expresses the reality or being of substance" (Prop. X, Schol.). The implications of this passage are these: The two attributes appear to the mind as being distinct from each other. In reality, however, they are one. For by Proposition X, attributes, like substance, are *summa genera* ("conceived through itself"). The two attributes must therefore be one and identical with substance. Furthermore, the two attributes have not been acquired by substance after it had been without them, nor are they conceived by the mind one after the other or deduced one from the other. They have always been in substance together, and are conceived by our mind simultaneously. Hence, the attributes are only different words expressing the same reality and being of substance.

Proposition XII is complementary to the definitions of substance and attribute. While the definition of attribute states affirmatively the subjective nature of attributes by declaring that they are only perceived by the mind, the proposition denies any independent reality to attributes by which the simplicity of the substance would be endangered. "No attribute of substance can be truly conceived from which it follows that substance can be divided." The conclusion is then reached in Proposition XIII, namely, that "substance absolutely infinite is indivisible."

Spinoza's demonstrations for both these propositions are practically the same. In both cases he begins with the same hypothetico-disjunctive proposition and proceeds to show in an identical manner that substance, because it is absolutely infinite, cannot be divided. It will be recalled that Spinoza's "absolutely infinite" has been shown to correspond to what the mediaevals called "essentially infinite." It is singularly worthy of notice that Spinoza's argument here against the divisibility of an *absolutely infinite* substance is the same as the mediaeval argument against the divisibility of an *essentially infinite* substance.

Spinoza's argument runs as follows:

I. If an absolutely infinite substance were divisible, the parts would either retain the nature of the whole or not.

II. If the parts retained the nature of the whole, there would then be many infinite substances, which is absurd.

III. If they did not retain the nature of the whole, then the whole would lose the nature of substance and cease to be.

The mediaeval argument against the divisibility of an essentially infinite substance, as given by Averroes, runs in a similar vein:

I. If an essentially infinite substance were divisible, the parts would either have the same nature as the whole or not.

II. If the parts had the same nature as the whole, then the parts of an infinite would be infinite, which is absurd.

III. If they did not have the same nature as the whole, then the whole would consist of heterogeneous parts and would thus lose its homogeneous and simple character.[1]

The discussion of attributes in this chapter has been confined to those phases of the problem which the exigencies of the interpretation of Propositions VII–X and XII–XIII required. Other phases of the problem will be discussed in the chapter on Extension and Thought.

---

[1] See Averroes' *Middle Commentaries* on *Physics*, III, 5, 204a, 20–32, and *Metaphysics*, XI, 10, 1066b, 11–21. Cf. my *Crescas' Critique of Aristotle*, p. 137, and note (d) on pp. 331–332.

CHAPTER VI

PROOFS OF THE EXISTENCE OF GOD

I. The Ontological Proof

THE first ten propositions of the *Ethics*, which precede Spinoza's proofs of the existence of God, are a challenge to mediaeval philosophers. The starting point is the definition of God, placed by Spinoza near the beginning of his work, which, as we have already shown, is an exact reproduction of a definition found in a standard work of a popular mediaeval Jewish philosopher.[1] Spinoza seems to address his imaginary opponents as follows:

All you mediaevals, to whatever school of thought you may belong, have builded your philosophies on the conception of a God epitomized by you in a formal definition which contains four characteristic expressions. You say that God is (1) an *ens* in the highest sense of the term, by which you mean that He is a being who exists necessarily. You also say that He is (2) "absolutely infinite," by which you mean that He is (3) "a substance consisting of infinite attributes," (4) "each of which expresses eternal and infinite essence" (Def. VI). God so defined you call absolute substance; you differentiate Him from the world which you call conditional substance, and then you declare that the relation between the absolute and the conditional substance is like that of creator to created. In opposition to you, I deny at the very outset the existence of a God outside the world and of His relation to the world as creator. Still, unaccustomed as I am

---

[1] *'Iḳḳarim*, II, 25. Cf. above, p. 118.

to dispute about mere names,[1] I shall retain your own term substance as a philosophic surrogate to the pious name God, and in your own terms I am going to unfold a new conception of the nature of God and of His relation to the world.

To begin with, I shall abandon your distinction between absolute substance and conditional substance, but shall use the term substance in that restrictive sense in which you use the expression absolute substance. Then, what you call conditional substance, or the world, I shall call mode. Furthermore, unlike you, I shall not describe the relation of substance to mode as that of creator to created, but rather as that of whole to part, or, to be more exact, as that of universal to particular (Defs. II and V; Axioms I and II; Prop. I).[2] The reason for my disagreeing with you on the question of the causal relation between God and the world is that I find your doctrine of creation, however you may try to explain it, an untenable hypothesis (Props. II–VI).[3] Barring this difference between us, a difference which, I must confess, is fundamental and far-reaching in its effect, I am going to describe my substance in all those terms which you make use of in describing your God. Like your God, my substance is (1) the highest kind of *ens*, for existence appertains to its nature (Prop. VII). (2) It is also absolutely infinite (Prop. VIII). (3) Furthermore, it consists of infinite attributes (Prop. IX). (4) Finally, each of its attributes expresses eternal and infinite essence (Prop. X).[4] I have thus described my substance in all those terms which you use in your formal definition of God. Consequently, as I am now to reproduce your proofs of the existence of God to prove the existence of my substance, I shall bracket together the terms God and substance and

[1] Cf. *Cogitata Metaphysica*, I, 3, quoted below. Cf. below, p. 190, n. 3.
[2] Cf. above, Chapter III.   [3] Cf. above, Chapter IV.
[4] Cf. above, Chapter V.

say: "God, or substance consisting of infinite attributes, each of which expresses eternal and infinite essence, necessarily exists" (Prop. XI). Having made it clear by this time what I mean by the term God, I am no longer afraid of being misunderstood. Hereafter I shall drop the term substance and use in its stead the term God. And so he does.

The expression *necessario existit*, which Spinoza uses in the eleventh proposition, is to be understood to have two meanings. In the first place, it means that it can be shown apodictically, by necessary, logical reasoning, that God must exist. In the second place, it means that the existence which is proved of God belongs to that class known as necessary existence as opposed to possible existence. In a passage in the *Cogitata Metaphysica*, I, 1, Spinoza points out the distinction between these two classes of existence: "From the definition of Being, or, if you prefer, from its description,[1] it is now easily seen that Being should be divided into Being which because of its own nature necessarily exists, or Being whose essence involves existence, and Being whose essence involves only possible existence." In the course of our subsequent discussion of the proofs, especially of the second proof, it will become clear that the purpose of this proposition is to state not only that God exists but also that His existence is of the kind known as necessary existence. This double purpose of the proofs of the existence of God is clearly brought out by Spinoza in his *Principia Philosophiae Cartesianae*, I, Proposition V, Demonstration: "The concept of God includes necessary existence. Therefore it is true to say

---

[1] Definition (ὁρισμός, ח׳, גדר) is to be distinguished from description (ὑπογραφή, רسم, רשם). Cf. Maimonides, *Millot ha-Higgayon*, Ch. 10. Spinoza's hesitancy as to whether Being (*ens*) has a definition or only a description reflects the question raised by Hillel of Verona in his Commentary on Maimonides' Twenty-five Propositions (Prop. 25) as to whether substance has a definition in view of the fact that it is a *summum genus*. Cf. my *Crescas' Critique of Aristotle*, p. 575.

that He has a necessary existence in himself, or that He exists."
Similarly Crescas in conclusion of his summary of Maimonides' proofs of the existence of God seems to emphasize that
the proofs demonstrate not only that God exists but that He
exists with an existence which is necessary *per se*.[1]

It will be well for us to state in Spinoza's own terms what
he is driving at in his proofs of the existence of God and what
he is trying to establish thereby. Spinoza himself would
have said that he was trying to determine by these proofs
what kind of being (*ens*) God is. For being — or rather the
ideas we have of being — is, according to Spinoza, of four kinds
— a classification which seems to be derived from a Hebrew
source. Some ideas are real, and these are ideas which have
an extra-mental object as their source; others are unreal,
and of these some are fictitious, mere figments of the imagination, composite pictures of things perceived and experienced; others are rational, mere modes of thought, such as
the universals known as genera and species; and still others
are merely verbal, because they exist neither in the intellect
nor in the imagination, such as chimeras and ideas conveyed
by expressions like "a square circle."[2] None of these unreal
ideas are ideas of things, for they have no real object as their

---

[1] *Or Adonai*, I, i, 32.

[2] *Cogitata Metaphysica*, I, 1.

The source of this classification is to be found in the Hebrew philosophic manual
Ruaḥ Ḥen, Ch. 5. According to the *Ruaḥ Ḥen*, there is the following classification
of being:

1. Real beings, דברים אמתיים, which exist outside the mind and of which we
can form an idea either in the mind or in the imagination.

2. Unreal beings, דברים שאינם אמתיים, which exist neither in the mind nor outside the mind. They are fictitious beings, having existence only in the imagination,
אלא שיש לענין ההוא מציאות בדמיון המאמין. Previous to this in the same chapter
they are also called "verbal beings," שאין שם רק דבור לבד. This class is subdivided into two parts:

a. Factitious beings which have no existence in reality, ויציר דברים שאינם
נמצאים כלל.

b. Factitious beings which not only have no existence in reality but whose nature

source, nor have they a counterpart outside the mind. Extra-mental existences only are real, and ideas in the mind are real only in so far as they represent those extra-mental existences. What Spinoza, therefore, is trying to establish by his proofs of the existence of God is that God is not a fictitious being, nor a verbal being, nor a being of reason, but a real being, who has existence outside our mind and who is the source and counterpart of the idea we have of Him. Substance, says Spinoza, is outside the intellect,[1] that is to say, it is not fabricated by the intellect. Only that conception of God, says he again, is a fiction which uses the name of God not in harmony with His real nature; [2] the true conception of God is that of "a body in nature whose idea is necessary in order to represent God immediately." [3]

In order to determine whether an idea is real or not one has to ascertain by means of the various approved sources of knowledge whether or not it has an extra-mental object

involves a contradiction, as the words "a square circle" או יציֵיר חרווח הדררית
הנמצאים בהפך תכונתם, כמו שידמה הגלגל מרובע.

3. Beings of reason, which exist only in the mind but have no existence outside the mind, as genera and species, ויש דברים גם כן שנמצאים בשכל, ואין להם מציאות כלל בעצמן חוץ לשכל, והם המינים ושאר הכללים הנבוהים.

The resemblance between this classification and that of Spinoza is striking. The only differences to be noted are as follows:

(1) The classification in *Ruaḥ Ḥen* applies the expression "verbal being" to both 2a and 2b. Spinoza applies it only to what in his classification corresponds to 2b.

(2) This classification considers the expression "a square circle" as something which is in the imagination. Spinoza says of a chimera, which to him is the equivalent of a "square circle," that it is neither in the intellect nor in the imagination (see *Cog. Met.*, I, 3).

Freudenthal is thus not quite right in saying that the distinction of *ens fictum*, *ens chimerae*, *ens rationis* and *ens reale* does not occur in Jewish philosophy. Cf. "Spinoza und die Scholastik" in *Philosophische Aufsätze, Eduard Zeller . . . gewidmet*, p. 103.

[1] Cf. *Ethics*, I, Prop. 4, Demonst.
[2] *Tractatus de Intellectus Emendatione*, § 54 (*Opera*, III, p. 20, note t).
[3] *Short Treatise*, Second Dialogue, § 12 (*Opera*, I, p. 34, ll. 15–17).

to correspond to it. Again and again Spinoza classifies the sources of knowledge. Not all of his classifications are of the same type; they are, however, all made up of various mediaeval classifications with some slight modifications of his own, as we hope to show in another chapter.[1] Roughly speaking, Spinoza maintains, clearly so in the *Short Treatise*, II, 1, that we may know things either directly or indirectly. Direct knowledge may be either sense perception in its many forms and derivations, or intuition, the latter of which is designated by Spinoza as "clear and distinct comprehension,"[2] "clear cognition,"[3] "intuitive science,"[4] or a perception "wherein a thing is perceived through its essence alone,"[5] that is to say, "intuitively, without any process of working."[6] Indirect knowledge consists of the inference of the unknown from the known, which is described by Spinoza as "true belief,"[7] "art of reasoning,"[8] or that mode of perception "wherein the essence of one thing is concluded from the essence of another."[9]

Now, according to Spinoza, any one of these sources of knowledge is sufficiently valid to establish the reality of any idea we happen to have. Intuition and logical inference are as valid proofs for the reality of ideas as direct sense perception; to Spinoza, in fact, they are more valid, for sense perception and imagination alone may lead to falsity.[10] Still, in

---

[1] Cf. below, Vol. II, Chapter XVI.

[2] *klaare en onderscheide bevatting. Short Treatise*, II, 1, § 2.

[3] *klaare Kennisse. Op. cit.*, II, 2, § 1.

[4] *scientia intuitiva. Ethics*, II, Prop. 40, Schol. 2.

[5] *ubi res percipitur per solam suam essentiam. Tractatus de Intellectus Emendatione*, § 19 (*Opera*, II, p. 10, l. 20).

[6] *sed intuitive, nullam operationem facientes. Ibid.*, § 24 (*Opera*, II, p. 12, ll. 13–14).

[7] *waar geloof. Short Treatise*, II, 1, § 2.

[8] *ratio. Ethics*, II, Prop. 40, Schol. 2.

[9] *ubi essentia rei ex alia re concluditur. Tractatus de Intellectus Emendatione*, § 19 (*Opera*, II, p. 10, l. 16). [10] *Ethics*, II, Prop. 41.

the proof of the existence of God in the history of philosophy, not all of these sources of knowledge were of use. Direct sense perception had to be eliminated, for, in the words of Scripture, if a proof-text is necessary, "Man shall not see me and live" (Exodus 33, 20). In fact, Spinoza explicitly states that this verse should be taken in its literal sense as an answer to Moses' request that God should show himself to him in some perceptible form,[1] which, it may be remarked incidentally, is an oblique criticism of Maimonides' interpretation of the verse as meaning that God's essence cannot be comprehended by the human intellect in denial of Moses' request that God should become known to him in His true essence.[2] Historically, therefore, the proofs of the existence of God had to fall back upon the kind of knowledge which is either direct like Spinoza's intuition, or indirect, that is, by way of logical reasoning.

In the history of religious philosophy both these methods of proving the existence of God, the direct and the indirect, were made use of. When theologians, for instance, appeal to revelation as a proof of the existence of God, either to an act of historical revelation in the past or to the constantly repeated revelations in the religious experience of chosen or gifted individuals, they make the knowledge of God something direct and immediately perceived. Similarly when Cicero[3] and, following him, others maintain that the idea of God is innate in man, they also make it an object of immediate apprehension. Likewise the argument from *consensus gentium* rests, in its ultimate analysis, on the assumption that God is an object of immediate knowledge.[4] But,

[1] *Tractatus Theologico-Politicus*, Ch. 2 (*Opera*, III, p. 40, ll. 12 ff.).
[2] *Moreh Nebukim*, I, 64, and I, 4.
[3] *De Natura Deorum*, I, 17, §§ 44-45; II, 4, § 12.
[4] *Ibid.*

on the other hand, the cosmological argument and the argument from design proceed on the assumption that God cannot be immediately known; He can become known only indirectly by the art of reasoning. To Spinoza, however, be it noted, God is an object of direct knowledge, for God, according to him, is known to us as an intuition, as a clear and distinct idea, which is adequate and true. "That existence belongs to the essence of God," says Spinoza, "we can clearly and distinctly understand" (*Short Treatise*, I, 1, § 1); "The knowledge of the eternal and infinite essence of God which each idea involves is adequate and perfect" (*Ethics*, II, Prop. XLVI); and "By adequate idea, I understand an idea which, in so far as it is considered in itself, without reference to the object, has all the properties or internal signs of a true idea" (*Ethics*, II, Def. IV). To Spinoza, therefore, the reality of the idea of God, that is to say, the existence of God, is self-evident as an immediate fact of knowledge, for we can have a knowledge of God which is "as clear as that with which we also know our body." [1]

But here a difficulty arises. To say that God's existence is immediately perceived as an intuition and to declare intuition as a valid source of knowledge, which establishes the reality of the intuited idea, is to start out with a major premise which would seem to require no further demonstration, and to which no further demonstration could add anything, least of all a demonstration in the Aristotelian sense. For a demonstration, according to Aristotle, is "a syllogism which produces science" [2] — and the science it produces in the conclusion must be something not known directly from the major premise. It has indeed been asked whether even in the deductive syllogism of Aristotle the conclusion ever

[1] *Short Treatise*, II, 19, § 14 (*Opera*, I, p. 93, ll. 20–22).
[2] *Analytica Posteriora*, I, 2, 71b, 17–18.

really adds anything to the major premise.[1] Still, while there may be some justification for Aristotle in reasoning from the universal to the particular and in trying to prove syllogistically that Socrates is mortal from the immediately known and undemonstrable premise that all men are mortal, — for, after all, there may be a real inference in the syllogism in so far as there may be a real difference between the particular and the universal, — there does not seem to be even this saving grace in Spinoza's proof where the subject and the predicate in both the major premise and the conclusion are practically the same. For what Spinoza is practically trying to do is to prove syllogistically that God is existent from the immediately known and undemonstrable premise that God is existent. Logically it is analogous to an attempt to prove the mortality of Socrates by the syllogism:

> The husband of Xanthippe is mortal,
> Socrates is the husband of Xanthippe,
> Therefore, Socrates is mortal,

in which there is no inference unless by Socrates' mortality here is meant that special kind of mortality which came to him as a result of the fact that he was the husband of Xanthippe. And yet Spinoza goes through all the motions of proving the existence of God. What need is there for proving that which at the very outset is assumed to be immediately known?

The answer that would naturally suggest itself is that we did not reproduce Spinoza's argument quite accurately, that the major premise in his syllogism does not in itself establish the existence of God; it only states the fact that we have an idea of God as an existent being, and the purpose of the syllogism therefore is to prove that our idea is real. We

[1] J. S. Mill, *System of Logic*, Bk. II, Chs. I and III.

should probably be referred to what is known as the ontological proof, to which class of reasoning most of Spinoza's proofs belong, and we should be reminded that in the ontological proof the major premise is always a statement of what our idea of God is and an assertion that our idea of God, whatever it be, whether of a greatest being, or of a most perfect being, or of a self-caused being, always involves existence, and that the purpose of the proof is to establish the reality of the idea. In refutation of this answer we may say that if the major premise is assumed not to establish the existence of God, then the conclusion does not establish it. Furthermore, we shall endeavor to show that in its classical formulation by the three authors with whom we shall chiefly concern ourselves here, Anselm, Descartes, and Spinoza, the reality of the idea of God was never sought to be proved by the syllogism, but it was already conceived to be established in the major premise by some other principle.

It is needless for us to repeat here in detail the stock objection to the ontological argument in its conventional formulation. The objection has become historically as famous as the proof itself. Generally speaking, it tries to point out that what the ontological proof establishes is that if God is conceived of as the greatest being, or the most perfect being, or a self-caused being, He must also be conceived of as existing outside the mind and cannot be conceived of as nonexistent. There is nothing in the proof, the objection continues, to show that the idea of God conceived of in any of those forms is not a fictitious and arbitrary idea fabricated by our mind. Now all these three protagonists of the ontological proof were aware of this objection, and they all tried to meet it squarely and directly. St. Anselm was challenged to answer it by Gaunilon, and he answered it. Descartes quotes the same objection from Thomas Aquinas and tries to rebut it.[1] Spinoza, too, was confronted with the stock objection by Oldenburg,[2] and he answered it.[3] Furthermore, he also quotes Thomas Aquinas as stating that "God cannot be proved *a priori*" and refutes that statement.[4] What is the force of all these answers, rebuttals, and refutations?

If we examine closely the answers given by St. Anselm, Descartes, and Spinoza to this most obvious objection, we shall find that they all try to show that the idea we have of God as an existing being does not depend for its proof upon the syllogism, but that its reality is immediately known, just as the reality of anything that is immediately perceived and experienced. God, they all seem to say, is an immediate object of knowledge, and the knowledge by which He becomes known to us is a valid source of knowledge. This is their proof for the existence of God. Nothing else is necessary to corroborate it. The kind of knowledge we have of God they hold to be as valid a proof for His existence as a miraculous revelation or a natural personal experience of His presence. There is no need to go further into this kind of immediate knowledge. As far as Spinoza is concerned, we shall discuss it fully in another chapter.[5]

That this is the meaning of the answer to the stock objection is clearly brought out in Descartes, and in his case the answer is generally so understood. The main point of his answer is that "whatever we clearly and distinctly perceive is true"[6] — true in the sense of its having objective reality,[7] of its not being an arbitrary and fictitious idea. The force of the ontological proof in Descartes, therefore, is its clearness and distinctness, its intuitive character, its immediacy

---

[1] *Primae Responsiones* (*Oeuvres*, VII, p. 115).
[2] Epistola 3.   [3] Epistola 4.
[4] *Short Treatise*, I, 1, § 10.   [5] Cf. below, Vol. II, pp. 155 ff.
[6] *Primae Responsiones* (*Oeuvres*, VII, p. 116).
[7] *Meditationes*, III (*Oeuvres*, VII, p. 46, ll. 8 f.).

after the manner of self-consciousness. It is this self-evident nature of the truth of the idea of God that distinguishes Descartes' ontological proof from his first proof in Meditation III, though both are alike in that they reason from the idea of God to His existence. In the first proof of Meditation III, the fact that we possess an idea of God is not in itself taken by Descartes to be a proof for His existence, for the idea might be arbitrary and fictitious. It is therefore necessary to establish the truth of the idea demonstratively, by reasoning from effect to cause, by showing that the idea we have of God could not have been produced except by a real object corresponding to it. In the ontological proof, on the other hand, the very nature of our idea of God is evidence of His existence, just as our thinking is evidence of our own existence and as our sense perception is evidence of the existence of the things perceived. It is not at all necessary to assume, as it is done, that Descartes' ontological proof is dependent upon his first and second proofs in Meditation III.[1] It is rather an independent proof, its basis being Descartes' theory of knowledge, according to which a clear and distinct idea like God is self-evidently true and contains objective reality.

Similarly Spinoza makes it unmistakably clear that his proof is primarily grounded upon the premise that God's existence is an immediate fact of our knowledge. In anticipation of the objection of Thomas Aquinas that "God cannot be proved *a priori*, because, indeed, He has no cause," he maintains that "God, however, the first cause of all things and even the cause of himself, manifests himself through himself."[2] The manifestation of God to us through

---

[1] Kuno Fischer, *Geschichte der neuern Philosophie*, I, 1 (3rd ed., Heidelberg, 1889), pp. 309 ff. Norman Smith, *Studies in the Cartesian Philosophy*, p. 58.

[2] *Short Treatise*, I, 1, § 10.

himself as evidenced by the clearness and distinctness and adequacy of the idea we have of Him directly and without any further reasoning proves His existence. Similar passages to the same effect are abundant in Spinoza's writings.[1]

If thus in both Descartes and Spinoza the ontological argument is really psychological, resting as it does upon the view that God is a direct object of our knowledge, can the same be asserted with equal certainty of St. Anselm's proof? On this point there exists a difference of opinion. On the one hand, attempts have been made to show that St. Anselm's argument is ultimately psychological like that of Descartes.[2] But, on the other hand, these attempts have been refuted on the ground that there is nothing in St. Anselm to warrant such a construction upon his argument.[3] In this entire controversy, however, one important passage in St. Anselm seems to have been lost sight of, namely, his answer to Gaunilon.

If we study the true meaning of Anselm's answer to Gaunilon's objection, we shall find that like Descartes and Spinoza he stresses the point that his ontological proof is based upon the premise that the existence of God is an immediate fact of consciousness. Gaunilon, as may be recalled, objected to the ontological proof by arguing that the idea of a being than whom a greater cannot be conceived no more proves the existence of God than the idea of an island than which a more excellent cannot be conceived proves the existence of that island. Anselm vehemently denies that there is

---

[1] See W. Apel, *Spinozas Verhältnis zum ontologischen Beweise* (Leipzig, 1911).

[2] Beda Adlhoch, "Der Gottesbeweis des hl. Anselm" in *Philosophisches Jahrbuch*, VIII–X (1895–1897), XV–XVI (1902–1903): "Verwegenheit also ist es nicht, wenn im Nachfolgenden zu beweisen versucht wird, das Argument sei ein psychologisches und geschichtsphilosophisches, kein ontologisches" (Vol. VIII, 1895, p. 56). See also G. Grunwald, *Geschichte der Gottesbeweise im Mittelalter*, pp. 31–33.

[3] Cf. C. Baeumker, *Vitelo*, p. 305.

any analogy between the idea of a being greater than all
other beings and the idea of an island more excellent than
all other islands, and exclaims: "But I call on your faith
and conscience to attest that this is most false." [1] We read
this answer and wonder. We say to ourselves: Simple Saint!
if the authority of faith and the dictates of a religious conscience are the ultimate arbiters in the controversy, why go
into all this trouble of proving the existence of God? Why
not quote Scripture and the church doctrine and be done
with it? There must therefore be some deeper meaning in
these simple words of Anselm. Is it not possible that in ap-
pealing to faith and to conscience Anselm is really invoking
the argument from revelation as attested by tradition by
which the existence of God is established as a fact of immediate personal experience? Such an argument from revelation
is common in Jewish philosophy,[2] and it may be considered
as partly psychological, in so far as the proof from revelation
derives its validity from the fact that it is an immediate experience, and partly historical and social, in so far as the
truth of the fact of revelation is attested by an unbroken
chain of tradition universally accredited within a certain
group.[3] It may thus be considered as the equivalent of the
argument from *consensus gentium*, which is also social and is
likewise ultimately based upon the immediacy of our knowledge of God, namely, the innateness of the idea of God.
Just as the general agreement of mankind is used by Cicero
as evidence that the idea of God is innate, so is the generally

---

[1] *Apologeticus*, Ch. 1.

[2] Cf. *Moreh Nebukim*, II, 23.

[3] Such a historical proof based upon revelation is referred to by Spinoza in
Tractatus Theologico-Politicus, Ch. 4 (*Opera*, III, p. 61, ll. 28–31): "The truth of
a historical narrative, however assured, cannot give us the knowledge nor consequently the love of God, for love of God springs from knowledge of Him, and knowledge of Him should be derived from common notions (*comminubus notionibus*), in
themselves certain and known."

accredited religious tradition within the group taken by the Jewish philosophers to prove the veracity of the fact of revelation.[1] Anselm thus says to Gaunilon that the idea we have of God is unlike the idea we have of a most excellent island. The latter may be arbitrary and imaginary; the former is a true and necessary idea, being based upon the immediate experience of God's existence in the act of revelation as attested by religious tradition universally accepted.

That the ontological proof must ultimately rest upon a psychological basis may also be gathered from one kind of opposition to that argument among the scholastics. There were those who attacked the validity of the proof on the ground of their denial of the major premise, maintaining that the idea of God as a being whose essence involves existence was not immediately perceived by everybody. It was only well-trained philosophers, they argued, who perceived it as an immediate truth. But admitting that philosophers did perceive it as an immediate truth, these opponents of the ontological proof admitted the validity of the ontological proof for philosophers.[2] The particular theory of knowledge involved in this sort of reasoning is that indirect knowledge may in the course of time become direct knowledge which is immediately accepted without the need of demonstration. Spinoza himself intimates this particular view when he says that the desire to know things by the third kind of knowledge may arise from the second kind of knowledge.[3] The same view seems to be reflected also in Descartes' statement that "those propositions indeed which are immediately deduced from first principles are known now by intuition, now by deduction, i.e., in a way that differs according to our

---

[1] Cf. my "Notes on Proofs of the Existence of God in Jewish Philosophy" in *The Hebrew Union College Annual*, I (1924), p. 577.

[2] C. Baeumker, *Vitelo*, p. 301.   [3] *Ethics*, V, Prop. 28.

point of view." [1] And so, when the knowledge of God's existence becomes immediate and direct, whatever its origin, the existence of God is said to be proved ontologically instead of demonstratively, for to prove the existence of God ontologically means to perceive it directly as a given fact. The immediacy of the knowledge of God's existence is fully explained by Spinoza toward the end of the Second Dialogue in the *Short Treatise*, and there, too, he seems to intimate that it is not all men that do have at first such an immediate knowledge of God. "However, I tell you this, that so long as we have not such a clear idea of God . . . we cannot truly say that we are united with God."

We have thus shown, I believe, that Spinoza as well as Descartes and Anselm starts his ontological argument with a major premise that God's existence is a fact of immediate knowledge. It is not necessary, as is generally done, to set up a straw-man in the form of an untenable ontological argument as it is conventionally stated, to riddle it through and through, and then to take up the defence of one particular favorite, either Anselm, or Descartes, or Spinoza, and claim that his particular argument is immune from such criticism on the ground that it is not "ontological" but rather "psychological." [2] The point we have been trying to make is that all these three protagonists of the so-called ontological argument are alike in this respect. They are all making use of a "psychological" argument, and their syllogism is tantamount to saying that we know directly, as we can know anything at all, that God exists. There is nothing in the conclusion of the syllogism that is not contained in the major premise. But if this is so, the question may be raised, not

---

[1] *Regulae ad Directionem Ingenii*, III (*Oeuvres*, X, p. 370, ll. 10–13).

[2] Adlhoch does this with reference to Anselm; Apel with reference to Spinoza; Descartes is singled out by everybody as an exception.

only against Spinoza, but against Anselm and Descartes as well, What is the significance of the syllogism in the ontological proof?

The answer is that the syllogism adds nothing to the major premise. But still it is not altogether redundant. It may be said that the function of the ontological proof is like that of the proposition of an analytical judgment, in which the predicate adds nothing to the subject, and still its use is not altogether unjustifiable. Perhaps the comparison can be put in the following manner. Just as propositions are either analytic or synthetic, so are syllogisms also either analytic or synthetic, and the relation of the analytical syllogism to the major premise is like that of the analytical proposition to the subject. To be more specific: The ontological proof for the existence of God is an analytical syllogism just as the proposition "God is existent" is an analytical judgment, and the relation of the syllogism in the ontological proof to the major premise is like the relation of the proposition "God is existent" to the subject "God." Neither of them adds anything to the contents of its respective subject or major premise with which it starts, but both of them analyze the contents of their respective subject and major premise.

It was not Kant who was the first to draw the distinction between analytical and synthetical judgments. It has been shown that the scholastics before him had recognized it and expressed it by the distinction between *per se nota* and *per aliud nota* or by similar other distinctions, such as *per se* and *per accidens* or *in materia necessaria* and *in materia contigenti*.[1] It can also be shown that it was not unknown to Arabic and Jewish philosophers, and having known that distinction, they asked themselves what kind of relation was expressed in an analytical proposition. That the relation

[1] Cf. P. Coffey, *The Science of Logic*, I, p. 70.

could not be real and hence the judgment could not be real they all seem to agree. They only seem to question whether there could be a justifiable logical relation which was not real. Thus in the proposition "God is existent," argues Avicenna, followed by a chorus of Jewish philosophers, since essence and existence are identical, the proposition is tautological, and is tantamount to saying "God is God." [1] And similarly Maimonides argues that in a proposition where the predicate is identical with the subject there is no real logical relation but only the explanation of a name.[2] Likewise Gersonides maintains that in the proposition "God is existent" the term "God" is a subject only "in discourse," not "in existence." [3]

All this may be considered as a sort of anticipation of John Stuart Mill's conclusion that an analytical judgment is only verbal, or that it is explicative, as others call it. And so may we also say of the analytical or ontological proof that it is only verbal and explicative. It is indeed true to say of an ontological proof what John Stuart Mill says of every form of Aristotle's deductive syllogism. It contains no real inference. It adds nothing to what is already known from the major premise. But still its use is justifiable. For it translates a conviction into an argument. It elicits a truth which is only implicitly contained in the major premise. It puts an immediate fact of consciousness in the form of a syllogistic reasoning. It resolves an idea into its component parts. Thus when Spinoza proves the existence of God ontologically, he does not pretend to arrive at a newly discovered fact, but rather to restate in formal language a fact already known.

---

[1] *Or Adonai*, I, iii, 1. Cf. above, p. 123.

[2] *Moreh Nebukim*, I, 51; cf. 52. Cf. above, p. 154.

[3] *Milḥamot Adonai*, III, 3. Cf. above, p. 151.

Truly speaking, if the ontological proof were to be put into a syllogistic formula in such a way as to bring out its entire force, it would have to be as follows:

Everything which is immediately perceived to exist exists.

God is immediately perceived to exist.

Therefore, God exists.

Now, none of the ontological proofs in their various forms as given by its three main exponents, Anselm, Decartes, and Spinoza, prove directly that God exists. What they prove is that the existence of God is known to us by a certain kind of immediate knowledge. Their various proofs can be reduced to the following syllogism:

If we have an idea of God as the greatest, or as the most perfect, or as a self-caused being, then God is immediately perceived by us to exist.

But we have an idea of God as the greatest, or as the most perfect, or as a self-caused being.

Therefore, God is immediately perceived by us to exist.

Their direct proof of the existence of God is their respective views that our immediate knowledge of God's existence which is implied in the idea we have of God as the greatest, or as the most perfect, or as a self-caused being is valid knowledge.

II. Spinoza's Four Proofs

The foregoing discussion of the nature of the ontological proof may serve as a general approach to the understanding of all of Spinoza's proofs of the existence of God. Whatever may be said in criticism of this mode of ontological reasoning hardly concerns those of us who are now mainly interested in the objective understanding of Spinoza's thought, rather than in passing criticism on it. It may perhaps be that the alleged immediacy of the idea of God is nothing but an after-thought of a departed traditional belief, just as the catless grin which Alice saw in Wonderland was nothing but an after-image of a departed grinning cat; or it may be that Spinoza is claiming "an arbitrary right to accept anything he pleases as self-evident"; [1] and it may perhaps also be, as we have been trying to show, that the reasoning by which it is sought to dissolve this idea into a syllogism, despite the cogency of its logical form, is nothing but the breaking up of a complex term into its component parts. But however slight this proof may appear to us, it certainly carried conviction to the mind of Spinoza and of others like him to whom an immediately and intuitively conceived idea by its very clearness and distinctness connoted as much reality as, aye even greater reality than, the undimmed perceptions of unimpaired senses. And perhaps we should be inclined to give more weight to this reasoning if we could only bear in mind that Spinoza's God is not the God of traditional theology, that his "God" is merely an appeasive term for the most comprehensive principle of the universe, which he supposed to be conceived apriorily as the ideal triangle, but unlike the ideal triangle, being the working principle of the universe and not its mere ideal pattern, its *a priori* conception involved an extra-mental reality which the *a priori* conception of a triangle did not. With these considerations looming before our mind, there remains for us only to deal with the external structure of the proofs, their origin, their individual history, their growth, and the final form in which they appear before us.

It may be recalled that Descartes has three proofs of the

[1] F. Pollock, *Spinoza*, p. 129.

existence of God, two of them in Meditation III[1] and a third in Meditation V, corresponding respectively to the three proofs in the *Discours de la Méthode*, IV,[2] in the *Principia Philosophiae*, I, 18–19, 20–21, and 14, and in the geometrical formulation of the arguments demonstrating the existence of God at the end of *Secundae Responsiones*, Propositions II, III, and I. The first two of these three proofs we shall designate respectively as the first and second proof of Meditation III, and the third as the ontological proof. All the proofs for the existence of God adduced by Spinoza in his various works may be traced to these three Cartesian proofs, and may be divided accordingly into three groups:

First, Descartes' first proof of Meditation III to be found in *Principia Philosophiae Cartesianae*, I, Proposition VI, and in the proof designated as *a posteriori* in *Short Treatise*, I, 1, and referred to also in a letter to Jelles (Epistola XL) and in a note to the *Tractatus de Intellectus Emendatione*, § 76 (*Opera*, II, p. 29, note a).

Second, Descartes' second proof of Meditation III to be found in *Principia Philosophiae Cartesianae*, I, Proposition VII, and in the third proof of *Ethics*, I, Proposition XI.

Third, Descartes' ontological proof to be found in *Principia Philosophiae Cartesianae*, I, Proposition V; in the *a priori* proof of *Short Treatise*, I, 1; in the first proof of *Ethics*, I, Proposition XI; and in letters to Blyenbergh (Epistola XXI) and Hudde (Epistola XXXIV).

The fourth proof in the *Ethics* is a modification of Descartes' second proof of Meditation III, and the second proof in the *Ethics*, we shall try to show, has been suggested by Descartes' ontological proof, but it contains many elements borrowed from mediaeval Jewish and Arabic philosophy.

---

[1] (1) *Oeuvres*, VII, p. 45, ll. 9 ff., (2) *ibid.*, p. 47, ll. 24 ff.
[2] (1) *Oeuvres*, VI, p. 33, ll. 25 ff., (2) *ibid.*, p. 34, ll. 24 ff., (3) *ibid.*, p. 36, ll. 4 ff.

We shall here deal with the four proofs of the *Ethics*, correlating with them the parallel proofs found in the other writings of Spinoza.

FIRST PROOF

What is mainly of interest to us in Spinoza's first proof in the *Ethics* and its parallels elsewhere is the various forms in which he reproduces Descartes' ontological argument. Spinoza does not summarize Descartes, he does not epitomize him, nor does he merely paraphrase him. He rather selects what he considers to be the salient features of Descartes' argument and moulds them into a form of his own. If we compare the various versions of Descartes' ontological proof as given by Spinoza, we shall find that the Demonstration of Proposition V in *Principia Philosophiae Cartesianae*, I, and the first part of the *a priori* proof in *Short Treatise*, I, 1, represent one type; that the proofs in Epistolae XXI and XXXIV and the second part of the *a priori* proof in *Short Treatise*, I, 1, introduced by the remark "otherwise also thus," represent another type; and that the first proof of Proposition XI in *Ethics*, I, represents a third type. How these three types of Descartes' ontological proof were chiselled out from the unhewn and rugged block of Descartes' rather discursive and informal discussion of the ontological proof can be best shown by trying to outline the salient features of Descartes' argument as they must have formulated themselves in Spinoza's mind.

The starting point of Descartes' argument is the presence of the idea of God in our mind. This idea of God, he contends, could not have reached our mind through the medium of our senses, nor is it a factitious idea, depending solely on our thought. We rather derive this idea of God, so to speak, from "the storehouse of our mind." [1] It is the first and fore-most of the clear and distinct and true ideas born within us.

But how do we know that the idea of God is not factitious? To this Descartes answers that we know it by the fact that the idea is unique and absolutely unlike any other idea, "for really I discern in many ways that this idea is not something factitious, and depending solely on my thought, but that it is the image of a true and immutable nature . . . because I cannot conceive anything but God himself to whose essence existence [necessarily] pertains." [2]

That existence pertains to the essence of God is known by us, according to Descartes, in two ways. In Meditation V, in *Principia Philosophiae*, I, 14, and in the geometrical formulation of the arguments demonstrating the existence of God at the end of *Secundae Responsiones*, Proposition I, he says that it is implied in our immediate idea of God as "a Being supremely perfect," [3] for since existence is perfection it must be included in that idea as something pertaining to the essence of God. In his *Primae Responsiones*, however, he declares that the pertinence of existence to essence in God is also implied in our idea of God as a self-caused being, or, as he expresses himself, in a being who possesses necessary existence, [4] for necessary existence is the equivalent of existence *per se*, [5] which, according to Descartes, means self-caused as well as causeless. [6] It is therefore natural for Descartes sometimes to leave out this intermediary step of

[1] *Meditationes*, V (*Oeuvres*, VII, p. 67, ll. 22 f.). Cf. *Meditationes*, III (*Oeuvres*, VII, p. 51, ll. 18 ff.).

[2] *Meditationes*, V (*Oeuvres*, VII, p. 68, ll. 10 ff.).

[3] *Meditationes*, V (*Oeuvres*, VII, p. 67, l. 9).

[4] *Primae Responsiones* (*Oeuvres*, VII, p. 117, ll. 5 ff.).

[5] See Gerhardt, *Die Philosophischen Schriften von Gottfried Wilhelm Leibnitz*, IV, p. 406: "Car l'Estre necessaire et l'estre par son Essence ne sont qu'une même chose."

[6] *Primae Responsiones* (*Oeuvres*, VII, pp. 109 ff.).

perfection or self-causation, by which we know that God's essence involves existence, and to speak of our immediate conception of God as that of a being whose essence involves existence.

Upon this assumption of the pertinence of existence to the essence of God Descartes builds his ontological proof. We find it in two forms.

In the first form, the major premise states that "all which I know clearly and distinctly as pertaining to this subject [i.e., of the innate idea] does really belong to it," [1] or as he puts it in *Primae Responsiones*, "That which we clearly and distinctly understand to belong to the true and immutable nature of anything, its essence, or form, can be affirmed of that thing." [2] The minor premise states that we clearly and distinctly understand that to exist belongs to the nature of God, and hence the conclusion that we can affirm of God that He exists. This is also the form used in the geometrical formulation of the arguments demonstrating the existence of God at the end of *Secundae Responsiones*, Proposition I. It is this form of the argument that is reproduced by Spinoza in Proposition V of *Principia Philosophiae Cartesianae*, I, and in the first part of the *a priori* proof of *Short Treatise*, I, 1, the phraseology of the *Primae Responsiones* being especially noticeable in the latter.

In the second form, Descartes draws a comparison between the idea of God and that of a triangle. Both have "a determinate nature, form, or essence, which is immutable and eternal." [3] That determinate nature, form, or essence in the case of the triangle is implied in its definition; but in the case of God it is implied in our idea of Him as all-perfection

---

[1] *Meditationes*, V (*Oeuvres*, VII, p. 65, ll. 17 ff.).
[2] *Primae Responsiones* (*Oeuvres*, VII, p. 118, ll. 22 ff.).
[3] *Meditationes*, V (*Oeuvres*, VII, p. 64, ll. 15 ff.).

or as self-causality. Thus from the definition of a triangle diverse properties follow, viz., "that its three angles are equal to two right angles, that the greatest side is subtended by the greatest angle, and the like." [1] Similarly from our idea of God as an all-perfect or self-caused being it follows "that an [actual] and eternal existence pertains to His nature." [2] The nerve of the argument, or, as Spinoza would say, the force of the argument (*vis argumenti*),[3] is the conclusion "that existence can no more be separated from the essence of God than can its having its three angles equal to two right angles be separated from the essence of a [rectilinear] triangle." [4] It is this form of the argument that is briefly restated by Spinoza in Epistola XXI, when he says: "If the nature of God is known to us, then the assertion that God exists follows as necessarily from our own nature as it follows necessarily from the nature of a triangle that its three angles are equal to two right angles." [5] In the second part of the *a priori* proof of *Short Treatise*, I, 1, it is reproduced rather incompletely: "The essences of things are from all eternity, and unto all eternity shall remain immutable. The existence of God is essence. Therefore, etc." The conclusion, in the light of our quotations from Descartes, should read as follows: Therefore, the essence and existence of God are together from all eternity, and unto all eternity shall remain unchanged, that is to say, existence can never be separated from the essence of God.

In the *Ethics*, Spinoza uses the first form of Descartes'

---

[1] *Meditationes*, V (*Oeuvres*, VII, p. 64, ll. 18 ff.).

The use of the triangle having its three angles equal to two right angles as an illustration for the idea of necessity is to be found in Aristotle, *Physics*, II, 9, 200a, 17 ff.

[2] *Meditationes*, V (*Oeuvres*, VII, p. 65, l. 24).

[3] Epistola 12 (*Opera*, IV, p. 62, l. 5).

[4] *Meditationes*, V (*Oeuvres*, VII, p. 66, ll. 8 ff.).   Cf. French version (*Opera*, IX, p. 52).   [5] Epistola 21 (*Opera*, IV, p. 130, ll. 4–7).

ontological proof with some modification. Reduced to a syllogism, the major premise therein is the statement that everything whose essence involves existence exists. The minor premise is the statement that God's essence involves existence. But the conclusion, that God exists, is arrived at indirectly by proving the contrary to be absurd. This is like the reasoning employed in St. Anselm's proof. In a letter to Schuller, Spinoza expresses a preference for this kind of proof, namely, the *reductio ad absurdum*, when the proposition is negative.[1] It is also to be noted that in this proof Spinoza finds that existence must pertain to the essence of God not in the idea of perfection, as does Descartes in Meditation V, but rather in the idea of self-causality, for Spinoza refers here to Proposition VII, the demonstration of which is based upon the premise that subtance, or, as he now calls it, God, cannot be produced by an external cause and must therefore be self-caused. But we have already seen that Descartes himself, in *Primae Responsiones*, makes self-causality the basis of the identification of essence and existence in God. There is therefore no foundation for the oft-repeated statement that Descartes bases his ontological proof on the idea of God as a most perfect being, whereas Spinoza bases his ontological proof on the idea of God as a self-caused being.[2] The two, as we have seen, are identified by Descartes himself.

In the light, however, of what we have said, namely, that the basis of the ontological proof is the assertion that we

---

[1] Epistola 64 (*Opera*, IV, p. 278, ll. 8 ff.): "deducendo rem ad absurdum." Cf. Epistola 63 from Schuller. See above, p. 97, and below, p. 378.

[2] It may be said that Leibniz advocated the substitution of "existence *per se*" for "perfection" as a criticism of Descartes, whereas Spinoza evidently did so as an interpretation of Descartes. Cf. A. Hannequin, "La preuve ontologique cartésienne défendue contre Leibnitz" in *Revue de Métaphysique et de Morale*, IV (1896), pp. 435, 436.

have a valid immediate perception of God's existence and
that the so-called ontological proofs merely show how our
valid immediate perception of God's existence is implied in
our idea of God as the greatest or the most perfect being,
or, in this particular proof, as a being whose essence involves
existence, Spinoza's first proof in the *Ethics* is really to be
reduced to the following syllogism:

> If we have a clear and distinct idea of God as a being
> whose essence involves existence, then God is im-
> mediately perceived by us to exist.
>
> But we have a clear and distinct idea of God as a
> being whose essence involves existence.
>
> Therefore, God is immediately perceived by us to
> exist.

SECOND PROOF

Against his own ontological proof based upon the insepara-
bleness of existence from the essence of God Descartes himself raises a difficulty which he considers of no little moment. "We are so much accustomed to distinguish existence
from essence in the case of other things," he says, "that we
do not with sufficient readiness notice how existence belongs
to the essence of God in a greater degree than in the case of
other things." [1] In order to remove this difficulty, Descartes
draws a distinction, or rather recalls an old distinction, between possible and necessary existence, declaring that "in
the concept or idea of everything that is clearly and distinctly
conceived, possible existence is contained, but necessary existence never, except in the idea of God alone." [2] It may be
here remarked that by necessary existence, as already pointed
out, is meant existence *per se*, which, according to Descartes

---

[1] *Primae Responsiones* (*Oeuvres*, VII, p. 116, ll. 9 f.).
[2] *Ibid.* (ll. 20 ff.).

himself, has a negative aspect in the sense of uncaused as well as a positive aspect in the sense of self-caused.[1] With this distinction drawn, Descartes substitutes the expression "necessary existence" for the mere word "existence" in his ontological proof, arriving at his conclusion that God exists not from the premise that existence is involved in the essence of God, but rather from the premise that necessary existence is involved in it. It will have been noticed that in his restatement of Descartes in *Principia Philosophiae Cartesianae*, I, Proposition V, Spinoza has already made use of this substitution, declaring that "the concept of God includes necessary existence," that is to say, necessary existence and not merely existence. In the *Short Treatise*, I, 1, however, and in the first proof in *Ethics*, I, Proposition XI, the term "existence" without the adjective "necessary" is used.

Now in the second proof in the *Ethics* Spinoza takes up again this new phrase "necessary existence" and builds around it a new proof. But why did Spinoza make a new proof out of it? Why did he not embody it in his first proof as did Descartes and as he himself did in his restatement of Descartes in his *Principia*? The answer would seem to be found in the fact that the phrase "necessary existence" had brought to Spinoza's mind the recollection of the mediaeval discussions about possible and necessary existence and of a mediaeval cosmological proof based upon that distinction, and all this appeared to him to warrant the framing of an entirely new and distinct proof. Thus Spinoza's second proof is of a composite nature. It is ontological and Cartesian in form, but its substance is enriched by borrowings from mediaeval sources. We shall attempt to disentangle this complicated and involved proof and reduce it to its simple constituent elements.

[1] See above, p. 180, n. 6.

In mediaeval Jewish philosophy, under the influence of Aristotle, a distinction is made between an internal cause, which resides in the nature of the thing itself, and an external cause, which resides outside of the thing. If the cause resides in the thing itself, an effect must follow from that cause unless there is an external impediment to prevent it. That external impediment may also be considered as a sort of cause, and thus we have a further distinction between a cause which produces existence and a cause which prevents or negates existence. Similar distinctions are familiar also to students of scholastic philosophy.[1] In Maimonides these distinctions are implied in the following statement: "Everything that passes from potentiality to actuality has something different from itself as the cause of its transition, and that cause is necessarily outside itself, for if the cause of the transition existed in the thing itself and there was no obstacle to prevent the transition, the thing would never have been in a state of potentiality but would have always been in a state of actuality."[2] In the commentaries upon this passage, distinct technical terms for the contrast between effective causes and impedimental causes are introduced.[3]

Then, again, in mediaeval Jewish philosophy, in the attempt to prove that God is everlasting and can never be

[1] For the distinction between external and internal cause (*causa extrinseca, causa intrinseca*), see *Metaphysics*, XII, 4, 1070b, 22–23; *Summa Theologica*, Prima Secundae, Quaest. 1, Art. 3, Obj. 1. See also *Principia Philosophiae Cartesianae*, I, Axiom 11. Cf. below, pp. 319 ff.

For the impedimental cause, see *Summa Theologica*, Pars I, Quaest. 115, Art. 6, Obj. 3: *Si effectus coelestis corporis non ex necessitate proveniat, hoc est propter aliquam causam impedientem.*

[2] *Moreh Nebukim*, II, Introduction, Prop. 18.

[3] See commentary of Shem-Tob on *Moreh Nebukim*, ad. loc.: מוֹצִיא, effective cause; מֵעִיק, מוֹנֵעַ (Arabic: عٰائِق. Cf. *Cuzari*, V, 20, p. 338, l. 19: עָאִיק = מוֹנֵעַ), impedimental cause. The impedimental cause is also mentioned by Avicenna in his *Al-Shifa'*. Cf. M. Horten, *Die Metaphysik Avicennas*, p. 267.

deprived of His existence, it is argued that God's existence could not be negated or taken away except by some cause, but that cause would have to be either like God himself or unlike himself; and as neither of these is possible, it is concluded that God's existence can never be negated. To quote: "God is everlasting, and will never cease to exist. For a being proved to have no beginning cannot pass away. Just as the coming of the non-existent into existence must have a cause, so also the disappearance of a thing from existence requires a cause. Nothing vanishes from existence on its own account, but on account of its opposite. God, however, has nothing opposite Him, nor, for that matter, anything like Him. For if anything were like Him in every respect, it would be identical with God himself and they could not therefore be described as two. As for assuming something opposite God to be the cause of His ceasing to exist, it is likewise impossible for the following reason. That opposite thing could not be without beginning, for it has already been proved that God's existence alone is without beginning, nor could it have been created, for everything created must be an effect produced by the eternal God; but, if so, how can the effect make its cause disappear?" [1]

Then, also, in mediaeval Jewish philosophy, in consequence of an Avicennian view, the origin of which I have discussed in another place,[2] a distinction is made between "necessary existence *per se*" and "possible existence *per se*." Necessary existence *per se* is that which Spinoza would call *causa sui*, something whose existence is independent of any cause.[3] "Everything that is necessary of existence in respect to its own essence has no cause for its existence in any man-

---

[1] *Cuzari*, V, 18, 5.
[2] Cf. my *Crescas' Critique of Aristotle*, pp. 109–112, 680 ff.
[3] Cf. above, p. 127; below, p. 252.

nor whatsoever." [1] Possible existence *per se* is that which owes its existence to some cause. "Everything that has a cause for its existence is in respect to its own essence only possible of existence, for if its causes exist, the thing likewise will exist." [2] Furthermore, the possible *per se* is said to become impossible in the absence of the cause upon which its existence depends, for "if its causes have never existed, or if they have ceased to exist, or if their causal relation to the thing has changed, then the thing itself will not exist." [3] But, still, when the cause from which it follows by necessity does exist, then the thing, though only possible by its own nature, is said to be necessary with reference to its cause. It may thus be said that within everything possible there is the distinction of being possible in itself but necessary with reference to its cause. According to this view, therefore, there is a fourfold classification of being, divided first into two main groups, into that which is causeless and hence necessary by itself and that which requires a cause for its existence, the latter of which being then subdivided into its three aspects, namely, possible in itself, necessary by its cause, and impossible in the absence of any cause. [4]

This fourfold classification of being is reproduced by Spinoza in *Cogitata Metaphysica*, I, 3, when he divides all things into necessary, impossible, possible, and contingent. Necessary existence, in Spinoza as in mediaeval philosophy, is exemplified by God. As an illustration for the impossible Spinoza mentions the "chimera," [5] which like the words "a

---

[1] *Moreh Nebukim*, II, Introduction, Prop. 20.

[2] *Ibid.*, Prop. 19.   [3] *Ibid.*

[4] See commentary of Shem-Tob on *Moreh Nebukim*, II, Introduction, Prop. 19.

[5] So also in Descartes, as, for instance, in the French version of Meditation III (*Oeuvres*, IX, p. 34). Aristotle's illustration of a non-existent being is a goat-stag (τραγέλαφος) and sphinx. Cf. *De Interpretatione*, I, 16a, 16–17; *Physics*, IV, 1, 208a, 30.

square circle" exists neither in the intellect nor in the imagination and is rightly called a verbal being. The term "possible" is used by Spinoza in the general sense of being brought about or being made necessary by a cause, and the term "contingent" is used by him to designate that aspect of the possible wherein it was said by the mediaevals to be possible in consideration of its own essence. "A thing is said to be possible when we understand its efficient cause, but do not know whether it is determined. Therefore, we may consider that to be possible which is neither necessary [i.e., by itself] nor impossible [i.e., by itself]. If now we attend merely to the essence of a thing and not to its cause, we say it is contingent; that is, when we consider anything between the extremes God and chimeras." That these two terms "possible" and "contingent" were meant by Spinoza for the two aspects of the possible as used by the mediaevals may be gathered from the context of the passage quoted and from parallel passages in the other works of Spinoza.[1] He then makes the following statement: "If any one wishes to call that contingent which I call possible and possible what I call contingent I shall not contradict him. For I am not accustomed to dispute about mere names. It will be sufficient if it is only admitted that these arise not because of something real, but only because of a deficiency in our perception (*defectus nostrae perceptionis*)."[2] The last statement is a repetition of what is said earlier in the same chapter: "For some, these two terms are considered defects of things, although, in truth, they are nothing more than a deficiency in our intellect (*defectus nostri intellectus*)."[3] The reference is no doubt to

[1] Cf. *Principia Philosophiae Cartesianae*, I, Prop. 7, Lemma 1, Nota 1; *Tractatus de Intellectus Emendatione*, § 53 (*Opera*, II, p. 19, ll. 30 ff.); *Ethics*, I, Prop. 33, Schol. 1; IV, Defs. 3 and 4. Cf. below, pp. 310, 399, 410.

[2] *Cogitata Metaphysica*, I, 3. Cf. *Metaphysics*, V, 30, 1025a, 24; below, p. 399, and Vol. II, pp. 13, 109, 160.   [3] Cf. *Ethics*, I, Prop. 33, Schol. 1.

the controversy between Avicenna and Averroes as to whether possibility is merely a conceptual aspect or a real property of being.[1] It is also to be noted that Spinoza's lofty declaration here in *Cogitata Metaphysica*, I, 3, that "I am not accustomed to dispute about mere names," as well as Blyenbergh's statement in one of his letters to Spinoza that "you have taught me that one must not quarrel over words," [2] is reminiscent of a similar expression used in Hebrew, Arabic, Latin, and Greek philosophic writings.[3]

Coming now to Spinoza's second proof in the *Ethics*, we find that it is replete with all those distinctions and lines of reasoning which we have abstracted from mediaeval sources. Spinoza refers to the distinction between an internal and an external cause when he speaks of a reason or cause which "must either be contained in the nature of the thing or lie outside it." [4] He also distinguishes between a positive cause and an impedimental cause when he says that if a thing

---

[1] See commentary of Shem Ṭob on *Moreh Nebukim*, II, Introduction, Prop. 19.

[2] Epistola 20 (*Opera*, IV, p. 101, ll. 4–5 and 24).

[3] Cf. Abraham Ibn Daud, *Emunah Ramah*, I, 6 (p. 20): . . . וקראנוהו אנחנו נפש ואתה אם לא ישר בעיניך זה השם, תשים לו איזה שם שתרצה, כי אין קפידא אצלנו בשמות. "We call soul *nefesh*. . . . If this name does not please you, call it by whatever other name you like, for we are not sticklers for names." Similarly Algazali in his *Tahafot al-Falasifat*, III (ed. Maurice Bouyges, p. 109, l. 9), says: فان لم تسموا هذا فعلا فلا مضايقة فى التسميات, which in the published Latin translation from the Hebrew version of Averroes' *Tahafot al-Tahafot* (*Happalat ha-Happalah, Destructio Destructionis*) is rendered as follows: "si autem non appellabilis hoc actionem non est disputatio de nominibus." (.ואם לא תקראו זה פעל, הנה אין לחץ בשמות) This translation was accessible to Spinoza. Descartes makes use of the same expression in a letter to Henry More. Cf. *Correspondance*, DXXXVII (*Oeuvres*, V, p. 269, ll. 25–26): "Ego vero non soleo quidem de nominibus disputare." Similar expressions occurring in Greek and in other Arabic sources are quoted by S. Horovitz in his *Die Psychologie bei den jüdischen Religions-Philosophen des Mittelalters*, p. 216, n. 13. As Greek examples he quotes from Alexander Aphrodisiensis, *Scripta Minora* (ed. Bruns), II, p. 183, l. 17: ὀνομάτων μὲν οὖν οὐδεὶς φθόνος, and from Galen, *Opera* (ed. Kühn), I, p. 155: ἡμεῖς δὲ οὐδὲν διαφερόμεθα πρὸς τοὺς, τὰ ὀνόματα ἐξαλλάττοντας.

[4] "Haec vera ratio seu causa vel in natura rei contineri debet, vel extra ipsam."

exists, "there must be a reason or cause why it exists; and if it does not exist, there must be a reason or cause which hinders its existence or which negates it." [1] Furthermore, he follows the main outline of the mediaeval argument for the everlastingness of God when he argues that if a reason or cause be granted "which hinders God from existing, or which negates His existence . . . it must be either in the nature itself of God or must lie outside it, that is to say, in another substance of another nature. . . . But substance possessing another nature could have nothing in common with God, and therefore could not give Him existence nor negate it." [2] Finally, he reproduces the mediaeval and his own classification of being into necessary, possible, and impossible when he states that "the nature of the thing itself shows the reason why a square circle does not exist . . . and the reason, on the other hand, why substance exists follows from its nature alone," [3] and when he further says that it is not from its own nature "but from the order of corporeal nature generally," i.e., its cause, that "it must follow, either that a triangle necessarily exists, or that it is impossible for it to exist." [4]

But more than this. There is a mediaeval proof for the existence of God based upon the distinction between necessary existence and possible existence which, as we shall now

---

[1] "Ratio, seu causa dari debet, cur existit; si autem non existit, ratio etiam, seu causa dari debet, quae impedit, quominus existat, sive quae ejus existentiam tollat."

[2] "Si . . . ratio . . . causa dari possit . . . quae impedit, quominus Deus existat, vel quae ejus existentiam tollat . . . ea, vel in ipsa Dei natura, vel extra ipsam dari deberet, hoc est, in alia substantia alterius naturae. . . . At substantia, quae alterius esset naturae, nihil cum Deo commune habere, adeoque, neque ejus existentiam ponere, neque tollere posset."

[3] "Ex. gr. rationem, cur circulus quadratus non existat, ipsa ejus natura indicat; . . . Cur autem contra substantia existat, ex sola etiam ejus natura sequitur."

[4] "At ratio, cur circulus vel triangulus existit, vel cur non existit, ex eorum natura non sequitur, sed ex ordine universae naturae corporeae; ex eo enim sequi debet, vel jam triangulum necessario existere, vel impossibile esse, ut jam existat."

proceed to show, served Spinoza as a pattern for his second proof. This mediaeval proof is one of the several forms of what is known as the cosmological proof. Spinoza, as we shall see, has changed it into an ontological proof.

In order to recreate the complete setting of this second proof of Spinoza, it is necessary for us to trace the development of the cosmological proof out of which it has arisen.[1] The cosmological proof is based upon the principle of causality, reasoning from effect to cause, which, when expressed in its most general terms, asserts that every form of coming into being or change requires a cause. The principle of causality alone, however, was not considered sufficient to be used as a proof for the existence of God. It had to be supplemented by some other principle. In Plato[2] that supplementary principle was the creation of the world. The cosmological proof as used by him may therefore be reduced to the following syllogism:

Everything that comes into existence must have a cause.

The world came into existence.

Therefore, the world must have a cause.

This form of the cosmological proof was also used by the Moslem Mutakallimun and their Jewish followers, among whom it was known as the proof from creation, though its identity with the Platonic proof from efficient causation was not always recognized.[3] With the denial of a created universe by Aristotle the cosmological proof assumed a new form. The principle of causality was still retained, but the theory of creation was replaced by the theory of the impos-

[1] Cf. my "Notes on Proofs of the Existence of God in Jewish Philosophy" in *The Hebrew Union College Annual*, I (1924), pp. 584 ff.

[2] *Timaeus* 28 A.

[3] See my "Notes on the Proofs of the Existence of God in Jewish Philosophy," *op. cit.*, p. 584, n. 44.

sibility of an infinite regress. In Aristotle two versions of this type of the cosmological proof occur, one couched in terms of motion and the other in terms of potentiality and actuality. Assuming the world to be a process of motion or a process of the actualization of the potential, and assuming also that both these processes require a cause and that there can be no infinite series of causes of any kind, the two forms of the proof run as follows:

A

Every series of things moved and moving must have an unmoved mover.

The world is a series of things moved and moving.

Therefore, the world must have an unmoved mover.

B

Every series of transitions from potentiality into actuality must have a cause which is pure actuality.

The world is a series of transitions from potentiality into actuality.

Therefore, the world must have a cause which is pure actuality.

The first of these versions is given by Aristotle in the Eighth Book of the *Physics*, the second in the *Metaphysics*.[1]

To these two Aristotelian versions of the cosmological proof Avicenna, and before him Alfarabi, added a third version couched in terms of possibility and necessity. This new version was introduced by them because they considered it to be more general and more universally applicable than the others. It will be noticed that this new version does not essentially differ from the other two, for motion, potentiality, and possibility are only different ways in which the principle of causality is expressed and are in a sense interchangeable

---

[1] *Metaphysics*, IX, 8, 1049b, 24 f., and XII, 7, 1072b, 3 f.

terms. In Greek the same term, δύναμις, means both potentiality and possibility, and Aristotle defines motion as the
actuality of that which is potential so far as it is potential [1]
and also as the actuality of that which is movable so far as
it is movable.[2] Maimonides, who besides the two Aristotelian
versions of the proof uses also the Avicennian version, introduces the latter by the following remark: "This is taken
from the words of Aristotle, though he gives it in a different
form." [3] From Maimonides it was taken over by Thomas
Aquinas, who makes use of it as the third of his five proofs
of the existence of God.[4] From him it was passed on into
modern philosophy, so that Kant uses the Avicennian version as his model cosmological proof. We shall endeavor to
show that this is also the basis of Spinoza's second proof.

The Avicennian version as reproduced by Maimonides —
for it was Maimonides from whom Spinoza most likely drew
his knowledge of it — is divided into two parts. In the first
part, it tries to establish the fact that in the universe among
all the things that actually exist there must be one which has
eternal existence, inasmuch as it is impossible either that all
things should be eternal or that all things should be transient.
In the second part, drawing upon the distinction between
necessary and possible (and also impossible) existence, it
tries to prove that the eternal being must have necessary
existence, that is to say, it must be independent of any cause,
or, as Spinoza would say, it must be *causa sui*. The proof
for this is based, again, as in Aristotle's versions, upon the
impossibility of an infinite regress. Reduced to its syllogistic
form, Avicenna's version of the proof runs as follows:

[1] *Physics*, III, 1, 201a, 10–11.
[2] *Physics*, III, 2, 202a, 7–8.
[3] *Moreh Nebukim*, II, 1.
[4] *Summa Theologica*, Pars I, Quaest. 2, Art. 3. Cf. *Contra Gentiles*, Lib. I, Cap. 13.

Every series of transitions from possible existence
   into necessary existence must have a cause which
   has necessary existence.

The world is a series of transitions from possible existence into necessary existence.

Therefore, the world must have a cause which has
   necessary existence.

A modification of the Avicennian proof was introduced
by Crescas.[1] Crescas denies the impossibility of an infinite
series of causes and effects and thereby removes one of the
premises of the Aristotelian proofs of the existence of God
in all of its forms. But still he retains the principle of
causality, maintaining that everything possible, i.e., everything which by its own nature may or may not exist, must
have a cause to give preference to existence over non-existence. That cause must itself be uncaused, that is, it must
have necessary existence. Once such a cause is given, argues
Crescas, it may have an infinite number of effects arranged
in a causal series, for infinity is not impossible.[2] How Crescas
conceived of this possibility does not concern us here.[3] Suffice
it to say that on the mere principle of causation, namely,
that any series of causes and effects, whether infinite or
finite, must have a first uncaused cause, Crescas establishes
a new cosmological proof for the existence of God. The
characteristic feature of this proof, in contradistinction to
the Aristotelian and the Avicennian, as will have been
noticed, is the elimination of the principle of the impossibility of an infinite series of causes and effects. But still like
the older Aristotelian proofs it retains the principle of causality, which principle is couched, as in Avicenna's proof, in
terms of possibility and necessity. Truly considered, Crescas'

---

[1] Or Adonai, I, iii, 2.   [2] Or Adonai, I, ii, 3.
[3] Cf. my Crescas' Critique of Aristotle, pp. 67–69, 490–497.

new proof is simply a restoration of the Platonic proof from efficient causation or of the proof from creation as used by Moslem and Jewish theologians, the only difference between them being that whereas the older proof starts with the conception of a universe created in time Crescas' proof starts with the conception of a universe which is only possible by its own nature. Reduced to its syllogistic formula, Crescas' proof runs as follows:

> Every series of possible beings must have a cause which is necessary being.
> The world is a series of possible beings.
> Therefore, the world must have a cause which is necessary being.

It is this proof of Crescas that Spinoza quotes, or rather paraphrases, in a letter to Meyer (Epistola XII) at the end of his lengthy refutation of the ancient arguments against infinity: "But here I should like it to be noted in passing that the more recent Peripatetics, as I at least think, misunderstood the argument of the Ancients by which they strove to prove the existence of God. For, as I find it in the works of a certain Jew, named Rab Ghasdai,[1] it reads as follows. If there is an infinite regression of causes, then all things which exist will be things that have been caused. But it cannot pertain to anything that has been caused that it should necessarily exist in virtue of its own nature. Therefore there is in nature nothing to whose essence it pertains that it should exist necessarily. But this is absurd: and there therefore also that.[2] Therefore the force of the argument lies not in the idea that it is impossible for the infinite actually to

---

[1] On this form of transliteration of Crescas' first name, see below, p. 295, n. 1.

[2] The original passage in the *Or Adonai*, I, iii, 2, reads as follows: "Whether causes and effects are finite or infinite, there is no escape from the conclusion that there must be something which is the cause of all of them as a whole, for if there were nothing but effects, those effects would have only possible existence *per se* and

exist, or that a regression of causes to infinity is impossible, but only in the impossibility of supposing that things which do not exist necessarily in virtue of their own nature, are not determined to existence by something which does exist necessarily in virtue of its own nature, and which is a cause, not an effect."

It is evident that Spinoza understood well the portent and significance of Crescas' proof. He only seems to be mistaken in its historical background when he describes it as a restoration of the original argument of the "ancients" (presumably Aristotle and his followers) which was corrupted by the misunderstanding of the "more recent Peripatetics" (presumably the scholastics). Quite the contrary, Crescas' argument is in direct opposition to the argument of those "ancients," though it may be considered, as we have pointed out, as a restoration of an argument still more ancient, namely, that of Plato.

We are now going to show how this cosmological proof of Avicenna couched in terms of possibility and necessity and as modified by Crescas by the elimination of the principle of the impossibility of an infinite series of causes and effects was taken up by Spinoza and remodelled into an ontological proof.

Just as Avicenna begins his proof with a classification of being, so Spinoza begins his proof with a classification of our ideas of being. Real beings, says Avicenna, fall, in the main, into two classes. There is one being, and one only, whose existence is necessary by his very nature; all others owe their existence to some external cause; in themselves they are only possible; but if the cause of their existence is present they

would thus need something to cause the preponderance of their existence over their non-existence. But that which would bring about this preponderance of their existence would be the cause of those effects, and that is what is meant by God."

are called necessary with reference to their cause, and if that cause is removed they become thereby impossible. Similarly Spinoza classifies our ideas of being with reference to their reality or existence as that which is necessary by its own nature and those which by their own nature are only possible, but become necessary by virtue of some cause from which they follow by necessity, or become impossible when that cause is absent. To this class belong our ideas of all beings which require a cause. Only one new class is introduced here by Spinoza, that which is impossible by its own nature, which is contrasted both with that which is necessary by its own nature and with that which is possible by its own nature. But this class, too, was not unknown to mediaeval Jewish philosophers, though Spinoza's immediate source may have been Descartes.[1] As an illustration of an idea whose existence is necessary by its own nature Spinoza cites substance or God. A square circle is his example of an idea whose existence is impossible by its own nature [2] — it is only a "verbal being," as he says elsewhere. The existence of a circle or a triangle is taken by him as a typical illustration of an idea which in itself has only possible existence and becomes either necessary or impossible according as the cause is present or absent.

Thus far Spinoza has been closely following Avicenna. But when on the basis of this classification of our ideas of

[1] Anything whose nature involves a self-contradiction is called impossible by its own nature and according to Jewish philosophers cannot be made possible even by God in the ordinary course of nature. Cf. Maimonides, *Moreh Nebukim*, I, 75, First and Fifth Arguments, and Descartes, *Meditationes*, VI (*Oeuvres*, VII, p. 71, ll. 18–20).

[2] Spinoza does not mention here the illustration of a chimera. Were it not for his note in *Cogitata Metaphysica*, I, 1, that "by chimera is understood a being which by nature involves a contradiction," one would be tempted to say that its impossibility is due only to the lack of proper causation and not to a self-contradiction in its nature.

being he attempts to construct a proof for the existence of God he leaves Avicenna behind. To begin with, like Crescas, he eliminates the impossibility of an infinite series of causes. But then he leaves Crescas, too. For Crescas still reasons cosmologically and *a posteriori*, from effect to cause, from the existence of things possible to the existence of a thing necessary. But Spinoza starts with an immediately perceived idea of a being whose existence is necessary by its own nature, the clearness and distinctness of which idea is in itself proof for its reality, and tries to resolve this immediately perceived truth into an analytical syllogism, which, as we have seen, is the main function of the ontological proof. The passage from the major premise to the conclusion is achieved, as in his first proof and as in Anselm's proof, by showing the absurdity of the contrary. Thus the Avicennian cosmological proof as modified by Crescas is transformed by Spinoza into an ontological proof after the manner of Descartes. Reduced to its syllogistic formula, Spinoza's second proof runs as follows:

> If we have a clear and distinct idea of God as a being whose existence is necessary by His own nature, then God is immediately perceived by us to exist.
>
> But we have a clear and distinct idea of God as a being whose existence is necessary by His own nature.
>
> Therefore, God is immediately perceived by us to exist.

The basis of the ontological proof, as we have seen, is our valid immediate perception of God's existence. This form of the proof merely shows how our valid immediate perception of God's existence is implied in our clear and distinct idea of God as a being whose existence is necessary by His own nature.

THIRD AND FOURTH PROOFS

It is almost an anti-climax to pass from that involved and complicated second proof of Spinoza to his third and fourth proofs which are based upon a single source, namely, Descartes' second proof in Meditation III. There is one phase, however, which is of interest, namely, Spinoza's endeavor to convert Descartes' proof from a cosmological argument, as it is reproduced by him in his third proof, to an ontological argument, as he gives it in his fourth proof. We have already seen how Spinoza has done it with another cosmological argument in his second proof. Generally speaking, it may be said that whatever any one may attempt to prove of God demonstratively, *a posteriori*, can also be proved of him ontologically, *a priori*, if it is assumed that the thing to be proved forms our immediate and self-evidently true idea of God. Now, in his second proof in Meditation III, Descartes takes the attributes of creation, conservation, or power, just as in his ontological proof he takes the attribute of perfection and self-causality, and argues that creation, conservation, or power must imply existence no less than perfection and self-causality. But there is the following difference, as it is at first assumed by Descartes, between creation, conservation, or power, on the one hand, and perfection and self-causality, on the other. The latter two are immediately perceived as our very idea of God and hence they yield an ontological proof, but the former are not immediately perceived as our very idea of God; they are derived demonstratively, *a posteriori*, from His actions, and hence they yield a cosmological proof. But here Spinoza seems to argue that power, too, is immediately perceived as our idea of God, just as perfection and self-causality in the view of Descartes, and as greatness in the view of Anselm. Why not then construct an ontological proof on the attribute of power? This reasoning marks the relation between the third and the fourth proofs of Spinoza. In his third proof Spinoza reproduces Descartes' second proof of Meditation III in its original cosmological form. In his fourth proof he converts it into an ontological proof. The relation between the third and fourth proofs is clearly brought out in Spinoza's own introductory words to the fourth proof: "In this last demonstration I wished to prove the existence of God *a posteriori*, in order that the demonstration might be the more easily understood, and not because the existence of God does not follow *a priori* from the same grounds."

But to come to the proofs themselves. Perhaps by way of general introduction I may say what I intend to do in the next few paragraphs. I intend to show, in the first place, that Descartes' second proof in Meditation III is only a modification of the traditional proof from creation. In the second place, I intend to explain why Descartes describes this proof either (*a*) as a proof from man's existence or (*b*) as a proof from man's conservation. In the third place, I intend to explain how it happens that this proof is restated by Spinoza in his third proof as a proof from power.

Descartes' second proof in Meditation III is described by himself as a proof from the individual's consciousness of his own existence to the existence of God.[1] It is thus a cosmological proof, reasoning from effect to cause, and, truly speaking, it is only verbally different from the proof of creation which, as has already been mentioned, was made use of by Plato and by Moslem and Jewish theologians as well as by Christian theologians.[2] The only difference between the old proof from creation and Descartes' second proof is

---

[1] *Meditationes*, III (*Oeuvres*, VII, p. 48, ll. 1 f.).
[2] John of Damascus, *De Fide Orthodoxa*, I, 3, First Proof.

that the older proof argues from the existence of the world
whereas Descartes argues from man's own existence or life.[1]
But this change in the vocabulary of the proof, or rather this
new additional vocabulary, is already to be found in the
writings of early authors. St. Augustine, for instance, in reproducing the argument from creation, says: "And therefore, whether we consider the whole body of the world . . .
or whether we consider all life . . . all can only be through
Him who absolutely is."[2] Similarly, Maimonides, in arguing for the existence of an eternal being in the universe, says:
"Consequently nothing whatever would exist [if all things
were transient]; but as we see things existing and find ourselves in existence, we conclude . . . there must be an eternal being that is not subject to destruction."[3] An analogy
between St. Augustine's contention that we have a consciousness of our own existence and a similar contention by
Descartes in his discussion of the nature of the human mind
has been pointed out by one of his objectors.[4]

These quotations are sufficient to show that the vocabulary used by Descartes in his second proof in Meditation III
has grown out of the older proof from creation. But it can
be further shown that there is a structural similarity between
the old argument from creation and Descartes' argument
from man's consciousness of his own existence. We have
already shown in a previous chapter [5] how the argument for
the creation of the world started with the tentative question

---

[1] Kuno Fischer designates Descartes' second proof as "anthropological."
Geschichte der neuern Philosophie, I, 1 (3rd ed., Heidelberg, 1889), p. 308.

[2] *De Civitate Dei*, VIII, 6: "Ac per hoc sive universi mundi corpus . . . sive
omnem vitam . . . nisi ab illo esse non posse, qui simpliciter est." This change in
the vocabulary of the argument is sometimes described as a change from a cosmological form to a psychological form. See C. Baeumker, *Vitelo*, pp. 320 ff.

[3] *Moreh Nebukim*, II, 1, Third Argument.

[4] *Objectiones Quartae* (*Oeuvres*, VII, p. 197, ll. 24 ff.).

[5] Cf. above, pp. 98 ff.

whether the world came into being by itself or by some external cause. Similarly, Descartes' proof from man's consciousness of his own existence begins with the question, "From whom do I then derive my existence? Perhaps from myself or from my parents, or from some other source less perfect than God?" [1] He concludes naturally that it must be derived from God.

Allied with the argument from creation is the argument from the divine government or conservation of the world.[2] This argument, instead of reasoning from the single and completed act of creation, reasons from divine providence, that is to say, from God's guidance and governance and conservation of the world. "Conservation" is a mediaeval term for the continuation of existence after the world was created,[3] and it is considered as direct an effect of God's causality as the act of creation itself.[4] This argument from divine government or conservation of the world is another form of cosmological reasoning, and it was considered as somewhat superior to the argument from creation, for it can be used even if the world is supposed to be eternal, inasmuch as God can be conceived as the governor of the world and the cause of its conservation without the world necessarily hav-

[1] *Meditationes*, III (*Oeuvres*, VII, p. 167, ll. 3 ff.).

[2] John of Damascus, *De Fide Orthodoxa*, I, 3, Second Proof: "Secunda ex earum conservatione et gubernatione. — Porro ipsa quoque rerum creatarum compages, conservatio, atque gubernatio, nos docent Deum esse, qui universum hoc coagmentarit, sustentet, et conservet, eique provideat." In John of Damascus this proof from conservation and government is distinguished from the proof of design as well as from the proof of creation. Cf. *Contra Gentiles*, Lib. I, Cap. 13, end.

[3] *Contra Gentiles*, Lib. III, Cap. 65: "Conservatio rei non est nisi continuatio esse ipsius."

[4] See *Moreh Nebukim*, I, 69: "Here I wish to show that God is the cause of every event that takes place in the world, just as He is the creator of the whole universe as it now exists." Again: "God, however, is himself the form of the universe, as we have already shown, and it is He who causes its continuance and permanency." Cf. *Ethics*, I, Prop. 24, Corol.; Epistola 18 (*Opera*, IV, p. 82, ll. 24 ff. and 4 ff.); Epistola 20 (p. 98, ll. 15 ff. and 33 ff.); *Meditationes*, III (*Oeuvres*, VII, p. 49, ll. 5 f.).

ing come into existence in time.¹ Thus we find that Descartes proposes a change in the form of his proof from man's existence or creation by transforming it into a proof from conservation, declaring that, even if we assume that we have always existed and need no author of our existence, we still need an author of our conservation.² It might therefore be said that Descartes' argument from man's existence corresponds to the argument from creation and his argument from man's conservation corresponds to the argument from divine government. Spinoza, in his *Principia Philosophiae Cartesianae*, I, Proposition VII, explicitly rejects the argument from existence and retains only the argument from conservation. Here in *Ethics*, I, Proposition XI, Third Proof, however, in summarizing Descartes' second proof in Meditation III, he continues to use the term "existence," which would seem to be a return to the "existence" form of Descartes' proof. But "existence" may mean both to "come into existence" and to "continue to exist." In this proof in the *Ethics* it may therefore be taken in the latter sense.

From the act of creation it is deduced, in mediaeval philosophy, that God possesses the attribute of power, or that He is omnipotent.³ Though wisdom and will may enter into the act of creation, still it is said that it is through "power" that God creates.⁴ It is for this reason that Descartes speaks of the "power" to create or to conserve, and Spinoza still

---

¹ The compatibility of the belief in the existence of God with the belief in the eternity of the universe is assumed by Maimonides. See *Moreh Nebukim*, I, 76, Sixth Argument: "But he seems to forget that we are at issue with those who, whilst they believe in the existence of God, admit at the same time the eternity of the universe."

² *Meditationes*, III (*Oeuvres*, VII, p. 49, ll. 12 ff.).

³ *Emunot we-De'ot*, II, 4; *Cuzari*, V, 18, 7-9.

⁴ *Ibid.* Cf. Thomas Aquinas, *Summa Theologica*, Pars I, Quaest. 9, Art. 2: "Omnes enim creaturae, antequam essent, non erant possibiles esse . . . sed per solam potentiam divinam, in quantum Deus poterat eas in esse producere."

more explicitly says: *"posse existere potentia est"* (*Ethics*, I, Proposition XI, Third Proof), and he also speaks of *"potentia conservandi"* (*Prin. Phil. Cart.*, I, Prop. VII, Lemma II). Descartes' second argument may therefore be referred to, as indeed Spinoza does seem to refer to it, as the argument from power, and it may be considered as one of the variations of the mediaeval arguments from creation or divine government.

Reduced to its syllogistic formula, Descartes' second argument in Meditation III as restated by Spinoza in his third proof may be given as follows:

> Everything that continues in its existence must have a cause.
>
> We and the world continue in our existence.
>
> Therefore, we and the world must have a cause.

This syllogistic form is clearly brought out in Spinoza's *Principia*. In the *Ethics* it is somewhat obscured, owing to Spinoza's predilection for indirect proof of the *reductio ad absurdum* type of argument. But it can be easily brought into accord with the argument employed in the *Principia*. It is an *a posteriori*, cosmological argument, pure and simple, only verbally different from the arguments from creation or government.

The proof in the form in which it is given in the *Ethics* may be fully unfolded as follows:

We have the idea of the existence of ourselves as finite beings and we also have the idea of the existence of God as an infinite being.

There are three possibilities as to the truth of these ideas. First, they are both false, and therefore "nothing exists."[1] Second, only the idea of our own existence is true, and

---

[1] "Ergo vel nihil existit."

therefore, "there is nothing which necessarily exists excepting things finite." [1]

Third, both ideas are true, and therefore a "being absolutely infinite also necessarily exists." [2]

The first of these possibilities is to be rejected, for "we ourselves exist." [3]

The second possibility is to be rejected, for "if, therefore, there is nothing which necessarily exists excepting things finite, it follows that things finite are more powerful than the absolutely infinite being, and this (as is self-evident) is absurd." [4] The force of this argument is to be understood in the light of Descartes' argument against our being ourselves the authors of our existence. Descartes' argument originally is that if we were ourselves the authors of our existence we should have endowed ourselves with every perfection of which we possessed any idea and which we include in our idea of God. Spinoza presents here the same argument in the form of a *reductio ad absurdum*. He proceeds as follows: If we exist and God does not exist, then we must exist "in ourselves," [5] that is to say, we must be the authors of our own existence. Therefore, the idea we have of our own existence is more powerful than the idea we have of God's existence, inasmuch as "inability to exist is impotence, and, on the other hand, ability to exist is power." [6] But we have set out with the assumption that we have an idea of God as as infinite being and of ourselves as finite beings. Hence, a self-contradiction.

[1] "Si itaque id, quod jam necessario existit, non nisi entia finita sunt."
[2] "Vel Ens absolute infinitum necessario etiam existit."
[3] "Atqui nos . . . existimus."
[4] "Si itaque id, quod jam necessario existit, non nisi entia finita sunt, sunt ergo entia finita potentiora Ente absolute infinito: atque hoc (*ut per se notum*) absurdum est."
[5] "Atqui nos, vel in nobis, vel in alio, quod necessario existit, existimus."
[6] "Posse non existere impotentia est, et contra posse existere potentia est."

Consequently, the third possibility must be true, and "therefore the being absolutely infinite, that is to say, God, necessarily exists." [1]

So much for Spinoza's third proof. We shall turn now to his fourth proof.

Suppose we say that our clear and distinct idea of God is that of a being of the highest power, i.e., of the highest power to create or to conserve, just as Anselm said that it is the idea of the greatest being and as Descartes himself said that it is the idea of the most perfect being or of a self-caused being. We should then be able to frame an ontological proof from the idea of God as the cause of existence or conservation. Descartes himself has already performed this conversion of his second proof into an ontological proof from "power" in the following passage in his *Primae Responsiones:* [2] "Further, because we cannot think of God's existence as being possible, without at the same time, and by taking heed of His immeasurable power, acknowledging that He can exist by His own might, we hence conclude that He really exists and has existed from all eternity; for the light of nature makes it most plain that what can exist by its own power always exists. And thus we shall understand that necessary existence is comprised in the idea of a being of the highest power, not by any intellectual fiction, but because it belongs to the true and immutable nature of that being to exist." Descartes thus has three forms of the ontological proof:

1. From the idea of a most perfect being.
2. From the idea of a self-caused being.
3. From the idea of a most powerful being.

What Spinoza is really trying to do in his fourth proof is

---

[1] "Ergo ens absolute infinitum, hoc est (*per Defin. 6.*) Deum, necessario existit."
[2] *Oeuvres*, VII, p. 119, ll. 11 ff.

simply to reproduce the third form of Descartes' ontological proof.

Reduced to a syllogism, Spinoza's fourth proof runs as follows:

> If we have a clear and distinct idea of God as a being of the highest power, then God is immediately perceived by us to exist.
>
> But we have a clear and distinct idea of God as a being of the highest power.
>
> Therefore, God is immediately perceived by us to exist.

Here, again, the proof merely shows how our valid immediate perception of God's existence is implied in our clear and distinct idea of God as a being of the highest power. The basis of the ontological proof, as we have said, is this valid immediate perception of God's existence.

There remains now only the last part of the Scholium of Proposition XI to be explained, the part which contains a provisional objection quoted in the name of "many persons" against "this demonstration." In order to simplify the discussion of this part of the Scholium, we shall preface it by a few general remarks.

First, the demonstration of which Spinoza says here that its force may not be easily grasped by many persons refers to the third proof and not to the fourth proof given at the beginning of the Scholium. It will have been noticed that the fourth proof is not given by Spinoza as an independent proof but as a Scholium to the third proof. And so when he says in that Scholium that "many persons, nevertheless, will perhaps not be able easily to see the force of this demonstration," the reference is to the third proof.

Second, the provisional objection raised in the Scholium is to be read in the light of Spinoza's discussion in his Scholium to Proposition VII in *Principia Philosophiae Carte-sianae*, I.

Third, the answer to this provisional objection is to be read in the light of Spinoza's Demonstration of Lemma I of the same Proposition in his *Principia*.

In the Scholium to Proposition VII in the *Principia*, Spinoza discusses Descartes' distinction between "difficult" (*difficile*) and "easy" (*facile*) creation or conservation. He interprets these terms as referring to the production of "more perfect" (*perfectius*) and "less perfect" (*imperfectius*) things respectively. In this Scholium to Proposition XI here in the *Ethics* Spinoza reproduces the same distinction, explaining the expression "more difficult to produce" (*factu diffi-ciliores*) as referring to that "to which they conceive more attributes pertain." By the same token we may say that "easy" production is the production of that to which they perceive less attributes pertain. We may thus further conclude that by his distinction between "more difficult" and "easy" production here Spinoza again means, as in the *Prin-cipia*, the distinction between the production of the "more perfect" and the production of the "less perfect."

With this distinction in view, says Spinoza, "many persons" will try to refute the third proof. The third proof, it will be recalled, starts with the hypothesis that we have two ideas, one of God as an infinite being and another of man as a finite being, and proceeds to argue that if man exists and God does not exist it will be contrary to the hypothesis. But these "many persons" will say, contends Spinoza, that the distinction between God and man as infinite and finite means a distinction between infinite perfection and finite perfec-tion or between having an infinite number and a finite num-ber of properties. But it has just been said that the difference between the "more perfect" and the "less perfect" corresponds respectively to the difference between "difficult" existence or production and "easy" existence or production. Accordingly, the existence denied of God and the existence affirmed of man are of two different kinds entirely, one being infinitely "difficult" existence and the other being "easy" existence. To deny therefore infinitely difficult existence of God while affirming easy existence of man does not imply a contradiction of our idea of God as an infinite or most perfect being. Quite the contrary, it is because we conceive of God as an infinite and most perfect being that His existence becomes infinitely difficult, and hence He does not exist, whereas man, being conceived as finite and imperfect, thereby has existence which is easy, and hence he does exist. Spinoza could have put into the mouth of these "many persons" the following illustration. Suppose we have two ideas, one of our possessing a million dollars and the other of our possessing one dollar. The first idea is more perfect than the second, inasmuch as more attributes or properties pertain to it. But because the idea of having a million dollars is more perfect their existence is more difficult and consequently they do not exist in our pocket, whereas the idea of having one dollar is less perfect; therefore its existence is easy and it does exist in our pocket.

To this provisional objection tentatively raised in the name of "many persons" Spinoza answers by recalling his old distinction between things "which are produced by external causes" [1] and things "which can be produced by no external cause." Of the former, he argues, it is indeed true to say that the greater the perfection the more difficult its existence and the smaller the perfection the easier the existence. Hence the idea of a million dollars has less possibility of existence than that of one dollar, for the perfection

---

[1] *Ethics*, I, Prop. 11, Schol. Cf. *Principia Philosophiae Cartesianae*, I, Prop. 7, Lemma I, Nota I.

as well as the existence of a million dollars is not intrinsic. The perfections of beings dependent upon external causes are themselves external perfections, and the more of them there are the more dependent the existence of the beings becomes upon external causes. "For whatever perfection or reality those things may have which are produced by external causes, whether they consist of many parts or of few, they owe it all to the virtue of an external cause, and therefore their existence springs from the perfection of an external cause alone and not from their own."[1] But if you have an idea of anything with a set of internal perfections, growing out of its own nature, then the possibility of its existence increases in proportion to the number of perfections, so that if we get an idea of an infinitely perfect being its existence becomes absolutely necessary. "In an idea or concept of everything, existence either as possible or as necessary is contained."[2] "For, as we cannot affirm existence of nothing, as we detract from the perfection of a concept and conceive its content to approach zero as its limit, so much do we detract from its possible existence. If we conceive this degree of perfection to be infinitely diminished, even to zero, it will contain no existence, or but an absolutely impossible one. On the other hand, if we increase this degree of perfection to infinity we conceive that it has the highest possible existence and so to be absolutely necessary."[3] This kind of internal perfection which grows out of the nature of things, as distinguished from external "marks of perfection which men from ignorance and tradition are accustomed to esteem as such,"[4] is to be understood only as "so much reality or being."[5] God, therefore, who is conceived as having an infinite number of perfections growing out of His own nature,

[1] *Ethics*, I, Prop. 11, Schol.

[2] *Principia Philosophiae Cartesianae*, I, Axiom 6. Cf. Prop. 7, Lemma I, Demonst.

[3] *Ibid.*, Prop. 7, Lemma I, Demonst.

[4] *Ibid.*, Prop. 7, Lemma I, Nota 2.

[5] *Ibid.*

has the most reality and being.[1] You cannot argue, as would those "many persons," that because God is infinitely perfect His existence is infinitely difficult, and hence He does not exist. Only external perfections may be said to increase the difficulty of existence; internal perfections, on the contrary, increase the possibility of existence. Such internal "perfection consequently does not prevent the existence of a thing, but establishes it; imperfection, on the other hand, prevents existence, and so of no existence can we be more sure than of the existence of the Being absolutely infinite or perfect, that is to say, God."[2]

To sum up our main conclusions: Historically there were two kinds of proofs for the existence of God, based upon two kinds of knowledge, indirect and direct. The indirect kind of knowledge gave us the various cosmological and teleological proofs. The direct kind of knowledge gave us the proofs based upon revelation, the innateness of the idea of God, and universal assent. The ontological proof as stated by Anselm, Descartes, and Spinoza is not an independent proof It is only a different way of formulating the old proofs based upon direct knowledge. In Anselm, it is a modified form of the argument from universal assent. In Descartes and Spinoza it is a modified form of the argument from the innateness of the idea of God.

Of the four proofs for the existence of God given by Spinoza in the *Ethics*, the *first* and *third* correspond respectively to Descartes' ontological proof in Meditation V and his cosmological proof in the second proof of Meditation III. Descartes' first proof in Meditation III is not reproduced by Spinoza in the *Ethics*, but is reproduced by him in the *Short Treatise* and in his *Principia Philosophiae Cartesianae*, and is referred to in his correspondence and in *De Intellectus*

---

[1] Cf. *Ethics*, I, Prop. 9.   [2] *Ethics*, I, Prop. 11, Schol.

Emendatione Tractatus. Spinoza's *second* proof in the *Ethics* is a modification of Descartes' ontological proof in Meditation V, enriched by elements borrowed from a cosmological proof in Hebrew philosophic sources. Spinoza's *fourth* proof in the *Ethics* is the conversion of his *third* proof, which is cosmological, into ontological form, which conversion was also made by Descartes himself.

The idea of God which is assumed in the ontological proof to imply existence is differently phrased in the different forms of the proof. In Anselm, it is the idea of the greatest being. In Descartes, it is the idea of the most perfect being, or of a self-caused being, or of the most powerful being. Spinoza's three ontological proofs — the *first*, *second*, and *fourth* proofs in the *Ethics* — make use of three descriptions which may be reduced to two. In the *first* proof, the idea of God is that of a being whose essence involves existence. In the *second* proof, it is that of a being whose existence is necessary *per se*. These two can be reduced to what Descartes described as a self-caused being. In the *fourth* proof, it is the idea of a being who is most powerful. This difference in terminology, however, is only verbal. Any other term, such, for instance, as the most real being (*ens realissimum*), can be used, if it is assumed to be that which is immediately perceived of God, without introducing anything new in the ontological proof. The recurrent claims for the discovery of new ontological proofs for the existence of God which we meet in philosophic literature generally prove, upon analysis, to be nothing but the substitution of some new terms for such older terms as the greatest, the most perfect, the self-caused, and the most powerful. Oftentimes, these so-called newly discovered ontological proofs are not even ontological, but rather disguised cosmological proofs.

CHAPTER VII

EXTENSION AND THOUGHT

I. The Framework of Spinoza's Universe

In our analysis of the *Ethics* so far we have found that of the first thirteen propositions twelve deal with the traditional problem of the nature of God, which we have discussed in the chapters on the definition, unity, and simplicity of substance, and one proposition deals with the proofs of the existence of God. The remaining propositions of the First Part of the *Ethics* similarly deal with a problem which in traditional philosophy would go under the title of the relation of God to the world. Spinoza starts out in Proposition XIV with a recapitulation of his denial, both in *Short Treatise*, I, 2, and in Propositions II–VI in the First Part of the *Ethics*, of the fundamental belief of all mediaeval philosophers that between God and the world there is a distinction of pure form and matter, the two constituting, as it were, two substances. "Besides God," he therefore maintains, "no substance can be nor can be conceived" (Prop. XIV). His demonstration of this proposition is again a summary of what he has already said in the *Short Treatise*, I, 2, and in Propositions II–VI, namely, if the world were of a nature absolutely distinct from that of God, all the difficulties which the mediaevals themselves had pointed out against the assumption of the existence of two deities [1] or against the assumption of the emanation of a material world out of an immaterial cause by the ordinary process of necessary causality [2] would recur and would be unanswerable (Dem-

---

[1] Cf. above, p. 83.   [2] Cf. above, p. 88.

onst.). He thus concludes that there cannot be anything in the nature of the universe, including matter, which is not in God himself, who according to all traditional opinions is the sole cause of the universe. "Hence it follows with the greatest clearness, firstly, that God is one, that is to say (Def. VI), in nature there is but one substance" (Corol. I). But this one substance or God, again according to all traditional opinions,[1] "is absolutely infinite" (*ibid.*), and therefore cannot be fully known by the finite intellect.[2] It is only the infinite intellect (*infinitus intellectus*),[3] i.e., the infinite intellect of God (*infinitus Dei intellectus*),[4] that can perceive everything which pertains to this one substance, that is to say, its infinite attributes. The finite "human mind can only get to know those things which the idea of an actually existing body involves, or what can be inferred from this idea."[5] But inasmuch as "this idea of the body neither involves nor expresses any other attributes of God than extension and thought,"[6] it follows that the human mind knows God "in so far only as He is considered under the attribute of extension"[7] and "under the attribute of thought, and not in so far as He is considered under any other attribute."[8] And so, just as his discussion of the impossibility of two substances in the *Short Treatise* culminates in the statement "that we posit extension as an attribute of God,"[9] so also here Spinoza concludes with the statement that "it follows, secondly, that the thing extended and the thing thinking are either attributes of God or affections of the attributes of God" (Corol. II).

---

[1] Cf. above, p. 117.　　　　　　[2] Cf. above, p. 142.
[3] *Ethics*, II, Prop. 7, Schol. (*Opera*, II, p. 90, l. 4).
[4] Epistola 66 (*Opera*, IV, p. 280, ll. 8–9).
[5] Epistola 64 (*Opera*, IV, p. 277, ll. 10–13).
[6] *Ibid.* (ll. 18–19).　　　　　　[7] *Ibid.* (ll. 23–24).
[8] *Ibid.* (ll. 28–29).　　　　　　[9] *Short Treatise*, I, 2, § 18.

The last expression, "or affections of the attributes of God," is a reference to the modal system of extension and thought, which Spinoza describes most fully and clearly in the *Short Treatise* [1] and his correspondence with Schuller. [2] The full scheme of Spinoza's system of extension and thought may be pieced together from these two main sources. In its bare outline it is as follows: There is, to begin with, substance or God with infinite attributes. Of these only two attributes are known to us, extension and thought. From these attributes there follows a series of modes, to wit, (1) immediate infinite modes, (2) a mediate infinite mode, and (3) finite modes. Of extension, the immediate infinite mode is motion-and-rest; of thought, the immediate infinite mode is the absolutely infinite intellect (*intellectus absolute infinitus*). Only one mediate infinite mode is specifically named by Spinoza, and that is the face of the whole universe (*facies totius universi*). He does not make it clear, however, whether it is a mode of extension or of thought or of both. The finite modes are the particular things (*res particulares*). Substance and its attributes are called by Spinoza *natura naturans*, the entire modal system of extension and thought is called by him *natura naturata*, and within the latter he distinguishes between the two classes of infinite modes, which he calls "general," and the single class of finite modes, which he calls "particular."

As a skeleton framework to hold together and to unify the fragmentary pieces of the visible universe, this scheme of Spinoza is to be regarded as one of the stages, an advanced stage, to be sure, in the long development of similar schemes since man began to distinguish between the visible and the invisible and to discern behind phenomenal sporadic changes

[1] *Ibid.*, I, 8–9.
[2] Epistolae 63–64.

a certain unity and a certain causal connection. Any attempt
to interpret this scheme of Spinoza as an adumbration of any
specific theories of modern science is justifiable in the same
sense as the Stoics were justified in transforming the gods
and goddesses of Olympia into the natural forces and moral
principles of their own philosophy, or as Philo and the mediaeval Jewish, Christian, and Moslem theologians were justified in investing the God and angels of the Bible with signif-
icances of their own philosophic principles. There is indeed
a justification in all such attempts at allegorical methods of
interpretation, whether applied to Homer, the Bible, or the
works of Spinoza, but only in so far as they are confined to
an effort to show that all these systems of myths, religion,
and philosophy were inspired by a common striving to see the
universe as a whole and to interpret it as a unit, and how in
reaching out for the truth they almost attained it. But the
allegorical method of interpretation becomes a perversion
of truth when confused with the method of historical research. The first step in understanding any author is to find
out what he means by what he says and how he came to
say it in a certain particular manner. In Spinoza's skeleton
framework of the universe, the terms used are those of traditional philosophy, and the concepts represented by these
terms, as well as the connection between them, are likewise
reminiscent of skeleton frameworks of the universe invented
by his predecessors. We happen to know also that philosophers throughout the ages have come to whatever new views
they have happened to arrive at as a result of criticism of
older views and a modification of the views criticized by
them. We have already seen how Spinoza's propositions in
the *Ethics* so far can be best explained as a criticism and
modification of his mediaeval philosophic background. We
shall therefore try to show how the entire scheme of Spinoza's

theory of extension and thought has grown out of a typical scheme held by mediaeval philosophers.

The mediaeval skeleton framework of the universe in its bare outline and without any discussion of its finer subtle points starts out, like that of Spinoza, with God who is infinite in His perfections; but unlike Spinoza's, it assumes God to be pure form, whose sole activity is thinking. The product of God's thinking is an Intelligence, which is likewise pure form and the activity of which is likewise thinking. But this Intelligence, owing to the dual aspect of its existence, being, on the one hand, necessary of existence, for it is the inevitable product of divine thinking, and, on the other hand, only possible of existence, for by its own nature and without a cause it could not have come into being, contains also a duality in its nature, the duality of necessity and possibility. Out of the necessary element in its nature there emanates another Intelligence, which is again pure form and the activity of which is again thinking; but out of its possible element there proceeds a sphere which is material and the activity of which is motion. As the astronomy of the Middle Ages posited a plurality of such concentric celestial spheres, the number of which varied according to different views but is generally spoken of as nine,[1] the process is repeated until we come to the last in the series of the concentric spheres, the so-called lunar sphere, and to the last in the series of the Intelligences, generally spoken of as the Tenth or Active Intelligence. This so-called Tenth Intelligence, like all the others, has in its nature the duality of possibility and necessity. Out of its possibility there arises the underlying general matter which is common to all the sublunar things and the nature of which is pure possibility and potentiality. Then by the motion of the spheres — their common circular

[1] Cf. *Moreh Nebukim*, II, 4.

motion as well as the particular variations in their common circular motion — this common underlying matter is predisposed for the assumption of the general as well as the particular forms by which the simple elements and the compound things are differentiated among themselves from each other. The forms themselves — from the primary forms of the four elements to souls and minds, which are also called forms — flow from the activity of the Tenth Intelligence,[1] which means that they ultimately flow from God.

Thus, according to this scheme, the entire universe is divided into matter and form. These two exist together in the physical part of the universe, but form exists apart from matter in the world of the Intelligences[2] and in God. While on the whole matter owes its existence to God as its ultimate cause, it does not come directly from God, inasmuch as God is pure form, and by a mediaeval principle, which may be formulated as *omne materiale e materiali*,[3] matter cannot arise from form. Matter arises somewhere in the process of emanation at a stage removed from God, and its origin is accounted for by what I have described elsewhere as "emergent emanation."[4]

In order to simplify the process of showing how Spinoza derived his own scheme from the mediaeval scheme, it is necessary for us to separate in the latter its essential from its non-essential elements. The essential element in the scheme is the main philosophic thesis that God is pure form and

[1] The most obvious sources from which Spinoza could have derived his knowledge of this mediaeval scheme are *Moreh Nebukim*, I, 72; II, 4; and Shem-Tob's commentary on *Moreh Nebukim*, II, 13.

[2] For a difference of opinion, however, with regard to the immateriality of the Intelligences, see below, p. 223.

[3] Cf. my paper, "The Problem of the Origin of Matter in Mediaeval Jewish Philosophy and Its Analogy to the Modern Problem of the Origin of Life," in *Proceedings of the Sixth International Congress of Philosophy*, p. 602.

[4] Cf. *ibid.*, pp. 603–604.

hence the material universe did not proceed from Him directly. The non-essential elements are the assumptions which happened to be part of the mediaeval scientific conception of the universe, namely, the theory of celestial spheres, the theory of the plurality of Intelligences, and the theory that the universe was finite in extent, being enclosed within an all-surrounding sphere. They were, however, not essential to the scheme itself. The non-essential character of these scientific assumptions in the mediaeval scheme is attested by the fact that in the history of philosophy, even before Spinoza, they had been eliminated or modified one by one without affecting the main philosophic thesis of the immateriality of God. The theory of the finite extent of the universe, which was an Aristotelian heritage in the history of philosophy, was attacked by Crescas [1] at the beginning of the fifteenth century, as it was again attacked by Bruno [2] about two centuries later, so that by the time of Spinoza the infinity of the universe was already treated as a philosophic commonplace. The theory of celestial spheres was eliminated from consideration in respectable scientific circles with the fall of the Ptolemaic astronomy in the sixteenth century, and even before that time two important features of that theory, namely, the difference between the matter and the motion of the celestial bodies and those of terrestrial bodies, had been disposed of by Crescas.[3] With the elimination of the celestial spheres there would necessarily have to follow the elimination of the plurality of the Intelligences, for the number of the Intelligences, according to the mediaeval view itself, was determined by the number of the spheres.[4] But still one Intelligence of pure form would have to remain

[1] Cf. my Crescas' Critique of Aristotle, pp. 115–117
[2] Cf. ibid., pp. 115, 118.   [3] Cf. ibid., pp. 118–120.
[4] Cf. Moreh Nebukim, II, 4.

for as long as the main thesis of God as pure form remained and for as long as the origin of the material world was explained not as an act of special creation out of nothing but as a process of emanation out of the substance of God. Thus the mediaeval scheme, stripped of its non-essential accessories and modified to fit the new scientific conceptions of the universe, must have presented itself to the mind of Spinoza as follows: There is God, a pure form, whose sole activity is thinking. The product of God's thought is an Intelligence, which is also pure form, but in the nature of which there is a duality of necessity and possibility. Out of this Intelligence emanates the physical universe, its matter out of the possibility of the Intelligence's nature, and its form, motion, and thought out of the necessity of the Intelligence's nature.

It is this main thesis, which on the whole had survived all the changing conceptions of the universe up to the time of Spinoza and from which the intermediary Intelligence was eliminated only whenever emanation gave place, as, for instance, in the case of Descartes, to a special act of creation out of nothing, that Spinoza constantly and repeatedly makes the subject of a frontal attack.[1] He does not dwell on the absurdity of the mediaeval theories of celestial spheres or on the plurality of Intelligences, for these were already dead issues in his own time and were not essential, as we have seen, to the main thesis. He does indeed discuss the problem of infinity, but not especially with reference to the infinite extent of the universe, but with reference to certain general aspects of the problem which were still vital issues in his own time, and he does it only in a letter in which he answers a question addressed to him and in a scholium to a proposition in which he refutes some unnamed opponents.[2] The

---

[1] Cf. above, Chapter IV.   [2] Cf. below, Chapter VIII.

main thesis, however, is attacked by him directly. He shows that if God is pure form, then the interposition of another form between God and the universe will not remove the difficulty of how matter could arise from form by the ordinary process of necessary causality.[1] As an escape from this difficulty he takes the bold step of making the material universe proceed by necessity directly from God, with the inevitable consequence that God himself becomes material, or, to use his own terms, extension becomes an attribute of God. In a letter to Oldenburg Spinoza seems to allude to this method of reasoning leading to his conclusion with regard to extension when he says: "And, on the other hand, things which they [the theologians], on account of their prejudices, regard as created, I contend to be attributes of God, and as misunderstood by them."[2]

The conclusion arrived at by Spinoza that God was material is not new in the history of philosophy. The most notable exponents of this view in European philosophy are the Stoics, who may have perhaps arrived at their materialism, like Spinoza, as a result of a criticism of the Platonic and Aristotelian dualism.[3] Though the Stoic view was not unknown to mediaeval Jewish philosophers, for in a work written in Arabic by an unknown Jewish or Moslem author and preserved in a Hebrew translation it is quoted in the name of Zeno, i.e., Zeno of Citium,[4] still none of them had ever attempted to bridge the gulf between God and the world by endowing God with materiality. Ibn Gabirol's *Fons Vitae*, to be sure, is said to have given rise to such a

---

[1] Cf. above, p. 91.   [2] Epistola 6 (*Opera*, IV, p. 36, ll. 21–23).

[3] This explanation for the Stoic materialism has been suggested by Zeller, but is rejected by him. Cf. Zeller, *Philosophie der Griechen*, III, 1 (4th edition), pp. 125 ff. English translation: *Stoics, Epicureans and Sceptics*, pp. 127 ff.

[4] See David Kaufmann, *Die Spuren Al-Batlajûsi's in der jüdischen Religions-Philosophie* (Budapest, 1880). Hebrew Text, p. 36, ll. 10 ff.

view in David of Dinant,[1] but this is far from being a true representation of the real view of Ibn Gabirol. Ibn Gabirol goes only so far as to assert, as do also Baḥya Ibn Pakuda [2] and Judah ha-Levi,[3] that the distinction of matter and form is also to be found in the Intelligences or angels, a view which was taken over from him by Duns Scotus and his followers and maintained by them against Thomas Aquinas. Leo Hebraeus refers to this view and ascribes it to Plato.[4] God himself, even according to Ibn Gabirol, was free of matter. Crescas, to be sure, comes near attributing extension to God when, after defining space as extension and assuming it to be infinite and the world to be in it, he quotes in support of his view the old rabbinic dictum that God is the place of the world.[5] Logically, if God is the place of the world and the place of the world is extension, God must have extension as one of His attributes. But Crescas stops short of drawing this daring conclusion. God still continues to be to him pure form, and in the problem of creation, in order to bridge the gulf between the immaterial God and the material world, he has to resort to the solution of endowing God with will and purpose and design. It is said that in Bruno there is an intimation that extension is one of God's attributes,[6] but if this really represents Bruno's reasoned-out view, then to say of Bruno, as does Pollock,

[1] Cf. Erdmann, *Grundriss der Geschichte der Philosophie*, §§ 192 and 188. But according to Albertus Magnus, David of Dinant's view that God is "principium materiale omnium" was due to the influence of Alexander of Aphrodisias: "Alexander etiam in quodam libello quem fecit de *Principio incorporeae et corporeae substantiae*, quem secutus est quidam David de Dinanto in libro quem scripsit de *Tomis*, hoc est, de divisionibus, dicit Deum esse principium materiale omnium" (*Summa Theologiae*, Pars I, Tract. IV, Quaest. 20, Membrum 2, Quaestio Incidens).

[2] *Ḥobot ha-Lebabot*, I, 6.

[3] *Cuzari*, IV, 3. Cf. commentaries *Ḳol Yehudah* and *Oẓar Neḥmad* on V, 18, 6.

[4] *Dialoghi d'Amore*, III, p. 244 (Bari, 1929). Cf. p. 246, where Avicebron is referred to.   [5] Cf. my *Crescas' Critique of Aristotle*, p. 123.

[6] Pollock, *Spinoza*, p. 104. Cf. *De la Causa*, III, p. 261, ll. 14–18 (ed. Lagarde).

that "he rejects the notion of formless matter" [1] is to put the wrong emphasis on his view. What should have been said is that he rejects the notion of matterless form. Clearer than all these intimations as to an extended God is the statement made by Henry More in a letter to Descartes, which reads: "God seems to be an extended thing." [2]

Spinoza, however, did not come to his view by merely adopting the statements of the Stoics or of Bruno or of More, or by merely carrying out to its logical conclusion the hint thrown out by Crescas. He had been forced to it, as we have shown in a previous chapter,[3] by the logic of the situation and as a result of his thorough and critical examination of the various mediaeval solutions of the problem of the rise of matter out of an immaterial God. Finding all the solutions of this difficulty under the theory of emanation unsatisfactory, and refusing to resort to the theory of creation *ex nihilo* or to the theory of the co-existence of an eternal matter alongside God, he was forced to the conclusion that God was not immaterial.

II. PROPERTIES, ATTRIBUTES, AND MODES

We have thus seen how the main outline of Spinoza's skeleton framework has developed out of the mediaeval framework. We shall now try to show in a similar manner the development of the individual parts within that framework — the infinity of God's attributes, the two known attributes of extension and thought, and the modal system under the two known attributes.

---

[1] *Ibid.*

[2] Descartes, *Correspondance*, DXXXI (*Oeuvres*, V, p. 238, l. 21): "Res enim extensa Deus videtur esse." Cf. Dunin-Borkowski, *Der junge De Spinoza*, pp. 359 ff.

[3] Cf. above, Chapter IV.

The infinity of God's attributes is implied throughout the mediaeval discussions of the nature of God, especially in the oft-repeated statement that God is indescribable.[1] A close and almost verbal resemblance to Spinoza's statement as to the infinity of attributes is to be found in Crescas, who, in discussing a certain Talmudic passage in which the excessive enumeration of divine attributes is discouraged, explains it on the ground that such an enumeration "would appear as an attempt to limit that which is infinite in number."[2] His pupil Joseph Albo puts it still more directly when he says: "It must be understood that the perfections which exist in God are unlimited in number, that is to say, they are infinite with reference to their plurality."[3] The term "perfection" is used here by Albo as synonymous with "attribute." With these mediaeval thinkers, to whom God was immaterial and separate from the world and to whom the attributes were expressions of divine perfections, it was only logical that they should insist not only upon the infinite degree of perfection of each attribute but also upon the infinite number of attributes. For them to say that God possessed an infinite number of attributes meant nothing more than to say that God's powers and perfections were inexhaustible. But with the gradual disappearance of the separation of God and the world, if not their complete identification, in the Renaissance philosophy, as for instance in the philosophy of Bruno, and with the general acceptance in opposition to Aristotle of the belief in an infinite number of worlds, the ascription of infinite attributes to God naturally assumed a new meaning. To the minds of some people it must have conveyed the idea of the existence of an infinite number of independent worlds.

[1] Cf. *Moreh Nebukim*, I, 59.
[2] *Or Adonai*, I, iii, 3 (p. 24a).
[3] *'Ikkarim*, II, 25. Cf. above, p. 117.

Thus Schuller asks of Spinoza whether or not "there must be constituted as many worlds as there are attributes of God." [1] Spinoza tries to set him aright on this point. In his answer to Schuller,[2] where reference is made to the Scholium to Proposition VII, Part II, and in other places where the infinite attributes are discussed,[3] Spinoza makes it quite clear that by infinite attributes he does not mean an infinite number of independent worlds, but rather an infinite number of aspects of one single infinite universe, analogous to the mediaeval conception of the infinite attributes of God.

The infinite attributes of God, however, are not known to us. Only some of them we are able to affirm of God, and even these, according to the mediaevals, do not tell us anything about the true essence of God. They are only inadequate terms by which we express the various ways in which God manifests himself through nature. The selection of attributes which are admissible of God constitutes one phase of the problem of attributes in mediaeval Jewish philosophy, and various lists have been drawn up by various philosophers. Saadia [4] enumerates life, power, and knowledge. Bahya Ibn Pakuda [5] mentions existence, unity, and eternity. Ibn Zaddik's [6] list contains existence, power, knowledge, abundance, justice, goodness, mercifulness, life, truth. Judah ha-Levi,[7] dividing attributes into actional, relational, and negational, mentions under them respectively the following groups: (a) making poor and rich, casting

---

[1] Epistola 63. [2] Epistola 64.

[3] Cf. *Short Treatise*, I, 1, § 8, note 3 (*Opera*, I, p. 17, ll. 33 ff.).

[4] *Emunot we-De'ot*, II, 4: חי, יכול, חכם.

[5] *Hobot ha-Lebabot*, I, 10: נמצא, אחד, קדמון.

[6] *'Olam Katan*, III (pp. 57 ff.): מציאות, גבור, חכם, עשיר, צדיק, מטיב, רחמן, חי, אמת.

[7] *Cuzari*, II, 1: (a) מוריש ומעשיר, משפיל אף מרומם, רחוח וחנון, קנא ונוקם, גבור, שדי; (h) ברוך ומבורך, מהולל, קדוש, רם ונשא; (c) חי, אחד, ראשון ואחרון.

down and exalting, merciful and gracious, jealous and re-
vengeful, strong, almighty; (*b*) blessed and praised, glorified,
holy, exalted and extolled; (*c*) living, one, first and last.
Abraham Ibn Daud [1] mentions eight: unity, truth, existence,
eternity, life, knowledge, will, and power, but concludes:
"We do not contend that there are no other attributes which
may be similarly affirmed of God, provided only that it be
made clear that they are to be understood in such a way as
to imply no plurality in His essence." [2] Descartes likewise
enumerates a similar list of attributes "in so far as they may
be known by the light of nature alone." [3] His list mentions
eternal, omniscient, omnipotent, the source of all goodness
and truth, creator of all things, and infinite perfection.

Spinoza does not altogether disregard these traditional
attributes of God. But they are not to him what he would
call "the proper attributes of God" [4] in the specific sense in
which he uses the term "attribute," namely, "that which
the intellect perceives of substance, as if constituting its essence." [5] They are called by him *propria*, "that is to say,
without them God would indeed be no God, but still it is
not they that constitute God: for they reveal nothing of the
character of substance, through which alone God exists." [6]
The contrast between attributes and properties is also implied in his opening statement in the Appendix to the First
Part of the *Ethics*, where he divides the contents of the First
Part into two problems, namely, (1) "the nature of God and
(2) its properties." [7] By "the nature of God" he means
there the attributes. Similarly in the *Tractatus de Intellectus*

---

[1] *Emunah Ramah*, II, iii (p. 52): ‏האחד, האמתי, הנמצא, הנצחי, החי, היודע,‏
‏הרוצה, היכול‏. [2] *Ibid.* (p. 56).
[3] *Principia Philosophiae*, I, 22.
[4] *Short Treatise*, I, 2, § 28. [5] *Ethics*, I, Def. 4.
[6] *Short Treatise*, I, 3, § 1, and note 1.
[7] Cf. above, p. 112.

Emendatione he says of "one" and "infinite" that "these are not attributes of God which set forth His essence."[1] These properties are further described by Spinoza either as being "an extraneous denomination, such as that He exists through himself, is eternal, one, immutable, etc.," or as having "reference to His activity."[2] What he means here by an "extraneous denomination" is not quite clear. But a passage in the *Cogitata Metaphysica* may throw light upon it. In that passage, using the traditional term "attribute" rather loosely in the sense of his own term "property," he enumerates the following eleven properties: eternity, unity, greatness, immutability, simplicity, life, understanding, will, power, creation, concurrence. These, he says, are divided by some into incommunicable (*incommunicabilia*) and communicable (*communicabilia*)[3] — a division which he characterizes as "more nominal than real," for all of them are to be incommunicable or homonymous, inasmuch as there can be no similarity in their meaning when applied to God and when applied to other beings. Spinoza himself divides them into those which explain God's "active essence" (*actuosam ejus essentiam*), such as "understanding, will, life, omnipotence, etc.," and those which only explain "His mode of existence" (*ejus modi existendi*), such as "unity, eternity, necessity, etc."[4] Now, in his correspondence, Spinoza speaks of the properties as being explanations of the expression necessary existence[5] or of the identity of essence and existence,[6] the latter of which, as we have shown, is itself derived from the nature of necessary existence.[7] Taking, therefore,

---

[1] § 76, note z (*Opera*, II, p. 29).   [2] *Short Treatise*, I, 2, § 29.

[3] This distinction has been traced by Freudenthal to Thomas Aquinas and Heereboord. Cf. "Spinoza und die Scholastik," in *Philosophische Aufsätze, Eduard Zeller . . . gewidmet*, p. 116.

[4] *Cogitata Metaphysica*, II, 11.

[5] Epistola 35.   [6] Epistola 83.   [7] Cf. above, pp. 126 ff.

all these passages together, we may conclude that the "extraneous denomination" is an explanation of God's "mode of existence" or of the expression "necessary existence." And thus Spinoza's properties correspond to what Maimonides described as (1) explanation of a name,[1] and (2) actions,[2] both of which are distinguished by him from essential attributes. In a letter to Oldenburg, evidently referring to these lists of attributes, Spinoza writes: "I say that many attributes which they [the theologians of his time] and all others at least who are known to me attribute to God, I regard as things created."[3] By "things created" (*creaturas*) he undoubtedly means what Maimonides calls "actions."

According to Joël the distinction between attributes and properties referred to by Spinoza is analogous to the distinction made by Crescas between essential attributes and attributes merely as intellectual conceptions.[4] The analogy is wrong on several grounds. First, the intellectually conceived attributes of Crescas may have a closer relation to Spinoza's definition of attributes[5] than to his definition of properties. Second, Crescas' intellectually conceived attributes imply a certain conceptual theory of universals which Spinoza's properties do not. Third, Crescas' intellectually conceived attributes, as I have shown, are one of several forms of anti-realistic conceptions of attributes in Jewish philosophy,[6] of which Maimonides' "explanation of a name" is an extreme type, and which, incidentally, may be traced to

---

[1] *Moreh Nebukim*, I, 51.

[2] *Ibid.*, I, 52.

[3] Epistola 6 (*Opera*, IV, p. 36, ll. 19–21).

[4] Joël, *Zur Genesis der Lehre Spinoza's*, pp. 19 ff.; Joachim, *A Study of the Ethics of Spinoza*, p. 42, n.

[5] Cf. above, p. 152.

[6] Cf. my "Crescas on the Problem of Divine Attributes" in *Jewish Quarterly Review*, n.s., VII (1916), pp. 1–44, 175–221. Cf. above, pp. 150 ff.

the nominal definition mentioned by Aristotle and described by him also as the explanation of a name.[1] The fact that Spinoza divides properties into those which are explanations of the expression necessary existence and those which describe actions shows quite clearly that they are traceable to what Maimonides describes as explanations of a name and actions.

But even as *propria*, not all the attributes that have been used by the mediaevals with reference to God are of interest to Spinoza. Many of them are only adjectives which happen to have been applied to God in the traditional literature of religion. Spinoza passes them by and confines himself only to those which are of a philosophic character. "We shall not trouble ourselves very much about the ideas that people have of God, but we shall only inquire briefly into what the philosophers can tell us about it." [2] Of these so-called philosophic *propria*, or, as he calls them here, "attributes which do not pertain to God," he reproduces a list which concludes with the phrase "and so forth": "A being existing through or of itself, cause of all things, omniscient, almighty, eternal, simple, infinite, the highest good, of infinite compassion." [3] In a foot-note to this passage, he describes these attributes which do not pertain to God as "certain modes which may be attributed to God" either in consideration of both his known attributes, such as eternal, self-subsisting, infinite, cause of all things, immutable, or in consideration of the attribute of thought only, such as omniscient, wise, etc., or in consideration of extension only, such as omnipresent, fills all, etc. A list of *propria* under the loose name of attributes is given in the *Cogitata Metaphysica*, namely, eternity, unity, greatness, immutability, simplicity, life, understand-

[1] *Analytica Posteriora*, II, 10, 93b, 29-37.
[2] *Short Treatise*, I, 7, § 2.   [3] *Ibid.*

ing, will, power, creation, concurrence.[1] In a letter to Hudde
he enumerates four *propria*, eternal, simple, infinite, indivisible, all of which are reduced by him to the single property of
perfection.[2] In a later letter to Hudde he refers not only
to these four properties but also to "the remaining similar
properties" and to their reduction by him to one property.[3]
In a letter to Tschirnhaus he mentions as properties the assertions "that He exists necessarily, that He is unique, immutable, infinite, etc."[4] In the Appendix to the First Part
of the *Ethics* there is an indirect reference to properties, of
which he mentions necessary existence, one, acting by the
necessity of His own nature, cause of all things, all things
being in Him, predestination.[5] A list of three *propria* is
given by him in the *Short Treatise*, namely, that God is
the cause of all things, divine providence, and divine predestination.[6]

These *propria*, which in traditional philosophy had passed
for divine attributes, do not according to Spinoza reveal
anything of the nature of God. Even in mediaeval philosophy they were taken, as a rule, as homonymous terms to be
understood in a sense entirely unrelated to their ordinary
meaning. It was well, indeed, for the mediaevals to give
up their inquiry about the nature of God at this point, for
to them God was absolutely distinct from the universe, as
pure form must be distinct from matter, and consequently
what they called attributes could not tell us anything of the
nature or essence of God or what God is. They told us only
what He is not or what He does in the world — the so-called

---

[1] *Cogitata Metaphysica*, II, 1–11. The origin of this list in various Latin sources
is given by Freudenthal, "Spinoza und die Scholastik," in *Philosophische Aufsätze
Eduard Zeller . . . gewidmet*, p. 110.
[2] Epistola 35.   [3] Epistola 36.   [4] Epistola 83.
[5] Appendix to *Ethics*, I.
[6] *Short Treatise*, I, 3, 5, and 6.

negative and actional interpretations of divine attributes.[1]
But according to Spinoza God is as material as the world,
and His essence, therefore, apart from His actions, does reveal itself in the nature of the physical universe. God or substance, to be sure, is unknown to us in His infinite fullness,
and even that part of Him which is known to us is known to
us only through attributes which are not substance itself but
only "that which intellect perceives of substance."[2] Still,
the intellect perceives them "as if constituting its essence,"[3]
that is to say, as if constituting the essence of substance.
While the mediaevals considered the essence of God unknown, because the knowledge gained of God's essence is
not so positive as the knowledge that one may gain, according to their theory of knowledge, of the essence of other
beings, Spinoza considered the essence of God in so far as
it could be known through nature as positive as, and even
more positive than, the knowledge one may gain, according
to his own theory of knowledge, of the essence of any particular being. One must therefore go, according to Spinoza,
to the physical universe, to consider its ways, and to be wise
as to the nature of God.

If we are to attempt to reconstruct hypothetically the
process of Spinoza's study of nature and of his reasoning
which ultimately led him to the discovery of the two known
attributes of God, we must assume that he started with the
Aristotelian method of classifying being. Three classifications of being are to be found in Aristotle, namely, the ten
categories, substance and accident, and matter and form.
Of these three classifications, the first must have been dismissed by Spinoza outright as something unuseful for his
purpose. Not only did it seem to him, as to others after

[1] *Moreh Nebukim*, I, 52.
[2] *Ethics*, I, Def. 4.   [3] *Ibid.*

him, to be logically faulty, but it is also reducible to lower
forms, for it is based upon the distinction of substance and
accident, the nine categories outside of substance being
nothing but an enumeration of various accidents casually
selected.[1] The classification of substance and accident, or
rather of substance and mode, to be sure, is used by Spinoza
as the ultimate classification of being in his own system,[2]
and rightly so, since in his own system only one substance is
assumed. In the system of Aristotle, however, where three
kinds of substances are assumed, the classification of substance and accident could not be ultimate, since substance
presupposes already the distinction of matter and form, for
the three substances in Aristotle are matter, form, and concrete things composed of matter and form.[3] Spinoza must
have therefore started his revision of the mediaeval scheme
with the last of the Aristotelian classifications of being,
namely, matter and form.

Then as a next step, we may assume, Spinoza must have
modified Aristotle's classification of matter and form to suit
his own particular theory of the materiality of God. In
Aristotle, as we have seen, matter and form are substances,
each of them existing "in itself." Though in concrete composite things form does not exist "in itself," [4] for it is inseparable from matter and cannot exist apart from matter,
still form can also be pure and exist "in itself" apart from
matter, as in the case of his own God. To Spinoza, however,
form could never be pure and exist apart from matter, for
even God, he has already shown, must be material. Matter
and form, therefore, could not be substances; they could be
only attributes of substance, and there could be only one
such substance, and that is God. Particular things are not

---

[1] Cf. above, p. 62.   [2] Cf. above, pp. 63 f.
[3] Cf. above, p. 67.   [4] Cf. above, p. 68.

substances. That they cannot be substances he has already shown from the very same terms used in the mediaeval definition of substance.[1]

Then Spinoza must have taken one further step and changed the terms "matter" and "form" into "extension" and "thought." The reason for his doing so will become clear to us when we consider the ambiguity of the old terms matter and form. In Aristotle and throughout the Middle Ages matter and form were correlative terms. They were applied simultaneously to everything within the hierarchy of beings that lie between the lowest matter and the highest form. They could not therefore be used by Spinoza in his own specific and restricted sense with reference to the two known attributes of God without leading to some confusion. It was in fact this multifariousness of meaning of the terms matter and form that led mediaeval philosophers to classify them according to their different applications and to label them by certain distinguishing adjectives, so that in Thomas Aquinas there are no less than fifty-one varieties of matter and no less than one hundred and twenty-one varieties of form.[2] In order therefore to avoid confusion, Spinoza had to find certain equivalents for matter and form which would have the traditional sanction of expressing the same contrast and which would also stand respectively for one traditional specific matter and for one traditional specific form.

Such two terms he found in extension and thought. The common matter underlying the four elements, according to Aristotle and his commentators, is something extended; in fact, it is the first kind of matter that is extended, and hence could be called extension. There is indeed a difference of opinion among his mediaeval commentators as to whether

---

[1] Cf. above, Chapter III.

[2] Cf. L. Schütz, *Thomas-Lexikon* (1895): "Materia" under c and "Forma" under b.

extension was the underlying common matter of the four elements itself or whether it was a sort of form of a still further inextended matter, in which case the underlying common matter of the four elements would be itself composed of matter and form, respectively known as prime matter (*materia prima*) and corporeal form (*forma corporeitatis*). The latter was the opinion of the leading Arabic and Jewish philosophers, such as Alfarabi, Avicenna, Algazali, Averroes, Joseph Ibn Ẓaddiḳ, Abraham Ibn Daud, and Joseph Ibn Aknin, though there was a difference of opinion among them as to the nature of the *forma corporeitatis*. The origin and history of this controversy about the *forma corporeitatis* have been discussed by me elsewhere.[1] Crescas, however, argues for the elimination of the inextended prime matter and makes the *forma corporeitatis* or extension itself at once the prime matter and the underlying common matter of the four elements.[2] The same view was also held, according to the testimony of Isaac Abrabanel, by his son Judah Abrabanel,[3] better known as Leo Hebraeus, author of the *Dialoghi d'Amore*. However it is, the common matter underlying the four elements was conceived to have extension as something inseparable from it, on which account it could be spoken of as extension. A further justification for the substitution of extension for matter by Spinoza was the fact that Descartes defined matter as extension,[4] though, perhaps, not in the same sense in which Crescas identified the two. The reason for Spinoza's substitution of thought for form is quite obvious, for the highest form or God is spoken of by Aristotle and throughout the Middle Ages as pure thought.

---

[1] Cf. my *Crescas' Critique of Aristotle* in the notes on pp. 579–590, of which a summary is given on pp. 99–101.

[2] *Ibid.*, pp. 102–104, 261–263; notes 26–32 on pp. 598–602.

[3] *Ibid.*, p. 600.

[4] *Principia Philosophiae*, II, 4, and cf. Spinoza, Epistola 83.

But "extension" and "thought" are abstract terms which "the intellect perceives of substance, as if constituting its essence."[1] It is only through their respective activities that they become manifest to our senses. Now, in Aristotle and throughout the Middle Ages God as pure thought was conceived as an active principle. Thought meant thinking, and that process of thinking is always active and is never in a state of quiescence. This is the trend of Aristotle's statements when he says of God's thought that it "thinks itself because it shares the nature of the object of thought. . . . For that which is capable of receiving the object of thought, i.e. the essence, is thought. And it is *active* when it *possesses* this object. Therefore the latter ⟨possession⟩ rather than the former ⟨receptivity⟩ is the divine element which thought seems to contain."[2] Maimonides re-echoes these statements when he declares that "God is the *intellectus*, the *intelligens*, and the *intelligibile*," and that "God is an intellect which always is in action."[3] Extension or matter, however, is different, according to Aristotle and the mediaevals and also Descartes;[4] it is never active, it is always passive. It is set into motion by an external agent, which ultimately terminates in God, who is the cause of motion in matter, but who is himself not matter and is not in motion. The view is most clearly set forth by Maimonides: "The principles of any individual compound substance are matter and form, and there must needs be an agent, that is to say, a mover which sets the substratum in motion, and thereby renders it predisposed to receive a certain form. The agent which thus predisposes the matter of a certain individual being is called

---

[1] *Ethics*, I, Def. 4.

[2] *Metaphysics*, XII, 7, 1072b, 19–23.

[3] *Moreh Nebukim*, I, 68.

[4] *Principia Philosophiae Cartesianae*, II, Prop. 12, and cf. Descartes, *Principia Philosophiae*, II, 36.

the immediate mover. Here the necessity arises of inquiring into the nature of motion, the moving agent and the thing moved. But this has already been explained sufficiently; and the opinion of Aristotle may be formulated in the words that matter is not the cause of its own motion.[1] This is the important proposition which leads to the investigation of the existence of the prime mover." [2]

Spinoza accepts the old philosophic view with regard to God's thought that it is the act of thinking and that God is therefore an intellect which is always in action. But he disagrees with the old philosophic conception of matter as something inert. In one of his letters he directly criticizes Descartes for maintaining that the variety of things can be deduced "from extension in no other way than by supposing that this was the effect produced in extension by motion which was started by God," [3] and gives as his own view that it must be "explained through an attribute, which expresses eternal and infinite essence." [4] Since according to his own view extension is an attribute of God just as thought is, extension must be active no less than thought, and just as thought is thinking so extension is motion, not motion imparted to it by an external agent, but something which expresses the activity of its own nature. These actional aspects of the attributes of extension and thought are what Spinoza calls immediate infinite modes.

---

[1] Cf. *Metaphysics*, I, 3, 984a, 21–25; XII, 6, 1071b, 28–30.

[2] *Moreh Nebukim*, II, Introduction, Prop. 25; *Crescas' Critique of Aristotle*, p. 315.   [3] Letter from Tschirnhaus (Epistola 82).

[4] Letter to Tschirnhaus (Epistola 83). Spinoza's statement that "matter is badly defined by Descartes as extension" is not to be taken literally as an objection to Descartes' identification of matter with extension. It is to be taken in connection with the entire letter of Tschirnhaus and as referring especially to the latter's restatement of the opinion of Descartes that the variety of things can be deduced "from extension in no other way than by supposing that this was the effect produced in extension by motion which was started by God." Cf. also the definition of matter in *Cogitata Metaphysica*, II, 10 (*Opera*, I, p. 269, ll. 31–33).

The immediate infinite mode of thought is designated by Spinoza in four ways. (1) Intellect (*Intellectus*, *Verstaan*).[1] (2) Absolutely infinite intellect (*intellectus absolute infinitus*).[2] (3) An infinite power of thought (*potentia infinita cogitandi*).[3] (4) The idea of God (*idea Dei*).[4] The term *intellectus* in the first two designations is to be understood here not only in the sense of the thinking subject but also in the sense of the act of thinking, that is to say, not only in the sense of the intellect, νοῦς, but also in the sense of intellection, νόησις, on the principle reproduced by Maimonides as the common opinion of the philosophers that "God is the *intellectus*, the *intelligens*, and the *intelligibile*" and that "all intellect is identical with its action; the intellect in action is not a thing different from its action, for the true nature and essence of the intellect is comprehension." [5] This principle is also reproduced by Spinoza.[6] When it is recalled that according to Spinoza there is no potential intellect but that every intellect is actual,[7] it will become clear how the term *intellectus*, which literally means the understanding subject, is used by him in the sense of the act of understanding. When, therefore, in the third designation he describes the infinite mode of thought as *potentia infinita cogitandi*, the term *potentia* is not to be taken in the sense of potentiality or faculty or the power to do something but in the sense of the power displayed in doing something, for ordinarily, as says Maimonides, "when we assume the intellect to be potential, we necessarily distinguish two things, the potential intellect and the potential intelligible object." [8]

---

[1] Letter from Schuller (Epistola 63), and *Short Treatise*, I, 9.
[2] Letter to Schuller (Epistola 64).   [3] Epistola 32 (*Opera*, IV, p. 173, l. 18).
[4] *Ethics*, II, Props. 3, 4, and 8. Cf. I, Prop. 21, Demonst.
[5] *Moreh Nebukim*, I, 68. Cf. below, Vol. II, pp. 24, 45.
[6] *Ethics*, II, Prop. 7, Schol. Cf. below, Vol. II, pp. 24, 45.
[7] *Ethics*, II, Prop. 48, Schol., and *Ethics*, I, Prop. 31, Schol.
[8] *Moreh Nebukim*, I, 68.

The active sense of the term *intellectus* is made clear by Spinoza himself in his description of the immediate infinite mode of thought in the *Short Treatise*. He says that "it has been from all eternity, and to all eternity will remain immutable. . . . It has one function, namely, to understand clearly and distinctly all things at all times." [1] The emphasis in these statements is on the terms "eternity," "immutable," and "at all times," and they reflect the following statements of Maimonides: "Now it has been proved that God is an intellect which *always* is in action, and that . . . there is in Him at no time a mere potentiality, that He does not comprehend at one time, and is without comprehension at another time, but He is an intellect in action *always*." [2] Spinoza continues to describe there the function of the infinite mode of thought as that "which produces invariably an infinite and most perfect satisfaction, which cannot omit to do what it does." [3] This seems to reflect Aristotle's description of the constant activity of the First Principle or God: "And its life is such as the best which we enjoy, and enjoy for but a short time. For it is ever in this state (which we cannot be), since its actuality is also pleasure . . . and the act of contemplation is what is most pleasant and best." [4]

The expression *idea Dei* we take to be the equivalent of the expression *intellectus absolute infinitus* as a description of the immediate infinite mode of thought. These two expressions, however, indicate two different aspects of that immediate infinite mode. The term *intellectus*, as we have seen, literally refers to the thinking subject, the νοῦς in Aristotle's enumeration of the threefold aspect of God's thinking, namely, the νοῦς, the νόησις, and the νοητόν or

[1] *Short Treatise*, I, 9, § 3.   [2] *Moreh Nebukim*, I, 68.
[3] *Short Treatise*, I, 9, § 3.
[4] *Metaphysics*, XII, 7, 1072b, 14–24.

νοούμενον, The term *idea* in *idea Dei* is a transliteration of εἶδος in the specific sense of εἶδος νοητόν (*forma intelligibilis*),[1] and hence it reflects the object of thought, the νοητόν or νοούμενον in Aristotle's threefold enumeration. But Inasmuch as in God, according to Aristotle, Maimonides, and Spinoza himself, the thinking subject, the act of thinking, and the object of thought are identical, the expressions *intellectus absolute infinitus* and *idea Dei* are identical in meaning, both designating the immediate infinite mode of thought.

That the relation between the "idea of God" and the "absolutely infinite intellect" was conceived by Spinoza to be like that of object of thought to the thinking subject, which, of course, in God are identical, may be shown from the following passage. In Proposition IV of *Ethics*, II, Spinoza says that "the idea of God . . . can be one only." In the Demonstration of this proposition he proves it by the contention that "the infinite intellect comprehends nothing but the attributes of God and His affections," which are all united in God as one. This passage makes it quite clear that the "idea of God" was considered by Spinoza to be related to the "infinite intellect" as the object of thought to the thinking subject with which it is identical. Another proof text may perhaps be found also in the following passage: "We must remember, besides, that our mind, in so far as it truly perceives things, is a part of the infinite intellect of God (Corol. Prop. XI, Part II), and therefore it must be that the clear and distinct ideas of the mind are as true as the ideas of God (*Dei ideae*)." [2] If in this passage the plural "*Dei ideae*" means the ideas of God in the "infinite intellect of God" rather than the ideas of God in "our mind," then it is quite evident that the relation between the "idea of

---

[1] *Metaphysics*, XII, 9, 1075a, 3–5. Cf. below, Vol. II, pp. 46–48, 93.
[2] *Ethics*, II, Prop. 43, Schol., end.

God" and the "infinite intellect of God," i.e., the absolutely infinite intellect, is like that between the clear and distinct ideas of our mind and our mind, that is to say, like the relation between the object of thought and the thinking subject, which two are identical in God.

Some students of Spinoza take the *idea Dei* as the mediate infinite mode of thought corresponding to the *facies totius universi* which they take as the mediate infinite mode of extension.[1] This view, however, is dictated only by the necessity of finding a special mediate infinite mode of thought in order to round out the symmetry of the modal system. No statement in Spinoza could be found which would definitely corroborate it. On the contrary, the following passage in the *Short Treatise* would seem to contradict it. Says Spinoza: "And since, as a matter of fact, nature or God is one being of which infinite attributes are predicated, and which contains in itself all the essences of created things, it necessarily follows that of all this there is produced in thought an infinite idea (*oneyndige Idea*), which comprehends *objective* the whole of nature just as it is *realiter*."[2] The "infinite idea" in this passage undoubtedly refers to the *idea Dei*, and from the context of the passage it is quite clear that it cannot be a mediate mode of thought, for right after this statement Spinoza says definitely: "Wherefore also, in the ninth chapter of the First Part, I called this idea a creation created immediately by God."[3] Furthermore, the use of the *idea Dei* in the Demonstration of Proposition XXI of *Ethics*, I, leaves no doubt that it is an immediate rather than a mediate mode of thought.[4]

---

[1] Pollock, *Spinoza*, pp. 187–188, referring also to Ed. Böhmer, "Spinozana," in *Zeitschrift für Philosophie und philosophische Kritik*, 42 (1863), pp. 107–116; Joachim, *A Study of the Ethics of Spinoza*, p. 94.

[2] *Short Treatise*, Appendix II, § 4 (*Opera*, I, p. 117, ll. 24–29)'.

[3] *Ibid.* (p. 117, ll. 29–31; p. 607, § 10).   [4] Cf. below, p. 378.

The immediate infinite mode of extension is designated by Spinoza in two ways: (1) Motion.[1] (2) Motion and rest.[2] The addition of rest to motion must have been suggested to him by Descartes, who speaks of motion and rest as "two diverse modes of a body in motion."[3] Whether Descartes himself meant by this addition that rest was a real entity, or whether he used it only as a rhetorical flourish, is a question which has been raised in connection with another passage in Descartes.[4] But it would seem that Spinoza had taken it to mean something positive, in opposition to Aristotle and the mediaevals, to whom rest was only the privation of motion.[5] The positive character of rest is affirmed by Spinoza when he says that "as is self-evident, the same force is required to give a body at rest a certain velocity as is required to bring the same body with that given velocity to rest,"[6] or when he says that "by force we understand the quantity of motion. . . . In bodies at rest by force of resistance we understand the quantity of rest."[7] It is interesting to note that Crescas in his criticism of Aristotle similarly maintains, though in a different sense, that there is a quantity of rest as there is a quantity of motion.[8] It has been suggested that by motion and rest Spinoza means energy in motion and energy in position, or kinetic and potential energy.[9]

---

[1] Letter from Schuller (Epistola 63), and *Short Treatise*, I, 9.

[2] *Short Treatise*, I, 2, § 19, note 7 (*Opera*, I, p. 25, ll. 26–27); II, notes to Preface; II, 19, § 6 (*Opera*, I, p. 90, ll. 26–27); II, 20, § 4, note 4 (*Opera*, I, p. 98, l. 35); Appendix II, § 15 (*Opera*, I, p. 120, l. 24); *Ethics*, I, Prop. 32, Corol. 2; Epistola 64; Meyer's Preface to *Principia Philosophiae Cartesianae* (*Opera*, I, p. 132, l. 13).

[3] *Principia Philosophiae*, II, 27.

[4] Pollock, *Spinoza*, p. 110.   [5] *Physics*, IV, 12, 221b, 12–13.

[6] *Principia Philosophiae Cartesianae*, II, Def. 8 (2).

[7] *Ibid.*, Prop. 22, Demonst., and Prop. 37, Corol. Cf. E. Schmitt, *Die unendliche Modi bei Spinoza* (Leipzig, 1910), p. 47, n. 2.

[8] Cf. my *Crescas' Critique of Aristotle*, pp. 287–288.

[9] Pollock, *Spinoza*, p. 113.

In the history of philosophy an immediate creation of God has been sometimes called a son of God. Thus Philo describes the intelligible world, which was an immediate creation of God and created by Him from eternity, as a son of God, whereas time, which is not an immediate creation of God but is the offspring of the cosmos, is described by him as a grandson of God.[1] This designation has gone over to Christian theology, and Spinoza refers to the Christian side of it elsewhere in his works.[2] But Philo's statement is also reproduced by Azariah dei Rossi,[3] and it is also reflected in Leo Hebraeus' *Dialoghi d'Amore*.[4] Following tradition, therefore, Spinoza characterizes the immediacy of these two infinite modes by saying of motion that it is "a son, product, or effect created immediately by God," and of understanding that it "is also a son, product, or immediate creation of God, created by Him from all eternity."[5]

Spinoza's God, though He can no longer be contrasted with the universe as the immaterial with the material, can still be contrasted with it as the simple whole with the aggregate whole. His God, as we shall show in the next chapter, is not identical with the physical universe. He transcends it in a certain special sense of the term transcendence.[6] And so, the aggregate totality of the physical universe, in so far as it is the necessary result of the activity of God's attributes of extension and thought, is called by Spinoza also an infinite mode of God, but in order to differentiate it from the other infinite modes he calls it a mediate infinite mode. This distinction between immediate and mediate infinite modes,

---

[1] *Quod Deus Sit Immutabilis*, VI, 31.
[2] *Cogitata Metaphysica*, I, 10; Epistola 73; *Ethics*, IV, Prop. 68, Schol.
[3] *Me 'or 'Enayim, Imre Binah*, Ch. 4, p. 100 (ed. Cassel).
[4] *Dialoghi d'Amore*, III, p. 244 (Bari, 1929).
[5] *Short Treatise*, I, 9, §§ 2–3.
[6] Cf. below, p. 322.

however, does not occur in all the writings of Spinoza. In
the *Short Treatise* he does not mention it. On the contrary,
the distinction drawn there is not between two kinds of infinite modes but rather between infinite modes, as motion
in extension and understanding in thought, and particular
things, the former of which are immediately created by God
whereas the latter are said to be created by God by a sub-
sidiary instrumental cause. God is therefore called by him
the proximate cause of the infinite modes but the remote
cause, in a certain sense, of the particular things.[1] But the
distinction between immediate and mediate infinite modes
is referred to several times in the *Ethics*,[2] and a mediate
infinite mode is specifically named by Spinoza in a letter to
Schuller.[3]

The name given by Spinoza to that mediate infinite mode
is "the face of the whole universe" (*facies totius universi*).[4]
The phraseology of this expression is reminiscent of the
Biblical manner of describing the totality or wholeness of
a certain extent of territory. Thus when the Bible wants to
say "over the entire earth," it says "upon the face of all the
earth," which in the Vulgate is translated by *super faciem
totius terrae* (Dan. 8, 5), or by *super faciem universae terrae*
(Gen. 7, 3, I Sam. 30, 16), or by *super faciem omnis terrae*
(II Sam. 18, 8, Zech. 5, 3). The term *facies* may also reflect
the Greek πρόσωπον in the sense of "person," for the Latin
facies as well as the Hebrew word for "face"[5] has acquired the
meaning of "person" under the influence of the Greek term.
Accordingly the *facies totius universi* may mean the whole
universe taken as an individual, in conformity with Spinoza's statement that "we may easily conceive the whole of

----

[1] *Short Treatise*, I, 3, § 2 (8). But cf. *Ethics*, I, Prop. 28, Schol.
[2] *Ethics*, I, Prop 23, Demonst.; Prop. 28, Schol.; Appendix (*Opera*, II, p. 80,
l. 17).   [3] Epistola 64.
[4] *Ibid.*   [5] ‏עָנִים‎.

nature to be one individual." [1] In coining or adopting this expression for the mediate modes, Spinoza may have also been influenced by the Cabalistic term "faces" (*parẓufim*, from πρόσωπον), which stands for the mediate emanations from the Infinite (*En Sof*), following from Him through the mediacy of the Sefirot. Abraham Herrera in his *Puerta del Cielo* refers to these mediate emanations as the "faces of the universe of the infinite." In the Spanish original, the phrase reads: "parzupim del mundo del ynfinito." [2] In the Hebrew version, the same term "parzupim," or rather "parzufim," is used.[3] In the abridged Latin version made from the Hebrew, the phrase reads: "Personæ Systematis(,) Infiniti." [4] Whether Spinoza had before him the Spanish original in manuscript or the Hebrew version printed in Amsterdam in 1655, twenty years prior to the writing of his letter to Schuller, dated "29 Julii, 1675," where the phrase "facies totius universi" occurs, it can be easily seen how Herrera's description of his mediate emanations by the phrase "*parzupim* of the universe of the infinite" suggested to him the phrase "facies totius universi" as a description of his own mediate infinite mode.

The expression "the face of the whole universe" is explained by Spinoza himself as meaning "the whole universe which, although it varies in infinite ways, yet remains always the same." [5] This explanation, it seems to me, may refer to two principles in Spinoza's philosophy.

In the first place, it may refer to the Cartesian and

---

[1] Scholium to Lemma 7, after Prop. 13 of *Ethics*, II.

[2] Cf. *Livro Quarto de La Puerta del Cielo De Abraham Cohen de Herrera*, Cap. 3, fol. 38b. MS. in the Library of the "Portugeesch Israëlietisch Seminarium Ets Haïm" in Amsterdam. A copy of this passage was made for me through the courtesy of the Librarian, Dr. J. S. da Silva Rosa.

[3] *Sha'ar ha-Shamayim*, II, 3: ‫ופרצופי עולם האין סוף‬.

[4] *Porta Cælorum*, II, 3, p. 45.

[5] Epistola 64.

Spinozistic principle of the preservation of the proportion of motion and rest.[1] According to this principle, the preservation of the proportion of motion and rest in the parts composing the body of an individual results in the preservation of the form (*forma*)[2] or shape (*figura*)[3] of that individual as a whole. Consequently the preservation of the proportion of motion and rest in the particular parts which compose the physical universe and constitute it as an individual whole will preserve the face (*facies*), i.e., the form (*forma*) and shape (*figura*), of the universe as a whole. As Spinoza says elsewhere: "Thus, if we advance *ad infinitum*, we may easily conceive the whole of nature to be one individual, whose parts, that is to say, all bodies, differ in infinite ways without any change of the whole individual."[4]

In the second place, it may refer to the principle of "the order and interdependence of nature as a whole" (*totius naturae ordo et cohaerentia*),[5] *facies* thus meaning *ordo et cohaerentia*. This principle is also spoken of by Spinoza as "the order of the whole of nature or the connection of causes" (*ordo totius naturae, sive causarum connexio*),[6] or as "the fixed and unchangeable order of nature or the chain of natural events" (*fixus et immutabilis naturae ordo sive rerum naturae concatenatio*),[7] or as "the concatenation of causes" (*concatenatio causarum*).[8] With reference to this principle, too, nature as a whole may be considered as an individual consisting of parts, "inasmuch as the power of nature is simply the aggregate of the powers of all her individual

---

[1] See Lemma 7, after Prop. 13 of *Ethics*, II. Cf. below, Vol. II, p. 69, n. 4.

[2] *Ethics*, IV, Prop. 39, Demonst.

[3] See Axiom 3 preceding Lemma 4, after Prop. 13 of *Ethics*, II.

[4] Scholium to Lemma 7, after Prop. 13 of *Ethics*, II.

[5] *Tractatus Theologico-Politicus*, Ch. 16 (*Opera*, III, p. 191, ll. 5–6).

[6] *Ethics*, II, Prop. 7, Schol.

[7] *Tractatus Theologico-Politicus*, Ch. 4 (*Opera*, III, p. 45, ll. 34–35).

[8] *Ibid.*, Ch. 4 (*Opera*, III, p. 58, l. 21).

components." [1] Now, this order of nature, according to Spinoza, may be explained either by the attribute of thought or by the attribute of extension, according as the component parts of the universe are considered either as modes of thought or as modes of extension.[2] By the same token, we may infer that according to Spinoza the order or the face of the whole universe may be also explained by the joint activity of both attributes, if the component parts of the universe are considered as modes of both thought and extension.

Consequently, the mediate infinite mode designated by Spinoza as "the face of the whole universe," if taken with reference to the principle of the preservation of the proportion of motion and rest, will be a mode of extension only, but if taken with reference to the principle of the order of the whole of nature, will be a mode of both extension and thought. As Spinoza does not say that "the face of the whole universe" is a mode of extension only and as he nowhere specifically mentions a mediate infinite mode of thought, we may conclude that "the face of the whole universe" is a mediate infinite mode of both extension and thought.

In our presentation of the system of infinite modes we have in some respects parted from the interpretations which one may find in the Spinoza literature, and in some other respects we have placed ourselves on the side of one class of interpreters as against that of another class.[3] Among the interpreters of Spinoza there are some who take the "face of the whole universe" to be only a mode of exten-

---

[1] *Ibid.*, Ch. 16 (*Opera*, III, p. 189, ll. 21–23).

[2] *Ethics*, II, Prop. 7, Schol.

[3] For a classification of the various interpretations of infinite modes, see E. Schmitt, *Die unendliche Modi bei Spinoza* (Leipzig, 1910), pp. 5 ff.

oion,[1] but in order to preserve the symmetry of extension and thought, they supply by conjecture the missing mediate infinite mode of thought out of other parts of Spinoza's writings. Two Spinozistic expressions have been borrowed to fill up that lacuna in Spinoza's list of infinite modes: (1) God's idea (*idea Dei*).[2] (2) "The constant form of reasoned thought or Necessary Logical laws."[3] Support for the first conjecture is adduced from the fact that certain descriptions of the *idea Dei* would seem to make it the ideal counterpart of the *facies totius universi*.[4] Martineau, who is the author of the second conjecture, does not adduce any textual support for his view. I am inclined to reject both these conjectures, for the following reasons. As we have already seen, the expression *facies totius universi* may include both the modes of extension and the modes of thought. Then, as we have also shown,[5] the *idea Dei* is an immediate mode of thought and the equivalent of the *intellectus absolute infinitus*. Finally, Martineau's "Necessary Logical laws" cannot be a mediate infinite mode parallel to the *facies totius universi*, for from a statement in Meyer's Preface to Spinoza's *Principia Philosophiae Cartesianae* it may be indirectly inferred that the "Necessary Logical laws" are parallel to "motion and rest" and consequently must be identical with the "absolutely infinite intellect" and are therefore an immediate infinite mode. The passage reads as follows: "And as the human body is not absolute, but its extension is determined according to natural laws of motion and rest, so also mind or human spirit is not

---

[1] See *ibid.*, p. 116, n. 4, where a list of authors holding different interpretations of the *facies totius universi* is given. Cf. Pollock, *Spinoza*, p. 188.

[2] Pollock, *Spinoza*, p. 187; Joachim, *A Study of the Ethics of Spinoza*, p. 94.

[3] Martineau, *A Study of Spinoza*, p. 200.

[4] Joachim, *op. cit.*, p. 95.

[5] Cf. above, pp. 239 ff.

absolute but is determined through ideas by natural laws of thought."[1]

In the philosophy of Aristotle and in the Aristotelian philosophy reproduced by the mediaevals sometimes for the purpose of refutation, a distinction is drawn between the universe as a whole and the particular things within it. The universe as a whole is said to be eternal and immutable, to have neither beginning nor end, never to have been different nor ever to change, but always to remain the same.[2] The particular things in the sublunary part of the universe, however, are different. They are called transient and are said to be subject to constant change[3] and to the process of generation and corruption.[4] Following tradition, Spinoza similarly distinguishes between the "general," which are the infinite modes, and the "particular," which are the particular things.[5] The infinite modes are described by him as eternal and immutable[6] and as remaining always the same,[7] whereas the particular things are described by him as "transient . . . which did not exist from all time, or have had a beginning"[8] and as "individual mutable things."[9]

But these transient things, according to the mediaeval Aristotelians, do not act sporadically and haphazardly. They are all subject to the necessary and immutable laws which govern the universe as a whole and the influence of which reaches every part of it. This view has been summed up in the following statement of Maimonides: "This whole order [of the universe], both above and here below, is never dis-

---

[1] Preface to the *Principia Philosophiae Cartesianae* (*Opera*, I, p. 132, ll. 12 ff.).
[2] *Moreh Nebukim*, II, 13, Third Theory.
[3] *Ibid.*, II, 10.   [4] *Ibid.*, II, 11.
[5] *Short Treatise*, I, 8.
[6] *Ibid.*, I, 9.   [7] Epistola 64.
[8] *Short Treatise*, II, 5, § 5 (*Opera*, I, p. 62, ll. 32 ff.). Cf. § 2 (p. 563).
[9] *Tractatus de Intellectus Emendatione*, § 100 (*Opera*, II, p. 36, l. 22).

turbed or interrupted, and nothing new is produced in it which is not in its nature and nothing happens in it which is contrary to law." [1] Furthermore, even according to Maimonides himself, to whom the world does not follow from God by mere necessity but by knowledge, God's eternal knowledge is of such a nature that in determining the changes in particular things it determines them in such a way that they follow "according to an imperishable and immutable order." [2] So also Spinoza maintains that the "individual mutable things" (*haec singularia mutabilia*) "are produced and are ordered" according to "fixed and eternal things" (*res fixae aeternaeque*), that is to say, the infinite modes, which are of an eternal and immutable nature. The sequence of individual mutable things is, therefore, "to be sought from fixed and eternal things only, and also from the laws inscribed in them, as it were in true codes." [3]

These fixed and eternal things, though they are themselves only modes which by definition can neither be nor be conceived without substance,[4] may still be considered with reference to the individual mutable things which are dependent upon them as substance is considered by Spinoza with reference to modes, that is to say, the individual mutable things can neither be nor be conceived without the infinite modes. The relation between them, therefore, is like that between substance and mode, namely, the relation between the whole and the part or between the universal and the particular.[5] This is the significance of the following passage: "It may indeed be said that these individual mutable things so intimately and essentially, if I may so speak, depend upon those that are fixed that the former without the latter can neither

---

[1] *Moreh Nebukim*, II, 13.   [2] *Ibid.*, III, 21.

[3] *Tractatus de Intellectus Emendatione*, § 101 (*Opera*, II, p. 36, ll. 35 ff.).

[4] *Ethics*, I, Def. 5.   [5] See above, pp. 74 ff.

be nor be conceived. Hence these fixed and eternal things, although they may be individual (*singularia*), nevertheless, on account of their presence everywhere and their extensive power, will be like universals to us, or so to speak, the *genera* of the definitions of individual mutable things, and proximate causes of all things." [1]

If this interpretation of the passage just quoted is correct, then the "fixed and eternal things" do not refer directly to substance or to attribute but only to the infinite modes, both the immediate and the mediate, though, of course, indirectly they may include also substance and attribute, inasmuch as they, too, are fixed and eternal and are the cause of the existence of the infinite modes. According to some interpreters of Spinoza, however, the fixed and eternal things refer directly to substance, attribute, and even finite modes. [2] The application of the expression "fixed and eternal things" to the infinite modes, that is to say, to the absolutely infinite intellect, motion and rest, and the face of the whole universe, reflects the expression "eternal things" which was applied by the mediaevals to the Intelligences, motion, and the universe as a whole, when these were assumed with Aristotle to be eternal. [3] The expression goes back to Aristotle himself. [4] Again, the characterization of the infinite modes as *singularia* in the passage quoted is in conformity with what we have said above, namely, that Spinoza's substance or God is in some respect transcending the universe and is a simple whole as contrasted with the universe, or, as he

---

[1] *Tractatus de Intellectus Emendatione*, § 101 (*Opera*, II, p. 37, ll. 3 ff.).

[2] For different interpretations of the meaning of the *res fixae et aeternae*, see E. Schmitt, *Die unendliche Modi bei Spinoza* (Leipzig, 1910), pp. 68–69.

[3] See my *Crescas' Critique of Aristotle*, pp. 287, 291, and note 18 on p. 645, note 31 on p. 662, note 32 on p. 663. The Hebrew expression underlying "eternal things" is: הדברים הנצחיים.

[4] τὰ ἀεὶ ὄντα, *Physics*, IV, 12, 221b, 3–4.

calls it, *natura naturata*, which is an aggregate whole. Consequently, substance is the only true whole or universal, and the infinite modes are in their relation to it only *singularia*.

In mediaeval philosophy a distinction is made between the possible *per se*, the possible *per se* but necessary in consideration of its cause, and the necessary *per se*. This distinction is based upon an Avicennian proposition which is reproduced by Maimonides as follows: "Everything that has a cause for its existence is in respect to its own essence only possible of existence, for if the causes exist, the thing likewise will exist, but if the causes have never existed, or if they have ceased to exist, or if their causal relation to the thing has changed, then the thing itself will not exist." [1] The origin, history, and implications of this proposition I have discussed elsewhere.[2] According to this threefold division of possibility and necessity, the particular things are called possible *per se*, the celestial spheres are called possible *per se* but necessary in consideration of their cause, and God is called necessary *per se* — a division based upon the Aristotelian division of the universe into the transiently movable, the eternally movable, and the eternally immovable.[3] Spinoza reproduces this mediaeval threefold division of possibility and necessity in different connections in several places in his works.[4] But here he applies it to his theory of infinite modes. He changes, however, the terms "possible" and "necessary" to "transient" and "eternal," with which, as we have seen, they are connected.[5] The particular things,

---

[1] *Moreh Nebukim*, II, Introd., Prop. 19; cf. my *Crescas' Critique of Aristotle*, p. 303.

[2] *Crescas' Critique of Aristotle*, pp. 109–111, 681–685.

[3] *Metaphysics*, V, 5, 1015a, 33–34. See *Crescas' Critique of Aristotle*, p. 109 and pp. 680 ff.

[4] See above, pp. 187 ff.

[5] Cf. my *Crescas' Critique of Aristotle*, pp. 109 ff. and 680 ff.

he says, are transient, i.e., possible *per se*. The infinite modes, while transient or possible *per se*, are not to be considered as transient or possible in consideration of their cause. God is eternal, i.e., necessary *per se*. "Now some objects are in themselves transient; others, indeed, are not transient by virtue of their cause. There is yet a third that is eternal and imperishable through its own power and might. The transient are all the particular things which did not exist from all time, or have had a beginning. The others are all those modes [marginal note adds: the general modes] which we have stated to be the cause of the particular modes. But the third is God." [1]

But while Spinoza operates on the whole with mediaeval conceptions and uses mediaeval terms, he always tries to emphasize the two points upon which he fundamentally differs from the mediaevals, namely, the necessity of God's causality and the denial of God's immateriality. This emphasis upon his two points of difference from the mediaevals may be discerned in the explanations he offers for the meaning of the old expression *natura naturans* as applied to God in contrast to *natura naturata* as applied to the world.

The distinction between God and the world, according to the mediaevals, is twofold. In the first place, God is the cause and the world His effect, and by cause they mean an intelligent cause, a creator, acting by design and with a purpose. In the second place, God is immaterial and the world material, so that God, if He is to be called substance at all,[2] is a substance beyond all substances, a superior or immaterial substance as against the world which consists of material substances. These two distinctions between God and the world are sometimes illustrated by the contrast be-

---

[1] *Short Treatise*, II, 5, § 5 (*Opera*, I, p. 62, ll. 28 ff.). Cf. § 2 (p. 563).
[2] Cf. above, p. 67.

tween the expressions *natura naturans* and *natura naturata*. Whatever the origin of these two expressions and whatever their variety of meanings,[1] it is sufficient for our present purpose to know that they were used by Thomas Aquinas in a sense which implied the two fundamental distinctions between God and the world as we have stated them. God, says he, is called *natura naturans* because He is "the universal cause of all things that happen naturally,"[2] by which he means, of course, that God is an intelligent and purposive cause. This universal cause, he says again in another place, belongs "to some superior substance, in which sense God is said by some to be *natura naturans*."[3] Spinoza seems to refer to this last passage when he says of the *natura naturans* that "the Thomists likewise understand God by it, but their *natura naturans* was a being (so they called it) beyond all substances."[4]

Now, Spinoza wanted to make use of these two expressions as respective designations of what in his philosophy corresponded to God and the world in mediaeval philosophy, namely, God and the modes. But still he did not want to use them in their old meaning by which they connoted a distinction between an intelligent cause and a premeditated effect or between an immaterial substance and a material substance. What did he do? He simply revised their meaning. Defining *natura naturans* as including substance and its attributes and *natura naturata* as including all the modes, the infinite as well as the finite,[5] he describes the differences between them in such terms that when we study them closely

---

[1] Cf. H. Siebeck, "Ueber die Entstehung der Termini *natura naturans* und *natura naturata*," in *Archiv für Geschichte der Philosophie*, 3 (1889–1890), pp. 370 ff.

[2] *Commentaria in Librum Beati Dionysii De Divinis Nominibus*, Caput 4, Lectio 21.

[3] *Summa Theologica*, Prima Secundae, Quaest. 85, Art. 6.

[4] *Short Treatise*, I, 8.   [5] *Ibid.*, I, 8; Epistola 9.

we discover that they are aimed directly against the Thomistic conception of the meaning of these expressions. In the first place, wishing to make it clear that, while he retains the original meaning of *natura naturans* as that of a universal cause, he does not mean by it an intelligent and purposive cause, Spinoza says that "by *natura naturans* we are to understand . . . God in so far as He is considered as a free cause," [1] by which he means to say, in so far as He acts by the necessity of His own nature,[2] whereas "by *natura naturata* I understand everything which follows from the necessity of the nature of God, or of any one of God's attributes." [3] In the second place, in opposition to the Thomists, who used the two expressions to designate a distinction between God as an immaterial substance and the world as a material substance, Spinoza, who denies finite substances and considers the distinction between God and the world as that between substance and mode, explains *natura naturans* by his own definition of substance and *natura naturata* by his own definition of mode. He thus says again: "By *natura naturans* we are to understand that which is in itself and is conceived through itself," whereas "by *natura naturata* I understand . . . all the modes of God's attributes in so far as they are considered as things which are in God, and which without God can neither be nor can be conceived." [4]

Another difference between Spinoza and the mediaevals, again growing out of his attribution of materiality to God, is his contention that the "two attributes may be conceived as really distinct — that is to say, one without the assistance of the other." [5] This passage, like so many other utterances

[1] *Ethics*, I, Prop. 29, Schol.
[2] *Ibid.*, I, Def. 7.
[3] *Ibid.*, I, Prop. 29, Schol.
[4] *Ibid.*, I, Prop. 29, Schol., and cf. Defs. 4 and 5.
[5] *Ibid.*, I, Prop. 10, Schol.

of Spinoza, is to be understood as a veiled criticism of the
mediaevals — in this case, of their conception of the interrelation of matter and form. According to Aristotle and the
mediaevals, though there exists a pure form, such as God
and the Intelligences, still in the physical universe matter
and form are only relative terms. Not only does not either
one of them exist without the other, but neither one of them
can be conceived without the other. Matter is matter only
with reference to some form, and form is form only with
reference to some matter. Furthermore, since God is pure
form, then matter, under the theory of emanation, must
ultimately have been produced by pure form, and it is form
which continues to be the active, producing principle in
matter. Matter itself is non-being; it is inert. It is form
which constitutes the existence of bodies,[1] and it is form
which sets matter in motion.[2] Form is said to exist in matter,
and matter is said to exist through form.[3] As against this,
Spinoza maintains that extension and thought, which in his
philosophy are the successors of matter and form,[4] are two
attributes of substance, existing in it together from eternity,
each having the same sort of existence as the other, and each
having its own independent form of activity, extension that
of motion and rest, and thought that of thinking. Unlike
form which produces motion in matter, thought does not
produce motion in extension. Motion is an activity of extension itself. Extension and thought, again, are not correlative terms, which cannot be conceived but through each
other; they can be conceived independently of each other
with reference to substance only. Nor does thought exist in
extension any more than extension exists through thought.

[1] Cf. my *Crescas' Critique of Aristotle*, pp. 257 ff.
[2] *Ibid.*, pp. 89, 299, 672–673.   [3] *Ibid.*, pp. 99, 257 ff., 577, n. 15.
[4] Cf. above, p. 234.

"For this is the nature of substance, that each of its attributes is conceived through itself, since all the attributes which substance possesses were always together, nor could one be produced by another; but each expresses the reality or being of substance."[1]

But still, though distinct from each other, extension and thought, again unlike matter and form, do not imply a plurality in the nature of substance. The reason why the mediaevals considered matter and form to constitute a plurality[2] wherever they existed together is not that they could be physically separated but that they were considered by them two distinct substances, each of which was supposed to exist in itself[3] and each of which was also supposed to be in contrast to the other, matter being potential, form actual, matter being the cause of corruption, form the cause of generation.[4] But according to Spinoza, extension and thought are not two substances but attributes of one substance, and they are only that "which intellect perceives of substance, as if constituting its essence."[5] There is no contrast between them of potentiality and actuality, or of imperfection and perfection. They are both expressing two different phases of the activity of substance, which in substance itself are one. Consequently, from the fact that the two attributes are conceived as distinct from each other it is not to be concluded that "they constitute two beings or two different substances"[6] after the manner of the Aristotelian and mediaeval matter and form. The independence of each attribute which Spinoza insists upon is merely to emphasize his denial of the interdependence of matter and form

---

[1] *Ethics*, I, Prop. 10, Schol.
[2] Cf. above, p. 113.
[3] Cf. above, p. 67.
[4] Cf. above, p. 236.
[5] *Ethics*, I, Def. 4.
[6] *Ibid.*, I, Prop. 10, Schol.

in mediaeval philosophy; it is not an independence which implies the reality of the attributes in their relation to substance or a reality in the difference between themselves, with the result that the unity of substance can no longer be logically maintained. The relation of the attributes to each other is of the same order as their relation to substance. Just as the difference between attribute and substance is only a conception of the human mind, so the difference between the attributes themselves is only a form of conception in the human mind, "for this is the nature of substance, that each of its attributes is *conceived* through itself." [1] It is in this sense only that the "two attributes may be *conceived* as really distinct — that is to say, one without the assistance of the other." [2]

Still, while extension is an attribute of God, it must not be confused with corporeality in the popular anthropomorphic conception of God. Spinoza dismisses this popular form of anthropomorphism which imagines "God to be like a man, composed of body and mind and subject to passion," without much ado, "for all men who have in any way looked into the divine nature deny that God is corporeal." [3] Behind this last statement there are the long discussions of the rabbis and of all the religious philosophers since Philo, who sought to spiritualize or to explain away the anthropomorphic expressions in certain portions of the Bible. Maimonides speaks for all of them when he emphasizes the importance of "God's incorporeality and His exemption from all passions," as doctrines "which must be explained to every one according to his capacity, and they must be taught by way of

---

[1] *Ibid.*   [2] *Ibid.*

[3] *Ibid*, I, Prop, 15, Schol. This Scholium belongs to Prop. 14; cf. Freudenthal, "Spinozastudien," in *Zeitschrift für Philosophie*, 108 (1896), p. 251, n. 2. The rest of this chapter is a discussion of the first part of this Scholium.

tradition to children and women, to the stupid and ignorant." [1]

The argument, however, which Spinoza reproduces in the
name of philosophers for the incorporeality of God does not
represent any of the standard philosophical arguments reproduced by Maimonides,[2] but it does represent the argument quoted with approval by Maimonides in the name of
the Kalam. The argument in Spinoza reads as follows:
"That He cannot be so they conclusively prove by showing
that by body we understand a certain quantity possessing
length, breadth, and depth, limited by some fixed shape;
and that to attribute this to God, a being absolutely infinite,
is the greatest absurdity." The Kalam argument in Maimonides reads as follows: "If God were corporeal, He would
be finite, which is true; and if He were finite, He would have
a certain dimension and a certain fixed shape, which is equally
a correct conclusion." [3] Spinoza's passage is clearly a paraphrase of Maimonides' passage with the additional inclusion
of the current definition of "body."

But the mediaevals, proceeds Spinoza, deny of God not
only body but also matter and extension in general, and thus
by removing from divine nature "substance itself, corporeal
or extended," they affirm "that it was created by God." This
leads Spinoza to a recapitulation of his arguments against
creation, namely: if God is pure form, how could matter
have arisen from Him? Of course, the mediaevals have their
different solutions of the problem of the origin of matter;
none of them sufficiently explains, however, "by what divine power it could have been created." This is quite a good
summary of his main points against creation.[4] He concludes,

---

[1] *Moreh Nebukim*, I, 35.   [2] *Ibid.*, and II, 1.
[3] *Ibid.*, I, 76, Third Argument.
[4] Cf. above, Chapter IV.

as he always does after an argument against creation, "that extended substance is one of the infinite attributes of God."

Spinoza then reproduces two arguments by which the philosophers have endeavored to prove the incorporeality of God:

"First, that corporeal substance, in so far as it is substance, consists, as they suppose, of parts, and therefore they deny that it can be infinite, and consequently that it can pertain to God." So far I have been unable to find the source of this argument in the form in which it is given here by Spinoza. My impression is that it is a composite argument made up of the following parts: (1) The standard argument for the incorporeality of God on the ground that God is one and indivisible, whereas corporeality implies composition and divisibility. Maimonides puts this argument as follows: "There is no unity unless one discards corporeality, for a corporeal thing is not one, but composed of matter and form, which are two distinct things by definition; and furthermore it is divisible." [1] Exactly the same argument is given by Descartes [2] and also by Spinoza in the *Short Treatise*. [3] (2) The Aristotelian denial of the existence of an infinite corporeal magnitude, [4] which is reproduced by Maimonides [5] and elaborately discussed by Crescas. [6] That this argument is of a composite nature may be inferred from the following statement with which Spinoza introduces it: "But for the sake of a fuller explanation, I will refute my adversaries' *arguments*, which, *taken altogether (omnia)*, come to this."

---

[1] *Moreh Nebukim*, I, 35.

[2] *Principia Philosophiae*, I, 23; *Principia Philosophiae Cartesianae*, I, Prop. 16. Cf. below, p. 268.

[3] *Short Treatise*, I, 2, § 18 (*Opera*, I, p. 24, ll. 12–15). Cf. below, p. 269.

[4] *Physics*, III, 5, 204a, 8 ff.; *Metaphysics*, XI, 10, 1066b, 1 ff.

[5] *Moreh Nebukim*, II, Introduction, Prop. I.

[6] *Or Adonai*, I, i, 1; I, ii, 1; cf. my *Crescas' Critique of Aristotle*, pp. 135 ff.

"Taken altogether" is undoubtedly a reference to the composite nature of the argument. A further proof that the argument as reproduced here in the *Ethics* is of a composite nature is the fact that in the *Short Treatise* [1] it is reproduced in its simple form, without any mention of infinity.

"A second argument is assumed from the absolute perfection of God. For God, they say, since He is a being absolutely perfect, cannot be passive; but corporeal substance, since it is divisible, can be passive." This argument, too, is found in Descartes [2] and in the *Short Treatise*,[3] and is implied in Maimonides' fourth proof for the existence, unity, and incorporeality of God from the concept of actuality and potentiality.[4]

The remaining parts of the Scholium to Proposition XV, which is taken up with a refutation of the alleged arguments against the possibility of an infinite corporeal substance, will be discussed in the next chapter.

---

[1] *Short Treatise*, I, 2, § 18 (*Opera*, I, p. 24, ll. 11–15).
[2] *Principia Philosophiae*, I, 23.
[3] *Short Treatise*, I, 2, § 18 (*Opera* I, p. 24, ll. 15–18).
[4] *Moreh Nebukim*, II, 1, Fourth Argument.

CHAPTER VIII

INFINITY OF EXTENSION

THE arguments of his "opponents" against the possibility of an infinite corporeal substance are introduced by Spinoza incidentally in connection with his discussion in the *Ethics* of the traditional rejection of extension as an attribute of God. The cause of this rejection, declares Spinoza, is to be found in the alleged incompatibility of extension with the infinity of the divine nature, for extension, assumed to be divisible and consisting of parts, cannot be infinite.[1] And thereupon Spinoza proceeds to adduce, as he says, "one or two," but actually three, of the "many examples" by which his opponents have tried to show, on the assumption of the divisibility of corporeal substance, that it could not be infinite. In the *Short Treatise*, however, this traditional argument for the rejection of extension as a divine attribute is reproduced without any reference to the problem of infinity. According to this earlier version of the argument, extension is said to be rejected as an attribute of God because, being divisible and consisting of parts, it is incompatible with the simplicity of the divine nature.[2] In both these places Spinoza's refutation of the argument is the same — an attempt to show that extension need not necessarily be divisible and composed of parts. This he does by drawing a distinction between extension as an attribute and extension as a mode and by showing that while the latter is divisible the

---

[1] *Ethics*, I, Prop. 15, Schol.: "First, that corporeal substance, in so far as it is substance, consists, as they suppose, of parts, and therefore they deny that it can be infinite, and consequently that it can pertain to God."

[2] *Short Treatise*, I, 2, § 18 (*Opera*, I, p. 24, ll. 11–15): "For since extension is divisible, the perfect being would have to consist of parts, and this is altogether inapplicable to God, because He is a simple being."

former is simple. In the *Short Treatise*[1] this distinction is clearly drawn; in the *Ethics*[2] there is only an emphasis on the indivisibility and simplicity of substance, with the implied inference that modes only are composed of parts and divisible. But here, again, in the *Short Treatise* the refutation aims to establish merely the simplicity of extension, whereas in the *Ethics* it aims to establish its infinity as well as its simplicity. In the *Ethics*, furthermore, Spinoza reinforces his refutation of his opponents by introducing a new distinction, namely, a distinction between quantity regarded "as it exists in the imagination" and quantity regarded "as it exists in the intellect," the former being "finite, divisible, and composed of parts" and the latter being "infinite, one, and indivisible" — a distinction, he says, which will be "plain enough to all who know how to distinguish between the imagination and the intellect."[3] Both these distinctions mentioned in the *Ethics* occur also in two different places in the *Tractatus de Intellectus Emendatione*. In one place there, Spinoza says that the idea of quantity, if the understanding (*intellectus*) forms it absolutely, is infinite, whereas the idea of quantity, if the understanding perceives it by means of a cause, is finite.[4] This distinction is undoubtedly identical with his distinction between extension as an attribute and extension as a mode, the former of which is infinite and the latter finite. In another place he speaks of the errors into which those "who do not accurately distinguish between intellect and imagination" easily fall, and he mentions as one of the errors their belief that extension must be finite.[5] Finally, these distinctions between substance and mode and between

---

[1] *Short Treatise*, I, 2, §§ 21–22 (*Opera*, I, p. 26, ll. 6–7).

[2] *Ethics*, I, Prop. 15, Schol. (*Opera*, II, p. 58, l. 16–p. 59, l. 1).

[3] *Ibid.* (*Opera*, II, p. 59, ll. 20–32).

[4] *Tractatus de Intellectus Emendatione*, § 108 (*Opera*, II, p. 39, ll. 4–14).

[5] *Ibid.*, § 87 (p. 32, l. 35–p. 33, l. 3).

intellect and imagination, with the addition of a third distinction, namely, that between the infinite and the indefinite, occur again in one of Spinoza's letters to Meyer.[1]

It is the purpose of this chapter to isolate the problem of the infinity of extension from the problem of the applicability of extension as an attribute of God, and to place this aspect of Spinoza's discussion of the problem of infinity, both the arguments of his unnamed opponents and also his criticism thereof, in the light of its historical setting. We shall deal here with certain texts of Crescas some of which have already impressed Joël and other students of Jewish philosophy with their obvious resemblance to certain passages in Spinoza's discussion of infinity.[2] As mere parallel passages they are interesting enough, if only to increase the number of such parallels that may be culled from the wide philosophic literature of the Middle Ages. It may perhaps be of somewhat greater significance if it is shown that even Spinoza's refutations are found among those offered by Crescas, but here, too, as we shall see, they may be found also in the works of other writers. But the matter grows in importance when we notice that the three "distinctions" mentioned by Spinoza in his letter remind one of three refutations by Crescas of three arguments which correspond respectively to the three "examples" of Spinoza. The matter becomes of still greater importance when, as we hope to show, Spinoza's entire discussion of the indivisibility of infinite extension is found to involve many difficulties which can be cleared up by the aid of a thorough understanding of Crescas' position on the same subject.

[1] Epistola 12.

[2] Cf. M. Joël, *Don Chasdai Creskas' religionsphilosophische Lehren*, p. 22, n. 1. Cross-references to Spinoza are also to be found in: M. Schreiner, *Der Kalâm in der jüdischer Literatur*, p. 27, n. 5; I. I. Efros, *The Problem of Space in Jewish Mediaeval Philosophy*, pp. 93, 97, 107; M. Waxman, *The Philosophy of Don Hasdai Crescas*, p. 40, n. 36.

It is safe to say that whomsoever in particular and directly Spinoza may have had in mind when assailing his opponents for denying the infinity of corporeal substance, it is ultimately the views and arguments advanced by Aristotle that he is contending with. Aristotle it was who boldly came out against the conception of an infinite which had been held by some of his predecessors, and it is in his writings that we find the most elaborate discussion of the subject. With a long array of arguments, in which all his characteristic theories of physics and metaphysics come into play, Aristotle exploded the theory of the existence of any possible phase of the infinite. This negation of the infinite, with the avalanche of arguments found in Aristotle's *Physics*, *Metaphysics*, and *De Caelo*,[1] had passed into the stock-in-trade of philosophic lore of mediaeval thought, where it played an important part, for it enters as an element into one of the chief proofs for the existence of God, namely, the cosmological proof based upon the assumption of the impossibility of an infinite regress. A few new arguments against infinity may have been added later, the old arguments of Aristotle may have been changed, garbled, misinterpreted, split up, and reclassified, but it is always to Aristotle that any mediaeval discussion of the impossibility of an infinite can be traced. It is, therefore, of the utmost importance for us to know to what extent the reasons attributed by Spinoza to his unnamed opponents for denying the infinity of corporeal substance do actually agree with what we know to be the views of Aristotle.

If we were to believe Spinoza, the main reason why Aristotle and his followers rejected infinity was their belief that corporeal substance is composed of parts. "Wherefore the whole heap of arguments," he says, "by which philosophers

[1] *Physics*, III, 4-8; *Metaphysics*, XI, 10; *De Caelo*, I, 5-7.

commonly endeavor to show that extended substance is finite, falls to the ground by its own weight, for all these arguments suppose that corporeal substance is made up of parts." [1] It would also seem that it is not the mere divisibility of extended substance that Spinoza understood to be the assumption underlying the arguments against infinity, but rather its divisibility into heterogeneous parts and its composition of those parts, so that extended substance, according to Spinoza, was not considered by his opponents as a continuous quantity. Thus he says: "Wherefore those who think that extended substance is made up of parts or of bodies really distinct from one another are talking foolishly, not to say madly. It is as though one should attempt by the mere addition and aggregation of many circles to make up a square, or a triangle, or something else different in its whole essence." [2] He furthermore compares the relation of the parts of which corporeal substance is supposed to be composed to that of points to a line. "In the same way, others, who have persuaded themselves that a line is made up of points, could also find many arguments by which they would prove that a line is not divisible to infinity." [3] Finally, Spinoza seems to imply that the assumption of the divisibility of corporeal substance, which is supposed to underlie the rejection of its infinity, is analogous to the belief in the discontinuity of nature as held by those who admit the existence of a vacuum, and thus he concludes the argument that "since, therefore, it is supposed that there is no vacuum in nature (about which I will speak at another time), but that all the parts must be united, so that no vacuum can exist, it follows that they cannot be really separated; that is to say,

---

[1] Epistola 12 (*Opera*, IV, p. 55, l. 16–p. 56, l. 1).
[2] *Ibid.* (p. 55, ll. 11–16).
[3] *Ibid.* (p. 56, ll. 2–4).

that corporeal substance, in so far as it is substance, cannot be divided." [1]

And yet how strangely un-Aristotelian are these views attributed by Spinoza to Aristotle. Aristotle, as we know him from his own writings, no more considered corporeal substance to consist of heterogeneous parts than a line to consist of points, for both body and line are to him continuous quantities and infinitely divisible. "It is impossible," he says, "that anything continuous should be composed of indivisibles; as, for instance, a line of points, since a line is a continued quantity, but a point is indivisible." [2] And what is true of a line is also true, according to Aristotle, of the other magnitudes, for "there is the same reasoning with respect to magnitude, time, and motion; for either each or no one of these consists of indivisibles and is divided into indivisibles." [3] Following out this line of reasoning, he concludes that "it is also evident that everything which is continuous is divisible into things always divisible." [4] And it is because of his belief in the continuity of corporeal substance that Aristotle rejects the existence of a vacuum and maintains "that there is not an interval different from bodies, either separable or actual — an interval which divides the whole body, so that it is not continuous, as Democritus and Leucippus say, and many other physicists — or even perhaps as something which is outside the whole body, which remains continuous." [5] Thus for every view ascribed by Spinoza to his opponents we may find in Aristotle a statement to the contrary.

Then there is another difficulty. Spinoza argues that his opponents denied the existence of an infinite because they

[1] *Ethics*, I, Prop. 15, Schol. (*Opera*, II, p. 59, ll. 16–19).
[2] *Physics*, VI, 1, 231a, 24–26.
[3] *Ibid.*, 231b, 18–20.   [4] *Ibid.*, 231b, 15–16.
[5] *Ibid.*, IV, 6, 213a, 31–213b, 2.

erroneously believed that infinite substance must be divisible, whereas he maintains that infinite substance is indivisible. Now, Aristotle himself discusses the possibility of an indivisible infinite substance, but, while admitting that there is an indivisible substance and that that substance can be called infinite, he argues that the term "infinite" when applied to that indivisible substance will not mean infinite except in the sense in which a voice is called "invisible," but that, he concludes, is not what he means by the term "infinite" when he investigates whether an infinite exists.[1] How then can Spinoza argue against those who deny the existence of an infinite and at the same time use the term "infinite" in a sense which is explicitly rejected by his opponents? Is he not committing here the fallacy of equivocation?

It has been suggested that in attacking his opponents for conceiving corporeal substance as an aggregate of distinct bodies it was Descartes whom Spinoza was aiming at.[2] In proof of this a passage is cited in which Descartes rejects extension as a divine attribute on account of its divisibility. A closer examination of this passage, however, will reveal that while it contains one of those arguments which Spinoza says are found "in authors, by which they endeavor to show that corporeal substance is unworthy of divine nature, and cannot pertain to it," [3] that argument is not used by Descartes to prove that corporeal substance cannot be infinite. Descartes simply endeavors to show that inasmuch as extension is divisible, and inasmuch as divisibility indicates imperfection, extension cannot be an attribute of God.[4] This

[1] *Ibid.*, III, 5, 204a, 8–14; *Metaphysics*, XI, 10, 1066b, 1–7.

[2] Cf. H. H. Joachim, *A Study of the Ethics of Spinoza*, p. 30, n. 1.

[3] *Ethics*, I, Prop. 15, Schol. (*Opera*, II, p. 58, ll. 13–16).

[4] *Principia Philosophiae*, I, 23: "Thus since in corporeal nature divisibility is included in local extension, and divisibility indicates imperfection, it is certain that God is not body." Compare Spinoza's *Principia Philosophiae Cartesianae*, I, Prop. 16.

exactly corresponds to the second of the two arguments which Spinoza ascribes, both in the *Ethics* and in the *Short Treatise*, to those who denied extension as an attribute of God.¹ It is in this sense only that Tschirnhaus said to Leibniz, evidently in the name of Spinoza, that Descartes erroneously attributed divisibility to extension.² But it does not mean that Descartes believed in the heterogeneity of matter and its divisibility into irreducible parts on account of which he had to deny its infinity. Quite the contrary, Descartes believed that matter, whose essence is extension,³ is infinite in extent.⁴ Furthermore, Descartes was far from considering corporeal substance to consist of parts really distinct from one another, for, by denying the existence of atoms ⁵ and of a vacuum,⁶ he held extension to be continuous and infinite in divisibility.⁷ Though he admits "that certain sensible bodies are composed of insensible particles," ⁸

---

¹ *Ethics*, I, Prop. 15, Schol. (*Opera*, II, p. 58, ll. 9–13): "A second argument is assumed from the absolute perfection of God. For God, they say, since He is a being absolutely perfect, cannot suffer; but corporeal substance, since it is divisible, can suffer: it follows, therefore, that it does not pertain to God's essence." *Short Treatise*, I, 2, § 18 (*Opera*, I, p. 24, ll. 13–15): "Moreover, when extension is divided it is passive, and with God (who is never passive, and cannot be affected by any other being, because He is the first efficient cause of all) this can by no means be the cause." See Wolf's note on p. 178. Cf. above, p. 260.

² "Extensionem non inferre divisibilitatem, inque eo lapsum esse Cartesium." Cf. K. I. Gerhardt, "Leibniz und Spinoza," in *Sitzungsberichte der königlich preussischen Akademie der Wissenschaften zu Berlin*, 1889, p. 1077, reprinted also in L. Stein, *Leibniz und Spinoza*, p. 283.

³ Cf. *Principia Philosophiae*, II, 4, and *Principia Philosophiae Cartesianae*, II, Prop. 2.

⁴ Cf. *Principia Philosophiae*, II, 21, and *Principia Philosophiae Cartesianae*, II, Prop. 6.

⁵ Cf. *Principia Philosophiae*, II, 20, and *Principia Philosophiae Cartesianae*, II, Prop. 5.

⁶ Cf. *Principia Philosophiae*, II, 16–19, and *Principia Philosophiae Cartesianae*, II, Prop. 3.

⁷ Cf. *Principia Philosophiae*, II, 34, and *Principia Philosophiae Cartesianae*, II, Prop. 5, Demonst.

⁸ *Principia Philosophiae*, IV, 201.

he himself takes great pains to point out that these parts are not indivisible and insists that his view has more in common with that of Aristotle than with that of Democritus.[1] All that we may gather, therefore, from Descartes' own statements is that, while extension is divisible and hence cannot be applied to God, it is not divisible into indivisible parts in the same way as, according to Spinoza's arguments here against his opponents, a line would have to be divisible if it were conceived to consist of points.

It was thus not Aristotle and his followers whom Spinoza could have meant when he ascribed to his opponents the discreteness of corporeal substance as the reason for their denying its infinity. Still less could he have meant Descartes, for Descartes not only like Aristotle believed in the continuity of extension, but also like Spinoza held it to be infinite. Unless, therefore, we are inclined to say that Spinoza willfully imposed upon his opponents views which they would disclaim or that he unwarily misunderstood their position, we are bound to look for some new meaning that may lie concealed behind his uttered words. We must particularly try to find out whether it is not possible that Spinoza uses here the terms "indivisible" and "divisible" in some special and generally unknown sense, for it is in the discovery of such a special, uncommon use of these two terms, it would seem, that we may find an answer to the questions raised by us. We must therefore acquaint ourselves thoroughly with the sources from which we have reason to believe Spinoza had drawn his knowledge of the ancient controversy about infinity in order to learn the exact meaning of the terms he uses, to fill out the gaps in his fragmentary statements, and to restate the full implications of his argument of which his words are sometimes mere suggestions.

[1] *Ibid.*, IV, 202.

Allowing ourselves to be guided by the gentle hand of Averroes through the uncharted texts of Aristotle's writings, for it was Averroes by whom Spinoza's predecessors had been so wisely guided in their pursuit of the same subject, we may restate for our purpose certain pertinent facts with regard to Aristotle's conception of infinity. (1) An infinite, by definition, must be divisible, for "if it is indivisible, it will not be infinite, unless in the same manner as voice is invisible. Those, however, who say that there is the infinite do not assert that it thus subsists, nor do we investigate it as a thing of this kind, but as that which cannot be passed through." [1] (2) A divisible infinite must be one of the following three: (*a*) A quantity existing as an accident in a corporeal subject. (*b*) An incorporeal quantity. (*c*) An incorporeal substance.[2] An accidental quantity existing in a corporeal subject is dismissed as something irrelevant to the conception of infinity under discussion. Then an incorporeal infinite quantity is dismissed on the ground that there is no incorporeal quantity. To quote Averroes: "It cannot be an incorporeal quantity, for since number and magnitude are inseparable from sensible objects, it follows that whatever is an accident of number and magnitude must likewise be inseparable, and infinity is such an accident, for finitude and infinity are two accidents existing in number and magnitude, inasmuch as the essence of number and magnitude is not identical with the essence of the infinite." [3] Finally, an infinite incorporeal substance is rejected on the ground of the

---

[1] *Physics*, III, 5, 204a, 12–14. Cf. *Metaphysics*, XI, 10, 1066b, 5–7.

[2] Cf. Averroes' Middle Commentary on the Physics, Book III, Summa iii, Chapter 4: "If the infinite is divisible, it must inevitably be an incorporeal quantity or a quantity existing in a subject or one of the incorporeal substances." Paraphrased also by Crescas, *Or Adonai*, I, i, 1 (p. 4a). Cf. my *Crescas' Critique of Aristotle*, pp. 137 and 330.

[3] Averroes, *loc. cit.* Paraphrased also by Crescas, *loc. cit.* (p. 4a–b). Cf. *Crescas' Critique of Aristotle*, pp. 137 and 330.

absurdities that would ensue if it were supposed to be divisible. We shall quote the argument on this last point in three versions:

In Aristotle the argument is given as follows: "It is also evident that it is not possible for the infinite to be, as subsisting in energy and as essence and a principle: for whatever part of it is assumed will be infinite, if it is partible: for the essence of infinite and the infinite are the same, since the infinite is essence or substance, and is not predicated of a subject. Hence it is either indivisible, or divisible into infinites. But it is impossible that there can be many infinites in the same thing. As air, however, is part of air, so likewise infinite is a part of infinite, if it is essence and a principle. It is, therefore, impartible and indivisible. But this is impossible, since it is infinite in energy; for it is necessary that it should be a certain quantum." [1]

Averroes' version of the same argument runs as follows: "After we have shown that the infinite cannot be an incorporeal nor a corporeal quantity, there is nothing left but that it should be an incorporeal substance, of the kind we affirm of soul and intellect, so that the thing assumed to be infinite, that is, described as infinite, and infinite being itself are one in definition and essence and not different in reason. However, if we assume the infinite to be of this kind, its essence thus being at one with its definition, then, as a result of its being infinite, we shall be confronted with the question whether it is divisible or indivisible. [In the first case,] if it be divisible, then the definition of a part and the whole of it will be the same in this respect, as must necessarily be the case in simple, homoeomerous things. But if this be so, then the part of the infinite will be infinite. For the parts must inevitably either be different from the infinite whole or not

---

[1] *Physics*, III, 5, 204a, 20-29. Cf. *Metaphysics*, XI, 10, 1066b, 11-19.

be different therefrom. If they be different, then the infinite
will be composite and not simple; if they be not different,
then the definition of the part will be the same as that of the
whole, for this reasoning must necessarily follow in the case
of all things that are homoeomerous. Just as part of air is
air, and part of flesh is flesh, so part of infinite is infinite,
forasmuch as the part and the whole in each of these are one
in definition and essence. If a difference is found in the parts
of homoeomerous bodies, it is due only to the subject which
is the receptacle of the parts and not to the form, for if we
imagine the form of a homoeomerous body without a subject,
the parts and the whole thereof will be the same in all respects
and without any difference. [In the second case,] if we say
that the infinite incorporeal substance is indivisible, which
must be the case of an incorporeal *qua* incorporeal, then it
cannot be said to be infinite except in the sense in which a
point is said to be infinite. In general, the treatment of the
existence of an incorporeal infinite is irrelevant to the subject under discussion." [1]

This Averroian version of Aristotle's argument is briefly
restated by Crescas in the following terms: "Again, we cannot help asking ourselves whether this incorporeal substance
is divisible or indivisible. If it is divisible, since it is also
incorporeal, simple, and homoeomerous, the definition of
any of its parts will be identical with that of the whole, and
since the whole is now assumed to be infinite, any part thereof
will likewise have to be infinite. But it is of the utmost
absurdity that the whole and a part thereof should be alike
[in infinity]. And if it is indivisible, which, indeed, as an incorporeal, it must be, we can no longer call it infinite, except
as a point is said to be infinite." [2]

[1] Averroes, *loc. cit.*, quoted in my *Crescas' Critique of Aristotle*, pp. 331–332.
[2] *Or Adonai, loc. cit.* (p. 4a). Cf. *Crescas' Critique of Aristotle*, p. 137.

The gravamen of this Aristotelian argument against an infinite incorporeal substance, as will have been gathered, is that if it were divisible its parts would each have to be either infinite or finite, neither of which is possible. It is this argument that is reproduced by Spinoza in his first "example": "If corporeal substance, they say, be infinite, let us conceive it to be divided into two parts; each part, therefore, will be either finite or infinite. If each part be finite, then the infinite is composed of two finite parts, which is absurd. If each part be infinite, there is then an infinite twice as great as another infinite, which is also absurd." [1] It will be recalled that it is by this very same reasoning that Spinoza has proved in Propositions XII and XIII that an infinite must be indivisible. [2]

It is simply a matter of ordinary good reasoning that any attempt at a refutation of Aristotle's arguments against infinity will have to proceed from his own premises and will have to use terms in his own sense. The infinite will have to be a quantitative term, "for it is necessary that it should be a certain quantum," [3] as Aristotle plainly puts it. It will have to be divisible. This at once renders it futile to seek to establish an infinite incorporeal substance which is not quantitative and not divisible and of which the use of the term infinite merely means its exclusion from the universe of finitude in the same sense as a point is said to be infinite. The infinite, the existence of which any criticism of Aristotle will seek to establish, will thus have to be an incorporeal quantity, inasmuch as an infinite quantity existing as an accident in a corporeal subject has been disposed of by Aristotle himself as something inconsistent with the conception of infinity. But an infinite quantity has been rejected

[1] *Ethics*, I, Prop. 15, Schol. (*Opera*, II, p. 57, ll. 28–33).
[2] Cf. above, pp. 156–157.   [3] Cf. quotation above, p. 272, n. 1.

by Aristotle on the ground that no incorporeal quantity exists. The first step, therefore, in proving the existence of an infinite will be to establish the existence of an incorporeal quantity. Furthermore, this incorporeal quantity, while it will be divisible in conformity with the definition of the term infinite, will at the same time also have to be homoeomerous, as everything incorporeal perforce must be, and consequently, as a second step, a way will have to be found by which the parts into which it is divisible will not each be infinite like the whole nor finite unlike the whole.

It is exactly this process of reasoning that is employed by Crescas in his criticism of Aristotle. Endeavoring to show that an infinite is possible, he first seeks to establish the existence of an incorporeal quantity. He does so by proving, by arguments which do not concern us here, that a vacuum does exist, not indeed within the universe, dispersed throughout the pores of bodies and thus breaking up their continuity, as was held by Democritus, but rather outside the universe, the view held by the Pythagoreans.[1] The vacuum is nothing but tridimensional extension, or, as Crescas calls it, "incorporeal dimensions" as contrasted with a plenum which is "corporeal dimensions."[2] The significance of this distinction may be fully appreciated when compared with the view of Aristotle. Tridimensionality, according to Aristotle, is either the essence of matter or a form of matter, for there is a difference of opinion among his commentators on that point.[3] In either case, tridimensionality is always corporeal, for even if it is a form of matter, as a form it cannot exist without matter. But to Crescas the vacuum outside the universe is tridimensionality which has an independent,

---

[1] Cf. my *Crescas' Critique of Aristotle*, pp. 53–60.

[2] *Or Adonai*, I, ii, 1 (p. 14b). Cf. *Crescas' Critique of Aristotle*, p. 187.

[3] Cf. *Crescas' Critique of Aristotle*, p. 101 and n. 18 on pp. 579–590. Cf. above, pp. 234–235.

incorporeal existence. Furthermore, this incorporeal tridimensionality, argues Crescas, is a continuous quantity, i.e., a
magnitude, inasmuch as it is described in terms of a continuous quantity rather than in those of a discrete quantity, for it
is said to be "great and small" rather than "much and few." [1]
As such it is infinite in divisibility. But Crescas argues also
that it must likewise be infinite in extent, "for if it had a
limit it would have to terminate either at a body or at another vacuum. That it should terminate at a body, however,
is impossible. It will, therefore, have to terminate at another
vacuum, and that will go on to infinity." [2]

But here Crescas seems to become conscious of the difficulty raised by Aristotle, in Averroes' version of the argument, against an infinite incorporeal substance. The infinite
vacuum is divisible, but it is also homoeomerous. This
being the case, the parts of the infinite vacuum will either
be identical with the whole in definition or not. If they are,
then the parts will each be infinite like the whole; if they are
not, then the whole will be composed of heterogeneous parts.
The passage in which Crescas refutes Aristotle's argument
and in which he also seems to touch upon this difficulty may
be given here in full: "We say that the argument is fallacious
and a begging of the question. For he who assumes the existence of an incorporeal infinite magnitude likewise affirms
the existence of an incorporeal quantity. By the same token,
it does not follow that the definition of the infinite would have
to apply to its parts, just as such reasoning does not follow
in the case of a mathematical line. Nor would there have to
be any composition in it except of parts of itself." [3]

This passage of Crescas is evidently meant to be a refuta-

---

[1] *Or Adonai*, I, II, 1 (p. 15a). Cf. my *Crescas' Critique of Aristotle*, p. 189.
[2] *Ibid.*
[3] *Or Adonai, loc. cit.* (p. 14a). Cf. *Crescas' Critique of Aristotle*, p. 179.

tion of the argument contained in the passage quoted above
from Averroes and of which Crescas himself has given a paraphrase. It will be recalled that Averroes argues against two
possible alternatives in the case where the infinite is assumed
to be both homoeomerous and divisible. First, if the parts
are each infinite like the whole, then the parts of an infinite
will be infinite, which is absurd. Second, if the parts are
each finite, then the infinite whole is composed of dissimilar
parts and is therefore no longer homoeomerous, which is
contrary to the assumption. Now, in this passage Crescas
evidently tries to answer both these alternatives. As against
the first, he seems to say that though the parts are assumed
to be of the same kind as the whole, they are not each infinite like the whole, for "it does not follow that the definition of the infinite would have to apply to all its parts, just
as such reasoning does not follow in the case of a mathematical line." As against the second, he seems to say that
though the parts are finite, the infinite whole would not be
composed of dissimilar parts, for "nor would there have to
be any composition in it except of parts of itself."

When we examine, however, this passage closely, we find
that its reasoning is not quite fully explained. In the first
place, Crescas does not fully explain why in an infinite
which is assumed to be homoeomerous and infinite in essence
the parts should not each be infinite like the whole. He
merely asserts that it would not have to be so in the case of
an infinite, just as something similar would not have to follow in the case of a mathematical line. But we may ask
ourselves: The infinite under discussion is infinite in its
essence just as a mathematical line is linear in its essence,
and since the parts of the line are linear like the whole, why
should not also the parts of the infinite be infinite like the
whole? In the second place, when Crescas, arguing appar-

only against the second alternative, tries to show that the
infinite would not be composed of dissimilar parts even if its
parts were each finite, he simply says "nor would there have
to be any composition in it except of parts of itself." What
is the meaning of this statement?

Joël, probably starting with the *a priori* belief that Crescas
must have used the analogy of the mathematical line in the
same way as it is used by Spinoza in his letter to Meyer,
paraphrases this passage as follows: "So wenig die Linie
aus Punkten bestehe, so wenig habe man sich die unendliche
Ausdehnung aus Theilen zusammengesetzt zu denken." [1]
This paraphrase seems to take the passage as a refutation of
an argument which assumes that the infinite is composed of
heterogeneous parts. But as we have seen, quite the contrary, the analogy of the mathematical line is meant to be
a refutation of that part of the argument, paraphrased by
Crescas himself from Averroes, in which it is urged that if
the infinite does not consist of heterogeneous parts, then the
parts of the infinite will each have to be infinite.

In order to get at the meaning of this difficult passage we
must call to our aid everything that was possibly known to
Crescas about a mathematical line and its definition and out
of this try to reconstruct imaginatively what he could have
meant by his allusion to a mathematical line as a solution
of the difficulty raised against the existence of an infinite.
Two main facts about a mathematical line must have been
known to Crescas. In the first place, he was acquainted with
Euclid's definitions of a line, of which there are two. But it
must have been the second of these definitions [2] with which
Crescas operated, for it is this second definition which is most
frequently quoted in the texts with which Crescas was ac-

---

[1] M. Joël, *Don Chasdai Creskas' religionsphilosophische Lehren*, p. 22.
[2] *Elements*, Book I, Def. 3.

quainted.[1] This definition reads: "The extremities of a line are points." In the second place, Crescas was well acquainted with Aristotle's statements that a line is a continuous quantity [2] and that "everything which is continuous is divisible into things always divisible." [3] According to these statements, then, a line is divisible into parts which are lines, and presumably a line can also be said to be composed of those lines into which it is divisible. Now the following question may be raised against these statements of Aristotle. Since the parts into which a line is divisible and of which they are also composed are according to Aristotle lines, they must also be defined as lines. But by Euclid's second definition of a line, the extremities of a line are said to be points. Consequently, if a line is divided into as well as composed of lines, a line must be also divided into and composed of points. But this is contrary to Aristotle's statement that a line is a continuous quantity and does not consist of points.[4]

This question must have undoubtedly been in the mind of Crescas when he made his allusion to the definition of a mathematical line. In his brief statement that the definition of the parts, of both the infinite and the line, is not identical with that of the whole and that both would not be composed except of parts of themselves, he gives us some clue as to what his answer to this question would be. He would answer it by saying that incorporeal quantities, which are continuous and homoeomerous like a mathematical line and the infinite vacuum, have no parts. Parts are to be found only in discrete quantities, such as number, which is made up of different units, or in corporeal continuous quantities where the parts differ from the whole in accidental qualities, as,

[1] Averroes' *Epitome of the Physics*, III (Hebrew version), p. 10b. Cf. Isaac Israeli, *Sefer Yesodot*, II, p. 45 (ed. Fried).

[2] *Physics*, VI, 1, 231a, 24.   [3] *Ibid.*, VI, 1, 231b, 15–16.

[4] *Ibid.*, VI, 1, 231a, 24–26.

for instance, the parts of an actual line which differ from the whole in length. If Aristotle does speak of a mathematical line as being infinitely divisible, the divisibility is merely in thought and in capacity; in reality infinite divisibility means nothing but a denial that the line consists of parts different from the whole. Or, to put the matter in other words, in the case of a discrete quantity, or of a corporeal continuous quantity, the whole is both divisible into parts and composed of those parts into which it is divisible; but in the case of an incorporeal continuous quantity, while the whole is infinitely divisible into parts, it is not composed of those parts into which it is infinitely divisible. In the case of the former, the parts are actual and co-exist with the whole; in the case of the latter, the parts are only potential and do not co-exist with the whole. This is what is behind Crescas' statement that the definition of the whole need not necessarily apply to the parts, for the parts are never actual and do never co-exist with the whole, and this is also what he means by saying that the whole is not composed "except of parts of itself," i.e., of parts which do not exist outside the whole or beside the whole. If Crescas had carried out his argument in full he would have drawn upon Aristotle's discussion as to "whether the formula [i.e., definition] of the parts must be present in the formula of the whole or not," [1] in the course of which discussion Aristotle says: "For even if the line when divided passes away into its halves, or the man into bones and muscles and flesh, it does not follow that they are composed of these as parts of their essence, but rather as matter; and these are parts of the concrete thing, but not of the form, i.e., of that to which the formula refers." [2]

---

[1] *Metaphysics*, VII, 10, 1034b, 23–24.

[2] *Metaphysics*, VII, 10, 1035a, 17–21. This interpretation of Crescas' passage is fully worked out in my *Crescas' Critique of Aristotle*, pp. 391–394.

In other words, to be divisible does not always mean to be composed.

The essential point in Crescas' answer to Aristotle's argument rests, as we have seen, upon the distinction between the vacuum outside the world and the plenum within it, or between incorporeal extension and corporeal extension. The answer given by Spinoza to the same argument, reproduced by him in his first "example," is based upon a similar distinction. What Crescas calls incorporeal extension or vacuum or space logically corresponds to what Spinoza calls extended substance or the attribute of extension, and what Crescas calls corporeal extension corresponds to what Spinoza calls the particular modes of extension.[1] To both of them, the former is infinite, whereas the latter is finite. Spinoza thus says in his letter to Meyer, and it is in answer to the first "example" mentioned in the *Ethics*, that the argument is based upon a failure to distinguish "between that which must be infinite from its very nature, or in virtue of its definition, and that which has no limits, not indeed in virtue of its essence, but in virtue of its cause."[2] From a comparison of his subsequent elaboration of this distinction in the letter with his corresponding discussion of the same distinction in the *Ethics*,[3] in the *Short Treatise*,[4] and in the *Tractatus de Intellectus Emendatione*[5] it is clear that the distinction is that between extension as an attribute and as a mode. That the latter is described by the expression "in virtue of its cause" may be explained by the fact that Spinoza regards the relation of substance to mode as that of cause to effect.[6]

---

[1] Cf. *Crescas' Critique of Aristotle*, pp. 116–118.
[2] Epistola 12 (*Opera*, IV, p. 53, ll. 2–5).
[3] *Ethics*, I, Prop. 15, Schol. (*Opera*, II, p. 58, l. 16–p. 59, l. 19).
[4] *Short Treatise*, I, 2, §§ 21–22 (*Opera*, I, p. 26, ll. 6–17).
[5] *Tractatus de Intellectus Emendatione*, §108 (*Opera*, II, p. 39, ll. 4–14).
[6] Cf. above, p. 76, and below, p. 324.

With his adoption of the old distinction between the two
kinds of extension, Spinoza also follows his predecessors in
his description thereof. But before we take up this point,
we have to explain Spinoza's use of the terms "indivisible"
and "divisible" in these descriptions. We have seen how the
term "divisible" may apply to three different kinds of divisibility. First, it may apply to what the mediaevals would call
an incorporeal continuous quantity, such as Crescas' vacuum
or a mathematical line, which is free of any accidents. This is
said to be divisible to infinity into parts which are homogeneous with the whole, that is to say, a vacuum into vacuums and
a line into lines. Second, it may apply to what the mediaevals
would call a corporeal continuous quantity which is subject
to qualitative or quantitative accidents. This is said to be
divisible into parts which while not generically different from
the whole differ from it and from one another by certain
qualitative or quantitative accidents. Thus, to use the illustration given by Averroes in the passage quoted above,
while parts of air are air and parts of flesh are flesh, the parts
differ from the whole and from one another in size or quality
or in some other accident. Third, it may apply to a discrete
quantity which is said to be divisible into parts which are
heterogeneous with the whole and of which the whole is composed. Now, the first of these three kinds of divisibility is
divisibility only in potentiality but not in actuality, for no
actual division into infinity is possible. To say therefore of
a thing that it is potentially infinitely divisible is tantamount
to saying that actually it is indivisible. In fact, Aristotle
himself, who defines a continuous quantity as that which is
infinitely divisible, describes such a quantity also as indivisible, on account of its not being infinitely divisible in actual-
ity. "Since, however, the term indivisible ($\dot{a}\delta\iota\dot{a}\iota\rho\epsilon\tau o\nu$) has
two meanings, according as a whole is not potentially divisi-

ble or is actually undivided, there is nothing to hinder us
from thinking an indivisible whole, when we think of length
(that being actually undivided)." [1] Drawing upon this passage of Aristotle, Thomas Aquinas similarly says: "Now the
indivisible is threefold, as is said in *De Anima*, III. First,
the continuous is indivisible, since actually it is undivided,
although potentially divisible. . . . The third kind of indivisible is what is altogether indivisible, as a point and unity,
which cannot be divided either actually or potentially." [2]

Now, in order to remove the difficulties we have pointed
out at the beginning of the chapter with regard to Spinoza's
reproduction of the views of his opponents and also in order
to make the infinite extension which Spinoza affirms to be
of the same kind with reference to divisibility as that which
Aristotle denies, we must assume that when Spinoza in his
arguments against Aristotle's denial of an infinite extension
insists that extension is indivisible he does not mean that it
is indivisible like a point, that is to say, indivisible even
potentially, but rather that it is indivisible like a continuous
quantity in Aristotle's own use of the term, which means
that it is indivisible in actuality. He is thus not arguing
against Aristotle from a new assumption which Aristotle
would not admit, but he is rather arguing against him from
Aristotle's own assumption. And, similarly, when he argues
that his Aristotelian opponents believe that extension is divisible and is composed of parts, he does not mean to say
that they believe that extension is divisible into, and com-

---

[1] *De Anima*, III, 6, 430b, 6–8.

[2] *Summa Theologica*, Pars I, Quaest. 85, Art. 8: "Dicitur autem indivisibile
tripliciter, ut dicitur in 3 de Anima (text. 23 et deinceps): uno modo sicut continuum
est indivisibile, quia est indivisum in actu, licet sit divisibile in potentia. . . .
Tertio modo dicitur indivisibile quod est omnino indivisibile, ut punctus et unitas,
quae nec actu nec potentia dividuntur" (quoted also by Schütz in *Thomas-Lexikon*
(1895), under "indivisibilis").

posed of, heterogeneous parts as if it were a discrete quantity; what he means to say is that, thinking as they do of extension only as that which is subject to accidental differences, they believe it to be divisible into parts which are quantitatively different from one another, and from such an assumption they argue against the existence of an infinite extension in the same way as one would argue against the infinite divisibility of a line or of matter if one started out with the assumption that a line is composed of points and that matter is composed of heterogeneous atoms dispersed in a vacuum. The point which I have been trying to make is this: When Spinoza charges his opponents with a belief that extension is divisible, he does not mean to say that extension is held by them to be divisible into indivisible parts. What he means to say is that in their use of the divisibility of extension as an argument against its infinity they failed to distinguish between extension as an attribute, or what the mediaevals would call an incorporeal extension, and extension as a mode, or what the mediaevals would call a corporeal extension. The former, because it is divisible into homogeneous parts, can be called indivisible, and can therefore be infinite. The latter, however, because it is divisible into parts which are quantitatively different, cannot be infinite.

The attribute of extension is described by Spinoza in the same terms in which the infinite incorporeal substance is described in the passage quoted above from Averroes. It is "infinite from its very nature, or in virtue of its definition" or "in virtue of its essence." [1] Like Crescas' incorporeal extension it is continuous and has no parts, for "part and whole are not true or real entities, but only things of reason, and consequently there are in nature [i.e., substantial extension]

[1] Epistola 12 (*Opera*, IV, p. 53, ll. 2-5).

neither whole nor parts." [1] It, therefore, "cannot be divided into parts, or can have no parts"; [2] but, as we have already pointed out, by this Spinoza simply means what Aristotle would have sometimes described as being continuous and infinitely divisible and what Crescas would have characterized as not being composed except of parts of itself. The mode of extension, on the other hand, is "composed of finite parts . . . and divisible" [3] just as any corporeal object, in the view of his predecessors, is divisible either into heterogeneous parts or into parts which are qualitatively or quantitatively different from each other. "Further," says Spinoza, "as regards the parts in nature, we maintain that division, as has also been said already before, never takes place in substance, but always and only in the modes of substance. Thus, if I want to divide water, I only divide the mode of substance, and not substance itself." [4] Similarly, in the passage quoted above from Averroes, we read: "Just as part of air is air, and part of flesh is flesh, so part of infinite is infinite, forasmuch as the part and the whole in each of these are one in definition and essence. If a difference is found in the parts of homoeomerous bodies [like air and flesh], it is due only to the subject which is the receptacle of the parts and not to the form, for if we imagine the form of a homoeomerous body without a subject, the parts and the whole thereof will be the same in all respects and without any difference." To be sure, Bruno, too, in his criticism of Aristotle's rejection of infinity dwells upon the absence of parts in the infinite, [5] but there is more in Spinoza's state-

---

[1] *Short Treatise*, I, 2, § 19 (*Opera*, I, p. 24, ll. 19–21).

[2] Epistola 12 (*Opera*, IV, p. 53, ll. 12–13).

[3] *Ethics*, I, Prop. 15, Schol. (*Opera*, II, p. 59, ll. 2–3).

[4] *Short Treatise*, I, 2, § 21 (*Opera*, IV, p. 26, ll. 6–11). The same illustration from water occurs also in *Ethics*, I, Prop. 15, Schol. (*Opera*, II, p. 59, l. 35–p. 60, l. 3).

[5] Cf. *De l'infinito universo et Mondi*, Dial. II, p. 337 (ed. Lagarde).

ment than in Bruno's, and the excess is strongly reminiscent of Crescas.

Thus when Spinoza maintains against Aristotle the existence of an infinite, indivisible extension, he does not reject Aristotle's conception of the infinite as something divisible. The indivisibility of his extension is not like the indivisibility of a point, but rather like the indivisibility which Aristotle sometimes applies to a continuous quantity which is otherwise described by him as infinitely divisible. Again, when he charges his opponents with considering extension as divisible and composed of distinct points, he does not mean that they held extension to be a discrete quantity, similar to the discreteness of a line if it were supposed to consist of points; he only means to say that, denying the existence of pure extension, they considered extension divisible and composed of parts on account of the qualitative or quantitative differences in the parts of the material subject in which it existed, and thus they argued against the infinity of extension in the same way as one could argue against the infinite divisibility of a line or of matter if one started with the assumption that a line was composed of points and that matter was made up of heterogeneous parts dispersed in a vacuum.

Against the existence of an infinite extension there is another argument the purpose of which is to show that the assumption of an infinite would give rise to the absurdity of one infinite being greater than another. This argument appears under various forms in many works of Hebrew and Arabic philosophic literature, and it also occurs in the writings of Bruno. We shall restate here two versions of this argument.

One version is found in Saadia,[1] in Gersonides, followed by Crescas, and in Bruno. In Gersonides, the argument is

---

[1] *Emunot we-De'ot*, I, 3, Eighth Theory (4).

illustrated by the movements of the heavenly spheres and is
aimed against the eternity and hence the infinity of time in
the past. Several propositions are assumed in this argument.
First, some of the heavenly spheres move faster than others.
Second, in the same given time, the fast-moving spheres perform a greater number of rotations than the slow-moving.
Third, one infinite cannot be greater than another. Out of
these propositions the argument may be formulated as follows: If time be infinite in the past, then the fast-moving
and slow-moving spheres will have performed an infinite
number of rotations. But since the number of rotations of
the fast-moving sphere must be greater than that of the slow-
moving, one infinite will be greater than another.[1] In Bruno's
argument the same difficulty is raised, but the illustration is
taken from the division of infinite distance into an infinite
number of paces (or feet) and an infinite number of miles.[2]
Spinoza's second "example" follows closely these two arguments, resembling in form more that of Bruno than that of
Gersonides. "Again, if infinite quantity is measured by
equal parts of a foot each, it must contain an infinite number
of such parts, and similarly if it be measured by equal parts

[1] *Milḥamot Adonai*, VI, i, 11 (pp. 341–342): "Having laid down these premises, I
contend that, if past time were infinite in quantity, it would follow that there could
be no swift motion and slow motion among the spheres. The argument runs as
follows: The number of rotations performed by the swift-moving sphere in the
past time, which is assumed to be infinite, must of necessity be infinite, and the
same must be true of the number of rotations performed by the slow-moving sphere.
But inasmuch as one infinite number cannot be greater nor smaller than another
infinite number, it will follow that no one sphere is of swifter motion than another,
for if one sphere moved more swiftly than another, the number of rotations of the
swift sphere would of necessity be greater."

This argument is reproduced in *Or Adonai*, III, i, 3 (p. 64a).

[2] *De l'infinito universo et Mondi*, Dial. II (p. 338): "El. Particolarmente di quello
che fa al proposito nostro de gl' infiniti passi, et infinite migla che uerrebono á fare
un infinito minore, et un' altro infinito maggiore nell' immensitudine de l'uniuerso."
Cf. on the same page: "la dimensione infinita non é meno de infiniti piedi, che de
infinite migla."

of an inch each; and therefore one infinite number will be twelve times greater than another infinite number." [1]

In his answer Bruno endeavors to show that in the infinite there can be no distinction of number and measure. "It is an absurdity to say that in the infinite one part is greater and another is smaller, and one part has a greater proportion to the whole and another a smaller." [2] Again: "In the innumerable and the immeasurable there is no place for more or less, few or many, nor for any distinction of number or measure." [3] A similar statement is also made by Galileo: "These are some of those difficulties which arise from discourses which our finite understanding makes about infinites, by ascribing to them attributes which we give to things finite and terminate, which I think most improper, because those attributes of majority, minority, and equality agree not with infinites, of which we cannot say that one is greater than, less than, or equal to another." [4] Exactly the same sort of answer is given by Crescas to Gersonides' argument, and, strangely enough, it contains some of the same expressions: "The fast spheres will, indeed, in a certain time perform the same number of rotations that slow spheres will perform in a greater time, when the number of their rota-

---

[1] *Ethics*, I, Prop. 15, Schol. (*Opera*, II, p. 57, ll. 33–37).

[2] *Op. cit.*, pp. 337–338: "Essendo che implica contradittione che ne l'infinito sia parte maggiore, et parte minore, et parte che habbia maggiore et minore proportione á quello."

[3] *De Immenso et Innumerabilibus*, II, 8 (*Opera Latina*, I, 1, p. 284):

> "Innumero nempe atque immenso non locus ullus
> Esse potest pluris, modici, pauci, atque minoris,
> Quae numeri et mensi discrimina cernimus esse."

(English translation quoted from J. Lewis McIntyre's *Giordano Bruno*, p. 188.)

[4] *Discorsi e Dimostrazioni matematiche intorno a due Nuove Scienze*, I, in *Le Opere di Galileo Galilei* (Firenze, 1890–1909), Vol. 8, p. 77, ll. 35 ff., quoted by Bertrand Russell in his *Scientific Method in Philosophy*, p. 192, from Tho. Weston's translation, p. 47.

tions is of such a kind as can be described by the terms much
and few, great and small, within a certain time limit, that is
to say, when both the number and the time are finite, and
this indeed is due to the fact that the fast sphere and the
slow sphere cannot perform the same number of rotations
in equal time. But when the time or the number of rotations
is infinite, neither of these can be described by the terms
much and few, great and small, equal and unequal, for all
these terms are determinations of measure, and measurability does not apply to an infinite. Hence, no absurdity will
ensue if both the fast and the slow spheres have performed
an infinite number of rotations in the past, inasmuch as the
number of their rotations cannot be properly described as
great and small and unequal." [1]

A similar distinction is to be discovered in Descartes' differentiation between the infinite and the indefinite. From the
illustrations he gives it is clear that by the indefinite he
means that whose parts cannot be expressed by any number.
He furthermore describes the indefinite as that which has
no limits only "in a certain sense," from which it may be
inferred that the real infinite is that which has no limits.
The difference between the indefinite and the infinite, according to Descartes, is therefore a difference between that
whose parts cannot be expressed by any number and that
which has no limits. By this distinction Descartes, like
Crescas and Bruno, disposes of such questions against the
existence of an infinite as, e.g., "whether the half of an infinite line is infinite." [2]

The other version of the argument is found in Avicenna, [3]

[1] *Or Adonai*, III, i, 4 (p. 67b).

[2] *Principia Philosophiae*, I, 26, and *Principia Philosophiae Cartesianae*, II,
Prop. 5, Schol.

[3] *Al-Najat*, II: *Physics* (Rome, 1593), p. 33, reproduced in Carra de Vaux's
Avicenne, p. 201.

Algazali,[1] Saadia and Baḥya,[2] Abraham ibn Daud,[3] and Altabrizi.[4] Crescas cites it in the name of Altabrizi in an abridged and modified form. We quote it here from Crescas: "Suppose we have a line infinite only in one direction. To this line we apply an infinite line [which is likewise infinite only in one direction], having the finite end of the second line fall on some point near the finite end of the first line. It would then follow that one infinite [i.e. the first line] would be greater than another infinite [i.e., the second line]. But this is impossible, for it is well known that one infinite cannot be greater than another." [5]

The refutation given by Crescas of this argument is again based upon the distinction between the infinite in the sense of the indefinite or of its being incapable of measurement and the infinite in the sense of its having no limits. To quote: "The impossibility of one infinite being greater than another is true only with respect to measurability, that is to say, when we use the term 'greater' in the sense of being greater by a certain measure, and that indeed is impossible because an infinite is immeasurable. In this sense, to be sure, the first one-side infinite line [in Altabrizi's argument] will not be greater than the second one-side infinite line, inasmuch as neither of them is measurable in its totality. Thus indeed the first line is not greater than the second, though it extends beyond the second on the side which is finite." [6] What Crescas is trying to do is to point out the possibility of an extension

---

[1] *Maḳaṣid al-Falasifah*, II, i (p. 126), quoted by me in *Crescas' Critique of Aristotle*, p. 347.

[2] *Emunot we-De'ot*, I, 3, Eighth Theory (3); *Ḥobot ha-Lebabot*, I, 5.

[3] *Emunah Ramah*, I, 4.

[4] Commentary on Maimonides' Twenty-five Propositions, Prop. I, quoted in my *Crescas' Critique of Aristotle*, pp. 145–146.

[5] *Or Adonai*, I, i, 1 (p. 5a–b). Cf. *Crescas' Critique of Aristotle*, p. 149.

[6] *Or Adonai*, I, ii, 1 (p. 15a). Cf. *Crescas' Critique of Aristotle*, pp. 190–191.

which is infinite in the sense that its parts cannot be equated with or explained by any number and still is not infinite in the sense that it has no limits. Such, for instance, are the lines in Altabrizi's argument, which are infinite on one side but finite on the other. When two such immeasurable but limited infinites are given, then while indeed one of them cannot be conceived as greater than the other in the sense that the total number of its parts can be expressed by a number which is greater, still it can be conceived as greater than the other in the sense that it can extend beyond the other on the limited side. The reason why one immeasurable infinite cannot be said to be greater than another, says Crescas, is that their parts cannot be expressed by any number and therefore the terms great and small are inapplicable to them.

It is, therefore, as a refutation of his second "example" in the *Ethics* that Spinoza in his letter to Meyer charges his opponents with the failure to make a distinction "between that which is called infinite because it has no limits, and that whose parts we cannot equate with or explain by any number, although we know its maximum and minimum," [1] concluding that, had they made such a distinction, "they would also have understood which kind of infinite can be conceived as greater than another infinite, without any complication, and which cannot be so conceived." [2] The wording of Spinoza's answer is strikingly reminiscent of both Crescas and Descartes.

Back again to Aristotle, by way of Averroes, Altabrizi, and Crescas, we must go for the source of Spinoza's third "example." In the *De Caelo*, Aristotle advances a series of arguments to prove from the circular movements of the heavenly spheres that the heavens cannot be infinite, for if they were infinite they could not revolve in a circle. One of these

---

[1] Epistola 12 (*Opera*, IV, p. 53, ll. 5–8).   [2] *Ibid.* (p. 53, ll. 14–15).

arguments, reproduced by Crescas from Averroes, runs as
follows: [1]

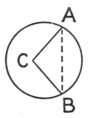

Let *ACB* be an infinite circle.
Let *CA* and *CB* be infinite radii.
Let *CA* revolve on its centre *C*.
Let *CB* be fixed.

If an infinite sphere could rotate upon itself, then *CA*
would sometimes have to fall on *CB*.

But the distance *AB* is infinite, and an infinite distance
cannot be traversed.

Consequently, *CA* could never fall on *CB*.

Hence, no infinite body could have circular motion.

An argument advanced by Altabrizi seems to be a modification of this Aristotelian argument. It is more general than
the Aristotelian argument in that it is detached from the
illustration of the movements of the spheres. Crescas reproduces it in the name of "one of the moderns" as a rein-
forcement of Aristotle's argument. In Crescas' restatement
it read as follows: "The same difficulty [according to this
version of the argument] would arise in the case of any two
lines emerging from a common point if they were supposed
to be infinite. The distance between any two such lines at
the point where they are intersected by a common chord
would undoubtedly increase in proportion to the extension
of the lines, and as the lines are assumed to be infinite, the
distance between them would likewise have to be infinite.

---

[1] *Or Adonai*, I, i, I (p. 7a). Cf. *De Caelo*, I, 5, 271b, 27–272a, 7; *Crescas' Critique
of Aristotle*, pp. 169 and 379–380.

But this is self-evidently impossible." [1] In almost exactly
the same terms Spinoza states his third "example." "Lastly,
if from one point of any infinite quantity it be imagined that
two lines, *AB*, *AC*, which at first are at a certain and determinate distance from one another, be infinitely extended, it
is plain that the distance between *B* and *C* will be continually increased, and at length from being determinate will be
indeterminable." [2]

In his answer Crescas again brings into play the distinction between the infinite and the indefinite. He endeavors
to show that while any given distance between any two points
in the infinitely extending lines must be finite, the distance
between them may be said to be infinite in the sense that
whatever distance we take there is always a greater distance
beyond it. It is analogous to what Aristotle says of magnitude and number that, while they are both finite in actuality
they are infinite in capacity, in so far as magnitude is infinitely divisible and number is infinitely addible. They are
in this sense infinite, "for the infinite is not that beyond
which there is nothing, but it is that of which there is always
something beyond." [3] To quote him in part: "To this the
opponent of Aristotle may answer that distance increases
[infinitely] in the same manner as number is said to increase
[infinitely], but it always remains limited. That the possibility of infinite increase is not incompatible with its being
actually limited may be seen from the case of infinite decrease, for the examination into contraries is by one and the
same science. [4] It has been demonstrated in the book on *Conic
Sections* that it is possible for a distance infinitely to decrease

[1] *Or Adonai*, *loc. cit.* Cf. *Crescas' Critique of Aristotle*, pp. 171 and 381–382.
[2] *Ethics*, I, Prop. 15 (*Opera*, II, p. 57, ll. 37 ff.).
[3] *Physics*, III, 6, 207a, 1–2.
[4] Cf. *Metaphysics*, XI, 3, 1061a, 19.

and still never completely to disappear.[1] It is possible to assume, for instance, two lines which, by how much farther they are extended, are brought by so much nearer to each other, and still will never meet, even if they are produced to infinity. If, in the case of decrease, there is a certain distance which always remains and does not disappear, *a fortiori* in the case of increase it should be possible for a distance, though infinitely increased, always to remain limited.[2] . . . This, to be sure, is remote from the imagination, but reason compels us to assume it."[3]

Now, Spinoza does not furnish us with any direct answer to the third "example," though his distinction between the infinite and the indefinite may apply to it. But when he says in his letter to Meyer that his opponents failed to distinguish, thirdly, "between that which we can only understand but cannot imagine, and that which we can also imagine,"[4] may we not assume that it is a reminiscence of the last statement by which Crescas concludes his lengthy refutation of the argument which is the exact prototype of the third "example"? Had Spinoza taken the trouble to give a full expression to what he had in mind when he quoted reminiscently this third distinction, he would undoubtedly have given us a paraphrase of this last quoted of Crescas' refutations, as he did, in part, at least, of his two other distinctions; or, perhaps, he would have gone still further and said

[1] Apollonius, *Conic Sections*, II, Theorem 13. See Munk, *Guide des Égarés*, I, p. 410, n. 2.

[2] *Or Adonai*, I, ii, 1 (p. 16a). Cf. *Crescas' Critique of Aristotle*, p. 207.

[3] *Or Adonai, loc. cit.* (p. 16b). Cf. *Crescas' Critique of Aristotle*, p. 211. That the last statement of Crescas about imagination and reason refers to the entire argument and not merely to the passage immediately preceding it may be gathered from Maimonides, who, speaking of the problem cited from the *Conic Sections*, similarly remarks. "This is a fact which cannot easily be conceived, and which does not come within the scope of the imagination" (*Moreh Nebukim*, I, 73, Prop. 10).

[4] Epistola 12 (*Opera*, IV, p. 53, ll. 8–10).

with a generous but rather patronizing gesture: *Nam, ut ipsam apud Judæum quendam Rab Ghasdaj* [1] *vocatum, reperio, sic sonat.* [2]

---

[1] The transliteration of Ḥasdai (חסדאי) by "Ghasdai" follows Spinoza's own method of transliterating the Hebrew *Ḥet* (ח) by *gh*. Cf. his *Compendium Grammatices Linguae Hebrææ*, Cap. II (*Opera*, I, p. 288, l. 18). The form "Jaçdai" (*Opera*, IV, p. 61, l. 35) which occurs in Leibniz's copy of the letter evidently represents the Spanish-Portuguese transliteration of the name. In old Spanish documents published by Fritz Baer in his *Die Juden im Christlichen Spanien*, I (1929), the name is usually written "Azday." But the following forms also occur: "Adzay" (p. 712), "Atzay" (pp. 499, 676), "Azay" (pp. 616, 723), "Azdray" (p. 1000), "nAzday" (p. 676), "Nazday" (p. 699). In these documents the personal name is generally followed by the surname "Cresques," but it occurs also without it (pp. 741, 1000), as here in Spinoza's letter. In Giovanni Francesco Pico della Mirandola's *Examen Doctrinae Vanitatis Gentium*, VI, 2, the name is transliterated "Hasdai" and is not followed by the surname. Nor is the surname given in the references to Crescas in the works of Isaac ben Shem-Ṭob and Shem-Ṭob ben Joseph ben Shem-Ṭob. Cf. my *Crescas' Critique of Aristotle*, pp. 32–33.

[2] Epistola 12 (*Opera*, IV, p. 61, ll. 17–18).

CHAPTER IX

THE CAUSALITY OF GOD

I. Materiality and Causality of God

AFTER recapitulating his position as to the materiality of God in Proposition XIV, Spinoza proceeds in logical order to state his conclusion that there is nothing in the material world which is not in God, or, to put it in the words of his own Proposition XV, "whatever is, is in God, and nothing can either be or be conceived without God." Taken by itself, this proposition would seem to be nothing but a repetition of the ordinary assertions of the omnipresence of God which are current in the literature of every religion. In fact, Spinoza himself acknowledges as much when he says that "like Paul, and perhaps also like all ancient philosophers . . . I assert that all things live and move in God, and I would dare to say that I agree also with all the ancient Hebrews as far as it is possible to surmise from their traditions." [1] By "all ancient philosophers" he undoubtedly refers not only to the Stoic poets Aratus and Cleanthes, to whom Paul himself refers in his statement "as certain also of your own poets have said," [2] and not only to the Stoics in general, whose God was material like the God of Spinoza, but also to those who like Aristotle conceived of God as immaterial, for, though immaterial and hence separated from the universe, that God was still He in whom the universe could be said to have its being, inasmuch as He was its formal, efficient, and final cause. [3] Similarly by the "ancient Hebrews" Spinoza does not refer only to the teachings

---

[1] Epistola 73.   [2] Acts 17, 28. Cf. Commentaries *ad loc.*   [3] Cf. below, p. 302.

of the Hebrew Bible but also, and perhaps more particularly, to the teachings of Judaism at the time of Paul, in its Palestinian and Hellenistic branches, for the omnipresence of God is emphasized by both of these branches of Judaism. The classic expression on this point, used by both the rabbis and Philo, is the statement which is quoted constantly in the Middle Ages by Jewish as well as Christian philosophers, namely, that God is the place of the world.[1] The belief in the omnipresence of God has continued to be a religious commonplace in Judaism as well as Christianity and Mohammedanism, and has been maintained by every shade of religious opinion, though, perhaps, not always without some slight shade of logical inconsistency. The most pertinent passage for our present purpose, both on account of its source and on account of its phrasing, is the following quotation from the Hymn of Unity, which is included in the Jewish liturgy: "Thou encompassest all and fillest all; and since Thou art all, Thou art in all. . . . Thou art not separated or detached from anything, nor is any place empty or devoid of Thee. . . . Thou art and existeth in all; all is Thine, and all is from Thee."[2]

But while the proposition taken by itself contains nothing new, it is used by Spinoza in a different sense. He himself alludes to that difference in its use when he says in his reference to Paul and all ancient philosophers that he agrees with their assertion, "though in another way." What the difference between them is becomes clear in Proposition XV, for this proposition is to be understood as a criticism of the mediaeval inconsistency in first affirming that all things are in God and then denying that matter is in God. For when

---

[1] *Genesis Rabbah* 68, 9 *et al.*, Philo, *De Somniis*, I, 11; Crescas, *Or Adonai*, I, ii, 1; Leibniz, *Nouveaux Essais*, II, 13, § 17. Cf. my *Crescas' Critique of Aristotle*, pp. 123, 201.   [2] *Shir ha-Yihud*, III.

the mediaevals reiterated their statements that God is all
and all is from God and in God, they had to make a mental
reservation with regard to matter. God was not matter, and
matter was not from God nor in God. Matter existed by the
side of God, according to Aristotle; it was created by God *ex
nihilo*, according to the generally accepted view of all the
three religions; it appeared somewhere in the process of
emanation, according to the emanationists. The statement
that God is all and all is from God and in God could not be
taken in its full and literal sense that "whatever is, is in God"
except by one who like Spinoza asserted that God was material.

But is it only this that Proposition XV means to assert,
namely, that matter as well as form is in God, or does it
mean more than this? Does it not mean a complete denial
of the separation of God from the world, with the inevitable
consequence of the disappearance of God as a distinct being
either in thought or in reality?

In the history of philosophy Spinoza's conception of God
has been characterized by different names. In his own day,
it was called deism of the type that flourished then in France,[1]
and it was also stigmatized as a disguised kind of atheism.[2]
When this imputation of atheism was renewed by Jacobi,[3]
Hegel quibbled about its being akosmism rather than atheism.[4] Novalis met the charge of atheism by declaring Spinoza
a God-intoxicated man [5] — a declaration which explains
Spinoza's profuse use of the term God rather than its meaning. The term pantheism is the one which has been most

---

[1] Epistola 42.   [2] Epistola 43.

[3] *Ueber die Lehre des Spinoza in briefen au den Herrn Moses Mendelssohn*, 1785.
Cf. Jacobi's *Werke* (1819), Vol. IV, 1, p. 216.

[4] *Encyclopädie der philosophischen Wissenschaften*, 1, § 50 (ed. Bolland), p. 74;
Vorlesungen über die Geschichte der Philosophie (ed. Bolland), p. 891.

[5] *Schriften* (ed. Paul Kluckhohn, Leipzig [1892]), Vol. III, p. 318, § 253.

often applied to it. Avenarius, who has stratified the writings of Spinoza on the basis of the use of the terms Nature, God, and Substance, just as the higher critics stratify the Pentateuch on the basis of the use of the terms Jehovah and Elohim, has discovered three phases in the development of Spinoza's pantheism, which he designates by the following terms: Naturalist All-in-one, Theistic All-in-one, and Substantive All-in-one [1] — a distinction in which one will find it hard to discover any difference. Windelband brushes all these subtleties aside and declares outright that Spinoza's conception of God is "complete and unreserved pantheism." [2]

The problem before us, however, is not to devise a fitting term by which Spinoza's conception of God can be adequately described, but rather to find out whether his God is absolutely identical with the aggregate totality of particular things or whether He does in some way transcend it. When we leave what others have said about Spinoza's God and turn to what he himself has said about Him, we find that the matter does not become any clearer. Though he makes reference to the characterization of his religion as one which "does not rise above the religion of the Deists," [3] he does not definitely disclaim it. Perhaps he saw no need of disclaiming it, since the author of that statement had done it himself when he said that "unless I am mistaken in my conjecture, this man does not include himself in the ranks of the Deists, and does not allow men to return to the least bit of religious worship." [4] Nor does he disclaim the charge of atheism except in so far as

[1] *Naturalistische All-Einheit, Theisitische All-Einheit, Substanzialistische All-Einheit.* Cf. R. Avenarius, *Ueber die beiden ersten Phasen des Spinozischen Pantheismus* (Leipzig, 1868).

[2] *Geschichte der Philosophie* (3rd edition), p. 336; English translation, *A History of Philosophy*, p. 409.   [3] Epistolae 42 and 43.

[4] Epistola 42.

the term meant in his time a man who is "wont to desire inordinately honors and riches." [1] No more conclusive than this evidence from silence are his positive statements. While in one place he asserts that "those who think that the *Tractatus Theologico-Politicus* rests on this, namely, that God and nature (by which they mean a certain mass, or corporeal matter) are one and the same, are mistaken," [2] in another place he asserts that "I could not separate God from nature as all of whom I have any knowledge have done," [3] and in still another place he identifies the terms God and nature.[4] All that one can with certainty gather from these passages is that while Spinoza did not identify God with nature conceived as an inert mass of matter, he did identify Him with it when conceived in all its infinite attributes. Nor, finally, can we get more light on the question from his statement that "the universe is God," [5] for here, too, the statement may merely mean, as may be judged from the context, "that all things [that is to say, including matter] emanate necessarily from the nature of God. [6] But does it also mean that God is nothing but the aggregate of particular things which constitute the universe?

Since the uttered statements of Spinoza do not throw any light on the question, we shall try the use of the historical critical method in order to solve our problem. We shall give an analysis of the salient features of the traditional conception of God which Spinoza constantly uses as the target for his criticism. We shall also try to find out what elements of it he criticized and ultimately rejected. Finally we shall try to reconstitute Spinoza's conception of God out of those

[1] Epistola 43.   [2] Epistola 73.
[3] Epistola 6.
[4] *Short Treatise*, 1, 2, § 12 (*Opera*, 1, p. 22, ll. 9–13).
[5] Epistola 43.
[6] *Ibid.*

elements of the traditional God which were left by him uncriticized.

The God of tradition whom Spinoza tries to dethrone is sometimes depicted by him disdainfully in all his anthropomorphic crudity as He was pictured in the minds of the vulgar.[1] But this may be considered only as an occasional departure from what is really his general practice. As a rule, the conception of God which he criticizes is that of the philosophers, of the "men who have in any way looked into the divine nature."[2] This conception of God is marked by two main characteristics, immateriality and causality. All the problems raised about the nature of God by philosophers throughout the Middle Ages can be grouped together under these two terms. The immateriality of God it is which gives rise to His unity, simplicity, immutability, and incomparability, out of which springs the complexity of problems which go under the general name of attributes. But such a conception of God's immateriality takes God completely out of the universe, which is not what the mediaeval philosophers wanted to do. And so, immediately after they establish the absolute immateriality of God, they turn around and try to introduce God back into the universe by establishing a certain causal relation between them. It is through the causality of God that the world comes into being and is ruled and guided by Him. God's omnipresence, omniscience, omnipotence, and benevolence of which they all speak are nothing but different ways of expressing the fact of divine causality. These, then, are the two main characteristics of the God of traditional philosophy. Now Spinoza's criticism of this conception of God in *Ethics*, I, falls into two parts, corresponding to these its two main characteristics, immate-

[1] E.g., *Ethics*, I, Prop. 15, Schol.
[2] *Ibid.*

riality and causality. The first fifteen propositions are all a criticism of the immateriality of God, culminating in Proposition XV in the statement that "whatever is, is in God," which, as we have shown, means that everything, including matter, is in God. Beginning now with Proposition XVI to the end of the First Part, he criticizes the old conceptions of the causality of God. In this chapter, however, we shall deal only with Propositions XVI–XVIII.

In order to be able to follow Spinoza's criticism, we must first give a formal statement of what the mediaevals meant by divine causality. Causes have been divided by Aristotle into four: the material, the formal, the efficient, and the final. Beginning with this commonplace of philosophy, the mediaevals asked themselves which of these causes God is. He cannot be the material cause, they said, for God is immaterial. He must therefore be the three other causes. Maimonides is worth quoting on this point. "It has been shown in the science of physics that everything, except the First Cause, owes its origin to the following four causes — the material, the formal, the efficient, and the final. These are sometimes proximate, sometimes remote, but each by itself is called a cause. They also believe — and I do not differ from their belief — that God, blessed be He, is the efficient, formal, and final cause." [1]

Now, in opposition to the mediaevals, as we have already seen, Spinoza makes God a material cause. Again, in opposition to the mediaevals, as we shall see subsequently, Spinoza unmakes God as the final cause. God then to him, if he were to retain the Aristotelian terminology, would be a material, formal, and efficient cause. But this terminology even in Aristotle was not unalterably fixed. The final and efficient causes are identified by him with the formal cause, and thus

[1] *Moreh Nebukim*, I, 69.

the only real contrast between causes is that of the material and formal.[1] This identification of the three causes is found also in Maimonides. "Aristotle has already explained that in natural things the efficient, formal, and final causes are identical."[2] We can readily see how in Spinoza's reasoning, with his discarding of the old Aristotelian terms matter and form, the old designation of causes as material and formal likewise disappears. "In creation," he says, "no other causes concur except the efficient one."[3] God is therefore spoken of by him as the efficient cause, for even as a material and formal cause, it is only through the active properties of extension and thought that God is conceived as cause. Efficient cause is thus to him the most applicable description of God, efficient in the most general sense of active and as the sum of all conditions that make for causality. There is a suggestion of this kind of reasoning in Spinoza's statement that "since substance is the principle of all its modes, it may with greater right be called active than passive."[4] But in order to show the difference between his conception of God as efficient cause and that of the mediaevals, he analyzes their conception of efficient cause and tries to show in what respect he departs from them.

In the *Short Treatise*, where an entire chapter is devoted to the explanation "that God is a cause of all things,"[5] Spinoza borrows a current eightfold classification of the Aristotelian efficient cause, which has been traced to the work of a Dutch philosopher by the name of Burgersdijck,[6]

---

[1] Zeller, *Philosophie der Griechen*, II, 2, pp. 327–330 (3rd edition). English translation, *Aristotle*, I, pp. 355–358.

[2] *Moreh Nebukim*, III, 13.

[3] *Cogitata Metaphysica*, II, 10 (*Opera*, I, p. 268, ll. 25–26).

[4] *Short Treatise*, I, 2, § 25 (*Opera*, I, p. 26, ll. 29–31).

[5] *Short Treatise*, I, 3.

[6] *Institutiones Logicae*, Lib. I, Cap. XVII. Cf. A. Trendelenburg, *Historische*

to show "how and in what sense God is a cause." This eight-fold classification, with the exception of the eighth, which appears later in the Scholium of Proposition XXVIII, is embodied in Propositions XVI–XVIII of *Ethics*, I. The correspondence between them, preliminary to our discussion of the meaning of these seven kinds of efficient cause, is herewith given: [1]

Ethics, I		*Short Treatise*, I, 3
Prop. XVI	7.	Universal cause
Prop. XVI Corol. 1	1.	Emanative, productive, active, efficient cause [2]
Prop. XVI Corol. 2	4.	Cause through himself (essential)
Prop. XVI Corol. 3 ...	6.	First, initial cause
Prop. XVII Corol. 1 ...	5.	Principal cause
Prop. XVII Corol. 2 ...	3.	Free cause
Prop. XVIII	2.	Immanent cause

However, while Spinoza has borrowed the scheme and terminology of the classification from Burgersdijck, he has made free use of it for his own purpose. The causes enumerated in this list are what the mediaevals themselves would have ascribed to God, but when used by Spinoza there is an implication that these causes are more truly applicable to his own conception of God's causality than to theirs.

But let us follow out this implied contention of Propositions XVI–XVIII that only God as conceived by Spinoza is in the true sense a *universal, efficient, essential, first, principal, free,* and *immanent* cause.

Beiträge zur Philosophie, Vol. III, p. 317 (Berlin, 1867); Ch. Sigwart, *Benedict de Spinoza's kurzer Tractat* (2nd ed.), p. 171; A. Wolf, *Spinoza's Short Treatise*, pp. 190 ff.

[1] Cf. Sigwart, *op. cit.*, p. 172. Sigwart seems to have overlooked the correspondence of Prop. 16 and Corollary 1 of Prop. 16 in the *Ethics* to the 7th and 1st classifications in the *Short Treatise*.

[2] *uytvloejende, daarstellende, doende, werkende.*

To the mediaevals, from the principle that God is a pure simple form and that "a simple element can produce only a simple thing" it appeared as an inevitable conclusion that, if necessary emanation was to be the theory explaining the origin of the world, the direct emanation from God must be one simple Intelligence and that matter must therefore emerge subsequently in the process.[1] According to this view, while God may indeed be considered as indirectly the cause of all the variety of material things, He is directly only the cause of one simple thing. In this sense, then, God is really what was called a *particular* cause as contrasted with a *universal* cause, for the latter kind of cause meant the ability to produce various things.[2] Thus while the mediaevals would undoubtedly insist upon calling God a universal cause,[3] they could not really call Him a universal cause in the strict sense of the term. But to Spinoza, since God is the direct cause of both extended modes and thinking modes, God can truthfully be called a universal cause.

Furthermore, Spinoza's God can be called a universal cause with more right than the God of the mediaevals for still another reason. Though the mediaevals believed like Spinoza that God is infinite, still they did not believe, for reasons we shall discuss later, that God ever did or ever will create all the infinite things which He has in His mind and which might be created.[4] The world is finite as contrasted with God who is infinite. Their God therefore was a *particular* and not a *universal* cause, since He did not create everything that was in His mind. But to Spinoza, just as from the two known attributes arise the known modes of the world, so also from the infinite attributes, which are unknown to us but which

[1] *Moreh Nebukim*, I, 22.   [2] *Short Treatise*, I, 3, § 2 (7).
[3] Cf. quotation from Thomas Aquinas, above, p. 254, n. 2.
[4] Cf. below, pp. 314 ff. and 411 ff.

exist and are conceived as an idea in the infinite intellect of
God, arise an infinite number of modes unknown to us.[1] The
world is as infinite as God, though only two of its modes are
known to us, and God therefore is a universal cause in the
true sense of the term. This is what lies behind Proposition
XVI. It is a denial of the mediaeval view that the world
is finite and not the fullest expression of God's being. If
the world were finite, he argues, then God could be called
only a particular cause and not a universal cause. But the
world is not finite, for "from the necessity of the divine
nature infinite numbers of things in infinite ways (that is
to say, all things which can be conceived by the infinite intellect) must follow" (Prop. XVI). Hence God can be truly
called a universal cause.

But in what manner do the modes follow from God? In
the Middle Ages it was said that they follow from God by
the process of emanation, and emanation was defined as a
special kind of efficient causation which applies exclusively
to the action of an immaterial agent upon a material object.[2]
"Inasmuch as it has been demonstrated that God is incorporeal and has also been established that the universe is His
work and that He is its efficient cause . . . we say that the
universe has been created by divine emanation and that
God is the emanative cause of everything that comes into
being within it."[3] God then is called by the mediaevals
the efficient cause only in a restricted sense, in the sense of
emanative cause. But to Spinoza, that distinction between
the act of a corporeal agent and the act of an incorporeal
agent does not exist. He therefore declares unqualifiedly
that "God is the efficient cause,"[4] that is to say, the efficient
cause in its general unrestricted sense. In the Short Treatise

---

[1] Cf. Epistolae 63, 64, and 66.
[3] Ibid.
[2] Moreh Nebukim, II, 12.
[4] Ethics, I, Prop. 16, Corol. 1.

he makes his point still clearer when he says that God can be called indifferently the "emanative," "productive," "active," or "efficient" cause, all of which "we regard as one and the same, because they involve each other." [1]

Probably the mediaevals themselves would subscribe to Spinoza's next statement that "God is cause through himself (*per se*, essentially), and not through that which is accidental (*per accidens*)." [2] But still, since the world of which they maintain God is the cause is unlike God in nature, God being immaterial and the world being material, then, despite their protestations, God must be considered not as an essential cause but as an accidental cause, for one of the meanings of essential cause, and the one which Spinoza has found in Bergersdijck and Heereboord, is that the cause produces something of its own kind. When the cause produces something which is not of its own kind, it is called accidental cause.[3] Consequently, since according to the mediaevals the world which was produced by God is not of His kind, for God is immaterial and the world is material, God then is only an accidental cause.

Similarly the mediaevals would whole-heartedly subscribe to Spinoza's fourth characterization of divine causality contained in his declaration that "God is absolutely the first cause." [4] In fact, God has been called the first cause ever since Aristotle. But behind this statement of Spinoza's that God is the "absolutely" first cause there is an unexpressed argument that the mediaevals could not with full right call

[1] *Short Treatise*, I, 3, § 2 (1).

[2] *Ethics*, I, Prop. 16, Corol. 2.

[3] Cf. Burgersdijck, *Institutiones Logicae*, Lib. I, Cap. XVII, Theor. XV–XVI; Heereboord, *Hermeneia Logica*, Lib. I, Cap. XVII, Quaest. XVI: "Similiter, cum animal sibi simile generat, dicitur causa per se generati animalis; cum generat monstrum, dicitur causa per accidens."

[4] *Ethics*, I, Prop. 16, Corol. 3.

their God an absolutely first cause. In the source used by
Spinoza, a distinction is made between two kinds of first
causes. One is called the absolutely first cause (*causa absolute prima*) and the other is called a first cause in its own kind
(*causa prima suo genere*). An absolutely first cause is described not only as a cause which is the first in a series of
causes, but also as one which is in no way dependent upon
anything else.[1] In fact, absolute independence of anything
else, whether external to God or within Him, is what the
mediaevals themselves insist upon when they describe God
as the first cause and as necessary existence.[2] It is with this
in mind that Spinoza argues here against the emanationists.
He seems to say: Inasmuch as according to the emanationists
God could not produce matter directly by himself but only
through His emanations, i.e., the Intelligences, God is dependent, as it were, on his own emanations. He is therefore
not an absolutely first cause. It is only Spinoza's God who
produces everything directly by the necessity of His own
nature and is in no way whatsoever dependent upon anything
else that can be rightfully called an absolutely first cause.

II. GOD AS FREE CAUSE

Besides *universal, efficient, essential,* and *first,* God is also a
principal and *free* cause.[3] With these Spinoza introduces
another one of his fundamental departures from mediaeval
philosophy. On the whole, Spinoza's views on the problem
of freedom may be treated under three headings: 1. The
definition of the terms "free" and "necessary." 2. How

---

[1] Cf. Burgersdijck, *Institutiones Logicae,* Lib. I, Cap. XVII, Theor. XXIX,
§§ 1–2; Heereboord, *Hermeneia Logica,* Lib. I, Cap. XVII, Quaest. XXVI; *idem.
Meletemata Philosophica, Disputationes ex Philosophia Selectae,* Vol. II, Disp. XVII.

[2] Cf. *Maḳaṣid al-Falasifah,* II, ii, 5–6 (pp. 139–140): "He [who is described as
having necessary existence] does not depend upon anything else." Cf. also *Emunah
Ramah,* II, 1 (p. 47), quoted below, Vol. II, p. 40.

[3] *Ethics,* I, Prop. 17 and Corol. 1–2; *Short Treatise,* I, 3, § 2 (3–5).

God is free. 3. How man is not free. Here in our interpretation of Proposition XVII we shall deal only with the first two topics, leaving the third topic to be discussed in our interpretation of the next group of propositions.

His own understanding of the terms free and necessary is made quite clear by Spinoza himself: "That thing is called free which exists from the necessity of its own nature alone, and is determined to action by itself alone. That thing, on the other hand, is called necessary, or rather compelled, which by another is determined to existence and action in a fixed and prescribed manner." [1] But how did Spinoza come to this definition? We shall try briefly and simply to explain the metaphysical and philological reasoning which had led Spinoza to formulate this definition.

The problem of freedom is sometimes discussed by the mediaevals as a problem of possibility. The question whether anything is absolutely free is thus stated as a question whether anything is absolutely possible. In Crescas, for instance, the headings over the chapters on freedom read: "An exposition of the view of him who believes that the nature of possibility exists," "An exposition of the view of him who believes that the nature of possibility does not exist." [2] There is a suggestion of this method of formulating the problem of freedom in the *Short Treatise* where in the chapter on "Divine Predestination" Spinoza raises the question "whether there are in nature any accidental things, that is to say, whether there are any things which may happen and may also not happen." [3] The phraseology used here by Spinoza reflects the Aristotelian definitions of the accidental and the possible. The former is reproduced by Crescas as that which "has in itself the possibility of being and of

<hr>

[1] *Ethics*, I, Def. 7.   [2] *Or Adonai*, II, v, 1–2.
[3] *Short Treatise*, I, 6, § 2.

not being"; [1] the latter is given by Aristotle himself as that which "may either be or not be." [2]

We have already called attention on several occasions to the mediaeval threefold division of possibility and necessity, namely, (1) possible *per se*, (2) possible *per se* but necessary in consideration of its cause, and (3) necessary *per se*. We have also called attention to the fact that Spinoza has made use of this threefold classification and that he has designated the possible *per se* by the term contingent and the possible *per se* but necessary in consideration of its cause by the general term possible. [3] Now, the question raised by the mediaevals through Crescas whether the nature of the possible exists really means whether pure possibility, i.e., possibility *per se*, exists. Crescas' answer is in the negative. There is nothing in nature which can be described as pure possibility, for for everything a cause can be found. So actually nothing in nature is possible *per se*; everything which is possible *per se* is necessary in consideration of its cause. Possible *per se* does not represent an actual thing in nature; it is only a logical distinction *secundum quid*. [4] It is this conception of the possible *per se* as merely a logical distinction *secundum quid* that must have led Spinoza to designate it by the term contingent, which, in Spinoza's definition of it, appears also as purely a logical distinction in things. According to this view, then, actually existent things fall only under two divisions, those which are necessary by their cause and those which are necessary by their own nature. These two meanings of necessary, in fact, correspond to two out of the five meanings that Aristotle attaches to the term. That which

[1] Or *Adonai*, I, i, 8. Cf. my *Crescas' Critique of Aristotle*, p. 249 and p. 551, n. 2; *Physics*, VIII, 5, 256b, 9–10.

[2] *Metaphysics*, IX, 8, 1050b, 11–12. Cf. *Crescas' Critique of Aristotle*, p. 551, n. 3.

[3] *Cogitata Metaphysica*, I, 3; *Ethics*, IV, Defs. 3–4. Cf. above, pp. 188 ff.

[4] Cf. *Or Adonai*, II, v, 3: . . . בבחינת . . . מה בצד.

is necessary by its cause corresponds to necessary in the sense which Aristotle describes as compulsory,[1] and that which is necessary by its own nature corresponds to necessary in the sense which Aristotle describes as that which cannot be otherwise.[2] What Spinoza does, then, in his definition of freedom in the *Ethics* is to simplify the terminology and to call that which is necessary by its own nature free and to call that which is necessary by its cause necessary or compelled. "True freedom," says Spinoza elsewhere, "is only, or no other than [the status of being] the first cause."[3] This on the whole corresponds to the mediaeval definition of freedom. "Free will," says Judah ha-Levi, "*qua* free will, has no compulsory cause."[4] Similarly Crescas defines free will as the ability "to will and not to will without an external cause."[5]

This definition of freedom is applied by Spinoza to God in Proposition XVII and its two Corollaries. Starting out in the proposition itself with the statement that God's action flows from His own nature and is without compulsion, he further explains in the first corollary that the compulsion comes neither from without nor from within Him, that is to say, God is what is generally called a *principal* cause, and concludes in the second corollary that only God is a *free* cause. All these would on their positive side seem to be merely a reassertion of views commonly held by mediaevals. But as elsewhere, Spinoza's statements here have also a negative side and are intended to emphasize something in opposition to the mediaevals. Fortunately, in this case, we do not have to guess what it is that he wants to emphasize and negate. He makes it clear for us in his Scholium.

---

[1] *Metaphysics*, V, 5, 1015a, 26.
[2] *Ibid.*, 34.
[3] *Short Treatise*, I, 4, § 5.
[4] *Cuzari*, V, 20.
[5] *Or Adonai*, II, v, 3 (p. 48b).

On the whole, the mediaevals would have subscribed to Spinoza's proposition that "God acts from the laws of His own nature only, and is compelled by no one." [1] In fact, in the Hymn of Unity, which is incorporated in the Jewish liturgy, we find a statement that reads almost like it: "Thou wast not compelled to perform Thy work, nor wast Thou in need of any help." [2] But still the mediaevals considered God's causality as an act of will, power, or intelligence. Will, power, and intelligence are the three terms which are generally used by mediaevals in connection with creation,[3] with the proviso, of course, that all the three are identical in God.[4] It is by means of will or power or intelligence that the mediaevals find themselves able to resolve all the difficulties about divine causality. The mediaeval philosophers, for instance, admit that God cannot "produce a square the diagonal of which is equal to its side, or similar other impossibilities." [5] Still when the question is raised that "to say of God that He can produce a thing from nothing is . . . the same as if we were to say that He could . . . produce a square the diagonal of which is equal to its side, or similar impossibilities," [6] or "what has made God create at one time rather than at another," [7] they answer to this question that "He willed it so; or, His wisdom decided so." [8]

As against this, Spinoza opposes his own view of causality, and in the process of unfolding it he emphasizes, allusively, to be sure, the distinction between his view and theirs. The

---

[1] *Ethics*, I, Prop. 17.

[2] *Shir ha-Yiḥud*, V.

[3] *Emunot we-De'ot*, II, 4; *Cuzari*, V, 18, 7–10; *Moreh Nebukim*, II, 18, Second Method. Cf. above, p. 204.

[4] *Moreh Nebukim*, II, 53. Cf. above, p. 155.

[5] *Ibid.*, II, 13, and cf. I, 75, 1; I, 75, 5; III, 15; *Emunot we-De'ot*, II, 13.

[6] *Moreh Nebukim*, II, 13, Second Theory

[7] *Ibid.*, II, 14. Cf. above, p. 100.

[8] *Ibid.*, II, 25. Cf. above, pp. 100 f.

fundamental difference, out of which all others arise, is his elimination of will and design from the causality of God. This is what he means when he says in the first corollary of Proposition XVII that "there is no cause, either external to God or within Him, which can excite Him to act." By a cause within God he means will and design. With the elimination of will and design from the nature of God, creation *ex nihilo* becomes an impossible act, as impossible as any of the things which the mediaevals themselves considered impossible, such, for instance, as the assumption that "God could bring about that it should not follow from the nature of a triangle that its three angles should be equal to two right angles." [1]

Then Spinoza takes up another point.

One of the reasons that led the mediaevals to attribute to God intelligence and will was the utter absurdity of the opposite alternative, for to deny them of Him would imply an imperfection in His nature. God, according to them, must be "free from imperfections," [2] and as a result of this, "we must remove from God anything that looks like an imperfection in Him." [3] Abraham Herrera, in his unpublished *Puerta del Cielo*, of which a printed Hebrew version has existed since 1655, puts the matter in the following way: "The eternal and omnipotent God, whom we call the First Cause, acts not from the necessity of His nature but by the counsel of His intellect, which is of the highest order, and by the choice of His free will," [4] for "to an Agent who is first and most perfect we must attribute that kind of action which on account of its superiority and priority excels any other kind of action; and that is the voluntary kind of action, for it is

---

[1] *Ethics*, I, Prop. 17, Schol.   [2] *'Ikkarim*, I, 15; *Moreh Nebukim*, I, 35.
[3] *'Ikkarim*, II, 7.
[4] *Sha'ar ha-Shamayim*, III, 6, beginning.

more perfect than all the natural and necessary actions and does in fact constitute their entelechy and the realization of their perfection." [1] It is undoubtedly to Herrera that Spinoza refers when he says: "I know, indeed, that there are many who think themselves able to demonstrate that intellect of the highest order and freedom of will both pertain to the nature of God, for they say that they know nothing more perfect which they can attribute to Him than that which is the chief perfection in ourselves." [2]

But Spinoza goes still further in his criticism of Herrera.

Herrera touches upon a question which had been constantly raised in the Cabala, namely, whether God could create the infinite number of things which are in His intellect or whether His power of creation was limited to that which He has created. The question is stated by Moses Cordovero as follows: "We shall raise a question by which some of the adepts in Cabala have been perplexed, namely, whether the Infinite, the King of Kings, the Holy One, blessed be He, has it in His power to emanate more than these Ten Sefirot or not, if we may express ourselves in this way. The question is a legitimate one, for inasmuch as it is of the nature of His benevolence to overflow outside himself, and inasmuch as it is not beyond His power, it may be properly asked why He has not produced thousands of millions of emanations. It should indeed be possible for Him to produce many times Ten Sefirot in the same way as He has produced this world." [3] In the discussion of this question by Herrera two points are made: First, that "if God had acted from His own nature and by necessity, He would have inevitably produced everything that is in His power, which would be infinite." [4] Sec-

---

[1] *Ibid.*, Argument IV.   [2] *Ethics*, I, Prop. 17, Schol.
[3] *Pardes Rimmonim*, II, 7.
[4] *Sha'ar ha-Shamayim*, III, 6, Argument III.

ond, since God has created by will and design, He has purposely created only a part of that which is in His intellect,
in order to be able to create other and more perfect things.
"We shall say briefly, that it is because He does not act by
the necessity of His infinite nature that the Infinite, blessed
be He, even though He is infinite, has not brought into existence or created an infinite number of things in an infinite
time, which He comprehends and includes in His immovable
eternity, nor has He produced them in infinite superficies,
positions, and places, into which His infinite power and
magnitude extend. He acts only by the freedom of His will
and purpose, and it is because of this that He has brought
into existence and created finite things in finite times and
in finite places, and to these things and into these things only
has He extended himself, so that He might be superior to
His creatures not only in an infinite degree of perfection but
also in infinite power, and if He ever wills He may create
other things more excellent and greater and in more suitable,
wider, and longer places and positions, all of which He comprehends and includes most perfectly in His eternity and
greatness. This view offers more easily [than any other view]
a vindication of the infinite power and nature of the First
Cause, namely, the view we have maintained that for every
one of the created things, however excellent it may be, He
is able to produce something more excellent." [1] A similar
argument is reproduced by Spinoza in the *Cogitata Metaphysica*. "If God acts from necessity, He must have created
a duration than which no greater can be conceived." [2]

That Spinoza had in mind the statements we have just reproduced from Herrera is evident from his following summary
of the views of his opponents: " But although they conceive

[1] *Ibid.*, III, 7.
[2] *Cogitata Metaphysica*, II, 10.

God as actually possessing the highest intellect, they nevertheless do not believe that He can bring about that all those
things should exist which are actually in His intellect, for
they think that by such a supposition they would destroy
His power. If He had created, they say, all things which are
in His intellect, He could have created nothing more, and this,
they believe, does not accord with God's omnipotence; so
then they prefer to consider God as indifferent to all things,
and creating nothing excepting that which He has decreed
to create by a certain absolute will." [1] Spinoza's own criticism of this solution of the problem is that it virtually sacri-
fices God's power in order to retain His perfection. "Therefore, in order to make a perfect God, they are compelled to
make Him incapable of doing all those things to which His
power extends, and anything more absurd than this, or more
opposed to God's omnipotence, I do not think can be
imagined." [2]

The mediaevals, after having gone to all the trouble of
ascribing to God intelligence and will, explain them away as
homonymous terms. They say "there is nothing in common
between His essence and our essence. . . . There is only
a resemblance between them in name, but in essence they
are different." [3] Similarly of will they say that "the term will
is homonymously used of man's will and of the will of God,
there being no comparison between God's will and that of
man." [4] Spinoza restates this view in great detail in the
Scholium to Proposition XVII, in the course of which he
explains the homonymous use of terms by the illustration of
the term "dog," which is used for "the celestial constellation
of the Dog and the animal which barks." [5] This illustration

---

[1] *Ethics*, I, Prop. 17, Schol.   [2] *Ibid.* Cf. below, pp. 411 ff.
[3] *Moreh Nebukim*, III, 20.   [4] *Ibid.*, II, 18, Second Method.
[5] A similar illustration is mentioned in *Cogitata Metaphysica*, II, 11.

is found in Philo [1] and in Maimonides and Averroes.[2]   The
introduction here on the part of Spinoza of the discussion
about the homonymity of will and intellect when applied
to God, which, as we have seen, is nothing but a restatement
of the common mediaeval view, would seem to be entirely
superfluous unless we assume that he wanted to make use
of it afterwards as a refutation of the mediaevals in their
attribution of will and intellect to God.   However, no such
refutation occurs in the Scholium.   Probably what Spinoza
meant to convey to the reader, though he does not definitely
say so, is that since intellect and will are to be applied to
God only homonymously, they are meaningless terms, and
consequently God's activity might as well be described as
following from the necessity of His nature.   This in fact
is what he argues in one of his letters: "Since . . . it is
admitted universally and unanimously, that the will of God
is eternal and has never been different, therefore they must
also admit (mark this well) that the world is the necessary
effect of the divine nature. . . .   For if you ask them whether
the divine will does not differ from the human will, they
will reply that the former has nothing in common with the
latter except in name;   moreover they mostly admit that
God's will, understanding, essence or nature are one and
the same thing." [3]   Spinoza's contention in this passage that
if the will of God is eternal then the world must be admitted
to be the necessary effect of the divine nature reflects Maimonides' elaborate arguments on the incompatibility of the
assumption of an eternal will of God and the belief in creation by design. [4]

[1] *De Plantatione Noe*, XXXVII, 155.

[2] Maimonides, *Millot ha-Higgayon*, Ch. 13; Averroes, *Epitome of the Isagoge*
(*Mabo* in *Kol Meleket Higgayon*, p. 2b). Cf. note in Klatzkin's Hebrew translation
of the *Ethics* (*Torat ha-Middot*), p. 348.

[3] Epistola 54.   [4] *Moreh Nebukim*, II, 21.

The opposite of will and design, in the Middle Ages, is not
only necessity but also chance. Thus Maimonides, in classifying the various theories of creation, mentions in opposition to intelligent creation not only the Aristotelian theory
of necessity but also the Epicurean view of accident and
chance.[1] The difference between chance on the one hand,
and will and necessity on the other, is that chance denies
the existence of a cause at all in creation, whereas will and
necessity both assume the existence of a cause, though each
conceives the cause to act in a different way. "But it would
be quite useless to mention the opinions of those who do not
recognize the existence of God, but believe that the existing
state of things is the result of accidental combination and
separation of the elements and that there is none that rules
or determines the order of the existing things."[2] Spinoza
similarly tries to differentiate between chance and necessity
in one of his letters and makes the interesting observation
that if God is assumed to act by a will whose laws are unknown to us, His activity really amounts to chance: "This
already impels me . . . briefly to explain my opinion on the
question whether the world was created by chance. My
answer is that, as it is certain that Fortuitous and Necessary
are two contrary terms, it is also clear that he who asserts
that the world is the necessary effect of the divine nature
also absolutely denies that the world was made by chance;
he, however, who asserts that God could have refrained from
creating the world is affirming, albeit in other words, that it
was made by chance."[3] So also in another letter Spinoza
asks his correspondent: "Tell me, I pray, whether you have
seen or read any philosophers who hold the opinion that the

---

[1] *Ibid.*, II, 13 and 20; cf. *Emunot we-De'ot*, I, 3, Ninth Theory; *Cuzari*, V, 20.
[2] *Moreh Nebukim*, II, 13.
[3] Epistola 54.

world was made by chance, that is, in the sense in which you understand it, namely, that God, in creating the world, had set himself a definite aim, and yet transgressed His own decree." [1] The implication of these statements is, as is quite evident, that the attribution of will to God really amounts to the denial of causality and to the explanation of the rise of things by chance.

III. The Meaning of Immanent Cause

His denial of chance or of causelessness is reaffirmed by Spinoza on several occasions in a positive way, as, for instance, when he says that "of every existing thing there is some certain cause by reason of which it exists." [2] He furthermore defines the cause of a thing by the statement that "if this [cause] did not exist it were impossible that the thing should exist," [3] which is reminiscent of Crescas' statement in his definition of a cause that "should the cause be conceived not to exist the effect could not be conceived to exist." [4] Now, causes, according to Aristotle, are either external (ἐκτός) to the thing [5] or present (ἐνυπάρχοντα) within the thing. [6] So also Spinoza on several occasions asserts that "we must look for this cause in the thing or outside the thing," [7] and on several other occasions he speaks of external and internal causes. [8]

What these internal and external causes are needs some explanation. Aristotle himself designates the material and formal causes as internal, whereas the efficient cause is de-

---

[1] Epistola 56.

[2] *Ethics*, I, Prop. 8, Schol.; cf. Epistola 34; *Short Treatise*, I, 6, § 2.

[3] *Short Treatise*, I, 6, § 4.

[4] Or *Adonai*, I, i, 3. Cf. my *Crescas' Critique of Aristotle*, p. 221.

[5] *Metaphysics*, XII, 4, 1070b, 23.   [6] *Ibid.*, 22.

[7] *Ethics*, I, Prop. 8, Schol. 2; *Short Treatise*, I, 6, § 4; Epistola 34.

[8] *Ethics*, I, Prop. 11, Schol.; III, Prop. 30, Schol.; *Ethics*, III, Affectuum Definitiones, 24, Expl.; Epistolae 34 and 60.

cribed by him as external,[1] But inasmuch as the efficient
cause is said by Aristotle to be sometimes the same as the
formal cause,[2] the efficient cause may thus according to him
be both an internal and external cause. Although Aristotle
does not give any concrete examples of what he means by
external and internal causes, such examples may be gathered
from his own writings as well as from the writings of his
followers.

Of an external cause the following are two examples:

First, a physical object which is spatially external to another physical object. Thus Maimonides, drawing upon
Aristotle, says that "everything must needs have a mover,
which mover may be either outside the object moved, as,
e.g., the case of a stone set in motion by the hand, or within
the object moved, as, e.g., the body of a living being," which
is moved by its soul.[3] In a passage corresponding to this
Aristotle says that "of those things which are moved essentially, some are moved by themselves (ὑφ' αὑτοῦ, i.e., by
an internal cause) and others by something else", [4] and later,
in explanation of things which are moved by something else,
he says: "Thus, a staff moves a stone, and is moved by a
hand, which is moved by a man." [5]

Second, an incorporeal being, like God, causing motion in
a corporeal object. In this case, says Maimonides, the term
"external" [6] is to be taken in the sense of "separate," [7] that
is to say, separate from body (χωριστὸς τοῦ σώματος) or incorporeal.

Similarly of an internal cause two examples may be found.

---

[1] *Metaphysics*, XII, 4, 1070b, 22 ff.   [2] *Physics*, II, 7, 198a, 24–26.
[3] *Moreh Nebukim*, II, Introduction, Prop. 17.
[4] *Physics*, VIII, 4, 254b, 12–14.   [5] *Ibid.*, VIII, 5, 256a, 6–8.
[6] חוץ, خارج = ἐκτός.
[7] *Moreh Nebukim*, II, 1: נבדל, مفارق = χωριστός[2].

First, the soul which exists in the body and is inseparable from the body and is the cause of its motion. We have already quoted above a statement from Maimonides where the soul is called an internal cause of motion. In a corresponding passage Aristotle similarly illustrates those things which contain in themselves the principle of motion by the example of the motion of an animal.[1]

Second, universal concepts such as genus with reference to species and both of them with reference to the individual essence. Genus and species combined make up a definition and are therefore related to the essence defined as cause to effect, for a good definition, according to Aristotle, must not only set forth the fact but it should also contain (ἐνυπάρχειν) and present the cause.[2] This Aristotelian view is implied in Maimonides' contention that God cannot be defined by genus and species on the ground that "there are no previous causes to His existence by which He could be defined."[3] Furthermore, since a definition according to Aristotle is of the form,[4] it may be called a formal or internal cause. It is to be noted that Aristotle uses the same term ἐνυπάρχειν in describing both the nature of the causality of the definition and the nature of the cause which he calls internal (ἐνυπάρχων). It is evident then that by internal cause he does not mean only a cause which inheres in the effect, but also a cause in which the effect inheres. The essential characteristic of an internal cause therefore is the fact that it is inseparable from its effect, either as the soul is inseparable from the body or as the definition is inseparable from the definiendum, for, as says Aristotle, the whole is in its

---

[1] Physics, VIII, 4, 254b, 15–16.

[2] De Anima, II, 2, 413a, 15. Cf. Analytica Posteriora, II, 10, 93b, 38 ff.

[3] Moreh Nebukim, I, 52. Cf. Munk, Guide des Égarés, I, p. 190, n. 3; Friedländer, Guide of the Perplexed, I, p. 178, n. 2.

[4] Metaphysics, VII, 11, 1036a, 28–29.

parts and the genus is in the species just as the parts are in the whole and the species is in the genus.[1]

Now, in the Middle Ages we meet with a contrast between the terms *transiens* and *immanens* in such expressions as *actio transiens* and *actio immanens* or *causa transiens* and *causa immanens*.[2] These two terms reflect Aristotle's external (ἐκτός) cause and internal (ἐνυπάρχων) cause. That this is so we have the testimony of Spinoza himself, who says: "immanent (*inblyvende*) or internal (*innerlyke*) cause (which is all the same to me)."[3] The term *immanens*, therefore, by analogy with Aristotle's term ἐνυπάρχων, describes not only a cause which resides in the effect but also a cause in which the effect resides, for the essential meaning of an immanent cause, as we have said, is its inseparability from its effect. The term *transcendens*, however, does not mean in the Middle Ages the same as *transiens*. It means to be logically greater or more general, especially to be logically greater and more general than the ten categories so as not to be contained under them.[4] In this sense it is used in the enumeration of the so-called *transcendentales* which are referred to by Spinoza.[5] The term *transcendens* is thus neither the synonym of *transiens* nor the opposite of *immanens*. In fact, in the case of an immanent cause of the second kind we have mentioned, i.e., immanent in the sense in which the genus is the immanent cause of the species, the cause, though immanent, may also be called transcendent in so far as it is more general than its effect. The conception of a

[1] Cf. *Physics*, IV, 3, 210a, 17 and 19.

[2] Cf. R. Eucken, *Geschichte der philosophischen Terminologie*, p. 204.

[3] *Short Treatise*, II, 26, § 7 (*Opera*, I, p. 110, ll. 22–23).

[4] Cf. W. Hamilton, *Lectures on Logic*, I, p. 198 (ed. 1866); C. Prantl, *Geschichte der Logik*, III, p. 245; R. Eucken, *Geschichte und Kritik der Grundbegriffe der Gegenwart*, pp. 79–80.

[5] *Ethics*, II, Prop. 40, Schol. 1; *Cogitata Metaphysica*, I, 6. Cf. below, Vol. II, pp. 123 f.

transcendent immanent cause is thus not a contradiction in terms.

In the light of this discussion, when Spinoza says here in Proposition XVIII that "God is the *causa immanens* and not *transiens* of all things," we may ask ourselves in which of their two senses does he use the terms *immanens* and *transiens*. It is quite clear that when he denies that God is a *causa transiens* of all things he means to say that God is neither a spatially external cause of all things nor a separate immaterial cause of all things. It is equally clear that when he affirms that God is the *causa immanens* of all things he does not mean that God is in all things after the analogy of the soul in the body in the Aristotelian manner of expres sion,[1] though among the Stoics God's immanence in the world is expressed in terms of His being the soul, the mind, or the reason of the world, and hence of His being in the world only as a part of it.[2] Proposition XIV of *Ethics*, I, where Spinoza says that all things are in God, and similarly the two Dialogues in the *Short Treatise*, where he likewise says that all things are in God as parts are in the whole, make it quite clear that the immanence of God does not mean that God is in all things as the soul is in the body, but rather that all things are in God as the less universal is in the more universal or, to use Spinoza's own expression, as the parts are in the

---

[1] The general misunderstanding of Spinoza's description of God as an immanent cause by taking it in the sense that God is a cause who resides in His effects after the analogy of the soul in the body occurs already in John Colerus' biography of Spinoza, published in Dutch in 1705: "In order to understand him, we must consider that . . . the immanent cause acts inwardly, and is confined without acting outwardly. Thus when a man's soul thinks of, or desires something, it is or remains in that thought or desire, without going out of it, and is the immanent cause thereof. In the same manner, the God of Spinoza is the cause of the universe wherein He is, and He is not beyond it." (English translation: *The Life of Benedict de Spinoza*, London, 1706, reprinted at The Hague, 1906, pp. 67–68.)

[2] Cf. Zeller, *Die Philosophie der Griechen*, III, 1, pp. 140–142; p. 151 (4th edition).

whole,[1] Spinoza's statement that God is the immanent cause
of all things is thus not an assertion that God is identical
with the aggregate totality of all things; it is only a denial
that God is the external and separable and hence immaterial
cause of all things. Inseparability from the effect, as we have
seen, is the essential characteristic of Aristotle's internal
cause. Spinoza makes the meaning of this term clear when
he defines the immanent cause negatively as that "which by
no means produces anything outside itself"[2] and as that in
which "the effect remains united with its cause in such a
way that together they constitute a whole."[3] When Spinoza
therefore says that all things are in God he means exactly
the same thing as when Aristotle says that man exists in
animal as a species in a genus.[4] And when he further says
that all things are in God as parts are in the whole he means
again exactly the same thing as when Aristotle says that the
"part is in the whole"[5] and as when Burgersdijck says that
"animal is a whole *per se* in respect to man and beast,"[6] that
is to say, the species man and beast exist in the genus animal
as parts in a whole. It is in this sense that God is the immanent cause of all things; He is their internal cause as the
genus is the internal cause of the species or the species of
the particulars and as the whole is the internal cause of its
parts. Now the universal, even though it does not exist
separately from the particulars, is not logically identical with
the sum of the particulars, for to Spinoza the universal is an
ens rationis, which means that it has a certain kind of conceptual existence, even though conceptual in the sense that it

---

[1] Cf. above, pp. 74 ff. Cf. also Epistola 32 to Oldenburg.

[2] *Short Treatise*, I, First Dialogue, § 12 (*Opera*, I, p. 30, ll. 24–25).

[3] *Ibid.*, Second Dialogue, § 3 (p. 31, ll. 20–22).

[4] *Physics*, IV, 3, 210a, 17–18   [5] *Ibid.*, 16.

[6] *Institutiones Logicae*, Lib. I, Cap. XIV, p. 52 (ed. Cambridge, 1680): "Animal
est totum [per se] respectu hominis et bestiae."

is *invented* by the mind, as we have shown in our discussion of his definition of attribute.[1] Consequently there is to be a corresponding conceptual distinction between God and the aggregate totality of modes. Being thus the immanent cause of all things in the sense that He is inseparable from them but still logically distinct from them, God may also be said to transcend them according to the old meaning of the term "transcendence," namely, that of being logically distinct and more general. With the totality of modes or what Spinoza calls the *facies totius universi* God is not identical; He is identical only with himself. With reference to the totality of modes God is therefore called an immanent cause, but with reference to himself He is called *causa sui*, which, as we have already shown,[2] means the denial of any kind of cause whatsoever, whether external or internal. This distinction implied in Spinoza's thought between one kind of whole, God, which transcends its parts and is their cause, and another kind of whole, the *facies totius universi*, which is the sum of its parts, is clearly stated by Proclus: "Every wholeness (ὁλότης) is either prior to parts or consists of parts. . . . A whole according to subsistence (καθ' ὕπαρξιν), therefore, is that which consists of parts, but a whole according to cause (κατ' αἰτίαν) is that which is prior to parts."[3]

But here a question may be raised. If God is related to the totality of modes as the universal to particulars or as the whole to the parts, then inasmuch as the universal as well as the whole has only conceptual existence, the existence of God which Spinoza has sought to establish is only a conceptual kind of existence, conceptual, presumably, in the sense of being *invented* by the mind. God is thus an *ens rationis*

---

[1] Cf. above, pp. 146 ff.   [2] Cf. above, p. 127.

[3] *Institutio Theologica*, LXVII (in *Plotini Enneades*, ed. Creuzer et Moser, Paris, 1855).

and not an *ens reale*. But this would seem to be contrary to the whole trend of Spinoza's proofs for the existence of God, which was to establish God as an *ens reale*.[1]

This question is raised by Spinoza himself in the First Dialogue in the *Short Treatise*. He puts it in the mouth of Desire. "Methinks," says Desire, "I see a very great confusion in this argument of yours; for, it seems you will have it that the whole must be something outside of or apart from its parts, which is truly absurd. For all philosophers are unanimous in saying that the whole is a second intention (*tweede kundigheid*), and that it is nothing in nature apart from human conception (*begrip*)."[2] The "second intention" is the scholastic *intentio secunda* which is applied to such universals as genus and species,[3] and what Desire is arguing is that God, who is said by Spinoza to be the whole, is nothing but an *ens rationis* or *intentio secunda* like a universal and God cannot therefore be, as Desire erroneously assumes Spinoza to say, "outside of or apart from its parts."

In his answer in the First Dialogue, speaking through the character of Reason, Spinoza first disclaims the imputation that he considers God as a whole "outside of or apart from its parts" by pointing out the difference between a transeunt and an immanent cause and by insisting that an immanent cause "by no means produces anything outside itself."

Then in the Second Dialogue, speaking through the character of Theophilus in answer to another question raised by Erasmus, he states that though the whole like the universal is an *ens rationis* there are two differences between them. First, "the universal (*algemeen*) results from various disconnected individuals, the whole, from various united in-

<hr>

[1] Cf. above, pp. 161 ff.

[2] *Short Treatise*, First Dialogue, § 10.

[3] Cf. R. P. M. Fernandez Garcia, *Lexicon Scholasticum Philosophico-Theologicum*, p. 361. Cf. below, Vol. II, p. 122.

dividuals." [1] Second, "the universal only comprises parts of the same kind, but the whole, parts both the same and different in kind." [2] These two differences, it may be remarked incidentally, reflect two of the several senses of the term whole discussed by Aristotle. Corresponding to Spinoza's description of the whole in the first difference, there is the following passage in Aristotle: "A whole (ὅλον) means . . . that which so contains the things it contains that they form a unity," in the sense of "making up the unity between them," as "the continuous and limited is a whole, when there is a unity consisting of several parts present in it." [3] Corresponding to Spinoza's description of the universal in the second difference, there is Aristotle's statement to the effect that the whole in the sense of the universal is said of a thing which comprises parts which are of the same kind and have common characteristics, "for universal (καθόλου), and, in short, that which is denominated as being a certain whole, are universal and a whole because they contain many things, are predicated of particulars, and are all one according to the predicate. Thus man, horse, and God are all of them one, because they are all living things." [4] Inasmuch as the whole and the universal despite their being both *entia rationis* are admitted by Spinoza to differ from one another on two points, we may also argue on behalf of Spinoza that this particular whole, namely God, though it may be called an *ens rationis* like any universal, differs from universals on still a third point, namely, that it is called an *ens rationis* only in the sense that its real existence can be *discovered* only by the mind, by the ontological proofs based upon the adequacy of the idea of God in our mind. In truth,

---

[1] *Short Treatise*, I, Second Dialogue, § 9.
[2] *Ibid.*
[3] *Metaphysics*, V, 26, 1023b, 27–28, 28–29, 32–33.
[4] *Ibid.*, 29–32.

however, God is an *ens reale*. Attributes, on the other hand, have no reality apart from God; they are said to be perceived by the intellect or the mind in the sense that they are *invented* by the mind.[1] Or, to make use of a modern distinction, God or substance or the whole is according to Spinoza a concrete or real universal, whereas attributes are according to him only abstract universals.

IV. God as Conscious Cause

Among the different terms describing God's causality which Spinoza has discussed, accepting some of them and rejecting others, the term "conscious" is not mentioned by him. We shall try to show that though Spinoza explicitly denies that God acts by will and design, insisting that He acts by the necessity of His own nature, he still admits that God is a conscious cause. In Aristotle as well as among the mediaeval philosophers, conscious causality by itself did not imply will and design, nor did it exclude necessity. Thus Aristotle's necessary activity of God, which was without design, was still a conscious sort of activity. The contemplation of himself is the activity which Aristotle ascribes to God.[2] This self-consciousness of God is furthermore described by Aristotle as an act of pleasure, for "the act of contemplation is what is most pleasant and best."[3] Still this conscious activity is a necessary sort of activity and is unaccompanied by will and design. Maimonides explains the difference between unconscious necessary activity and conscious necessary activity as follows: A cause is said to act by necessity and unconsciously when the effect follows from it "in the same manner as the shadow is caused by a body, or heat by fire, or light by the sun." A cause is said to act

---

[1] Cf. above, pp. 146 ff.   [2] *Metaphysics*, XII, 9, 1074b, 33-35.
[3] *Ibid.*, XII, 7, 1072b, 24.

by necessity but consciously when the effect is said to follow from it in the same way as "when we say that the existence of the intellect necessarily implies the existence of
the intelligible object, for the former is the efficient cause of
the latter in so far as it is an intelligible object." But
Maimonides goes further and explains that although Aristotle
admitted consciousness on the part of God, and ascribed to
Him a certain self-satisfaction with His activity, "we do not
call this design and it has nothing in common with design,"
inasmuch as "it is impossible for Him that He should wish
to be different." "For example, man is pleased, satisfied,
and delighted that he is endowed with eyes and hands, and
it is impossible that he should desire it to be otherwise, and
yet the eyes and hands which a man has are not the result of
his design, and it is not by his own determination that he
has certain properties and is able to perform certain actions."[1]

This would seem to be also the position of Spinoza. God
is a necessary cause acting without will and design but still
a conscious cause. Not only does Spinoza's theory of the
attribute of thought and his belief in the unity of nature
point to that conclusion,[2] but his description of the function
of that infinite mode of thinking as producing invariably
"an infinite or most perfect satisfaction"[3] is almost a verbal
reproduction of Aristotle's or Maimonides' characterization
of the consciousness of the activity of God. Indeed Spinoza
denies of God the emotions of joy and sorrow when he says
that "God is free from passions, nor is He affected with any
affect of joy or sorrow,"[4] but this merely means that the consciousness he ascribes to God must be unlike our own consciousness — a view which was commonly held by the
mediaevals. Indeed in the *Cogitata Metaphysica* he refers

---

[1] *Moreh Nebukim*, II, 20.   [2] Cf. below, Vol. II, pp. 13 ff. and p. 337.
[3] *Short Treatise*, I, 9, § 3.   [4] *Ethics*, V, Prop. 17. Cf. below, Vol. II, pp. 283 ff.

to "personality" (*personalitas*) as a term which theologians apply to God and dismisses it as something of which he is unable to form a clear and distinct concept. Still he makes it quite clear that God knows himself and that His understanding by which He knows himself does not differ from His will and power by which He created the world,[1] that is to say, God is conscious of himself, but His consciousness of himself does not imply design and purpose.

[1] *Cogitata Metaphysica*, II, 8. In connection with this attempt to solve the problem of the consciousness of Spinoza's God, compare the discussions in the following works: A. Trendelenburg, *Historische Beiträge zur Philosophie* (1855), II, pp. 59 ff.; C. Sigwart, *Spinoza's neuendeckter Tractat von Gott, dem Menschen und desen Glückseligkeit* (1866), pp. 94–95; M. Joël, *Zur Genesis der Lehre Spinoza's* (1871), pp. 13–17; G. Busolt, *Die Grundzüge der Erkenntnisztheorie und Metaphysik Spinozas* (1875), pp. 117 ff.; F. Pollock, *Spinoza* (1880), pp. 352 ff.; J. Martineau, *A Study of Spinoza* (1882), pp. 334 ff.; E. E. Powell, *Spinoza and Religion* (1906), pp. 47 ff.; E. Lasbax, *La Hiérarchie dans l'Univers chez Spinoza* (1919), pp. 187 ff.; H. Höffding, *Spinoza Ethica* (1924), pp. 49–50.

CHAPTER X

DURATION, TIME, AND ETERNITY

THE next group of propositions of Part I and the subsequent parts of the *Ethics* are strewn with references to eternity and duration. By way of general introduction we shall discuss here Spinoza's definitions of these two terms, and with them also his definition of time.

I. THE STORY OF DURATION

When Spinoza's contemporary Locke discovered that there is some reason in the general impression that duration, time, and eternity "have something very abstruse in their nature," he suggested a way out of the difficulty by tracing them right to "their originals," by which he meant, as he proceeded to explain, "sensation and reflection," which to him were the original sources of all our knowledge.[1] An equal abstruseness confronts one in reading the variety of statements in which Spinoza contrasts the terms duration, time, and eternity. In our attempt to clear up this abstruseness, we may perhaps equally follow Locke's advice to turn right to the originals of these terms — not indeed to the originals in the sense of what Spinoza considered as the sources of our knowledge, but rather to the originals in the sense of the literary sources on which Spinoza drew in his discussions of the meaning of these terms. Here no less than in the other problems which we have already examined Spinoza operated with terms and ideas which had been long in vogue in the philosophic literature with which he was acquainted, modi-

[1] Locke, *Essay Concerning Human Understanding*, II, 14, § 2.

fying them whenever he had reason to do so and turning
them to new uses in his own particular scheme of reasoning.
The task which we have set ourselves in this chapter, therefore, is to analyze briefly the historical background of the
meaning of duration, time, and eternity, to show that there
are certain common principles underlying all the mediaeval
discussions on the meaning of these terms, however differently expressed they may be in language and phraseology,
to collect all the historical strands, and out of them to weave
together Spinoza's conception of duration, time, and eternity.

In Plotinus' elaborate discussion on time there is a historical survey of all the views that make time dependent
upon motion. Among these he reproduces Aristotle's view on
time which in his paraphrase reads that "time is the number
or measure of motion." [1] The original definition of time by
Aristotle, in its *locus classicus*, reads in full that "time is
this, the number of motion according to prior and posterior."[2]
The addition of the term "measure" by Plotinus may be explained on the ground that the term number in the definition
is, according to Aristotle himself, not to be taken in its ordinary meaning,[3] and that the term measure is sometimes substituted by Aristotle for the term number.[4] Rejecting the
Aristotelian definition of time, Plotinus defines it as something independent of motion. Perhaps it will help us to
understand how time is conceived by him apart from motion if we recall that motion does not appear in the first
two of Plotinus' emanated stages of being, which in order of
priority are: (1) the Intelligence (νοῦς), (2) the universal
soul (ψυχὴ τοῦ κόσμου), and (3) the all-encircling celestial
sphere (περιφορά). Motion appears only in the sphere, but

---

[1] *Enneads*, III, vii, 8 (ed. Creuzer et Moser, Paris, 1855). For ed. Volkmann
(Leipzig, 1883) raise chapter numbers by one in all subsequent references to *Enneads*.
[2] *Physics*, IV, 11, 219b, 1-2.   [3] *Ibid.*, 4-9.   [4] *Ibid.*, IV, 12, 221b, 7.

time appears, according to Plotinus, in the universal soul. Repeating Plato's statement, which appears also in a modified form in Philo, that time is the image of eternity,[1] Plotinus identifies time with the life of the universal soul[2] in contradistinction to eternity, which is identified by him with the life of the Intelligence.[3] Now, the life of the universal soul has a certain kind of extension (διάστασις)[4] and succession (ἐφεξῆς).[5] It is varied (ἄλλη)[6] in its nature. It is a process of transition from one act of thought (διάνοια) to another,[7] the unity of which exists only by virtue of a certain kind of continuity (συνέχεια).[8] It is a continuous acquisition of existence (προσκτώμενον . . . ἐν τῷ εἶναι).[9] All these characterizations of the life of the universal soul are true also of time, which is identical with that life. It is "the life (ζωή) of the soul consisting in the movement by which she passes from one state of life (βίος) to another,"[10] or, it is "the length of the life" of the soul, "proceeding in equal and similar changes advancing noiselessly," and "possessing a continuity of energy" (συνεχὲς τὸ τῆς ἐνεργείας ἔχον).[11]

But this kind of time which proceeds "in equal and similar changes advancing noiselessly" cannot by itself become fixed and definite; it cannot be measured and divided into definite portions.[12] For time to be measured and divided there must be an external standard of measurement, which external standard is the movement of the all-encircling sphere. "So that if some one should say that the movement of the sphere,

---

[1] Timaeus 37D; Enneads, III, vii, Procemium; Philo, De Eo, Quis Rerum Divinarum Heres Sit, XXXIV, 165, and De Mutatione Nominum, XLVII, 267.

[2] Enneads, III, vii, 10.   [3] Ibid., III, vii, 2, end.

[4] Ibid., III, vii, 10 (p. 177, l. 29).

[5] Ibid. (l. 25).   [6] Ibid. (l. 28).

[7] Ibid. (l. 27).   [8] Ibid. (l. 42).

[9] Ibid. (l. 47).   [10] Ibid. (ll. 32–33).

[11] Ibid., III, vii, 11 (p. 178, ll. 3–4).

[12] Ibid. (ll. 30–31).

after a certain manner, measures time as much as possible, by its quantity indicating the corresponding quantity of time, which cannot in any other way be grasped or conceived, he indeed will not adduce an absurd explanation of time." [1] The time which we use, then, in our daily course of life is essentially the same as the time which is an image of eternity; it differs from it not in kind but only in degree, in that it is a certain definite portion of it, measured off by the movement of the sphere. Thus, in opposition to Aristotle, Plotinus maintains that time, i.e., the time which we use in our daily course of life, is only measured or made manifest by motion, but it is not generated by motion.[2] And in still another respect Plotinus differs from Aristotle. According to Aristotle, time is primarily defined as the measure of motion, though he declares that in a secondary sense it may also be said that time is measured by motion.[3] But according to Plotinus, time is primarily measured by motion. "Hence some philosophers have been induced to say that time is the measure of motion instead of saying that it is measured by motion." [4] Finally, it is Plotinus' contention that inasmuch as time is within the universal soul, the universe, which is said to move within the universal soul, may on that account also be said to move and to have its being within time.[5]

What we get out of this analysis of Plotinus' discussion of time is that there are two kinds of time. One is indefinite time; the other is definite time. Both of these kinds of time are genetically independent of motion. They are essentially the same: the life of the world soul and an image of eternity. But definite time has some connection with motion in so

---

[1] *Ibid.* (ll. 48–52).

[2] *Ibid.* (ll. 52–54).

[3] *Physics*, IV, 12, 220b, 14 16. Cf. Crescas' *Critique of Aristotle*, p. 646, n. 22.

[4] *Enneads*, III, vii, 12 (p. 179, ll. 21–23).

[5] *Ibid.*, III, vii, 10 (p. 177, ll. 21–23); 11 (p. 178, l. 26).

far as it is measured by it. The main contrasts between the
Aristotelian and the Plotinian definitions of definite time are
thus twofold: (1) according to Aristotle time is generated
by motion; according to Plotinus, time is only made manifest by motion; (2) according to Aristotle, time is the measure of motion; according to Plotinus, time is measured by
motion.

Plotinus, as will have been noticed, uses the same term
time for both definite time and indefinite time. But an enigmatic passage in the Encyclopaedia of the Iḥwan al-Ṣafa,[1]
which we are going to show to contain a formulation of Plotinus' definition of time, supplies us with a special term for
indefinite time.

The Iḥwan al-Ṣafa enumerate four definitions of time.
Two of them, the second and third in their enumeration,
read as follows: "It is also said that time is the number of
the motions of the celestial sphere; or, it is said that time is
a duration which is numbered by the motions of the celestial
sphere." [2] The first of these definitions is clearly the Aristotelian definition reproduced only in part, as in Plotinus, and
with the use only of the original term number. The second
definition, it will be noticed, is just the reverse of the first.
In the first, it is time which numbers motion; in the second,
it is motion which numbers time. The contrast, then, is just

[1] The development of the conception of duration in Arabic and Hebrew philosophic texts presented in the succeeding pages has already been discussed by me
on several occasions in the following places: "Note on Crescas' Definition of Time"
in the *Jewish Quarterly Review*, n. s., X (1919), pp. 1–17. This was revised,
amplified, and incorporated in the notes to Prop. XV in *Crescas' Critique of Aristotle*,
especially in note 9 on pp. 636–640 and in note 23 on pp. 651–658, and in the Introduction on pp. 93–98. It was also used by me in "Solomon Pappenheim on Time
and Space and His Relation to Locke and Kant" in *Jewish Studies in Memory of
Israel Abraham* (1927), pp. 426–440. The subject is presented here in revised, enlarged, and new form.

[2] Fr. Dieterici, *Die Naturanschauung und Naturphilosophie der Araber*, pp. 14–
15; Arabic text: *Die Abhandlungen der Ichwân Es-Safâ*, p. 35.

like the one made by Plotinus between his definition and that
of Aristotle. Again, like Plotinus this definition also implies
that there are two kinds of time, one indefinite and the other
definite, and that the indefinite time becomes definite by
the motion of the sphere. But more than Plotinus, this definition gives a special name to the indefinite time. It calls
it duration. If we assume then, as we are certainly justified
in doing, that the Iḫwan al-Ṣafa's definition is a brief formulation of Plotinus' lengthy discussion on time, then we may
restate Plotinus' conception of time as follows: The essence
of time is duration, which is independent of motion and
exists within the universal soul. Time is only a definite and
fixed portion of duration determined by motion.

If this is true, then we may consider Plotinus as the source
of a variety of definitions of time which occur alike in mediaeval Arabic, Hebrew, and Latin sources as well as in modern
philosophy and in which the term duration, sometimes under
the guise of other terms, appears as something independent
of motion. Such definitions, of course, do not always reproduce Plotinus accurately or even follow him completely.
They are changed, modified, become combined with other
definitions, and completely lose their original form. But
they can always be traced, I believe, to Plotinus, and with a
little effort their variations from the original Plotinian definition can always be accounted for. I shall try to reproduce a
few examples of the variety of forms which this Plotinian
definition of time has assumed in Arabic, Hebrew, Latin, and
other philosophic writings down to the time of Spinoza.

We shall first deal with Arabic and Hebrew texts, and then
with texts in Latin and other languages.

In surveying the Arabic and Hebrew philosophic texts we
may discover three sets of definitions in which the influence
of Plotinus is recognizable or the term duration is made use

of. In the first set, the Plotinian conception of time, either with the mention of the term duration or without it, is used, as in the Iḫwan al-Ṣafa, in opposition to the Aristotelian definition. In the second set, the Plotinian conception of time, again either with the mention of the term duration or without it, is used in combination with the Aristotelian definition, and as supplementary to it. In the third set, the term duration is embodied within the phraseology of a current definition of time which, not unlike that of Aristotle, made time dependent upon notion.

Of the first set of definitions we have an example in Saadia's reference to one who "imagines that time is external to the sphere and that the world is within it." [1] From the context it is unmistakably clear that the contention of this definition is that time is by its nature independent of motion and that it has been put forward in opposition to the definition of Aristotle. The statement that "time is external to the sphere and the world is within it" is reminiscent of similar statements made by Plotinus, namely, that "the sphere exists and is moved within time" (ἐν χρόνῳ γάρ καὶ αὕτη καὶ ἔστι καὶ κινεῖται)[2] or that the activity of the soul constitutes time and "the universe is within time" (ὁ δὲ ἐν χρόνῳ).[3]

A similar allusion to the Plotinian conception of time as opposed to that of Aristotle is found in Altabrizi. He enumerates four definitions of time. Three of these either identify time with motion or make it belong to motion. But one of these, the fourth one, states that time is neither a body nor anything belonging to a body.[4] This, it seems to me, is

[1] *Emunot we-De'ot*, I, 4.

[2] *Enneads*, III, vii, 11 (p. 178, ll. 17–18).

[3] *Ibid.* (l. 26).

[4] Commentary on Maimonides' Twenty-five Propositions, Prop. 15. Cf. my *Crescas' Critique of Aristotle*, pp. 635–636, 656.

merely another way of saying that time is neither motion nor anything belonging to motion, for body is that which alone has motion. To deny that time is dependent upon motion is, therefore, merely to repeat Plotinus' contention against Aristotle.

An echo of the Plotinian conception of time may be also found in Crescas. Openly rejecting the Aristotelian definition, he defines time as "the measure of the duration of motion or rest between two instants."[1] He furthermore indicates the significance of this definition as an attempt to free time from motion when he says, again in opposition to Aristotle, that as a result of his new definition, time exists only in the soul. It may be remarked here that by "soul" Crescas does not mean the universal soul of Plotinus, but rather the human soul. But when Crescas further argues, as a consequence of his definition of time, that there had existed time prior to the creation of the world,[2] the implication is that prior to the creation of the world time, or rather duration, existed in the mind of God as did eternity according to the views of Philo and Plotinus. Time in the created world, however, is essentially not different from time or duration before the creation of the world. It is not generated by motion, but only measured by motion. Crescas could thus repeat with Philo and Plotinus that time is an image of eternity.

Of the second set of definitions we have a good example in Maimonides. Though following Aristotle in saying that time is an accident of motion[3] and hence could not have existed prior to the creation of the world, Maimonides states that we may have in our mind an idea of a certain duration which

---

[1] Or Adonai, I, ii, 11. Cf. my Crescas' Critique of Aristotle, pp. 289, 651–658, 93–98.   [2] Ibid.

[3] Moreh Nebukim, II, Introduction, Prop. 15.

existed prior to the creation of the world. He calls that duration a "supposition or imagination of time but not the reality
of time." [1] Maimonides' "supposition or imagination of
time" seems to be the same as Plotinus' "image of eternity,"
i.e., a duration which is independent of motion. But whereas
Plotinus' "image of eternity" is time itself and is essentially
of the same nature as eternity in so far as both are independent of motion, Maimonides' "imagination of time" is
essentially different from time; it is only a pseudo-time, inasmuch as it is independent of motion, whereas time, properly so called, is generated by motion. The Plotinian time is
thus combined by Maimonides with the Aristotelian time and
made to supplement it.

The view of Maimonides is adopted by Albo, and is restated by him in a new way. He says there are two kinds of
time. One is "unmeasured duration which is conceived only
in thought and which existed prior to the creation of the
world and will continue to exist after its passing away."
This he calls "absolute time," in which there is no distinction
of equal and unequal or of before and after, and which he
identifies with what Maimonides has described as an "imagination of time." The other kind of time is that which is
"numbered and measured by the motion of the sphere, to
which are applicable the distinctions of before and after,
of equal and unequal." [2] These two kinds of time, as I have
said in the case of Maimonides, are undoubtedly the result
of a combination of the Aristotelian time and the Plotinian
time.

Examples of the third set of definitions are to be found in
the works of several authors. Saadia has two versions of a
definition which belongs to this type: (1) "Time is nothing

[1] *Ibid.*, II, 13.
[2] '*Ikkarim*, II, 18. Cf. my *Crescas' Critique of Aristotle*, p. 658.

but the extension of the duration of bodies." [1] (2) "The essence of time is the duration of these existent things." [2] Abraham bar Ḥiyya, in whose text there is a doubtful reading of one word, gives a definition of time which like the definitions of Saadia reads either (1) "that time is nothing but the extension of existent things" or (2) "that time is nothing but a term signifying the duration of existent things." [3] Similarly Algazali gives a definition, evidently meant by him to be a paraphrase of Aristotle's definition, which reads that "time is a term signifying the duration of motion, that is to say, the extension of motion." [4] It will be noticed that the common element in all these definitions is the use of the terms extension and duration and that these terms extension and duration are used in connection with "bodies," or "existent things," or "motion," all of which means the same thing, for by "existent things" here is meant "bodies," and "bodies" have "motion." All these definitions, despite their use of the term duration, or extension, imply the dependence of time upon motion, and may be traced, I believe, to a definition the phrasing of which reads that time is the extension (διάστημα) of motion, and which is attributed by Plutarch and Stobaeus to Plato and by Simplicius to Zeno and is included by Plotinus among the definitions which make time dependent upon motion. [5]

Throughout my discussion of Arabic and Hebrew texts I have used the term duration. Now, this term, derived from the Latin *durare*, literally, "to be hardened," and hence, "to continue, to last, to remain," has been used in the Middle

---

[1] *Emunot we-Deʻot*, II, 11.   [2] *Ibid.*, I, 4.

[3] *Hegyon ha-Nefesh*, I, p. 2a.

[4] *Maḳaṣid al-Falasifah*, II, iii (p. 192).

[5] Cf. *De Placitis*, I, 21, and *Eclogae*, I, 8, in Diels, *Doxographi Graeci*, p. 318; Simplicius on *Categories* in Zeller, *Philosophie der Griechen*, III, 1, p. 184, n. 6 (4th edition); *Enneads*, III, vii, 6.

Ages in a certain technical sense in connection with time. In Arabic and in Hebrew, no more than in Greek, however, is there any term of the same derivative technical meaning which is etymologically of the same origin. But the texts which I have discussed contain three Arabic and eight Hebrew terms which, though etymologically unconnected with the Latin *duratio*, can be shown from their context and implications to have the same technical meaning as the Latin *duratio*. These three Arabic and eight Hebrew terms can be arranged etymologically in three groups.[1] (1) The terms in the first group all go back to a root meaning "to stretch, to extend," and are used in philosophic Arabic and Hebrew as some of the equivalents of the Greek διάστασις, "extension," which, as we have seen, occurs in Plotinus as one of the characteristics of indefinite time. (2) The term in the second group comes from a root meaning "to join, to keep together," and is the equivalent of the Greek συνέχεια, "continuity," which, again as we have seen, occurs in Plotinus as one of the characteristics of indefinite time. (3) The terms in the third group go back to roots meaning "to remain, to survive, to exist," and are the equivalents, though not etymologically of the same origin, of the Greek συνέχεια, and reflect the expressions of continuity and existence used by Plotinus in connection with indefinite time. The importance of this philological digression will come out in our discussion of Latin texts which we now begin.

---

[1] The three groups of terms are as follows:

I. مدّة (Iḥwan al-Ṣafa and Algazali), עת, מדה (Hebrew translations of Algazali). امتداد (Maimonides), המשך (Samuel Ibn Tibbon's translation of Maimonides and Albo), איכות (Ḥarizi's translation of Maimonides).

II. بقاء (Saadia), קיום, השארות (Judah Ibn Tibbon's translation of Saadia), עמדה (Abraham bar Ḥiyya).

III. התדבקות (Crescas).

Cf. my *Crescas' Critique of Aristotle*, pp. 638, 639, 655, 656.

In Latin philosophic texts, as far as I have been able to examine them, we find on the whole the conception of duration combined in a variety of manners with the Aristotelian definition of time. A good example of it is to be found in Augustine's treatment of time.

Augustine starts out by saying that time is that "by which we measure the motion of bodies." [1] In this he is certainly following the phraseology of Aristotle. But he does not stop with this. He soon asks himself what time is in itself. [2] In this again he is repeating a question raised by Aristotle. [3] He then proceeds to show that time cannot be identical with the motion of a body, [4] in which again Aristotle himself would agree with him, for to Aristotle time is only an accident of motion but is not motion itself. [5] But still it would seem that Augustine means to deny by his statement more than the identification of motion and time. It would seem that he means to make time more independent of motion than was done by Aristotle, though still not altogether independent of motion as was done by Plotinus. That time was not according to Augustine altogether independent of motion and hence purely subjective in its nature is evidenced by the fact that when he suggests that time is a certain kind of "stretching out" (*distentio*) he immediately adds that he does not know of what it is a stretching out and marvels "if it be not of the mind itself." [6] His answer to this is in the negative. It is not of the mind itself, he says in effect, but it is rather *in* the mind. "In thee it is, O my mind, that I measure my times." [7] Time indeed is the measure of motion, as said Aristotle, but it is not motion itself but

---

[1] *Confessions*, XI, 23.
[2] *Ibid.*, XI, 23 and 26.
[3] *Physics*, IV, 10, 217b, 32.
[4] *Confessions*, XI, 24.
[5] *Physics*, IV, 10, 218b, 9–18.
[6] *Confessions*, XI, 26.
[7] *Ibid.*, XI, 27.

only the memory of motion that time measures. "In thee, I say, do I measure times. The impression which things make in thee as they pass by doth still remain, even when the things themselves are gone, and this impression it is which, being still present, I measure." [1] Thus a connection of time with motion is assumed by Augustine, but a connection not with motion that is still present, but with the image of motion which exists in the mind after the motion itself is gone. This is far from the purely ideal conception of time which interpreters of Augustine generally attribute to him. It is certainly unlike the purely ideal conception of time which we find in Plotinus and Crescas and in the pseudo-time or duration which according to Maimonides and Albo existed prior to the creation of the world. It is nothing but a modification of Aristotle's definition of time which must have been suggested to Augustine by Aristotle's own contention that in some respect time exists only in the soul. [2]

For our immediate purpose, however, the chief importance of Augustine's discussion of time consists in the term *distentio* which he uses on several occasions in describing the nature of time. [3] In this word *distentio*, it seems to me, we may discern a technical term used as the equivalent of *duratio*. The term *distentio* is the equivalent of the Greek διάστασις, and it will be recalled that terms meaning "stretching out" traceable to the Greek διάστασις were used in Arabic and Hebrew texts for duration and that the term διάστασις itself is used by Plotinus as one of the characteristics of his indefinite time or duration.

The use of the concept of duration in connection with the Aristotelian definition of time is to be found in the writings

[1] *Ibid.*
[2] *Physics*, IV, 14, 223a, 16–23.
[3] *Confessions*, XI, 23, end, and 26.

of almost all the leading scholastics. Confining ourselves only to what is common to all of them, we may discern in them the following general characteristics. Duration is assumed by them as a genus of which time is a species, for they speak of duration as being of three kinds, (a) eternity, (b) aevum, and (c) time.[1] While time is generally defined after Aristotle as being the measure of motion, duration is conceived as something independent of motion. Two definitions of duration may be discerned in their writings. One reads that duration is the permanence or perseverance or continuation of existence.[2] The other reads that it connotes a certain succession.[3] Both these expressions, "permanence or perseverance or continuation of existence" and "succession," as will be recalled, are used by Plotinus among his characterizations of his indefinite time, and the first of these expressions is the underlying meaning of some of the terms used by Arabic and Hebrew authors for the concept of duration. One

[1] Cf. Suarez, *Disputationes Metaphysicae*, Disp. L, Sec. III, 1: "Primo, ac praecipue dividitur duratio in creatam et increatam. Duratio increata est aeternitas simpliciter dicta." . . . Sec. V, 1: "Duratio igitur creata dividi potest primo in permanentem et successivam. . . . Dividitur ergo ulterius duratio creata permanens in durationem immutabiliter natura sua permanentem, quae aevum appellatur, et in eam quae licet permanens sit." . . . Sec. VIII, 1: "Agimus ergo de duratione habente continuam successionem, de qua Philosophi disputant cum Aristotele in 4. Phys. eo quod tempus, Physicum motum consequi videatur." Cf. also Marc. Anton. Galitius, *Summa Totius Philosophiae Aristotelicae ad mentem S. Bonaventurae*, Pars I, Lib. IV, Tract. II, Quaest. III: "Tres durationes communiter a Doctoribus assignari solere, omnibus in scholis versatis patentissimum esse opinor."

[2] Cf. Suarez, *op. cit.*, Disp. L, Sec. I, 1: "Dicitur enim durare res, quae in sua existentia perseverat: unde duratio idem esse censetur, quod permanentia in esse." Bonaventura, *Commentaria in Quatuor Libros Sententiarum*, Lib. II, Dist. XXXVII, Art. I, Quaest. II: "Continuatio in esse non est aliud quam duratio."

[3] Cf. Suarez, *op. cit.*, Disp. L, Sec. II, 1: "Est ergo prima opinio Ochami, et Gabrielis supra dicentium, durationem distingui ab existentia, quia existentia significat absolute, et simpliciter rem esse extra suas causas: duratio vero dicit existentiam connotando successionem, cui vel coexistat, vel possit coexistere res, quae durare dicitur: vel aliter, quod duratio dicat existentiam, quatenus apta est ad coexistendum successioni." Cf. also Léon Mahieu, *François Suarez*, p. 374.

gets, however, the impression that these typical scholastics did not consider duration as something purely subjective, any more than Augustine did. Whatever they believed the relation of duration to its object to be, they seem to have attached to it some kind of objectivity. All their discussions on that point would seem to be attempts at different interpretations of Aristotle's statement that time, in so far as it is the number of motion and not motion itself, is in the soul.[1]

The scholastic distinction between duration and time appears also in the discussions of Descartes and Locke. Duration is defined by Descartes as a mode of consideration of the perseverance in the existence of a thing.[2] Whether the thing is moved or unmoved it has duration, and duration of the same kind. Time, however, applies only to things in motion, and is defined by him as the measure of motion.[3] Locke follows on the whole the same tradition, but instead of defining duration, like Descartes, as the perseverance in existence, he defines it as the distance (= extension, διά-στασις) between any parts of that succession furnished to us by the train of ideas which constantly succeed one another in the understanding.[4] It will have been noticed that the two characteristic expressions used by Descartes and Locke in their definitions of duration, namely, "perseverance in existence" and "succession," correspond exactly to the two definitions of duration which we find among the scholastics and which can be traced to Plotinus. Furthermore, if we substitute Plotinus' "soul" for Locke's "understanding," we shall find that Locke's characterization of duration is reminiscent of Plotinus' characterization of indefinite time.

---

[1] *Physics*, IV, 14, 223a, 16–23.
[2] *Principia Philosophiae*, I, 55.
[3] *Ibid.*, and I, 57.
[4] *Essay Concerning Human Understanding*, II, 14, §§ 1–3.

This idea of succession which constitutes duration, continues Locke, is not derived from motion.[1] Time, however, is connected with motion, and is defined by him as duration measured by motion.[2]

The cumulative effect of all these definitions of time in the Greek, Arabic, Hebrew, and Latin philosophic traditions, from Plotinus down to Locke, stands out clearly in its main outline. There is duration. This duration is not generated by motion. It is something generated in the mind. In Plotinus it is said to be in the universal soul. In Augustine it is identified with memory or the impression of things gone that remains in the mind. In Maimonides and Albo, who call it either an imagination of time or absolute time, it is also said to be something which is formed in our mind. In Crescas, time is similarly said to be in the soul. In Locke it is said to be in the human understanding, consisting of the train of ideas within it. Furthermore, this duration exists apart from the physical world. In Saadia it is said to be external to, that is to say apart from, the sphere. In Altabrizi, it is said not to belong to anything corporeal. In Maimonides, Crescas, and Albo it is said to have existed prior to the creation of the world. In Descartes and Locke it is said to apply to things which have no motion. Finally, this duration is considered as something indefinite and indeterminate. Time is generally taken to differ from duration. Though there is no general agreement as to whether time is generated by motion or not, it is generally agreed that time applies to things which have motion. It is considered as a definite portion of motion, and this definiteness, it is generally admitted, is attained by its being measured by motion.

[1] *Ibid.*, § 6.   [2] *Ibid.*, §§ 17 and 19.

II. Duration and Time in Spinoza

It is in this mould of thought that we must cast Spinoza's expressions on duration and time. In presenting the subject, we shall first deal with those aspects of duration in which it is contrasted with time, leaving for subsequent discussions all the other aspects of it in which it is contrasted with eternity.

The fullest definition of duration is given by Spinoza in the *Cogitata Metaphysica*.[1] "Duration," it reads, "is the attribute under which we conceive the existence of created things, in so far as they persevere in their own actuality." Substantially it reëchoes one of the two types of definitions of duration which we have reproduced above from scholastic authors and in which *continuatio in esse, permanentia in esse,* and *in sua existentia perseverat* are the expressions indiscriminately used.

The immediate literary source of Spinoza, however, would seem to be found in the following statement of Descartes: "We merely think that the duration of each thing is a mode under which we shall conceive this thing, in so far as it perseveres to exist."[2]

Still when we compare closely Spinoza's definition with that of Descartes we shall notice three differences. First, Descartes calls duration a "mode," whereas Spinoza calls it an "attribute." Second, Descartes only says in so far as it perseveres to "exist," whereas Spinoza uses first the term "existence" like Descartes, but then adds the term "actuality" in the statement "in so far as they persevere in their own actuality." Third, Descartes simply says "thing," whereas Spinoza speaks of "created" things. The question

---

[1] *Cogitata Metaphysica*, I, 4.
[2] *Principia Philosophiae*, I, 55.

before us is whether it was merely as a matter of free para-
phrasing that Spinoza happened to make these three verbal
changes or whether there was some well thought out reason
which led him to introduce them.

With respect to the substitution of the term attribute for
mode, we shall try to show that it was done by Spinoza at
the suggestion of Descartes himself.

While in his formal definition Descartes calls duration a
mode, elsewhere he refers to it indiscriminately as belonging
either to "modes of things" (*rerum modos*) or to "affections
of things" (*rerum affectiones*).[1] Modes and affections are used
by Descartes as interchangeable terms, both of them in contrast, on the one hand, to "things" and, on the other hand,
to "eternal truths which have no existence outside our
thought."[2] Now, according to Descartes, while the terms
modes, qualities (or affections), and attributes are on the
whole analogous in meaning, still they are used in different
senses when they are considered with reference to their application to substance.[3] Consequently, though in his formal
definition of duration, as we have seen, he uses the term
"mode" and elsewhere he also refers to it as an "affection,"
he insists that the most proper term to be used in connection with it is "attribute." "And even in created things
that which never exists in them in any diverse way, like
existence and duration in the existing and enduring thing,
should be called not qualities or modes, but attributes."[4]

---

[1] My statement is based upon the following consideration. In *Principia Philosophiae*, I, 48, Descartes divides all objects into A (1), things, or (2), affections of
things, and B, eternal truths having no existence outside our thought. Then he
proceeds to say: "Of the things we consider as real, the most general are substance,
duration, order, number." I take it that of these four examples, the first, substance,
is an illustration of A (1), things, whereas the other three, duration, order, number,
are illustrations of A (2), affections of things. Later in 56, instead of "things and
affections of things," he uses the expression "things or modes of things."

[2] *Ibid.*, I, 48.   [3] *Ibid.*, I, 56.   [4] *Ibid.*

Spinoza thus had very good reason for substituting the term "attribute" for "mode" in the definition of duration. Still occasionally he slips back to the use of the term "affection," which to him as to Descartes is synonymous with "mode."[1] Thus in the following passage he says: "For, as was noted in the first Part of the discussion, duration is an affection (*affectio*) of existence."[2]

Similarly, Spinoza had a very good reason for introducing the term "actuality" to explain the term "existence." The term "existence," when used by Spinoza or his predecessors in the definition of duration, was meant to emphasize two things. In the first place, it was meant to emphasize that it was *existence* and not *motion* that was required for the conception of duration, inasmuch as duration was independent of motion. This, as we have seen, is the common characteristic of duration throughout the history of that term. Descartes makes himself explicit on that point when he says, "For we do not indeed apprehend that the duration of things which are moved is different from that of things which are not moved."[3] In the second place, it was meant to emphasize that there is no duration in beings which have no existence, as, for instance, fictitious beings and beings of reason. Suarez definitely excludes from duration "ficta" and "entia rationes."[4] Now, the word "existence" by itself would perhaps have been sufficient as an emphasis of the second point. Still, in order not to leave any room for doubt, Spinoza adds the phrase "in so far as they persevere in their own *actuality*," that is to say, the existence must be an actual existence and not one which is only in thought. It is not impossible that in phrasing this definition Spinoza was

[1] Cf. below, Vol. II, pp. 193–194.
[2] *Cogitata Metaphysica*, II, 1 (*Opera*, I, p. 250, ll. 13–14).
[3] *Principia Philosophiae*, I, 57.
[4] Suarez, *op. cit.*, Disp. L, Sec. I, 1.

directly influenced by Suarez, who insists that duration is to
be attributed to a thing which exists in actuality.[1] The same
idea that duration requires an actually existent object is expressed by Spinoza also in the following manner: "Duration
is an affection of existence, not of the essence of things."[2]
By "essence" he means the concept of a thing which may
or may not have existence outside our mind. In the same
vein he also says: "The duration of our body does not depend upon its essence . . . nor upon the absolute nature
of God . . . but . . . the body is determined to existence
and action by causes. . . . The duration, therefore, of our
body depends upon the common order of nature and the
constitution of things."[3] The dependence of duration upon
actually existing things is clearly expressed in the following
passage: "Before creation no time and duration can be
imagined by us. . . . Hence duration presupposes that things
either have been created before it or at least exist with it."[4]
It may be recalled that Plotinus gives as one of the characteristics of his indefinite time or duration that it is "a continuity
of energy."[5] "Energy" may mean there "actuality" as well
as "activity."

By the same token, the introduction by Spinoza of the
qualifying term "created" in the expression "of the existence
of *created* things" had a certain definite purpose. Indeed
Suarez uses it also in connection with duration.[6] But Spinoza
means by it something different. By the term "created"
Spinoza does not mean here the traditional conception of

---

[1] *Ibid.*: "Igitur in universum *durare* solum tribuitur rei actu existenti, et prout
existens est." Cf. Galitius, *op. cit.*, Pars I, Lib. IV, Tract. II, Quaest. I, § 2: "Duratio est permanentia rei in suo esse actuali, quieto, et perfecto."

[2] *Cogitata Metaphysica*, II, 1.

[3] *Ethics*, II, Prop. 30, Demonst. On essence and existence, see also below, p. 383.

[4] *Cogitata Metaphysica*, II, 10.

[5] See above, p. 333.

[6] See quotation above, p. 344, n. 1.

creation with its inevitable implication of coming into being in time *ex nihilo*. What he means by it is that the things conceived as having duration must have their existence dependent upon a cause, irrespective of the question whether they had a beginning in time or not. Or, as Spinoza himself says, duration is to be attributed to things "only in so far as their essence is to be distinguished from their existence," [1] that is to say, in so far as their existence is not necessary by their own nature but must be brought about by a cause. If this is the meaning of Spinoza's statement, we can find a historical background for it. It corresponds to the contention of Suarez that even if the angels or the heavens were assumed to have been created by God from eternity, they would still have duration, inasmuch as they would still have been called created beings in so far as their existence is conditioned by a cause. [2]

Spinoza's definition of duration as an attribute, or mode, or affection of existence may bring up the question of the relation of duration to existence. Are they identical, or is there some difference between them? and if the latter, what is the difference? To be sure, Spinoza does not raise this question explicitly. But the question had been raised by the scholastics, and Spinoza must have been conscious of it, for some statements in his writings, as we shall try to show, seem to aim at it. The question as to "how duration is related to existence," as stated by Suarez, reads: "whether it is something distinct from the thing itself, or whether it is completely identical with it." [3] Three views are reported.

---

[1] *Cogitata Metaphysica*, II, 1. Cf. use of "created" below, p. 383, n. 5.

[2] *Op. cit.*, Disp. L, Sec. III, v: "Unde si Deus creasset angelum, ut coelum ab aeterno, non esset in eo durationis principium, et nihilominus duratio eius creata esset, et essentialiter differens ab aeternitate."

[3] *Op. cit.*, Disp. L, Sec. I, 1: "Hinc ergo nascitur difficultas, quomodo duratio ad existentiam comparetur; an scilicet, sit aliquid distinctum ab ipsa re, aut prorsus idem sit." Cf. Galitius, *op. cit.*, Pars I, Lib. IV, Tract. II, Quaest. II: "An duratio realiter differat ab existentia?"

According to some, duration and existence differ from each other *in re* and *realiter*, that is to say, they are separable and each of them can be conceived without the other.[1] Others, as Bonaventura, Bañez, and other Thomists, consider the difference between them as a *modal* difference, like that which exists between a substance and a mode or between two modes.[2] Suarez, Scotus, Occam, and Biel, however, consider duration and existence as being *inseparable* though *distinct* from each other, the distinction between them being one of reason.[3] Similarly Descartes, after discussing the three kinds of distinction, the real, the modal, and that of reason (*ratione*), the last of which he defines as that "between substance and some one of its attributes without which it is not possible that we should have a distinct knowledge of it," [4] concludes that "because there is no substance which does not cease to exist when it ceases to endure, duration is only distinct from substance by reason." [5] Evidently drawing upon these discussions, Spinoza likewise says: "From which it clearly follows that duration is distinguished from the whole existence of a thing only *by reason*. For, however much duration you take away from any thing, so much of its existence you detract from it." [6]

In the light of this statement, when Spinoza chose to define duration as an "attribute" of existence, he used the term attribute in the strictly technical sense in which he defines it in the *Ethics*, namely, as a purely subjective aspect of the thing of which it is used. This is an indirect corroboration of our interpretation of Spinoza's attribute as something purely subjective.

[1] Suarez, *op. cit.*, Disp. L, Sec. II.
[2] Cf. Léon Mahieu, *François Suarez*, pp. 372 f.; Galitius, *loc. cit.*
[3] Cf. Léon Mahieu, pp. 373 f.
[4] *Principia Philosophiae*, I, 60 and 62.
[5] *Ibid.*, I, 62.   [6] *Cogitata Metaphysica*, I, 4.

In the passage just quoted, Spinoza, as will have been noticed, uses the expression "the whole existence of a thing" when he wishes to prove that duration differs from existence only by reason. The expression "the whole of existence" implies, of course, that there may be a part of existence and hence a part of duration. This leads Spinoza in the passage quoted to introduce his definition of time. It is possible, he says, to take off a certain portion of the duration of a thing. But "in order to determine this we compare it with the duration of those things which have a fixed and determinate motion, and this comparison is called time." [1] Or as he says in another place: "No one doubts, too, that we imagine time because we imagine some bodies to move with a velocity less, or greater than, or equal to that of others." [2] Here then we have a definition of time in terms of duration the like of which we have already met in Plotinus, in the Arabic Iḥwan al-Ṣafa, in the Jewish Crescas, and in many scholastics. Spinoza's contemporary Locke, as we have seen, restates it. His immediate source, however, must again have been Descartes in the following passage: "But in order to comprehend the duration of all things under the same measure, we usually compare their duration with the duration of the greatest and most regular motions, which are those that create years and days, and these we term time." [3]

Essentially, thus, time and duration, according to Spinoza, are the same. Time is not a new attribute of things, it is not different from the attribute of duration, nor does it add anything to duration. It is only a definite portion of duration measured by motion. Thus Descartes: "Hence this [time] adds nothing to the notion of duration, generally taken, but a mode of thinking." [4] And so also Spinoza:

[1] *Ibid.*
[2] *Ethics*, II, Prop. 44, Schol.
[3] *Principia Philosophiae*, I, 57.
[4] *Ibid.*

"Therefore, time is not an affection of things but only a mode of thought or, as we have said, a being of reason; it is a mode of thought serving to explain duration." [1]

Thus duration is a mode of existence, and time is a mode of duration. It is analogous to the successive relations between time, motion, and body in Aristotle. Motion, according to the mediaeval Aristotelian phraseology, is an accident of body and time is an accident of motion. [2] Substitute the terms duration and existence respectively for motion and body and the term mode for accident and you get a perfect analogy.

The upshot of all this discussion is this. Everything which may be conceived of as existing or as not existing, depending upon some cause for its existence, has existence superadded to its essence. Such a thing is called by Spinoza a created thing. Now, existence of a thing merely means the fact that the concept which we form in our mind of a thing has an object outside our mind to correspond to it. The concept is the essence of the thing, the outside reality is the existence of the thing. Now the mind in which the concept is formed does not create the existence. The existence is given. But when the mind comprehends that given existence, it comprehends it as something enduring, as something persevering in its actuality, and it cannot perceive it otherwise. Existence does not appear to the mind as a point, but as some sort of extension. This conception of the mind of the external existing object as something persevering in its own actuality, or, in other words, this attribute under which we conceive existence, is that which is called duration. Duration thus refers only to things which have existence, and then only to the existence of such things and not to their essence. "It

[1] *Cogitata Metaphysica*, I, 4.
[2] *Moreh Nebukim*, II, 13, First Theory.

should be noted under duration, as it will be of use when below we are discussing eternity, that it is conceived as greater and less and *as if it were* composed of parts, and then only as an attribute of existence and not of essence." [1] Note the expression "*as if it were* composed of parts," for duration according to Spinoza is a continuous quantity and does not consist of discrete parts such as moments.[2] Or, again, Spinoza speaks of duration as "existence considered in the abstract, as if it were a certain kind of quantity." [3]

If we were now to compare Spinoza's and Aristotle's conceptions of time with respect to the problem of their subjectivity and objectivity, we should find that there is little difference. Both assume time to be partly real and partly ideal. In so far as Aristotle's motion and Spinoza's existence are outside the mind, the former's time and the latter's duration are real. In so far as the measure of time of Aristotle and the duration of Spinoza are conceptions of the mind, they are both ideal. In fact the same dual nature of time we shall find throughout the mediaeval definitions, despite the controversies among their various proponents on that point. None of the mediaevals believed in the absolute ideality of time. Not even Augustine went as far as that. The only place where we find a conception of absolutely ideal time is where time can be conceived to exist in a mind which has existence without a body and without a physical world to draw its thoughts from, such as God and Plotinus' universal soul. Of such a nature is the time of Plotinus, the time of Crescas, in its existence prior to the creation of the world, the imagination of time of Maimonides, and the absolute time of Albo.

[1] *Cogitata Metaphysica*, I, 4.
[2] *Epistola* 12.
[3] *Ethics*, II, Prop. 45, Schol.

Exactly the same definitions of duration and time which have been found in the *Cogitata Metaphysica* are to be found in Spinoza's letter to Meyer.[1] Using there the term "modes" as the equivalent of the expression "created things" in the *Cogitata Metaphysica*, meaning thereby something whose essence does not necessarily involve existence, he says that duration is that by means of which "we can only explain the existence of modes." He then goes on to say that from the fact that we can determine duration, there arises time for the purpose of determining duration, concluding that time is merely a mode "of thinking or, rather, of imagining."[2] The additional phrase "or, rather, of imagining" is of no special significance here. It is probably nothing but a reminiscent expression of Hobbes' statement that "time is a phantasm of motion." [3] Hobbes himself meant by phantasm not "imagination" as opposed to "thought," but rather imagination in the general sense of not being "the accident or affection of any body" and of not being "in the things without us, but only in the thought of the mind."[4] This is exactly what Spinoza meant by suggesting "imagining" as an alternative for "thinking." It is not impossible, too, that the use of the term "imagining" by Spinoza is a faint reminiscence of the Platonic and Plotinian saying that time is the "image" of eternity.

Duration is thus assumed by Spinoza to have two characteristics. First, the existence of an object which is said to be conceived under the attribute of duration must be only a possible existence, depending upon God as its efficient cause,[5] which he describes in the *Cogitata Metaphysica* by the term "created things" and in his letter to Meyer by the

---

[1] *Epistola* 12.
[2] *Ibid.* (*Opera*, IV, p. 57, ll. 7–8): "cogitandi, seu potius imaginandi Modos."
[3] *Elementa Philosophiae*, Pars II, Cap. VII, § 3.
[4] *Ibid.*   [5] See below, Vol. II, pp. 80 ff.

term "mode." This differentiates duration from eternity, which we shall discuss later. Second, duration is to be conceived as unlimited, unmeasured, and undetermined. This differentiates duration from time. These two characteristics of duration are contained in the term "indefinite" which Spinoza uses in his definition of duration in the *Ethics*. "Duration," he says, "is the indefinite continuation of existence." [1] Note incidentally his use of the term "continuation," which, as will be recalled, like the terms "permanence" and "perseverance," is used by the scholastics in their definition of duration. In the explanation to this definition in the *Ethics* Spinoza, it seems to me, is trying to bring out the double meaning of the term "indefinite" as corresponding to the two characteristics of duration. In so far as duration applies to existence which is not necessary by its own nature, Spinoza says, "I call it indefinite because it cannot be determined by the nature itself of the existing thing." In so far as duration is unlimited and unmeasured and is, as we have seen above, "the whole existence of a thing" and not merely a portion of it, Spinoza says that he calls it indefinite "because it cannot be determined . . . by the efficient cause, which necessarily posits the existence of the thing but does not take it away." By the "efficient cause" he means here God, who is described by him as "the efficient cause of all things which can fall under the infinite intellect." [2] The implication of the statement here that if duration were not indefinite God would have been taking away (*tollit*) the existence of the thing can be explained by the statement in the *Cogitata Metaphysica* that "however much of duration you take away (*detrahis*), so much of its existence do you take away from it." [3]

---

[1] *Ethics*, II, Def. 5. [2] *Ethics*, I, Prop. 16, Corol. 1.
[3] *Cogitata Metaphysica*, I, 4.

Time, as we have seen, does not differ essentially from duration; it is only a limited portion of duration. Spinoza thus sometimes speaks of duration as "indefinite time" (*tempus indefinitum*), and contrasts it with "finite time" (*tempus finitum*), "limited time" (*tempus limitatum*), and "definite time" (*tempus definitum*).[1] And, *vice versa*, he speaks also of time as "determinate duration" (*duratio determinata*).[2] It is for this reason that Spinoza sometimes speaks of "duration or time"[3] as if the two terms meant to him the same thing. In this indeed Spinoza is really reverting to Plotinus' use of the term time and also to those Jewish philosophers who used the term time for that motion-free time which, as we have been trying to show, is known in scholasticism under the name of duration.

III. Eternity

The term eternity started on its career in the history of philosophy with two meanings. Like the twofold meanings with which so many of our other philosophic terms have started their historical careers, they may be designated the Platonic and the Aristotelian. Briefly stated, the difference between these two meanings is as follows. To Plato eternity is the antithesis of time and it means the exclusion of any kind of temporal relations. To Aristotle eternity is only endless time. The question before us is, how did it happen that eternity, which prior to Plato, for all we know, had meant simply endless time, came to mean with Plato the exclusion of time?

The answer to this question seems to be that the term eternity has acquired its new meaning in Plato from the nature of the eternal beings to which it was exclusively ap-

---

[1] *Ethics*, III, Prop. 8 and Demonst.   [2] *Ethics*, I, Prop. 21, Demonst.
[3] *Ethics*, I, Def. 8.

plied by him. Beginning as an adjective of those eternal beings, designating only one of their characteristics, namely, that of ceaseless existence, it came to be used, as it so often happens with terms, as a surrogate for those beings. Those "eternal beings" became simply "the eternals" by the same process that "port wine" became simply "port." The adjective eternal thus became with Plato a substantive, the eternals. In this capacity of a substantive, the term eternal was used by Plato not only in the sense of ceaseless existence but as inclusive of all the other properties which characterized those beings for which the term eternal substituted. The new and enlarged concept formed out of the term eternity as a surrogate became in fact a sort of epitome of all the characteristics by which the ceaseless existing beings were differentiated from the other kinds of beings. In other words, it epitomized to Plato all the essential differences between his world of ideas and his world of sense.

This process of investing the term eternity with all the connotations of the eternal beings to which it happened to be exclusively applied went on, as we shall try to show, throughout the history of philosophy, and it is the tracing of this process that constitutes the history of the term.

To Plato the differences between the world of ideas and the world of sense may be summed up, for our present purpose, under two headings. In the first place, the world of ideas is beginningless, whereas the world of sense had a beginning in an act of creation. In the second place, the world of ideas is immovable, immutable, and indivisible, whereas the world of sense is subject to motion, change, and division. The ideas, therefore, which alone in the opinion of Plato were eternal in the original sense of beginningless became the Eternals, and the term eternity, because of its exclusive application to the ideas, came to include in its meaning all the other characteristics of the ideas. Eternity thus came to stand in Plato for permanence, unity, Immutability, identity, and indivisibility. It was no longer infinite time, but rather freedom from any sort of temporal relations, for time to Plato, as later to Aristotle, was connected with motion. The relation of time to eternity was conceived by him as that of the world of sense to the world of ideas. Time was thus described by him as the moving image of eternity.[1]

To Aristotle, however, there was more than one kind of beginningless being. The universe as a whole, the celestial spheres, motion, the immaterial Intelligences, and the Immovable Mover were all eternal in the sense of having no beginning and no end. Eternity, therefore, had with him as many meanings as the number of beings to which it was applied. When applied to the universe or to the movable spheres, eternity meant nothing but infinite time, and this was inseparable from motion. For while indeed, argues Aristotle, the object which has infinite motion cannot truly be described as being in time, which in the strict technical sense of the term means to be comprehended by time and transcended by it, it is still described by him as being *in* time in the less technical sense of being *with* time, that is to say, of being when time is.[2] When, however, eternity is applied to immovable beings, as God or the Intelligence, it of necessity means a negation of temporal relation, for there can be no time when there is no motion. While Aristotle himself does not say anything on this subject beyond the statements that the universe, circular motion, the spheres, and God are all eternal, this inference is certainly to be derived from his statements.[3]

[1] *Timaeus*, 37 D.   [2] *Physics*, IV, 12, 221a, 9–11.
[3] Cf. my *Crescas' Critique of Aristotle*, pp. 287, 646, n. 91. Cf. also Aristotle's discussion of the meaning of αἰών in *De Caelo*, I, 9, 279a, 22–33.

To Plotinus as to Aristotle there is more than one kind of being which has a beginningless existence, for the process of emanation is continuous and therefore the sphere is as eternal, in the sense of having no beginning, as the universal soul, as the intelligible world, as the Intelligence, and as the One or God. But unlike Aristotle he does not apply the term eternity to all of these types of being. Rather like Plato he applies it exclusively to what in his system corresponds to the world of ideas in the system of Plato, to the intelligible world, to the Intelligence and the One. Eternity according to him is identical with God.[1] It is the life of the Intelligence. It is "life consisting in rest, identity, uniformity, and infinity."[2] The universal soul, however, has no eternity but time, or, as we have preferred to call it, indefinite time or duration, whereas the sphere and everything that is moved with it and through it has definite time. Though time is endless to Plotinus, still it is not eternity, for eternity, as in Plato, is essentially of a different nature than time and is an exclusion of any kind of temporal relation.

Among Jewish and Arabic philosophers, the Aristotelian and Plotinian Intelligences as well as the Plotinian universal soul became the Intelligences, the number of which were determined by the number of the celestial spheres and which were identified with the angels of the Bible and functioned as the cause of the motion of the celestial spheres.[3] But with their rejection of the Plotinian emanation and their acceptance in its place of the theory of creation, God became the only being who had endless existence and thereby He also became the exclusive possessor of the attribute of eternity. Eternity could then have been used by them as a

---

[1] *Enneads*, III, vii, 4 (ed. Creuzer et Moser, Paris, 1855).
[2] *Ibid.*, 10 (p. 177, ll. 34–35).
[3] Cf. above, p. 218.

surrogate to God and as an epitome of all His attributes. Still the problem of creation was for them a vital subject of discussion and in the course of that discussion they had to deal with Aristotle's theory of the eternity of the world and of motion, and this called for the use of the term eternal in its Aristotelian sense of infinite time. Thus the term eternity had to be used by them both with reference to God and with reference to other beings which were supposed by Aristotle to be of endless existence. The result was that the term eternity had for them two meanings, again the Platonic and the Aristotelian. On the one hand, it meant the exclusion of time; on the other, it meant infinite time. Owing to this double meaning of the term, Jewish philosophers always took great pains to explain that when eternity is applied to God it does not mean infinite time but rather freedom from temporal relations.

We may illustrate this generalization by a brief analysis of the discussion of the attribute of eternity which occurs in the writings of some of the leading Jewish philosophers. It usually takes the form of an explanation of the terms "first" and "last," the use of which is the Biblical way of expressing the eternity of God,[1] that is to say, eternity *a parte ante* and *a parte post*. In their explanation of these Biblical terms, Jewish philosophers endeavor to emphasize that these two terms should not be taken literally to mean beginningless and endless time but should be taken rather as implying God's exclusion from any kind of temporal relation.

Both Baḥya and Maimonides insist upon this point and suggest that the term "first" should be taken as a negation either of God's having anything prior to Him, as Baḥya expresses himself,[2] or of His having been created, as Mai-

---

[1] Cf. Isaiah 44, 6.   [2] *Ḥobot ha-Lebabot*, I, 6.

monides puts it.[1] Similarly, Judah ha-Levi speaks of God as transcending all relations of time and explains the terms "first" and "last" not as affirmations of literal priority and posteriority but rather as negations of God's having been preceded by anything and of His ever coming to an end.[2] A most interesting passage for our purpose is that of Abraham Ibn Daud where eternity is directly identified with immovability and immutability. "When we ascribe to God the attribute 'eternal,' we only mean thereby that He was immovable, that He is immovable, and that He will be immovable. You already know that by motion we mean change from one state to another."[3] Crescas, though on account of his defining time as duration independent of motion he has no objection to the use of divine attributes which imply duration,[4] follows Maimonides in interpreting the term "first" in the sense of being "uncreated."[5]

The most interesting passage for our purpose, however, is that of Albo. "First" and "last," he says, mean absolute independence of any temporal relations.[6] Albo, as we have already seen, distinguishes between two kinds of time: one, absolute time or duration, which is infinite, and the other, definite time, which is finite. Eternity as applied to God, according to him, excludes duration as well as definite time.[7] The reason given by him why God alone of all beings is described as eternal is that God alone of all beings has necessary existence by virtue of His own nature, whereas all other beings have only possible existence by their own nature.[8]

[1] *Moreh Nebukim*, I, 57.   [2] *Cuzari*, II, 2.

[3] *Emunah Ramah*, II, iii (pp. 54–55).

[4] *Or Adonai*, I, iii, 3 (p. 23b). Cf. my "Crescas on the Problem of Divine Attributes" in the *Jewish Quarterly Review*, New Series, VII (1916), pp. 181–182.

[5] *Or Adonai*, I, iii, 3 (p. 24b). Cf. my "Crescas on the Problem of Divine Attributes," p. 207, n. 111.   [6] *'Ikkarim*, II, 18.

[7] *Ibid.*   [8] *Ibid.*

Or to put it in other words, eternity is applied to God, according to Albo, because in God essence and existence are identical.[1] Eternity is, therefore, defined by Albo as identity, uniformity, and immutability,[2] terms which remind us of those used by Plotinus as well as Plato in his characterization of eternity.

The use of eternity as a description of necessary existence *per se*, i.e., of the identity of essence and existence, may be also found in Altabrizi. Among the four definitions of time which he adduces there is one which reads that "time exists in itself, is neither a body nor anything belonging to a body, but is something which has necessary existence by virtue of itself." [3] I have suggested elsewhere that the last statement was taken from the Plotinian definition of eternity and was misapplied by Altabrizi to time.[4]

In exactly the same sense is the term eternity used in mediaeval Latin philosophic texts. It is applied exclusively to God and it is defined as the exclusion from any temporal relations. If other beings are assumed to have an endless existence, they are not described as eternal but by some other term. If the same term eternal is applied also to other beings, then the term when applied to God is said to have a special meaning. In either way, eternal as applied to God means more than the mere negation of beginning and end. It means immovability and necessity of existence.

The contrast between eternity and time as that between permanence and motion is suggested by Augustine when he speaks of eternity as the "ever-fixed" (*semper stantis*) and of time as the "never-fixed" (*numquam stantis*),[5] or when he says that "time does not exist without some kind of

---

[1] *Ibid.*   [2] *Ibid.*

[3] Altabrizi, Commentary on Maimonides' Twenty-five Propositions, Prop. 15.

[4] Cf. my *Crescas' Critique of Aristotle*, p. 662, n. 29.

[5] *Confessions*, XI, 11.

change caused by motion, while in eternity there is no change." [1] Boethius expresses the distinction between eternity and infinite time in the following statement: "Philosophers say that ever (*semper*) may be applied to the life of the heavens and other immortal bodies. But as applied to God it has a different meaning." [2] Though the world, according to Aristotle, "never began nor were ever to end, and its life did endure with infinite time, yet it is not such that it ought to be called eternal." [3] In order not to confuse eternity with infinite time he suggests two different terms for them. "Wherefore, if we will give things their right names, following Plato, let us say that God is eternal and the world perpetual." [4]

The views of Augustine and Boethius are re-echoed throughout the history of mediaeval philosophic writers. Eternity and time are considered to be of essentially different natures, and in order to take care of the duration of beings which can be described by neither eternity nor time, the term *aevum* is generally used. A list of scholastic views on eternity is given by Suarez. [5] But for our present purpose Suarez' own view on eternity is of significance, for, like Albo, he identifies it with necessary existence *per se*. He argues that eternity is not only a negation of God's having been created, or of His having a beginning and end, or of His being subject to motion and change, but that it has a positive meaning in so far as it expresses the necessity of the existence of God by His own essence, i.e., the identity of His essence and existence. [6]

---

[1] *De Civitate Dei*, XI, 6.
[2] *De Trinitate*, IV, ed. Stewart and Rand, pp. 20–21.
[3] *Consolatio Philosophiae*, V, 6, ed. Stewart and Rand, pp. 400–401.
[4] *Ibid.*, pp. 402–403.
[5] *Disputationes Metaphysicae*, Disp. L, Sec. III.
[6] *Ibid.*, Disp. L, Sec. III, x.

A similar definition also occurs in Abraham Herrera's cabalistic work *Puerta del Cielo*. The author quotes Plato, Plotinus, Boethius, Torquato Tasso, and Ficino on the meaning of eternity. He himself defines it as his contemporary Suarez and as Albo do, as meaning existence which is necessary by its own nature, or the identity of essence and existence, for, as he says, "every essence that is necessary and *per se* is eternal." [1]

Whatever sources Spinoza had consulted about eternity he must have received the following general impression. Eternity as applied to God does not mean merely endless time. It is used as an epitome of the main distinguishing characteristics by which God is differentiated from other beings. These distinguishing characteristics are summed up under two headings, both going back to Aristotle. First, God is immovable, whereas everything else is movable, and hence eternity is said to mean immovability, immutability, permanence, indivisibility, and all the other negations that go with it. Second, God has necessary existence, whereas other beings have only possible existence. Accordingly eternity is also said to mean, as in Albo, Suarez, and Herrera, the necessary existence of God or, which is the same thing, the identity of essence and existence in Him. Following these traditional views on eternity, Spinoza gives his own definition of the term.

To begin with, eternity is not merely beginningless and endless time or duration. "It cannot therefore be explained by duration and time, even if duration be conceived without beginning or end." [2] Indeed, in common speech, we speak of the eternity of the world when we mean its eternal duration in time, but this is an erroneous use of the term. It is

---

[1] *Sha'ar ha-Shamayim*, III, 4.
[2] *Ethics*, I, Def. 8, Expl.

only because of a defective terminology that "we say that the world has existed from eternity." [1] As we have seen, Boethius has already tried to remedy this defect by introducing the use of the term perpetual. An equally defective use of the term eternity, says Spinoza, is when it is used with reference to things which do not exist, as when we say "that the essence of things is eternal, although we do not think of the things as ever existing." [2] The reference in this passage is undoubtedly to the use of the term eternal with reference to the axiomatic truths which exist only as concepts of the mind, as, for instance, in the expression "eternal truths" used by Descartes. The particular Cartesian passage which Spinoza had in mind is probably the following: "When we apprehend that it is impossible that anything can be formed of nothing, the proposition *ex nihilo nihil fit* is not to be considered as an existing thing, or the mode of a thing, but as a certain eternal truth which has its seat in our mind, and is a common notion or axiom." [3]

Thus eternity, like duration and time, refers only to things which exist, or, as Spinoza would call them, real beings. But inasmuch as real beings are divided, according to Spinoza, into those "whose essence involves existence," i.e., God or Substance, and those "whose essence involves only a possible existence," [4] eternity, says Spinoza, applies only to the first kind of real being. Accordingly Spinoza reverts to a definition of eternity the like of which we have found in Albo, Suarez, and Herrera. Now, in Spinoza's terminology the expression essence involving existence has the same meaning as *causa sui* or being causeless or infinite — infinite in the sense of undetermined by a cause. [5] Hence Spinoza defines eternity as an "attribute under which we conceive the in-

---

[1] *Cogitata Metaphysica*, II, 1.   [2] *Ibid.*   [3] *Principia Philosophiae*, I, 49.
[4] *Cogitata Metaphysica*, I, 1.   [5] Cf. above, pp. 127, 138.

finite existence of God." [1] "Infinite" is used here in the
sense of causeless, in contrast to "created," which, as we have
seen, is used by him in his definition of duration in the sense
of "caused." [2] Similarly in a letter to Meyer he says that
eternity is the only term which explains the existence of
substance, and hence it means "the infinite enjoyment of
existence, or (in awkward Latin) essendi." [3] Here, too, by infinite existence he means existence undetermined by a cause.
The expression *existendi* or *essendi fruitio* undoubtedly reflects the expression *plentitudo essendi* which is used by
Suarez in his definition of eternity.[4] The same implication
is also to be found in his formal definition of eternity in the
Ethics, which reads as follows: "By eternity I understand
existence itself (*ipsam existentiam*), so far as it is conceived
necessarily to follow from the definition alone of the eternal
thing." [5] I take the *ipsam* in *ipsam existentiam* not only as
a reflexive and emphatic pronoun but in the sense of *existentiam per se* or *per essentiam*, the equivalent of the expression
ipsius esse per essentiam which occurs in Suarez' definition
of eternity.[6]

The existence of God to which alone, then, eternity applies differs from the existence of all other beings, according
to Spinoza, not only in that it is identical with His essence
but also in that it is known and demonstrated in a different
manner from that of the existence of other beings. There
are three ways in which the existence of a thing may be
known, according to Spinoza: the way of perception, the

---

[1] *Cogitata Metaphysica*, I, 4.   [2] Cf. above, p. 351.

[3] Epistola 12: "hoc est, infinitam existendi, sive, invita latinitate, essendi
fruitionem."

[4] Suarez, *Disputationes Metaphysicae*, Disp. L, Sec. III, x: "Est enim aeternitas
duratio ipsius esse per essentiam: unde sicut ille esse est ipsa plentitudo essendi,
ita aeternitas est (ut ita dicam) ipsa plentitudo durandi."

[5] *Ethics*, I, Def. 8.

[6] Cf. quotation in note 4 above.

way of reason, and the way of intuition — his well-known three stages of knowledge. Now, in the case of all other beings, their existence is known by the first two kinds of knowledge, either by direct perception or by indirect proof *a posteriori*. The existence of eternal truths, the axioms and common notions, are perceived directly as intuitions, or what Descartes would call innate ideas.[1] Spinoza thus says: " By eternity I understand existence itself, so far as it is conceived necessarily to follow from the definition alone of the eternal thing, for such existence, like the essence of the thing, is conceived as an eternal truth." [2] The comparison with eternal truths is meant to bring out the fact that the existence of God which is identical with His essence is intuitively known as the essence of the eternal truths. But there is a difference between the eternal God and the eternal truths. In the eternal God there are both essence and existence, though the two are identical. In the eternal truths there is only essence; there is no existence in them.[3]

In Albo's discussion of the eternity of God, we have seen, not only time but also duration is excluded as an admissible attribute of God. In scholastic philosophy, however, the admissibility of duration as a fitting attribute of God was a mooted point. Suarez quotes Aureolus as being opposed to the attribution of duration to God. He himself is in favor of it.[4] Spinoza likewise raises the question in *Cogitata Metaphysica*, II, 1, and like Albo and Aureolus he denies the applicability of duration to God. The passage in which the discussion is contained, however, seems to refer to certain definite texts which at the present writing I am unable to identify.

[1] Cf. below, Vol. II, pp. 155 ff.   [2] *Ethics*, I, Def. 8, and Expl.
[3] Cf. above, p. 367, notes 2 and 3.
[4] Suarez, *op. cit.*, Disp. L, Sec. III, 11.

CHAPTER XI

MODES

PROPOSITIONS XIX to XXXVI, despite their external appearance of disjointedness and incongruity, have in reality, like all the other groups of propositions we have already treated, a logical order of sequence. They fall into six groups, dealing with the following topics: I. Eternity of God (Props. XIX–XX). II. Infinite and Eternal Modes (Props. XXI–XXIII). III. The Nature of Modes in General (Props. XXIV–XXVII). IV. Finite Modes (Props. XXVIII–XXIX). V. Intellect, Will, and Power (Props. XXX–XXXV). VI. Purposelessness (Prop. XXXVI and Appendix). All these six topics may be subsumed under one general topic which, like that of the preceding group of propositions (Props. XV–XVIII), is the causality of God, Propositions XIX–XXIX dealing with the effects of God's causality, that is to say, modes, and Propositions XXX–XXXVI and Appendix dealing with the necessary and purposeless nature of God's causality. Furthermore, not only are the propositions under each of these topics logically coherent in themselves, but there is also a logical transition from one topic to another.

The subject of Propositions XIX–XXIX is the description of the modal system of the universe. Having already dealt with the nature of God and His attributes, His existence and His causality, Spinoza now undertakes to present a complete and systematic view of his conception of the modes. If we may use here Spinoza's own expressions which we have already discussed previously but which in the *Ethics* are not

introduced by Spinoza until later in the course of the propositions under consideration, we may say that the *Ethics* so
far has dealt with *natura naturans*; from now on it will deal
with *natura naturata*. In our chapter on Extension and
Thought we have already discussed quite fully Spinoza's
system of modes as they are treated by him in his writings
outside the *Ethics*. That chapter may serve us now as a
general introduction to the subject. In this chapter we shall
draw upon it only in so far as it will be necessary for us to
explain the order and the meaning of the propositions before
us, but we shall give fuller consideration to those phases
of the problem which appear for the first time in these
propositions.

To describe the modal system of the universe or, in simpler
language, the world as it is seen, perceived, and thought
of by us, the most natural method for Spinoza would have
been to start with that which we ordinarily think of as directly
known to us, namely, individual things, and work up gradually to that which we ordinarily think of as known to us only
indirectly. He could have done so without the sacrifice of
the use of his own terminology. He could have started with
an enumeration and classification of individual things or
finite modes and then reduced them to two classes, extended
things and thinking things. He could have then considered
the totality of these individual things as constituting the
infinite physical universe and called it by his own expression
"the face of the whole universe" and described it in his own
way as a mediate infinite and eternal mode. He could have
then explained the behavior of the finite modes within the
totality of the universe on the basis of two principles, motion-
and-rest, on the one hand, and understanding, on the other,
and described these again in his own way as immediate infinite and eternal modes. Then he could have gone further

and shown how these two activities are the expressions of two aspects of a single self-subsistent whole transcending the aggregate totality of the individual modes and called that transcendent whole substance and the two aspects, of which motion-and-rest and understanding are expressions, the attributes of extension and thought. To have done so Spinoza would have followed the *a posteriori* method used by Aristotle and by his adherents in the Middle Ages. But Spinoza considered himself bound by the self-imposed *a priori* reasoning of his geometrical method. Substance is more immediately known to us, according to him, than the individual things, and the source of knowledge by which it is known to us is the most reliable. From the definition of substance the nature of the entire universe follows by necessity as the properties of a triangle follow from the definition of a triangle. Spinoza, therefore, preferred to start with substance or God and to work gradually downward to individual things. Spinoza is reported to have remarked to Tschirnhaus that while most philosophers begin with creatures he began with God [1] — a remark which, it must be said, describes only his method of exposition but not necessarily the manner in which he has arrived at his scheme.

But departing though he did from most philosophers, Spinoza was not altogether without a model.

His model is the theory of emanation. This theory of emanation with its initial monism is not only taken by him as a model for his own system in preference to the dualism which is implied in the Aristotelian theory of the eternal co-existence of the universe with God, but, as we have seen on several occasions, it is also used by him as the main target

[1] See K. I. Gerhardt, "Leibniz und Spinoza," in *Sitzungsberichte der königlich preussischen Akademie der Wissenschaften zu Berlin*, 1889, p. 1077. Cf. below, Vol. II, p. 4.

of his criticism. There are, of course, fundamental differences between the prototype and the copy, chief among which is the nature of God, which is pure thought according to the emanationists but is both thought and extension according to Spinoza. Barring this fundamental difference between them, the respective schemes in both systems are parallel to each other. There is God as the starting point of both systems. The two immediate infinite and eternal modes in Spinoza, namely, the absolutely infinite intellect and motion-and-rest, correspond respectively to the Intelligences and the circular motion of the spheres in emanation. Spinoza's "face of the whole universe" corresponds to the outermost celestial sphere which encloses the totality of the physical universe according to the emanationists, with the difference that the former was considered as infinite whereas the latter was considered as finite. And then, within the universes of both these systems there are individual things.

Another important element of emanation retained by Spinoza is its terminology. When choosing his terms carefully, he always speaks of things as following (*sequi*) from the nature of God or from His attributes. This reflects the terms "proceeding"[1] and "following by necessity"[2] which are generally used in Hebrew philosophic literature in connection with the process of emanation. Even when he uses some other term, such as that God "acts" (*agit*)[3] or "to be produced" (*produci*) by God,[4] it is to be understood in the sense that it follows by necessity from the nature of God. The term cause which Spinoza applies to God is likewise to be understood in the logical and geometrical sense, that is to

---

[1] יצא. Cf. *Emunah Ramah*, II, iv, 3.

[2] يلزم, יתחייב. Cf. *Moreh Nebukim*, II, 22.

[3] *Ethics*, I, Prop. 17; IV, Praef.

[4] *Ibid.*, I, Prop. 28, Schol.

say, in the sense in which the premise of a syllogism is said to be the cause of its conclusion and the definition of a triangle is said to be the cause of its properties. The term "cause" (*causa*) to Spinoza means the same as the term "reason" (*ratio*), which two terms are sometimes connected by him by the co-ordinating conjunction "or,"[1] so that the causality he affirms of God is not meant to be understood as implying temporal sequence.[2] In this respect, indeed, his conception of God's causality corresponds exactly to that of the emanationists as it is characterized by Maimonides in the following passage: "It is clear that when Aristotle says that the first Intelligence necessarily follows from God, that the second necessarily follows from the first, and the third from the second . . . he does not mean that one thing was first in existence and then out of it came the second as a necessary result. . . . By the expression 'it necessarily follows' he merely refers to the causal relation; he means to say that the first Intelligence is the cause of the existence of the second, the second of the third, and so on   ; but none of these things preceded another, or has been in existence, according to him, without the existence of that other. It is as if one should say, for example, that from the primary qualities there follow by necessity roughness, smoothness, hardness, softness, porosity, and solidity, in which case no person would doubt that though . . . the secondary qualities follow necessarily from the four primary qualities, it is impossible that there should exist a body which, having the primary qualities, should be denuded of the secondary ones."[3] The same idea, it may be added, is reflected in Spinoza's use

---

[1] *Ibid.*, I, Prop. 11, Demonst. 2 (*Opera*, II, p. 52, l. 31 *et pass.*); IV, Praef. (*Opera*, II, p. 206, l. 26).

[2] Cf. Joachim, *A Study of the Ethics of Spinoza*, p. 54, n.

[3] *Moreh Nebukim*, II, 21.

of the expression prior in nature [1] or prior in causality [2] which he applies to God.

But whatever the differences between his God and the God of tradition, Spinoza seems to say at the beginning of this new chapter in the *Ethics* that his God does not differ from the traditional God in the matter of eternity. "God is eternal," or, since God's attributes are nothing but certain aspects of His essence, "all His attributes are eternal." [3] Now, eternity in the history of philosophy, as we have shown, meant three things. In the first place, it meant necessary existence *per se*, or the identity of essence and existence. In the second place, it meant immutability. Then, in the third place, it meant, at least in Spinoza's assertions that the eternal existence of God is an eternal truth, to be immediately known as an intuition. [4] In the first two propositions of this new chapter in the *Ethics*, therefore, Spinoza reiterates these three implications of the term eternity. In the first place, it means necessary existence *per se*, or the identity of essence and existence, "for God is substance, which necessarily exists, that is to say a substance to whose nature it pertains to exist," [5] and furthermore, "the existence of God and His essence are one and the same thing." [6] In the second place, eternity means immutability, hence "it follows that God is immutable, or (which is the same thing) all His attributes are immutable." [7] In the third place, the eternal existence of God may be called an eternal truth in so far as it is immediately known as an intuition, for "the existence of God, like His essence, is an eternal truth." [8] It is in this respect only,

---

[1] *Ethics*, I, Prop. 1. Cf. above, p. 77.

[2] *Ibid.*, I, Prop. 17, Schol. (*Opera*, II, p. 63, l. 7): "prior causalitate."

[3] *Ibid.*, I, Prop. 19.   [4] Cf. above, p. 369.

[5] *Ethics*, I, Prop. 19, Demonst.

[6] *Ibid.*, I, Prop. 20.   [7] *Ibid.*, Corol. 2.

[8] *Ibid.*, I, Prop. 19, Schol.; Prop. 20, Corol. 1.

and not in respect of lack of reality, that Spinoza calls the
existence of God an eternal truth.[1]

Again, preserving the vocabulary of emanation, Spinoza
speaks of his modes as things which follow from God. But
inasmuch as unlike the emanationists Spinoza does not take
God to be pure thought but rather as possessing an infinite
number of attributes of which the two known ones are
thought and extension, he does not speak of a single mode
following from God but rather of various modes following
respectively from the various attributes. Still like the emanationists he insists that each mode following from an attribute
must be similar to the attribute from which it follows in
certain essential characteristics. These essential characteristics he sums up in two terms, eternal and infinite. By the
term eternal in its application to modes, however, he does not
mean eternity in all the three senses which it has in its application to God. For one thing, it cannot mean necessary existence *per se* or the identity of essence and existence, for the
modes have no necessary existence *per se* and their existence
is not identical with their essence. For another thing, it
cannot mean the immediate perception of the modes as an
eternal truth, for they are known only through their cause.
"Eternal" in this case means only to be immutable, or to exist
forever, as Spinoza directly expresses himself in Proposition
XXI, or to have indeterminate existence or duration, as he
indirectly expresses himself in the Demonstration of Proposition XXI where he describes the opposite of it to have "determinate existence or duration." Similarly by the term
infinite which he applies to this mode he does not mean infinity in the sense of causelessness, for the modes have God
as their cause. "Infinite" in this case means to be the most
perfect, the most complete and the greatest of its kind, that

[1] Cf. above, pp. 367, 369.

is to say, that which cannot be limited by another thing of the same nature, or what Spinoza elsewhere describes as the "infinite in its own kind." [1] That this is what Spinoza means by the term infinite as applied to modes may be gathered from the first part of the Demonstration of Proposition XXI. It is in the light of these remarks, therefore, that we may understand the full meaning of Proposition XXI: "All things which follow from the absolute nature of any attribute of God must *forever exist*, and must be *infinite*; that is to say, through that same attribute they are *eternal* and *infinite*." What he means to say is this: They are eternal only in the sense of existing forever or of being immutable, and they are also infinite only in the sense of being unlimited by another thing of the same attribute.

It is true, of course, that since by eternal and infinite when applied to the immediate modes Spinoza does not mean the same as when these terms are applied to God, he could just as well have said in Proposition XXI that all things which follow from the absolute nature of any attribute of God *cannot* be eternal and infinite. But he chose to phrase his proposition in positive terms evidently because he wanted to emphasize the ever-existence and the infinite perfection of these immediate modes, for it is in these respects that he will want later to differentiate them from individual things or finite modes. Another plausible reason for his choosing to phrase the proposition in positive terms is that by affirming that the modes are infinite in perfection he indirectly hit at the mediaevals who contended that "the existence of an infinite effect is impossible, for, were it to exist, it would be like its cause." [2]

The Demonstration of Proposition XXI follows Spinoza's favorite method of demonstration by proving the impossibil-

[1] *Ibid.*, I, Def. 6, Expl. Cf. above, p. 136.
[2] Abraham Herrera, *Sha'ar ha-Shamayim*, V, 12.

ity of the opposite,[1] namely, the impossibility "that in some attribute of God something which is *finite* and has a *determinate existence or duration* follows from the absolute nature of that attribute." For the purpose of his discussion he takes up the mode of the attribute of thought, which he designates here by the name of the "idea of God" (*idea Dei*) but by which he means the same as by what he describes elsewhere as the "absolutely infinite intellect," [2] and asks the reader to observe that the same reasoning is true of the other immediate modes, such, for instance, as motion-and-rest in the attribute of extension. But note how carefully this demonstration is constructed. It falls into two parts, corresponding to the two terms used in the proposition, namely, infinite and eternal. In the first part he tries to show that the immediate modes cannot be finite. In the second part he tries to show that they cannot have a "determinate duration."

The immediate modes which in Proposition XXI Spinoza has shown to be eternal and infinite are designated by him n Proposition XXII as the modification (*modificatio*) by which attributes are modified, and he tries to show also that the mediate mode, which he elsewhere designates by the name of the "face of the whole universe," [3] must likewise be eternal and infinite, in the particular sense, of course, in which, as we have seen, he uses these terms with reference to modes. But instead of the term eternal which we should expect here he uses now the expression to exist necessarily (*necessario existere*), by which, however, he means the same thing. Evidence that by the expression to exist necessarily in this proposition he means the same as by the term eternal in the preceding proposition may be found in the following passage in the demonstration of the next proposition: "If

<hr/>

[1] Cf. above, pp. 97, 183.   [2] Cf. above, pp. 238 ff.
[3] Cf. above, p. 344.

a mode, therefore, be conceived to exist necessarily and to be infinite, its necessary existence and infinitude must be concluded from some attribute of God or perceived through it, in so far as it is conceived to express infinitude and necessity of existence, that is to say, eternity." [1] In the light of these remarks, we may now read Proposition XXII: "Whatever follows from any attribute of God, in so far as it is modified by a modification which through the same attribute exists necessarily and infinitely, must also exist necessarily and infinitely." What he means to say is this: The modes which follow from the immediate modes must be eternal and infinite like the immediate modes themselves. Thus there are two kinds of eternal and infinite modes, namely, immediate and mediate.

In our discussion of the preceding two propositions, for the sake of clearness and in view of the fact that we have already given a complete discussion of the subject in a previous chapter, we have used the terms immediate modes and mediate modes. Spinoza himself, however, has so far used neither of these terms. In fact, in none of the propositions proper of the *Ethics* has he so far used the term mode. He has always spoken generally of things following from God or from the nature of any of God's attributes, though the term affection (*affectio*) in the sense of mode has been used by him in a proposition. [2] To introduce the term mode and to distinguish among modes which are infinite and eternal between those which are immediate and those which are mediate is the purpose of Proposition XXIII. In this proposition, dealing again with the infinite and eternal modes and using again the term "to exist necessarily" for "eternal," he introduces for the first time the term "mode": "Every mode which exists

---

[1] *Ethics*, I, Prop. 23, Demonst.
[2] *Ibid.*, I, Prop. 1; cf. Prop. 4, Demonst.

necessarily and infinitely must necessarily follow either from the absolute nature of some attribute of God, or from some attribute modified by a modification which exists necessarily and infinitely," which the Demonstration explains to mean "either immediately or mediately" and refers in connection with the former to Proposition XXI and in connection with the latter to Proposition XXII. These two references make it clear that Proposition XXI deals with immediate infinite and eternal modes whereas Proposition XXII deals with mediate infinite and eternal modes.

Thus in these three propositions we have an outline of Spinoza's theory of infinite and eternal modes and of their classification into immediate and mediate. But the names of these modes are not given by him. He mentions here the name of only one of these immediate infinite and eternal modes, and this, too, only indirectly, namely, the idea of God in thought. Another name for this immediate infinite and eternal mode as well as all the names of the other infinite and eternal modes is supplied by Spinoza, as we have already seen, in one of his letters.[1]

In our statement that the term eternal when applied to modes does not mean the same as the term eternal when applied to God, especially in so far as in the later case the term means the necessary existence *per se* or the identity of essence and existence, we have anticipated Propositions XXIV–XXVII. It is evidently because in the preceding propositions Spinoza has given no hint of this changed meaning of the term except only, as we have suggested, indirectly when he speaks in Proposition XXI of existing forever as an alternative of eternal, or when he speaks in the Demonstration of the same proposition of "determinate existence or duration" as the opposite of eternity, that he now feels

[1] Cf. above, p. 216.   Cf. pp. 238, 242, 244.

that an explanation of the term eternal as applied to modes is due. And so immediately after he has completed his outline of his theory of the infinite and eternal modes he proceeds to say that these modes, though called eternal, have no necessity at all of their own nature but that in everything they are and in everything they do they are to be considered as having been determined by God as their cause. Now, the causality of God, it may be recalled, has been described by Spinoza by seven characteristic terms, among which he mentions the following three, namely, that God is (1) an efficient cause, (2) an immanent cause, and (3) a free cause.[1] As distinguished from God in these three respects the modes are now shown by Spinoza in Propositions XXIV, XXV, and XXVI to be dependent upon Him as their efficient cause, their immanent cause, and their free cause.

In the first place, he says in Proposition XXIV, God is the efficient cause of the modes. But before we go further with the proposition, we must point out the relation between Spinoza's use of the term efficient cause and the use of the same term by the mediaevals. In Maimonides, for instance, the term efficient cause means primarily the cause that brings things into being, and is distinguished by him from the term formal cause which means the cause that preserves the existence of things after their having come into being. God is, however, according to him both the efficient and the formal cause of the universe, inasmuch as God is both the cause of the commencement of the existence of things and the cause of the continuance of the existence of things. Thus arguing against those who maintained that the world could continue to exist even without God once it had been produced by God, he says that "they would be right, if God were only the

---

[1] Cf. above, pp. 304 ff.

efficient cause and if the continuance of the existence of the produced thing were not dependent upon Him. . . . God, however, is himself the form of the universe, as we have already shown, and it is He who causes its continuance and permanence." [1] The same idea that God is both the cause of the creation and the cause of the permanence of the universe runs throughout scholastic philosophy, though a different terminology is used. In Thomas Aquinas the cause of the permanence of the universe is called *causa essendi*, whereas the cause of the creation of the universe is called *causa fiendi*.[2] In Duns Scotus both these causes, which he calls *causa conservans* and *causa producens* respectively, are said to be subdivisions of the efficient cause.[3] Similarly Descartes speaks of God not only as the cause of the creation of the world but also as the cause of its conservation.[4]

Reflecting this historical background and using, like Duns Scotus, the term efficient cause to include both the cause of creation and the cause of conservation, Spinoza says that modes are dependent upon God as their efficient cause, for inasmuch as "the essence of things produced by God does not involve existence," [5] "God is the cause not only of the commencement of the existence of things, but also of their continuance in existence." [6] In the course of his discussion Spinoza refers to the scholastic expression *causa essendi*, mentioned by us before, as a description of the continuance of the existence of things. *Essendi*, in the scholastic use of the term, means *existendi*, as has been pointed out by Spinoza himself in a letter to Meyer,[7] and is therefore to be translated

[1] *Moreh Nebukim*, I, 69.

[2] *Summa Theologica*, Pars I, Quaest. 104, Art. 1, Conclusio and ad 2.

[3] *In Octo Libros Physicorum Aristotelis Quaestiones*, Lib. II, Quaest. 8, No. 5.

[4] *Meditationes*, III (*Oeuvres*, VII, p. 49, ll. 12 ff.).

[5] *Ethics*, I, Prop. 24.   [6] *Ibid.*, Corol.

[7] Epistola 12 (*Opera*, IV, p. 55, l. 3). Cf. above, p. 108, n. 4, and p. 141, n. 4.

by "existence" rather than by "essence," though the latter resembles it more closely etymologically.

In the second place, Spinoza wants to say, the modes are dependent upon God as their immanent cause. He does not, however, say so in these very words. What he says reads that "God is the efficient cause not only of the existence of things, but also of their essence." [1] But we shall try to show how in Spinoza's mind to say that God is the cause of the essence of things was the equivalent of saying that God is the immanent cause of things.

The essence of things in Aristotle and throughout the subsequent history of philosophy meant the concept of things as it is formed by its definition. Thus the essence of man is animality and rationality, inasmuch as man is defined as a rational animal. But animality, which is the genus of man, is considered by Aristotle as the cause of man, and that kind of cause, as we have shown, is called an immanent cause in the sense that the effect resides in it. [2] Consequently, if the Aristotelian theory of definition is followed, namely, that a thing is defined by its genus, it may be said that the genus is the cause of the essence of the species, or, to express it differently, the essence of the species is dependent upon the genus as its immanent cause. Now, Spinoza rejects this Aristotelian theory of definition, "although," he says, "all the logicians admit this," [3] and sets up in its place a new theory according to which modes or things "which do not exist through themselves" [4] or which are "created" [5] are to be defined "only through the attributes whose modes they are, and through which, as their genus, they must be

---

[1] *Ethics*, I, Prop. 25.   [2] Cf. above, pp. 323 ff.
[3] *Short Treatise*, I, 7, § 9.
[4] *Ibid.*, § 10.
[5] *Tractatus de Intellectus Emendatione*, § 96 (*Opera*, II, p. 35, l. 12).   Cf. above, pp. 350–351.

understood," [1] or, as he sometimes says, through their "proximate" [2] or "efficient" [3] cause. According to this theory, man is not defined as a rational animal but rather as a combination of the modes of God's attributes of extension and thought, or, as Spinoza himself says, "the essence of man consists of certain modifications of the attributes of God." [4] Still, while Spinoza differs from his predecessors as to the nature of a definition, he does not differ from them as to the meaning of the term essence. The essence of a thing is still to him the concept of a thing attained by what he considers to be the definition of a thing, namely, the attributes of which the thing is a mode, for "a definition, if it is to be perfect," he says, "must explain the innermost essence of a thing." [5] But the attributes are said by Spinoza himself to be related to the *definiendum* as its genus and consequently as its immanent cause. [6] Spinoza is thus enabled to speak of the attributes or of substance or of God, just as his predecessors speak of the genus, as the cause of the essence of the *definiendum*, or, rather, as the immanent cause of the *definiendum*. But still, unlike the Aristotelian definition which merely states what a thing is but does not affirm that it exists, [7] Spinoza's theory of definition maintains that a definition affirms what a thing is as well as that it exists, for "given the definition of a thing, there should be no possibility of questioning whether it exists." [8] Though he says elsewhere that "the essence of things produced by God does not involve existence," [9] he does not mean that there is a possi-

[1] *Short Treatise*, I, 7, § 10.
[2] *Tractatus de Intellectus Emendatione*, § 96 (*Opera*, II, p. 35, l. 13).
[3] Epistola 60 (*Opera*, IV, p. 270, l. 22).
[4] *Ethics*, II, Prop. 10, Corol.
[5] *Tractatus de Intellectus Emendatione*, § 95 (*Opera*, II, p. 34, l. 29).
[6] Cf. above, pp. 324, 328.   [7] Cf. above, p. 124.
[8] *Tractatus de Intellectus Emendatione*, § 97 (*Opera*, II, p. 35, ll. 31–32).
[9] *Ethics*, I, Prop. 24.

bility of questioning whether they exist; he only means that their existence is not determined by their own nature but by their cause. Consequently, unlike the genus in the Aristotelian definition, the attributes, or substance, or God, or the proximate or the efficient cause in Spinoza's definition are the causes of both the existence and the essence of the thing defined. Hence in wishing to say that the modes are dependent upon God as their efficient cause Spinoza says in Proposition XXV that "God is the efficient cause not only of the existence of things, but also of their essence."

In the third place, says Spinoza, modes are dependent upon God as their only free cause. We already know that by the term free cause Spinoza means that "which exists from the necessity of its own nature alone, and is determined to action by itself alone," [1] and that when he speaks of God as being the only free cause [2] he means that God alone "acts from the laws of His own nature only, and is compelled by no one." [3] The modes, on the other hand, not being free, are determined in their action by some cause. This conclusion with regard to modes is summed up by Spinoza in two statements in Proposition XXVI, first, in a positive statement, "a thing which has been determined to any action was necessarily so determined by God," and second, in a negative statement, "that which has not been thus determined by God cannot determine itself to action."

Now this proposition, both in its positive and in its negative statements, would on the whole have been admitted by the mediaeval Jewish theologians and philosophers. In the Talmudic literature there occur such sayings as "everything is in the control of God," [4] "everything is foreseen," [5]

[1] *Ibid.*, I, Def. 7.   [2] *Ibid.*, I, Prop. 17, Corol. 2.
[3] *Ibid.*, I, Prop. 17.
[4] *Berakot* 33b, and parallels.
[5] *Abot*, III, 15.

and "no one on earth bruises his finger, unless it is decreed in heaven." [1] In the philosophic literature it is generally maintained that everything has a cause which ultimately goes back to God as the first cause. Thus Judah ha-Levi sums up the position of Jewish philosophers by saying that whatever one may think of freedom of the will, it is generally admitted that nothing happens which does not come either directly or indirectly under the decree or determination of God. [2] Similarly Maimonides maintains "that God is the efficient cause of the particular events that take place in the world, just as He is the efficient cause of the universe as a whole as it now exists." [3] But still, while they would have admitted both these parts of the proposition, they would have insisted that man has freedom of the will. The Talmudic statement that "everything is in the control of God" adds "except the fear of God," [4] and the statement that "everything is foreseen" adds "yet freedom of choice is given." [5] Similarly in the philosophic literature the principle of freedom of the will is maintained. Now this freedom of the will, according to its protagonists, does not exclude the omniscience and hence the foreknowledge of God. How these two can be reconciled constitutes the problem of the freedom of the will. Various solutions of this problem are offered. It is sometimes said that while God has foreknowledge of man's choice it does not determine that choice, for God's knowledge is not causative. [6] Or it is admitted that God has no foreknowledge of man's choice, but it is argued that such a lack of foreknowledge is no defect in God. [7] Sometimes it is argued that while indeed both the principle of man's

[1] *Ḥullin* 7b.
[2] *Cuzari*, V, 20.
[3] *Moreh Nebukim*, I, 69.
[4] *Berakot* 33b.
[5] *Abot*, III, 15.
[6] *Emunot we-De‘ot*, IV, 4; *Cuzari*, V, 20.
[7] *Emunah Ramah*, II, vi, 2 (p. 96).

freedom and the principle of God's foreknowledge are to be admitted, there is no contradiction between them, for God's knowledge is a homonymous term and is absolutely unlike human knowledge.[1] Now, all these, Spinoza must have argued in his mind, are a sort of specious reasoning and special pleading which do not really remove the essential difficulty. To say that God's knowledge is not causative or that God has no foreknowledge is to deny God's omnipotence and omniscience, and to say that God's knowledge is different from ours is tantamount to an admission that the problem is unsolvable. If God's omnipotence and omniscience are to be maintained, then God must be the cause of every future event and He must also have foreknowledge of that event. If despite this it is maintained that man has freedom of the will, then it means that man can render indeterminate that which has been determined by God. It is this pointed argument against the mediaeval position on the freedom of the human will that Spinoza had in mind when he said in Proposition XXVII that "a thing which has been determined by God to any action cannot render itself indeterminate."

Spinoza has thus explained the two sets of infinite and eternal modes, those which immediately follow from the attributes of God and those which follow from His attributes in so far as they are modified already by the immediate modes. But the world which Spinoza has undertaken to describe does not consist wholly of infinite and eternal modes. The modes which come directly under our observation are what Spinoza calls individual things (*res singulares*), and these are neither infinite in the perfection of their nature nor eternal in the duration of their existence. They are rather imperfect and transient things. Consequently, after having shown in Proposition XXV that God is the efficient cause not

---

[1] *Moreh Nebukim*, III, 20.

only of the existence of the infinite and eternal modes but also of their essence, he derives therefrom in the Corollary of the same proposition that "individual things are nothing but affections or modes of God's attributes, expressing those attributes in a certain and determinate manner." The implication of this statement is that God is also the cause of the existence and of the essence of finite modes. When in the next proposition he states in a general way that God is the cause of the action of a thing, he similarly means to assert that God is the cause of the action of the infinite and eternal modes as well as of the finite and transient modes. Thus individual things, like the infinite and eternal modes, follow from God and are determined by God in their existence, essence, and action.

But if individual things follow from God, then, since God is infinite, where does their finiteness come from? It will be recalled that both in his criticism of the emanationist explanation of the rise of matter out of an immaterial God [1] and in his own argument for the infinity and eternity of the immediate and mediate modes [2] Spinoza insisted upon strict adherence to the principle of necessary causality, namely, that the effect must be like the cause, so that cause and effect are mutually implicative concepts and one can be known by the other.[3] How then on the basis of this principle can Spinoza assert that finite things follow from the infinite God? Spinoza is thus now confronted with the same problem as the emanationists when these latter found themselves called upon to explain the rise of matter — the problem which Spinoza thought he had solved for good when he endowed God with the attribute of extension. The

[1] Cf. above, Chapter IV
[2] Cf. above, pp. 377–378.
[3] *Ethics*, I, Def. 4. Cf. above, p. 90.

problem now returns to him not in the form of how material things arose from an immaterial cause but rather in the form of how finite things arose from an infinite cause.

That Spinoza was conscious of this problem is quite evident. In the Second Dialogue in the *Short Treatise* he puts it in the mouth of Erasmus, who asks, if "the effect of the inner cause cannot perish so long as its cause lasts; . . . how then can God be the cause of all things, seeing that many things perish?" The same problem is again stated by him, not indeed directly in the form of a question but rather indirectly in the form of a positive statement, in the Demonstration of Proposition XXVIII in *Ethics*, 1: "That which is finite and which has a determinate existence could not be produced by the absolute nature of any attribute of God, for whatever follows from the absolute nature of any attribute of God is infinite and eternal." In both these places the same solution for the problem is offered. In the Second Dialogue of the *Short Treatise*, Erasmus, speaking for Spinoza, says that "God is really a cause of the effects which He has produced immediately, without any other conditions except His attributes alone; and that these cannot perish so long as their cause endures; but that you cannot call God an inner cause of the effects whose existence does not depend on Him immediately, but which have come into being through some other thing, except in so far as their causes do not operate, and cannot operate, without God, nor also outside Him, and that for this reason also, since they are not produced immediately by God, they can perish." The same explanation is given by Spinoza himself in *Short Treatise*, I, 8, where he says that the individual things are produced by the "general mode," which expression is used by him there to include both the immediate and mediate infinite modes, though he mentions there only the immediate modes.[1] Similarly in the Scholium to Proposition XXVIII of *Ethics*, I, Spinoza maintains that God is the absolutely proximate cause (*causa absolute proxima*) of the immediate infinite modes, that He is only the proximate cause in its own kind (*causa proxima in suo genere*) of the mediate infinite modes, but that in distinction to these, though not in the literal sense of the term, He is the remote cause (*causa remota*) of the individual things.[2] In addition to all this, he also says in Proposition XXVIII as follows: "An individual thing, or a thing which is finite and which has a determinate existence, cannot exist nor be determined to action unless it be determined to existence and action by another cause which is also finite and has a determinate existence, and again, this cause cannot exist nor be determined to action unless by another cause which is also finite and determined to existence and action, and so on *ad infinitum*." Taking all these passages together we may restate Spinoza's explanation of the rise of finite things as follows: Finite things follow directly from finite causes. These finite causes are infinite in number and form an infinite series of causes and effects. This infinite series of finite causes follows from the mediate infinite mode. This mediate infinite mode follows from the immediate infinite modes, which, in their turn, follow directly from God.

[1] Cf. above, pp. 216, 249.

[2] From the reading of the opening lines of the Scholium as given in Gebhardt's edition (*Opera*, II, p. 70, ll. 2–4; cf. editor's discussion on p. 352), it is clear that "quaedam a Deo immediate produci debuerunt" (l. 2) refers to the immediate infinite modes and that "et alia mediantibus his primis" (ll. 3–4) refers to the mediate infinite modes. When, therefore, Spinoza says later "that of things immediately produced by God He is the proximate cause absolutely, and not in their own kind" (ll. 5–7), it may be inferred that of the mediate infinite modes God is the proximate cause in their own kind. The distinction between these two senses of proximate cause is found in Heereboord's *Meletemata Philosophica, Disputationes ex Philosophia Selectae*, Vol. II, Disp. XXII. Cf. also above, p. 308.

The analogy between this explanation of the rise of finite things in the system of Spinoza and the explanation for the rise of material things in the system of emanation is quite complete. Just as the emanationists speak of material things as "proceeding" or as "following by necessity" from God, so also Spinoza speaks of finite things as "following" from God.[1] Just as the emanationists start out with the principle that "the direct emanation from God must be one simple Intelligence, and nothing else," [2] so also Spinoza starts out with the principle that "whatever follows from the absolute nature of any attribute of God is infinite and eternal." [3] Just as the emanationists account for the rise of material things by interposing immaterial Intelligences between God and matter, so also Spinoza accounts for the rise of finite things by interposing infinite modes between God and finite modes. Finally, just as the emanationists arrange all the material things, from the celestial spheres to the lowest of sublunar existences, in a series of causes and effects, so also Spinoza arranges all the finite modes in a series of causes and effects. The only difference between them is that according to the emanationists, who follow Aristotle in his denial of an infinite series of causes and effects,[4] this series is finite, whereas according to Spinoza, who, by his own statement,[5] admits with Crescas the possibility of an infinite series of causes and effects,[6] this series is infinite. The gist of both these explanations is that material things and finite things which cannot be conceived to follow directly from God can be conceived to follow indirectly from Him if we only inter-

[1] Cf. above, p. 373.   [2] *Moreh Nebukim*, II, 22.

[3] *Ethics*, I, Prop. 28, Demonst.

[4] *Metaphysics*, II, 1, 993a, 30 ff.

[5] Epistola 12. Cf. above, pp. 195 ff.

[6] Cf. my *Crescas' Critique of Aristotle*, pp. 68–69; 225–229; 490, n. 13; 496, n. 21.

pose between these material or finite things and God a buffer
of intermediate causes.

But still it is hard to see how a buffer of intermediate
causes can solve the problem. For, truly speaking, any explanation offered in solution of the problem of the rise of
finitude in Spinoza or of the rise of matter in emanation must
not only show that finitude or matter does not come directly
from the infinite or the immaterial cause but it must also
show how either one of these can come at all, seeing that
all things, according to both these systems, must ultimately
be traced to the infinite or the immaterial God as their prime
cause. This is the very reasoning employed by Maimonides
in rejecting necessary emanation,[1] and this is also the very
reasoning by which Spinoza was forced to the conclusion
that God is material.[2] The absence of any attempt on the
part of Spinoza to explain his position on this point, or, as
it may be phrased, the absence of any explicit statement of
a principle of individuation (*principium individuationis*) in
the philosophy of Spinoza, makes one wonder whether this
failure of his to offer any explanation was not due to the
fact that he did not think it was necessary for him to do so.
He may have felt quite justified in dispensing with such an
explanation for either one of the following two reasons —
either because he relied upon his readers to be able to find
among the several solutions evolved in the course of the history of philosophy by the various monistic systems, in explanation of their common difficulty as to how the many
arose from the one, a solution which would apply to his own
particular problem as to how the finite arose from the infinite,
or because he relied upon them to discover for themselves
some essential difference between his own particular kind of

[1] *Moreh Nebukim*, II, 22. Cf. above, p. 106.
[2] Cf. above, Chapter IV.

monism and the other kinds of monism by which the former was rendered immune to the difficulty which required a special principle of individuation for its solution. We shall, therefore, first canvass the various solutions of the common difficulty of monistic systems to see if any of them could be used by Spinoza, and then, in the event of our failure to find any solution which could be suitably used by him, we shall try to see if there is not something about Spinoza's conception of God which disposes of that common difficulty of monistic systems without any recourse to a special principle of individuation.

One of the explanations of the origin of the many which is common to monistic systems in the history of philosophy is to regard the many as unreal and as having only an illusory existence. In European philosophy this tendency appears with the Eleatics and recurs under different forms in the various idealistic systems. Some interpreters of Spinoza take his finite modes to be of a similar nature. But passages [1] in which Spinoza couples "affections" with "substance" as the two things which exist outside the mind, in contrast to attributes which he uses as an alternative term for substance, clearly indicate that he considered the modes as something having reality outside the mind like substance itself, and as being unlike the attributes, which he considered only as aspects under which substance appears to our mind. The only difference that Spinoza finds between the reality of substance and the reality of modes is that the former is due to the necessity of its own nature whereas the latter is due to the existence of substance. The finite modes are no less real to him than the infinite and eternal modes.

Another explanation which occurs in the history of philosophy in answer to the problem of how the many arose from

---

[1] *Ethics*, I, Prop. 4, Demonst.; Prop. 28, Demonst.

the one or the individual from the general consists in an attempt to accredit all these to matter. According to this explanation, all that is necessary is to account for the origin of matter, but once matter is accounted for, either by the theory of its co-eternal existence with God or by the process of emanation or by the belief in a special act of creation *ex nihilo*, there is a ready explanation for all the change, corruptibility, divisibility, individuality, and in fact for all the changing phenomena of the visible world. It is thus that mediaeval philosophers speak for Aristotle and for themselves of matter as the principle of individuation. Spinoza, however, could not offer matter as his principle of finitude, for if matter is taken as a principle of individuation it is only because it is considered as something which by its very nature is potential, passive, imperfect, and is consequently the cause of divisibility and corruptibility. But Spinoza's matter, being extension and an infinite attribute of God, is none of these,[1] and cannot therefore out of its own nature become the principle of finitude.

Still another explanation occurs in the history of philosophy which has a direct bearing upon Spinoza's problem here, for the problem which the explanation was meant to solve is formulated as here by Spinoza in terms of the rise of the finite from the infinite. This explanation may be designated by the Cabalistic Hebrew term *Zimzum*,[2] i.e., contraction. The theory of *Zimzum* has a long history and is susceptible of various philosophic rationalizations, but we shall quote here a brief statement of its original and unadulterated meaning from Abraham Herrera's *Puerta del Cielo*. Starting with the statement that "from an infinite power, it would seem, an infinite effect would necessarily have to follow," Herrera proceeds to say with the Cabalists that "in a certain

---

[1] Cf. above pp. 237, 257.   [2] צמצום.

manner God had contracted His active force and power in order to produce finite effects." [1]   It must have been with reference to this problem of the rise of the finite from the infinite that Solomon Maimon made in one of his works the cryptic remark that the view of Spinoza "agrees with the opinion of the Cabalists on the subject of *Zimzum*." [2]   In his autobiography, Solomon Maimon similarly calls attention to the analogy between Spinoza and the Cabalistic principle of *Zimzum* in the following passage: "In fact, the Cabala is nothing but an expanded Spinozism, in which not only is the origin of the world explained by the contraction (*Einschränkung = Zimzum*) of the divine being, but also the origin of every kind of being, and its relation to the rest, are derived from a special (*besondern*) attribute of God." [3]   However, Spinoza could have made no use of this theory of contraction in the solution of his problem of the rise of the finite from the infinite, for *Zimzum* as a solution of the problem implies that the infinite cause is an intelligent agent, and it is in this sense that it is generally used among the Cabalists, but to Spinoza, who insists upon the necessary nature of the divine causality, such an assumption is entirely inadmissible. To quote again from Herrera: "The second reason on account of which it is possible for us to maintain that the Infinite had in some manner contracted and limited himself in order to enable himself to produce finite and limited emanations is that the act of contraction is an act by means of His intelligence and His will." [4]

Finally, among the various formulations of the theory of

[1] *Sha'ar ha-Shamayim*, V, 12.

[2] Cf. Solomon Maimon's Hebrew commentary *Gib'at ha-Moreh* on *Moreh Nebukim*, I, 74.

[3] *Salomon Maimon's Lebensgeschichte von ihm selbst beschrieben*, Part I, Ch. XIV (1792), p. 146. English translation by J. C. Murray, Boston, 1888.

[4] *Sha'ar ha-Shamayim*, V, 12.

emanation which are advanced as explanations of the problem of the origin of matter there is one which, by analogy
with one of the present-day solutions of the problem of the
origin of life known as "emergent evolution," we may call
"emergent emanation."[1] It assumes indeed, as do all theories
of emanation, that God is immaterial and that matter does
not therefore arise directly from God. Still it does not arise
from anything external to God. Nor does it arise by the will
of God. It arises because in the process of emanation a new
cause inevitably makes its appearance. This new cause does
not proceed from God nor does it come from without, but
is the necessary concomitant of a new relation which, not
present in God, appears in the first Intelligence by the very
nature of its being an emanation and hence, unlike God,
having only possible existence. This theory says in effect that
matter is not the resultant of spiritual causes, but rather an
emergent, arising as something unpredictable out of a new
relation which makes its appearance in the emanated Intelligence. Now such an unpredictable new relation appears also
in Spinoza's immediate infinite modes, and it appears in them
by the very circumstance that their existence is dependent
upon God as their cause, and hence, unlike God, they have
only possible existence. Out of this new relation or condition,
not present in God but present in the immediate infinite
modes, Spinoza might say, there arise the finite modes.
Logically this would be a tenable explanation. But if we
assume this explanation to have been satisfactory to Spinoza
to account for the rise of finite modes from an infinite God,
why should he not have accepted it also as satisfactory to
account for the rise of material things from an immaterial

---

[1] Cf. my paper "The Problem of the Origin of Matter in Mediaeval Jewish
Philosophy and its Analogy to the Modern Problem of the Origin of Life" in *Proceedings of the Sixth International Congress of Philosophy* (1926), pp. 602 ff.

God? What then becomes of his main argument against the immateriality of God? If Spinoza did refuse to accept this sort of reasoning as an explanation of the rise of matter out of an immaterial cause, we must assume that he would also refuse to accept it as an explanation of the rise of finite modes out of an infinite cause.

Inasmuch as none of these historical solutions could be fittingly used by Spinoza, let us now look for some difference between Spinoza and the emanationists — a difference that would be sufficiently valid to dispose of the difficulty with which we are now contending.

Such a difference can be found if we only free Spinoza from the encumbrance of the traditional terminology which he affects, for, in truth, while he uses emanationist terms he does not mean by them exactly what the emanationists mean. When the emanationists speak of things as "proceeding" from God or as "following by necessity" from God,[1] they really mean that there is an actual egression of something from within God which on its departure from God assumes a nature unlike that of God. Though that departure is not in time nor in space, still logically the world follows from God in some order of succession and is outside of God. The Intelligences are thus conceived as proceeding from God and the spheres as proceeding from the Intelligences, and within the spheres appears matter which is not contained in God. In such a conception of succession, the appearance of matter, indeed, has to be accounted for. When Spinoza, however, describes the modes as following (*sequi*) from God or as being produced (*produci*) by God, or when he speaks of God as acting (*agit*) or as a cause, all these expressions, as we have shown above,[2] mean nothing but that the modes are contained in the substance as the conclusion of a syllogism is

---

[1] Cf. above, p. 373.   [2] Cf. above, p. 373.

contained in its premises and as the properties of a triangle are contained in its definition.[1] There is no such thing as the procession of the finite from the infinite in Spinoza. God or substance is to him an infinite logical crust which holds together the crumbs of the infinite number of the finite modes, and that crust is never broken through to allow the crumbs to escape or to emanate. Infinite substance by its very nature contains within itself immediate infinite modes, and the immediate infinite modes contain within themselves mediate infinite modes, and the mediate infinite modes contain within themselves the infinite number of finite modes, which last are arranged as a series of causes and effects. In such a conception of an all-containing substance there can be no question as to how the finite came into existence out of an infinite any more than there can be a question as to how substance came into existence. Substance is *causa sui*, and its nature is such that it involves within itself three orders of modes — immediate infinite, mediate infinite, and finite. The question as to how things come into existence can logically appear only within the finite modes, and the answer to this, as given by Spinoza, is that each finite mode comes into existence by another finite mode, and so on to infinity, but the entire infinite series is ultimately contained in God, who is *causa sui*, through the mediate and immediate infinite modes. Things are finite by the very fact that they are parts of a whole which is infinite.

Spinoza has thus proved that both the infinite modes and the individual things are determined by God in three respects, viz., in their existence, in their essence, and in their action. As a result of this he concludes in Proposition XXIX that "in nature there is nothing contingent, but all things are determined from the necessity of the divine nature to

[1] Cf. *Ethics*, I, Prop. 17, Schol., and above, p. 90.

exist and act in a certain manner." Three statements are
contained in this proposition. In the first place, it denies
contingency, or, as he calls it elsewhere, the existence of
"accidental things," which are defined by him as those
things which have "no cause"[1] or of which, through "a
deficiency in our knowledge . . . the order of causes is concealed from us."[2] Accidental things arc similarly defined
by Aristotle as those things which have no determinate
cause.[3] In the second place, since there are no accidental
things in nature but everything in nature is determined in
its existence and action by a cause, there is no freedom in
nature, if by freedom is meant, as it is defined by Spinoza,
that which exists and acts by its own nature and without
any other cause.[4] In the third place, all the causes in nature
are traceable to one cause, which is the necessity of the divine
nature. This concludes Spinoza's treatment of the modes.
Taking now all the modes together, the finite as well as the
infinite, he contrasts them with substance and attributes,
calling the former *natura naturata* and the latter *natura
naturans*.[5] Similarly in the *Short Treatise* he makes the same
classification at the beginning of his treatment of the modes.[6]
But we have already discussed this matter quite fully in the
chapter on Extension and Thought.[7]

---

[1] *Short Treatise*, I, 6, § 2. Cf. above, p. 318.

[2] *Ethics*, I, Prop. 33, Schol. 1. Cf. *Cogitata Metaphysica*, I, 3, and above, p. 189.

[3] *Metaphysics*, V, 30, 1025a, 24.

[4] Cf. *Ethics*, I, Def. 7.

[5] *Ibid.*, I, Prop. 29, Schol. Cf. above, p. 390, n. 1.

[6] *Short Treatise*, I, 8.

[7] Cf. above, pp. 253 ff.

CHAPTER XII

NECESSITY AND PURPOSELESSNESS

I. Intellect, Will, and Power

THE statement in Proposition XXIX that there is nothing contingent in nature, that everything is determined by a cause, and that the causes are traceable to God reflects on the whole the mediaeval philosophic position. When Crescas raises the question whether pure possibility exists in nature, he sums up the case for the negative by the statement that "in the case of all things that are subject to generation and corruption, their existence is necessarily preceded by four causes . . . and when we inquire again into the existence of these causes, it is also found that they must necessarily be preceded by other causes . . . and when we look for other causes for these causes, the same conclusion follows, until the series of causes terminate at the Prime Being who is necessary of existence." [1] Similarly Maimonides states that "when we have found for any existing thing those four causes which are in immediate connection with it, we find for them again causes, and for these again other causes, and so on until we arrive at the first causes," and then finally at God. [2] But the mediaevals, after having asserted the existence of this causal nexus, try to break the nexus at two points, by introducing a certain kind of design in the causality of God and a certain amount of freedom in the action of man. Spinoza will therefore now try to eliminate both design in God and freedom in man and will insist upon an un-

[1] *Or Adonai*, II, v, 2. Cf. above, p. 309.
[2] *Moreh Nebukim*, I, 69.

interrupted sequence of causal continuity. Here in the last seven propositions and Appendix of the First Part of the *Ethics*, which deals with God, he tries primarily to eliminate design in God; later in the last two propositions of the Second Part, which deals with man, he tries to eliminate freedom in man.

The design in God's actions, especially in the act of creation, is expressed by the mediaevals in terms of certain attributes which they find to be implied in the divine act of creation. Thus Saadia derives from the fact of creation that God has life, power, and knowledge.[1] Judah ha-Levi derives from the same fact that God has knowledge, power, life, and will.[2] Maimonides insists that creation must be an act of will and design,[3] which, according to his own statements, imply also life, knowledge, and power.[4] These four attributes then are what according to the mediaevals raise the actions of God above a mere mechanical process and make His causality the result of will, intelligence, and purpose.

In desiring to show that the causality of God is a necessary process Spinoza subjects these attributes to a critical examination with a view to finding out what they may actually mean when applied to God. He does this in two ways. First, he tries to prove that on the showing of the understanding of the meaning of the attributes of intellect, life, and power by the mediaevals themselves God's action must be a necessary action. This method of attack he has followed above in the Scholium to Proposition XVII. Second, unfolding his own conception of these attributes of intellect, will, and power, he again tries to show that God's action is a necessary action. This is what he is proposing to do now in Propositions XXX–XXXIV before us.

---

[1] *Emunot we-De'ot*, II, 4.
[2] *Cuzari*, V, 18, 7–9.
[3] *Moreh Nebukim*, II, 19 and 21.
[4] *Ibid.*, II, 19; I, 53.

In both these places, it will be noticed, Spinoza deals only with three out of the four attributes enumerated by the mediaevals, mentioning only intellect, will, and power, but leaving out life. The reason for his not mentioning life may perhaps be found in the fact that Spinoza defines life as "the power (*vim*) through which things persevere in their existence," and "moreover, the power by which God perseveres in His existence is nothing else than His essence." [1] Now, the "ability to exist" is defined by Spinoza himself as "power" (*potentia*).[2] Consequently, life (*vita*), according to Spinoza, is power (*potentia*). It may therefore be concluded that the omission of the attribute of life by Spinoza in the propositions before us is due to the fact that he has included it under the attribute of power.

In his first kind of argument in the Scholium to Proposition XVII, as we have already seen, Spinoza has arrived at the conclusion that, from the point of view of those who believe that intellect, will, and power pertain to the nature of God, it would have to follow that "God's intellect, will, and power are one and the same thing." On the whole, this represents exactly the views of Saadia, Maimonides, and the other Jewish philosophers, all of whom maintain that these attributes are one and the same in God. To quote a short passage from Maimonides: "You must know that wisdom [i.e., intellect] and life [and for that matter also will and power] in reference to God are not different from each other."[3] Similar statements as to the identity of intellect, will, and power in God are made by Spinoza in his *Cogitata Metaphysica*,[4] and there, too, he is merely repeating the common mediaeval view. In the Scholium to Proposition XVII,

[1] *Cogitata Metaphysica*, II, 6.   [2] *Ethics*, I, Prop. 11, Demonst. 3.
[3] *Moreh Nebukim*, I, 53. Cf. quotations from Saadia and Albo above, p. 155.
[4] *Cogitata Metaphysica*, II, 7, note, and 8.

therefore, he tries to establish the necessity of God's causality by arguing from this commonly accepted mediaeval view and contending that if intellect and will pertain to the essence of God and are one, then these attributes must be homonymous terms, and hence meaningless terms, and consequently to say that God acts by intelligence and will is tantamount to saying that God acts by necessity.[1]

But here in these Propositions XXX–XXXIV Spinoza tries to establish this necessary causality of God not by arguing from the generally accepted mediaeval view but by arguing against it. In the first place, he seems to say, the three attributes by which the mediaevals try to characterize the causality of God are not of the same order. Indeed, "the power of God is His essence itself,"[2] but as for intellect and will, they do not pertain to the essence of God. Intellect and will, which are the same,[3] are nothing but modes of God. What kind of mode the intellect, or, rather, the absolutely infinite intellect, is, has already been explained by Spinoza. It is the immediate mode of thought corresponding to motion and rest, which are the immediate mode of extension.[4] So is also will an immediate mode of thought. Consequently, "will and intellect are related to the nature of God as motion and rest,"[5] except that will and intellect are the immediate mode of the attribute of thought whereas motion and rest are the immediate mode of the attribute of extension. Now, the attribute of thought in its self-conscious activity has as the direct object of its knowledge the essence of God himself and through God's essence also the modes.[6]

[1] Cf. above, p. 317.   Cf. also Bruno, *De l'infinito universo et Mondi*, Dial. I, p. 316, ll. 21-31 (ed. Lagarde).   [2] *Ethics*, I, Prop. 34.   Cf. Prop. 17, Schol.

[3] *Ethics*, II, Prop. 49, Corol.; *Tractatus Theologico-Politicus*, Ch. 4 (*Opera*, III, p. 62, ll. 28–29).   [4] Cf. above, p. 216.

[5] *Ethics*, I, Prop. 32, Corol. 2.

[6] Cf. below, Vol. II, p. 17.

The intellect, however, not pertaining to the essence of God
and being only a mode of thought, cannot have the essence of
God as the object of its knowledge. But still, the object of
its knowledge must be something that exists outside the intellect itself. Since, however, outside the intellect there is
nothing but God or (which is the same thing by Def. IV)
His attributes and their modes,[1] and since furthermore the
intellect cannot comprehend the essence of God himself,
the object of its knowledge must be the attributes of God
and their affections, not only the attribute of thought, of
which it is itself a mode, and the modes of thought, but also
the attribute and modes of extension.[2] This is what is meant
by Proposition XXX: "The actual intellect, whether finite
or infinite," that is to say, whether the human intellect or
the absolutely infinite intellect, "must comprehend the attributes of God and the affections of God, and nothing else."

The terms "actual intellect" (*intellectus actu*) and "potential intellect" (*intellectus potentia*) used by Spinoza in this
proposition are a mediaeval heritage, and are to be found in
Arabic, Hebrew,[3] and Latin philosophy, but ultimately go
back to Aristotle's νοῦς ἐνεργείᾳ (or ἐντελεχείᾳ) and νοῦς δυνά-
μει, and these are to be distinguished from the terms "active
intellect" (*intellectus agens*) and "passive intellect" (*intellectus passivus*) which go back to the Greek νοῦς ποιητικός
and νοῦς παθητικός.[4] The terms "actual" and "potential"
describe two states of the intellect, one before the act of
thinking, when the intellect is a mere capacity, and the other

---

[1] *Ethics*, I, Prop. 4, Demonst.   [2] Cf. above, pp. 142 f.

[3] The Hebrew and Arabic terms are: (1) השכל בפועל, العقل بالفعل;
(2) השכל בכח, العقل بالقوّة.

[4] The corresponding Hebrew and Arabic terms are: (1) השכל הפועל,
العقل المنفعل; (2) השכל הנפעל, العقل الفعال.
Cf. below, Vol. II, p. 14.

in the act of thinking, when the intellect is an actuality. The nature of these two states of the intellect is discussed by Aristotle in *De Anima*, III, 4, the most pregnant passage in which is the following: "The intellect is in a manner potentially all objects of thought, but is actually none of them until it thinks." [1] An elaborate discussion of this distinction is also to be found in Maimonides in a chapter which has been drawn upon by Spinoza on several occasions.[2]   But, as Spinoza himself says, he uses the expression "actual intellect" not because he agrees with Aristotle and the mediaevals that there is a "potential intellect" but rather for the purpose of emphasizing the fact that the intellect is to him always that which Aristotle and the mediaevals would describe as actual, "that is to say, the act of understanding itself (*ipsa scilicet intellectione*)." [3]

Furthermore, says Spinoza, since intellect and will are modes whereas power is identical with the essence of God, intellect and will belong to *natura naturata*, whereas power, by implication, may be said to belong to *natura naturans*. Hence the significance of Proposition XXXI, that "the actual intellect, whether it be finite or infinite, together with will, desire, love, etc., must be referred to the *natura naturata* and not to the *natura naturans*." The mention of desire and love in this proposition together with will and intellect is in accordance with Spinoza's habit of referring to desire and love as modes either of will [4] or of thought.[5] Will and intellect, it may be recalled, are considered by Spinoza as modes of thought and as identical with each other.

Spinoza's denial of will as pertaining to the essence of God and his relegation of it to the realm of modes leads him

---

[1] *De Anima*, III, 4, 429b, 30–31.
[2] *Moreh Nebukim*, I, 68.   Cf. above, pp. 238–239; below, Vol. II. pp. 24, 45.
[3] *Ethics*, I, Prop. 31, Schol.
[4] *Short Treatise*, II, 2, § 4, and 16, § 8.   [5] *Ethics*, II, Ax. 3.

directly to a denial of the mediaeval attribution of freedom
of the will to God. As a prelude to what the mediaevals
meant by attributing freedom of will to God, we may first
make clear what they meant by will and by freedom of the
will in general. The best definition of will for our present
purpose is that given by Maimonides. "The true essence of
the will is the ability to will and not to will." [1] Practically
the same definition is also given by Descartes: "The faculty
of will consists alone in our having the power of choosing to
do a thing or choosing not to do it (that is, to affirm or deny,
to pursue or to shun it)." [2] Spinoza, as we shall show on a
later occasion, reproduces this definition when he says that
"by will I understand a faculty of affirming or denying." [3]
The implication of this definition is that there is no will unless
there is that possibility of choice between willing and not
willing. An eternal and immutable will, therefore, is a contradiction in terms, according to Maimonides. [4] As a result
of this definition, no act of the will can be an eternal and immutable act; it must have a beginning and end or it must
be an intermittent act. Now, proceed the mediaevals, if
the changes which by definition must occur in any act of the
will are brought about by external causes the will is said to
be not free. But if they are brought about without any external causes but by the very nature of the will itself, then
the will is called free. "Free will," says Judah ha-Levi, "*qua*
free will, has no compulsory cause." [5] Similarly Crescas defines absolutely free will as the ability "to will and not to will
without an external cause." [6] These definitions, in fact, cor-

---

[1] *Moreh Nebukim*, II, 18, Second Method.
[2] *Meditationes*, IV (*Oeuvre*, VII, p. 57, ll. 21–23).
[3] *Ethics*, II, Prop. 48, Schol.; *Short Treatise*, II, 16, § 2. Cf. below, Vol. II,
      p. 167.
[4] *Moreh Nebukim*, II, 21.
[5] *Cuzari*, V, 20.
[6] *Or Adonai*, II, v, 3 (p. 48b).

respond to Spinoza's own definition of freedom.[1] But while in nature in general, it is admitted by the mediaevals, there is no such free will, and while in the case of man the question of freedom constitutes one of their major problems of philosophy, with reference to God, they all maintain that He acts from the freedom of His will. Says again Maimonides: "If this will pertained to a material thing, so that the object sought after by means of that will was something outside the thing, there would then be a will which would change according to obstacles and newly arising circumstances. But the will of an immaterial being, which in no sense has for its object any other thing, is unchangeable, and the fact that it now wills one thing and tomorrow it wills another thing does not constitute a change in the essence of the being nor does it lead to the assumption of the existence of another cause [external to it]."[2] As against this the position taken by Spinoza may be summed up as follows: Granted that God is free, that freedom cannot be called freedom of the will; for will, he maintains, cannot pertain to the essence of God.

The argument for the inadmissibility of will in God is given in Proposition XXXII. Will, says Spinoza, cannot pertain to the essence of God. It is only an infinite mode, identical with the infinite intellect, following immediately from the attribute of thought. Being a mode of thought, it is determined by thought as its cause, just as the finite will of any individual being is determined by a series of causes, which series is infinite, according to Spinoza himself, or finite, according to the mediaevals.[3] Having a cause, will can no longer be called free. Hence, "the will cannot be called a free cause, but can only be called necessary."[4]

---

[1] *Ethics*, I, Def. 7. Cf. above, p. 311.   [2] *Moreh Nebukim*, II, 18.
[3] Cf. above, p. 196.
[4] *Ethics*, I, Prop. 32, and Demonst.

Furthermore, it follows "that God does not act from freedom of the will," [1] for will does not pertain to His essence
but is only a mode which by its very nature must have
a cause and cannot therefore be free. To say that God acts
from freedom of will has no more meaning than to say that
God acts from freedom of motion, since both are modes
respectively of the attributes of thought and extension. [2]

One of the implications of the mediaeval view that God
acts from freedom of will is that the world could have been
produced by God in another manner and in another order
than that in which it has been produced. A brief statement
of this view is to be found in Herrera's *Puerta del Cielo*.
In his fourth argument in proof that God acts from freedom
of the will he says that "such free action was the beginning
of all the things which were produced and caused by God
when it was so decreed by His will, and by the same token
God could have omitted to bring them into existence or
He could have brought other things into existence, and
even now after having brought these things into existence,
He can still change them, destroy them, and then bring
them back into existence, all according to His free choice
and will." [3]

But perhaps still more pertinent for our present purpose
are the statements made by Maimonides, in which he contrasts Aristotle's theory of necessity with his own theory of
creation by will and design, for in these statements we shall
find the background not only of the view which Spinoza rejects but also the view which he adopts as his own. Restating Aristotle's view, Maimonides says that "it is the view
of Aristotle that this universe proceeded from the Creator by
way of necessity, that God is the cause and the world is the

[1] *Ibid.*, Corol. 1.   [2] *Ibid.*, Corol. 2.
[3] *Sha'ar ha-Shamayim*. III. 6.

effect, and that this effect is a necessary one; and just as it cannot be explained why God exists or how He exists in this particular manner, namely, being one and incorporeal, so it cannot be asked concerning the whole universe why it exists or how it exists in this particular manner. For it is necessary that the whole, i.e., the cause as well as the effect, should exist in this particular manner; it is impossible for them not to exist, or to be different from what they actually are. This leads to the conclusion that the nature of everything remains constant, and that nothing changes its nature in any way." [1] As against this Maimonides maintains as his own view that "we who believe in creation must admit that God could have created the universe in a different manner as regards the causes and effects contained in it." [2] Or again: "We, however, hold that all things in the universe are the result of design, and not merely of necessity. It is possible that He who designed them may change them and conceive another design. Not every design, however, is subject to change, for there are things which are impossible by their nature and cannot be altered, as will be explained." [3] The exceptions referred to here by Maimonides are those things which he himself and other mediaevals consider as impossible on account of their involving a contradiction in their definition, such as, e.g., a square the triangle of which is equal to its side. [4]

With this as his background Spinoza formulates his own view in Proposition XXXIII, aligning himself with Aristotle as against Maimonides: "Things could have been produced by God in no other manner and in no other order than that in which they have been produced." Direct references to controversies on this point are made by him in his *Short*

[1] *Moreh Nebukim*, II, 19.
[2] *Ibid.*, III, 13.
[3] *Ibid.*, II, 19. Cf. 17.
[4] Cf. above, p. 312, n, 5.

Treatise.[1] In the *Short Treatise*, furthermore, there is a passage parallel to the demonstration of this proposition.[2] Here in the *Ethics* the most important part of the discussion is given in two Scholia. In the first Scholium Spinoza explains the meaning of the terms "necessary," "impossible," "possible," and "contingent," which we have already discussed on several occasions.[3] But the introduction of these terms right after the proposition, which is undoubtedly directed against the passage we have quoted above from Maimonides, is significant, for in that passage of Maimonides, as we have seen, reference is also made to the nature of the impossible. Spinoza seems to challenge Maimonides as follows: You say that while indeed in nature there are certain things which are impossible, there is nothing in it which is absolutely necessary, but everything in it is possible or contingent, inasmuch as everything in nature, according to you, can be changed or come into existence without any previous cause but by the mere will of God. As against you I say that in nature there are only things impossible and things necessary, but nothing that is absolutely possible or contingent.

The second Scholium falls into three parts, as follows: (1) From the beginning of the Scholium to "Neither is there any need that I should here repeat those things which are said in the Scholium to Proposition XVII" (*Opera*, II, p. 74, l. 20–p. 75, l. 3). (2) From "But for the sake of those who differ from me" to "and hence . . . God's intellect and will . . . must have been different, which is absurd" (*Opera*, II, p. 75, l. 3–p. 76, l. 3). (3) From "Since, therefore, things could have been produced by God in no other manner or order" to the end of the Scholium (*Opera*, II, p. 76, l. 4–l. 34).

---

[1] *Short Treatise*, I, 4, § 3 and § 7 (*Opera*, I, p. 37, ll. 16 ff., p. 38, ll. 30 ff.).
[2] *Ibid.*, § 7 (p. 38, ll. 33 ff.).   [3] Cf. above, pp. 188 ff.

In the first part Spinoza deals with a problem which he has already dealt with before in the Scholium to Proposition XVII, but he restates it here in a different form. On the previous occasion the problem was presented by him in the form of a question as to whether God has produced all the things which are actually in His intellect. Here the problem is presented by him in the form of a question as to whether God has produced all the things in as high a degree of perfection as they are actually in His intellect. In a somewhat similar way the problem is stated in the *Cogitata Metaphysica*: "If God created a duration so great that no greater could be given He necessarily diminished His own power." [1] Both these phases of the problem, however, are combined by him into one in the *Short Treatise* when he says: "But now, again, there is the controversy whether, namely, of *all* that is in His idea, and which He can realize so *perfectly*, whether, I say, He could omit to realize anything, and whether such an omission would be a perfection in Him." [2] In the passage from Herrera, which I have quoted as the literary background of Spinoza's discussion in the Scholium to Proposition XVII,[3] it may also be noticed that the two phases of the problem are combined. Not only does Herrera say that only a limited number of those things which are in the intellect of God have been produced by Him, but he also maintains that this limited number of things produced are not of the highest degree of perfection, for God, according to him, can still produce things of higher perfection. In his argument in the first part of the Scholium here Spinoza repeats in the main the arguments employed by him in the first part of the Scholium to Proposition XVII; he only changes the term omnipotence for perfection. His opponents say, he argues here, that if the

---

[1] *Cogitata Metaphysica*, II, 10.   [2] *Short Treatise*, I, 4, § 3.

[3] Cf. above, pp. 314 ff.

things produced by God are of the highest perfection, then God could no longer produce things which are more perfect, and if He could not do so, it would be an imperfection in Him. As against this Spinoza contends, in effect, that, quite the contrary, it is the perfection of God that must lead one to say that the things already produced by Him are of the highest perfection, for if He could have produced more perfect things and did not produce them, then His failure to produce them would have to be accounted for by some imperfection in His nature, the imperfection either of incompetency or of ill-will. A similar argument is put in the mouth of Aristotle by Maimonides in the following passage: "For, according to this theory, God, whom every thinking person recognizes to be endowed with all the kinds of perfections, is in such a relation to the existing beings that He cannot change in them anything. . . . Aristotle says that God does not try to make any change, and that it is impossible that He should will anything to be otherwise from what it is. If it were possible, it would not constitute In Him greater perfection; it might, on the contrary, from some point of view, be an imperfection." [1]

In the second part of the Scholium here Spinoza takes up again the main proposition, namely, "that things could be created in no other mode or order by Him," and tries to prove it against his opponents from their own admission "that will pertains to God's essence." Now, the main point in this premise admitted by his opponents, if we take Maimonides as its chief exponent, is that while the will of God is co-eternal with God, the world is not eternal, for will by its very nature means the ability to will to do a thing at one time and not to will to do it at another time,[2] and to adopt

---

[1] *Moreh Nebukim*, II, 22.   Cf. Bruno, *De l'infinito universo et Mondi*, Dial. I, p. 317, ll. 1 ff. (ed. Lagarde).   [2] *Ibid.*, II, 18.

one course or the other by an act of decree or decision; but, they contend, inasmuch as in the case of God the decree or decision is entirely independent of anything external to Him, it does not produce any change in His essence. As against this Spinoza raises the following question: This decree (*decretum*)[1] of God to make things in the manner and order in which they are, when did it take place? There are three possible assumptions: (1) It could have taken place shortly *before* the things were produced by God. (2) It could have co-existed with God from eternity, without any possibility of its being changed even by the will of God. (3) It could have co-existed with God from eternity, but with the possibility of its being subject to change by the will of God prior to His having produced the things. Spinoza, in the course of his discussion, examines all these three assumptions and tries to show either that they are untenable or that they prove just the opposite of what his opponents have set out to prove.

To begin with, the first assumption is untenable even according to the mediaevals themselves, for, according to Maimonides and others, prior to creation there was no time; what there was then may be called an "imagination of time" or, if you choose, eternity, in which there is no *before* nor *after*.[2] Spinoza thus says: "But since in eternity there is no *when* nor *before* nor *after*, it follows . . . that . . . God had not existed before His decrees, and could never exist without them."[3]

Then, proceeds Spinoza, if the second assumption be true, it will prove his own contention against his opponents.

---

[1] Hebrew and Arabic equivalent: גזירה قدر, قضا. (*Cuzari*, V, 19; *Moreh Nebukim*, III, 17).

[2] '*Ikkarim*, II, 18. Cf. above, p. 339.

[3] *Ethics*, I, Prop. 33, Schol. 2 (*Opera*, II, p. 75, ll. 12-15).

If things have come into existence exactly in the manner in which it had been decreed by God from eternity and if God could not have changed that decree, then "things could have been produced by God in no other manner and in no other order than that in which they have been produced."[1] This second assumption, it may be remarked, seems to reflect the following statement in Heereboord: "What God does in time He has decreed from eternity."[2] But Spinoza seems to differ from Heereboord as to the meaning of this statement. According to Heereboord, this statement does not mean that "God accomplishes things in time in the order in which He has decreed them from eternity";[3] it only means that "God produces in time the things which He has decreed from eternity and He produces them as He has decreed to produce them."[4] According to Spinoza, the order as well as the nature of things has been decreed from eternity. In Proposition XXXIII he speaks of the unchangeability of the manner (*modus*) and order (*ordo*) in which things have been produced, and in Scholium II, evidently in direct opposition to Heereboord, he speaks of both the nature of things (*rerum natura*) and their order (*ordo*)[5] as having been decreed by God from eternity.

There is nothing left therefore for his opponents but to adopt the third assumption, namely, that God himself could have changed His eternal decree prior to the creation of the world so that the world could have been created otherwise than the way it had been decreed from eternity. As

[1] *Ibid.*, II, Prop. 33.

[2] *Meletemata Philosophica, Disputationes ex Philosophia Selectae*, Vol. II, Disp. XXIV, IX: "Uti quid Deus facit in tempore, ita ab aeterno decrevit."

[3] *Ibid.*: "Quo ordine res Deus decrevit ab aeterno, eo in tempore exequitur."

[4] *Ibid.*: "Quas res decrevit ab aeterno et quales decrevit facere, eas et tales in tempore facit."

[5] *Opera*, II, p. 75, ll. 16–17, 20.

against this, Spinoza raises four objections, which, it must
be said, have not passed unnoticed by the mediaevals themselves.

First, it implies that prior to creation there could have
been a change in God's will and hence also in His intellect
with which His will is identical. Maimonides himself has
discussed this problem and admits that such a change in
God's will is possible inasmuch as it is not determined by
any external cause.[1]

Second, if such a change in God's will was possible before
creation, why should it not be possible now after creation?
Here, too, Maimonides would say that if God willed it and
if it served any purpose He could change the order of nature
even after its creation, except in things which are impossible
by their own nature and would involve a contradiction in
their definition.[2]

Third, Maimonides as well as all other philosophers agrees
"that God is an intellect which always is in action, and that
there is in Him no potentiality at all."[3] But to say that
God changes His will or intellect implies a change from potentiality to actuality, which is contrary to their own premise. This argument, too, has been discussed by Maimonides,
who tries to show that in an incorporeal agent a change
from non-action to action does not imply a transition from
potentiality to actuality. "The active intellect may be
taken as an illustration. . . . It is an evident fact that
the active intellect does not act continually . . . and yet
Aristotle does not say that the active intellect is changeable,
or passes from a state of potentiality to that of actuality,
although it produces at one time something which it has not

[1] *Moreh Nebukim*, II, 18. Cf. above, pp. 101 ff.

[2] *Ibid.*, II, 19; III, 25. Cf. above, p. 312.

[3] *Ibid.*, I, 68. Cf. above, p. 239.

produced before." [1] In fact, Spinoza himself makes use of this statement of Maimonides in the *Short Treatise*. "Furthermore, of such an agent who acts in himself it can never be said that he has the imperfection of a patient, because he is not affected by another; such, for instance, is the case with the intellect." [2]

Fourth, Maimonides and all the other mediaevals admit that God's will and intellect are identical with His essence. [3] To say therefore that His will could change would imply that His essence could also change. This, too, is answered by Maimonides. "Similarly it has been shown by us that if a being [like God] acted at one time and did not act at another, this would not involve a change in the being itself." [4]

In the third part of the Scholium Spinoza combines all the three phases of the problem and asserts (1) that "things could have been produced by God in no other manner or order," (2) that God created "all things which are in His intellect," and (3) that the things created were created "with the same perfection as that in which they exist in His intellect." All these three principles are included in what Spinoza calls necessity, by which he means that things cannot be otherwise than what they are, that they cannot be more than they are, and that they cannot be more perfect than they are. The mediaeval views which are in opposition to this conception of necessity are divided by Spinoza into two classes. The first class is characterized by him as the view which makes everything dependent upon "the will of God alone" (*Dei tantum voluntas*) or upon "a certain indifferent God's will" (*indifferens quaedam Dei voluntas*) or upon God's "good pleasure" (*ipsius beneplacitum*). According to this

[1] *Ibid.*, II, 18, First Method.
[2] *Short Treatise*, I, 2, § 24 (*Opera*, I, p. 26, ll. 23–26).
[3] *Moreh Nebukim*, I, 53 and 68. Cf. above, pp. 155, 317, 402.
[4] *Ibid.*, II, 18, Second Method.

view not only are things in themselves neither perfect nor imperfect, but they are also neither good nor evil. They are so only by the will of God alone, and therefore if God had willed He could have made them otherwise. The second class is characterized by him as the view of those "who affirm that God does everything for the sake of the good." Spinoza's characterization of these two mediaeval views reflects again Maimonides' discussion of the difference between the view of the Mohammedan Ashariya and his own view. According to the Ashariya everything is the result of God's will alone; according to Maimonides, it is the result of both will and wisdom. The essential difference between these two views is the question whether the things created by God and the commandments revealed by Him are the work of an arbitrary will or whether they are created and revealed for the sake of some purpose.[1] "Purpose" is another word used by Maimonides for what Spinoza calls here "the good," for, as says Maimonides, "we call 'good' that which is in accordance with the object we seek."[2] Similarly Heereboord says that "the good is the formal reason of the final cause."[3] All these go back to Aristotle's definition of the good as "that which all things aim at."[4]

In Maimonides' own words the Asharian view is described as the view of those thinkers "who assume that God does not produce one thing for the sake of another, that there are no causes and effects, but that all His actions are the direct result of the will of God, and no purpose can be found for them, nor can it be asked why He has made this and not that; for He does what pleases Him, and it is not to be considered as the result of some kind of wisdom."[5]

[1] *Ibid.*, III, 25 and 26.　　　　[2] *Ibid.*, III, 13.
[3] *Meletemata Philosophica, Disputationes ex Philosophia Selectae*, Vol. II, Disp. XXIII, 11: "Bonitas ergo formalis ratio est causae finalis."
[4] *Nicomachean Ethics*, I, 1, 1094a, 3.　　　　[5] *Moreh Nebukim*, III, 25.

His own view is described by him as follows: "The things which God wills to do are necessarily done; there is nothing that could prevent the realization of His will. God, however, wills only that which is possible; not indeed everything that is possible, but only such things as His wisdom decrees upon." [1] "The only question to be asked," says Maimonides in another place, "is this: What is the cause of this design? The answer to this question is that all this has been made for a purpose which is unknown to us." [2]

In criticizing both these views, Spinoza dismisses the first one by summarizing his previous contention that a change in God's will is unthinkable. Still, though he is opposed to this view, he considers it nevertheless "at a less distance from the truth" than the second view, which he proceeds to refute in the following statement. "For these seem to place something outside of God which is independent of Him, to which He looks while He is at work as to a model, or at which He aims as if at a certain mark. This is indeed nothing else than to subject God to fate, the most absurd thing which can be affirmed of Him. . . . Therefore it is not worth while that I should waste time in refuting this absurdity."

There is more hidden away in this statement than what it seems to convey to the mind of the casual reader. We may try to unfold all its implications by making Spinoza address Maimonides directly and speak out all that was in the back of his mind when he gave utterance to this statement. Spinoza seems to address Maimonides as follows:

You say that things do not depend upon an arbitrary will of God but upon a rational will, which you call wisdom, so that everything created by God has a purpose. God, then, is guided by a purpose or by His Wisdom, the nature of

[1] *Ibid.*   [2] *Ibid.*, II, 19.

which you say is unknown to us, but which you maintain is not external to Him. It is well for you to seek refuge out of the difficulties into which your own philosophy so often leads you by pleading ignorance. But those predecessors of yours, the rabbis, aye, and the philosophers, too, whose traditional teachings, from which you refuse to depart, are responsible for all your philosophical difficulties, did confess to know what that divine Wisdom was and the purpose for which all things were created. They say that the Wisdom, which speaks in person in the eighth chapter of the Book of Proverbs, is the Torah, or the Law of Moses, and it is the Torah which is regarded by them as the purpose for which the world was created.[1] Furthermore, this Torah, though not considered in Judaism to be eternal, existed, according to its beliefs, before the creation of the world, and it is said that God consulted it as to the creation of the world,[2] and that it served Him as a sort of model according to which the world was created; as the rabbis say: "God looked into the Torah and created the world."[3] Not only your rabbis but also your philosopher Philo speaks of Wisdom and of the Logos in the same way as the rabbis speak of the Torah, namely, as divine instruments of creation.[4] Of course, you yourself do not take these statements literally. You insist upon identifying Wisdom with the essence of God. But it is these traditional utterances about Wisdom in the sense of the Torah that really lie behind your statements that things were created for some unknown purpose and by some un-

---

[1] Or *Adonai*, II, vi, 4, quoting as proof-text the rabbinic dictum אלמלא תורה לא נתקיימו שמים וארץ (*Pesaḥim* 68b), which he evidently takes to mean "but for the Torah, heaven and earth would not have come into existence." The dictum, however, may mean "but for the Torah, heaven and earth would not continue to exist."   [2] *Pirke de-Rabbi Eliezer*, Ch. 3.

[3] *Genesis Rabbah*, I, 1, and parallels.

[4] *De Eo: Quis Rerum Divinarum Heres Sit*, XLI, 199; *De Cherubim et Flammeo Gladio*, XXXV, 124 ff. Cf. Drummond, *Philo Judaeus*, II, pp. 205–206.

known divine wisdom. Stripped of this metaphysical garb with which you have clothed these ancient utterances, your own statements "seem to place something outside of God which is independent of Him, to which He looks while He is at work ·as to a model, or at which He aims as if at a certain mark."

But furthermore, Spinoza seems to say to Maimonides, if the Torah is that which God consulted and by which God was guided in creating things, then your God is governed by a Torah or Wisdom or Logos just as some philosophers, say the Stoics, maintain that the world is governed by fate (*fatum*, ἡ εἱμαρμένη). "This indeed is nothing else than to subject God to fate." This by itself makes Spinoza's statement intelligible enough. But there may be even more than that in it. The Stoics speak of fate as the Logos of the universe.[1] Similarly Philo refers to the Logos as that "which most men call fortune (τύχη),"[2] fortune probably being here an interchangeable term with fate.[3] What Spinoza therefore would seem to say to Maimonides is this: Since the Stoic and the Philonic Logos, which is sometimes used as the equivalent of Wisdom or your Torah, is called fate, when God is said to be ruled by the Torah or Wisdom or the Logos, He is really said to be ruled by fate. In fact Campanella combines the terms "wisdom" and "fate" when he speaks of the maintenance of things by the power of God or necessity, by His wisdom or fate (*fatum*), and finally by His love or ordinance.[4]

---

[1] Cf. Zeller, *Philosophie der Griechen*, III, 1, p. 161, n. 2 (4th ed.). English translation: *Stoics, Epicureans, and Sceptics*, p. 161, n. 3.

[2] *Quod Deus Sit Immutabilis*, XXXVI, 176.

[3] Cf. Francis Bacon, *De Augmentis Scientiarum*, III, 4 (*Works*, London, 1857, Vol. I, p. 569): "quas uno nomine *Fatum* aut *Fortunam* vocabant."

[4] Reproduced by Erdmann, *Grundriss der Geschichte der Philosophie*, I, § 246. 4, based upon Campanella's *Philosophia Universalis*, VI, Proem.

Now Spinoza would not shrink from the use of the term "fate" in its strictly Stoic sense of a universal and inscrutable law that governs all things. In fact in *Short Treatise*, I, 6, he practically uses the term "fate" when he describes the contents of the chapter in which he denies the existence of any accidental things by the title "On Divine Predestination." But what he insists upon saying here is that while all things and all actions, in so far as they follow with inevitable necessity from the nature of God, may be said in a certain sense to have a fatalistic necessity, God himself must be conceived as absolutely free and as not being subject to any fate. This distinction evidently was difficult to be grasped by his correspondents, and on several occasions in letters to Ostens and Oldenburg Spinoza felt called upon to explain himself. To quote a few characteristic passages from these letters: "The basis of his argument is this, that he thinks that I take away God's liberty, and subject Him to fate. This is entirely false. For I assert that all things follow with inevitable necessity from the nature of God, just as all assert that it follows from the nature of God that He understands himself." [1] Again: "I want to explain here briefly in what sense I maintain the fatalistic necessity of all things and of all actions. For I do in no way subject God to fate, but I conceive that everything follows with inevitable necessity from the nature of God, just as all conceive that it follows from the nature of God himself that He should understand himself." [2]

Unlike intellect and will, which do not pertain to God, power, as we have already pointed out, is admitted by Spinoza to pertain to the essence of God and to be identical with His essence. Hence Proposition XXXIV: "The power of God is His essence itself." Power, as we have elsewhere

[1] Epistola 43.   [2] Epistola 75.

remarked, means to Spinoza the ability to exist and the ability to bring things into existence.[1] Hence Spinoza defines God's power here in the demonstration of the proposition as that "by which He himself and all things are and act." From this definition of power and from its identity with the essence of God Spinoza tries to solve again the problem which he has discussed in Scholium II to Proposition XVII and in the third part of the Scholium to Proposition XXXIII, namely, whether God created all things which are in His intellect. His answer is in the affirmative. Hence Proposition XXXV: "Whatever we conceive to be in God's power necessarily exists." In the *Short Treatise* he expresses the same view by saying: "We deny that God can omit to do what He does." [2]

II. FINAL CAUSES

It may be recalled that the mediaevals apply the term "cause" to God in three out of its four Aristotelian senses. God is to them the efficient, formal, and final cause, but not the material cause, of the world.[3] In opposition to them, Spinoza made God also the material cause of the world, and by further reducing the formal to the efficient cause, he has throughout his discussion of the causality of God, from Proposition XV to XXXV, elaborated in great detail his conception of the efficient causation of God. In the course of his discussion he has also refuted the views of those who, having denied the principle of causality altogether, attributed the succession and change of things either to chance [4] or to the direct intervention of God's arbitrary will.[5] The latter view, which is discussed by him in the last part of

---

[1] Cf. above, pp. 204–205.
[3] Cf. above, p. 302.
[5] Cf. above, pp. 416 ff.
[2] *Short Treatise*, I, 4, § 1.
[4] Cf. above, p. 318.

Scholium II to Proposition XXXIII, led him to touch upon the problem of final causation, without, however, going into a full discussion of the problem. Now, at the conclusion of the first Part of the *Ethics*, Spinoza wanted to come out with a formal denial of the mediaeval view as to the existence of final causes in nature.[1] But following his general custom in the propositions of the *Ethics*, instead of directly opposing the mediaevals, he states his own position in positive terms, but in such a manner as to contain an indirect denial of the commonly accepted belief in final causes.

The oppositional views in the history of philosophy to final causes may be summed up under two headings. First, the view that everything is the result of the arbitrary will of God, which, as we have seen, Maimonides attributes to the Mohammedan Ashariya. Second, the view that everything is the result of chance and accident, which, again, Maimonides attributes to the Epicureans.[2] Spinoza, as we have seen, has discussed both these views and rejected them.[3] The method by which he now tries in Proposition XXXVI to reject final causes altogether is by reducing every final cause to an efficient cause. When two events constantly and repeatedly succeed one another, he seems to say, it is not to be explained in terms of final causes, namely, that the first event aims at, or is made to serve, the second event as its purpose, but it is to be explained rather solely in terms of efficient causes, namely, that the second event follows by necessity from the nature of the first event, for "nothing exists from whose nature an effect does not follow." This method of eliminating final causes by reducing them to

---

[1] On the general problem of final causes in the philosophy of Spinoza, see Peter Brunner, *Probleme der Teleologie bei Maimonides, Thomas von Aquin und Spinoza* (Heidelberg, 1928).

[2] *Moreh Nebukim*, II, 13. Cf. above, p. 318.

[3] Cf. above, pp. 416 ff.

efficient causes is already indicated in the *Cogitata Meta-physica*: "Second, I say that in creation no causes concur except the efficient one. I might have said that creation negates or excludes all causes except the efficient." [1] A still clearer statement to the same effect occurs in the Preface to *Ethics*, IV: "A final cause, as it is called, is nothing, therefore, but human desire. . . . Therefore, having a house to live in, in so far as it is considered a final cause, is merely this particular desire, which is really an efficient cause." [2] This in fact is nothing but a logical corollary from Aristotle's own denial of design and purpose in God's causality, which Spinoza seems to be stressing in this proposition against Aristotle. For Aristotle, though he denies design and purpose in the causality of God, still maintains that there are final causes in nature, a logical inconsistency which Maimonides makes much of in his defence of the belief in creation. [3] Thus both Maimonides and Spinoza see the inconsistency in Aristotle's attempt to uphold the existence of final causes in nature while denying at the same time the existence of design in God, but as they are in disagreement as to which of these two premises is correct, they arrive at two diametrically opposite conclusions. Maimonides starts with the Aristotelian premise that there are final causes in nature and therefore argues, as against Aristotle, that there must be design in the causality of God. Spinoza, on the other hand, starts with the Aristotelian premise that there is no design in the causality of God and therefore argues, also against Aristotle, that there cannot be final causes in nature. This denial of final causes by Spinoza re-echoes, on the whole, Francis Bacon's condemnation of the search of final

[1] *Cogitata Metaphysica*, II, 10.
[2] *Opera*, II, p. 207, ll. 2–4 and 9–11.
[3] *Moreh Nebukim*, II, 20 ff.

causes in the realm of physics.[1] But unlike Bacon, who admits that final causes are "true and worthy to be inquired in metaphysical speculations"[2] and that they are perfectly compatible with efficient or physical causes, "except that one declares an intention, the other a consequence only,"[3] Spinoza eliminates them even from metaphysical speculations.

If this is the meaning of the last proposition, then the Appendix to Part I, which deals exclusively with the problem of final causes, is, with the exception of the introductory paragraph, really a scholium to the last proposition of Part I. In the Appendix, Spinoza starts out with a restatement of that "which men commonly suppose" with regard to final causes. The passage which follows falls into two parts and betrays the influence of two different sources. The first part restates the view of those who hold "that all things in nature, like men, work for (*propter*) some end; and indeed it is thought to be certain that God himself directs all things to some sure end (*ad certum aliquem finem*)." The immediate source of this view is the following passage in Heereboord: "All natural things work for (*propter*) some end, or, rather, they work to some end, since they are directed by God to an end pre-determined for each thing (*ad finem singulis praefixum*)."[4] The second part of the passage adds "for it is said that God has made all things for man, and man that he may worship God." The immediate source of this statement seems to be a combination of the following passages in Saadia and Maimonides. Saadia's passage reads as follows: "Should it occur to one to ask for what reason

[1] *De Augmentis Scientiarum*, III, 4.

[2] *Ibid.*, III, 4 (*Works*, London, 1857, Vol. I, p. 570; Vol. IV, p. 364).

[3] *Ibid.*

[4] *Meletemata Philosophica, Disputationes ex Philosophia Selectae*, Vol. II, Disp. XXIV, II, § 1: "Res omnes naturales agunt propter finem, aut potius aguntur ad finem, quatenus a Deo diriguntur ad finem singulis praefixum."

did God create all these things, three answers may be given.
. . . The third answer is that He created the beings for their
own benefit so that He might direct them in that benefit and
they might worship Him." [1] In another place Saadia states
that "although we observe that the created beings are many
. . . the end of all of them is man."[2] Maimonides' passage,
in which there seems to be an allusion to the statements
quoted from Saadia, reads as follows: "But of those who
accept our theory that the whole universe has been created
from nothing, some hold that the inquiry after the purpose
of creation is necessary, and assume that the universe was
only created for the sake of man's existence, that he might
worship God."[3] It must, however, be remarked that, contrary to what may be inferred from Spinoza's statement
here, neither Saadia nor Maimonides is in the least dogmatic about this view. Maimonides definitely rejects the
view that the universe exists for man's sake and that man
exists for the purpose of worshipping God, and gives as his
own view that "we must in continuing the inquiry as to the
purpose of creation at last arrive at the answer that it was
the will of God or that His wisdom decreed it."[4] Even Saadia
gives as his first answer to the question as to the purpose of
creation the view "that God created things for no purpose at
all . . . for God is above any consideration of external
purpose."[5]

Spinoza's own discussion of the problem is divided by
himself into three parts. First, how man came to the idea
of final causes. Second, arguments against the existence of
final causes. Third, certain erroneous conceptions to which
the idea of final causes gave rise.

[1] *Emunot we De'ot*, I, 1   [2] *Ibid.*, IV, Introduction.
[3] *Moreh Nebukim*, III, 13.   [4] *Ibid.*
[5] *Emunot we-De'ot*, I, 4.

In his account of the origin of the belief in final causes and his explanation of the question "why all are so naturally inclined to embrace it," Spinoza does nothing more than transform the reasons which his predecessors had used as arguments for the existence of final causes into motives for their belief in final causes. He seems to say to them: Your so-called arguments for the existence of final causes are nothing but the expressions of your desires and wishes which you put in the form of logical arguments. Or to put it in other words, Spinoza tries to show that what the mediaevals call reasons are only different forms of rationalization.

Take the conception of final causes in human actions, Spinoza seems to argue, and you will find that even there, where final causes are generally assumed to exist beyond any shadow of a doubt, their existence may be questioned. For what basis is there for this general belief that man does everything for an end, if not the belief that man is free to choose from two alternatives that which is profitable to him. Let us then consider what is meant by this freedom of choice. The best description, Spinoza would seem to argue, is to be found in Saadia, who says that it is a matter of common observation that "man feels that he can speak or remain silent, seize or set loose, and all this without being conscious of any force that could restrain him from carrying out his desire."[1] Freedom then is that feeling of being able to choose without being conscious of any compulsion to make the choice. This choice, furthermore, is supposed to be made in consideration of a certain end which man has in view, and it is this supposition of an end which is generally taken to establish the existence of final causes in human action. But, says Spinoza, is it not possible that the consciousness of freedom

[1] *Ibid.*, IV, 4.

is only a delusion based upon the ignorance of the true causes that really determine one's action, and therefore the belief that one acts for a certain purpose or final cause is also a delusion based upon an ignorance of the real causes, which are always efficient causes, that really necessitate one's action? "It will be sufficient," says Spinoza, "if I take here as an axiom that which no one ought to dispute, namely, that man is born ignorant of the causes of things, and that he has a desire, of which he is conscious, to seek that which is profitable to him. From this it follows, firstly, that he thinks himself free . . . and, secondly, it follows that man does everything for an end."

It must, however, be remarked that Spinoza had been anticipated by Crescas in the suggestion that the consciousness of freedom may be a delusion. In discussing the argument for freedom from the fact that man is not conscious of any compulsion in making a decision, Crescas says that "though man, in making a choice, is unconscious of any compulsion and restraint, it is quite possible that, were it not for some cause that compels him to choose one of the alternatives, he would desire both alternatives alike." [1]

Spinoza continues with the same method of argument with which he had started. Taking the traditional philosophic evidences for design in nature from which the mediaevals tried to prove creation and the existence of an intelligent deity, he transforms them into psychological motives which have induced man to attribute the delusions of his own freedom and of the purposiveness of his own actions to nature and God. The traditional philosophic view is summed up by Maimonides in the following passage: "Aristotle repeatedly says that nature produces nothing in vain,[2] that is to

[1] *Or Adonai*, II, v, 3.
[2] *De Caelo*, I, 4, 271a, 33; *De Anima*, III, 9, 432b, 21.

say, every natural action must necessarily have a certain object. Thus, Aristotle says that plants were created for the sake of animals; and similarly he shows in the case of some other things that one exists for the sake of the other. This is still more obvious in the case of the organs of animals. Know that the existence of such a final cause in the various parts of nature has compelled philosophers to assume the existence of a primal cause apart from nature, namely, that which Aristotle calls the intelligent or divine principle, which divine principle creates one thing for the purpose of another. And know also that to those who acknowledge the truth, the greatest of all arguments for the creation of the world is that which has been demonstrated with regard to natural things, namely, that every one of them has a certain purpose and that one thing exists for the sake of another." [1] All this, says Spinoza, is simply a projection of man's own purposes into the actions of other human beings and into nature, for "by his own mind he necessarily judges that of another" and thus also "it comes to pass that all natural objects are considered as means for obtaining what is profitable." Furthermore, since man has falsely considered these things as means to some end, he thought "it was impossible to believe that they had created themselves," and so again by an analogy of his own experience he inferred "that some ruler or rulers of nature exist, endowed with human liberty, who have taken care of all things for him, and have made all things for his use." The allusions in this passage to the passages quoted from Maimonides are quite apparent. Spinoza finally concludes his argument with a condemnation of the Aristotelian principle quoted by Maimonides, namely, that "nature does nothing in vain," as an attempt to show "that nature, the gods, and man are alike mad."

[1] *Moreh Nebukim*, III, 13.

One would naturally expect that in discussing design in nature Spinoza would resuscitate the old problem of evil which philosophers before him had found at variance with the assumption of design and providence in nature. Spinoza introduces this problem with an enumeration of the so-called physical evils which are similarly discussed by Maimonides in connection with the problem of final causes and design,[1] and in connection with the problem of divine knowledge.[2] The evils which Spinoza happens to mention, "storms, earthquakes, diseases," are reminiscent of the list of evils mentioned by Gersonides, in which are included evils which arise "from the mixture [i.e., diseases] . . . earthquakes, storm, and lightning." [3] But when Spinoza pretends to reproduce the mediaeval explanation of evil by saying that "it was affirmed that these things happened because the gods were angry either because of wrongs which had been inflicted on them by man, or because of sins committed in the method of worshipping them," he does not do justice to their case. Maimonides, Gersonides, and others had more subtle solutions for the problem of evil.

This explanation that physical evil is a divine retribution for moral evil or sin, which Spinoza rightly or wrongly reproduces as the only or the chief explanation that had been advanced for the problem, leads him to revive the old question, already raised in the Bible, especially in the Book of Job, and repeated throughout the history of Jewish religious literature as well as in the literature of other religions, namely, that our observation does not confirm the belief that physical evil is proportionate to moral evil, for "experience," says Spinoza, "daily contradicted this, and showed

---

[1] *Ibid.*, III, 12.   [2] *Ibid.*, III, 16, end.

[3] *Milḥamot Adonai*, IV, 3 (pp. 160–161); Introduction to his Commentary on Job.

by an infinity of examples that both the beneficial and the injurious were indiscriminately bestowed on the pious and the impious." Parallel passages in which the problem is stated in similar terms can be picked up at random in almost any mediaeval work dealing with this problem. But I shall quote here only the following passage from Crescas: "The great difficulty which cannot be solved completely . . . is the ill-order which is believed to exist in the world from the fact of our observation that many worthy people are like the dust at the feet of unworthy ones, and, in general, the question why there is a righteous man who fares badly and a wicked man who fares well, a question by which prophets and philosophers have been perplexed unto this day." [1]

Many solutions are offered for this problem. Maimonides, for instance, enumerates four theories, the Aristotelian, the Scriptural or his own, the Mutazilite, and the Asharian, and finds that Job and his three friends, Eliphaz the Temanite, Bildad the Shuite, and Zophar the Naamathite, are respectively the spokesmen of these four views. [2] Spinoza seems to sum up all the solutions of the problem in the following general statement: "Hence it was looked upon as indisputable that the judgments of the gods far surpass our comprehension." It is quite possible that this is all that the various solutions ultimately amount to. Strictly speaking, however, the solution mentioned here by Spinoza as typical of all the solutions would, according to Maimonides, represent only the view of Zophar the Naamathite or of the Ashariya.

In the second part of the Appendix we may discern four arguments against final causes.

[1] *Or Adonai*, II, ii, 2 (p. 35b). Cf. *Moreh Nebukim*, III, 19; *Milḥamot Adonai*, IV, 2 (p. 156).
[2] *Moreh Nebukim*, III, 17 and 23.

The first two arguments seem to be directed against two statements made by Heereboord. First, "the end is prior in intention to the means."[1] Second, "God . . . works in a most eminent way for an end, not one which is outside himself . . . God has done all things for His own sake . . . not that He stood in need of those things which He made . . . which view the scholastics explain in the following manner: God has done all things for an end, not of want but of assimilation," that is to say "in order to benefit other things which are outside himself,"[2] by assimilating them to himself, i.e., by making them like himself. Now, in the *Cogitata Metaphysica*, where Spinoza does not choose to enter into controversy with those "who ask whether God had not determined for himself beforehand an end for the sake of which He had created the world," he is quite willing to say that "a created object is one which presupposes for its existence nothing except God," and to supplement this statement by the explanation that "if God had predetermined for himself some end, it evidently was not independent of God, for there is nothing apart from God by which He was influenced to action."[3] But here in the *Ethics* he rejects any conception of end, even if it be nothing apart from God himself. Heereboord's first statement which declares the priority of the end to the means is characterized by Spinoza as one which "altogether turns nature upside down," for it makes the things which are im-

---

[1] *Meletemata Philosophica, Disputationes ex Philosophia Selectae*, Vol. II, Disp. XXIV, VIII: "Finis est prior in intentione quam media."

[2] *Ibid.*, Disp. XXIV, VI–VII: "Deus . . . modo eminentissimo agit propter finem, non qui extra se sit. . . . Deus omnia fecit propter se . . . non quod istis, quae fecit, indigeret . . . quod Scholastici enunciarunt hoc modo; Deus omnia fecit propter finem, non indigentiae, sed assimilationis, . . . ut bene aliis faciat, quae sunt extra se, rebus." Cf. Baensch's note to this passage in his translation of the *Ethics*.

[3] *Cogitata Metaphysica*, II, 10.

mediately produced by God to exist for the sake of things produced by Him last. The second statement is simply dismissed by him as a verbal quibble and he insists that "if God works to obtain an end, He necessarily seeks something of which He stands in need," and thus "this doctrine does away with God's perfection."

The third argument deals with the scholastic theory of the concurrence of God (*concursus Dei*), of which there is an elaborate discussion in Heereboord.[1] This theory, which is repeatedly stated by Descartes in several different connections,[2] is explained in Spinoza's restatement of Descartes to mean that "each single moment God continually creates things as if anew," from which it follows "that things in themselves have no power to do anything or to determine themselves to any action."[3] A similar explanation of Descartes' principle is given by Blyenbergh in a letter to Spinoza: "Following your assertion, creation and preservation are one and the same thing, and God makes not things only, but also the motions and modes of things, to continue in their own state, that is, concurs in them." From this Blyenbergh infers "that nothing can happen against the will of God."[4] Here in the *Ethics* he illustrates the theory of concurrence by the following example: "For, by way of example, if a stone has fallen from some roof on somebody's head and killed him, they will demonstrate in this manner that the stone has fallen in order to kill the man. For if it did not fall for that purpose by the will of God, how could so many circumstances concur through chance (and a num-

---

[1] *Meletemata Philosophica, Disputationes ex Philosophia Selectae*, Vol. I, Disps. VII–XII.

[2] *Principia Philosophiae*, II, 36. For other references to Descartes and parallel passages in scholastic authors, see Gilson, *Index Scholastico-Cartésien*, 81, and cf. 110–112.

[3] *Cogitata Metaphysica*, II, 11.   [4] Epistola 20.

ber often simultaneously do concur)?"[1] He concludes by characterizing the exponents of this view in the following words: "And so they all fly to God, the refuge for ignorance."[2] A similar description of the Asharian view that every occurrence is determined by the direct intervention of God's absolute will is given by Maimonides in the following passages: "For example, when a storm or gale blows, it causes undoubtedly some leaves of a tree to drop, breaks off some branches of another tree, tears away a stone from a heap of stones, raises dust over herbs and spoils them, and stirs up the sea so that a ship goes down with the whole or part of her contents."[3] Now the Mohammedan Ashariya "admit that Aristotle is correct in assuming one and the same cause [the wind] for the fall of leaves [from the tree] and for the death of a man [drowned in the sea]. But they hold at the same time that the wind did not blow by chance; it is God that caused it to move; it is not therefore the wind that caused the leaves to fall; each leaf fell according to the divine decree; it is God who caused it to fall at a certain time and in a certain place; it could not have fallen before or after that time or in another place, as this had previously been decreed."[4]

The fourth argument[5] is directed against the alleged evidence of design that may be discerned in the structure of the human body. Cicero makes use of this sort of evidence. "But we may yet more easily comprehend that the world was given by the immortal gods to men, if we examine thoroughly into the structure of the body and the form and perfection of human nature."[6] Among the several examples

---

[1] *Opera*, II, p. 80, l. 35–p. 81, l. 2.   [2] *Ibid.*, p. 81, ll. 10–11.
[3] *Moreh Nebukim*, III, 17, Second Theory.
[4] *Ibid.*, Third Theory.
[5] *Opera*, II, p. 81, ll. 11 ff.
[6] *De Natura Deorum*, II, 54, § 133.

which indicate design in the structure of the human body
he mentions the delicate structure of the eye, which he describes in some detail.[1] The same evidence is used also by
Maimonides. Like Cicero, he illustrates it by a description
of the structure of the eye, and then concludes: "In short,
considering the humor of the eye, its membranes and nerves,
with their well-known functions, and their adaptation to the
purpose of sight, can any intelligent person imagine that all
this is due to chance? Certainly not . . . but is according
to our view the result of the action of an intelligent being."[2]
Spinoza's answer to this alleged evidence of design is that
it is based on ignorance, for "when they behold the structure
of the human body, they are amazed; and because they are
ignorant of the causes of such art, they conclude that the
body was made not by mechanical but by divine or supernatural art." Note the difference between Maimonides'
passage and Spinoza's passage in the choice of an oppositional
term to "intelligent being" or "divine art." In Maimonides
the oppositional term is "chance," i.e., without any cause;
in Spinoza it is "mechanical art," i.e., necessary efficient
causation. Maimonides, however, was not ignorant of "mechanical art" as a possible alternative for "chance" in opposition to "intelligent being," for between his premise that
the structure of the eye could not be the work of chance and
his conclusion that it must be the work of an intelligent
agent he inserts the statements that "this is an artistic organization" and that "nature has no intelligence and no organiz-
ing faculty, as has been accepted by all philosophers," and
it is in consequence of this that we must assume that it is
the work of an intelligent agent. In short, Maimonides
maintains that the artistic organization of the structure of

---

[1] *Ibid.*, II, 57, § 142.
[2] *Moreh Nebukim*, III, 19.

the eye eliminates not only the assumption of "chance" but also the assumption of a "mechanical art," and points to a "divine art" as its only possible explanation.

In the third part of the Appendix Spinoza shows how from the conception of final causes and from the belief that all things are made for man there has been formed the conception of good, evil, order, confusion, heat, cold, beauty, and deformity. Here, too, Spinoza is transforming a statement used by those who believe in the existence of final causes into an argument against them. The statement which must have given rise to Spinoza's argument here is found in Heereboord. He says: "The end produces the means; not only does it produce them, but it also endows them with goodness, measure, and order." [1] In his criticism of this statement Spinoza is trying to establish the principle that good and evil in all their variety of forms are only relative to man — "they do not reveal the nature of anything in itself, but only the constitution of the imagination." This is not an especially new view. Maimonides has fully developed it, and the following are a few characteristic expressions used by him: "Evils are evils only in relation to a certain thing. . . . All evils are privations. . . . It cannot be said of God that He directly creates evil. . . . His works are all perfectly good." [2] In letters to Blyenbergh Spinoza uses almost the same expressions as Maimonides: "But I for my part cannot admit that sin and evil are something positive . . . for the evil in it [Adam's disobedience] was no more than a privation of a more perfect state which Adam had to lose through that action." [3] "I think that I have sufficiently shown that that which gives its form to evil, error, or crimes does not con-

---

[1] *Meletemata Philosophica, Disputationes ex Philosophia Selectae*, Vol. II, Disp. XXIII, VII: "Finis causat media, nec causat solummodo, sed dat illis bonitatem, mensuram, et ordinem."   [2] *Moreh Nebukim*, III, 10.
[3] Epistola 19 (*Opera*, IV, p. 88, ll. 10–11; p. 91, ll. 4–6).

sist in anything which expresses essence, and that therefore it cannot be said that God is the cause thereof." [1] Similarly in *Cogitata Metaphysica* he repeats the words of Maimonides in saying that "a thing considered in itself is called
neither good nor evil, but only in respect to another being,
which it helps to acquire what is desired, or the contrary." [2]

The direct influence of Maimonides upon Spinoza's treatment of evil is evident beyond any doubt in *Short Treatise*,
I, 4. Spinoza raises there the question how it is possible for
a perfect God to permit confusion to be seen everywhere in
nature. The term "confusion" reflects the expression "absence of order" used by Maimonides [3] and its similar expression "ill-order" which occurs frequently in Gersonides
and Crescas. [4] Spinoza denies that there is real confusion in
nature. What we call confusion is simply a deviation from
certain general ideas which we have set up as exemplars of
perfection. He then dismisses the existence of general ideas,
referring in the course of his discussion to those who say
that "God has no knowledge of particular and transient
things, but only of the general, which in their opinion are
imperishable," and concludes that "God then is the cause
of, and providence over, particular things only." Now,
Maimonides, in a similar way, after discussing the problem
whether Providence extends only to the species or also to
the individuals, [5] proceeds to say that "species and other
general ideas are only things of reason, whilst everything
that exists outside the mind is an individual object, or an
aggregate of individual objects. This being granted, it must
be further admitted that the divine influence, which exists

---

[1] Epistola 23. [2] *Cogitata Metaphysica*, I, 6.
[3] *Moreh Nebukim*, III, 19: העדר סדור, انتظام‎ عدم‎.
[4] *Milḥamot Adonai*, IV, 2 (p. 156); *Or Adonai*, II, ii, 2 (p. 35b): רוע הסדור.
[5] *Moreh Nebukim*, III, 17.

in union with the human species, that is, the human intellect, is that which exists in union with the individual intellects, that is to say, that which emanates in Reuben, Simeon, Levi, and Judah." [1] More especially, Spinoza's reference to "those who follow Aristotle," who "say that these things are not real things, only things of reason," would seem to draw upon Maimonides' statement "that species and other general ideas are only things of reason."

This conception of the relativity of good and evil is expressed by Spinoza in the *Short Treatise* by the statement that they are "entities of reason" (*entia rationis*) as opposed to "real entities" (*entia realia*), for among the entities of reason, he says, are included all relations, and "good and evil are only relations." [2] Here in the *Ethics*, however, Spinoza goes still further and calls good and evil "entities (*entia*) not of the reason (*rationis*) but of the imagination (*imaginationis*)."

The Appendix is concluded by Spinoza with the question "why God has not created all men in such a manner that they might be controlled by the dictates of reason alone." [3] The question is an old one. Judah ha-Levi, for instance, puts it in this way: "Would it not have been better or more commensurate with divine wisdom, if all mankind had been guided in the true path?" [4] Descartes, too, has raised it. "And, finally, I must also not complain that God concurs with me in forming the acts of the will, that is the judgment in which I go astray." [5] But "I nevertheless perceive that God could easily have created me so that I never could err, although I still remained free and endowed with a limited

---

[1] *Ibid.*
[2] *Short Treatise*, I, 10. Cf. above, pp. 161–162.
[3] *Opera*, II, p. 83, ll. 26–27.
[4] *Cuzari*, I, 102.
[5] *Meditationes*, IV (*Oeuvres*, VII, p. 60, ll. 26–28).

knowledge." [1] Spinoza has raised the same question also in the *Short Treatise*: "Against all this others object: how is it possible that God, who is said to be supremely perfect, and the sole cause, disposer, and provider of all, nevertheless permits such confusion to be seen everywhere in nature? Also, why has He not made man so as not to be able to sin?" [2] The question was also addressed to Spinoza in a letter by Blyenbergh. [3]

Two answers to this question given by Descartes are made use of by Spinoza.

First, Descartes denies that acts of error and sin have any positive existence with reference to God, for "these acts are entirely true and good, inasmuch as they depend on God." [4] This answer is followed by Spinoza in the *Short Treatise*, in his letter to Blyenbergh, [5] and in the Second Part of the *Ethics*. [6] To quote the *Short Treatise*: "As regards the other [objection], why God has not made mankind so that they should not sin, to this it may serve [as an answer], that whatever is said about sin is only said with reference to us." [7]

Second, Descartes maintains that error and sin were made possible by God for the special purpose of adding to the perfection of the universe as a whole. "And it is easy for me to understand that, in so far as I consider myself alone, and as if there were only myself in the world, I should have been much more perfect than I am, if God had created me so that I could never err. Nevertheless I cannot deny that in some sense it is a greater perfection in the whole universe that cer-

---

[1] *Ibid.* (p. 61, ll. 9–11).
[2] *Short Treatise*, I, 6, § 6.
[3] Epistola 22 (*Opera*, IV, p. 142, ll. 26 ff.).
[4] *Meditationes*, IV (*Oeuvres*, VII, p. 60, ll. 28–29).
[5] Epistola 23 (*Opera*, IV, p. 147, ll. 1 ff.).
[6] Props. 33 and 35. Cf. below, Vol. II, pp. 111 ff.
[7] *Short Treatise*, I, 6, § 8.

tain parts should not be exempt from error as others are than
that all parts should be exactly similar." [1]   This answer in
the form in which it is given by Descartes is not reproduced
by Spinoza, and he did not reproduce it for the self-evident
reason that he did not believe that anything was created by
God for any purpose, even for the perfection of the universe
as a whole.   But there is in Spinoza an answer which upon a
close examination appears to be only a revised form of this
answer of Descartes.   Error and sin exist in the world, he
argues in effect, not because they are to contribute to the
perfection of the whole universe but because their exclusion
from the world would be contradictory to the conception of
God as infinitely great and powerful.   Given a God whose
greatness and power are infinite, he seems to argue, such a
God must be able to produce by the necessity of His nature
everything conceivable, and that includes also sin.   This is
the meaning of the following concluding passage in the
Appendix: "I give but one answer: Because to Him material was not wanting for the creation of everything, from
the highest down to the very lowest grade of perfection; or,
to speak more properly, because the laws of His nature were
so ample that they sufficed for the production of everything
which can be conceived by an infinite intellect." [2]

[1] *Meditationes*, IV (*Oeuvres*, VII, p. 61, ll. 17–23).
[2] *Opera*, II, p. 83, ll. 27–32.

THE PHILOSOPHY OF SPINOZA

VOLUME II

CHAPTER XIII

BODY AND MIND

I. God and Man

THE contrast between God and the world which the mediaevals expressed in terms of immateriality and materiality or of immovability and movability provided them also with a basis for the distinction between metaphysics and physics. Metaphysics, as the science of things immaterial and immovable, dealt with God and His attributes, or, to use Aristotle's own definitions, it dealt with "something eternal and immovable and separable [from body]"[1] or with "being *qua* being — both what it is and the attributes which belong to it *qua* being."[2] Physics, on the other hand, dealt with the material and movable objects of the world, or, to use again Aristotle's own definition, it dealt "with things which are inseparable from bodies but not immovable."[3] It is this distinction between God and the world or metaphysics and physics which as a rule underlies the main divisions of the theoretical part of philosophy in mediaeval systematic works. In these mediaeval works, however, though logically the order of reasoning proceeds from physics to metaphysics, sometimes the order of these two topics is reversed, and metaphysics, on account of its superior importance, is placed first.[4] Thus, for instance, Avicenna in his *Al-Shifa'* and *Al-*

---

[1] *Metaphysics*, VI, 1, 1026a, 10–11; *De Anima*, I, 1, 403b, 15–16.

[2] *Metaphysics*, VI, 1, 1026a, 31–32.

[3] *Ibid.*, 13–14.

[4] On the order of the sciences, see my paper "The Classification of Sciences in Mediaeval Jewish Philosophy," in *Hebrew Union College Jubilee Volume* (1925), pp. 285 ff.

Najat places physics first, whereas Algazali and Shahrastani in their restatements of Avicenna's philosophy place metaphysics first. In most of these mediaeval systematic works, furthermore, the theoretical part of philosophy is preceded by a treatise on logic, which was considered as an auxiliary discipline intended to serve as an introduction to philosophy; in some instances, as in the case of Saadia's *Emunot we-De'ot*, the opening sections contain a discussion of the theory of knowledge. The same principle of division underlies also Descartes' *Principia Philosophiae*, but the First Part, though embodying a great deal of what is traditionally included under metaphysics, is described by the author himself as a discussion "Of the Principles of Human Knowledge," corresponding, evidently, to the introductory treatises on logic in mediaeval systematic works.

This variety of forms in the literary arrangement of systematic works on philosophy was especially noted by Spinoza, and while on the whole he was to divide his own systematic works into the two conventional divisions, God and the world, or metaphysics and physics, he set out to depart from the most prevalent and logical practice, though not without precedent, by treating of God first — a departure which was necessary for him in order to keep up his literary pretension that his entire philosophy was evolved from his conception of God. To Tschirnhaus this departure seemed to be of great significance, for in a conversation with Leibniz about the *Ethics* of Spinoza he is reported to have said that most philosophers begin with creatures, Descartes began with the mind, but Spinoza began with God.[1] Now in Spinoza the old contrast between God and the world as that between the immaterial

---

[1] Cf. K. I. Gerhardt, "Leibniz und Spinoza," in *Sitzungsberichte der königlich preussischen Akademie der Wissenschaften zu Berlin*, 1889, p. 1077. On the plan of the *Ethics*, see R. McKeon, *The Philosophy of Spinoza*, pp. 90–92.

and the material disappeared, and in its place a new contrast appeared, namely, that between the infinite and the finite. By the same token, the old Aristotelian distinction between the subject-matter of metaphysics and the subject-matter of physics as that between the immaterial and the material also disappeared. In Spinoza's new terminology the subject-matter of metaphysics would be the infinite and the subject-matter of physics would be the finite. It is in these terms, therefore, that Spinoza describes the contents of the two main divisions, God and the world, or metaphysics and physics, which constitute his *Ethics* and *Short Treatise*: "Having in the first part discoursed on God and on the universal and infinite things, we shall proceed now, in the second part, to the treatment of particular and finite things." [1] Or, "I pass on now to explain those things which must necessarily follow from the essence of God or the Being eternal and infinite." [2]

Had Spinoza in the latter parts of these two works intended to write an encyclopaedia of the physical sciences, he would have proceeded probably along the lines of the traditional mediaeval encyclopaedists, which ultimately go back to the classification of Aristotle's writings. Corresponding to the traditional classification of the universe into translunar and sublunar regions, Spinoza would have divided his modes into infinite and finite or into general *natura naturata* and particular *natura naturata*, and just like the mediaevals, who treat of the Intelligences, of the Spheres, and of the universe as a whole under metaphysics, Spinoza would have included the treatment of the "absolutely infinite intellect," of "motion and rest," and of "the face of the whole universe" [3]

---

[1] *Short Treatise*, II, Preface, § 1.
[2] *Ethics*, II, Praef.
[3] Cf. above, Vol. I, pp. 238–247.

under metaphysics. Taking only the finite modes or the particular *natura naturata* as properly belonging to the field of physics, he would have grouped them together into the three traditional realms of nature, and under each of these he would have studied the various sciences according to their traditional classification, and among these he would have included psychology, which since Aristotle had been a part of the physical sciences. Man, on the whole, would have been studied by him as a part of the animal kingdom. But in man he would have discovered a certain aspect of psychology which is peculiar to him as a human being and by which he has been traditionally set apart from the rest of the animals, and that is mind. Again, in the individual human behavior and in the social history of man he would have discovered certain peculiar elements which have given rise to the sciences known through Aristotle as ethics, economics, and politics.

These are the main topics which Spinoza would have treated in the *Ethics* had his purpose been to write a comprehensive treatise on the nature of the physical universe and on the beings that inhabit it. But the main object of Spinoza's work, after he has discussed God in the First Part, is, as he himself says, "to consider those things only which may conduct us as it were by the hand to a knowledge of the human mind and its highest happiness." [1] He therefore confines himself to those things "which concern man." [2] His subject is thus the higher phases of human psychology and certain phases of human conduct, corresponding roughly to the Third Book of Aristotle's *De Anima*, which deals with mind, and to the main problem of Aristotle's *Nicomachean Ethics*, which is to define the meaning of human happiness.

[1] *Ethics*, II, Praef.
[2] *Short Treatise*, II, Preface, § 1.

In singling out man from the innumerable particular things in nature, Spinoza was not motivated by the belief that man occupies a place which is unique in nature, but rather was he motivated by the belief that man is a part of nature and that he epitomizes in himself, as it were, the whole of nature. The idea of man as a miniature universe or microcosm is old in literature, and the analogy between the constitution of the human body and the universe is frequently resorted to by mediaeval philosophers. There is a suggestion of this analogy in Plato when he speaks of the world as a perfect animal in unity,[1] and refers to the structure of man as an imitation of the spherical form of the universe.[2] Aristotle, too, throws out a hint in the same direction when he speaks of animals as the "small world" ($\mu\iota\kappa\rho\hat{\omega}\ \kappa\acute{o}\sigma\mu\omega$) and of the universe as the "great one" ($\mu\epsilon\gamma\acute{a}\lambda\omega$).[3] Similarly Plotinus refers to animals as microcosms.[4] It is probably with reference to these sources that the Iḥwan al-Ṣafa begin their detailed analogies between man and the universe by quoting from unnamed sages to the effect that the universe is a great man[5] and that man is a small universe.[6] The analogy appears in the works of many Jewish philosophers — Ibn Gabirol,[7] Joseph Ibn Ẓaddiḳ,[8] and Judah ha-Levi.[9] Most important of all is the long chapter devoted to this analogy by Maimonides.[10] These Jewish philosophers had before them not only the precedents of Greek and Arabic philosophers but also

---

[1] *Timaeus* 30D.   [2] *Ibid.* 44D.

[3] *Physics*, VIII, 2, 252b, 26–27.

[4] *Enneads*, IV, iii, 10 (ed. Creuzer et Moser, Paris, 1855, p. 205, l. 40; ed. Volkmann, Leipzig, 1884, Vol. II, p. 22, ll. 12–13).

[5] Dieterici, *Die Lehre von der Weltseele*, p. 27.

[6] Dieterici, *Die Anthropologie der Araber*, p. 41.

[7] *Fons Vitae*, III, 2 (pp. 77, 24–78, 4); III, 58 (p. 208); *Liḳḳute Meḳor Ḥayyim*, III, 6 and 44.

[8] *'Olam Ḳaṭan*, Introduction (p. 2).

[9] *Cuzari*, IV, 3.

[10] *Moreh Nebukim*, I, 72. See Munk, *Guide des Égarés*, I, p. 354, n. 1.

those of the rabbis, who for homiletical purposes made use of the correspondence between the parts of the universe and the parts of the human body.[1] It is my purpose to show that the first thirteen propositions in the Second Part of the *Ethics* are built on this old analogy between the macrocosm and the microcosm. Propositions I–IX describe the macrocosm, whereas Propositions X–XIII describe the microcosm, showing wherein the two are alike and wherein they differ. Had Spinoza written his *Ethics* after the manner of rabbis and scholastics, he would have started the Second Part with a statement somewhat as follows: Part II. Chapter I. Wherein we shall discuss the nature of the human mind and its relation to body, showing that in man, the microcosm, mind and body are related to each other after the analogy of the relation between thought and extension in God, the macrocosm, blessed be He.

II. Extension and Thought in God

Like other philosophers before him, and repeating his own statement in the First Part of the *Ethics*,[2] Spinoza begins the Second Part with the proposition that "thought is an attribute of God."[3] This conception of God as thought runs throughout the history of philosophy. It is the chief characteristic of Aristotle's Prime Mover [4] as well as of Plotinus' One. To both Aristotle and Plotinus thought was not something extraneous to God's essence or inherent within His essence, but rather something identical with His essence, and to them this conception of the identity of God's essence with thought presented no difficulty at all. In the Middle

---

[1] *Abot de-Rabbi Nathan*, Ch. 31.
[2] *Ethics*, I, Prop. 14, Corol. 2.
[3] *Ibid.*, II, Prop. 1.
[4] *Metaphysics*, XII, 7, 1072b, 28.

Ages, however, when affirmations about God were required to have the significance of logical judgments, an overscrupulous logical conscience caused philosophers to wonder how it was possible in a logical synthetic judgment to predicate of God that which was identical with His essence. This was the crux of the problem of divine attributes.[1] The difficulty was overcome, at least by some, by the theory that though metaphysically the attribute is identical with God, logically, when used as a predicate in a proposition, it expresses only a subjective judgment of mankind about Him. In this sense also, as we have already shown,[2] Spinoza uses the term "attribute," and it is in this sense that he says here that "thought is an attribute of God" (Prop. I). But lest one of the unwary, misguided by the variegated meaning of the term "attribute," be tempted to take it to mean something added to, or inherent within, the essence of God, he immediately explains himself by saying, in effect, that by the attribute of thought he means nothing but that "God is a thinking thing" (*ibid.*).

The demonstration of Proposition I contains two parts — the Demonstration proper and a Scholium. In the Demonstration, Spinoza tries to prove the existence of thought as an attribute of God from the fact that "individual thoughts, or this and that thought," exist in the world. In the Scholium, he tries to prove the same thing "from the fact that we conceive an infinite thinking Being." What Spinoza really means to say is this: The nature of God is to be established by the same proofs that are employed for the establishment of His existence. God is that which the proofs for His existence show Him to be. He cannot be otherwise or

---

[1] Cf. my "Crescas on the Problem of Divine Attributes," in *Jewish Quarterly Review*, n.s., VII (1916), 1–44, 175–221. Cf. also above, Vol. I, Chapter V.

[2] Cf. above, Vol. I, pp. 146 ff.

less or more than what is warranted by these proofs. Now, the proofs of the existence of God, historically, are in a general way of two kinds, — cosmological, reasoning from effect to cause, or ontological, reasoning from the idea of God to His existence, — the latter being the kind of proof which Spinoza himself employs in Proposition XI of the First Part. So, Spinoza says here in effect, by whatever method you try to prove the existence of God, the proof will establish God as a thinking thing. If you employ the cosmological method, then the fact that there exist in the world before us individual thoughts will lead you, by the general method employed in cosmological proofs, to the existence of a prime thought which is the cause of all other thoughts — just as in Aristotle, for instance, the fact that there exist in the world individual movements will lead you to the existence of a prime mover. And if you employ the ontological method, then the very fact that we have a clear and distinct idea of an infinite thinking being proves his existence.

But while in Proposition I Spinoza merely restated the old conception of God, in Proposition II he shows wherein he differs from his predecessors. To his predecessors God was thought only, without any admixture of materiality, or extension, as Spinoza prefers to call it. To Spinoza God is both extension and thought. Hence Proposition II: "Extension is an attribute of God, or God is an extended thing." Not only individual thoughts are traceable to God as their source, but also individual extended things can be traced directly to God and can be shown to have their existence in God.

Spinoza offers no detailed argument in proof of this second proposition. He only says that its demonstration is of the same character as that of the first proposition. But let us try to work out the application of the twofold demonstration of the first proposition to this proposition.

Cosmologically, Spinoza would say, the fact that individual extended things exist in the world before us must lead us to the attribution of extension to God. Otherwise, we should be unable to account for the origin of matter or extension. Should we try to account for it, we should have to resort to the theory of a special creation *ex nihilo*, or to the theory of emanation, or to the theory of an eternal matter existing beside God and constituting, as it were, a second substance. But I have already shown that all these theories are untenable.[1] You will, of course, say that the impossibility of an infinite regress, which is the mainstay of the cosmological proof in its Aristotelian version, makes it necessary for us to assume that God is immovable and hence incorporeal. But I have already referred you to a certain Jew, named "Rab Ghasdai," who has shown how the cosmological proof can be restated without the assumption of the impossibility of an infinite regress.[2]

And if you follow the ontological argument, Spinoza would continue to say, then I maintain that our idea of God as an infinite being conceives Him to be infinite both as thought and as extension. All your arguments against the possibility of an infinite extension are due, as I have already pointed out, to a failure to make three fundamental distinctions in the conception of the infinite. According to my own view, it is possible to conceive of an infinite extension, if that infinite is infinite by its own nature, if it is infinite in the sense that it has no limits, and if it is something which can be understood even though it cannot be imagined.[3]

Having restated his conception of God as a thinking and extended thing, Spinoza now proceeds to explain the relation

---

[1] Cf. above, Vol. I, Chapter IV.
[2] Epistola 12. Cf. above, Vol. I, pp. 196–197, 295, n. 1.
[3] *Ibid.* Cf. above, Vol. I, Chapter VIII.

of God to the world and His knowledge of the world. Some of the things he is going to say are again a repetition of what he has already said before. But he evidently feels the need of repeating himself in order to give a complete outline of the parallel between the macrocosm and the microcosm. We shall therefore follow in his footsteps and try to comment upon everything he says, even at the risk of repeating some of the things we have already said before in this book.

In the Middle Ages three views existed with regard to the relation of God to the world and His knowledge of it.

According to one view, God is the arbitrary creator of the world who, having created it, is the arbitrary ruler of it. The creation of the world as well as its governance is thus considered as the exercise of two faculties in God, as it were, free will and power. These two faculties of God are conceived after the manner of the faculties of free will and power in man, except that they are infinitely superior to those of man and absolutely arbitrary, being independent of any external conditions and circumstances. This view, which is primarily the uncritical opinion of the common masses of believers, was presented as a philosophical system by a certain branch of the Moslem Kalam, of which the best restatement and criticism are to be found in Maimonides.[1] According to this view, God's will and power are conceived as absolute, unlimited, and unchecked by any rule. Creation, as a free exercise of will and power, is furthermore a continuous act, and every event is a direct creation of God. Existence is a succession of specially created events. It is analogous to the theory of divine concurrence alluded to elsewhere by Spinoza,[2] though, I must say, the two views are not neces-

---

[1] *Moreh Nebukim*, I, 73–76; III, 17, Third Theory. Cf. the presentation of this view of the Kalam in Roth, *Spinoza, Descartes, and Maimonides*, pp. 80 ff.

[2] Appendix to *Ethics*, I. Cf. above, Vol. I, p. 433.

sarily identical, for the Kalam denies not only natural causality but also uniformity of action in nature, inasmuch as it
assumes God's will to be absolutely arbitrary, whereas divine
concurrence does not necessarily assume God's will to be absolutely arbitrary; it is rather an intelligent will; and hence,
barring the possibility of miracles, divine concurrence does not
deny uniformity of action in nature.[1] Spinoza characterizes all
such views as views which make everything dependent upon
chance[2] and deny natural causality altogether.

As the extreme opposite of this is the view which considers God as the necessary cause of the universe and the
events within it as rigidly following from Him by laws of
necessity, allowing no room for chance, spontaneity, and
miracles.[3] Though God is not altogether a blind cause according to this view, for self-consciousness is one of His
characteristics,[4] still He has no direct knowledge of the
particular things outside himself. If He knows them at all,
He knows them only indirectly through His knowledge of
His own self. This view is ascribed by Maimonides to
Aristotle, and in its Neoplatonized form in which it is presented by Maimonides it may be restated as follows: Beginning with God as a simple being, all things emanate from
Him by necessity. Now, God himself as a thinking thing
has only himself as the object of His thought, but inasmuch
as He is the ultimate source of the emanation of everything
within the world, He has also knowledge of everything outside himself. To quote a statement from Alfarabi which is the
source of many similar statements throughout Jewish philosophy: "The Prime Being has an idea of His own essence;

---

[1] Cf. below, pp. 333–335.
[2] Epistola 54. Cf. above, Vol. I, pp. 318 ff.
[3] *Moreh Nebukim*, II, 25.
[4] *Ibid.*, II, 20. Cf. above, Vol. I, pp. 329 ff.

but inasmuch as His own essence is in a certain respect identical with all the existent beings, by forming an idea of His own essence He forms, in a certain respect, an idea also of all the existent beings." [1] Or to quote a similar passage from Gersonides: "Inasmuch as it must be necessarily assumed that God knows His own essence according to the rank He holds in the order of existence, and inasmuch as His own essence is of such a nature that all things emanate from it according to a certain order of gradation, it must be concluded that God knows all things that emanate from Him, for if He did not know them, then His knowledge of His own essence would be a defective sort of knowledge." [2] Maimonides, too, states the same view in the following passage: "And inasmuch as He knows himself and comprehends His greatness and glory and truth, He knows everything and nothing is hidden from Him." [3] Thus also Leo Hebraeus, speaking of those who identify the actual intellect (*l'intelletto attuale* = νοῦς ἐνεργείᾳ) with God — by which he evidently means the Active Intellect (*l'intelletto agente* = νοῦς ποιητικός) [4] which according to Alexander of Aphrodisias is identical with God — says that the actual intellect or God, by comprehending himself, knows all other things (*vedendo se medesimo, tutti conosce*). [5]

Between these two opposite extremes there is the mediating view of Maimonides, which admits will in God but considers His will not as arbitrary but as intelligent and purposive and as being limited by self-imposed laws. While creation according to this view is an act of will, that will had

---

[1] *Sefer ha-Haṯḥalot* in Filipowsky's *Sefer ha-Asif* (1849), p. 4.

[2] *Milḥamot Adonai*, III, 4 (p. 138).   [3] *Mishneh Torah, Yesode ha-Torah*, II, 9.

[4] Cf. above, Vol. I, p. 404. If the *Dialoghi d'Amore* was written originally in Hebrew (cf. above, Vol. I, p. 12, n. 2), the confusion might have arisen by mistaking הפועל for בפועל in השכל הפועל.

[5] *Dialoghi d'Amore*, I, p. 42 (Bari, 1929).

a certain purpose, unknown to us, in the creation of the world, and the created world, though under direct divine providence, is still governed by laws of causality.[1] God knows all the particular things directly, but with a knowledge which is absolutely unlike ours.[2]

Disregarding Maimonides' mediating view altogether, Spinoza takes up in the Scholium to Proposition III the two extremely opposite views, those of the Kalam and Aristotle, rejecting the former and espousing the latter.

The first view is accurately restated by Spinoza in all its essential features. It conceives the "power of God" as "free will," and it compares God's power to the power "of kings." "All existent things" are accordingly considered as "contingent," that is to say, without cause, and as dependent upon chance. He describes this view as that of the "common people." Though he does not undertake a detailed refutation of it, he furnishes us with a good outline of such a refutation.

In the first place, he seems to say, if the coming of the world into being was an act of free will, then the world must have come into being in time, prior to which time it did not exist; and hence prior to that time God did not exercise His power. But, argues Spinoza, "it is as impossible for us to conceive that God does not act as that He does not exist."

In the second place, he seems to say again, if God's exercise of power is an intermittent action, as must needs be implied in the theory of creation, then by analogy of human power, with which God's power is compared by the common people, God's failure to exercise His power must be accounted for either by an inability to supply certain conditions necessary for the exercise of that power or by an inability to overcome certain obstacles. And so, argues Spinoza, "I could show besides not only that the power which the common

---

[1] Cf. Munk, *Guide des Égarés*, I, p. 287, n.   [2] *Moreh Nebukim*, III, 20.

people ascribe to God is a human power (which shows that they look upon God as a man, or as being like man), but that it also involves weakness."

Both these arguments, it must be said, were known to mediaeval philosophers. In fact, they are the stock arguments which are brought up in the Middle Ages whenever the problem of creation is discussed. In Maimonides they occur in the following passages: "They also try to reduce the theory of creation to an absurdity, by saying: How could God ever have been inactive without producing or creating anything in the infinite past?"[1] Furthermore, inactivity in human beings implies weakness or want of power, for "if an agent is active at one time and inactive at another, it is because of obstacles or of needs which arise or are within him. . . . As, however, God has no needs . . . and no obstacles . . . there is no reason why God should be active at one time and inactive at another. On the contrary, He must be always active in the same manner as He is always in existence."[2] Note the similarity between this last expression and the statement in Spinoza's first argument that "it is as impossible for us to conceive that God does not act as that He does not exist."

The view which Spinoza advances as his own in the same Scholium contains some points of agreement with the Neoplatonized Aristotelian view of mediaeval philosophy as well as some essential points of difference. The points in which he agrees with it are: (1) that the world follows from God by necessity and not by will and design; (2) that God knows himself; and (3) that He knows all things which follow from himself. The points on which he differs from the older view are as follows: According to the Neoplatonized Aristotelian

---

[1] *Ibid.*, II, 14, Seventh Method.
[2] *Ibid.*, Sixth Method.

view, God is only a thinking thing; His only activity is that
He understands himself; and the only thing that follows
from Him directly is a pure Intelligence or an intellect. According to Spinoza's own view, God is not only a thinking
thing, but also an extended thing and an infinite number of
other unknown things; His activity consists not only in that
He understands himself through His being a thinking thing,
but also in an infinite number of other activities which He
exercises through His possessing the attribute of extension
and an infinite number of other attributes; and, finally, the
things that follow from Him directly consist not only in an
intellect, which is only the immediate mode of thought, but
also in motion and rest, which are the immediate modes of
extension, and in an infinite number of other things, which
are the immediate modes of the other infinite attributes. All
this is implied in the following statement of the Scholium:
"God does everything with that necessity with which He
understands himself; that is to say, as it follows from the
necessity of the divine nature that God understands himself
(a truth admitted by all), so by the same necessity it follows
that God does an infinitude of things in infinite ways."
What Spinoza means to say is this: just as according to
emanationists, to whom God is pure thought, it follows from
the necessity of His nature that He knows himself, so according to his own view, which conceives of God as possessing
also extension and an infinite number of other attributes,
it follows from the necessity of the nature of God that He
does an infinite number of things. But, furthermore, God's
knowledge of His essence must include, as is admitted by the
mediaevals themselves, a knowledge of everything that proceeds from His essence; it follows therefore, in Proposition
III, that "in God there necessarily exists the idea of His
essence, and of all things which necessarily follow from His

essence." The term "idea," as we shall explain hereafter,[1] means the form of a thing which is the immediate object of cognition.

The mediaeval assertion that God knows particulars has given rise to three difficulties, due to three characteristics of particular things, namely, that they are many, that they are non-existent, and that they are material. Similar difficulties must have been felt by Spinoza to follow also from his own assertion in Proposition III that God knows not only himself but also "all things which necessarily follow from His essence." The solution of these difficulties is given by him in Propositions IV, VIII, and IX.

The first difficulty from the multiplicity of particular things is briefly formulated by Maimonides as follows: "It is impossible," he says, "that God's knowledge should include any plurality." [2] The problem is more elaborately stated by Gersonides: "If God apprehended these things, then, inasmuch as the intellect becomes actualized by what it knows and identified with it, it would follow that God instead of being simple would have an internal plurality, by reason of the plurality of the ideas which are apprehended by Him and with which His essence becomes identified." [3]

Several solutions are given of this difficulty. One solution is that God's "knowledge is directly connected with the species and only indirectly extends to individual members of the species." [4] Spinoza refers to this view in the *Short Treatise*, but rejects it on the ground that species or universals have no existence, and concludes that God's knowledge

---

[1] Cf. below, pp. 46 ff.

[2] *Moreh Nebukim*, III, 20.

[3] *Milḥamot Adonai*, III, 2 (4) (p. 122), paraphrased in *Or Adonai*, II, i, 2 (p. 29a).

[4] *Moreh Nebukim*, III, 20 (cf. III, 16). Narboni *ad loc.* identifies it as the view of Avicenna.

of things which follow from Him must be a knowledge of particulars.[1]

Another solution is that while God knows the things which are outside himself, or, rather, which follow from himself, directly as particulars, He knows them by one single and simple kind of knowledge, so that they are apprehended by Him as one single idea. Two versions of this solution may be discerned, one in Maimonides and the other in Gersonides. Maimonides states it laconically as a principle that "God's knowledge is one, though it embraces many different kinds of objects,"[2] and if the question is raised how this is possible, his answer is that this is one of the five ways in which God's knowledge differs from human knowledge, for, according to him, the term "knowledge" when applied to God is to be understood in a homonymous sense. Gersonides disagrees with Maimonides on the homonymity of the term "knowledge," and, in fact, on the homonymity of all the attributes, when applied to God, and though like Maimonides he admits that particular things are apprehended by God as one single idea, he maintains that in a smaller degree — an incomparably smaller degree — particular things may be so apprehended also by human beings.[3] His explanation of the process of the unification of the particular things into one single idea is given in the following passage: "From the premise that God knows [particular] things it would not necessarily have to follow that there would be a plurality in His essence. The order in which these things proceed from God reduces them to a unity, that is to say, in a certain aspect these things are one, as we have mentioned many times before. It is with reference to this aspect that God appre-

---

[1] *Short Treatise*, I, 6, § 7.
[2] *Moreh Nebukim*, III, 20.
[3] *Milḥamot Adonai*, III, 5 (1) (p. 147).

hends them." [1] A fuller and clearer statement of the same view is contained in the following paraphrase of Gersonides' passage by Crescas: "The solution of this problem may be easily accomplished with the aid of what has just been said, namely, that God's knowledge which is identical with His essence is the cause of the existence of everything outside himself. The [idea of the] general order [2] which is in God, even though it comprehends many objects, is still one idea, inasmuch as the many objects are comprehended in it only in so far as they are successively the entelechy of one another, in which respect they are all reduced to unity. . . . It is therefore clear that God comprehends all things in a manner in which they are one in Him, and consequently no plurality occurs in His essence." [3]

In the light of these quotations, it is evident that it is in anticipation of the question how God in His simplicity of nature could comprehend a plurality of modes that Spinoza states in Proposition IV that "the idea of God, from which infinite numbers of things follow in infinite ways, can be only one." It should be noted that in this proposition the statement that "infinite numbers of things follow in infinite ways" from the "idea of God" is rather loosely used. More correctly it should be said, as in Proposition III, that they follow from the essence of God. We shall presently show that while the "idea of God" comprehends a knowledge of all the attributes and their modes, it is really an immediate mode only of the attribute of thought, and hence the cause only of the modes of thought, and consequently infinite

[1] *Ibid.*, III, 4 (4) (p. 141).

[2] Hebrew הסדור הכולל, which corresponds to the oft-recurrent expression הסדור המושכל אשר בנפש השם יתברך, "the conceptual order which is in God's mind" (III, 4 (3), p. 141 and elsewhere). Hence my bracketed addition in the translation of the text.

[3] *Or Adonai*, II, i, 2 (p. 29b).

numbers of *thinking* things only follow from it in infinite ways. Later in the Corollary to Proposition VII Spinoza indicates quite clearly that from the "idea of God" only ideas follow, for he says: "Whatever follows formally [i.e., objectively in the modern sense] from the infinite nature of God, follows from the idea of God, in the same order and in the same connection objectively [i.e., subjectively in the modern sense] in God." The meaning of the term "idea of God" we have explained above.[1]

Now, this "idea of His essence" which exists in God as a single "idea of God," though it is an immediate mode only of the attribute of thought,[2] comprehends a knowledge of the essence of God not only under the attribute of thought but also under the attribute of extension, as well as under all the other infinite attributes. Similarly it comprehends a knowledge of "all things which necessarily follow from His essence,"[3] whether they be modes of thought or of extension or of any of the other unknown infinite attributes. This view is explicitly stated by Spinoza in the *Short Treatise* when he says that "the most immediate mode of the attribute which we call thought contains *objective* [i.e., subjectively] the formal [i.e., objective] essence of all things. . . . And since, as a matter of fact, nature or God is one being of which infinite attributes are predicated, and which contains in itself all the essences of created things, it necessarily follows that of all this there is produced in thought an infinite idea, which apprehends *objective* [i.e., subjectively] the whole of nature just as it is *realiter*."[4] In short, this statement amounts to saying that the attribute of thought in its activity of knowing apprehends the attribute of extension as well as

---

[1] Cf. above, Vol. I, pp. 239 ff.   [2] Cf. above, Vol. I, pp. 239 ff.
[3] *Ethics*, II, Prop. 3.
[4] *Short Treatise*, Appendix II, § 3 (*Opera*, I, p. 117, ll. 18 ff.).

the modes of extension. This would seem to contradict
Spinoza's own previous statement that these two attributes
must be conceived "as really distinct" from one another.[1]
In order therefore to obviate this seeming contradiction,
Spinoza proceeds in Propositions V–VII to draw a distinction between the attributes as they are conceived by us and
the attributes as they really are in God. The former phase
of the attributes is dealt with by him in Propositions V and
VI; the latter, in Proposition VII.

The attributes as they are conceived by us are conceived
by us each one "through itself (*per se*)," "as really distinct
— that is to say, one without the assistance of the other." [2]
God appears to us as a "thinking thing" and as an "extended thing," [3] and these two are conceived by us as if
they were two natures in God, one independent of the other.
From each of these independently conceived attributes there
appears to us to follow by necessity, according to Spinoza,
an independent series of modes. Unlike the mediaevals, to
whom extended modes follow ultimately from God who is
only a thinking thing, Spinoza maintains that from God as
a thinking thing only thinking modes can follow; extended
modes must follow from God as an extended thing; and so
also must every other possible mode follow from an attribute
of the same kind.

This is the contention of Propositions V and VI. God as
a thinking thing, he says, "can form an idea of His own
essence, and of all things which necessarily follow from it," [4]
and consequently, "the formal being of ideas recognizes
God for its cause in so far only as He is considered as a thinking thing." [5] But, on the other hand, "the formal being of

---

[1] *Ethics*, I, Prop. 10, and Schol.   [2] *Ibid*
[3] *Ibid*, II, Props. 1 and 2.
[4] *Ibid*., II, Prop. 5, Demonst.   [5] *Ibid*., II, Prop. 5.

things which are not modes of thought does not follow from
the divine nature because of His prior knowledge of these
things." [1] Quite the contrary, it must follow from some other
attribute. The formal being of extended modes, for instance, will thus have to follow from the attribute of extension, for "just as ideas follow from the attribute of thought,
in the same manner and with the same necessity the objects
of ideas follow and are concluded from their attributes." [2]
Consequently, "the modes of any attribute have God for
a cause only in so far as He is considered under that attribute
of which they are modes, and not in so far as He is considered
under any other attribute." [3]

In God, however, Spinoza goes on to say in Proposition
VII, the attributes are not something distinct from one
another, for "substance thinking and substance extended are
one and the same substance, which is now comprehended
under this attribute and now under that. Thus, also, a mode
of extension and the idea of that mode are one and the same
thing expressed in two different ways." [4] Since thought
and extension, whether as attributes of substance or as
modes of those attributes, are only two different aspects of
one and the same thing, they form two mutually implicative series, so that "the order and connection of ideas
is the same as the order and connection of things." [5]
Without acting upon one another, mind and body, by virtue
of their being modes of attributes which only appear to be
two but in reality are one, are so well co-ordinated that there
is a perfect correspondence between their actions. [6] When
therefore Spinoza says in Proposition VI that "the modes of
any attribute have God for a cause only in so far as He is

[1] *Ibid.*, II, Prop. 6, Corol.   [2] *Ibid.*
[3] *Ibid.*, II, Prop. 6.   [4] *Ibid.*, II, Prop. 7, Schol.
[5] *Ibid.* II, Prop. 7.   [6] Cf. below, pp. 189 ff.

considered under that attribute of which they are modes,"
he does not mean to imply that the attributes and their
modes exist as something really distinct in the essence of
God; he only means that "when things are *considered* as
modes of thought, we must explain the order of the whole
of nature or the connection of causes by the attribute of
thought alone, and when things are *considered* as modes of
extension, the order of the whole of nature must be explained
through the attribute of extension alone, and so with the
other attributes." [1]

In the course of his discussion in the Scholium to Proposition VII Spinoza tries to explain how "a mode of extension
and the idea of that mode are one and the same thing expressed in two different ways" or "manifested through different attributes" by quoting a philosophic truism "which
some of the Hebrews," he says, "appear to have seen as if
through a cloud" to the effect that "God, the intellect of
God, and the things which are understood by God (*resque
ab ipso intellectus*) are one and the same thing." The reference is to Maimonides, who speaks of the "well-known principle enunciated by the philosophers with regard to God that
He is the *intellectus*, the *intelligens*, and the *intelligibile*, and
that these three things in God are one and the same, and do
not in any way constitute a plurality." [2] In Aristotle this
principle is stated in the following passages: "As the intellect
(νοῦς) thinks (νοεῖ) itself because it shares the nature of the
object of thought (νοητοῦ); for it becomes an object of
thought in coming into contact with and thinking its object,
so that thought and object of thought are the same." [3]

---

[1] *Ethics*, II, Prop. 7, Schol.

[2] *Moreh Nebukim*, I, 68; cf. *Mishneh Torah, Yesode ha Torah*, II, 10; Ibn Ezra's
commentary on Exodus 34, 6; *Cuzari*, V, 12.

[3] *Metaphysics*, XII, 7, 1072b, 19–21.

Again, "as, then, intellect (νοῦς) and the object of thought
(νοουμένου) are not different in the case of things that have
not matter, they will be the same, i.e., the act of intelligence (νόησις) will be one with the object of thought." [1]

Two observations in connection with this indirect reference to Maimonides are in place here.

First, in the original passage of Maimonides four terms are
identified: *Deus, intellectus, intelligens,* and *intelligibile* or,
as this last term is expressed in Spinoza's terminology, *res
ab ipso intellectae.* In Spinoza's passage, however, only three
terms are identified: *Deus, intellectus, res ab ipso intellectae;*
Maimonides' term *intelligens,* for which the Greek equivalent
is νόησις in the corresponding passage in Aristotle, is omitted
by Spinoza. The explanation for this omission would seem
to be that Spinoza, by removing the distinction between
intellectus potentia and *intellectus actu* not only in God but
in all beings,[2] has been using the term *intellectus* in the
sense of *intelligens,* i.e., *intellectus actu.* We have already
shown on other grounds that the term *intellectus* as used by
Spinoza in connection with the immediate infinite and eternal
mode of thought is to be understood in this sense.[3]

Second, in quoting Maimonides' statement as to the identity of *God, intellect, intelligens,* and *intelligibile,* Spinoza
makes free use of it in its application to his own particular
conception as to the nature of the relation of an idea of an
object to the object itself. Originally in Maimonides all
that the statement means is that in the case of any intellect
which is in action — and God is an intellect which is always

---

[1] *Ibid.,* XII, 9, 1075a, 3–5. The corresponding terms in Hebrew and Arabic are:
(1) νοῦς, שכל, عقل; (2) νόησις, משכיל, عاقل; (3) νοητόν, νοούμενον, מושכל,
معقول.

[2] *Ethics,* I, Prop. 31, Schol. Cf. above, Vol. I, pp. 404 f.

[3] Cf. above, Vol. I, pp. 338 f.

in action — the idea which exists in the intellect of an external object and the act of forming that idea by the intellect are one and the same thing with the intellect itself. Maimonides illustrates it by the example of a tree existing in nature and the idea of that existing tree, the latter of which is in the human intellect when in action as it is eternally in God, who is an intellect always in action. "It is therefore clear to you that the thing comprehended is the abstract form of the tree, and at the same time it is the intellect passed into action. The intellect and the intelligible form of the tree are not two different things, for the intellect in action is nothing but that which is comprehended, and that agent by which the form of the tree has been turned into an intelligible and abstract object, namely, the intellectual faculty of the human soul, is undoubtedly the intellect passed into action." [1] Now, all that this statement means is that the idea, or intelligible form in Maimonides' terminology, of the tree in the actual intellect of man or in God is identical with that intellect and its action or with God and His action. It does not mean that the tree as it exists in nature and the idea of that tree in the actual human intellect or in God are one and the same thing manifested through different attributes. Quite the contrary, Maimonides would say with Aristotle, the tree which exists in nature and the idea, or rather intelligible form, of the tree are two substances, one being the concrete individual thing, which is one of the three Aristotelian substances, and the other being its form, which is likewise one of the Aristotelian substances. [2] It is only according to Spinoza's own denial of the existence of finite substances that the tree and the idea of the tree are one and the same thing manifested through different attributes. Or, to take Spino-

---

[1] *Moreh Nebukim*, I, 68.
[2] Cf. above, Vol. I, p. 67, and below, p. 35.

za's own example of a circle instead of Maimonides' example of a tree, and to quote his own words: "For example, the circle existing in nature and the idea that is in God of an existing circle are one and the same thing, which is manifested through different attributes."

It is perhaps because of this his different application of the principle quoted from Maimonides that Spinoza refers to it as "a truth which some of the Hebrews appear to have seen as if through a cloud."

A second difficulty which the mediaevals have found in the attribution to God of a knowledge of particular things outside himself is that it would involve a knowledge of things which are non-existent. For particular things are transient events, now being non-existent, then coming into existence, and then again passing out of existence; but still, if God's knowledge of particular things is assumed, we must also assume "that all these new things that arise are known to Him before they take place," and so "this theory will lead to the conclusion that God's knowledge extends to things not in existence." [1] Knowledge of non-existent things, however, was objectionable to the mediaevals on two main grounds. First, it was not true knowledge, if by truth is meant the correspondence of the idea in the mind to an object outside the mind.[2] Second, in the event the non-existent object became existent, it would imply a change in the essence of the knower.[3]

Here, too, in answer to this question, Maimonides simply states the principle that God's knowledge includes things not in existence, and describes it as one of the five ways in which God's knowledge differs from human knowledge.[4] He

---

[1] *Moreh Nebukim*, III, 20. Cf. also 16.   [2] Cf. below, p. 98.

[3] *Or Adonai*, II, i, 2 (p. 29a); *Milḥamot Adonai*, III, 2 (6) (pp. 122–123).

[4] *Moreh Nebukim*, II, 20.

makes, however, the reservation that "we contend that it is not impossible that God's knowledge should have for its object a thing which does not yet exist, but the existence of which God foresees and is able to effect. It is only that which does not exist at all that is absolute non-existence for God's knowledge and cannot be the object of that knowledge, just as our own knowledge cannot have as its object that which is non-existent for us." [1] Gersonides, on the other hand, differing from Maimonides as to the nature of God's knowledge of particulars and as to the homonymity of the term "knowledge" when applied to God, explains God's knowledge of particular non-existent things on the ground that they are comprehended in the general order of nature of which God has an idea. "As for the second objection, namely, that God's knowledge would include non-existence, it is groundless according to our own conception as to the nature of God's knowledge of particulars. Our contention that God knows particulars only in so far as they are ordered under that knowledge related to the conceptual order of these things which exists in the mind of God and which exists there always, rather than to things themselves which come into being, inasmuch as He does not acquire His knowledge from the things, but, quite the contrary, the things acquire their existence from the knowledge which He has of them, that is to say, their existence is produced as an effect from the order of these things which is conceived as an idea in the mind of God. This being the case, it does not follow that [by knowing particulars] God's knowledge would be based upon non-existence; quite the contrary, it would be based on something which exists always in the same state and without any change." [2]

[1] *Ibid.*
[2] *Milḥamot Adonai*, III, 5 (2) (pp. 147–148).

Operating with the same terms and following the same
processes of reasoning, Spinoza tries to explain in Proposition VIII in what sense God can be said to know non-existent individual things. Perhaps the best way of puzzling out
the meaning of this proposition is by trying to find some
equivalence between the different terminologies of Spinoza
and the mediaevals.

Like Maimonides, Spinoza would divide all non-existent
things into those which are non-existent but capable of
existence and those which are non-existent and can never
become existent. These latter are those impossibilities the
non-existence of which, according to both Maimonides and
Spinoza, does not impair the omnipotence of God,[1] and by
the same token, their unknowability to God does not impair
His omniscience. For, again, according to both Maimonides
and Spinoza, only those non-existent things are known to
God which, while non-existent now, may become existent in
the future.

Now, these kinds of possible but as yet non-existent
things would be called by the mediaevals "potential things."
Spinoza calls them "formal essences" (*essentiae formales*).
The essence of a thing, as we have already seen, is the concept of a thing apart from its existence outside the human
mind.[2] But still, while having no existence outside the human
mind, non-existent things are contained in something outside
the human mind. As to that something in which they are
contained, there is a difference of opinion. According to the
mediaevals, who considered these possible but as yet non-
existent things as potential existences, their potentiality is
contained in matter, which has existence outside the human
mind, and the informing principle, which is ultimately to

[1] *Ethics*, I, Prop. 33; *Moreh Nebukim*, III, 15. Cf. above, Vol. I, pp. 312, 313.
[2] Cf. above, Vol. I, pp. 124, 383 ff.

bring these potential things into actual existence, is contained in the examplar and idea in the mind of God, or, as Gersonides states this view, it is the conceptual order of nonexistent things in the mind of God which endows them with existence.[1] Spinoza, however, by discarding the distinction between matter and form as a distinction between potentiality and actuality, and by making both extension and thought, the heirs of matter and form, attributes of God, finds that "the formal essences of individual things or modes," that is to say, non-existent individual things, "are contained in the attributes of God." Then, again, according to Gersonides, God knows these possible but as yet nonexistent things only in so far as they are comprehended in the "conceptual order of these things which exists in the mind of God."[2] Similarly, according to Spinoza, "the ideas of nonexistent individual things or modes are apprehended in the infinite idea of God."

In contradistinction to the "formal essences" of individual things which do not exist outside the human mind and which are only "contained in the attributes of God," there are things which exist outside the human mind. These are the individual things which constantly come into being, exist for a while, and pass away; in short, the things which have duration. It is these things that are generally spoken of as existent individual things; and it is they that form the object of what is generally called knowledge. Of such existent individual things Spinoza states in the Corollary to Proposition VIII that they "are said to exist, not only in so far as they are included in God's attributes, but in so far as they are said to have duration," and "their ideas involve existence through which they are said to have duration." Whether

[1] *Milḥamot Adonai*, III, 4 (3) (p. 141).
[2] *Ibid.*

God knows such existent individual things and in what manner He knows them constitute the mediaeval problem of
divine knowledge. To repeat briefly what we have said
above: Some philosophers have maintained that God does
not know particulars; that He only knows universals. This
view is rejected by both Maimonides and Gersonides; [1] they
both agree that God knows particulars. They differ, however, as to the manner of His knowing them. To Maimonides,
God knows them *qua* particulars, but with a knowledge
which is absolutely unlike human knowledge. To Gersonides,
God knows them only in so far as they are united as a whole
and are included in the idea in the mind of God. Spinoza,
too, maintains that God knows particulars, and, like Maimonides, he openly refutes those who maintain that God
knows only universals. [2] As to the manner in which God
knows the particulars, his view is analogous to that of Gersonides, whose discussion on the subject, as we have been
trying to show, forms the literary background of Proposition VIII.

That Spinoza's reasoning in Proposition VIII, which we
have just explained, reflects the text of Gersonides may be
seen from the Scholium. Spinoza is trying there to illustrate
the manner in which non-existent things can be known by
the example of a circle in which there is contained an infinite number of rectangles equal to one another. A similar
illustration is suggested by Gersonides when he says that
"our knowledge may be actual even when the object of that
knowledge is non-existent, as is the case in many of the mathematical figures of which we have a knowledge even though
they have no existence at all outside the soul." [3]

---

[1] *Moreh Nebukim*, III, 18; *Milḥamot Adonai*, III, 4 (pp. 137–138).
[2] *Short Treatise*, I, 6, § 7. Cf. above, Vol. I, pp. 437–438.
[3] *Milḥamot Adonai*, III, 2 (2) (p. 127).

A third objection raised by the mediaevals against God's knowledge of particulars is derived from the view that the fundamental contrast between God and things is a contrast between the immaterial and the material. The immaterial, the immovable, the non-temporal, the most perfect, and the simple, it is argued, can have no knowledge of that which is material, movable, temporal, imperfect, and manifold.[1] To Spinoza, with the disappearance of the old contrast between the immaterial and the material, the objection presented itself in the form of a question as to how the infinite can have a knowledge of the finite. This question is raised by Spinoza in Proposition IX. It is analogous to the question, raised by him before in Proposition XXVIII of Part I, as to how the infinite can be the cause of the finite. The answer in both cases is the same.[2] God as the infinite immanent cause, immanent in the sense of the whole in which the infinite causally interrelated effects reside as parts,[3] is the cause of the ideas of the finite things in so far only as they are indissoluble parts of an infinite series of causes and effects within His attribute of thought. God is thus not the immediate cause of the ideas of the individual things, but rather their remote cause, in the restricted sense of the term "remote" which Spinoza has suggested elsewhere.[4] Directly, the idea of each individual thing has for its cause the idea of another individual thing, and so on *ad infinitum*. God is the cause of these individual ideas only in so far as they are united into an infinite whole. And so also He knows the individual things directly only as an infinite whole, and only indirectly as finite individuals. The solution is analogous to Gersonides' theory that God knows the particulars only in so far as they are included in the universal order which forms

---

[1] *Ibid.*, III, 2 (1–4) (p. 122).
[2] Cf. above, Vol. I, pp. 397–398.
[3] Cf. above, Vol. I, pp. 323 ff.
[4] *Ethics*, I, Prop. 28, Schol.

a united whole. And so, starting with Proposition IX that
"the idea of an individual thing actually existing has God
for a cause, not in so far as He is infinite, but in so far as He
is considered to be affected by another idea of an individual
thing actually existing, of which idea also He is the cause in
so far as He is affected by a third, and so on *ad infinitum*,"
he concludes in the Corollary that God in a similar manner
knows the individual things within that infinite series, "for
a knowledge of everything which happens in the individual
object of any idea exists in God in so far only as He possesses
the idea of that object."

III. Body and Mind in Man

With Proposition X Spinoza begins his discussion of the
microcosm, trying to show the resemblances as well as the
differences between man and God. Just as God is a single
substance manifested through the attributes of extension and
thought, so is man a single individual thing composed of the
two modes of body and mind. Furthermore, just as God
knows himself and through that knowledge knows the things
that follow from himself, so man knows himself and through
that knowledge knows the things outside himself. In the
same manner he finds an analogy between the interrelation
of extension and thought in God and the interrelation of
body and mind in man. But there are also differences
between them, and the first fundamental difference which
he discusses is that between the relation of extension and
thought to God and the relation of body and mind to man.
God is a substance in whom extension and thought are attributes. Logically, then, God is the underlying subject of
these two attributes, without himself being composed of
them. But man is not a substance, and logically he is not
the underlying subject of body and mind; he is rather him-

self composed of body and mind. This is the reason why
Spinoza starts his discussion of man in Proposition X with
the statement that "the being of substance does not pertain
to the essence of man, or, in other words, substance does
not constitute the form of man." Not satisfied with a mere
denial that man is a substance, he proceeds in the two Scholia
and the Corollary of this proposition, as well as in the
Preface to Part II of the *Short Treatise*, to refute in detail
the views of his predecessors who maintained that man is
a substance.

In traditional philosophy, as we have already seen, the
term "substance" was applied to several things — matter,
form, any concrete object consisting of matter and form,
and in an equivocal sense also to God.[1] The difference between the concrete object as substance and God as substance is that the former is material and of a composite
nature, whereas the latter is immaterial and of an absolutely
simple nature. According to this view, man is, like any
other concrete object, a substance consisting of matter and
form, in fact of a hierarchy of matters and forms, and in his
case there is a particular matter and form called body and
soul. The relation of man to God is like that of any particular
thing within the physical universe or of the physical universe
as a whole, namely, the relation of the thing created to the
agent that has created it. In opposition to this conception
of man, Spinoza reiterates his own view that the term "substance" is to apply to God alone, that nothing that is finite
can be called substance, that particular things are to be
called modes, and that modes exist in the substance as particulars in a universal, in the sense that they are conceived
through the substance. "I by no means think that man, in

[1] Cf. above, Vol. I, pp. 67–68.

so far as he consists of spirit, soul,[1] or body, is a substance. Because, already at the beginning of this book, we proved (1) that no substance can have a beginning; (2) that one substance cannot produce another; and lastly (3) that there cannot be two like substances." [2] "Hence it follows that the essence of man consists of certain modifications of the attributes of God, for the being of substance does not pertain to the essence of man (Prop. X, Pt. II). It is therefore something (Prop. XV, Pt. I) which is in God, and which without God can neither be nor be conceived, or (Corol. Prop. XXV, Pt. I) an affection or mode which expresses the nature of God in a certain and determinate manner." [3]

But Spinoza goes further than this in his argument against the traditional application of the term "substance" to man. The concrete individual man, and for that matter any concrete object, is according to the Aristotelian philosophy not only one substance but a complexity of substances. By himself, as a particular concrete object, man is what Aristotle calls a first substance, consisting of matter and form, each of which is also a substance. Then man belongs to the genus animal and the species rational, which two are also substances, the species being called by Aristotle second substance and the genus being called by him, by implication, third substance.[4] According to this view, then, man is substance not only because he is a concrete being, but also because he consists of matter and form, and belongs to a genus and species.

---

[1] These two terms "spirit, soul" (*geest, ziele*) probably reflect the two Latin terms *spiritus* and *anima* or *mens*. In J. Van Vloten's Latin translation of the *Short Treatise* (*Ad Benedicti de Spinoza Opera quae supersunt omnia Supplementum*, Amsterdam, 1862, p. 88) these two terms are translated by *spiritus, mens*. Cf. below, p. 44, n. 1.

[2] *Short Treatise*, II, Preface, § 2.

[3] *Ethics*, II, Prop. 10, Corol.

[4] *Categories*, 5, 2a, 11 and 14. Cf. Grote, *Aristotle* (1872), I, p. 96.

Matter and form, furthermore, are included by Aristotle among the causes of man: "The cause of man," he says, "is the elements in man, viz. fire and earth as matter, and the peculiar form." [1]

Spinoza criticizes one by one these various uses of the term "substance" in connection with man.

In the first place, says Spinoza, what you call the matter and form of man, that is to say, the elements out of which the human body is composed and the peculiar shape and figure it possesses, are not substances, but only modes of extension, for all that man "has of form, motion, and other things, are likewise [modes] of the other attribute which is attributed by us to God." [2] They cannot be substances, because they do not conform to Aristotle's own definition of substance. For according to Aristotle a substance by definition must possess four characteristics, namely, (a) it must be that which exists in itself and does not exist in a subject, or, if it does exist in a subject, (b) it must be the cause of the existence of that subject, (c) it must also constitute the limits which define the individuality of the subject, and (d) it must be its essence.[3] Now, we have already seen how Spinoza's formal definition of substance in Definition III of the First Part of the *Ethics* implies an argument to show that matter and form cannot be substances, on the ground that they cannot truly be said to exist in themselves.[4] Now, in his arguments that man is not a substance he is trying to show that in man matter and form cannot be substances, on the ground that they cannot truly be said to be the causes of the existence of their subject, to define individuality of it,

---

[1] *Metaphysics*, XII, 5, 1071a, 13–14.

[2] *Short Treatise*, II, Preface, § 3 (*Opera*, I, p. 53, ll. 6–8).

[3] For these four characteristics of substance, see my *Crescas' Critique of Aristotle*, pp. 102–103, and note 9 on pp. 573–576.

[4] Cf. above, Vol. I, Chapter III.

and to be its essence. "And although from this, [namely], that the nature of man can neither be, nor be understood, without the attributes we ourselves admit to constitute substance, some try to prove that man is substance, yet this has no other ground than false supposition. For, since the nature of matter or body existed before the form of this human body existed, that nature cannot be peculiar to the human body, because it is clear that during the time when man was not, it could never belong to the nature of man." [1] And again: "For since it is possible for more men than one to exist, therefore that which constitutes the form of man is not the being of substance." [2]

In the second place, continues Spinoza, man is not a substance by virtue of the genus and species which are generally supposed to constitute his definition, for genus and species, according to Spinoza's own theory of definition,[3] "do not belong to the nature of definition." Man, being only a mode, or a thing which does not exist through itself, or a thing which is created, must be defined through his proximate or efficient cause which is God, or through the attributes whose mode he is, and it is these attributes, namely extension and thought, and not the universals animality and rationality, that may be considered as the genera through which man is defined or understood, for, as says Spinoza, "the second [kind of definitions] are those [of things] which do not exist through themselves, but only through attributes whose modes they are, and through which as their genus they must be understood." [4]

But here Spinoza seems to become conscious of a difficulty. If God or His attributes of thought and extension are to

---

[1] *Short Treatise*, II, Preface, § 4.   [2] *Ethics*, II, Prop. 10, Schol. [1].
[3] Cf. above, Vol. I, pp. 383 ff.
[4] *Short Treatise*, I, 7, § 10. Cf. above, Vol. I, pp. 383 ff.

take the place of the genus animality and the species rationality in forming the definition of man, then God must bear the same relation to man in Spinoza's new conception of a definition as animality and rationality in the old Aristotelian conception of a definition. Now, animality and rationality, in the old conception of a definition, are said to constitute the nature or the essence of man; they are what are called the essential attributes of man; and consequently they are said to pertain to the essence or nature of man, for according to the generally accepted view, held by those whom Spinoza describes as "they" [1] or as "many people," [2] "that pertains to the essence of a thing without which the thing can neither be nor be conceived." [3] Consequently, according to Spinoza's conception of a definition, God should pertain to the essence or nature of man. This view that man as well as all other beings is of the essence or nature of God is reflected in such statements by John Scotus Erigena as "God is the essence of all things" [4] and all things "participate in the essence" [5] of God, or in such a statement by Amalric of Bena as "God is the essence of all created beings." [6] According to Hieronymus Zanchius, the view that man is of the essence of God is traceable to the heresies of the Manichaeans and the Priscillians.[7] But Spinoza is opposed to this view, and, if his con-

[1] *Ibid.*, II, Preface, § 5 (*Opera*, I, p. 53, l. 19).

[2] *Ethics*, II, Prop. 10, Schol. [2].

[3] *Ibid.* The same statement occurs also in the *Short Treatise* (*loc. cit.*), but with the use of the term "nature" instead of "essence."

[4] *De Divisione Naturae*, I, 3: "Ipse namque omnium essentia est."

[5] *Ibid.*, I, 12: "Est igitur Principium . . . Principium quia ex se sunt omnia, quae essentia participant."

[6] Gerson, *De Concordia Metaphysicae cum Logica* in *Opera Omnia* (Antwerpiae, 1706), Vol. IV, Col. 826 B: "Dixit [Almaricus] enim Deum esse essentiam omnium creaturarum." Cf. R. Eisler, *Wörterbuch der philosophischen Begriffe* (1927), under "Gott," Vol. I, pp. 584–585.

[7] *De Operibus Dei intra Spacium Sex Dierum Opus*, Pars III, Liber II, Caput VI: *De Unione Animae cum Corpore*, Thesis II: "At Deus non est in nobis, neque ut

ception of the relation of God to the world is to be described
as pantheism, it is pantheism of a different kind. While
indeed he considers man as well as all other beings as modes
of the attributes of thought and extension of God, he does
not consider them as being in a literal sense of the same essence as God. As we shall see later, in his definition of mind,
he considers mind only as a part of the infinite intellect of
God, but not of the essence of God.[1]

In answer to this difficulty Spinoza tries to show that the
view commonly held by "many people" as to the meaning
of pertaining to the essence of anything is erroneous even on
their own ground. For those "many people" admit that
"God is the sole cause both of the essence and of the existence of all things," and to prove that this is a commonly
accepted view Spinoza quotes, evidently from Descartes,
the scholastic expression that God is a cause both *secundum
fieri* and *secundum esse*.[2] Consequently, if their conception
as to the meaning of pertaining to the essence of things were
correct, they would have to believe "either that the nature
of God belongs to the essence of created things, or that
created things can be or can be conceived without God," or,
"which is more probable," they would have to admit that
"there is no consistency in their thought."[3]

But, concludes Spinoza, their conception of the meaning
of pertaining to the essence of anything is wrong. For,
argues he, to pertain to the essence of a thing implies a
mutual relationship and dependence between the thing itself

---

materia, neque ut forma: alioqui essemus de essentia Dei: quae fuit haeresis Mani-
chaeorum et Priscillianistarum" (3rd ed., 1602, p. 792).

[1] Cf. below, pp. 49 ff.

[2] Cf. Descartes, *Quintae Responsiones* (*Oeuvres*, VII, p. 369, ll. 22–23): "Deus
est causa rerum creatarum, non modo secundum fieri, sed etiam secundum esse."
See Lewis Robinson, *Kommentar zu Spinozas Ethik*, I, p. 295. Cf. above, Vol. I,
p. 382.

[3] *Ethics*, II, Prop. 10, Schol. [2].

and that which pertains to its essence. "I say that to the essence of anything pertains that . . . without which the thing can neither be nor be conceived, and which in its turn cannot be nor be conceived without the thing." [1] God, therefore, does not pertain to the essence of man or of any created thing, even though He constitutes its definition, for the causal relation between God and His creatures is not mutual, because while everything is dependent upon God for its essence and existence, God is independent of anything. In this, indeed, Spinoza reechoes an old-established principle, for one of the characteristics of God as a being whose existence is necessary *per se* is that He is a being "upon whom the existence of all things is dependent, but whose existence is independent of anything else." [2]

This seems to me to be the full meaning of the argument contained in the two Scholia and the Corollary of Proposition X as well as in the Preface to *Short Treatise*, II. But obviously the statement in the Second Scholium and the parallel statement in the *Short Treatise* that "many people say that that pertains to the essence of a thing without which the thing can neither be nor be conceived, and they therefore believe either that the nature of God belongs to the essence of created things, or that created things can be or can be conceived without God," refers to some definite text. What text it was I have so far been unable to discover. But we can gather some idea as to its content. Probably it was some pantheistic argument where the problem of the relation of God to the universe was presented in the form of a disjunctive proposition that God is either the essence of all things or that He is outside and above all things. Or, perhaps, it was some

[1] *Ibid.*, II, Def. 2. Cf. Prop. 10, Schol. [2], and *Short Treatise*, II, Preface, §5.
[2] *Emunah Ramah*, II, i (p. 47). Cf. *Maḳaṣid al-Falasifah*, II, ii, 5–6 (pp. 139–140), quoted above, Vol. I, p. 308, n. 2.

theological treatise where the problem of Christology was presented in the form of a disjunctive proposition that the Father and the Son are either homoousious or heteroousious.

Man, then, as a whole is not a substance, nor are his soul and body, taken individually, substances. Man is a combination of two modes. "All that he has of thought are only modes of the attribute of thought," and "all that he has of form, motion, and other things, are likewise" modes of the attributes of extension.[1] Or, as he expresses it in the *Ethics*, "the essence of man consists of certain modifications of the attributes of God."[2] These modifications are mind and body, the human mind being "a part of the infinite intellect of God,"[3] and the human body being "a mode which expresses in a certain and determinate manner the essence of God in so far as He is considered as a thing extended."[4] The relation between these two is like that between the thinking substance and the extended substance; they are one and the same thing expressed in two different ways.[5] This is what Spinoza has set out to prove, and accordingly in Propositions XI-XIII he discusses with reference to man every point which he has previously discussed in Propositions I-IX with reference to God, concluding with the Corollary in Proposition XIII: "Hence it follows that man is composed of mind and body."

But what is mind, or, rather, the "human mind" (*mens humana*), as Spinoza calls it here? The answer to this question is given by Spinoza in Propositions XI, XII, and XIII. Gradually, stage by stage, he adds one statement to another,

[1] *Short Treatise*, II, Preface, § 3.
[2] *Ethics*, II, Prop. 10, Corol.
[3] *Ibid.*, II, Prop. 11, Corol.
[4] *Ibid.*, II, Def. 1. Cf. Meyer's Preface to *Principia Philosophiae Cartesianae* quoted in Epistola 24.
[5] *Ethics*, II, Prop. 7, Schol.

out of which there emerges in the end his definition of the
human mind.

Spinoza begins his definition of the mind in Proposition XI
with the statement that "the *first thing* which forms the
actual being of the *human mind* is nothing else than the *idea*
of an *individual* thing *actually* existing." I have italicized
six terms in this proposition as being of special significance.
The subject of his inquiry, as will be noticed, is described by
Spinoza not as "soul" (*anima*) or "intellect" (*intellectus*),
but as the "human mind" (*mens humana*). The question
may therefore be asked: In what sense does Spinoza use this
term "mind" qualified by the term "human"? And of this
human mind he wants to know not only the thing which forms
its being, but the "first thing" (*primum*) which forms its
"actual" (*actuale*) being. Is there any significance in the use
of these two qualifying adjectives? Then, the first thing
which forms the actual being of the human mind is described
by him as an "idea" (*idea*) of something. What does he
mean exactly by the term "idea"? Finally, that idea which
is the first thing which forms the actual being of the human
mind is said by him to be the idea not merely of a thing existing but of an "individual" (*singularis*) thing "actually"
(*actu*) existing. What is the purpose of the use of these two
qualifying terms?

Ordinarily the term "soul" when qualified by the term
"human" is used as the antithesis of both animal and vegetable soul and refers to the rational faculty of the soul, or
the intellect. Such is the significance of the qualifying term
"human," to mention but two examples, in Maimonides [1]
and in Thomas Aquinas.[2] In the latter the term "mind"

---

[1] *Moreh Nebukim*, II, 1: נפש האדם באדם. From the context it is clear that it
refers only to the intellect.

[2] *Summa Theologica*, Pars I, Quaest. 75, Art. 2: "animam humanam, quae
dicitur intellectus vel mens."

without the qualifying adjective "human" means also the same thing,[1] though it is sometimes used by him to include also the faculties of will and memory.[2] Similarly Descartes uses the term "human soul" in the sense of "mind." [3] Among the philosophers of the Renaissance the terms *animus* and *mens* [4] were used as designations of the individual human soul, which was considered as being of divine origin and separable from the body, in contradistinction to the term *spiritus*, which was used as a designation of the vital force which was inseparable from the body,[5] thus on the whole the term *spiritus* corresponding to the sensitive faculties in Aristotle and the terms *animus* and *mens* corresponding to the rational faculty in Aristotle. It is probably with reference to this contrast of terms that Descartes says that he prefers the term *mens* to *anima*, on the ground that the latter "is equivocal and is frequently applied to what is corporeal." [6] Verulam, according to the testimony of Spinoza, "often uses 'intellect' (*intellectus*) for 'mind' (*mens*), in which respect he differs from Descartes." [7] Now Spinoza, as we know, rejects the existence of absolute faculties in the soul, declaring that the so-called faculties "are either altogether fictitious, or else are nothing but metaphysical or universal entities."[8]

[1] Cf. quotation in the preceding note.

[2] *Quaestiones Disputatae de Veritate*, Quaest. X, Art. I, ad 7: "mens non est una quaedam potentia praeter memoriam, intelligentiam et voluntatem, sed est quoddam totum potentiale, comprehendens haec tria."

[3] Cf. *Meditationes, Synopsis* (*Oeuvres*, VII, p. 14, l. 16), and French version (VIII, p. 10): "Mais que l'esprit [=*mens*], ou l'ame de l'homme (ce que ie ne distingue point), est immortelle de sa nature."

[4] Cf. Telesius and Campanella in Erdmann, *Grundriss der Geschichte der Philosophie*, I, § 243.3; § 246.5.

[5] Cf. *ibid.*, § 246.5.

[6] Cf. Def. 6 in *Rationes Dei Existentiam etc.* at the end of *Secundae Responsiones* (*Oeuvres*, VII, p. 161).

[7] Epistola 2 to Oldenburg.

[8] *Ethics*, II, Prop. 48, Schol.

Nor, for aught we know, does he in the *Ethics* make any distinction between the vital and the intellectual forces of the soul as constituting different faculties, though in the *Short Treatise* he does say that man consists "of spirit (*geest* = *spiritus*), soul (*ziele* = *anima, mens*), or body." [1] Accordingly Spinoza uses the terms "mind" (*mens*) and "human mind" (*mens humana*) and "soul" (*anima*) in the *Ethics* [2] and the term "soul" (*anima*) throughout the *Tractatus de Intellectus Emendatione* in the most general sense, and every one of these terms is to be understood to include all those functions which traditionally were considered as constituting the faculties of the human soul.

Now, these faculties of the human soul, or, rather, of the animal soul in general, are divided by Aristotle as well as by the mediaevals into perceptive and motive. Thus says Aristotle: "There are two different characteristics by which the soul is principally defined; firstly, motion from place to place, and secondly, thinking and judging and perceiving by the senses." [3] And thus also Judah Ha Levi, speaking for the mediaevals, says that "all the faculties of a living being are either perceptive or motive." [4] Of these two classes of faculties, the perceptive are considered by Aristotle as being prior to the motive, for intelligence is one of the causes of motion. "Both these, then," says Aristotle, "are causes of locomotion, intelligence and appetency." [5] And Abraham Ibn Daud puts it more directly: "Of these two classes of

---

[1] *Short Treatise*, II, Preface, § 2. The "spirits" (*geesten*), i.e., animal spirits (*spiritus animales*), are again mentioned in *Short Treatise*, II, 11, § 2; 19, §§ 11 f.; 20, § 2, § 3, § 5; 22, § 7. Cf. *Ethics*, V, Praef. (*Opera*, II, p. 278, ll. 9 ff.). Cf. above, p. 35, n. 1.

[2] Cf. *Ethics*, II, Prop. 11, and Epistola 32 (*Opera*, IV, p. 174, l. 3): "mens humana"; *Ethics*, III, Prop. 57, Schol. (*Opera*, II, p. 187, l. 15): "idea seu anima"; V, Praef. (p. 270, l. 4). "anima seu mens."

[3] *De Anima*, III, 3, 427a, 17–19. Cf. 9, 432a, 15–17.

[4] *Cuzari*, V, 12.   [5] *De Anima*, III, 10, 433a, 13.

faculties the one which is prior in living beings is perception." [1] With this prevalent view about the priority of the
perceptive faculties to the motive in the background, Spinoza
significantly begins his definition of the human mind by
saying that the *first thing* which forms the actual being of the
human mind is not what is generally described as the motive
faculties, but rather that which is described as the perceptive
faculties, or which he himself describes as the idea of something. The significance of this part of his definition will
appear in our discussion of Spinoza's theory of emotions.

Within perception itself, whether it be sensation or cognition, there is according to Aristotle and his followers a distinction of potential and actual perception. The difference
between these two kinds of perception consists in the respectively different relations of the agent and the act of the perception to the object of the perception. In potential perception, the agent or the faculty of perceiving as well as the
act of perceiving differs from the object perceived. In actual
perception they are all identical. "Now actual knowledge,"
says Aristotle, "is identical with the thing known." [2] And
again: "In a manner the soul is all existent things. For they
are all either objects of sensation or objects of thought; and
knowledge and sensation are in a manner identical with
their respective objects." [3] This view is re-echoed by Maimonides in his statements that "the intellect in action is
nothing but the thing comprehended" and that "the intellect in action is not a thing different from its action." [4]

Now, Spinoza has abolished this distinction between the
actual and the potential. Mind is to him always actual,
just as intellect is to him always actual. When it happened

---

[1] *Emunah Ramah*, I, 6 (p. 26).   [2] *De Anima*, III, 7, 431a, 1–2.
[3] *Ibid.*, 8, 431b, 21–23.
[4] *Moreh Nebukim*, I, 68. Cf. above, Vol. I, p. 238.

that twice in succession he used the expression "actual intellect," he at once made haste to explain that it was not meant to indicate that a potential intellect exists but rather that intellect is always actual.[1] Similarly in his definition of the term "idea" he preferred the use of the term "conception" to that of "perception," on the ground, he says, that "the name perception seems to indicate that the mind is passive in its relation to the object; but the word conception seems to express the action of the mind."[2] Since the mind is thus always actual, the object of the knowledge of the mind will, according to Spinoza, always be identical with the mind. Consequently, in setting out to define "mind," Spinoza speaks of the object of the mind as that "which forms the *actual* being of the human mind," that is to say, as that which is identical with the human mind, which, according to him, is always actual.

This object of the knowledge of the mind which is identical with the mind itself is, furthermore, according to Aristotle, not the matter of a thing, but rather its form. "It follows," says Aristotle, "that the faculties must be identical, if not with the things themselves, then with their forms. The things themselves they are not, for it is not the stone which is in the soul, but the form of the stone."[3] The Greek word for "form" used in this passage of Aristotle is εἶδος, from which we get the Latin and our own term "idea." Now, in the Latin philosophic terminology, though the term *forma* has on the whole supplanted the term *idea* in its Aristotelian sense, still the term "idea" has been retained for that particular form which is the object of knowledge,[4] or what is

---

[1] *Ethics*, I, Props. 30 and 31, Schol. Cf. above, Vol. I, p. 404.
[2] *Ibid.*, II, Def. 3, Expl.   [3] *De Anima*, III, 8, 431b, 28–432a, 1.
[4] *Summa Theologica*, Pars I, Quaest. 15, Art. 1: "idea enim Graece, Latine forma dicitur; unde per ideas intelleguntur formae aliarum rerum praeter ipsas res existentes."

called the intelligible form. Descartes retains the same use
of the term when he says that "idea is a word by which I
understand the form of any thought."[1] This meaning of
the term "idea" is on the whole retained also by Spinoza
when he says in Definition III of Part II, "By idea, I understand a conception of the mind which the mind forms because it is a thinking thing." Still it will appear in the course
of our discussion that the term "idea" did assume with him
a wider meaning, and it was used by him not only in the
sense of *forma intelligibilis*, but also in the sense of *forma
imaginabilis* and *forma sensibilis*,[2] and this despite his statement that "by ideas I do not understand images (*imagines*)
which are formed at the back of the eye, or, if you please,
in the middle of the brain, but rather conceptions of thought
(*cogitationis conceptus*)."[3] This denial of his that images
are to be called ideas is therefore to be taken with some
reservation and as reflecting the following statement of
Descartes: "And thus it is not only images depicted in the
imagination that I call ideas; nay, to such images I here
decidedly refuse the title of ideas, in so far as they are pictures
in the corporeal imagination, i.e., in some part of the brain.
They are ideas only in so far as they constitute the form of
the mind itself that is directed towards that part of the
brain."[4] Consequently, following the Aristotelian view that

---

[1] Def. 2 in *Rationes Dei Existentiam etc.* at the end of *Secundae Responsiones*
(*Oeuvres*, VII, p. 160).

[2] Cf. W. Hale White's translation of *Tractatus de Intellectus Emendatione*, Preface, pp. ix–x.

Klatzkin in his Hebrew translation of the *Ethics* (*Torat ha-Middot*) quite rightly
translates *idea* by מושכל, i.e., *intelligibile*. Though it is not an exact translation of
idea, it renders its meaning correctly in places where *idea* stands for *forma intelligibilis* (εἶδος νοητόν, צורה מושכלת).

[3] *Ethics*, II, Prop. 48, Schol.

[4] Def. 2 in *Rationes Dei Existentiam etc.* at the end of *Secundae Responsiones*
(*Oeuvres*, VII, p. 160).

it is the form of a thing and not its matter that is identical with the soul, Spinoza says that the first thing which is identical with the actual human mind is the *idea* of a thing; the term "idea" here is used by him in the most general sense, comprehending what Aristotle would call the sensible, imaginable, and intelligible form of a thing. Since the mind or the soul is identical with the idea, Spinoza sometimes uses the expression "idea or soul" (*idea, seu anima*).[1]

This, it appears to me, is how Spinoza has arrived at his definition of the mind as the idea of the body. It is nothing but a new way of restating the Aristotelian definition of the soul as the form of the body. It is not impossible that in his use of the term "idea" instead of "form" Spinoza was influenced by Francis Glisson and John Marcus Marci, both of whom use the term "idea" in their definition of soul.[2] But, as we have seen on several other occasions, we must differentiate between the reasoning which leads Spinoza to certain conclusions and the phraseology in which he clothes those conclusions. A dependence in the latter does not necessarily mean a dependence in the former.

But that thing the form of which is the object identical with the *actual* mind, again according to Aristotle, must itself be actual, for "knowledge and sensation, then, are subdivided to correspond to things. Potential knowledge and sensation answer to things which are potential, actual knowledge and sensation to things which are actual."[3] Furthermore, that thing must be *finite*, for an infinite actual object does not exist,[4] nor can it be known.[5] Thus also Spi-

---

[1] *Ethics*, III, Prop. 57, Schol. (*Opera*, II, p. 187, l. 15).

[2] Cf. Dunin-Borkowski, *Der junge De Spinoza*, pp. 384 f., 392.

[3] *De Anima*, III, 8, 431b, 24–26.

[4] *Physics*, III, 4–8; *De Caelo*, I, 5–7; *Metaphysics*, XI, 10; *Moreh Nebukim*, II, Introduction, Prop. 1. Cf. my *Crescas' Critique of Aristotle*, pp. 135 ff.

[5] *Physics*, I, 4, 187b, 7; *Moreh Nebukim*, III, 16. Cf. above, Vol. I, p. 139.

noza maintains here that the idea which forms the actual being of the mind must be the idea "of an *individual* thing *actually* existing." In the Demonstration he makes it quite clear that he means by it that the object cannot be a "non-existent thing" nor "an infinite thing." In these two respects, then, the microcosm differs from the macrocosm, for in the latter case the object of God's knowledge is "all things which follow necessarily from His essence," [1] the number of which is infinite,[2] and within which are also included "non-existent individual things." [3]

Since it is the idea or the form of a thing which constitutes the human mind, "it follows that the human mind is a part of the infinite intellect of God." [4] This reflects on the whole the view generally held in mediaeval philosophy, especially among the emanationists, according to which all forms are bestowed upon matter by the so-called Active Intellect, which is in direct line of emanation from the thinking activity of God. Judah ha-Levi expresses this view quite neatly when he says that "philosophers were forced to acknowledge that these forms could only be given by some divine being, which they call the form-giving Intelligence"; [5] though in another place he qualifies this statement by referring to "others who assert that the powers and qualities of minerals are the product of combination only, and consequently do not require forms of divine origin. The latter kinds of forms are only necessary for plants and animals to which a soul is attributed." [6] The significance of this statement of Spinoza that "the human mind is *a part of the infinite intellect of God*" is to be found both in what it directly affirms and in what it indirectly denies. It directly affirms that the human mind is what the mediaevals would describe as being of divine

---

[1] *Ethics*, II, Prop. 3.   [2] *Ibid.*, II, Prop. 4.   [3] *Ibid.*, II, Prop. 7.
[4] *Ibid.*, II, Prop. 11, Corol.   [5] *Cuzari*, V, 4.   [6] *Ibid.*, V, 10.

origin. But it seems indirectly to deny that it is what some mediaevals would describe as being a part of God's essence itself. It is a part only, Spinoza seems to say, of the infinite intellect of God, which corresponds to what the mediaevals call the Active Intellect. Thus also one of Spinoza's teachers, Manasseh ben Israel, argues vehemently against the view held by certain Jewish as well as non-Jewish philosophers that the human mind is a part of God's own essence, admitting only that it is a spiritual being of divine origin and of the same order of excellence as angels.[1] Of Hebrew sources for the view that the soul is a part of God's essence itself, Manasseh ben Israel mentions two Cabalistic works, *Shefa' Ṭal*, Introduction, (by Shabbethai Sheftel Horwitz), and *Pardes Rimmonim*, XXIV, 13, by Moses Cordovero. The "gentile philosophers" who were of the same view are not named by Manasseh ben Israel. But the following names occur in Albertus Magnus: Xenophanes, the Pythagoreans, Alexander (of Aphrodisias), and David of Dinant.[2] Hieronymus Zanchius similarly denies that the soul is a part of the essence of God, but evidently he would also deny that it was a part of the Active Intellect or of Spinoza's infinite intellect of God, for he explicitly denies that it is a part of the essence of angels, insisting that in each individual human being the soul is created by God *ex nihilo*.[3] In the light of this discussion one can appreciate the vagueness with which Descartes

---

[1] Cf. *Nishmat Ḥayyim*, II, 9. Cf. also *Emunot We-De'ot*, VI, 1.

[2] Albertus Magnus, *Summa Theologiae*, Pars II, Tract. XII, Quaest. 72, Membrum 4, Art. 2. Cf. Thomas Aquinas, *Contra Gentiles*, Lib. II, Cap. 85: "Quod anima non est de substantia Dei."

[3] *De Operibus Dei intra Spacium Sex Dierum Creatis Opus*, Pars III, Liber II, Cap. V: *De Origine Animorum*, Thesis I: "Animae humanae neque ab Angelis, neque ex Dei substantia . . . conditae fuerunt"; Thesis II: "Singulorum hominum animae, et unius et eas nihilo creari, a Deo, probabilius est" (3rd ed., 1602, pp. 760 and 765). Cf. above, p. 39. Zanchius also denies that the soul arises "*per traducem*" (*ibid.*, after Thesis I, p. 763; cf. p. 759, before Thesis I) or "*ex traduce*" (cf.

has phrased his statement that "the human mind has in it something that we may call divine." [1]

Furthermore, the form of the thing which according to Aristotle is the object of sensation and knowledge and identical with the mind is not something static and eternally fixed like a Platonic idea; it is, rather, constantly changing, as is the matter of the thing in relation to which it is the form. It is thus that Aristotle maintains that "sensation," of which the form of a thing is the object, "consists in being moved and acted upon, for it is held to be a species of qualitative change." [2] And what is true of sensation is true also of knowledge. "The soul is said . . . to perceive and to think; and all these states are said to be motions." [3] Spinoza expresses the same view when he says in the *Short Treatise* that "as the idea comes from the existence of the object, therefore according as the object changes or perishes, so the idea must change or perish." [4] Consequently, since it is the idea of an object which constitutes the actual being of the mind, "whatever happens in the object of the idea constituting the human mind must be perceived by the human mind." [5] In this respect, the microcosm is like the macrocosm, for "a knowledge of everything which happens in the individual object of any idea exists in God." [6] But there is the following difference between them. God has a knowledge of them "in so far only as He possesses the idea of that object." [7]

Index). Similarly Spinoza says: "Hoc satis constat, illam non esse *ex traduce*" (*Cogitata Metaphysica*, II, 12).

[1] *Regulae ad Directionem Ingenii*, IV (*Oeuvres*, X, p. 373, ll. 7–8): "Habet enim humana mens nescio quid divini."

[2] *De Anima*, II, 5, 416b, 33–35.

[3] *Ibid.*, I, 4, 408b, 2–4. A contradictory statement concerning knowledge is to be found in *Physics*, VII, 3, 247a, 16–247 b, 1. Cf. my *Crescas' Critique of Aristotle*, note 20 on pp. 547–548.

[4] *Short Treatise*, Appendix II, § 7 (*Opera*, I, p. 118, ll. 21–24).

[5] *Ethics*, II, Prop. 12.   [6] *Ibid.*, II, Prop. 9, Corol.   [7] *Ibid.*

Man has a knowledge of them because the idea is "united with the object." [1]

But what is that individual finite thing actually existing which Spinoza has so far referred to as the primary object of the idea which constitutes the human mind? Now, Aristotle would have said that it is external objects, for sensation, which is the primary stage in the process of cognition, is impossible without external objects. [2] Indeed, Aristotle raises the question why there should not be sensation without external objects. "The question arises," he says, "why there is no sensation of the senses themselves; that is, why they produce no sensation apart from external sensibles." [3] But his answer remains in the negative. In opposition to this, Spinoza maintains that the first thing the mind is aware of, or the first thing of which the idea forms the actual being of the mind, is not external things, but man's own body. In the *Short Treatise* he states this view quite plainly when he says that of the influences that the body exercises upon the soul the most important one is "that it causes the soul to become aware of it, and through it also of other bodies," [4] so that "the first thing which the soul gets to know is the body." [5] Again, in a letter to Schuller he maintains that "the human mind can only get to know those things which the idea of an actually existing body involves, or what can be inferred from this idea." [6] If we were to restate Spinoza's view in the language quoted above from Aristotle, we could say that Spinoza maintains that there is a sensation of the senses themselves. Hence Proposition XIII: "The object of the idea constituting the human mind is a body, or a cer-

---

[1] *Short Treatise*, Appendix II, § 7 (*Opera*, I, p. 118, l. 25).
[2] *De Anima*, II, 5, 417a, 2 ff.   [3] *Ibid.*, 2–4.
[4] *Short Treatise*, II, 19, § 13.
[5] *Ibid.*, § 14.   [6] Epistola 64.

tain mode of extension actually existing, and nothing else."
In this, again, the microcosm is partly like the macrocosm
and partly unlike it. Like God, who knows His own essence,[1] man knows his own body; but whereas God knows
at once His own essence and all things which necessarily
follow from His essence,[2] man knows primarily his own
body, and only secondarily, as we shall see,[3] things which
are external to his body. Again, God knows His own essence in all the infinity of its attributes; but the human mind
as a mode of thought knows primarily only the body which
is a mode of extension. For man, unlike God, is not a single
substance of which mind and body are attributes, but He
is "composed of mind and body."[4]

But, though man is composed of mind and body as if these
two were distinct things and independent of each other, still
"the human mind is united to the body,"[5] that is to say,
it is inseparable from it. This must be considered the essential point in Spinoza's theory of the mind — its inseparability from the body. It runs counter to the entire trend of
the history of philosophy down to his time, for everybody
before him, for diverse reasons, insisted upon the separability of mind from body.

This general insistence among mediaeval philosophers upon
the separability of soul from body, or at least upon the separability of certain faculties of the soul from body, irrespective of their views as to the nature of the soul itself, had its
origin, I believe, in three sources: first, the Biblical account of the origin of the soul as an inbreathing from God
in the human body, which in post-Biblical Judaism, and

---

[1] *Ethics*, II, Prop. 3.   [2] *Ibid.*
[3] Cf. below, Chapter XIV.
[4] *Ethics*, II, Prop. 13, Corol.
[5] *Ibid.*, Schol.

hence in Christianity, whether independently or under the influence of foreign ideas, developed into a dichotomy of soul and body; second, the Platonic view of the soul as something immaterial and eternal and distinct from body; third, the various attempts on the part òf the commentators of Aristotle to make the rational faculty of the soul something separable from body — attempts which probably took rise in Aristotle's own statement that while "the soul . . . cannot be separated from the body . . . there is, however, no reason why some parts should not be separated." [1] This attempt started with Themistius, who considered the Aristotelian hylic or passive intellect ($\nu o\hat{v}s$ $\pi a\theta\eta\tau\iota\kappa\acute{o}s$) as something separable from body. [2] An essentially similar, though much modified, view was held also by Averroes. [3] It is against the latter that Thomas Aquinas maintains "that the possible intellect of man is not a separate substance." [4] Even those who rejected this interpretation of the passive intellect have introduced between it and the active intellect the so-called acquired intellect "which is not a power inherent in the body but is separated from the body with a true separation." [5] Though this acquired intellect is not mentioned in Aristotle, it was used in mediaeval expositions of the Aristotelian psychology as an interpretation of his views, and it may be considered as an outgrowth of Aristotle's actual intellect ($\nu o\hat{v}s$ $\dot{\epsilon}\nu\epsilon\rho\gamma\epsilon\acute{\iota}a$ or $\dot{\epsilon}\nu\tau\epsilon\lambda\epsilon\chi\epsilon\acute{\iota}a$), to which Spinoza has referred in Part I, Propositions XXX and XXXI, by the term *intellectus actu*. [6] It would seem that it was in accordance with the general line of the development of discussions of this kind that among the Renaissance philosophers a distinction grew up

---

[1] *De Anima*, II, 1, 413a, 3–7.
[2] *Milḥamot Adonai*, I, 1. Cf. Munk, *Guide des Égarés*, I, note on pp. 306 ff.
[3] *Ibid.*   [4] *Contra Gentiles*, Lib. II, Cap. 59
[5] *Moreh Nebukim*, I, 72.
[6] Cf. above, Vol. I, p. 404.

between *spiritus* and *animus* or *mens* and that those who denied the separability of *spiritus* from body admitted the separability of *animus* or *mens* from body, the latter two terms corresponding on the whole to the Aristotelian rational faculty of the soul.

Now, all these views as to the separability of the soul or of the intellect come into play in almost any discussions of the nature of the soul by mediaeval philosophers, whether writing in Arabic, in Hebrew, or in Latin, and irrespective of what the formal definition of the soul may be. The insistence upon the separability of the soul was essential for them, if they wanted to give a rational explanation of immortality. Though the separability of the soul from body does not necessarily imply its immateriality, for it can be separable from body even if it be material, provided it is of a different matter than that of the body, still the prevalent opinion among the mediaevals was that it was immaterial, and among the emanationists it was considered, like all the other forms, as directly emanating from the divine thinking.[1]

It is against this prevalent view of the separability of the soul, and especially against the emanationists' view that the soul is an emanation of God's thinking and hence separable from the body, that Spinoza comes out in his statement that the "human mind is united to the body."[2] This statement means more than a mere assertion that the soul is united to the body; it means that the soul is inseparable from the body. We can clearly see all the arguments with which this statement is charged. Spinoza seems to address his opponents as follows: You maintain that the human soul, or at least that faculty of it which you call the acquired intellect, is separable from the body. What is your reason for that? It is be-

[1] Cf. above, Vol. I, p. 218.
[2] *Ethics*, II, Prop. 13, Schol.

cause, you say, the acquired intellect, as an emanation from God, who is pure thought and unlike body, must likewise be unlike body. Its union with the body does not make it a part of the body. It has an existence apart from the body, being an immaterial substance in contradistinction to the body which is a material substance. Now, I agree with you that the human mind, "in so far as it understands (*intelligit*)," — and according to me it always understands,[1] and is what you would call an actual or an acquired intellect, — "is an eternal mode of thought,"[2] or that it "follows from the divine nature,"[3] or that it is "a part of the infinite intellect of God."[4] But so according to me is also the human body a mode of God's attribute of extension and follows from the divine nature. And consequently, according to my way of reasoning, just as in God the attribute of thought is inseparable from the attribute of extension, so in man the mode of thought, i.e., mind, is inseparable from the mode of extension, i.e., body. Thus starting with the very same premise, that soul has its origin in the divine nature, we arrive at different conclusions as to its relation to body, all because we hold fundamentally different views with regard to the nature of God.

But whether the human soul is separable from body or not, soul as such is not considered either by the mediaevals or by Spinoza as something which is unique to man. According to the Aristotelian traditions of the mediaevals, soul is a species of form (εἶδος),[5] being only an advanced stage in the hierarchy of forms which run throughout nature and of which every individual thing is possessed. It is only a special

---

[1] *Ibid.*, I, Prop. 31, Schol.
[2] *Ibid.*, V, Prop. 40, Schol.
[3] *Ibid.*, V, Prop. 36, Schol.
[4] *Ibid.*, II, Prop. 11, Corol. Cf. V, Prop. 40, Schol.
[5] *De Anima*, II, 2, 414a, 13–14.

name given to that particular form which appears in plants, animals, and men, and which is manifested by the functions of nutrition, growth, reproduction, locomotion, sensation, and reason, the last of these functions being given the special name of intellect. If therefore we define soul as the form of the body, and if we substitute the general term "form" for the special kind of form called soul, we can see how, according to Aristotle and the mediaevals, the possession of a soul in the general sense of form is not unique in man, inasmuch as everything in nature possesses some kind of form. It is in this sense that Cabalists, in a generally misunderstood passage, speak of a "mineral soul" in addition to the customary vegetable, animal, and rational souls.[1] It is in this sense also undoubtedly that Renaissance philosophers like van Helmont, Telesius, and Bruno held the doctrine of *omnia animata*. It is not to be inferred, however, that all those who espoused this doctrine necessarily meant to attribute life and consciousness to all things. Van Helmont, for one, meant by it, with reference to metals, only a certain principle of cohesion, and, with reference to plants, only a certain composite humor; it is only with reference to animals and man that he meant by it a substantial vital principle.[2] In some instances, to be sure, the expression *omnia animata* may indeed point to a doctrine of panpsychism, with its implication that all matter is living, but unless there is some definite evidence assuring the accuracy of such an interpretation the expression is to be taken as nothing more than a general annunciation that the term *anima* in a variety of different meanings denotes something which exists in all things, in the same manner as the term "form" in a variety of different meanings

---

[1] נפש הדומם. Ḥayyim Vital, *Sha'are Ḳedushshah*, III, 1. Cf. I. Misses, "Spinoza und die Kabbala," in *Zeitschrift für exacte Philosophie*, VIII (1889), p. 364.

[2] Cf. G. S. Brett, *A History of Psychology*, Vol. II, p. 188.

is said by Aristotle to denote something which exists in all things.

This is what I understand to lie behind Spinoza's utterance that all things are animate. Spinoza seems to address the Aristotelian philosophers as follows: If soul and intellect are merely different grades of form, what need is there for you to use these three terms? Your manner of speaking of things in the mineral kingdom as having only form, and of things in the vegetable and animal kingdoms as possessing a soul, and of man as possessing an intellect, merely tends to produce in the mind of the student and reader the impression of a discontinuity in nature, of realms standing distinct and quite apart from each other, whereas in truth these three terms merely describe a gradation of stages in the succession of forms. Would it not be better, then, to take one single term such as "mind" or "soul" and apply it to all things which in traditional philosophy would be said to possess form? And so, after his discussion of the definition of the human mind, Spinoza concludes in the Scholium to Proposition XIII that "these things which we have proved hitherto are altogether general, nor do they refer more to man than to other individuals, all of which are animate, although in different degrees." This statement that all things are animate, as we have been trying to show, does not point to a panpsychistic conception of nature. The animateness which Spinoza ascribes to all things, as we have explained, merely means that the term "soul" (anima), and not the implication of life and consciousness which that term has, should be applied to all things. The term "soul" as he uses it here does not necessarily imply life and consciousness. When he says in the same passage that things are animate "in different degrees" he means that certain things which he would describe as animate do not possess life and consciousness. All that he means by his statement that all things are animate in different degrees is exactly what Aristotle would have meant by saying that all things have forms in different degrees. In the place of the old term "form," as we have already seen, Spinoza uses the term "idea" in the sense of the intelligible, imaginable, and sensible forms, which according to Aristotle himself are the objects respectively of cognition, imagination, and perception,[1] and it is because that of all things there are such forms or ideas in God that all things may be said to be animate. "For of everything there necessarily exists in God an idea of which He is the cause, in the same way as the idea of the human body exists in Him; and therefore everything that we have said of the idea of the human body is necessarily true of the idea of any other thing. We cannot, however, deny that ideas . . . differ from one another, and that one is more excellent and contains more reality than another."[2]

But what are the demarcations between the different degrees of animateness? The signs of demarcation between the different degrees of animateness which Spinoza assigns to all things, as well as between the different ideas of things which according to him exist in God, are not definitely explained by him. But a study of what the signs of demarcation were according to the mediaevals between the different forms which all things possessed and a comparison of them with some of the characteristic features of the human mind according to Spinoza will furnish us with a fairly clear idea of what he considered to be the differences in the degree of animateness of things and also of what he considered to be the differences in the ideas that exist of them in God. Now, according to the mediaevals, the chief stages in the hierarchy

[1] Cf. above, pp. 46–48.
[2] *Ethics*, II, Prop. 13, Schol.

of forms are, first, the form which endows matter with corporeality or tridimensionality (*forma corporeitatis*), then the
form which endows the simple four elements with their specific distinguishing characteristics (*forma elementalis*), then
the form of composite objects (*forma mixtionis*), then the
form which endows plants with the functions of nutrition,
growth, and reproduction (*forma vegetabilis*), then the form
which endows animals with the power of sensation (*forma
sensitiva*), and, finally, the form which endows man with
the power of reason (*forma humana sive intellectiva*). There
is no doubt that Spinoza would classify his ideas in some
such manner as the mediaevals classified their forms, differing from them perhaps somewhat in so far as he differed
from them in his conception of nature and in the classification of the objects of nature. But on the whole he would
follow the same principle of classification, arranging the ideas
according to the order of their corresponding objects, for,
as he himself says, "we cannot, however, deny that ideas like
objects themselves differ from one another,"[1] the differences
between the former corresponding respectively to the differences between the latter. But it happens that on the difference between the idea or the soul of the human body and the
ideas or souls of other individual things we have some definite
information in Spinoza. It is consciousness. While like the
ideas of all other things, which are the forms and functions
and the essences of things, the form and function and essence
or idea of the human body exists in God, still it differs from
the idea of everything else in that it is conscious of its own
body. This consciousness of the body, which the idea of
the human body possesses, constitutes the first activity of the
human mind, and in this the human mind or soul differs
from the minds and souls of all other things, which according

[1] *Ibid.*

to Spinoza can be called animate. Just as in Aristotle the animal soul differs from the vegetable soul in that it is endowed with sensation, i.e., a consciousness of the existence of other bodies, so in Spinoza the idea of the human body which exists in God differs from the ideas of all other individual things which exist in God in that it is conscious of its own body. That consciousness is not to be imputed to all things, even though they are all described by Spinoza as being "animate," may be inferred indirectly from his discussion of the delusion of freedom in a letter to Schuller. "Conceive, if you please," he writes, "that a stone while it continues in motion thinks, and knows that it is striving as much as possible to continue in motion." [1] The implication is quite clear that the stone, though included among all things described as "animate," is not necessarily assumed to be conscious of its own body and its affections. And just as there is a difference between the idea of the human body and the idea of all other individual objects, so also there must be differences between the ideas of all those other individual objects.

Recapitulating now the main points which have so far been brought out in Spinoza's definition of soul as compared with that of the Aristotelian tradition, we find both points of resemblance and points of difference between them. His predecessors begin their investigation of the soul by asserting that all things have forms, sometimes also called by the name of ideas. Spinoza similarly begins by saying that of all things there are ideas. The forms, according to his predecessors, are of different degrees. According to Spinoza, too, the ideas are of different degrees. But whereas according to his predecessors the forms of certain things, beginning with plants, are called soul, and forms of still other things,

[1] Epistola 58 (*Opera*, IV, p. 266, ll. 13–15).

beginning with man, are called intellect, according to Spinoza all ideas may be called soul and consequently all things may be said to be animate. He retains, however, the term "intellect" as strictly applying to the ideas of man, and does not use it with reference to the ideas of beings of a lower grade. Again, according to his predecessors, the forms come directly from the divine nature, whereas the matter originates outside of the divine nature, and consequently they held that certain forms, either the human soul as a whole or certain parts of the human intellect, are separable from the human body. According to Spinoza, however, both the forms and the so-called matter come directly from the divine nature, one from the attribute of thought and the other from the attribute of extension, and consequently, since thought and extension are inseparable in God, soul and body are inseparable in man. Finally, the fundamental difference between the human soul and all other souls is that the former is conscious of its own body.

But what is it that creates these differences between the various grades of forms or ideas or souls both in Aristotelianism and in Spinoza? Or, in other words, why should the human form possess sensation and thought in addition to nutrition, growth, and reproduction and the vegetable form possess only nutrition, growth, and reproduction? and then, again, why should the mineral form be without even these last three functions? The mediaevals answer this question by the statement that the forms, though all of them of divine origin, differ in their excellence and perfection by reason of the differences in the material objects upon which they are bestowed. Though all material objects, they say, consist of the same four elements, still they become differentiated and distinguished from one another by reason of the difference in the arrangement and disposition of these elements which are in constant change and motion. "As the fifth element in its entirety is constantly in circular motion, there arises therefrom in the elements a compulsory movement whereby they are forced out of their respective natural localities . . . so that there arises an intermixture of the elements . . . in which they act and react upon each other. The elements thus intermixed undergo a change, so that there arises from them first various kinds of vapors; afterwards the several kinds of minerals, all the species of plants, and many species of living beings, according to the complexion of the mixture." [1] Similarly Descartes says that "there is therefore but one matter within the universe . . . but all the variation in matter, or diversity in its forms, depends upon motion," and he ascribes this view to the "philosophers," i.e., Aristotle and his followers, who "have said that nature was the principle of motion and rest." [2] Now, of these various mixtures, which are the result of the motion of the elements, one is more excellent than another, and accordingly there is a difference in the excellency of their forms. "The finer this mixture is, the nobler is the form proper for it in which the divine wisdom manifests itself in a higher degree." [3] This accounts not only for the variety of forms in the inanimate world but also for the variety of souls and their faculties in the animate world. "That portion of the matter which has been purified and refined . . . has received the faculty of growth. . . . That portion of it which has been further purified . . . has received the faculty of sensation. . . . The portion which has been still further purified . . . has been endowed with the intellectual faculty." [4]

[1] *Moreh Nebukim*, I, 72.
[2] *Principia Philosophiae*, II, 23. Cf. *Physics*, II, 1, 192b, 20–23.
[3] *Cuzari*, V, 10.
[4] *Moreh Nebukim*, III, 17, Second Theory.

In exactly the same way Spinoza explains the differences between the various ideas of things and their superiority to one another. "We cannot, however, deny that ideas, like objects themselves, differ from one another, and that one is more excellent and contains more reality than another, just as the object of one idea is more excellent and contains more reality than another. Therefore, in order to determine the difference between the human mind and other things and its superiority over them, we must first know, as we have said, the nature of its object, that is to say, the nature of the human body. . . . In proportion as one body is better adapted than another to do or to suffer many things, in the same proportion will the mind at the same time be better adapted to perceive many things. . . . We can thus determine the superiority of one mind to another." This leads Spinoza to "say beforehand" what he describes as "a few words upon the nature of bodies." His discussion is given in the form of a series of Axioms, Lemmas, Definitions, a Scholium, and Postulates which are interposed by him between the Propositions XIII and XIV. We shall try to show that his "few words upon the nature of bodies" follow a certain well-defined traditional outline.

IV. THE NATURE OF BODIES

The study of the human body in mediaeval philosophy begins with a classification of bodies in general. There are, to begin with, simple bodies. These are the four elements. The term "simple bodies" [1] by which Aristotle as well as the mediaevals designates the elements is an indication of their character. Then there are composite bodies. These are all the bodies which come under our observation in the phys-

---

[1] ἁπλᾶ σώματα, פשוטים גשמים. *De Caelo*, III, 1, 298a, 29. Cf. my *Crescas' Critique of Aristotle*, p. 337, n. 20. Cf. also *Ruaḥ Ḥen*, Ch. 8.

ical world.[1] Thus referring to this classification Aristotle says, "the body must be either simple or composite."[2] Furthermore, composite bodies consist either of similar or of dissimilar parts.[3] In fact, this is the formal division followed in some mediaeval compendiums of philosophy.

Spinoza follows the same traditional method of philosophers. The series of Axioms, Lemmas, Definitions, Scholium, and Postulates between Propositions XIII and XIV fall into three distinct divisions:

I. The first two and second two Axioms with the intervening three Lemmas deal, as he himself says, with "simplest bodies" (*de corporibus simplicissimis*).[4]

II. Beginning with the Definition and through Axiom III and Lemmas IV–VII, he deals with composite bodies consisting of similar parts. "Up to this point we have conceived an individual to be composed merely of bodies which are distinguished from one another solely by motion and rest, speed and slowness, that is to say, to be composed of the most simple bodies."[5]

III. Beginning with the Scholium to Lemma VII and through the six Postulates, he deals with composite bodies consisting of dissimilar parts, or, as he himself says, with "an individual of another kind, composed of many individuals of diverse natures."[6]

These simple bodies or elements in Aristotle are conceived to be either at rest or in motion. They are at rest when they are in their proper localities; they are in motion when they are outside their proper localities.[7] "Each of the four ele-

---

[1] Cf. my *Crescas' Critique of Aristotle*, p. 163.
[2] *De Anima*, III, 12, 434b, 9–10.   [3] Cf. *Crescas' Critique of Aristotle*, p. 159.
[4] Axiom 2 of the second group of Axioms after Lemma 3 (*Opera*, II, p. 99, l. 23).
[5] Scholium to Lemma 7.   [6] *Ibid.*
[7] As to what these proper localities are, see my *Crescas' Critique of Aristotle*, note 64 on pp. 445–446.

ments occupies a certain position of its own assigned to it by
nature . . . and they remain at rest in their natural places.
When one of them is moved from its place by some external
force, it returns towards its natural place as soon as that
force ceases to operate. For the elements have the property
of moving back to their place."[1] Furthermore, motion is
either slow or fast, which is determined either by the medium
through which the motion takes place or by the weight of
the object in motion.[2] Finally, these simple elements are
called substances, each of which consists of matter and form
which are also called substances. Thus, inasmuch as the
simple elements differ in form, the differences between them
may be designated as differences in respect of substance.
Similarly, inasmuch as what they have in common is matter,
they may be said to have a common substance.

Of these mediaeval statements Spinoza retains all those
which he can make use of in his own system, even in some
modified sense, but rejects all those which are incongruous
with his own fundamental principles. He is thus not unwilling to say with the mediaevals that "all bodies are in a
state of either motion or rest" and that "every body moves,
sometimes slowly, sometimes quickly"; but still, in attributing to every body motion and rest he does not mean exactly,
like the mediaevals, that the elements are at rest when in
their natural places and in motion when out of their natural
places, but rather, like Descartes, that "movement and rest
are merely two diverse modes of a body in motion."[3] But
he rejects the application of the term "substance" to matter
and form and the simple bodies which consist of them. Consequently, in opposition to the mediaevals who regard their

[1] *Moreh Nebukim*, I, 72. Cf. *Crescas' Critique of Aristotle*, pp. 141, 161; note 22
on pp. 337–338; note 23 on pp. 410–414.
[2] Cf. *Crescas' Critique of Aristotle*, note 32 on p. 340.
[3] *Principia Philosophiae*, II, 27. Cf. above, Vol. I, p. 242.

simple bodies, the Aristotelian four elements, as distinguished from one another both in respect to motion and in respect to substance, i.e., form, Spinoza says of his own simple bodies, molecules, or whatever else they may have been called by him, that "bodies are distinguished from one another in respect of motion and rest, quickness and slowness, and not in respect of substance." [1] Similarly the thing which the Aristotelian simple bodies have in common, i.e., matter, is not a substance; for if, indeed, "all bodies agree in some respects," [2] it is not because they all have a common substance, namely, matter, but because "they involve the conception of one and the same attribute," [3] namely, extension, and also because "they are capable generally of motion and of rest, and of motion at one time quicker and at another slower." [4]

Again, partly following the mediaevals and partly departing from them, Spinoza states in Lemma III the principle of the causality of motion. In Aristotle this principle is expressed in the statement that "it is necessary that whatever is moved should be moved by something." [5] But while that something must again be moved by something, the series of causes cannot go on infinitely,[6] for "the existence of an infinite number of causes and effects is impossible."[7] Spinoza is quite willing to agree with the mediaevals that "a body in motion or at rest must be determined to motion or rest by another body, which has also been determined to motion or rest by another." [8] But in direct opposition to the mediaevals

[1] Lemma 1. [2] Lemma 2.
[3] Ibid., Demonst. [4] Ibid.
[5] Physics, VII, 1, 241b, 24. Cf. Moreh Nebukim, II, Introduction, Prop. 17; Crescas' Critique of Aristotle, pp. 297–299, 668–675.
[6] Moreh Nebukim, II, 1 and 12.
[7] Ibid., II, Introduction, Prop. 3. Cf. Metaphysics, II, 2, 994a, 1 ff.; Crescas' Critique of Aristotle, pp. 221 ff., 479 ff.
[8] Lemma 3. As for the additional term "rest," see above, Vol. I, p. 242.

who deny the possibility of an infinite series of causes he concludes his statement with "and so on *ad infinitum.*"[1] As we have already seen in the proofs of the existence of God, Spinoza, like Crescas, admitted the possibility of an infinite series of causes and effects, provided the entire series was immanent within an infinite uncaused cause.[2]

The restatement of this ancient principle of the causality of motion in Lemma III leads Spinoza to restate in the Corollary to that Lemma what is known as Newton's First Law of Motion which has already been formulated by Galileo [3] and is given by Descartes under the name of the "first law of nature." [4] This again leads him to a restatement in Axioms I and II of two other laws of motion, both of which are taken from Descartes.[5]

Composite bodies, continues Spinoza, are made up of the union of simple bodies, either of a similar or of a dissimilar nature, and may be considered as complete individual aggregate units, to be distinguished from other units of the same kind by the nature of the union of the simple bodies.[6] Such composite bodies are divided by Spinoza into three classes, (1) hard, (2) soft, and (3) fluid,[7] each of these terms being described by him somewhat after the manner of Descartes.[8] The simple bodies constituting the composite body may undergo a variety of changes. If these simple

---

[1] *Ibid.*   [2] Cf. above, Vol. I, pp. 195 ff.

[3] *Discorsi e Dimostrazioni matematiche intorno a due Nuove Scienze*, IV, in *Le Opere di Galileo Galilei* (Firenze, 1890–1909), Vol. 8, p. 268, ll. 13 ff.

[4] *Principia Philosophiae*, II, 37; *Principia Philosophiae Cartesianae*, II, Prop. 14, Corol.

[5] The two axioms correspond respectively to the following passages in Descartes: (1) *Principia Philosophiae*, II, 45–53; *Principia Philosophiae Cartesianae*, II, Props. 24–31. (2) *Principia Philosophiae*, II, 49; *Principia Philosophiae Cartesianae*, II, Prop. 28, Rule 4.

[6] Definition.   [7] Axiom 3.

[8] *Principia Philosophiae*, II, 54 ff.

constituent bodies are of a similar nature, three kinds of changes are possible in them within the composite body, and they are described by Spinoza in Lemmas IV, V, and VI. If they are of a dissimilar nature, many other kinds of changes, he says, are possible in them within the composite body.[1] But whatever changes the simple constituent body may undergo within the composite body, the latter as a whole remains unchanged in form and retains its original nature.[2] "Thus, if we advance *ad infinitum*, we may easily conceive the whole of nature to be one individual, whose parts, that is to say, all bodies, differ in infinite ways without any change of the whole individual."[3] This is a reproduction of the Cartesian principle of the preservation of the proportion of motion and rest in the universe.[4]

As with the whole of nature or the macrocosm, so also with man, the microcosm. Man is a composite individual consisting of parts which are dissimilar in nature.[5] Of these parts, some are fluid, some soft, and some hard [6] — a classification which is reminiscent of Maimonides' statement, in his comparison between the macrocosm and the microcosm, that the variety of parts of which the universe consists corresponds to the variety of parts of which man consists, namely, solid parts, humors (i.e., fluids), and gases.[7] In the remaining four postulates Spinoza enumerates some of the physiological changes that may be wrought in the human body through external bodies and, conversely, the power of man to work changes in external bodies. Man may be

[1] Scholium after Lemma 7.
[2] Lemma 7.   [3] *Ibid.*
[4] Cf. *Principia Philosophiae*, II, 36; *Principia Philosophiae Cartesianae*, II, Props. 13 and 14.
[5] Postulate 1.   [6] Postulate 2.
[7] *Moreh Nebukim*, I, 72. Literally, the last term is to be translated "spirits." On its meaning, see Munk, *Guide des Égarés*, I, p. 355, n. 1.

affected in numerous ways by his contact with external bodies.[1] He may be further affected by external things through his absorption of food which is transformed into parts of his own body.[2] The effect of external bodies upon man may remain even after the cause of it has been removed.[3] Finally, just as man is affected by external bodies, man may also affect external objects by his power to move and arrange them in many ways.[4] These postulates, as we shall see in the next chapter, come into play in Spinoza's theory of imagination and memory.[5]

[1] Postulate 3.   [2] Postulate 4.
[3] Postulate 5.   [4] Postulate 6.
[5] Cf. below, pp. 80 ff.

CHAPTER XIV

THE COGNITIVE FACULTIES

In Aristotle as well as in all the mediaeval treatises on the soul which were inspired by his *De Anima*, the definition of the soul is followed by a discussion of its faculties, which are divided into two kinds, the cognitive and the motive.[1] Under the cognitive there comes first sensation. This is followed by common sense, then by imagination in its various forms, and then by memory, all of which, in mediaeval treatises, are subsumed under the general title of internal senses, corresponding to the external senses of sensation. Then comes reason, or the intellectual faculty. It is this threefold classification of the faculties of knowledge that underlies Spinoza's restatement of Descartes' division of all modes of perception (*omnes modos percipiendi*) into sensation, imagination, and pure cognition (*sentire, imaginari, et pure intelligere*).[2] In some philosophical and theological treatises, furthermore, in addition to these three kinds of knowledge which have their ultimate source in external material things, there is mention also of a kind of knowledge which is not derived from external material things. This is invariably described by such terms as "intuition," "innate ideas," "prophetic gift," or "divine inspiration." Not all these kinds of knowledge are considered of equal validity, and thus a distinction is made between true knowledge and false knowledge. Finally, after the discussion of the cognitive faculty, the

---

[1] Cf. *De Anima*, III, 3, 427a, 17 ff.; 9, 432a, 15 ff. Cf. *Cuzari*, V, 12; *Emunah Ramah*, I, 6. Cf. above, p. 44.

[2] *Principia Philosophiae Cartesianae*, I, Prop. 15, Schol.; cf. *Principia Philosophiae*, I, 32.

discussion of the motive faculty is taken up. Under this, desire and will, as distinguished from sense and intelligence, make their appearance.

This is a brief outline of topics in their conventional order as they occur in representative works of mediaeval philosophy, and this outline, we shall see, is also followed by Spinoza in Propositions XIV–XLIX of the Second Part of the *Ethics*. Had Spinoza written the *Ethics* in the manner of rabbis and scholastics, he would have prefaced this portion of his work with the following statement:

Part II, Chapters II–V. Wherein we shall deal with what is generally called the faculties or functions of the soul, for having given in Chapter I the definition of the human mind and its relation to the body, we deem it fit to explain in Chapters II–V what its faculties or functions are. We shall deal in these four chapters with the following main topics:

A. Cognitive Faculties:

Ch. II. External Senses (Props. XIV–XVI); Internal Senses (Props. XVII–XVIII); Consciousness and Reason (Props. XIX–XXIII).

Ch. III. Truth (Props. XXIV–XL).

Ch. IV. The Three Kinds of Knowledge (Prop. XL, Schol. II–Prop. XLVII).

B. Motive Faculty:

Ch. V. Will (Props. XLVIII–XLIX).

I. SENSATION

In the account of the process of sensation as given by Aristotle, three essential elements are involved. In the first place, there must be an external object to stimulate the sentient faculty into activity.[1] In the second place, the external

---

[1] *De Anima*, II, 5, 417a, 2 ff.; 417b, 25.

object through its contact, either directly or indirectly,[1] with the sense-organ produces a certain affection (πάθος) or movement (κίνησις), so that "sensation consists in being moved and acted upon, for it is held to be a species of qualitative change (ἀλλοίωσις)."[2] In the third place, in sensation it is the sensible forms apart from their matter that are impressed upon the sense and are received by it.[3] Now all these three elements, which we have selected from Aristotle's long and intricate discussions about the process of sense-perception, stand out quite conspicuously in Spinoza's discussion of sensation in Propositions XIV–XVI. But in addition to these elements taken from Aristotle one also notices in these three propositions certain assertions which are not found in Aristotle or which are diametrically opposed to the views of Aristotle. Especially noticeable as a departure from Aristotle is Spinoza's reiteration that the mind's awareness of its own body precedes its awareness of other bodies, which is quite the opposite of what Aristotle would seem to say. These additional elements not found in Aristotle, as well as these divergences from Aristotle, we shall now try to show, can be traced to the influence of Telesius and Descartes.

Telesius himself says of his own account of sensation that it is unlike that of Aristotle.[4] But as in the case of so many others who had set out to disagree with Aristotle, the points of agreement between Telesius and Aristotle are more numerous than those on which they disagree. Often the differences between him and Aristotle, as Cicero said of the differences between Zeno and Aristotle,[5] are merely in a change

---

[1] *Ibid.*, II, 11, 423b, 2 ff.   [2] *Ibid.*, II, 5, 416b, 33–35.

[3] *Ibid.*, II, 12, 424a, 17–19.

[4] *De Rerum Natura*, VII, 2 (Roma, 1923, Vol. III, p. 4): "Quoniam non, quo nobis modo, Aristoteli itidem sensus fieri videtur."

[5] Cicero, *De Finibus*, IV, 9, § 21.

of terminology. Corresponding to Aristotle's distinction
between the Active Intellect in its interpretation according
to Alexander of Aphrodisias as identical with God and the
human soul as a whole, Telesius distinguishes between what
he calls the divine soul in man and the natural soul or the
spirit.[1] Again, like Aristotle, he maintains that it is with the
latter alone that psychology is concerned, and that it is by it
alone that sensation and all the other forms of natural cognition are to be explained. Indeed, Telesius departs from Aristotle's view that the sensitive faculty of the soul is located
in the heart. But he is merely following Galen when he states
that the location of the natural soul or spirit is in the brain.[2]
The brain, however, he says, while it is the chief location of
the spirit, does by no means confine it in itself, for as a matter of fact the spirit or the natural soul extends to the other
parts of the body — the spinal cord, the nerves, arteries,
veins, and the covering membranes of the internal organs.[3]
Again, as in Aristotle, the process of sensation in Telesius is
assumed to involve three elements. (1) External objects
acting upon the spirit through contact with the body in
which the spirit is located. (2) An affection or a responsive
movement produced thereby in the spirit. (3) The perception of these by the spirit. Accordingly, Telesius defines
sensation as the perception by the spirit, first, of its own
affection by the external things which act upon it, and second,
of the action of the external things. But unlike Aristotle, he
considers the perception of the spirit's own affection by the
action of the external objects to come before its perception

---

[1] Cf. J. Lewis McIntyre, "A Sixteenth Century Psychologist," in *The British
Journal of Psychology*, I (1904), p. 66, referring to *De Rerum Natura*, I, 8, and II,
25.

[2] Cf. Galen, *De Usu Partium Corporis Humani*, Liber III, Cap. XI (*Opera
Omnia*, ed. Kühn, Vol. III, p. 242); Gershon ben Solomon, *Sha'ar ha-Shamayim*,
XII, 1 (p. 75b).   [3] McIntyre, *op. cit.*, p. 67.

of the action of the external objects themselves. To quote: "Sense is thus the perception of the action of things and of the impulses of the air, and also the perception of the spirit's own affections and changes and movements — but especially the latter. For the spirit perceives the former [the action of things] only because it perceives itself to be affected, changed, or set in motion by them." [1]

Descartes' account of sensation bears the same relation to that of Aristotle as the account given by Telesius. Like Telesius, Descartes considers the brain as the principal seat of the mind, though the mind is united with the whole body. The mind, he says, "not only understands and imagines, but also perceives." The "perceptions of the senses, or, in common language, sensations," are explained by him as "diverse affections of our mind" which arise from certain movements which are excited in the brain "by means of the nerves which are extended like filaments from the brain to all the other members with which they are so connected that we can hardly touch any part of the human body without causing the extremities of some of the nerves spread over it to be moved." [2] He then sums up his discussion of the process of sensation in the statement that "the diversities of these sensations depend firstly on the diversity in the nerves themselves, and then on the diversities of the motions which occur in the individual nerves. We have not, however, so many individual senses as individual nerves; it is enough merely to distinguish seven chief different kinds, two of which belong to the internal sense, and five to the external." [3] What these two internal senses are he does not specify here. He speaks rather vaguely of "the passions or affections of

[1] *De Rerum Natura*, VII, 2 (Vol. III, p. 4, ll. 9–14) and McIntyre, *op. cit.*, p. 71.
[2] *Principia Philosophiae*, IV, 189; *Passions de l'Ame*, I, 12 ff.
[3] *Principia Philosophiae*, IV, 190.

the mind" and "the natural appetites." But in his correspondence he seems to include under the internal senses "imagination, memory, etc."[1] Imagination and memory are as a rule included within the ordinary mediaeval fivefold classification of the internal senses.

This, then, is the general background of Spinoza's treatment of sensation in Propositions XIV–XVII.

If in Propositions XIV–XVI we take Spinoza's "human mind" to be a substitution for Telesius' "natural soul" or "spirit," we get in them a description of the process of sensation similar to that given by Telesius. To begin with, "the human body is affected in many ways by external bodies."[2] This statement combines the first two elements of sensation as laid down by Telesius as well as by Aristotle and Descartes, namely, the action of an external object upon the soul, and an affection created in the soul or spirit by that action. Then, in the second place, "the human mind must perceive everything which happens in the human body."[3] This, again, corresponds to one part of the third element in sensation as laid down by Telesius, namely, the perception by the spirit of its own affections and movements. This perception of the human mind of the affections of the body by external bodies Spinoza would undoubtedly have called sensation, if he had wanted to use that term. Instead, however, in Proposition XIV he merely describes that process, without naming it. He says: "The human mind has an aptitude to the perception of many things, and its aptitude increases in proportion to the number of ways in which its body can be disposed."

---

[1] *Correspondance*, XLVI (*Oeuvres*, I, p. 263, ll. 6–8). Though Descartes does not definitely say there that imagination and memory belong to the internal senses, it may be inferred from the fact that after mentioning "les cinq sens" he proceeds to say: "L'anatomise maintenant les testes de divers animaux, pour expliquer en quoy consistent l'imagination, la memoire etc."

[2] *Ethics*, II, Prop. 14, Demonst.   [3] *Ibid.*

The similarities in expression to the passages quoted above from Descartes are quite evident. What Spinoza means to say is that the mind "not only understands and imagines, but also perceives," and that the diversities in these perceptions correspond to the diversities in the physiological processes in the body. Whether Spinoza would continue to follow Descartes and the entire philosophic tradition in reducing the diversities of sensation to the traditional five external senses, there is no way of telling. But that he has followed Descartes partly in reducing the internal senses to two will be shown later.

These varieties of sensation, Spinoza proceeds to say, are grouped together in our mind and form what is called a perception. The difference between elementary sensations and perception was known to Aristotle and his mediaeval followers. According to them, perception was attributed to a special sense which differed from the five senses to which sensation was attributed. This special sense is called by Aristotle the common sense (κοινὸν αἰσθητήριον, *sensus communis*), whose organ is the heart and one of whose functions is described by him as the unifying principle whereby things are perceived as wholes.[1] But Spinoza seems to have done away with this special sense, as on the whole he has done away with the dissection of the mind into distinct faculties, and with the elimination of this special sense of perception he has also eliminated the actual difference between perception and simple sensations. Sensations, according to him, do not come to us in their elementary and isolated forms; they come to us as parts of complex relations or perceptions. In his definition of sensation in Proposition XIV, therefore, he does not speak of the mind's aptitude to experience any particular

---

[1] *De Juventute*, 3, 469a, 11–12; *De Sensu*, 7, 449a, 3 ff. Cf. W. A. Hammond, *Aristotle's Psychology*, Introduction, p. liii.

simple sensation, but rather of its aptitude "to the perception of many things," that is to say, to the simultaneous perception of many things. The mind's knowledge of its own body, which Spinoza has laid down as the first stage in the mind's knowledge, is therefore something composite in its nature; it is a perception which is made up of many elementary sensations. He thus says in Proposition XV: "The idea which constitutes the formal being of the human mind is not simple, but is composed of a number of ideas."

But while Spinoza, like Telesius, considers sensation, or rather perception, as beginning with a knowledge of the affections and movements within one's own body, he believes, again like Telesius, that this knowledge of the nature of one's own body involves also a knowledge of the nature of the external bodies by which one's own body is affected and by which it is set in motion. He thus says in Proposition XVI: "The idea of every way in which the human body is affected by external bodies must involve the nature of the human body, and at the same time the nature of the external body." From this proposition he draws two Corollaries. The First Corollary states that our knowledge of external things is to be regarded as caused by our knowledge of our own bodies: "Hence it follows, in the first place, that the human mind perceives the nature of many bodies together with that of its own body." The emphasis in this Corollary is that the perception of the nature of the external bodies can exist only together with that of one's own body, inasmuch as the former is caused by the latter. It reflects the statement quoted above from Telesius that "the spirit perceives the former [the action of external things] only because it perceives itself to be affected, changed, or set in motion by them." It may perhaps also reflect Descartes' contention that nothing is conveyed to the brain by the nerves from the external bodies "excepting the local motion of the nerves themselves," so that there is nothing known of the external objects by the senses but their figure, magnitude, or motion.[1] The Second Corollary states that our knowledge of external things is only relative to ourselves: "It follows, secondly, that the ideas we have of external bodies indicate the constitution of our own body rather than the nature of external bodies."

Still, though affirming that sensation is relative to ourselves and that consequent y no two sensations of the same thing experienced by two different individuals can be exactly the same, Spinoza does not thereby affirm the purely subjective nature of sensation. There is always an external object, as real as we ourselves are real, that is to say, as real as modes in general are real, which are the cause of our sensations. "If the human body be affected in a way which involves the nature of any external body, the human mind will contemplate that external body as actually existing or as present."[2] How much of the nature and reality of the external object is conveyed to us by sensation, this statement does not tell us, and it would be idle to speculate on the basis of it as to what Spinoza really thought of this problem. He may have held like Descartes that "there is nothing known of external objects by the senses but their figure, magnitude, or motion." [3] We know that like many others he held that sense-perception is not always reliable; [4] but at the same time he considered sense-perception to be a clear indication that external objects exist and are not the mere projection of our own consciousness. While the senses indeed may deceive us as to the nature of things, he argues in one place, we

[1] *Principia Philosophiae*, IV, 198.   [2] *Ethics*, II, Prop. 17.
[3] *Principia Philosophiae*, IV, 198.
[4] Cf. *Tractatus de Intellectus Emendatione*, § 78 (*Opera*, II, p. 30, ll. 2 ff.).

can still gain by the means of them a true knowledge of the nature of things if we only acquire a true knowledge of the senses themselves and know in what way they operate. "It is known that the senses are sometimes deceived, but it is only known confusedly. It is not known in what manner they deceive, and if after doubt we acquire a true knowledge of the senses and know in what way by their instrumentality objects are represented at a distance, doubt is again removed." [1]

II. Imagination and Memory

The seventeenth proposition, however, concludes with the proviso ". . . until the human body be affected by an affect which excludes the existence or presence of the external body," and then in the Corollary and in the Scholium Spinoza proceeds to state that the affects of the external objects upon the human body persist in the mind even after the disappearance of those external objects. In these statements Spinoza passes from his discussion of the experiences of the external senses to the experiences of the so-called internal senses. Now, the internal senses in mediaeval philosophy are variously enumerated; the most common enumeration given of them is, however, that of five, corresponding to the five external senses. But Descartes, as we have seen, speaks only of two internal senses, and these are identified by him especially with imagination and memory. And so also here in the next two propositions, wishing to deal with the internal senses, Spinoza especially discusses imagination and memory, which are the two internal senses mentioned by Descartes.

The subject-matter of Propositions XVII and XVIII is to some extent indicated by Spinoza himself. Though in Proposition XVII and in its Corollary Spinoza merely de-

[1] *Ibid.* (p. 30, ll. 6–10).

scribes a psychological process without naming it, toward the end of the Scholium he adds that "in order that we may retain the customary phraseology, we will give to those affections of the human body, the ideas of which represent to us external bodies as if they were present, the name of the images of things." Then, again, in Proposition XVIII he uses the term "remember" (*recordabitur*), and the term "memory" (*memoria*) is afterwards mentioned in the Scholium. Imagination and memory are thus by Spinoza's own designation the subject-matter of Propositions XVII and XVIII respectively. This, however, is to be taken only as a general description of the contents of these two propositions. More specifically, as we shall try to show, Proposition XVII deals with both imagination and memory, and Proposition XVIII does not deal with memory, but rather with recollection, which is a special kind of memory.

In Aristotle and throughout the Middle Ages the terms "memory" and "imagination" were used to describe two mental processes which were alike in every essential respect and were only slightly distinguishable from one another. Both these terms, according to them, indicated the retention by the mind of the image of a thing which was once present to our senses but is no longer present. Moreover, "in reply to the question to what part of the soul memory is to be ascribed," Aristotle answers that "it is plain that it belongs to the same part as imagination." [1] Imagination, in fact, is according to Aristotle the source of memory. "Memory, even the memory of concepts, does not take place without an image," [2] he says, "and the objects of memory, essentially, are the same as the objects of imagination." [3] The most characteristic difference between them, however, says he, is

---

[1] *De Memoria*, 1, 450a, 22–23.   [2] *Ibid.*, 12–13.
[3] *Ibid.*, 23–24.

that in memory the image of the thing gone is accompanied
by a consciousness that it is a copy of something actually
seen before, which thus involves a perception of time, whereas
in imagination there is not that consciousness.[1] Furthermore, from the various restatements of Aristotle's discussion
of imagination in mediaeval Arabic and Hebrew philosophic
texts it appears that a distinction is to be drawn between
two kinds of imagination which may be designated respectively by the terms "retentive imagination" and "compositive imagination,"[2] corresponding to what is called today
reproductive and productive imagination. These two forms
of imagination are briefly described by Maimonides in the
following passage: "The imaginative part of the soul is
that faculty which [a] retains the impressions of the sensibly
perceived objects after the latter have ceased to be in contact with the senses which had perceived them, and [b] puts
together some ideas with others and separates some ideas
from others, as a result of which it happens that this faculty
puts together things which have been perceived with things
that have never been perceived and the perception of which
is entirely impossible."[3] Now this definition of retentive
imagination does on the whole serve also as a definition of
memory, and it is for this reason, as I hope to show elsewhere, that in some Arabic and Hebrew texts retentive
imagination and memory have been identified, or, rather,
confused.

Suggestions of this distinction between retentive and
compositive imagination may be discovered in the various

[1] *Ibid.*, 1, 449b, 24 ff.

[2] Cf. *Emunah Ramah*, I, 6 (p. 29), on difference between מצייר and מדמה
ומחשב. Cf. S. Landauer, "Die Psychologie des Ibn Sina," in *Zeitschrift der Deutschen Morgenländischen Gesellschaft*, 29 (1875), p. 400, n. 4; S. Horovitz, *Die Psychologie bei den jüdischen Religions-Philosophen des Mittelalters*, p. 247, n. 85.

[3] *Shemonah Perakim*, Ch. 1.

scattered passages which occur in the writings of Spinoza, though no formal distinction is drawn by him between them. Referring to imagination as the so-called common sense,[1] with which indeed imagination is sometimes identified by Aristotle [2] and by mediaeval Arabic, Hebrew,[3] and Latin [4] writers, as well as by Descartes,[5] Spinoza defines it in three independent passages which, by the analogy of the passage quoted from Maimonides, may be reduced to two definitions of imagination, as follows: First, "an imagination is an idea by which the mind contemplates any object as present." [6] In this passage, it will be noticed, there is no implication that the thing imagined does not represent an existent object as it really is. Second, "those things . . . are commonly said to be imagined, although we clearly understand that the thing is not as we picture it to be,"[7] and furthermore "a fancy . . . arises from putting together diverse confused ideas which belong to diverse things and operations in nature." [8] In these two passages, it will be noticed, the thing imagined does not represent an existent object as it really is, but an artificial picture made up of different things observed. It is quite obvious that the first of these two definitions is a general definition of retentive imagina-

[1] *Tractatus de Intellectus Emendatione*, § 82 (*Opera*, II, p. 31, ll. 9–10).

[2] *De Memoria*, I, 450a, 10–11.

[3] To mention only two texts both of which exist in Arabic as well as in Hebrew: (1) *Mizan al-'Amal* [IV], p. 19; *Mozene Zedek*, IV, p. 30: خِيَال, כח דמיוני = حِسّ, مُشتَرَك ; חוש משותף; (2) *Cuzari*, V, 12, p. 312, ll. 17–18; p. 313, ll. 14–15: قُوَّة הרגשה משתתפת, حَاتَة مُشتَرِكَة = כח יצורי, مُتَصَوَّرَة.

[4] Eustachius a S. Paulo, *Summa Philosophiae*, III: *Physica*, Pars III, Tract. III, Disput. III, Quaest. III: *De sensu Communi*; quoted also by Gilson, *Index Scolastico-Cartésien*, p. 265, No. 411, and by Robinson, *Kommentar zu Spinozas Ethik*, I, p. 318, n.

[5] *Meditationes*, II (*Oeuvres*, VII, p. 32, ll. 18–19).

[6] *Ethics*, V, Prop. 34, Demonst.

[7] *Tractatus de Intellectus Emendatione*, § 56 (*Opera*, II, p. 21, ll. 3–5).

[8] *Ibid.*, § 64 (p. 24, ll. 26–28).

tion, whereas the second is a definition of compositive imagination.

Similarly Spinoza's conception of the relation between imagination and memory is like that we have found in the passages quoted above from Aristotle. To him as to Aristotle imagination is the source of memory, and consequently in many places of his writings Spinoza uses these two terms as alternatives, as, e.g., "imaginatur, vel recordatur,"[1] "imaginatio, sive memoria,"[2] "imaginatio, seu memoria."[3] That, following Aristotle, he considered imagination the source of memory is also made clear by Spinoza in a passage in which he says that while memory may be "strengthened by the help of the intellect," still it is not in need of the intellect, for it is also strengthened "by the force with which the imagination or that sense called common is affected by some individual corporeal thing."[4] What he means to say is exactly what we have quoted above[5] from Aristotle, that "memory, even the memory of concepts, does not take place without an image," and that "the objects of memory, essentially, are the same as the objects of imagination." Perhaps a still more apposite passage in Aristotle is this: "Consequently, memory concerns the faculty of thought accidentally and the primary power of sense essentially."[6] Still, with all these close relationships between memory and imagination, like Aristotle, Spinoza points out that memory differs from imagination in that it is associated with a consciousness of time duration: "What, then, is memory?" he asks; and he answers: "It is nothing else than the sensation of impressions on the brain

---

[1] *Ethics*, II, Prop. 40, Schol. [1] (*Opera*, II, p. 121, ll. 26–27).
[2] *Ibid.*, III, Prop. 2, Schol. (p. 144, l. 25).
[3] *Ibid.*, V, Prop. 34, Schol. (p. 302, l. 1).
[4] *Tractatus de Intellectus Emendatione*, §§ 81–82 (*Opera*, II, p. 31, ll. 3–4, 9–11).
[5] P. 81, notes 2 and 3.
[6] *De Memoria*, 1, 450a, 13–14.

accompanied with attention to the definite duration of the sensation." [1] The corresponding passages in Aristotle read: "All memory implies a time elapsed." [2] "Whenever one actually remembers having seen or heard, or learned something, he includes in this act, as we have already observed, the consciousness of 'formerly'; and the distinction of 'former' and 'latter' is a distinction in time." [3]

A contrast between imagination and memory, it seems to me, can also be discovered in the following passage. "But in order that we may retain the customary phraseology," he says, "we will give to those affections of the human body, the ideas of which represent to us external bodies as if they were present, the name of the images of things (*rerum imagines*), although they do not actually reproduce (*referunt*) the figures of the things (*rerum figurae*)." [4] Now what does Spinoza mean by this contrast between *rerum imagines* and *rerum figurae*?

In answer to this question we may remark at first that in a corresponding passage in Descartes where "to imagine" is defined as "nothing else than to contemplate the figure or image of a corporeal thing (*rei corporeae figuram, seu imaginem*)" [5] the terms "image" and "figure" are used synonymously rather than antithetically. Etymologically, these two terms would seem to reflect the several terms by which Aristotle describes the form of imagination (φάντασμα) and of memory (μνημόνευμα), such as ζωγράφημα,[6] πάθος,[7] τύπος,[8] γραφή,[9] εἰκών.[10] In fact, in one of the Latin translations of

---

[1] *Tractatus de Intellectus Emendatione*, § 83 (*Opera*, II, p. 31, ll. 20–22).

[2] *De Memoria*, 1, 449b, 28.

[3] *Ibid.*, 19–22.

[4] *Ethics*, II, Prop. 17, Schol. (*Opera*, II, p. 106, ll. 7–9).

[5] *Meditationes*, II (*Oeuvres*, VII, p. 28, ll. 4–5).

[6] *De Memoria*, 1, 450a, 29–30.

[7] *Ibid.*, 30.   [8] *Ibid.*, 1, 450b, 16.

[9] *Ibid.*   [10] *Ibid.*, 1, 451a, 15.

Aristotle, as we shall see anon, the term τύπος is translated by *figura*. Here in Spinoza, however, it would seem that the terms "image" and "figure" are not used as synonyms but rather as contrasting terms. What that contrast is may perhaps be explained by a consideration of the following passages in which Aristotle draws a distinction between imagination and memory.

Aristotle first raises the question "whether one remembers the affection (πάθος) or the thing from which the affection is derived." [1] His answer is that the memory-image is both. "In so far as it is regarded in itself, it is only an object of contemplation (θεώρημα, *speculamentum*) or a phantasm (φάντασμα, *phantasma*); but when considered as relative to something else, it is, as it were, a likeness (εἰκών, *imago*) and a mnemonic token (μνημόνευμα, *memoriale*)." [2] He then concludes the definition of memory by saying that it is "the state of a phantasm (φαντάσματος, *phantasmatis*) related as a likeness (εἰκόνος, *imaginis*) to that of which it is a phantasm (φάντασμα, *phantasmatos*)." [3] The implication is that memory, in contradistinction to imagination, is not a mere phantasm (φάντασμα), that is to say, a mere affection (πάθος), but is the likeness (εἰκών) of a thing. But previous to these passages, in discussing the possibility that memory may only be an affection (πάθος), he speaks of it as "an impression (τύπος) or picture (γραφή) within us." [4] Now, in an old Latin translation of Aristotle which was accessible to Spinoza τύπος is translated by *figura*,[5] and the terms φαντάσματος and εἰκόνος are translated respectively by the vague and non-telling

---

[1] *De Memoria*, 1, 450b, 12–13.
[2] *Ibid.*, 25–27.
[3] *Ibid.*, 1, 451a, 15–16.   [4] *Ibid.*, 1, 450b, 16.
[5] *Aristotelis Omnia Quae Extant Opera* . . . (Venetiis, apud Iuntas), Vol. VI, Pars II (1574), fol. 18va H: "Et, si est simile sicut figura aut pictura in nobis huius ipsius sensus. . . ."

phantasmatis and *imaginis.*[1] It is quite conceivable, then, that by some confusion of terms Spinoza has transformed Aristotle's contrast between φάντασμα and εἰκών into a contrast between *imago* and *figura*, or it is also possible that in some Latin reproduction of this Aristotelian passage the term εἰκών was rendered by *figura*, and thus when he says that imagination gives us only the *rerum imagines* and not the *rerum figurae* he means to say that in this respect imagination is unlike memory, for the latter, according to Aristotle, gives us the *rerum imagines* (reflecting the Greek φάντασμα) in the sense of *rerum figurae* (reflecting the Greek εἰκών), whereas the former gives us the *rerum imagines* not in the sense of *rerum figurae* but in the sense of affection (πάθος), impression (τύπος), or picture (γραφή) within us.

This, then, is in the main the outline of Spinoza's conception of imagination and memory and their relation to each other. Accordingly, when, without mentioning the word "imagination," Spinoza says in the Corollary to Proposition XVII that "the mind is able to contemplate external things by which the human body was once affected as if they were present, although they are not present and do not exist," he describes in a general way both imagination and memory.

In the Demonstration of the Corollary Spinoza gives a physiological explanation of imagination, of which he says in the Scholium: "This may indeed be produced by other causes, but I am satisfied with having here shown one cause through which I could explain it, just as if I had explained it through the true cause." Though the explanation is based upon certain physiological notions of his own time,[2] its gen-

---

[1] *Ibid.*, fol. 18vb, M: "Quid igitur est memoria, et meminisse dictum est, quod phantasmatis ut imaginis, cuius phantasma est habitus."

[2] Cf. Descartes' explanation of the internal sensations in *Principia Philosophiae*, IV, 190.

eral outline follows that of Aristotle's explanation of imagination. The gist of Aristotle's explanation is that the affections produced in the sense-organ by an external object are communicated to the blood, where they continue to persist, and then from the blood they are conveyed to the heart, which is the seat of imagination. There they become images.[1] Except for taking the brain instead of the heart as the seat of imagination, Spinoza's explanation follows a similar outline. Through the movements of the "fluid parts of the human body," that is to say, the blood, or the animal spirits, which are the most subtle parts of the blood,[2] the affection caused in the sense-organ by an external body is retained even after the removal of the body, and "it often strikes upon the softer parts," that is to say, upon the nerves and brain. There images are formed.

The term which Spinoza uses throughout his writings for the kind of memory we have just discussed is *memoria*, and for the verb he uses *recordari*.[3] This term represents the Greek μνήμη. But Spinoza uses also another term, that of *reminiscentia*,[4] which is used in mediaeval Latin in the sense of recollection as distinguished from memory, and it represents the Greek ἀνάμνησις. Now, recollection is a conscious reproduction of a memory. According to Averroes, it differs from memory in that it is not a continuous experience and is therefore not associated with a consciousness of time or duration. "The difference between recollection and memory consists in this: Memory refers to that which has always been in the mind from the time it was comprehended in the

---

[1] *De Somniis*, 3, 461a, 1 ff. Cf. Hammond, *Aristotle's Psychology*, Introduction, p. lviii.

[2] Cf. Descartes, *Les Passions de l'Ame*, I, 10.

[3] *Ethics*, II, Prop. 40, Schol. [1]: "imaginatur, vel recordatur" (*Opera*, II, p. 121, ll. 26–27); cf. III, Prop. 2, Schol. (p. 144, ll. 11, 12, 13).

[4] *Tractatus de Intellectus Emendatione*, § 83 (*Opera*, II, p. 31, ll. 22–23).

past to the present time; recollection refers to that which has been forgotten. Recollection therefore is an interrupted memory; memory is a continuous recollection."[1] Similarly Spinoza differentiates recollection from memory by the fact that it is not associated with the consciousness of temporal duration. "For in the case of recollection the mind thinks of that sensation, but without regard to its continuous duration, and so the idea of that sensation is not the duration itself of the sensation, that is to say, the memory itself."[2] Recollection, furthermore, is explained by Aristotle as being dependent upon association. "Acts of recollection happen when one movement has by nature another that succeeds it in regular order. If this order is necessary, it is evident that whenever a subject experiences the former of two movements thus connected, it will experience the latter. . . . Whenever, therefore, we are recollecting, we are experiencing certain of the antecedent movements until finally we experience the one after which customarily comes that which we seek."[3] Such associations, Aristotle further explains, are produced by three conditions, namely, (1) similarity, (2) contrast, and (3) contiguity,[4] which, according to Aristotle's use of the term "contiguous" ($\sigma\acute{v}\nu\epsilon\gamma\gamma\upsilon s$), means contiguity either of space or of time. Now, in Proposition XVIII the process of remembering dealt with is described by Spinoza as a form

---

[1] *Averrois Paraphrasis in Librum De Memoria et Reminiscentia* in *Aristotelis Omnia Quae Extant Opera* . . . (Venetiis, apud Iuntas,) Vol. VI, Pars II (1574), fol. 21ra BC:

"Rememoratio autem differt a conservatione. quia conservatio est illius, quod semper fuit in anima, postquam fuit comprehensum: memoratio autem est eius, quod fuit oblitum. et ideo rememoratio est conservatio abscisa: servatio autem est rememoratio continua."

My translation of this passage follows the Hebrew text (MS. Jewish Theological Seminary), which differs somewhat in its phraseology from the Latin text.

[2] *Tractatus de Intellectus Emendatione*, § 83 (*Opera*, II, p. 31, ll. 22–25).

[3] *De Memoria*, 2, 451b, 10–13; 16–18.

[4] *Ibid.*, 19–20.

of association, and he especially describes the process of association by temporal contiguity:[1] "If the human body has at any time been simultaneously affected by two or more bodies, whenever the mind afterwards imagines one of them, it will also remember (*recordabitur*) the others." Consequently, though the term used in this proposition for remembering is *recordari*, it is clear that the mental process described there is that of recollection. And so also in the Scholium, though Spinoza speaks there of *memoria*, it is quite clear that he uses that term in the sense of *reminiscentia*, for the process which he describes there in detail is that of the association of ideas. In fact, his very opening statement in the Scholium is suggestive of a statement in Aristotle's explanation of recollection. Spinoza says: "It is nothing else than a certain concatenation of ideas, involving the nature of things which are outside the human body, a concatenation which corresponds in the mind to the order and concatenation of the affections of the human body." Aristotle similarly says: "When one wishes to recollect, this is what he will do: he will try to obtain a beginning of movement whose sequel shall be the movement which he desires to reawaken. . . . For just as things are to each other in order of succession, so also are the mnemonic movements."[2]

III. Consciousness and Reason

Knowledge of any kind, according to Aristotle, whether it be sense-perception, or imagination, or reason, has for its object a certain form. When, for instance, in actual sensation and reasoning the sensitive and rational faculties are said to be identical with their objects, it is not with the things themselves that they are identical, but rather with

---

[1] Cf. below, pp. 213–214.
[2] *Ibid.*, 2, 451b, 29–452a, 2.

their forms.[1] "The things themselves they are not, for it is not the stone which is in the soul, but the form of the stone."[2] Similarly, imagination is the persistence of these immaterial forms in the mind, "for mental images are like present sensation, except that they are immaterial."[3] So also reason has for its object certain forms, for "to the thinking soul images serve as present sensations,"[4] the images of the thinking soul, of course, being immaterial. These three stages of knowledge, viz., sensation, imagination, and reason, are so related to each other that the lower is indispensable to the higher and the higher implies the lower. "Imagination, in fact, is something different both from perception and from thought (διανοίας), and is never found by itself apart from sensation, any more than is belief (ὑπόλη-ψις) apart from imagination."[5] Since it is the forms of things that constitute the objects of sensation and cognition, "the intellect," according to Aristotle, "is the form of forms (εἶδος εἰδῶν), and sensation the form of sensibles (εἶδος αἰσ-θητῶν)."[6] In this way, according to Aristotle's method of reasoning, the sensible forms may be regarded as the matter of the imaginative forms and the imaginative forms as the matter of the intelligible forms.

Moreover, according to Aristotle, consciousness is a concomitant fact of sensation no less than of knowledge. We not only see, but we are conscious of the fact that we see; we not only know, but we know that we know. The consciousness of the sensations is attributed by Aristotle to one of the activities of the common sense. "There is also a kind of

---

[1] *De Anima*, III, 8, 431b, 24–28.   [2] *Ibid.*, 431b, 28–432a, 1.

[3] *Ibid.*, 432a, 9–10.

[4] *Ibid.*, III, 7, 431a, 14–15.

[5] *Ibid.*, III, 3, 427b, 14–16. On the meaning of "belief" (ὑπόληψις) in the sense of "thought" (διάνοια) in this passage, see Hicks, *ad loc*.

[6] *Ibid.*, III, 8, 432a, 2–3.

common faculty," says Aristotle, "that is associated with all the particular senses, by virtue of which one is conscious that one sees and hears."[1] The same he also says of knowledge: "The mind itself is included among the objects which can be thought."[2] The association of consciousness with sense-perception and thought is stated by Themistius in the following passage: "When a man perceives whiteness he is conscious of the fact that he perceives the whiteness, and when he knows that the angles of a triangle are equal to two right angles he is conscious of the fact that he knows it."[3] The same view is repeated in the works of mediaeval philosophers. Judah ha-Levi includes among the endowments of the soul its knowledge of itself.[4] Abraham Ibn Daud explicitly makes consciousness associated with sensation, imagination, and thought. "For the ass and the ox and the other animals, when they see, see only with their eyes, but are not conscious of the fact that they are endowed with the perfection of sight and are exercising it. When they are deprived of that perfection, they are similarly unconscious of the fact that they are missing something; they simply do not see. Similarly when they imagine, they are not conscious of the fact that it is an imagination, or when they apprehend something instinctively, they are not conscious of the fact that it is only an instinctive apprehension. Man alone thinks in abstract ideas and has an idea of his idea."[5] Similarly Shem-Tob Falaquera restates Aristotle's view as follows:

[1] *De Somno*, 2, 455a, 15–16; cf. *De Anima*, III, 2, 425b, 12.

[2] *De Anima*, III, 4, 430a, 2–3.

[3] *Themistii in Aristotelis Metaphysicorum Librum Lambda Paraphrasis*, ed. Samuel Landauer, Hebrew text, p. 29, ll. 30–32; Latin text, p. 33, ll. 33–36: "quippe homo albedinem apprehendens iam animo concepit se albedinem percepisse, pariterque cum intellegit angulos trianguli aequales esse duobus angulis rectis, *iam intellexit* percepitque hoc intellexisse."

[4] *Cuzari*, V, 12. Cf. Commentaries *Kol Yehudah* and *Ozar Neḥmad, ad loc.*

[5] *Emunah Ramah*, I, 7 (p. 35).

"Reason is an immaterial substance . . . it conceives itself as an idea."[1]

Scraps of statements like those of which we have constructed the preceding two paragraphs must have been floating in the mind of Spinoza as he drew up Propositions XIX–XXIII. What he wanted to say we can easily conjecture. He wanted to say that we do not know things in themselves, but only the ideas or forms of things. Furthermore, he wanted to say that sensation is transformed and becomes reason when instead of having for its object the forms of things it has for its object the forms of forms of things or the ideas of ideas. Finally, he wanted to say that our knowledge is always associated by a consciousness of it on our part. In the *Tractatus de Intellectus Emendatione* Spinoza uses terms and expressions which betray their origin in the passages we have quoted, though he does not use them in exactly the same connection. Trying there to show that the mind by its native force is an instrument for the creation of ideas, he says that we begin with a true idea, as, e.g., the idea of Peter. This on the whole corresponds to Aristotle's εἶδος αἰσθητῶν, though the relation of the idea to the object in this particular passage of Spinoza, as we shall see presently, is not the same as the relation of the idea or form to the sensible object in Aristotle. Then this idea of Peter becomes the object of another idea which Spinoza calls the "idea of the idea" (*idea ideae*), corresponding to Aristotle's εἶδος εἰδῶν. Furthermore, the idea, when it becomes the object of another idea, is described by Spinoza as "something intelligible" (*quid intelligibile*),[2] which again corresponds to νοητὸν εἶδος, which is implied in a passage of Aristotle[3] and which is ex-

---

[1] *Sefer ha-Nefesh*, Ch. 14. Cf. *De Anima*, III, 4, 430a, 2 ff.

[2] *Tractatus de Intellectus Emendatione*, § 34 (*Opera*, II, p. 14, l. 24).

[3] *De Anima*, III, 4, 429a, 15–18.

plicitly used by the mediaevals in the expression *forma intelligibilis*. The only apparent difference between Spinoza's
use of *idea ideae* in this passage and Aristotle's use of εἶδος
εἰδῶν in the passage referred to is that Spinoza uses it in the
sense of one idea being the object of another idea, whereas
Aristotle uses it in the sense of one idea being the form of
another idea. But the difference is inconsequential, for inasmuch as Aristotle as well as Spinoza maintains that "that
which thinks and that which is thought are identical,"[1] to
say that one idea is the object of another and to say that one
idea is the form of another is to say exactly the same thing.
In fact, Spinoza himself in the *Ethics* uses the expression
idea ideae in the sense of the "form of the idea (*forma ideae*)."[2]
This *idea ideae* in the sense of both consciousness and rational knowledge is also described in Spinoza by the terms
"reflective knowledge" (*cognitio reflexiva*) and "reflective
idea" (*idea reflexiva*), terms which are of scholastic origin.[3]
In one place he thus says: "Whence it may be gathered that
method is nothing else than reflective knowledge (*cognitio
reflexiva*) or the idea of an idea";[4] and in another place he
says: "Lastly, now that we have explained what feeling
(*gevoel, sensus*) is, we can easily see how this gives rise to a
reflective idea (*weerkeerige Idea, idea reflexiva*), or the knowledge of oneself, experience, and reasoning."[5] In still another
place Spinoza describes consciousness without designating it
by a special term, but includes it under the general term
gevoel, sensus, which indeed reflects the variety of meanings
which historically the term *sensus* had.[6] Spinoza thus says:

---

[1] *Ibid.*, 430a, 3–4.   [2] *Ethics*, II, Prop. 21, Schol.

[3] Thomas Aquinas, *Opusculum de Principio Individuationis*: "et ideo omnis
cognitio sua de se ipsa proprie est reflexa."

[4] *Tractatus de Intellectus Emendatione*, § 38 (*Opera*, II, p. 15, ll. 29 ff.).

[5] *Short Treatise*, Appendix II, § 17 (*Opera*, I, p. 121, ll. 8–11).

[6] Cf. L. Schütz, *Thomas-Lexikon* (1895), under *sensus*. Cf. also below, p. 202:
συνείδησις = *sensus*.

"And this change in us, resulting from other bodies acting upon us, cannot take place without the soul, which always changes correspondingly, becoming aware of the change. And this change is really what we call feeling (*gevoel, sensus*)." [1]

But let us now see how these views on the relation between sensation and reason and on the relation of consciousness to both of them are unfolded by Spinoza in the *Ethics* in the propositions under consideration.

Sensation, which, as Spinoza has already said, begins with a knowledge of one's own body, is the only channel through which a knowledge of the body and its existence is attained. What sensation conveys to the mind, he now wants to say, is not the body itself, or its matter, as Aristotle would say, but ideas of its affections, or, as Aristotle would say, its sensible form. This is exactly what Spinoza says in Proposition XIX: "The human mind does not know the human body itself, nor does it know that the body exists, except through ideas of affections by which the body is affected." In the *Tractatus de Intellectus Emendatione* he expresses the same view somewhat differently when he says that by means of vague experience (*experientia vaga*) "nothing of natural objects is ever perceived save accidents." [2] By "accidents" there he means what he describes here in the *Ethics* as "affections by which the body is affected."

But wishing now to say that the human mind knows not only the body but knows also itself, Spinoza reverts to his accustomed analogy between the macrocosm and the microcosm. God, he says in Proposition XX, knows not only the human body but also the human mind. "There exists in God the idea or knowledge of the human mind, which fol-

---

[1] *Short Treatise*, II, Preface, § 2, note 1 (13) (*Opera*, I, p. 52, ll. 30–33).

[2] *Tractatus de Intellectus Emendatione*, § 27 (*Opera*, II, p. 13, ll. 3–4).

lows in Him, and is related to Him in the same way as the Idea or knowledge of the human body." By analogy with the macrocosm, the microcosm, too, i.e., man, has not only a knowledge of his body, but also of his own mind. He thus says in Proposition XXII: "The human mind not only perceives the affections of the body, but also the ideas of these affections." But between these two propositions Spinoza has inserted Proposition XXI, in which he explains the nature of this idea or knowledge of the human mind. In the first place, the expression "idea or knowledge of the human mind (*mentis humanae . . . idea, sive cognitio*)," which he has used in Proposition XX, is explained by him in the Scholium to Proposition XXI as being identical with the expression "idea of the idea (*idea ideae*)," which, as we have seen, is of Aristotelian origin. The interchangeability of these two expressions may be explained by the fact that the idea according to both Aristotle and Spinoza is identical with the mind, on account of which, as we have seen, Spinoza has defined the mind as the idea of the body. In the second place, coming even closer to the historical use of the Aristotelian *idea ideae*, he says again, in the same Scholium, that the idea of the idea means the "form of the idea (*forma ideae*)." This use of the term "form" as a designation of a higher idea in its relation to a lower idea which is the former's object of knowledge suggests at once that the higher ideas are related to the lower ideas as forms in any successive series of forms are generally conceived by Aristotle to be related to one another, that is to say, the relation of a higher form to a lower form is analogous to the relation of form to matter or of mind to body. Spinoza thus says in Proposition XXI: "This idea of the mind is united to the mind in the same way as the mind itself is united to the body."

The upshot of this discussion is that all knowledge, from

sensation to reason, barring only intuitive knowledge, of which Spinoza will speak later, and also the consciousness that is associated with sensation, imagination, and reason, have their source in sense-perception. In Aristotle this view is expressed in the following passage: "But, since apart from sensible magnitudes there is nothing, as it would seem, independently existent, it is in the sensible forms that the intelligible forms exist. . . . And for this reason, as without sensation a man would not learn or understand anything, so at the very time when he is actually thinking he must have an image before him."[1] Spinoza clinches the same view in Proposition XXIII: "The mind does not know itself except in so far as it perceives the ideas of the affections of the body." By the mind's knowledge of itself in this proposition he refers to consciousness as well as to the rational activity of the mind, for the rational activity of the mind begins with the mind's ability to know itself and to conceive of general ideas as existing apart from particular bodies.[2] Spinoza thus introduces here reason, or what he calls later the second kind of knowledge. [3]

[1] *De Anima*, III, 8, 432a, 3–9.
[2] Cf. *Short Treatise*, Appendix II, § 17, and above, p. 94.
[3] Cf. below, Chapter XVI.

CHAPTER XV

TRUTH

THE standard theory of truth in the Middle Ages is that of correspondence. It is derived from Aristotle, who gives it in many places of his writings, from among which the following passage may be quoted: "To say of what is that it is, and of what is not that it is not, is true." ¹ It is restated by Averroes in his *Epitome of the Metaphysics*.² Among Jewish philosophers it is reproduced in the oft-repeated formula that truth is the correspondence of that which is in the mind with that which is outside the mind.³ In scholastic philosophy we have Thomas Aquinas' quotations from various authors in which the correspondence theory of truth is expressed in a variety of ways, among which is also included a quotation from Isaac Israeli's *Liber de Definitionibus* that "veritas est adaequatio rei et intellectus." ⁴

But Aristotle has another definition of truth the real significance of which has not been fully recognized. It differs from the first definition based upon the correspondence theory. Originally in Aristotle it reads as follows: "Everything that is true must in every respect agree with itself."⁵

---

¹ *Metaphysics*, IV, 7, 1011b, 27.

² "Secundo dicitur de vero, quod, scilicet, ita se habet in intellectu, quemadmodum extra intellectum." Cf. *Averrois Epitome in Librum Metaphysicae* in *Aristotelis Omnia Quae Extant Opera* . . . (Venetiis, apud Iuntas), Vol. VIII (1574), fol. 357va I.

³ Narboni on *Moreh Nebukim*, II, 14 (p. 31a); *Or Adonai*, II, i, 2 (p. 29a). Cf. also *'Olam Ḳaṭan*, III (p. 58): "The definition of truth is that a thing is [said to be] what it [really] is."

⁴ *Quaestiones Disputatae de Veritate*, Quaest. I, Art. I. Cf. *Summa Theologica*, Pars I, Quaest. 16, Art. 2.

⁵ *Analytica Priora*, I, 32, 47a, 8.

In this form it is also reproduced by Averroes [1] and Gerson-ides.[2] In some Hebrew texts, however, self-evidence rather than self-consistency is given as a criterion of truth. Thus Narboni defines truth as something which is self-evident.[3] Sometimes self-evidence and self-consistency are combined to form the criterion of truth. Thus Crescas says that "truth is evident by itself and consistent with itself in all points." [4] From a study of the contexts in which these definitions occur, it is clear that the internal criterion of truth, self-consistency and self-evidence, is not to be taken as contradictory to the external criterion of correspondence. It is to be taken rather as supplementary to it, applicable especially to concepts and to judgments about concepts where correspondence with reality cannot be ascertained except by such criteria as self-evidence and self-consistency. In scholastic philosophy, several definitions of truth which would come under what is called here the internal criterion of truth are reproduced by Thomas Aquinas, the most impor-tant of which for our purpose, on account of their phrasing, are Augustine's definition that "truth is that whereby is made manifest that which is" and Hilary's definition that "truth is that which makes being clear or manifest." [5]

These two theories of truth are reproduced by Spinoza separately and independently of each other in several places in his works. The first theory is reproduced by him in the statement that "a true idea must agree with that of which it is the idea (cum suo ideato)." [6] The second theory, in its

---

[1] *Philosophie und Theologie von Averroes*, ed. M. J. Müller, Arabic text, p. 7, l. 8.

[2] *Milḥamot Adonai*, VI, i, 15 (p. 358).

[3] Commentary on *Moreh Nebukim*, II, Introduction, Prop. 8.

[4] Cf. my *Crescas' Critique of Aristotle*, p. 199, and n. 79 on p. 456.

[5] *Summa Theologica*, Pars I, Quaest. 16, Art. 1: "Augustinus . . . *De Vera Re-ligione*, Cap. 36 . . . Veritas est qua ostenditur id quod est; et Hilarius . . . Lib. V *De Trinitate*, ante med. . . . Verum est declarativum aut manifestativum esse."

[6] *Ethics*, I, Axiom 6.

self-evidence form, is reproduced by him in such statements as "truth is self-evident,"[1] "truth needs no mark,"[2] "truth is the standard of itself,"[3] "truth reveals itself,"[4] or "truth is the index of itself."[5] The same theory in its self-consistency form is reproduced by him in the statement that "truth does not conflict with truth."[6] A free but accurate version of the second theory, both in its self-evidence and in its self-consistency form, is given by Spinoza in the following passage: "If anybody had been led by good fortune to proceed in this way in the investigation of nature, that is to say, by acquiring ideas in their proper order according to the standard of a given true idea, he would never have doubted of their truth, because the truth, as we have shown, is self-evident and all things would have flowed spontaneously towards him."[7] The two theories of truth, the external and internal, are brought together by Spinoza in his *Cogitata Metaphysica*. After explaining that the correspondence theory of truth had its origin in popular speech, from which it "was then borrowed by philosophers for denoting the correspondence of the idea with that of which it is the idea (*cum suo ideato*)," he proceeds to enumerate what he calls "the properties of truth or of a true idea." He mentions two properties: "1. That it is clear and distinct. 2. That it is beyond all doubt, or, in a word, that it is certain."[8] "Clearness" and "distinctness" and "certainty" are nothing but

---

[1] *Tractatus de Intellectus Emendatione*, § 46 (*Opera*, II, p. 18, l. 2): "Veritas se ipsam patefacit."

[2] *Ibid.*, § 36 (p. 15, l. 15): "Veritas nullo egeat signo."

[3] *Ethics*, II, Prop. 43, Schol. (*Opera*, II, p. 124, l. 38): "Veritas sui fit norma."

[4] *Short Treatise*, II, 15, § 3 (*Opera*, I, p. 79, l. 6): "De Waarheid, en zig zelfs . . . openbaart."

[5] *Epistola* 76 (*Opera*, IV, p. 320, l. 8): "Est enim verum index sui."

[6] *Epistola* 21 (*Opera*, IV, p. 126, l. 30): "Veritas veritati non repugnat."

[7] *Tractatus de Intellectus Emendatione*, § 44 (*Opera*, II, p. 17, ll. 16–20).

[8] *Cogitata Metaphysica*, I, 6.

other terms for self-evidence. Similarly in a letter to de Vries, while discussing the distinction between two kinds of definition, Spinoza indirectly alludes to the two criteria of truth: "Therefore, a definition either explains a thing as it exists outside the understanding . . . or else a definition explains a thing as it is conceived or can be conceived by us."[1] Of the former, he says previously, it "ought to be true,"[2] whereas "the latter need not be," that is to say, it need not be true in the sense of corresponding to something outside the understanding, for while the truth of the former is to be tested by its correspondence to an external object, the truth of the latter consists in its internal consistency.

In the *Ethics* Spinoza designates the second kind of truth, namely, that which is tested by the internal criterion, by the term "adequate," as distinguished from the first kind of truth, which is tested by the external criterion. "By adequate idea, I understand an idea which, in so far as it is considered in itself, with reference to the object, has all the properties or internal signs of a true idea. I say internal, so as to exclude that which is external, the agreement, namely, of the idea with that of which it is the idea (*cum suo ideato*)."[3] In a letter to Tschirnhaus he makes this distinction between true and adequate still clearer: "I recognize no other difference between a true and an adequate idea than that the word 'true' refers only to the agreement of the idea with that of which it is the idea, while the word 'adequate' refers to the nature of the idea in itself; so that there is really no difference between a true and an adequate idea except this extrinsic relation."[4]

In this definition of adequate idea here in the *Ethics*

---

[1] Epistola 9 (*Opera*, IV, p. 43, ll. 11 ff.).   [2] *Ibid.* (l. 1).
[3] *Ethics*, II, Def. 4 and Expl.
[4] Epistola 60.

Spinoza only refers to "the properties or internal signs of a true idea," without telling us what they are. But in the passage quoted previously from the *Cogitata Metaphysica* he mentions two properties: (*a*) clearness and distinctness, and (*b*) certainty. Now, the first of these properties, namely, clearness and distinctness, is also used by Descartes as a criterion of truth,[1] and Spinoza refers to it indirectly in another place in the *Ethics* when he says that an adequate cause is one "whose effect can be clearly and distinctly perceived by means of the cause."[2] The second of these properties of a true idea, namely, certainty, is mentioned by Spinoza also in several other places in his works. In the *Short Treatise* he says: "Any one who is in the possession of the truth cannot doubt that he possesses it."[3] In the *Tractatus de Intellectus Emendatione*, in the discussion of the properties of the intellect, he similarly says: "It involves certitude, that is to say, it knows that things are formally as they are contained in it objectively."[4] In the Scholium to Proposition XLIX of the Second Part of the *Ethics*, however, he warns against the confusion of the absence of doubt, which assent to false ideas may involve, and real certainty, which is the mark of a true idea. "A false idea, therefore, in so far as it is false, does not involve certitude. Consequently, when we say that a man acquiesces in what is false and does not doubt it, we do not say that he is certain, but merely that he does not doubt, that is to say, that he acquiesces in what is false, because there are no causes sufficient to make his imagination waver."

The cumulative impression of these statements about the

[1] *Meditationes*, III (*Oeuvres*, VII, p. 35, ll. 8 ff.).
[2] *Ethics*, III, Def. 1.
[3] *Short Treatise*, II, 15, § 3 (*Opera*, I, p. 79, ll. 9–11).
[4] *Tractatus de Intellectus Emendatione*, § 108 (*Opera*, II, p. 38, ll. 32–33).

internal criteria of truth — clearness and distinctness and certainty — is that they are used by Spinoza in two senses.

First, they are used by Spinoza as supplementary to the external criterion of correspondence. In this sense, they are again subdivided into two usages. In the first place, they are used as means or evidence of establishing the agreement between the idea and its ideate. Thus in the passage quoted from the *Tractatus de Intellectus Emendatione*, speaking of the properties of the intellect, he says that the intellect "involves certitude, that is to say, it knows that things are formally as they are contained in it objectively."[1] In the second place, they are used to indicate a subjective necessity and conviction on the part of him who asserts the truth of correspondence. The assertion that a thing is as it really is, is in itself not a true assertion unless the one who has made it is certain of it and does not simply guess at it. "If any person says that Peter, for example, exists, and does not know that he exists, that thought, so far as that person is concerned, is false, or if it be preferred so to speak, is not true, notwithstanding that Peter may actually exist. Nor is the proposition that Peter exists true excepting for the man who knows certainly that Peter exists."[2] A similar insistence upon the consciousness of certainty as an element in truth may be also discerned in the following statements of Descartes: "But it is certain that we shall never take the false as the true if we only give our assent to things that we perceive clearly and distinctly. . . . It is also quite certain that whenever we give our assent to some reason which we do not exactly understand, we either deceive ourselves, or, if we arrive at the truth, it is only by chance, and thus we cannot be certain that we are not in error."[3]

[1] *Ibid.*
[2] *Ibid.*, § 69 (p. 26, ll. 21–25).
[3] *Principia Philosophiae*, I, 43–44.

Second, the internal criteria of truth are used by Spinoza as something independent of correspondence in its ordinary meaning of the agreement between what is in the mind with what is outside the mind. According to this sense of the internal criteria of truth, for an idea to have all the intrinsic signs of truth does not imply that it must be a copy of something which actually happens to exist outside the mind. To be sure, for an idea to be true it must agree with the reality of its ideate. But the reality with which a true idea must agree is not necessarily an external object; it may be its ideal nature conceived by the mind as something necessary in itself, or as something which follows by necessity from that which is conceived as necessary by itself, or as something which follows necessarily from its own nature and definition. While the external criterion of truth establishes the correspondence of an idea with an ideate of which it is a copy, the internal criterion of truth establishes the correspondence of an idea with an ideate in which it is implied. In the latter case, the true idea may be an idea implied as a conclusion in its premises, or as the properties of a triangle in its definition, or as the attributes of God in His essence. "For as regards what constitutes the form of truth, it is certain that true thought is distinguished from false thought not only by an external but mainly by an internal mark; as, for example, if a workman has rightly conceived any structure, although the thing has never existed and will never exist, his thought is nevertheless true, and the thought is the same whether the thing exists or not."[1] Correspondence here means agreement with the reality of its own nature, in so far as it is contained within its own nature and follows from its own nature. "Moreover, from the last thing we have said, namely, that the idea must altogether agree with

[1] *Tractatus de Intellectus Emendatione*, § 69 (*Opera* II, p. 26, ll. 17–21).

its formal essence, it is clear that in order that our mind may exactly reproduce the pattern of nature it must draw all its ideas from that idea which reproduces the origin and fountain of the whole of nature, so that it may also become the source of other ideas."[1] The building properly conceived by the architect is a true idea because, in so far as it is properly constructed, it is a faithful image of the nature of a building, and in fact may become the source of other ideas of buildings. There are thus true ideas, "the object of which we know with perfect certainty depends upon our power of thinking, and has no object in nature."[2] It is internal truth in this second sense that Spinoza describes as adequate in his formal definition of the term "adequate" given in the *Ethics* which we have quoted above. It is interesting to note that in almost similar terms and using the same illustration of an architect's conception of a building Thomas Aquinas describes the nature of what has been called here the internal criterion of truth: "Hence, everything is said to be absolutely, in so far as it is directed to an intellect from which it depends, and thus it is that the works of men's hands are said to be true as being directed to our intellect. For a house is said to be true that expresses the likeness of the form in the architect's mind."[3] Again, "a craftsman is said to produce a false work, if it falls short of the proper operation of his art."[4]

With this definition of internal truth or adequate ideas, Spinoza now proceeds to find out what ideas in our mind are true or adequate in this sense. Now, Descartes, after laying down the "general rule that all things which I per-

---

[1] *Ibid.*, § 42 (p. 17, ll. 3–7).
[2] *Ibid.*, § 72 (p. 27, ll. 12–13).
[3] *Summa Theologica*, Pars I, Quaest. 16, Art. 1.
[4] *Ibid.*, Pars I, Quaest. 17, Art. 1.

ceive very clearly and very distinctly are true,"[1] raises the question, "What then were these things?"[2] He then proceeds to test one by one the things known to us in order to determine whether they are clearly and distinctly perceived. He mentions at first external things, or "objects which I apprehend by means of the senses";[3] then he mentions the general belief "that there are objects outside of me from which these ideas proceed, and to which they are entirely similar";[4] after that he mentions certain things "very simple and easy in the sphere of arithmetic or geometry," such as "that two and three together make five";[5] and finally he mentions the certainty of the truths that I am and that there is a God.[6] Spinoza proceeds here in a similar manner to investigate which ideas are adequate and which are not. Directly challenging Descartes, he seems to say: I agree with you that we have no clear and distinct knowledge of external things (Props. XXIV–XXVI), but I do not agree with you that we have a clear and distinct knowledge that we ourselves exist (Props. XXVII–XXXI). The only clear and distinct knowledge that we have is the following: (1) Ideas which are related to God (Prop. XXXII). (2) Simple ideas (Prop. XXXIV). (3) Common notions and the ideas which may be deduced from them (Props. XXXVII–XL).

But let us work out these propositions in detail.

To begin with, he says, the knowledge of the component parts of the human body is not adequate knowledge, that is to say, it is not a knowledge which is self-evident and clearly and distinctly understood, for all that the mind knows about them is their behavior, but not their nature, and their behavior, being the result of a complicated system of causes,

---

[1] *Meditationes*, III (*Oeuvres*, III, p. 35, ll. 14–15).
[2] *Ibid.* (l. 18).   [3] *Ibid.* (l. 19).   [4] *Ibid.* (ll. 26–27).
[5] *Ibid.* (p. 35, l. 30–p. 36, l. 2).   [6] *Ibid.* (p. 36, ll. 16 ff.).

cannot be immediately known with clearness and distinctness. In fact, one must understand the entire order of nature before one is able to understand the working of the component parts of the human body.[1]

Nor does the human mind have an adequate knowledge of external bodies, for external bodies are known to us only through the affection of our own body, and then, too, only in so far as they are perceived by the senses. But there is more to be known about external bodies than what is inadequately revealed of them by sensation.[2] In fact, the very existence of external bodies is perceived by us only by the manner in which they affect our own body.[3] But inasmuch as most of the bodies which have once affected us and of which we speak as knowing them are not always present to our sensuous perception, our knowledge of them is only a sort of imagination, and such imaginary knowledge is not adequate knowledge.[4]

Since the mind has no adequate idea of the component parts of its own body nor of the external bodies which affect it, it has no adequate knowledge of its own body itself,[5] nor of the affections of its own body,[6] nor of itself or of the idea of itself.[7]

---

[1] *Ethics*, II, Prop. 24: "The human mind does not involve an adequate knowledge of the parts composing the human body."

[2] *Ibid.*, II, Prop. 25: "The idea of each affection of the human body does not involve an adequate knowledge of an external body."

[3] *Ibid.*, II, Prop. 26: "The human body perceives no external body as actually existing, unless through the ideas of the affections of its body."

[4] *Ibid.*, II, Prop. 26, Corol.

[5] *Ibid.*, II, Prop. 27: "The idea of any affection of the human body does not involve an adequate knowledge of the human body itself."

[6] *Ibid.*, II, Prop. 28: "The ideas of the affections of the human body, in so far as they are related only to the human mind, are not clear and distinct, but confused."

[7] *Ibid.*, II, Prop. 28, Schol., and Prop. 29: "The idea of the idea of any affection of the human body does not involve an adequate knowledge of the human mind."

All these propositions are finally summed up by Spinoza in the statement that "the human mind, when it perceives things in the common order of nature, has no adequate knowledge of itself, nor of its own body, nor of external bodies, but only a confused and mutilated knowledge."[1]

The reason why the mind has no adequate idea of all these things is that it perceives them for the most part as disconnected fragments of reality and does not grasp them in their totality as part of the entire reality. This fragmentary conception of things is designated by Spinoza by the expression the "common order of nature" (*communis naturae ordo*). Under this conception of nature things appear as being related to each other externally (*externe*) by a chance coincidence (*fortuito occursu*), and not internally (*interne*) by a universal concatenation of causes by which alone many diverse things are capable of being perceived simultaneously in their mutual relations of differences, agreements, and oppositions.[2] When things are viewed as part of the common order of nature and not as depending upon their essence or upon the absolute nature of God, they are said to have duration or an indefinite continuation of existence,[3] for the continuation of existence is called indefinite when "it cannot be determined by the nature itself of the existing thing nor by the efficient cause."[4] Consequently, since the mind is said to have only inadequate knowledge both of its own body and of external bodies it also has only inadequate knowledge both of the duration of its own body[5] and of the duration of individual things which are outside its own body.[6] It is this

---

[1] *Ibid.*, II, Prop. 29, Corol., and cf. Schol.

[2] *Ibid.*, II, Prop. 29, Schol.

[3] *Ibid.*, II, Prop. 30, Demonst.   [4] *Ibid.*, II, Def. 5.

[5] *Ibid.*, II, Prop. 30: "About the duration of our body we can have but a very inadequate knowledge."

[6] *Ibid.*, II, Prop. 31: "About the duration of individual things which are outside us we can have but a very inadequate knowledge."

method of viewing things as belonging to the common order
of nature that is meant when it is said that things are contingent and corruptible. For when things are said to be contingent or corruptible it does not mean that their coming
into existence or their passing out of existence comes about
without a cause; it only means that we have no adequate
knowledge of them in their true causal relations, that is to
say, that through "a deficiency in our knowledge" we are
unable to view them in their mutual relations as a whole.[1]

Having explained what ideas are inadequate, Spinoza
now proceeds to explain what ideas are adequate. But inasmuch as adequate ideas are by definition ideas which are
clear and distinct, and clearness and distinctness are the
internal criteria of truth, he uses the term "true" in place of
the term "adequate."

To begin with, the idea of God and all other ideas relating
to God are true ideas. The truth of these ideas is not tested by
the external standard of correspondence, for the knowledge
of the existence of God is not demonstrated cosmologically,
but rather ontologically, that is to say, by the self-evidence
of the idea as attested by its clearness and distinctness. By
this internal evidence and not by anything external do we
know that God is not a fictitious being or a being of reason, but a real being. Since the truth of our idea of God
depends upon the native power of the intellect alone, everything that can be deduced from the idea of God is equally
true. "For if we suppose the intellect to have perceived
some new being which had never existed, as some imagine
the intellect of God before He created things (a perception
which could not possibly arise from any object), and if we
also suppose the intellect to deduce other perceptions legiti-

---

[1] *Ibid.*, II, Prop. 31, Corol. Cf. *Ethics*, I, Prop. 33, Schol. 1; above, Vol. I, p. 189;
below, p. 160.

mately from the first, all those thoughts would be true and determined by no external object, but would depend solely on the power and the nature of the intellect."[1] And so Spinoza concludes here in Proposition XXXII that "all ideas, in so far as they are related to God, are true."

Furthermore, inasmuch as our thinking is a mode of God's attribute of thought, it follows, in Proposition XXXIII, that "in ideas there is nothing positive on account of which they are called false." What Spinoza is trying to deny by this proposition is the assumption that the mind has a certain freedom to conceive ideas arbitrarily. To assume this would be analogous to the assumption that the body has a certain freedom to act arbitrarily. The reason why Spinoza rejects the former assumption with reference to the mind is the same as that for which he rejects the latter assumption with reference to the body. It would break up the continuity and the necessary concatenation of causes in the process of nature. It would imply, as he puts it in the Preface of the Third Part of the *Ethics*, that "man disturbs rather than follows her [nature's] order." It would set the mind and the body free from the universal order of nature, from God; it would make them act independently of the infinite series of causes that proceed from God; and it would thus virtually declare them to be causes of themselves like God. This is the underlying thought of a statement in which Spinoza criticizes the view of some unnamed authors, among whom he undoubtedly also meant to include Descartes:[2] "They say that the mind can by its own strength create sensations or ideas which do not belong to things, so that in a measure they make it out to be a God."[3] This last statement is undoubt-

[1] *Tractatus de Intellectus Emendatione*, § 71 (*Opera*, II, p. 27, ll. 3 9).
[2] Cf. *Principia Philosophiae*, I, 31, *Principia Philosophiae Cartesianae*, I, Prop. 15, Schol.; *Meditationes*, IV.
[3] *Tractatus de Intellectus Emendatione*, § 60 (*Opera*, II, p. 23, ll. 15-17).

edly directed against Descartes' assertion that the principle
of free will "in a certain measure renders us like God in
making us masters of ourselves."[1] "Moreover," says
Spinoza, "they assert that we, or our mind, has such freedom that it can control us, or itself, and indeed its own
freedom."[2] Spinoza denies all this, for according to him
every movement of the body is a mode of the attribute of
extension and every idea in the mind is a mode of the attribute of thought. In a certain sense, Spinoza's statement in
Proposition XXXIII that "in ideas there is nothing positive
on account of which they are called false" may also be said
to reflect the questions raised by Thomas Aquinas whether
falsity exists in things and also whether it exists in the intellect.[3] Spinoza's argument in the Demonstration that there
can be no falsity in ideas themselves because ideas are modes
of God's thought and in God's thought there can be no falsity
is similar to the argument by Thomas Aquinas that there
can be no falsity in things themselves because "truth is said
to exist in things by conformity to the Divine Intellect . . .
in so far as it imitates it. But everything, in so far as it exists,
imitates God. Therefore everything is true without admixture of falsity." [4] Descartes expresses the same view in the
statement that "our errors cannot be imputed to God." [5]
Now in the light of all these passages, Proposition XXXIII
assumes the form of a syllogism as follows: If in ideas there
is something positive on account of which they are called

---

[1] *Les Passions de l'Ame*, III, 152.

[2] *Tractatus de Intellectus Emendatione*, § 60 (*Opera*, II, p. 23, ll. 17–19).

[3] *Summa Theologica*, Pars I, Quaest. 17, Art. 1: "Utrum falsitas sit in rebus";
Art. 3: "Utrum falsitas sit in intellectu."

[4] *Ibid.*, Art. 1: "3. Praeterea, verum dicitur in rebus per comparationem ad
intellectum divinum (ut supra dictum est, quaest. 16, art. 1), in quantum imitatur
ipsum. Sed quaelibet res, in quantum est, imitatur Deum. Ergo quaelibet res vera
est absque falsitate."

[5] *Principia Philosophiae*, I, 36.

false, then we must assume either that the mind has the power and freedom to conceive ideas which are false and is therefore the cause of its own actions like God, or that falsity is caused directly by God. But either of these alternatives is impossible. Therefore, "in ideas there is nothing positive on account of which they are called false."

In the second place, Spinoza wants to say, simple ideas are true, inasmuch as they are clear and distinct. Now, in the original passage in the *Tractatus de Intellectus Emendatione* where Spinoza first makes the statement about the clearness and distinctness and hence the truth of simple ideas, he does not use the expression "simple ideas"; the expression he uses there is "the idea of a simple object." "If the idea be that of an object perfectly simple (*simplicissimae*) it can only be clear and distinct."[1] In a later passage, however, he uses the expression "simple idea" (*idea simplex*), and as examples of it he mentions the ideas of a semicircle, motion, and quantity. "Hence it follows that simple thoughts cannot be other than true, such, for example, as the simple idea of the semicircle, of motion, of quantity, etc."[2] But it would seem that within these simple ideas used by him in the sense of ideas of simple objects Spinoza further distinguishes between those ideas which are formed absolutely (*absolute*) and those which are formed from other ideas, for in still another passage he distinguishes between motion and quantity, both of which have been described by him, in the passage quoted, as simple ideas, by saying that the intellect "forms the idea of quantity absolutely (*absolute*), and not by attending to other thoughts; but it forms the ideas of motion only by attending to the idea of quan-

---

[1] *Tractatus de Intellectus Emendatione*, § 63 (p. 24, ll. 20–21).

[2] *Ibid.*, § 72 (p. 27, ll. 28–30). Descartes similarly mentions "figure, extension, motion, etc.," as illustrations of a simple idea. Cf. *Regulae ad Directionem Ingenii*, XII (*Oeuvres*, X, p. 418, ll. 17–18).

tity."[1] Here in Proposition XXXIV he evidently uses the expression "absolute idea" (*idea . . . absoluta*) as the equivalent of a simple idea in the general sense of an idea of a perfectly simple (*simplicissima*) object. He thus says: "Every idea which in us is absolute, that is to say, adequate and perfect, is true." This view as to the truth of simple ideas may be traced to the following statements of Aristotle: "The process of thinking indivisible wholes belongs to a sphere from which falsehood is excluded. . . . Falsehood, in fact, never arises except when notions are combined." [2] This Aristotelian passage is also the basis of Descartes' statements that "there can be no falsity save in the last class — that of the compounds made by the understanding itself" [3] and that "simple natures are known *per se* and are wholly free from falsity." [4] Thomas Aquinas, too, says that "falsity of the intellect is concerned with the composition of the intellect alone." [5]

Ideas which are not true are classified by Spinoza in the *Tractatus de Intellectus Emendatione* into fictitious ideas (*ideae fictae*), false ideas (*ideae falsae*), and doubtful ideas (*ideae dubiae*).[6] The common element in all these untrue ideas is that they are composite and not simple and that they arise in the imagination and not in the intellect. "We have shown that fictitious, false, and other ideas derive their origin from the imagination, that is to say, from certain fortuitous (if I may so speak) and disconnected sensations, which do not arise from the power itself of the mind." [7]

---

[1] *Ibid.*, § 108 (p. 38, l. 34–p. 39, l. 3).

[2] *De Anima*, III, 6, 430a, 26–430b, 2.

[3] *Regulae ad Directionem Ingenii*, VIII (*Oeuvres*, X, p. 399, ll. 14–16).

[4] *Ibid.*, XII (p. 420, ll. 14–15).

[5] *Summa Theologica*, Pars I, Quaest. 17, Art. 3: "Quia vero falsitas intellectus per se solum circa compositionem intellectus est."

[6] *Tractatus de Intellectus Emendatione*, § 77 and § 84 (*Opera*, II, p. 29, l. 19; p. 32, l. 4).　　　　　[7] *Ibid.*, § 84 (p. 32, ll. 5–8).

With respect to doubtful ideas, as with respect to fictitious and false ideas, Spinoza furthermore says that "doubt is never produced in the mind . . . if there be only a single idea in the mind." [1] Though in Proposition XXXV Spinoza deals specifically with false ideas, what he says there applies equally to the other untrue ideas.

In his explanation of what falsity is, Spinoza also explains what it is not. It is not, in the first place, anything positive. What Spinoza means by this has already been explained in Proposition XXXIII. Nor, in the second place, does it consist in absolute privation (*absoluta privatio*). What Spinoza means by this is that falsity is not a natural limitation of man as is, for instance, his inability to fly or to live under water. For it is the mind, which is capable of thinking truthfully, that sometimes thinks falsely, and not the body, which is incapable of thinking at all. A parallel passage to this is found in Descartes: "For error is not a pure negation, but is a lack of some knowledge which it seems that I ought to possess." [2] A still more elucidating passage in Descartes is this: "It is very true that whenever we err there is some fault in our method of action, or in the manner in which we use our freedom; but for all that there is no defect in our nature, because it is ever the same whether our judgment be true or false." [3] Nor, in the third place, does it consist in absolute ignorance (*absoluta ignoratia*). It consists rather in a knowledge which man ought to know and does know, but knows wrongly. Falsity then is error, which two terms are used interchangeably by Spinoza [4] as well as by Descartes. [5]

---

[1] *Ibid.*, § 78 (p. 29, ll. 26–27).

[2] *Meditationes*, IV (*Oeuvres*, VII, p. 54, l. 31–p. 55, l. 3). Quoted also by Lewis Robinson, *Kommentar zu Spinozas Ethik*, I, p. 339.

[3] *Principia Philosophiae*, I, 38.

[4] *Tractatus de Intellectus Emendatione*, § 64, note b, and § 66 (*Opera*, II, p. 24, and p. 25, ll. 20–28); *Ethics*, II, Prop. 35, Demonst.

[5] *Meditationes*, IV.

Such error or falsity cannot arise in absolute or simple ideas; [1] it arises, as do fictitious ideas, "from putting together diverse confused ideas which belong to diverse things and operations in nature." [2] In this, indeed, he follows Aristotle, whose statement we have quoted above. [3] Or again, "falsity consists solely in the affirmation concerning anything of something which is not contained in the concept we have formed of the thing." [4]

The cause of such error and falsity is relative human ignorance. Imagination has free play only where there is not the restraining control of knowledge. If the necessity or the impossibility of a thing which depends upon external causes were known to us, says Spinoza, "we could imagine nothing concerning it." [5] Or, "if any God or anything omniscient exists, it is impossible for it to fancy anything," [6] that is to say, to have erroneous knowledge based on fancy. It is for this reason that "the less men know nature, so much the more easily they can fancy many things." [7] The ignorance from which all confusion arises is of a threefold nature. First, "the mind knows a whole or a complex only in part." Second, "it does not distinguish the known from the unknown." Third, "it considers simultaneously without any distinction the many things which are contained in each object." [8] Of these three types of ignorance, the first type, which consists in knowing things only in a partial and fragmentary manner, is probably what Spinoza always refers to as mutilated ideas. Evidence for this may be found in his use of the expres-

---

[1] Cf. above, p. 112, in our comments on Prop. 34.
[2] *Tractatus de Intellectus Emendatione*, § 64 (*Opera*, II, p. 24, ll. 27–28).
[3] Cf. above, p. 113.
[4] *Tractatus de Intellectus Emendatione*, § 72 (p. 27, ll. 26–28).
[5] *Ibid.*, § 53 (p. 20, ll. 4–6).
[6] *Ibid.*, § 54 (p. 20, ll. 7–8).
[7] *Ibid.*, § 58 (p. 22, ll. 21–22).
[8] *Ibid.*, § 63 (p. 24, ll. 16–20).

sion "mutilated and, as it were, fragmentary" (*mutilatas quasi, et truncatus*).¹ The second and third types, which consist in the failure to perceive distinctions between things, are probably what Spinoza always refers to as confused ideas. He thus says here in Proposition XXXV: "Falsity consists in the privation of knowledge, which inadequate, that is to say, mutilated and confused, ideas involve." Similarly toward the end of the unfinished *Tractatus de Intellectus Emendatione* he concludes that "false ideas and ideas of imagination . . . are considered as such solely through defect of our knowledge."² To illustrate how through ignorance man is led into error and falsity Spinoza cites two examples, one from the delusion of freedom and the other from the misjudgment of the distance of the sun.³ A misjudgment about the size of the sun as an illustration of falsehood is similarly used by Aristotle in the following passage: "But there are false imaginings concerning things of which we hold at the same time a true conception. For example, the sun appears to us only a foot in diameter, but we are convinced that it is larger than the inhabited world."⁴ In the course of his remarks on the delusion of freedom Spinoza alludes to those who pretend to know what the will is and in what manner it moves the body "and devise seats and dwelling-places of the soul."⁵ The allusion is principally to Descartes' theory of the pineal gland, by means of which the mind by the mere exercise of the will is said by him to be able to move the body,⁶ and which is also considered by him as the seat and dwelling-place of the soul.⁷

---

¹ *Ibid.*, § 73 (p. 28, l. 4).   ² *Ibid.*, § 110 (p. 40, ll. 5–7).
³ *Ethics*, II, Prop. 35, Schol. Cf. *Ethics*, IV, Prop. I, Schol.
⁴ *De Anima*, III, 3, 428b, 2–4.
⁵ *Ethics*, II, Prop. 35, Schol.
⁶ *Ibid.*, V, Praef.
⁷ Cf. *Les Passions de l'Ame*, I, 32.

Ideas then are not false in themselves. They become false only as a result of their being merely a broken-up fragment of a whole idea which in itself is true, or of their being the outcome of a confused combination of simple ideas which in themselves are true, and this mutilation and confusion of the ideas are due merely to ignorance and to a failure to see things as a whole in their mutual relationships or to a failure to analyze a complex idea into its component simple parts.[1] "For we have seen that the motion of a semicircle is false, as a disconnected affirmation in the mind, but that it is true if it be joined to the concept of a globe, or to the concept of any cause determining such motion."[2] As for the ideas themselves, which thus become mutilated or confused as a result of ignorance, they arise in our mind because our mind is a mode of God's attribute of thought. "Moreover if, as is self-evident, it belongs to the nature of a thinking being to form true or adequate thoughts, it is certain that inadequate ideas arise in us solely because we are part of some thinking being, whose thoughts, some in their completeness and others in part only, form our mind."[3] It is this which Spinoza means to say here in Proposition XXXVI: "Inadequate and confused ideas follow by the same necessity as adequate or clear and distinct ideas."

The third class of ideas which are true or adequate, says Spinoza, are common notions and ideas which follow by logical reasoning from common notions. This thought is developed by him in Propositions XXXVII-XL. But inasmuch as the meaning of common notions is not explained until the first Scholium to Proposition XL, we shall first discuss this Scholium and then return to the propositions.

---

[1] *Tractatus de Intellectus Emendatione*, § 63 (*Opera*, II, p. 24. ll. 20 ff.).

[2] *Ibid.*, § 73 (p. 28, ll. 5–8).

[3] *Ibid.*, § 73 (p. 28, ll. 8–13).

Demonstrative reasoning as expressed in any syllogism, according to Aristotle, must start with premises which are "true, primary, immediate, more known than, prior to, and the causes of the conclusion."[1] These premises which are the immediate propositions (προτάσεις ἄμεσοι) of a syllogism are called by him axioms, with which are correlated definitions, and hypotheses,[2] corresponding roughly to the first principles enumerated by Euclid at the beginning of his *Elements*. In Euclid, however, the axioms are called common notions (κοιναὶ ἔννοιαι).[3] Similarly in Arabic and Hebrew philosophic texts the Euclidian axioms are designated by such terms as "first notions" and "known notions." [4] In Latin philosophic texts, the expression "communes animi conceptiones" is used in place of axioms by Boethius, Casiodorus, John of Salisbury,[5] and Alanus de Insulis (or, rather, Nicolaus of Amiens).[6] Descartes, too, speaks in one place of axioms or common notions (*Axiomata sive communes notiones*)[7] and in another place refers to axioms as common notions.[8] Meyer in his Preface to Spinoza's *Principia Philosophiae Cartesianae* similarly speaks of "Axiomata, seu communes animi Notiones." [9]

Bearing all this in mind, Spinoza says significantly, "I have thus explained the origin of those notions which are

---

[1] *Analytica Posteriora*, I, 2, 71b, 21–22.   [2] *Ibid.*, 72a, 1–24.

[3] Cf. T. L. Heath, *The Thirteen Books of Euclid's Elements*, I, p. 221.

[4] ידיעות נודעות, ראשונות, מושכלות ראשונות (*Millot ha-Higgayon*, Ch. 8; *Ruaḥ Ḥen*, Ch. 3); cf. my *Crescas' Critique of Aristotle*, p. 465, n. 109.

[5] Cf. John of Salisbury, *Policraticus* (ed. C. C. I. Webb, Oxford, 1909), VII, 7, 649c, where references are given by the editor to Boethius, *Euclidis Geometriae Interpretatio*, I, and to Casiodorus, *De Artibus et Disciplinis Liberalium Litterarum*, Ch. 6.

[6] Cf. *De Arte seu de Articulis Catholicae Fidei*, Prologus, in Migne, *Patrologia Latina*, Vol. 210, Col. 597. Cf. below, p. 148, no. 3.

[7] *Rationes Dei existentiam . . . More Geometrico Dispositae* at end of *Secundae Responsiones* (*Oeuvres*, VII, p. 164, ll. 25–27).

[8] *Principia Philosophiae*, I, 13.

[9] *Opera*, I, p. 127, l. 19.

called common, and which are the foundations of our reasoning (*ratiocinii*)," and immediately after that he refers to these common notions as axioms or notions (*axiomatum, sive notionum*).[1] We have in this passage, then, a restatement of what Aristotle conceived to be demonstrative knowledge (ἀποδεικτικὴ ἐπιστήμη).[2] But instead of Aristotle's ἀποδεικτικὴ ἐπιστήμη Spinoza uses here the term *ratiocinium*. Descartes, more like Aristotle, speaks of the common notion as that out of which demonstrations are framed.[3] And these foundations of reasoning, Spinoza says, again following Aristotle, are the indemonstrable common notions or axioms.

But "common notions" or "axioms" are not the only immediately known propositions which form the premises in syllogisms. There are others. Maimonides in his treatise on logical terminology enumerates four: (1) sensible perceptions, (2) first notions, (3) generally known opinions, and (4) opinions accepted on the authority of one or more of the chosen few.[4] The difference between the first two of these four and the last two is stated by Maimonides as follows: The first two are *common* to all men, whereas the last two are confined to certain groups and classes of people. From the fact that the first two kinds of immediate propositions are described by Maimonides as "common" to all men, it is quite clear that his "first notions" or "axioms" and "sensible perceptions" are subdivisions of what are otherwise called "*common* notions." The third and fourth kinds of immediately known propositions named by Maimonides correspond on the whole to what Aristotle designates as prob-

---

[1] *Ethics*, II, Prop. 40, Schol. 1 (*Opera*, II, p. 120, ll. 15–17).

[2] *Analytica Posteriora*, I, 2, 71b, 20.

[3] *Principia Philosophiae*, I, 13: "Invenit etiam communes quasdam notiones, et *ex his* varias demonstrationes componit."

[4] (1) המושכלות הראשונות (2) [المحسوسات] ;המורגשות, המוחשים [المعقولات]
.[المقبولات] המקבלות (4) ;[المشهورات] המפרסמות (3) [الاول]

abilities (τὰ ἔνδοξα), and which are described by him as those opinions "which appear to all, or to most men, or to the wise; and to these, either to all, or to the greater number, or to such as are especially renowned and illustrious."[1] Not all these four classes of immediately known propositions, adds Maimonides, are of equal usefulness in the formation of a syllogism. Those based upon common notions, both first notions and sensible perceptions, are the most useful, for they produce a demonstrative syllogism. Those based upon generally known opinions produce a dialectic syllogism. Those based upon opinions accepted on authority produce a rhetorical syllogism or the enthymeme. In addition to all these, says Maimonides, there are propositions which are ill-founded and untrue and which produce sophistic syllogisms. All these statements of Maimonides reflect on the whole Aristotle's distinction between demonstration, on the one hand, and dialectic, rhetorical, and sophistic syllogisms, on the other.[2]

Evidently bearing this chapter of Maimonides in mind, Spinoza says that he could, if he would, "distinguish those notions which are more useful than others, and those which are scarcely of any use; those which are common; those which are clear and distinct only to those persons who do not suffer from prejudice; and, finally, those which are ill-founded."[3]

But the resemblance between this Scholium of Spinoza and the chapter in the Maimonides treatise on logical terminology goes still further. Maimonides makes a distinction between axioms, or what he calls "first notions," and "second notions."[4] "First notions" are illustrated by him by three

---

[1] *Topics*, I, 1, 100b, 21–23.   [2] *Ibid.*, 100a, 25 ff.; *Rhetoric*, I, 2.
[3] *Ethics*, II, Prop. 40, Schol. 1.
[4] מושכלות שניות ,מושכלות ראשונות.

examples taken from Euclid's list of common notions and
definitions: "The whole is greater than the part; [1] two is an
even number; [2] things which are equal to the same thing
are also equal to one another."[3] "By second notions,"
Maimonides says, "I refer to the geometrical constructions
and astronomical calculations which are all true notions, for
they are demonstrated by premises which for the most part
approximate first notions." What he means to say is that
"second notions" are the theorems of Euclid's *Elements* and
of Ptolemy's *Almagest* which, while really deduced from first
notions by means of a demonstration, are to be treated as if
they were immediately known.[4] The expression "second
notions" in the sense of conclusions derived by means of
demonstration from first notions, or notions which are like
first, occurs also in other Hebrew philosophic texts. For
example: "And they [the first notions] are the principles of
those intellectual disciplines which are arrived at by means
of demonstrative reasoning. The latter are the conclusions
of the former, i.e., the first notions, and are called second
notions, or third [notions], or fourth [notions], or even higher
than that, depending upon the number of propositions required in each case under consideration."[5] Again: "It is
not to be assumed that what to the philosopher is a second
notion is to the prophet a first notion, as some people think,
for if that were the case, then the philosopher's knowledge
of a given thing would be more perfect than that of the
prophet, inasmuch as he would know the thing in its causes
whereas the prophet would not know it in its causes."[6] To

[1] *Elements*, I, Common Notion 5.   [2] *Ibid.*, VII, Def. 6.
[3] *Ibid.*, I, Common Notion 1.
[4] Cf. quotation from Descartes on immediately deduced conclusions, below,
p. 130 n. 1.
[5] *Ruaḥ Ḥen*, Ch. 3.
[6] *Milḥamot Adonai*, Introduction (p. 4).

know a thing in its causes means here to know a thing by demonstration from self-evident premises.

Bearing again this chapter of Maimonides in mind, Spinoza makes another significant statement: "Moreover, it would be manifest whence these notions which are called second (*notiones . . . secundae*) . . . have taken their origin." In the light of our preceding discussion it is quite evident that by "notiones secundae" Spinoza means here the conclusions in demonstrative syllogisms. This makes his use of the expression *secundae notiones* unlike the scholastic use of the expressions *secundae intentiones* or *secundae notiones* with which Spinoza's expression here is generally identified.[1] The scholastic expressions refer to such concepts as genus, species, difference, and their like, by which mental relations are established between such universal concepts as man and animal, which are called by the scholastics *primae intentiones* or *primae notiones*.[2] The scholastic *secundae intentiones* or *secundae notiones* are called so because they were based upon the *primae intentiones* or *primae notiones*, which are universals. But inasmuch as universals are discussed by Spinoza later in the same Scholium without referring to them as *primae intentiones* or *primae notiones*, it is quite evident that there is no connection between his *secundae notiones* and the scholastic *secundae notiones* or *secundae intentiones*, or at least the meaning of the expression has been modified by Spinoza under the influence of its use by Maimonides. The expression "second notion" (*tweede kundigheid*) in its original scholastic meaning, however, is used by Spinoza in the *Short Treatise*.[3]

[1] Cf. note *ad loc.* in Baensch's translation of the *Ethics* (p. 283), and Lewis Robinson, *Kommentar zu Spinozas Ethik*, I, p. 346.

[2] Cf. P. Coffey, *The Science of Logic*, I, pp. 31 32; R. P. M. Fernandez Garcia, *Lexicon Scholastico-Theologicum*, p. 361, s.v. "intentio secunda."

[3] First Dialogue, § 10.

If we assume that Spinoza's expression "second notions" means the same as that of Maimonides and of the other Hebrew philosophic authors, then the passage following his mention of "second notions," which I have left out from my quotation above, is to be given a meaning which is different from that which is generally given to it. The entire passage in Latin reads as follows: "Praeterea constaret, unde notiones illae, quae secundas vocant, et consequenter axiomata, *quae* in *iisdem* fundantur, suam duxerunt originem." Naturally, the italicized *quae* in the quotation is taken to refer to "axiomata" and the italicized *iisdem* to "notiones . . . secundas," and the passage is generally translated as follows: "Moreover, it would be manifest whence these notions which are called second, *and consequently the axioms which are founded upon them*, have taken their origin." But in view of the use of the expression "second notions" in Maimonides and other Hebrew writings with which I have shown Spinoza's use of the expression to agree, one would expect here the italicized statement to read *and consequently the axioms upon which they are founded*. To be sure, the text may be translated this way even as it now reads, though it would be rather awkward to take *quae* to refer to "notiones . . . secundas" and *iisdem* to "axiomata."[1] But it is not impossible that in some manner the text has been corrupted here from its original reading: *in quibus eaedem fundantur*.

Closely related to the common notions are the scholastic six transcendentals (*transcendentales*),[2] of which Spinoza mentions here only three: Being (*ens*), Thing (*res*), Something (*aliquid*). The other three transcendentals, Unity (*unum*), Truth (*verum*), and Goodness (*bonum*), are, however,

[1] Strangely enough, two translations, both in English, that of Elwes and that [of Boyle] in Everyman's Library, render the passage as here suggested.

[2] Cf. W. Hamilton, *Lectures on Logic* (1866), I, p. 198; Prantl, *Geschichte der Logik* (1867), III, p. 245.

mentioned by him elsewhere.[1] These are differentiated by Spinoza from the common notions. The transcendentals, like universals, are confused and inadequate ideas, whereas the common notions, both primary and secondary, are adequate ideas. Though both universals and common notions ultimately rest upon sense-perception, still they differ from one another. The difference between them is threefold. In the first place, the ordinary universals, "such as Man, Horse, Dog, etc.," are formed by imagination and memory [2] — a view which agrees with that of Aristotle.[3] The common notions, on the other hand, are formed by the mind itself. In the second place, the universal is not an idea of what is truly proper and common to all things, but only an image of that upon "which all of them agree in so far as the body is affected by them . . . that is to say, by each individual."[4] The common notions, on the other hand, are ideas in the mind of "that which is common and proper to the human body, and to any external bodies by which the human body is generally affected."[5] In the third place, the universals "are not formed by all persons in the same way, but they vary in each case according to the thing by which the body is more frequently affected, and which the mind more easily imagines or remembers."[6] The common notions, on the other hand, "are common to all men,"[7] that is to say, are conceived by all men in the same way. It is because of these differences between them, maintains Spinoza, that universals are confused and inadequate ideas, whereas the com-

[1] *Cogitata Metaphysica*, I, 6, and cf. end of I, 5.

[2] *Ethics*, II, Prop. 40, Schol. 1 (*Opera*, II, p. 121, ll. 12 ff.).

[3] Cf. *Analytica Posteriora*, II, 19, 99b, 36–100a, 14.

[4] *Ethics*, II, Prop. 40, Schol. 1 (*Opera*, II, p. 121, ll. 18–21).

[5] *Ibid.*, II, Prop. 39.

[6] *Ibid.*, II, Prop. 40, Schol. 1 (*Opera*. II, p. 121, ll. 24–27).

[7] *Ibid.*, II, Prop. 38, Corol.

mon notions are clear and distinct and adequate ideas. But yet, despite these differences between "common notions" and "universals," Spinoza sometimes loosely refers to common notions as universals, as when, for instance, he describes the knowledge deduced from common notions as an inference from some universal (*ab aliquo universali*)[1] or as universal knowledge (*cognitio universalis*).[2]

The immediate propositions with which demonstrative reasoning must begin are divided by Aristotle into those which are proper only to certain special sciences and those which are common to all the sciences.[3] Inasmuch as the sciences differ according to the subject-matter of which they treat,[4] the immediate propositions within each science must be common to all the things included within that particular science. Now, it is my purpose here to show that the common notions of which Spinoza treats in Propositions XXXVII–XL are the immediate propositions which belong only to the study of bodies and not to that of God, or, as Aristotle would have said, they are the axioms of physics and not of theology or metaphysics. Evidence for this assertion is to be found in the following statement in the Scholium to Proposition XLVII, where Spinoza says that though both God and the common notions are known to all, "the reason why we do not possess a knowledge of God as distinct as that which we have of common notions is, that we cannot imagine God as we can bodies." This statement makes it quite clear that Spinoza's common notions are the primary principles only of the science of bodies or of physics. Within this science of bodies, however, says Spinoza after Aristotle, the common notions are those primary principles

---

[1] *Tractatus de Intellectus Emendatione*, § 19 (*Opera*, II, p. 10, l. 18).
[2] *Ethics*, V, Prop. 36, Schol. Cf. below, p. 138.
[3] Cf. Grote, *Aristotle*, I, pp. 305, 309, 341.
[4] Cf. above, p. 3.

which are based upon "that which is common to everything, and which is equally in the part and in the whole" and "forms the essence of no individual thing." [1]

But what are these common notions of the science of physics? Here again we must look for aid in Aristotle. Physics, according to him, deals with things which are inseparable from bodies and are movable.[2] Bodies have certain common properties which he calls common sensibles (κοινὰ αἰσθητά), under which he includes motion, rest, figure, magnitude, number, and unity.[3] Now in Lemma II, to which Spinoza refers after mentioning the common notions in Proposition XXXVII, bodies are said to have three things in common: they are (1) a mode of extension, and they are capable (2) of motion and (3) of rest. Similarly in the *Tractatus Theologico-Politicus* Spinoza says that "in the examination of natural phenomena we try first to investigate what is most universal and common to all nature — such, for instance, as motion and rest, and their laws and rules."[4] Inasmuch as it is quite clear from these passages that at least two of Aristotle's six common sensibles, namely, motion and rest, are specifically mentioned by Spinoza as common notions, and inasmuch as the remaining four, namely, figure, magnitude, number, and unity, can be regarded as modes of extension in which according to Spinoza all bodies agree, it may be inferred that Spinoza's common notions reflect Aristotle's common sensibles and that these common sensibles are used by Spinoza in the sense of the common notions or axioms of the science of physics.

These common notions, Spinoza proceeds to argue in Proposition XXXVIII, are adequately perceived, that is to say,

[1] *Ethics*, II, Prop. 37.
[2] *Metaphysics*, VI, 1, 1026a, 13-14. Cf. above, p. 3.
[3] *De Anima*, III, 1, 425a, 14-16; cf. II, 6, 418a, 17-18.
[4] *Tractatus Theologico-Politicus*, Ch. 7 (*Opera*, III, p. 102, ll. 21-24).

they are clear and distinct and immediate. Thus also the premises in a syllogism must be according to Aristotle and Maimonides immediately perceived, and this includes also premises which are based upon sense-perception, provided the sense-perception is sound.[1] But sense-perception, according to Aristotle, may be considered in two ways: first, the act of sense-perception (αἰσθάνεται), and second, the content of sense-perception (αἴσθησις), and while the former is of the particular, the latter is of the universal, i.e., of that which is common to everything.[2] Furthermore, the universals are described by Aristotle as things which cannot be divided (τὰ ἀμερῆ),[3] that is to say, things which are equally in the part and in the whole. Finally, these kinds of universals which are the content of sense-perception are according to Aristotle common to all men, for out of sense-perception, which is innate in all animals, there arises in man memory, experience, and finally universals.[4] All these points are reflected in Proposition XXXVIII and the Corollary: "Those things which are common to everything, and which are equally in the part and in the whole, can be only adequately perceived. . . . Hence it follows that some ideas or notions exist which are common to all men."

Since the common notions are ultimately based upon sensible perceptions, they will naturally begin, as sense-perception as a whole does according to Spinoza, with a knowledge of our own body, and will include a knowledge of external things only in so far as the former is affected by the latter. Hence Proposition XXXIX: "There will exist

---

[1] Cf. above, pp. 119 f.

[2] *Analytica Posteriora*, II, 19, 100a, 17.

[3] *Ibid.*, 100b, 2. In the two Latin translations of Averroes' Long Commentary on the *Analytica Posteriora*, made from the Hebrew, this term is translated by (1) *quae non partitur*, and (2) *quae non dividitur*.

[4] *Analytica Posteriora*, II, 19, 99b, 36–100a, 9.

in the human mind an adequate idea of that which is common and proper to the human body, and to any external bodies by which the human body is generally affected — of that which equally in the part of each of these external bodies and in the whole is common and proper." These common notions, therefore, derived as they are from sensible perception, are not limited in number, for the elements which things have in common are far greater than we usually perceive in our limited knowledge or, rather, in our ignorance. Were our knowledge perfect we could see how all things which appear different to us unite in God. The common notions therefore grow in number with the increase of our knowledge of nature. Spinoza expresses this view very neatly in the *Tractatus de Intellectus Emendatione* when he says that "the more things the mind knows the better it understands its own powers and the order of nature."[1] Here in the Corollary to Proposition XXXIX he expresses the same view in the statement, "Hence it follows that the more things the body has in common with other bodies, the more things will the mind be adapted to perceive."

Summing up our discussion as to Spinoza's use of the expression "common notions," we can trace its development in the mind of Spinoza out of certain statements in the writings of Aristotle. Whether the view he had of the subject is complete and accurate and one that would be acceptable to a modern student of the subject, does not interest us. What is of importance is that it represents an impressionistic picture which Spinoza could have got by reading the works of Aristotle and Maimonides. It is a picture based upon the Aristotelian theory of syllogism as outlined by Maimonides. In the mind of Spinoza this outline presented itself in the following diagram:

---

[1] *Tractatus de Intellectus Emendatione*, § 40 (*Opera*, II, p. 16, ll. 21–22).

The foundations of our reasoning (*ratiocinii nostri funda-menta*) are immediately known premises which are divided as follows:

A. Notions common to all men:
　　1. Sensible perceptions.
　　2. Axioms, subdivided into
　　　　(*a*) First notions.
　　　　(*b*) Second notions.
B. Notions common to some men:
　　1. Generally accepted opinions.
　　2. Authoritatively accepted opinions.
C. Ill-founded opinions.

Of these, as we have seen, Spinoza mentions explicitly A.2 (*a*) (*b*) and alludes indirectly to B and C.

These common notions form the premises in syllogisms from which by the proper application of the rules of logic conclusions can be derived. Given in the premises common notions which are true and given a syllogism which is formally correct, the conclusion will be true, for, as says Aristotle, "from true premises it is not possible to draw a false conclusion."[1] Similarly Spinoza seems to argue that since there is an inevitable necessity of truth in a conclusion drawn from true premises, the conclusion is no less clear and distinct than the premises. Formally one may speak of the premise as being immediately known and of the conclusion as being mediately known by means of a middle term. But in reality the conclusion is known simultaneously with the premise. "If a thought be true," says Spinoza, "the mind will easily proceed to deduce without any interruption things which are true."[2] The emphasis is here on the expression "without

---

[1] *Analytica Priora*, II, 2, 53b, 7–8.
[2] *Tractatus de Intellectus Emendatione*, § 104 (*Opera*, II, p. 37, ll. 34–35).

any interruption." So also Descartes argues that though remote conclusions are known only by deduction and first principles are known by intuition, still "it is possible to say that
those propositions indeed which are immediately deduced
from first principles are known now by intuition, now by
deduction, i.e., in a way that differs according to our point
of view." [1] Again, it is one of the functions of the intellect
"that it perceives some things or forms some ideas absolutely,
some ideas from others." [2] Here, again, the premises which
are known absolutely and the conclusions which follow from
the premises are both the activity of the same function of the
mind and are both perceived simultaneously. Hence Proposition XL: "Those ideas are also adequate which follow in
the mind from ideas which are adequate in it." The emphasis
here is that both the conclusion and premises are knowledge
of the same order and validity. In Descartes there is a somewhat similar statement: "Mind perceives these and other
facts to be true so long as the premises from which they are
derived are attended to." [3] Furthermore, maintains Descartes, "deduction, or the pure illation of one thing from
another . . . cannot be erroneous when performed by an
understanding that is in the least degree rational." [4]

[1] *Regulae ad Directionem Ingenii*, III (*Oeuvres*, X, p. 370, ll. 10–15).
[2] *Tractatus de Intellectus Emendatione*, § 108 (p. 38, ll. 34 ff.).
[3] *Principia Philosophiae*, I, 13.
[4] *Regulae ad Directionem Ingenii*, II (*Oeuvres*, X, p. 365, ll. 4–7).

CHAPTER XVI

THE STAGES OF KNOWLEDGE

In his preceding propositions Spinoza has dealt with three kinds of knowledge. Broadly speaking they are: (1) Sensation, imagination, and memory (Props. XIV–XVIII). (2) Ratiocinative knowledge (Props. XXXVII–XL), under which Spinoza enumerated its three constituent elements: (*a*) simple ideas and (*b*) common notions, both of which form the basis of ratiocination, and (*c*) conclusions drawn from them. (3) Knowledge of ideas in so far as they are related to God (Prop. XXXII). Of these three kinds of knowledge, the first was declared by him to be inadequate, whereas the second and third were declared by him to be adequate. Now as if to summarize the result of his discussion in the preceding propositions and to prepare us for his fuller description of the contents of the second and third kinds of knowledge in Propositions XLIII–XLVII, he gives us a formal classification of the three kinds of knowledge (Prop. XL, Schol. II) and an evaluation of them (Props. XLI–XLII). Similar classifications occur in the *Short Treatise*[1] and in the *Tractatus de Intellectus Emendatione*.[2]

What strikes one most in these classifications is the inconsistency in the use of the terms "three" and "four." In the *Tractatus de Intellectus Emendatione* Spinoza explicitly states that the modes of perception (*modos percipiendi*) are

---

[1] *Short Treatise*, II, 1. The following two terms are used by Spinoza in describing the classes of knowledge: (1) modes (*manieren, modos*), *Short Treatise*, II, 4, § 1 (*Opera*, I, p. 59, l. 5); *Tractatus de Intellectus Emendatione*, § 18 (*Opera*, II, p. 10, l. 3); (2) kinds (*genera*), *Ethics*, II, Prop. 40, Schol. 2 (*Opera*, II, p. 122, l. 15).

[2] *Tractatus de Intellectus Emendatione*, §§ 18 ff. (*Opera*, II, p. 10).

four. In the *Ethics* he actually divides knowledge (*cognitio*) into four kinds (*genera*), but by treating the first and the second only as two modes of regarding things (*utrumque res contemplandi modum*) under one kind of knowledge designated by a single term, he refers to the first three of his original four kinds of knowledge as "these two kinds of knowledge," thus making altogether a threefold classification. In the *Short Treatise* he first enumerates only three, but by subdividing the first into two parts he really has a fourfold classification. In fact, in another place in the *Short Treatise* he refers to his division of ideas "into four kinds," [1] and in still another place he speaks of what he has previously designated the third kind of knowledge as the "fourth, and last, kind of knowledge." [2]

The explanation for this, I think, is to be found in Saadia, whose passage on the sources of knowledge will be shown in the course of our discussion to be the model upon which Spinoza formed his own classification. Saadia begins with a general statement that the sources of knowledge are three. He enumerates them as follows: (1) Sense-perception. (2) Knowledge of reason, i.e., self-evident knowledge. (3) Knowledge by [logical] necessity. But after enumerating and describing these three sources of knowledge he says, "We shall add to these a fourth source . . . namely, reliable tradition," which he describes as being based upon the first three.[3] Whatever other influences may have entered into Spinoza's discussion of his classification of knowledge, Saadia's classification is undoubtedly responsible for its

[1] *Short Treatise*, II, 4, § 9.   [2] *Ibid.*, II, 22, § 1.

[3] *Emunot we-De'ot*, Introduction. For similar other classifications of the sources of knowledge among Jewish philosophers, see my paper "Notes on the Proofs of the Existence of God in Jewish Philosophy," in *Hebrew Union College Annual*, I (1924), pp. 578–580. The sources dealt with there are: *Hobot ha-Lebabot*, I, 10, *Cuzari*, V, 12; *'Olam Katan*, I, i; *Moreh Nebukim*, II, 33, supplemented by I, 51, and *Millot ha-Higgayon*, Ch. 8.

main outline. Not only are his kinds of knowledge, as we shall show, identical with those enumerated by Saadia, but his predilection for a threefold classification, which is the result of a combination of the equivalents of Saadia's first and fourth sources of knowledge into one, reflects the method employed by Saadia, who similarly begins with a threefold classification and then as an afterthought adds a fourth class, not as an independent source of knowledge, but rather as one based upon the others. Fourfold classifications of knowledge occur in Plato.[1] Aristotle enumerates various classifications,[2] all of which, however, as we shall see in the sequel, are reducible to the threefold classification of Spinoza. Threefold classifications of knowledges seem to have been in vogue among the Jews, Moslems, and Christians alike. Thus also Algazali speaks of three kinds of knowledge: reason, religion, and sense-perception.[3] Among Christian authors threefold classifications occur in the writings of Clement of Alexandria,[4] Maximus Confessor,[5] Erigena,[6] Gilbert,[7] Hugo of St. Victor,[8] Alanus (or Nicolaus of Amiens),[9] Richard of St. Victor,[10] and Nicolaus of Cusa.[11]

[1] *Republic*, VI, 511D, and VII, 533E: νόησις (νοῦς, ἐπιστήμη), διάνοια, πίστις, εἰκασία (cf. E. Zeller, *Die Philosophie der Griechen*, II, 1 (4th ed.), p. 637, n. 3).

[2] *Analytica Posteriora*, II, 19, 100b, 7–8; δόξα, λογισμός, ἐπιστήμη, νοῦς; *De Anima*, III, 3, 428a, 4–5: αἴσθησις, δόξα, ἐπιστήμη, νοῦς; *Metaphysics*, XII, 9, 1074b, 35–36; ἐπιστήμη, αἴσθησις, δόξα, διάνοια; *Nicomachean Ethics*, VI, 3, 1139b, 16–17: τέχνη, ἐπιστήμη, φρόνησις, σοφία, νοῦς, ὑπόληψις, δόξα (cf. J. Geyser, *Die Erkenntnistheorie des Aristoteles*, p. 141).

[3] *Mizan al-ʿAmal* [XXIV], p. 117; *Mozene Ẓedeḳ*, XXIV, p. 150.

[4] πίστις, γνῶσις, ἐπιστήμη. Cf. Erdmann, *Geschichte der Philosophie*, I, § 136.

[5] *Sensus, ratio, intellectus*. Cf. *ibid.*, § 146.

[6] *Sensus externus* and *sensus internus* (διάνοια), *ratio* (λόγος), *intellectus* or *animus* (νοῦς). Cf. *ibid.*, § 154.2.

[7] *ratio* (physics), *disciplinalis speculatio* (mathematics), *intellectus* (theology). Cf. *ibid.*, § 163.4.

[8] *cogitatio, meditatio, contemplatio*. Cf. *ibid.*, § 165.4.

[9] *opinio, fides, scientia*. Cf. *ibid.*, § 170.2, and see quotation below, p. 148, n. 3.

[10] *cogitatio* (*imaginatio*), *meditatio* (*ratio*), *contemplatio* (*intelligentia*). Cf. *ibid.*, § 172.3.   [11] *sensus, ratio, intellectus*. Cf. *ibid.*, § 224.2.

The first kind of knowledge, as we have seen, is subdivided by Spinoza into two forms. We shall refer to them as first form and second form, according to the order in which they occur in the *Short Treatise* and the *Ethics*. In the *Tractatus de Intellectus Emendatione* their order is reversed.

The first form of the first kind of knowledge is described by Spinoza as knowledge (1) from sense-perception (*per sensus . . . perceptiones*),[1] (2) from experience (*ondervinding*),[2] or (3) from vague experience (*experientia vaga*).[3] Sense-perception is named as a source of knowledge in all the classifications in mediaeval texts which we have referred to above. The term "experience" is mentioned by Maimonides as a kind of immediate knowledge which may form the basic premise of a syllogism, though it is not included in his original list of primary and immediately known premises, which, as we have seen, includes only four, namely, sense-perception, first notions, generally known opinions, and opinions accepted on authority.[4] As an illustration of knowledge by experience Maimonides mentions the knowledge that scammony[5] causes diarrhoea and that gallnut causes constipation. These illustrations of Maimonides are in fact nothing but a specified paraphrase of Aristotle's statement that "to have a judgment that when Callias was ill of this disease this did him good . . . is a matter of experience."[6] Algazali, too, mentions the illustration from scammony; but he adds two others, namely, that fire burns and that wine intoxicates.[7] Among the several illustrations given by

---

[1] *Ethics*, II, Prop. 40, Schol. 2.   [2] *Short Treatise*, II, 1, § 2.

[3] *Tractatus de Intellectus Emendatione*, § 19 (*Opera*, II, p. 10, l. 11); *Ethics*, II, Prop. 40, Schol. 2.

[4] Cf. above, p. 119.

[5] אן[ל]שקמוניא, השקמוניא (*Millot ha-Higgayon*, Ch. 8), السقمونيا (Algazali, *Maḳaṣid al-Falasifah*, I, 4, p. 52).

[6] *Metaphysics*, I, 1, 981a, 7–9.

[7] *Loc. cit.* See above, n. 5.

Spinoza of experience there is one of a similar nature, dealing as it does with the efficacy of the application of certain means for the obtaining of certain ends: "Again through vague experience I also know that oil is the proper food for feeding flame, and that water is fit for extinguishing it."[1] Now experience (ἐμπειρία) is said by Aristotle to arise from sense-perception through memory. "So out of sense-perception comes to be what we call memory, and out of frequently repeated memories of the same thing develops experience; for a number of memories constitute a single experience."[2] He distinguishes it from art in that "experience is knowledge of individuals, art of universals."[3] This Aristotelian explanation of experience is generally followed by the mediaevals, but they try to show that certain experiences are the result of both sense-perception and intellect. Thus Comtino in his commentary on Maimonides' treatise on logical terminology says that "propositions based upon experience are made up of propositions based upon sensible perceptions and intellectual notions, as has been stated by Algazali, for when we say that fire burns, scammony causes diarrhoea, and wine intoxicates, while it is the senses which perceive repeatedly, time after time, that the imbibing of wine is followed by intoxication, it is reason which judges that this sequence of events must come to pass by necessity, for if it came to pass only by chance it would not occur in the majority of cases,[4] and as a result there becomes ingrained in

---

[1] *Tractatus de Intellectus Emendatione*, § 20 (*Opera*, II, p. 10, ll. 27 ff.).

[2] *Analytica Posteriora*, II, 19, 100a, 3–6. Cf. *Metaphysics*, I, 1, 980b, 28 ff.

[3] *Metaphysics*, I, 1, 981a, 15–16.

[4] Cf. *Physics*, II, 5, 196b, 10–13: "First then we observe that some things always come to pass in the same way, and others for the most part. It is clearly of neither of these that chance is said to be the cause, nor can the effect of chance be identified with any of the things that come to pass by necessity and always, or for the most part."

the mind a knowledge of this fact upon which it can rely."[1] Descartes, too, describes experience in a way which suggests the mediaeval modification of Aristotle's description. He says: "Matter of experience consists of what we perceive by sense, what we hear from the lips of others, and generally what reaches our intellect either from external sources or from that contemplation which our mind directs backwards on itself (*ex sui ipsius contemplatione reflexa*)."[2] Spinoza's description of experience reflects this Aristotelian description as restated by Descartes, and this is the significance of his statement that experience is "from individual things, represented by the senses . . . to the *intellect*."[3] As for the expression "vague experience," it is to be found in Bacon.[4]

The second form of the first kind of knowledge is described by Spinoza as knowledge (1) from hearsay (*hooren zeggen*),[5] (2) from hearing (*ex auditu*),[6] (3) from some sign (*ex aliquo signo*),[7] or (4) from signs (*ex signis*).[8] The expressions "from hearsay" and "from hearing" reflect Saadia's fourth source of knowledge, which we have translated above "tradition" but which literally means "saying."[9] Another Hebrew word for tradition literally means "hearing."[10] The two words "hearing" and "saying" occur together in a Talmudic passage.[11] Tradition is one of the things that Spinoza means by

---

[1] See Comtino's Commentary on *Millot ha-Higgayon*, Ch. 8, and *Maḳaṣid al-Falasifah*, I, 4 (pp. 52–53).

[2] *Regulae ad Directionem Ingenii*, XII (6) (*Oeuvres*, X, pp. 422, l. 25–423, l. 1).

[3] *Ethics*, II, Prop. 40, Schol. 2.

[4] Cf. *Novum Organum*, I, c. Cf. W. Hale White's translation of the *Tractatus de Intellectus Emendatione*, Preface, p. xii, n. 1.

[5] *Short Treatise*, II, 1, § 2.

[6] *Tractatus de Intellectus Emendatione*, § 19 (*Opera*, II, p. 10, l. 9).

[7] *Ibid.*

[8] *Ethics*, II, Prop. 40, Schol. 2.

[9] הגדה.

[10] מפי השמועה, *Sanhedrin* 88a.

[11] אין אומרים שמועה והגדה. *Mo'ed Ḳatan* 23a.

"hearing" and "hearsay." The term "sign" in the sense of words heard or written, and hence of the ideas formed of them, has been ascribed to Occam, from whom, it has been suggested, Spinoza borrowed it.[1] But there is a passage in Aristotle which may be considered the source of Occam as well as of Spinoza. "Spoken words," says Aristotle, "are the signs (σύμβολα, *signa* in the Latin translations accessible to Spinoza) of mental experience, and written words are the signs of spoken words."[2] Similarly Hobbes speaks of names as the "signs" of our "conceptions."[3] What is more significant still is the fact that Hobbes calls them arbitrary (*arbitraria*) signs in contradistinction to natural (*naturalia*) signs.[4] So also Spinoza qualifies his "from some sign" in the *Tractatus de Intellectus Emendatione* by the statement "which everyone may name as he pleases (*quod vocant ad placitum*)."[5] Descartes, too, without using the word "sign," seems to refer to what Aristotle and Spinoza call signs when he says that "we observe that words, whether uttered by voice or merely written, excite in our minds all sorts of thoughts and emotions."[6] Spinoza's contemporary Locke likewise says: "There are two sorts of signs commonly made use of, viz., ideas and words."[7] The fullest explanation of signs is given by Spinoza in the following passage. After stating that "words are part of the imagination, that is to say, we form many conceptions according to the manner in which words

---

[1] *Quaestiones super Analytica Posteriora*, I, 37, p. 403 A, quoted by W. Eichberg in his *Untersuchungen über die Beziehungen der Erkenntnislehre Spinozas zur Scholastik mit besonderer Berücksichtigung der Schule Okkams* (Borna-Leipzig, 1910), p. 20, n. 19.

[2] *De Interpretatione*, 1, 16a, 3–4.

[3] "Nomina, ut definitum est, disposita in oratione, signa sunt conceptuum." *Elementa Philosophiae*, Pars I, Cap. II, § 5, p. 15 (*Opera*, I, London, 1839).

[4] *Ibid.*, § 2, p. 13.   [5] § 19 (*Opera*, II, p. 12, ll. 9–10).

[6] *Principia Philosophiae*, IV, 197.

[7] *Essay Concerning Human Understanding*, IV, 5, § 2.

are loosely combined in the memory from some disposition of the body," he adds. "It is to be noted also that they are formed according to the caprice and notions of the vulgar, so that they are nothing but signs of things as they exist in the imagination, and not as they exist in the intellect."[1]

The second kind of knowledge, while mentioned in the *Short Treatise*, given a name, and illustrated by an example, is not described there. The nearest we get there to a description of this kind of knowledge is the statement that it is not confined to "the experience of a few particulars" and that it examines things "in the light of true reason."[2] But in the *Tractatus de Intellectus Emendatione* it is introduced first by the general statement that this kind of knowledge arises "when the essence of a thing is deduced from another thing." Then this kind of deduction is subdivided into two forms: (1) "when we . . . infer the cause from the effect," and (2) "when we make an inference from some universal which is always accompanied by some property." In the *Ethics* it is described by a statement which is to be taken as a parallel to the second form of deduction mentioned in the *Tractatus de Intellectus Emendatione*. It reads as follows: "From our possessing common notions and adequate ideas of the properties of things." The expression "common notions" in this passage of the *Ethics* is undoubtedly the same as the expression "some universal" in the passage in the *Tractatus de Intellectus Emendatione*. It is therefore with reference to this second form of deduction that Spinoza describes the second kind of knowledge as universal knowledge (*cognitio universalis*) in the Scholium to Proposition XXXVI of the Fifth Part of the *Ethics*.[3]

[1] *Tractatus de Intellectus Emendatione*, §§ 88–89 (*Opera*, II, p. 33, ll. 8–15). Cf. below, p. 174, n. 2.

[2] *Short Treatise*, II, 1, § 3 (*Opera*, I, p. 55, ll. 4–6).

[3] *Opera*, II, p. 303, l. 19. Cf. below, p. 150, n. 5.

The first form of deduction under Spinoza's second kind of knowledge, the deduction of cause from effect, corresponds exactly to what Saadia in his classification of the sources of knowledge describes as knowledge by [logical] necessity. Saadia illustrates it by many examples, the simplest of which is that where there is smoke there is fire.[1] Another example cited by Saadia reads as follows: "As, e.g., in order not to deny the plainly evident functioning of the soul [i.e., sensation, etc.] we are forced to admit that man has a soul, even though we do not perceive it."[2] Similarly Spinoza illustrates the deduction of cause from effect in the second kind of knowledge as follows: "We deduce from some other thing in this way: when we clearly perceive that we are sensible of a particular body and no other, then we clearly deduce, I say, from that perception that our mind is united to that body, and that the union is the cause of that sensation." In a note explaining this passage Spinoza comes still closer to Saadia's statement. "By that union," he says, "we understand nothing except the sensation itself, which is an effect, from which we conclude a cause of which we understand nothing."[3] Furthermore, Saadia, after mentioning a few other complicated examples which require a knowledge of mathematics and astronomy, concludes with the following words of warning: "Having explained the nature of logically necessary knowledge, we deem it fit to mention some precautions which would safeguard this kind of knowledge from fallacies, for most of the discords among men and the diversity of their arguments arise in and from this kind of reasoning."[4] Similarly Spinoza comments in a note to his illus-

---

[1] *Emunot we-De'ot*, Introduction.

[2] *Ibid.*

[3] *Tractatus de Intellectus Emendatione*, § 21 and note g (*Opera*, II, p. 11, ll. 3–7).

[4] *Emunot we-De'ot*, Introduction.

tration of the deduction of cause from effect that "such a conclusion, although it may be certain, is nevertheless not sufficiently safe, unless great precautions are taken."[1]

The second form of deduction under Spinoza's second kind of knowledge, namely, the deduction of a conclusion from a premise in a syllogism, is described by him, as we have seen, in two passages. In the *Tractatus de Intellectus Emendatione* he describes it as "an inference from some universal which is always accompanied by some property."[2] This passage seems to be simply a description of the composition of the major premise of a syllogism, such as "all men are mortal," in which "all men" is Spinoza's "some universal" and "mortal" is his "some property" by which the universal is accompanied. The passage in the *Ethics*, namely, "from our possessing common notions and adequate ideas of the properties of things,"[3] is similarly a description of the major premise, with the added emphasis that the relation of the predicate to the subject in it must be adequately known, that is to say, immediately known and in need of no demonstration. The statement in Proposition XL of the Second Part of the *Ethics* that "those ideas are also adequate which follow in the mind from ideas which are adequate in it" evidently refers to this second form of deduction, namely, the deduction of a conclusion from a premise.

The third kind of knowledge is described in the *Short Treatise* as that which is the "result of clear and distinct conception." In the *Tractatus de Intellectus Emendatione* it is described as that which arises "when a thing is perceived through its essence alone, or through the knowledge of its proximate cause." In Scholium II to Proposition XL of the

[1] *Tractatus de Intellectus Emendatione*, § 21, note h (*Opera*, II, p. 11).
[2] *Ibid.*, § 19 (p. 10, ll. 18-19).
[3] *Ethics*, II, Prop. 40, Schol. 2.

Second Part of the *Ethics* it is called intuitive science (*scientia intuitiva*), and is described as knowledge which advances "from an adequate idea of the formal essence of certain attributes of God to the adequate knowledge of the essence of things." The same description is repeated almost verbatim in the Demonstration of Proposition XXV of the Fifth Part of the *Ethics*, and it is restated in the Scholium to Proposition XXXVI of the Fifth Part of the *Ethics* as a knowledge which follows "from the divine nature, and continuously depends upon God." In the Scholium to Proposition XLVII of the Second Part of the *Ethics* it is described as follows: "Hence we see that the infinite essence and the eternity of God are known to all; and since all things are in God and are conceived through Him, it follows that we deduce from this knowledge many things which we can know adequately, and that we can thus form that third kind of knowledge."

Taking all these passages together, we get four characteristics of the third kind of knowledge. *First*, it is knowledge which is deduced from "an adequate idea of the formal essence of certain attributes of God" or from "the divine nature" or from "the infinite essence and the eternity of God." *Second*, it arises "when a thing is perceived through its essence alone." *Third*, it arises when a thing is perceived "through the knowledge of its proximate cause." *Fourth*, it is the "result of clear and distinct conception." Now we shall try to show that when Spinoza says in the *second* of these characteristics that it is the knowledge of a thing when perceived "through its essence alone" he means the same as when he says in various ways in the *first* of these characteristics that it is a knowledge of God or His attributes, that when he says in the *third* of these characteristics that it is the knowledge of a thing when perceived "through the knowledge of its proximate cause" he means here by "proximate cause" God or His attributes, and that when he says in the *fourth* of these characteristics that it is the "result of clear and distinct conception" he means it to be a summary of all the other three characteristics. Finally, we shall try to show that by all these characterizations of the third kind of knowledge Spinoza means to say that it is knowledge attained from what he would call a true definition.

The passage by which I shall try to prove my statements in the preceding paragraph is Spinoza's discussion of the nature of a definition in the *Tractatus de Intellectus Emendatione* and its parallel discussion in the *Short Treatise*. In the *Tractatus de Intellectus Emendatione* Spinoza distinguishes between the definition of an uncreated thing and the definition of a created thing.[1] By an uncreated thing he means a thing that is in itself (*in se*) or is the cause of itself (*causa sui*).[2] This, of course, refers to God and His attributes. In the *Short Treatise* this kind of definition is explicitly said to be "of those attributes which pertain to a self-subsisting being . . . for, since they exist as attributes of a self subsisting being, they also become known through themselves."[3] Furthermore, this kind of definition is said to be of a thing which is "understood through its essence alone."[4] From all this it is clearly seen that the *second* characteristic mentioned above of the third kind of knowledge, namely, that it is the knowledge of a thing when perceived "through its essence alone," is identical with its *first* characteristic, namely, that it is knowledge deduced "from an adequate idea of the formal essence of certain attributes of God" or "from the divine nature" or from "the infinite essence and the eternity of God."

[1] *Tractatus de Intellectus Emendatione*, §§ 96 ff. (*Opera*, II, p. 35).
[2] *Ibid.*, § 92 (p. 34, ll. 10–11).   [3] *Short Treatise*, I, 7, § 10.
[4] *Tractatus de Intellectus Emendatione*, § 92 (*Opera*, II, p. 34, ll. 11–12).

By a created thing, which is the subject of the other kind
of definition, Spinoza means any mode or particular thing,
using here, of course, the term "created" not in its specific
sense of creation but in the general sense of having a cause
for its existence. We have already shown that this use of the
term is made by Spinoza elsewhere.[1] Of the definition of
created things Spinoza simply says that it must "include
the proximate cause."[2] But what does he mean by proximate cause? In the *Tractatus de Intellectus Emendatione* he
illustrates it by the definition of a circle, which is defined
"as a figure which is described by any line of which one ex-
tremity is fixed and the other movable."[3] This would seem
to imply that Spinoza means by this kind of definition what
is generally known as a genetic, constructive, or causal
kind of definition, or whatever else this kind of definition is
called. Accordingly, by a proximate cause he would seem
to mean the process by which a thing is produced. In the
Short Treatise, however, he narrows it down to only one kind
of causal definition. He describes it there as the definition of
things "which do not exist through themselves, but only
through the attributes whose modes they are."[4] The context
of the passage makes it quite clear that by "attributes" he
means the attributes of God. Accordingly, by a proximate
cause he would seem to mean God and His attributes, who is
the cause of all things and is their proximate and not their
remote cause.[5]

This apparent inconsistency between these two quoted
passages, however, can be removed by the distinction which
Spinoza makes, though with not as much clearness as one

---

[1] Cf. above, Vol. I, pp. 350–351, 383.

[2] *Tractatus de Intellectus Emendatione*, § 96 (*Opera*, II, p. 35, ll. 12–13).

[3] *Ibid.*, § 96 (p. 35, ll. 13–15).

[4] *Short Treatise*, I, 7, § 10.

[5] *Ethics*, I, Prop. 28, Schol.

would have wished him to make, between figures and other
entities of reason (*figurae, et caetera entia rationis*) and physical entities and realities (*entia physica, et realia*).[1] In the
case of the former, such as the definition of a circle, the proximate cause means the process by which the circle is produced. In the case of the latter, the proximate cause means
God and His attributes, who is "the cause of all things."[2]
Spinoza thus argues that we may deduce "all our ideas
from things physical or from real entities, by advancing as
strictly as possible according to the sequence of causes from
one real entity to another real entity,"[3] for "it is apparent
we can understand nothing of nature without at the same
time making our knowledge of the first cause, that is to say,
of God, more ample."[4]

It is evident, therefore, that by the *third* characteristic
mentioned above of the third kind of knowledge, namely,
the knowledge of a thing when perceived "through the knowledge of its pròximate cause," Spinoza means the knowledge
of a thing attained through the knowledge of God and His
attributes.

It is thus the knowledge attained from the definition of a
thing, either the definition of an uncreated thing or the definition of created things, that forms knowledge of the third
kind. It is these two definitions that are reproduced by
Spinoza in disguised languages in the passages collected
above from the *Tractatus de Intellectus Emendatione*, the
Ethics, and the *Short Treatise*. When he says in the *first* and
second characteristics mentioned above that the third kind
of knowledge is knowledge deduced from "an adequate idea
of the formal essence of certain attributes of God"[5] or from

---

[1] *Tractatus de Intellectus Emendatione*, § 95 (*Opera*, II, p. 35, ll. 5–6).
[2] *Ibid.*, § 99 (p. 36, l. 10).   [3] *Ibid.*, § 99 (p. 36, ll. 10-17).
[4] *Ibid.*, § 92, note f (p. 34).   [5] Cf. above, p. 141.

"the divine nature"[1] or from "the infinite essence and the
eternity of God,"[1] or that it arises "when a thing is perceived
through its essence alone,"[1] he means by all these statements
that it is knowledge derived from the definition of a thing
uncreated. When, on the other hand, he says in the *third*
characteristic that it is knowledge arising when a thing is
perceived "through the knowledge of its proximate cause,"
he means by it that it is knowledge derived from the definition of things created. But when he says in the *fourth*
characteristic that it is the "result of clear and distinct
conceptions,"[1] he means by it knowledge derived from a
definition in general, be it a definition of a thing uncreated
or of things created.

These three kinds of knowledge are described by Spinoza
by the following groups of terms: (1) Belief (*geloof*),[2] opinion
(*waan, opinio*),[3] or imagination (*imaginatio*).[4] (2) True belief
(*waar geloof*),[5] belief,[6] or reason (*reeden, ratio*).[7] (3) Clear
knowledge (*klaare kennisse*),[8] knowledge (*weten, kennisse*)[9]
or intuitive science (*scientia intuitiva*).[10] All these terms can
be shown to have been used by other philosophers in the
senses in which Spinoza used them.

The terms "belief" and "opinion" reflect respectively the
Greek ὑπόληψις and δόξα, which, like Spinoza's first kind of
knowledge, are used by Aristotle as designations of a knowledge which is based upon sense-perception and imagination

---

[1] Cf. above, p. 141.
[2] *Short Treatise*, II, 1, § 2.
[3] *Ibid.*, II, 2, §§ 1-2; *Ethics*, II, Prop. 40, Schol. 2.
[4] *Ethics*, II, Prop. 40, Schol. 2.
[5] *Short Treatise*, II, 1, § 2, and 14, § 2 (*Opera*, I, p. 77, l. 4).
[6] *Ibid.*, II, 2, §§ 1-2.
[7] *Ibid.*, II, 14, § 2 (*Opera*, I, p. 77, l. 4).
[8] *Ibid.*, II, 2, §§ 1-2.
[9] *Ibid.*, II, 4, § 1, note 1 (*Opera*, I, p. 59, l. 28), and 14, § 1 (p. 77, l. 7).
[10] *Ethics*, II, Prop. 40, Schol. 2.

and hence may be false.[1] The term "belief" alone may reflect also Plato's *πίστις*.[2] The terms "imagination" and "opinion" reflect the Greek λογισμός and δόξα, which, as we shall see later,[3] have been translated into Latin by "imagination" and "opinion" and were used by Aristotle as designations of a kind of knowledge which, again like Spinoza's first kind of knowledge, may be false. If we are right in assuming that Aristotle's ὑπόληψις and δόξα are etymologically the sources of Spinoza's "belief" and "opinion," then the contrast between Spinoza's first and second kinds of knowledge corresponds to Aristotle's contrast between ὑπόληψις, δόξα and τέχνη, ἐπιστήμη, φρόνησις, σοφία, νοῦς.[4] Furthermore, within the last five Aristotelian terms one may also discover some suggestion for Spinoza's distinction between the second and third kinds of knowledge, ἐπιστήμη, corresponding to the second kind of knowledge, and νοῦς, corresponding to the third kind of knowledge.

The term "belief" which is used by Spinoza for the first kind of knowledge is also used by him, either with or without the qualifying adjective "true," as a designation for the second kind of knowledge. If, as we have suggested, "belief" reflects Aristotle's ὑπόληψις, then the twofold use of this term by Spinoza reflects the twofold meaning of ὑπόληψις in Aristotle. In one sense, ὑπόληψις means approximately the same as δόξα, and it corresponds therefore to the first kind of knowledge in Spinoza. In another sense, it means scientific or demonstrative knowledge, and it corresponds therefore to the second kind of knowledge in Spinoza.[5] Spinoza's

---

[1] *De Anima*, III, 3, 427b, 14–16; *Nicomachean Ethics*, VI, 3, 1139b, 17–18. Cf. J. Geyser, *Die Erkenntnistheorie des Aristoteles*, pp. 141–142.

[2] Cf. above, p. 133, n. 1.   [3] See below, p. 151.

[4] *Nicomachean Ethics*, VI, 3, 1139b, 15 ff.

[5] Cf. J. Geyser, *Die Erkenntnistheorie des Aristoteles*, pp. 147 ff.; R. D. Hicks on *De Anima*, III, 3, 427b, 16.

qualified expression "true belief," accordingly, will reflect Aristotle's expression "vehement belief" (ὑπόληψις σφοδρά), and Spinoza's description of "belief" in its second sense as "things . . . known to us through the *conviction* or *persuasion* (*overtuyginge*) of our understanding that it must be so and not otherwise"[1] will reflect Aristotle's identification of πίστις with ὑπόληψις σφοδρά.[2] By the same token, if one wishes to push the inquiry still further, the expression "true belief" may also reflect Plato's δόξα ἀληθής.[3] It is also possible, as has been suggested by Joël,[4] that the use of the expression "true belief" as a designation for the second kind of knowledge with the definition that "belief is a strong proof based on reasons, whereby I am convinced in my mind that the thing is really, and just such, outside my understanding, as I am convinced in my mind that it is,"[5] is based upon Crescas' statement that "belief is nothing but the conviction that the thing is outside the soul as it is in the soul,"[6] or as Maimonides says: "By belief we do not understand that which is uttered with the lips but that which is apprehended by the soul, the conviction that the object [of belief] is exactly as it is apprehended."[7] This conception of "belief," which in Maimonides is explicitly applied to matters religious, seems to me to be in opposition to Descartes' statement that "belief (*fides*) in these things [i.e. matters that have been divinely revealed], as all belief in obscure matters, is an action not of our intelligence (*ingenii*), but of our will."[8]

The term "reason" (*ratio*) in Spinoza's second kind of

---

[1] *Short Treatise*, II, 2, § 2 (*Opera*, I, p. 55, ll. 23–26).
[2] *Topics*, IV, 5, 126b, 18. Cf. Geyser, *op. cit.*, p. 148.
[3] *Timaeus* 51D.
[4] Joël, *Zur Genesis der Lehre Spinoza's*, pp. 63–64.
[5] *Short Treatise*, II, 4, § 1, note 1 (*Opera*, I, p. 59, ll. 23–25).
[6] *Or Adonai*, II, v, 4 (p. 49b).
[7] *Moreh Nebukim*, I, 50.
[8] *Regulae ad Directionem Ingenii*, III (*Oeuvres*, X, p. 370, ll. 21–22).

knowledge represents the Greek λόγος, which in the sense of ratiocination is the basis of Aristotle's scientific knowledge (ἐπιστήμη), that is to say, knowledge based upon demonstrative reasoning.

The term "knowledge" or "clear knowledge" used by Spinoza for his third kind of knowledge etymologically reflects the Greek ἐπιστήμη, which is used by Aristotle in the sense of Spinoza's second kind of knowledge. Evidently Spinoza uses this term loosely as the equivalent of Aristotle's νοῦς in the sense of immediate knowledge. Or it may reflect Plato's use of the term ἐπιστήμη as the equivalent of νοῦς.[1]

The term "intuitive science" in Spinoza's third kind of knowledge is borrowed directly from Descartes, who uses the term "intuitus" as the opposite of both "inductio" and "deductio."[2]

These three terms, "opinion," "belief," and "knowledge," as designations of three stages of knowledge, arranged in the same order as in Spinoza but used in a different sense, are found in the following passage of Alanus (or Nicolaus of Amiens): "Belief (*fides*) stands therefore at least above opinion (*opinio*), but below knowledge (*scientia*)."[3]

In a conversation with Leibniz about Spinoza's *Ethics*, Tschirnhaus designates the three kinds of knowledge by *sensualis, pragmativa* (*-ca?*), and *intuitiva*.[4] The first and third

---

[1] Cf. above, p. 133, n. 1.

[2] *Regulae ad Directionem Ingenii*, III (*Oeuvres*, X, p. 368, ll. 12–13); IV (p. 372, l. 16).

[3] "Fides igitur utique super opinionem sed infra scientiam." *De Arte seu Articulis Catholicae Fidei*, I, xvii, in Migne, *Patrologia Latina*, Vol. 210, Col. 601. This work is now ascribed to Nicolaus of Amiens. Cf. M. Grabmann, *Geschichte der scholastischen Methode* (1911), II, pp. 459 ff.

[4] The conversation was published by K. I. Gerhardt, "Leibniz und Spinoza," in *Sitzungsberichte der königlich preussischen Akademie der Wissenschaften zu Berlin*, 1889, pp. 175 ff. Cf. p. 177: "nam aliam esse sensualem, aliam pragmativam (-cam?), aliam intuitivam."

terms are quite clear. As for the second term, *pragmativa*, if it is not a corruption of some such term as *ratiocinativa*, it may have here the meaning of laborious or demonstrative knowledge, i.e., mediate knowledge arrived at by a process of reasoning as opposed to the immediate knowledge of *intuitiva*, after the analogy of the various shades of meanings of πραγματεία, *a philosophical argument*, πραγματευτέος, *to be labored at*, the Byzantine meaning of πραγματικός, *arduous, difficult, troublesome*, and the *pragmaticus* of the Roman writers used in the sense of one who suggested arguments to public speakers and advocates.[1] In a similar connection does the Latin equivalent of πρᾶγμα, *negotium*, occur in Ibn Gabirol's *Fons Vitae*, where the immediate or intuitive knowledge of the intellect is described as a knowledge *sine inquisitione, sine negotio*.[2] Int he corresponding passage in the Epitome Campililiensis of the *Fons Vitae*, instead of *sine negotio* the expression used is *sine . . . fatigatione*.[3]

There are certain distinguishing characteristics which differentiate the three kinds of knowledge from one another. The first kind of knowledge is based upon sense-perception and is formed by means of imagination and memory. The second kind of knowledge, which consists of common notions and of conclusions derived from common notions, is likewise based upon sense-perception, but it is formed by the activity of the mind itself. The third kind of knowledge is entirely free from sense-perception and is formed both in the mind and by the mind. Again, like the first kind of knowledge and like the common notions in the second kind of knowledge, the third kind of knowledge is also a direct and

---

[1] Cf. Liddell and Scott, *Greek-English Lexicon*, 7th ed.; E. A. Sophocles, *Greek Lexicon of the Roman and Byzantine Periods*.

[2] *Fons Vitae*, III, 48 (p. 187); cf. below, p. 156.

[3] *Ibid.* (p. 369).

immediate sort of knowledge. It differs, however, from conclusions in the second kind of knowledge in that the latter
is mediate knowledge, deduced by syllogistic reasoning and
by means of a middle term from common notions, whereas
the former is immediate knowledge which is implicit in the
very nature and essence of the thing. Spinoza seems to express this distinction by saying, evidently with reference to
the distinction between the second and the third kinds of
knowledge, that in the former we reason "from universal
axioms alone (*ab axiomatibus solis universalibus*)," whereas in
the latter we form our thoughts "from some given definition
(*ex data aliqua definitione*)." [1] Now, the difference between
drawing conclusions from "universal axioms" and forming
thoughts from "some given definition," according to Aristotle, is this: In the case of the former, the knowledge is derived indirectly, syllogistically, and by means of a middle
term; in the case of the latter it is derived directly as the
unfolding of something which is implicit in the definition.[2]
Furthermore, an axiom is a universal, whereas a definition,
according to Aristotle, is neither a particular nor a universal.[3] Spinoza says somewhat in a similar way that the
definition deals with some particular affirmative essence
(*essentia aliqua particularis affirmativa*),[4] whereas axioms are
described by him as being universal. Hence in another
place he refers to the third kind of knowledge as knowledge of
individual objects (*rerum singularium cognitio*) and to the
second kind of knowledge as universal knowledge (*cognitio
universalis*).[5]

[1] *Tractatus de Intellectus Emendatione*, §§ 93–94 (*Opera*, II, p. 34, ll. 20–24).
[2] *Analytica Posteriora*, II, 10, 94a, 10 ff.
[3] *Ibid.*, I, 10, 77a, 4.
[4] *Tractatus de Intellectus Emendatione*, § 93 and § 98 (*Opera*, II, p. 34, l. 19; p. 36, ll. 3–4).
[5] *Ethics*, V, Prop. 36, Schol. (*Opera*, II, p. 303, ll. 17 and 19). Cf. above, p. 138.

The evaluation of the validity of these three kinds of knowledge is given by Spinoza in Proposition XLI: "Knowledge of the first kind alone is the cause of falsity; knowledge of the second and third orders is necessarily true." This proposition re-echoes the general view of philosophers throughout history which is formulated by Aristotle in the following statement: "Now of the thinking states by which we grasp truth, some are unfailingly true, others admit of error — δόξα, for instance, and λογισμός, whereas ἐπιστήμη and νοῦς are always true."[1] The exact meaning of some of the Greek terms in this passage is a debatable point, and they have been variously translated. But in two Latin translations made from the Hebrew of Averroes' Long Commentary on the *Analytica Posteriora*, published with Aristotle's works, the following Latin translations of the Greek terms are given: δόξα, *phantasia, imaginatio;* λογισμός, *opinio, computatio;* ἐπιστήμη, *sapientia, scientia;* νοῦς, *intellectus.*[2] From this commentary of Averroes, which was accessible in many editions, the passage quoted from Aristotle was taken to mean that imagination and opinion (δόξα and λογισμός), i.e., Spinoza's first kind of knowledge, admit of error, whereas discoursive knowledge (ἐπιστήμη) and intuition (νοῦς), i.e.,

---

[1] *Analytica Posteriora*, II, 19, 100b, 5–8. Cf. *Nicomachean Ethics*, VI, 3, 1139b, 15–18.

[2] The two Latin translations, one by Abraham de Balmes and the other by Giovanni Francesco Burana, of Averroes' interpretation of the Aristotelian passage in question read as follows:

ABRAHAM DE BALMES	BURANA
"Habitus autem qui in mente sunt, qui veraces sunt, quidam eorum sunt semper veraces; et quidam sunt, qui mendacium admittunt, prout sunt phantasia et opinio. Qui vero semper est verax, ipse est intellectus, et sapientia."	"Ex habitibus vero, qui sunt in intellectu, quibus verificamus, aliqui sunt veri semper, aliqui vero suscipiunt falsum, quemadmodum imaginatio et computatio: verus autem semper est intellectus et scientia."

(*Aristotelis Omnia Quae Extant Opera* . . . (Venetiis, apud Iuntas), Vol. I, Pars II (1574), fol. 567 r).

Spinoza's second and third kinds of knowledge, are unfailingly true.

But note that Spinoza does not say in Proposition XLI that the first kind of knowledge is false. He only says that it is the cause of falsity (*falsitatis causa*), that is to say, it may lead to falsity. Similarly in the *Short Treatise* he describes it as being merely "subject to error."[1] Aristotle, too, says of the two terms δόξα and λογισμός, which he includes under what corresponds to Spinoza's first kind of knowledge, that they only admit of falsity (ἐπιδέχονται τὸ ψεῦδος).[2] Descartes, too, while speaking of deduction and intuition, which correspond to Spinoza's second and third kinds of knowledge, as "the most certain routes to knowledge," refers to all the other modes of knowledge, which Spinoza would put under his first kind of knowledge, merely "as suspect of error and dangerous."[3] Sense-perception, imagination, and opinion Spinoza would admit are not always false. They only *may* be false, owing to the unreliability of our senses. What is it then that serves as a judge to decide which of our sense perceptions, or imaginations, or opinions are true and which are false? It is not the first kind of knowledge itself, says Spinoza, which verifies its own perceptions, but it is the second and third kinds of knowledge. Hence Proposition XLII: "It is the knowledge of the second and third, and not that of the first kind, which teaches us to distinguish the true from the false." Thus the second and third kinds of knowledge are not only sources of true knowledge by their own right, but they are also the criteria of the truth of the knowledge of the first kind.

But while the second and the third kinds of knowledge are the criteria of the first kind, Spinoza now wants to say in

---

[1] *Short Treatise*, II, 1, § 2.   [2] *Analytica Posteriora*, II, 19, 100b, 7.
[3] *Regulae ad Directionem Ingenii*, III (*Oeuvres*, X, p. 370, ll. 16–19).

Proposition XLIII that the mind itself is the criterion of the second and third kinds of knowledge. But before we take up this proposition we shall first discuss a passage in Aristotle which may be considered as the source of this proposition, and then we shall discuss certain passages in the *Tractatus de Intellectus Emendatione* which seem to reflect that source.

Demonstrative knowledge, the kind of knowledge which Spinoza describes as second, must, according to Aristotle, begin with certain principles which are undemonstrable and immediately known. Were it not so, he argues, then one demonstration would require another demonstration, and the other still another, and so on to infinity, which is impossible.[1] The primary premises of syllogisms must therefore be known immediately by the intellect (νοῦς).[2] As a result of this, "intellect (νοῦς, intuition) will be the originative source of demonstrative knowledge (ἐπιστήμη)."[3]

Spinoza proceeds in the same manner to prove that his second kind of knowledge rests ultimately upon the third kind, i.e., the power of the mind itself. Like Aristotle he denies the possibility of an infinite regress of demonstrations. "To this end, we must first consider that there is here no search *ad infinitum;* that is to say, in order that the best method of discovering the truth may be found, there is no need of another method for investigating the method of investigating the truth, and in order that the second method may be investigated there is no need of a third, and so on *ad infinitum*, for in this way we shall never arrive at a knowledge of the truth, nor indeed at any knowledge."[4] This second kind of knowledge must ultimately rest upon the intellect,

[1] *Analytica Posteriora*, I, 3, 72b, 5–22; cf. II, 19, 100b, 12–14.
[2] *Ibid.*, II, 19, 100b, 12. [3] *Ibid.*, 100b, 15.
[4] *Tractatus de Intellectus Emendatione*, § 30 (*Opera*, II, p. 13, ll. 17–23).

which "by its own native force forms for itself intellectual instruments by which it acquires additional strength for other intellectual works, and from these works other instruments or power of further discovery, and thus by degrees advances until it reaches the pinnacle of wisdom."[1] But "there must before everything else exist in us a true idea which is as it were an innate instrument."[2] The test of such a true idea is its self-evidence, and the certainty which it provokes in the mind of those who possess it, for "the mind acts according to certain laws, and as if, so to speak, it were a sort of spiritual automaton,"[3] with the result that one of the functions of the mind is "that it involves certitude,"[4] that is to say, it knows truth when it presents itself to it. Consequently, "if anybody had been led by good fortune to proceed in this way in the investigation of nature, that is to say, by acquiring ideas in their proper order according to the standard of a given true idea, he would never have doubted of their truth, because the truth, as we have shown, is self evident and all things would have flowed spontaneously towards him." [5]

All this reasoning, the Aristotelian background and his own statements in the *Tractatus de Intellectus Emendatione*, lies behind Proposition XLIII: "He who has a true idea knows at the same time that he has a true idea, nor can he doubt the truth of the thing." In the Scholium to this proposition he explains the nature of the internal criterion of truth as distinguished from the external, and he uses phrases and expressions which are similar to those used by him in the *Tractatus de Intellectus Emendatione*.

[1] *Ibid.*, § 31 (p. 14, ll. 4–7).
[2] *Ibid.*, § 39 (p. 16, ll. 13–14).
[3] *Ibid.*, § 85 (p. 32, ll. 24–25).
[4] *Ibid.*, § 108 (p. 38, l. 32).
[5] *Ibid.*, § 44 (p. 17, ll. 16–20).   Cf. above, pp. 99 ff.

There is, however, a difference between the second and the third kind of knowledge. Although both these kinds of knowledge are formed by the mind and are tested by the mind itself for their validity and truth, still they differ in one fundamental respect. The common notions of Spinoza's second kind of knowledge, like the immediate premises in Aristotle's demonstrative knowledge,[1] are ultimately in their final analysis traceable to sense-perception. They are considered to be the work of the intellect only because it is the intellect which transforms these sense-perceptions into scientific universal notions. Spinoza's third kind of knowledge, however, is of a different nature. It has no connection with sense-perception at all. It is "formed purely by the mind," says Spinoza, "and not by fortuitous movements of the body."[2] It is generated within the mind itself, because the human mind is part of the infinite intellect of God. "We must remember, besides," says Spinoza, "that our mind, in so far as it truly perceives things, is part of the infinite intellect of God (Corol. Prop. XI, Pt. II), and therefore it must be that the clear and distinct ideas of the mind are as true as those of God."[3]

Now what is the nature of this third kind of knowledge? The term "intuitive" by which it is described merely explains that it is immediate. Immediacy, according to Descartes, is the essential characteristic of intuition as a source of knowledge.[4] But what is its source, and how does it arise?

The so-called innate ideas would naturally suggest themselves to our mind as something similar to Spinoza's third kind of knowledge. However, the term innate ideas is in itself

[1] *Analytica Posteriora*, II, 19, 99b, 20 ff.
[2] *Tractatus de Intellectus Emendatione*, § 91 (*Opera*, II, p. 34, ll. 3–4).
[3] *Ethics*, II, Prop. 43, Schol.
[4] Cf. *Regulae ad Directionem Ingenii*, III (*Oeuvres*, X, p. 368, ll. 14 ff.).

a vague term and has been used by historians as a description for a variety of kinds of knowledge which differ in origin
and nature. First, Aristotle's primary principles (ἀρχαί) or
immediate premises (προτάσεις ἄμεσοι) are sometimes spoken
of as innate despite the fact that he himself definitely says
that they are neither inherent (ἐνοῦσαι) nor not-inherent
(οὐκ ἐνοῦσαι)[1] in us, but that they are developed by our mind
out of our capacity of sense-perception. Second, Plato's
theory of reminiscence is also sometimes spoken of as a
theory of innate ideas,[2] though Plato's knowledge has a
definite external, though a super-sensible, source, namely, the
world of ideas. Third, Cicero speaks of the idea of God as
being innate in the sense that it is generated in the mind itself, it is congenital with man, and has neither an external
sensible or external super-sensible source.[3] In the Middle
Ages Jewish philosophers, too, speak of a sort of immediate
knowledge which is generated in the mind and is independent of sense-perception. Thus Ibn Gabirol says that
" the action of the intellect is the apprehension of all the intelligible forms in no-time and in no-place, without any investigation (inquisitione), without any labor (negotio), and
without any other cause except its own essence, for it is completely perfect."[4] But even this passage does not definitely
make it clear that there is no external super-sensible source
of this knowledge of the intellect, for the intelligible forms
which the intellect comprehends seem to have come from
somewhere and are not generated by the mind itself. Similarly other Jewish philosophers, speaking of Aristotle's immediate propositions or axioms or primary notions, as they
call them, say that they come to the mind by divine inspira-

---

[1] *Analytica Posteriora*, II, 19, 99b, 25 and 30–32.
[2] Cf. P. Janet et G. Séailles, *Histoire de la Philosophie* (12th ed., Paris, 1921), p. 118.   [3] *De Natura Deorum*, I, 17, § 44; II, 4, § 12.
[4] *Fons Vitae*, III, 48 (p. 187); *Likkute Mekor Ḥayyim*, III, 30.

tion.[1] But here, again, does this mean that they are implanted in the mind by God, or does it mean that they are formed out of sense-perception with the assistance of divine inspiration? In either case, they have an external source, though, as in Plato, it may be only a super-sensible external source. The same is probably also true of the innate ideas which are mentioned by the Schoolmen. Even with regard to the chief exponent of innate ideas in modern philosophy, Descartes, we cannot be altogether certain what he means by them. One of his innate ideas, at least, the idea of God, has a super-sensible external source, namely, God.

Now, what is the exact meaning of Spinoza's third kind of knowledge? It is quite certain that, unlike the so-called innate ideas of Aristotle, it has no external sensible source. But is it like the innate ideas of Plato and of the mediaevals, which have a super-sensible external source? Or is it like the Ciceronian innate ideas, having no external source at all? No direct answer to this question is given by Spinoza. The only passage which seems to have a bearing upon it is that in which he denies the Platonic theory of recollection,[2] from which it may be inferred positively that the third kind of knowledge is not a form of recollection, but it sheds no light on the question as to whether it is without any super-sensible external source at all. The cumulative effect of Spinoza's utterances on this subject, however, is that his third kind of knowledge combines in itself elements of both these meanings of innate ideas. In so far as the human mind is part of the infinite intellect of God, it gets its ideas from God; the ideas of the third kind of knowledge are thus the equivalent of those kinds of innate ideas which have a super-sensible

[1] *Cuzari*, V, 12; *Emunah Ramah*, II, iv, 1 (pp. 58 and 60). Cf. my paper "Notes on the Proofs of the Existence of God in Jewish Philosophy" in *Hebrew Union College Annual*, I (1924), pp. 581–582.

[2] *Ethics*, V, Prop. 23, Schol. Cf. below, p. 296.

source. Spinoza thus says in his description of the third kind of knowledge that "we must remember, besides, that our mind, in so far as it truly perceives things, is a part of the infinite intellect of God (Corol. Prop. XI, Pt. II), and therefore it must be that the clear and distinct ideas of the mind are as true as those of God." [1] But on the other hand, inasmuch as the God of Spinoza is not an external cause from whom the human mind emanates or by whom it is created, but is rather an immanent cause within which the human mind is contained [2] or a whole of which the human mind is a part, to say that the human mind gets its ideas from God means that the ideas are generated within it and do not come from any source which may be called external in any sense whatsoever.

With this explanation of the nature of the second and third kinds of knowledge, Spinoza proceeds to enumerate the things which are included under these two kinds of knowledge.[3] Under the second kind of knowledge he is going to mention only the common notions [4] which form the basis of knowledge derived from them by the art of reasoning. Now these common notions, as we have already shown, when taken only with regard to physical bodies, are the modes of extension, i.e., motion and rest and their laws and rules, which are common to all things.[5] Motion and rest are what Spinoza calls the immediate infinite and eternal modes of extension, and they are also called by him the fixed and eternal things.[6] It is these which in Propositions XLIV–XLVI Spinoza identifies with the common notions — one of the three subject-matters of the second kind of knowledge. The task of enumerating the subject-matter of the third class

---

[1] *Ibid.*, II, Prop. 43, Schol. [2] Cf. above, Vol. I, p. 323.
[3] For the subject-matter of the first kind of knowledge, see above, pp. 106–109.
[4] For simple ideas and conclusions, see above, pp. 112–113, 117, 129–130.
[5] Cf. above, p. 126. [6] Cf. above, Vol. I, pp. 242, 251.

of knowledge is not a long one, for, as Spinoza says elsewhere, "the things which I can as yet understand by this
kind of knowledge are very few." [1] This statement seems to
be directly aimed at Descartes, who, after enumerating several examples of intuitive knowledge, such as man's knowledge of the fact that he exists, and that he thinks; that the
triangle is bounded by three lines only, and the sphere by
a single superficies, concludes that "facts of such a kind are
far more numerous than many people think, disdaining as
they do to direct their attention upon such simple matters." [2]
Spinoza does not seem to think that the objects of the third
kind of knowledge are numerous. Leaving out mathematical
concepts and other entities of reason, of which he treats
elsewhere and gives several illustrations,[3] especially that
of the rule of three,[4] and confining himself to what he calls
elsewhere "physical entities and realities,"[5] he mentions in
Proposition XLVII the "knowledge of the eternal and infinite essence of God."

But let us now work out the details of Propositions XLIV–
XLVII. From the time of Aristotle particular sublunar
things were regarded as having a double aspect. In themselves they were regarded as transient things, generated and
corruptible, subject to chance and accident, and hence by
their own nature only contingent. But regarded as part of
the entire universe they are both eternal and necessary.
Their matter is an eternal matter and their motion is an
eternal motion, and that eternal motion of theirs proceeds
directly by necessity from the Prime Mover, and follows

---

[1] *Tractatus de Intellectus Emendatione*, § 22 (*Opera*, II, p. 11, ll. 18–19).

[2] *Regulae ad Directionem Ingenii*, III (*Oeuvres*, X, p. 368, ll. 22–27).

[3] Cf. above, p. 144.

[4] *Tractatus de Intellectus Emendatione*, à 22 (*Opera*, II, p. 12, ll. 7–14). *Ethics*, II,
Prop. 40, Schol. 2.

[5] Cf. above, pp. 126, 144.

thence by an unbroken causal nexus. When we call something accidental or contingent we do not mean that it has no
cause, but that its cause is an indefinite one or that it cannot
be definitely determined by our knowledge.[1] In the Middle
Ages that sort of double aspect of things is spoken of as a
distinction in things between their being possible in themselves and their being necessary with reference to their cause
— a distinction which we have discussed before on several
occasions and to which, as we have seen, Spinoza makes several references.[2]

Now, this way of viewing things in their causal connection, as something necessary and eternal, is the act of the
intellect, which, says Maimonides, represents things "in
their true form as well as in their causal relations," whereas
"imagination," he continues, "has none of these functions,
for it only perceives the individual and the compound in
that aggregate condition in which it presents itself to the
senses."[3] Spinoza draws a similar distinction between intellect and imagination. Imagination sees things only in
their fragmentary and unrelated condition, or it puts together "diverse confused ideas which belong to diverse
things and operations in nature."[4] It is the imagination, too,
through which "we look upon things as contingent with
reference to both the past and the future."[5] But reason
(ratio), which is one of Spinoza's technical terms for the second kind of knowledge,[6] sees things in their necessary and
eternal aspect. Hence Proposition XLIV and Corollary II:

---

[1] *Metaphysics*, V, 30, 1025a, 24. Cf. above, p. 109, and Vol. I, p. 189.

[2] Cf. above, Vol. I, pp. 188 ff.; 310.

[3] *Moreh Nebukim*, I, 73, note to Prop. 10.

[4] *Tractatus de Intellectus Emendatione*, § 64 (*Opera*, II, p. 24, ll. 27–28). Cf.
above, pp. 82 ff.

[5] *Ethics*, II, Prop. 44, Corol. 1.

[6] *Ibid.*, II, Prop. 40, Schol. 2. Cf. above, p. 145.

"It is not of the nature of reason to consider things as contingent, but as necessary" and "it is of the nature of reason to perceive things under a certain form of eternity (*sub quadam aeternitatis specie*)."

These necessary and eternal aspects of things, Spinoza proceeds to say, are the immediate infinite modes: motion and rest under extension, and the absolutely infinite intellect under thought. These infinite modes, again, are what Spinoza calls the "fixed and eternal things," without which, as without substance, individual things "can neither be nor be conceived," and which, "on account of their presence everywhere and their extensive power, will be like universals to us, or, so to speak, the *genera* of the definitions of individual mutable things, and the proximate causes of all things." [1] What he means to say is that the infinite modes are related to all things as genera in the traditional conception of a definition are related to the things defined in terms of genus and species, or as proximate causes in Spinoza's own conception of a definition are related to things defined in terms of proximate causation. [2] Hence Proposition XLV: "Every idea of any body or actual existing thing necessarily involves the eternal and infinite essence of God," or, as he states it more specifically elsewhere, the "idea of the body neither involves nor expresses any other attributes of God than extension and thought." [3] It is through these infinite modes or the "fixed and eternal things" that the individual things are best known and understood, for "while it seems to be by no means easy to arrive at a knowledge of these individual things, for to conceive all things simultaneously is a work far beyond the strength of the human intellect," [4] it is possible for man to

---

[1] *Tractatus de Intellectus Emendatione*, § 101 (*Opera*, II, p. 37, ll. 4–9).
[2] Cf. above, Vol. 1, pp. 383 ff.   [3] Epistola 64.
[4] *Tractatus de Intellectus Emendatione*, § 102 (*Opera*, II, p. 37, ll. 10–12).

have an adequate and perfect knowledge of the necessary and eternal aspect of the individual things, of the so-called "fixed and eternal things," or the motion and rest of bodies and their laws and rules, and even of the minds of bodies. Hence Proposition XLVI: "The knowledge of the eternal and infinite essence of God which each idea involves is adequate and perfect." This, then, constitutes the subject-matter of the second kind of knowledge.

As for the subject-matter of the third kind of knowledge, it is the knowledge of God. Such a knowledge is immediate, clear, and distinct, for we could have no true knowledge at all unless we possessed a "standard of truth," which is, "in fact, a being single and infinite, in other words, it is the sum total of being, beyond which there is no being found."[1] We know that such a being exists by proofs generally called ontological, which really means that we know Him immediately and directly and on the principle that "if such a Being did not exist, it could never be produced"[2] in our mind. Hence Proposition XLVII: "The human mind possesses an adequate knowledge of the eternal and infinite essence of God." This is the subject-matter of the third kind of knowledge.

In conclusion Spinoza tries to show the difference between our knowledge of the common notions, which belongs to the second kind of knowledge, and our knowledge of God, which belongs to the third kind of knowledge. Both are immediate knowledge. Both are knowledge which is formed by the mind. Both are knowledge which is common to all men.[3] But still there is a difference between them. The common notions are formed by the mind from that which the body has in common with other bodies,[4] whereas the idea of God arises in the

---

[1] *Ibid.*, § 76 (p. 29, ll. 16–18).   [2] *Ibid.*, § 76, note a (p. 29).
[3] *Ethics*, II, Prop. 38, Corol., and Prop. 47, Schol.
[4] *Ibid.*, Prop. 39.

mind itself by virtue of its being a part of the infinite intellect of God. It is because of this that "men do not possess a knowledge of God as distinct as that which they have of common notions," for "they cannot imagine God as they can bodies." The ordinary knowledge that men have of God is erroneous knowledge, arising as it does from their habit of attaching "the name of God to the images of things which they are accustomed to see, an error they can hardly avoid, inasmuch as they are continually affected by external bodies."[1]

Let us now outline the result of our discussion in these last two chapters of Spinoza's classification of the various types of knowledge:

A. Inadequate knowledge, which includes:
    I. First kind of knowledge, consisting of
        (*a*) Sense perception, experience, vague experience;
        (*b*) Hearsay, hearing, some sign, signs.
B. Adequate knowledge, which includes:
    II. Second kind of knowledge, consisting of
        (*a*) Simple ideas and
        (*b*) Common notions, and
        (*c*) Deductions drawn therefrom, either as
            (1) Cause from effect or as
            (2) Conclusion from premises.
    III. Third kind of knowledge, derived either from the
        (*a*) Definition of a created thing, or from the
        (*b*) Definition of an uncreated thing, i.e., the idea of God and ideas related to God.

---

[1] *Ibid.*, Prop. 47, Schol.

CHAPTER XVII

WILL

In the plan which Spinoza had in mind for the *Ethics*, the Second Part, which deals with man, was to conclude with a denial of human freedom of the will, just as the First Part of the *Ethics*, which deals with God, concludes with a denial of divine will, its freedom and its purposiveness. But in order to deny freedom of the will one must first explain what is generally meant by will. And so in the remaining two propositions of the Second Part Spinoza begins in Proposition XLVIII with a statement of his main topic, namely, the denial of the freedom of the will, and then passes on, in the Scholium to this proposition and in Proposition XLIX, to a discussion of the general nature of will. In our presentation of the views of Spinoza on these two points, we shall start with the latter point. In fact, this is Spinoza's method of procedure in the corresponding chapters in the *Short Treatise* (Part II, Chapters XVI–XVIII). Before we try to ascertain whether the "well-being of a perfect man" is attained "voluntarily or of necessity," he says, "it is necessary to inquire what the will is." [1]

In Aristotle the nature of will is determined by its relation to sensation and thought, on the one hand, and to desire, on the other. Neither sensation nor thought, according to Aristotle, affirms or negates. Sensation merely asserts that there is an object, and thought merely asserts that there is an image of an object. "Sensation, then," says Aristotle, "is analogous to simple assertion or to simple ap

[1] *Short Treatise*, II, 16, § 1.

prehension by thought," [1] and "to the thinking soul images serve as present sensations." [2] "The speculative intellect," he says again, "thinks nothing that is practical and makes no assertion about what is to be avoided or pursued." [3] It is desire which converts the simple assertions of the sense and of the intellect into affirmations and negations, and it is this which prompts pursuit and avoidance. Now the original Greek term ὄρεξις, for which we have used the English "desire" as a translation, literally means propension or inclination, and it is this literal meaning of the term which describes its nature according to Aristotle. Desire itself is an inclination to and hence a pursuit of what has already been determined for it as pleasant, or as good, or as true; and, contrariwise, it is an avoidance of what has already been determined for it as painful, or as evil, or as false. But that which determines whether a thing is pleasant, good, or true is not desire itself, but rather sensation, imagination, or intellect. Sensation or imagination determines whether a thing is pleasant or painful, the practical intellect determines whether a thing is good or evil, and the speculative intellect determines whether a thing is true or false. [4] The determination by the rational part of the soul, i.e., the practical or speculative intellect, that a thing is good or true is called will (βούλησις), whereas the determination by the irrational part of the soul, i.e., sensation and imagination, that a thing is pleasant is called concupiscence (ἐπιθυμία). [5] But as the pleasant may be bad and false and still the soul unguided by the rational faculty may pursue it, concupiscence is called an irrational desire, as contrasted with will

[1] *De Anima*, III, 7, 431a, 8.
[2] *Ibid.*, 14–15.
[3] *Ibid.*, III, 9, 432b, 27–28.
[4] *Ibid.*, III, 7, 431b, 6–12; cf. *Nicomachean Ethics*, VI, 2, 1139a, 27–31.
[5] *De Anima*, III, 9, 432b, 5–6.

which is a rational desire. Neither of these two, however, is distinct either from sense and intellect, on the one hand, or from desire, on the other. Only in the manner of their being (τὸ εἶναι) do they differ, that is to say, the differences between them are only essential or logical.[1]

These Aristotelian views on will are reflected in Spinoza. On the whole, we may reduce all of Spinoza's utterances on will to three main assertions. (1) There is a difference in some respect between will and desire. (2) Will is only a universal concept, and not a real entity. (3) Will is identical with intellect. All these three assertions, we shall try to show, are directly taken from Aristotle or can be indirectly traced to him.

In the first place, Spinoza reproduces in *Short Treatise*, II, 17, Aristotle's views on the meaning of ὄρεξις, βούλησις, and ἐπιθυμία. Using for these three Greek terms respectively the Latin terms *cupiditas*, *voluntas*, and *voluptas*, he says quite properly, though with some hesitation as to its accurateness, that "according to Aristotle's definition, desire appears to be a genus containing two species . . . whence it appears to me that by desire (or *cupiditas* [= ὄρεξις]) he means any inclination, be it towards good, be it towards evil; but when the inclination is only towards what is or appears to be good . . . he calls it *voluntas* [= βούλησις] or good will; while, if it is bad . . . he calls it *voluptas* [= ἐπιθυμία] or bad will." This fundamental distinction between will and desire as that between an affirmation of what is good and a mere inclination toward it, which Spinoza reproduces in this chapter of the *Short Treatise* in the name of Aristotle, runs throughout his statements in its preceding

---

[1] *Ibid.*, III, 7, 431a, 13–14, 19–20. For the meaning of τὸ εἶναι, see G. Rodier's note on *De Anima*, II, 1, 412b, 11, in his *Aristote, Traité de l'Ame* (1900), Vol. II, p. 180.

chapter. "The power to affirm and deny is called will," [1] whereas "desire, we have said, is the inclination which the soul has towards something which it chooses as a good." [2] The will, he says again, is "regarded as affirmation or decision." [3] Finally, in a long passage in which he restates the view of "those who maintain that there is a will," he says that the will "is only the activity of the understanding whereby we affirm or deny something about a thing, with regard to good or evil . . . while desire is the inclination, which we only subsequently feel, to advance it." [4] Thus also Descartes states that "the faculty of will consists alone in our having the power of choosing to do a thing or choosing not to do it (that is, to affirm or deny, to pursue or to shun it)." [5]

In the *Ethics* Spinoza similarly restates the same fundamental distinction between will (*voluntas*) and desire (*cupiditas*), though it would seem that, unlike his statements in the *Short Treatise*, where the affirmations and denials of the will are those concerned with good and evil, or what Aristotle would call the affirmations and denials of the practical intellect, in the *Ethics* the affirmations and denials of the will are those concerned with truth and falsehood, or what Aristotle would call the affirmations and denials of the speculative intellect. Spinoza thus says: "By the will (*voluntas*) I understand a faculty . . . by which the mind affirms or denies that which is true or false, and not a desire (*cupiditas*) by which the mind seeks a thing or turns away from it." [6]

---

[1] *Short Treatise*, II, 16, § 2 (*Opera*, I, p. 80, ll. 22–23).

[2] *Ibid.*, § 2 (p. 80, ll. 18–19).

[3] *Ibid.*, § 2, note 1 (p. 80, l. 24). In this note he tries to show how will differs from the first and second kinds of knowledge.

[4] *Ibid.*, § 8 (p. 84, ll. 18–28).

[5] *Meditationes*, IV (*Oeuvres*, VII, p. 57, ll. 21–23). Cf. above, Vol. I, p. 406.

[6] *Ethics*, II, Prop. 48, Schol.

It is this restriction of will to decisions of the speculative intellect with regard to questions of truth and falsehood that is hinted at by Spinoza in the following passage: "This effort (*conatus*), when it is related to mind alone, is called will (*voluntas*), but when it is related at the same time to mind and body, is called appetite (*appetitus*)," which, as he proceeds to explain, does not differ in its essential meaning from desire (*cupiditas*).[1] But even in the *Ethics* he occasionally uses "will" with reference to the decisions of the practical intellect, as when he uses, for instance, the expression "will (*voluntas*) or desire (*appetitus*) of doing good." [2]

The second point that Spinoza tries to make about the nature of will is to deny that it exists as something real in nature. As real entities in nature there are only certain individual volitions, for which the term "will" is used only as a general name. In the *Short Treatise* he describes will, and sometimes also intellect, invariably as "an *ens rationis*, and not an *ens reale*," [3] or as "not a thing in nature, but only a fiction (*verzieringe*)," [4] or as a universal.[5] And what is true of will, he says in the *Ethics*, is also true of understanding (*intelligendi*), desiring (*cupiendi*), loving (*amandi*), and the other faculties. They are "either altogether fictitious (*fictitias*), or else are nothing but metaphysical or universal entities (*entia metaphysica, vel universalia*)." [6] "The intellect and will, therefore, are related to this or that idea or volition as rockiness is related to this or that rock, or as man is related to Peter or Paul." [7] This conception of intellect and will as universals of the anti-realistic type is not to be

---

[1] *Ibid.*, III, Prop. 9, Schol.
[2] *Ibid.*, III, Prop. 27, Corol. 3, Schol.
[3] *Short Treatise*, II, 16, § 4 (*Opera*, I, p. 83, l. 4).
[4] *Ibid.*, § 4 (ll. 6–7).   [5] *Ibid.*, § 3, note 2 (p. 81, l. 19).
[6] *Ethics*, II, Prop. 48, Schol.
[7] *Ibid.*; cf. Epistola 2 (*Opera*, IV, p. 9, ll. 14–16).

taken as something in opposition to Aristotle, but rather as an interpretation and development of Aristotle's views. Despite his use of the term "faculty" (δύναμις) in connection with intellect and will, Aristotle did not consider them to have any greater reality than such universals as rockiness and man. His rejection of Plato's conception of the trichotomy of the soul,[1] his insistence upon the unity of the soul,[2] his statement that there is no soul apart from the powers of the soul such as nutrition, appetency, sensation, locomotion, and understanding, any more than there is figure apart from triangle, quadrilateral, and the rest,[3] and finally his contention that the appetitive function (ὀρεκτικόν) and will (βούλησις) are only essentially or logically different from the sensitive faculty and the faculty of thought (διανοητική)[4] — out of all these one could develop the view upheld by Spinoza that the faculties of will and understanding are only universals. This view that the soul and its faculties are nothing but universals and, to use Spinoza's pointed characterization, "are related to this or that idea or volition as rockiness is related to this or that rock, or as man is related to Peter or Paul,"[5] could have also been inferred from Aristotle's statement that "in a manner the soul is all existent things, for they are all either objects of sensation or objects of thought; and knowledge and sensation are in a manner identical with their respective objects."[6]

It is also the Aristotelian contention that rational desire or will is only essentially or logically distinguished from thought that must have given rise to Spinoza's third point

---

[1] *De Anima*, I, 5, 411b, 5 ff.; III, 9, 432b, 3 ff.
[2] *Ibid.*, II, 2, 413b, 13 ff.; II, 3, 414b, 20 ff.
[3] Cf. *ibid.*, II, 3, 414b, 20–22; I, 1, 402b, 5–8.
[4] Cf. *ibid.*, III, 7, 431a, 13–20; III, 9, 432b, 3–6.
[5] *Ethics*, II, Prop. 48, Schol.　　　[6] *De Anima*, III, 8, 431b, 21–23.

about will, namely, that "the will and intellect are one and the same."[1] When Aristotle says, for instance, that "pursuit and avoidance in the sphere of desire correspond to affirmation and denial in the sphere of the intellect,"[2] and when he further says that "with speculative thought, which is not concerned with action and production, right and wrong functioning consist in the attainment of truth and falsehood respectively,"[3] it is quite legitimate to infer from his statements that the will, which is defined by Spinoza in the *Ethics* as the faculty "by which the mind affirms or denies that which is true or false,"[4] is "only a certain mode of thought, like the intellect,"[5] and that "in the mind there is no volition or affirmation and negation excepting that which the idea, in so far as it is an idea, involves."[6] The full explanation of this view is clearly given in the Demonstration of Proposition XLIX of the Second Part of the *Ethics*. In the *Short Treatise* he states it in the following terms: "The understanding is purely passive; it is an awareness, in the soul, of the essence and existence of things; so that it is never we who affirm or deny something of a thing, but it is the thing itself that affirms or denies, in us, something of itself."[7] The first part of this passage is only a restatement of the view we reproduced above from Aristotle that intellect itself neither affirms nor denies, but that it merely asserts the existence of an image of an object.[8]

---

[1] *Ethics*, II, Prop. 49, Corol.

[2] *Nicomachean Ethics*, VI, 2, 1139a, 21–22.

[3] *Ibid.*, 27–29.

[4] *Ethics*, II, Prop. 48, Schol. Cf. above, p. 167.

[5] *Ibid.*, I, Prop. 32, Demonst. That will is only a mode of thought is also maintained by Descartes. Cf. *Correspondance*, LXXIII bis (*Oeuvres*, I, p. 366, ll. 3–5): "Car vouloir, entendre, imaginer, sentir, etc., ne sont que des diverses façons de penser."   [6] *Ibid.*, II, Prop. 49.

[7] *Short Treatise*, II, 16, § 5 (*Opera*, I, p. 83, ll. 13–17).

[8] Cf. above, pp. 164–165.

In the light of what we have shown before, as may be recalled, that in mediaeval philosophy will and intellect are
as a rule identified in God, and that Spinoza refers to this
as the view of "those who have maintained that God's intellect, will, and power are one and the same thing," [1] his
insistence here upon the identity of will and intellect in man
assumes the form of a challenge to his opponents. You say,
he argues, that will and intellect, though identical in God,
are still two distinct faculties in man. I contend that in man
no less than in God they are identical, for by the very same
proof-texts from Aristotle that you can justify their identity
in God I can also justify their identity in man.

In the *Short Treatise*, however, he goes still further and
discusses the view of those who would have intellect and will
two different faculties in man. According to his restatement
of this view, — and he must have had Descartes, among
others, in mind,[2] — understanding and will are regarded by
its proponents as "necessarily distinct, and really distinct
substances." But "as the soul is said to direct these two
substances," Spinoza argues, "it must be a third substance."
But "all these things are so confused," he says, "that it is
impossible to have a clear and distinct conception about
them."[3] The main trend of his criticism of this view is to
show that by conceiving soul, understanding, and will as
distinct entities or substances it will be difficult to establish a satisfactory relation between them and to explain
adequately how they act upon one another and are acted
upon by one another.[4]

These, then, are three points which Spinoza established
with regard to the nature of the will. First, will, as dis-

---

[1] *Ethics*, I, Prop. 17, Schol. Cf. above, Vol. I, p. 317.
[2] Cf. *Principia Philosophiae*, I, 32-35.
[3] *Short Treatise*, II, 16, § 3, note 2 (*Opera*, I, p. 81, ll. 21-26).
[4] *Ibid.*, § 3, note 2 (p. 81, l. 27-p. 82, l. 21).

tinguished from desire, is the faculty of the affirmation or
donial of that which is true or false. Second, like intellect,
will is only a universal of the anti-realistic type: there is no
will apart from the individual volitions, just as there is no
intellect apart from the individual ideas. Third, will and intellect are one and the same thing. Spinoza now returns to
his main problem, to show that the will is not free,[1] and with
this also to deny the freedom of other faculties, such as understanding, desiring, loving, etc.,[2] all of which, like will, are
only modes of thought.[3]

The argument by which Spinoza proves here the impossibility of freedom is the stock argument of the mediaevals,
which has already been used by him in the Demonstration
of Proposition XXXII of the First Part of the *Ethics*. The
argument is based upon the principle of causality. It is
summed up in the statement that every affirmation or act
of the will must be determined by a cause, which must in its
turn be determined by another cause, and so on *ad infinitum*.[4] This necessarily leads to the conclusion that all affirmations and acts of the will are caused not by themselves
but by God, who is the ultimate cause of everything.[5] This
conception of God as the cause of all things does not imply
a belief in God as creator, for even if creation is denied and
the world is assumed to be eternal, God is still to be conceived of as the cause of the world, for "the same activity
is required of God in order to maintain a thing in existence
as to create it." [6] Since no affirmation or act of the will can
be brought about without a cause, the will is not free, for

---

[1] *Ethics*, II, Prop. 48.   [2] *Ibid.*, II, Prop. 48, Demonst.   [3] *Ibid.*, II, Axiom 3.
[4] Cf. *ibid.*, II, Prop. 48, Demonst.; *Short Treatise*, II, 16, § 3 (*Opera*, I, p. 81,
l. 4–p. 82, l. 2); Epistola 2 (*Opera*, IV, p. 9, ll. 16–20).
[5] Cf. above, pp. 110 ff.
[6] *Short Treatise*, II, 16, § 3, note 2 (*Opera*, I, p. 82, ll. 24 25). Cf. above, Vol. I,
pp. 203–204.

by definition "that thing is called free which exists from the necessity of its own nature alone, and is determined to action by itself alone." [1] This argument, which Spinoza applies first to will, is applied by him also to understanding, desire, and the other modes of thought. In the *Ethics* he simply says concerning the latter that "in the same manner it is demonstrated that in the mind there exists no absolute faculty of understanding, desiring, loving, etc." [2] In the *Short Treatise*, however, he restates the argument in its special application to desire. [3] The conclusion at which he arrives is that there is no freedom either in the conceptions formed by the mind, or in the affirmations or denials about the truth or falsehood of these conceptions, or in the pursuit or avoidance by the mind of good or evil. [4]

The Scholium to Proposition XLIX with which the Second Part concludes corresponds to the Appendix with which the First Part concludes. In the symmetrical construction of the first two parts of the *Ethics*, the First Part, about God, concludes with a discussion of design, which is a certain phase of the alleged freedom of the divine will, and the Second Part, about man, similarly concludes with a discussion of certain phases of the alleged freedom of the human will. That in the First Part the concluding discussion is called Appendix and in the Second Part it is called Scholium makes only a verbal difference. We have shown above that with the exception of the first paragraph in the Appendix, which discusses the general problem of the First Part, the Appendix is really a Scholium to the last proposition. Similarly, here, though the Scholium belongs to the last proposition, or rather to the last two propositions, the opening of it is really an Appendix to the Second Part, discussing as it does its

---

[1] *Ethics*, I, Def. 7.
[2] *Ibid.*, II, Prop. 48, Demonst.
[3] *Short Treatise*, II, 17, § 5.
[4] *Ethics*, II, Prop. 49.

central problem, namely, that of truth and falsehood. Furthermore, just as the Appendix was divided by Spinoza himself into three parts, so the Scholium here is divided by him into three parts: I. A few additional remarks on the question of freedom. II. Objections and answers with regard to Spinoza's own view on freedom. III. Some advantages of his own view on freedom.

In his additional remarks he points out that one of the reasons why men are led to the belief in the freedom of the will, and especially to the belief in the freedom of affirming and denying, is their failure to distinguish between images, words, and ideas.[1] Elsewhere he has succinctly summarized the relation between these three terms in his statement that words "are nothing but signs of things as they exist in the imagination, and not as they exist in the intellect."[2]

The objections against his view on will and its freedom which Spinoza discusses here are four in number.

The first objection is based upon the assumption that will extends more widely than the intellect, and is directed against Spinoza's view that will is indistinguishable from the intellect. Here in the *Ethics* Spinoza reproduces this assumption anonymously, but in letters to Oldenburg[3] and Blyenbergh[4] he describes it as the view of Descartes.[5] His answer to this objection is twofold. First, while admitting that "will extends itself more widely than the intellect, if by the intellect we understand only clear and distinct ideas," he denies that it extends itself more widely "than the perceptions or the faculty of conception (*perceptiones, sive*

---

[1] *Ibid.*, II, 16, § 6 (*Opera*, I, p. 83, ll. 18–30).
[2] *Tractatus de Intellectus Emendatione*, § 89 (*Opera*, II, p. 33, ll. 13–15). Cf. above, pp. 137–138.   [3] Epistola 2 (*Opera*, IV, p. 9, ll. 5–6).
[4] Epistola 21 (*Opera*, IV, p. 129, ll. 28–32).
[5] *Principia Philosophiae*, I, 35; *Principia Philosophiae Cartesianae*, I, Prop. 15, Schol.; *Meditationes*, IV (*Oeuvres*, VII, p. 56, l. 26–p. 57, l. 5).

concipiendi facultas)" or that it is to be assumed "to be infinite any more than the faculty of feeling (*sentiendi facultas*)." What he means to say is that will may extend itself more widely than intellect, if the term "intellect" is
taken in its narrow sense of the thinking faculty, but it does
not extend itself more widely than intellect if this term is
taken in the general sense of mind (*mens*) or soul (*anima*)
with which it is identified by Spinoza.[1] Second, he shows
that the assumption, starting out with a failure to distinguish
between will as a universal and will as a real entity or faculty
of the soul, lapses into the further fallacy of transferring the
implications of the term taken in the former sense to the
term taken in its latter sense.

The second objection, directly aimed at the denial of the
freedom of the will, belongs to that class of arguments in
favor of the freedom of the will which are generally described,
whenever the problem is discussed, as arguments from experience. Thus Crescas describes one class of arguments for
freedom as being based upon the common observation that
many things depend upon will,[2] and similarly Suarez introduces his second class of arguments for freedom by the
statement: "*Secundo argumentari possumus ab experientia.*"[3]
The particular argument from observation or experience
which Spinoza reproduces here anonymously is again, in a
letter to Blyenbergh,[4] ascribed by him to Descartes.[5] It is
based upon the generally accepted belief as to "the possibility of suspending our judgment, so as not to assent to the
things we perceive." In answer to this objection, Spinoza
denies that "we have the power of suspending judgment,"

---

[1] Cf. above, pp. 43–44.   [2] *Or Adonai*, II, v, 3 (p. 47b).

[3] *Disputationes Metaphysicae*, Disp. XIX, Sec. II, xiv.

[4] Epistola 21 (*Opera*, IV, p. 131, l. 33–p. 132, l. 1).

[5] *Principia Philosophiae*, I, 39; *Principia Philosophiae Cartesianae*, I, Prop. 15.
Schol.

and declares that the suspension of judgment "is in truth a perception and not free will."

The third objection is aimed at his view that the affirmation or the denial of truth or goodness about a thing is the act of a will which is identical with the intellect,[1] that is to say, it is involved in the idea of the thing and is not, as is maintained by Descartes,[2] the act of a will within us outside the intellect and the idea of the thing. Now, the objection runs, ideas differ with respect to their perfection, reality, or truth — a view maintained by Descartes[3] and reproduced previously by Spinoza.[4] Accordingly, if affirmations of truth and falsehood about a thing were involved in the idea of the thing, one affirmation should contain more reality than another. Furthermore, the affirmation of something that is true should require a greater power than the affirmation of something that is false. But this is not so, for "one affirmation does not seem to contain more reality than another," and "it does not appear that we need a greater power for affirming a thing to be true which is true than for affirming a thing to be true which is false." And so Spinoza concludes: "This also seems to point to a difference between the will and the intellect." In his answer Spinoza first denies the assertion that one affirmation does not contain more reality than another, maintaining that in some respect "the individual affirmations differ just as the ideas differ." He then also denies the assertion that the power of thinking required for the affirmation of that which is false is equal to the power of thinking required for the affirmation of that which is true.

[1] Cf. *Ethics*, II, Prop. 49, Demonst.; *Short Treatise*, II, 16, § 2. "Goodness" only is mentioned in *Short Treatise*, but see above, pp. 167–168.

[2] *Notae in Programma* (*Oeuvres*, VIII, p. 363, ll. 16–20): "ipsum actum judicandi, qui non nisi in assensu, hoc est, in affirmatione vel negatione consistit, non retuli ad perceptionem intellectus, sed ad determinationem voluntatis."

[3] *Meditationes*, III (*Oeuvres*, VII, p. 40, ll. 7 ff.).   [4] *Ethics*, I, Prop. 9.

Falsity, he rephrases a previous statement, is non-being, or, as he has phrased it previously, it "consists in the privation of knowledge, which inadequate, that is to say, mutilated and confused, ideas involve." [1] The affirmation of that which is false to be true, therefore, does not require any power at all, inasmuch as it consists only of a privation of knowledge.

A similar objection against the same view, though differently stated, is given in the *Short Treatise* as follows: "If it is not we, but the thing itself, that makes the affirmation and denial about itself in us, then nothing can be affirmed or denied except what is in agreement with the thing; and consequently there is no falsity." [2] The answer given there by Spinoza is the same as here. Falsity, he says, consists in the fact that "when we happen to know something or a part of an object, we imagine that the object (although we only know very little of it) nevertheless affirms or denies that of itself as a whole," [3] or in other words, "falsity consists in the privation of knowledge, which inadequate, that is to say, mutilated and confused, ideas involve." [4] This passage in the *Short Treatise*, II, which occurs in Chapter XVI, where the question of the freedom of the will is discussed, is, according to Freudenthal, [5] to be transferred to Chapter XV, where the question of truth and falsehood is discussed. But, as we have seen, the substance of this passage is analogous to that of Spinoza's third objection and answer which occurs in the *Ethics* in connection with the problem of the freedom of the will. So we have reason to believe that this passage in the *Short Treatise* rightly belongs in Chapter XVI.

---

[1] *Ibid.*, II, Prop. 35.

[2] *Short Treatise*, II, 16, § 7 (*Opera*, I, p. 83, ll. 30–34).

[3] *Ibid.*, § 7 (p. 84, ll. 5–10). [4] *Ethics*, II, Prop. 35.

[5] "Spinozastudien," in *Zeitschrift für Philosophie und philosophische Kritik*, 108 (1896), p. 278.

The fourth objection against free will is the famous argument from an ass perishing of hunger and thirst when placed at an equal distance from food and drink, which is attributed to Johannes Buridanus. The argument is reproduced by Spinoza also in the *Cogitata Metaphysica* (Part II, Chapter XII), where he summarizes philosophic views without necessarily subscribing to them. The gist of the argument as restated here by Spinoza is that since a man placed in such a state of equilibrium would not perish, man must be endowed with free will. In answer to this objection, Spinoza contends that given a man placed in such a state of equilibrium and without any internal or external motives or incentives or causes to determine his action, the man, like the ass, would certainly perish of hunger and thirst. But — and here we may conclude the unfinished argument of Spinoza — inasmuch as there will always be present other external motives or incentives or causes to determine action, and especially the internal motive of the conatus for self-preservation,[1] neither ass nor man will perish under such circumstances. In the case a man does perish under such circumstances, says Spinoza, then "if you ask me whether such a man would not be thought an ass rather than a man, I reply I do not know; nor do I know what ought to be thought of a man who hangs himself, or of children, fools, and madmen." The mention of "a man who hangs himself" is an allusion to his view that there is no conatus for self-destruction as there is for self-preservation, and that every act of self-destruction must be explained on the ground of external circumstance.[2] The mention of "children, fools, and madmen" as examples of persons acting in an irresponsible manner seems to reflect the stereotyped Talmudic phrase "deaf-mute, madman, and

[1] Cf. below, pp. 195 ff.   [1] Cf. below, pp. 197–198, 237.

child" [1] which is constantly used as an illustration of an irresponsible agent. But the direct source of these three examples of unintelligent human beings is to be found in Maimonides' statement that while the doctrine of the incorporeality of God is to be explained to every trained and intelligent person according to his capacity, it is to be taught only as a matter of tradition to "children, women, fools, and those who are bereft of reason." [2] Barring "women," the three examples used by Spinoza are identical with those used by Maimonides, and are given by him in the same order.

That these four objections are not all that can be urged against his denial of free will is admitted by Spinoza himself when he says that "there may be other objections besides these." Some such additional objections are to be found in a letter addressed to Spinoza by Tschirnhaus[3] and in Spinoza's answer to that letter addressed to Schuller,[4] and also in the *Short Treatise*.[5]

The third part of the Scholium is described by Spinoza himself as dealing with "some of the advantages of this doctrine" or as showing "what service to our own lives a knowledge of this doctrine is." In the corresponding chapter of the *Short Treatise* (Part II, Chapter XVIII), "this doctrine" is more fully explained by the proposition that man, "being a part of the whole nature, on which he depends, and by which also he is governed, cannot of himself do anything for his happiness and well-being."

---

[1] חרש שוטה וקטן. Cf. *Mishnah, Baba Ḳama*, VIII, 4.

[2] *Moreh Nebukim*, I, 35. The terms used by Maimonides are: לקטנים ולנשים ולסכלים, ולחסרי השכל. The terms used by Spinoza are: "pueri, stulti, vesani, etc." (*Opera*, II, p. 135, ll. 30–31).   [3] Epistola 57.

[4] Epistola 58.

[5] *Short Treatise*, II, 16, § 8 (*Opera*, I, p. 84, ll. 14 ff.).

CHAPTER XVIII

EMOTIONS

IMAGINE that the impish spirit which had induced Spinoza to break up his orderly, systematic, and clear-cut thinking into disconnected and mystifying geometric propositions had still further induced him to write the last three parts of the *Ethics* in some cryptic language, so that we were now faced with the task of deciphering these propositions in addition to explaining them. But imagine also that by some sane promptings Spinoza had included within parentheses after all the technical terms in these parts of his work their respective equivalents in some language in which the traditional vocabulary of European philosophy has been preserved — say, Greek, Latin, Arabic, or Hebrew. Then, even before we could read a single word in them, we should have been able to determine the nature of these parts of the *Ethics* and the type of literature to which they belong, and this by merely observing the terms included within the parentheses. We should at once have placed them among books on ethics which from the time of Aristotle down to Spinoza's own time dealt with the emotions of the soul, its virtues and vices, and the final happiness of man. Whatever book of that type of literature we take, — be it Aristotle's *Nicomachean Ethics*; the various books containing the teachings of the Stoics, such as the philosophical writings of Cicero, Diogenes Laertius' life of Zeno, or Stobaeus' *Eclogae*; the numerous mediaeval ethical works written in Hebrew and Latin; or the works of philosophers after the mediaeval period, such, for instance, as the First Part of Hobbes' *Leviathan* or the Second and Third Parts of Descartes' *Les Passions de l'Ame*,

— we shall find in it lists of emotions and virtues which are practically the same as those enumerated here by Spinoza.

But if, following the methods pursued by Grotefend and Champollion in their discoveries of the keys to the Babylonian cuneiform and Egyptian hieroglyphic, we ultimately succeeded in deciphering this imaginary cryptic language of Spinoza, we should soon discover that despite the sameness of terminology there is a great difference in these specifically ethical parts of the *Ethics* and the traditional ethical works which served Spinoza as a model. The difference is stated by Spinoza himself in his Preface to the Third Part. His predecessors, he says, considered actions and appetites as virtues and vices which are to be bewailed, laughed at, mocked, or detested.[1] He is to consider them as certain facts in the causality of nature which are to be studied and understood. "I shall consider human actions and appetites," he says, "just as if I were considering lines, planes, or bodies."[2]

This method, however, as Spinoza himself avers, is not altogether new. He refers to "very eminent men . . . to whose labor and industry" he confesses himself to be "much indebted,"[3] and he mentions especially Descartes, who, he says, strove "to explain human emotions by their primary causes."[4] The reference is to *Les Passions de l'Ame*, which he mentions later in the Preface to the Fifth Part by the title of its Latin translation, *Passiones Animae*. Among the "very eminent men" he undoubtedly meant to include also Aristotle and the mediaeval philosophical writers on ethics, all of whom, as a rule, tried to trace human conduct to its psychological basis, carrying out Aristotle's dictum that the

[1] *Ethics*, III, Praef. (*Opera*, II, p. 137, ll. 15–18).
[2] *Ibid.* (p. 138, ll. 26–27).
[3] *Ibid.* (p. 137, ll. 20–22.)　　　　[4] *Ibid.* (p. 138, ll. 1–2).

student of politics, and for that matter also the student of ethics in general, must know the facts about the soul.[1]

But traditional philosophy from Aristotle to Descartes, even when it treated emotions as "natural things which follow the common laws of nature," [2] and even when it tried to find a psychological basis for human conduct, still differentiated between emotions and virtues. The difference between these two is stated by Aristotle himself. We are called good or bad, and we are praised or blamed, he says, on the ground of our virtues or vices, but we are neither called good or bad nor praised or blamed on the ground of our emotions ($\pi\acute{\alpha}\theta\eta$).[3] That this is to be so, says Aristotle further, is to be explained by the fact that the emotions do not imply choice ($\pi\rho o\alpha\acute{\iota}\rho\varepsilon\sigma\iota\varsigma$), which is deliberate desire or will ($\beta o\acute{\upsilon}\lambda\eta\sigma\iota\varsigma$),[4] whereas virtue and vice are the result of choice and will.[5] But while Aristotle perhaps may not have meant by "choice" the existence of a will which is free and autonomous, his successors made freedom of the will the basis of human conduct and of virtue and vice. Thus Descartes, evidently reflecting Aristotle's definition of virtue, maintains that "it is for those actions alone which depend on this free will that we may with reason be praised or blamed."[6] It is with reference to this that Spinoza argues that inasmuch as Descartes believed in the freedom of the will, he "believed that the mind is absolute master over its own actions," [7] and therefore actions, as differentiated from emotions, constituted virtues and vices, to be called good or bad and to be praised or blamed. The difference between emotions and virtues and vices is also

---

[1] *Nicomachean Ethics*, I, 13, 1102a, 18–19.
[2] *Ethics*, III, Praef. (*Opera*, II, p. 137, ll. 8–10).
[3] *Nicomachean Ethics*, II, 5, 1105b, 25–1106a, 2.
[4] *Ibid.*, III, 3, 1113a, 9–10.   [5] *Ibid.*, II, 5, 1106a, 2–4.
[6] *Les Passions de l'Âme*, III, 152. Cf. *Principia Philosophiae*, I, 37.
[7] *Ethics*, III, Praef. (*Opera*, II, p. 137, l. 26–p. 138, l. 1).

implied in many other statements of Descartes, as, for example, when he says that "pride and abjection are not only vices, but also passions," [1] whereas ingratitude is not a passion but only a vice.[2] But, argues Spinoza, if the freedom of the will is denied, the difference between emotions and virtues automatically disappears. Human actions, like human emotions, are inevitably determined by causes. They are not to be detested or scoffed at, but rather to be understood "by the universal laws and rules of nature."[3]

What we have, then, are not natural and causally determined phenomena called emotions, on the one hand, and free actions called virtues and vices, on the other, but rather the welter of blind emotions in conflict with one another and the victory of some of them over others. There is no vice, "for nothing happens in nature which can be attributed to any vice of nature, for she is always the same and everywhere one." [4] And man, in respect to what is generally called vice as well as in all other respects, is a part of nature; [5] he is not within her as "a kingdom within a kingdom" nor as one who "disturbs rather than follows her order." [6] What men call vice is simply "impotence (*impotentia*) and want of stability," [7] and this "impotence of man to govern or restrain the effects I call servitude." [8] By the same token, what men call virtue is simply power (*potentia*), for by "virtue and power, I understand the same thing; that is to say (Prop. VII, Part III), virtue, in so far as it is related to man, is the essence itself or nature of the man in so far as it has the power of effecting certain things which can be

---

[1] *Les Passions de l'Ame*, III, 160.
[2] *Ibid.*, III, 194.
[3] *Ethics*, III, Praef. (*Opera*, II, 138, ll. 17–18).
[4] *Ibid.* (ll. 11–13).
[5] *Ibid.*, IV, Prop. 4.
[6] *Ibid.*, III, Praef. (*Opera*, II, p. 137, ll. 11–12).
[7] *Ibid.*, IV, Prop. 18, Schol.
[8] *Ibid.*, IV, Praef. (*Opera*, II, p. 205, ll. 7–8).

understood through the laws of its nature alone." [1] Since the determining factor in this conflict between the emotions is reason, or mind, or intellect, the difference "between true virtue and impotence may, from what has already been said, be easily seen to be this — that true virtue consists in living according to the guidance of reason alone; and that impotence therefore consists in this alone — that man allows himself to be led by things which are outside himself, and by them to be determined to such actions as the common constitution of external things demands, and not to such as his own nature considered in itself alone demands." [2] "Impotence" and "passion" are therefore sometimes used by Spinoza as synonymous terms. [3] It may be remarked that the term "servitude" (*servitus*) used by Spinoza as a description of what is generally called "vice" or "sin" and what he calls "impotence," just as its opposite term "liberty" used by him later, [4] is borrowed from New Testament as well as rabbinic theology and reflects the expression "servant of sin" (*servus peccati* in the Vulgate). [5]

Had Spinoza written his *Ethics* in the manner of the rabbis and scholastics, he would have prefaced the last three parts of the *Ethics* with a statement somewhat as follows:

Having dealt in the previous parts of our work with what is generally known as theoretical philosophy, we shall now

---

[1] *Ibid.*, IV, Def. 8.   [2] *Ibid.*, IV, Prop. 37, Schol. 1.

[3] *Ibid.*, V, Prop. 20, Schol.: "impotentia, seu passio" (*Opera*, II, p. 293, l. 26).

[4] Cf. below, p. 311.

[5] John 8, 34; Romans 6, 17. Cf. also *Sukkah* 52b and Rashi's and Gersonides' commentaries on Proverbs 29, 21, according to which the verse is to be translated and interpreted as follows: "He that delicately bringeth up his *servant* (i.e., his Evil *Yezer* or Impulse; cf. below, p. 326) from a child shall have him become a *master* at the length." In Gersonides, still more closely analogous to Spinoza's use of the term "servitude," the terms "servant" and "master" in this verse are taken to refer not to the theological "Evil *Yezer*" but rather to the psychological "appetitive faculty bent on pursuit of bodily desires" as opposed to "reason" by which man, he adds, ought to let himself be guided.

deal with practical philosophy, or what is known as ethics, politics, and economics. Following the order of topics which are generally included under ethics, we shall divide the subject into three parts: first, the emotions (Part III); second, the so-called virtues and vices (Part IV); third, final bliss (Part V). In fact, such an outline of the last three parts of the *Ethics*, though differently phrased, occurs toward the end of the Preface to Part III. It reads as follows: "I shall, therefore, pursue the same method in considering the [*a*] nature [Part III] and [*b*] strength [Part IV] of the emotions and [*c*] the power of the mind over them [Part V] which I pursued in our previous discussion of God [Part I] and the mind [Part II], and I shall consider human actions and appetites just as if I were considering lines, planes, or bodies." [1]

The fifty-nine propositions of the Third Part of the *Ethics* fall into four groups, dealing with the following topics:

I. Actions and Passions (Props. I–III).

II. The Conatus and the Primary Passive Emotions (Props. IV–XI).

III. Derivative Passive Emotions (Props. XII–LVII).

IV. Active Emotions (Props. LVIII–LIX).

I. Actions and Passions

In his treatise on *Les Passions de l'Ame* Descartes begins his discussion of the emotions with a definition of the terms "action" and "passion." Following Aristotle, he defines the two terms as referring to one and the same event occurring or happening anew which with respect to the agent is called an action and with respect to the recipient or patient is called a passion.[2] The distinction between action and passion is to be found also in the thoughts which constitute the func-

---

[1] *Ibid.*, III, Praef., end.
[2] *Les Passions de l'Ame*, I, 1.

tions of the soul. The actions of the soul are "all forms of one will (*voluntas, voluntates*), because we find by experience that they proceed directly from our soul, and appear to depend on it alone." The passions of the soul are "all those kinds of perception or forms of knowledge which are found in us, because it is often not our soul which makes them what they are, and because it always receives them from the things which are represented by them." [1]

Among these passions of the soul Descartes further distinguishes two classes: (1) those which have the soul itself as a cause, such as the perception of that which is willed or imagined by the action of the soul itself, and (2) those which have the body as a cause, [2] especially those which "come to the soul by the intermission of the nerves." [3]

Those which have the body as a cause are again divided by Descartes into three classes: (1) those which relate to things which are external to us, such as the various sense perceptions, (2) those which relate to our body, or to some of its parts, such as hunger, thirst, and pain, and (3) those which relate to the soul only as if they were in the soul itself, [4] although "they are caused, maintained, and fortified by some movement of the spirits." [5] By the "spirits" he means the "animal spirits" or the "very subtle parts of the blood." [6]

It is this last subdivision of the passions, namely, that which has the body as a cause but is related solely to the soul, that Descartes specifically identifies with the emotions. The passions of the soul are therefore defined by him as "perceptions, or sensations, or emotions of the soul which are related especially to it, and which are caused, maintained, and fortified by some movement of the spirits." [7]

---

[1] *Ibid.*, I, 17.

[2] *Ibid.*, I, 19.

[3] *Ibid.*, I, 21 and 22.

[4] *Ibid.*, I, 23, 24 and 25.

[5] *Ibid.*, I, 29.

[6] *Ibid.*, I, 10.

[7] *Ibid.*, I, 27, quoted in *Ethics*, V, Praef.

Inasmuch as the passions of the soul are caused by the body, and "what in the soul is a passion is in the body commonly speaking an action," Descartes proceeds to examine "the difference which exists between soul and body in order to know to which of the two we must attribute each one of the functions which are within us." [1] The method by which this difference can be ascertained is formulated by him as follows: "All that we experience as being in us, and that to observation may exist in wholly inanimate bodies, must be attributed to our body alone," but "all that which is in us, and which we cannot in any way conceive as possibly pertaining to a body, must be attributed to our soul." [2]

With these preliminary remarks Descartes proceeds to explain the functions of the body and their relation to the functions of the mind. Denying at the very outset that the soul supplies movement and heat to the body,[3] he proceeds to give a brief but detailed description of "the whole method in which the bodily machine is composed," [4] and of "all the functions which pertain to the body alone." [5] On the whole, movement is the function of the body and thought is the function of the mind, and the two are independent of each other. Still, by the movements of the animal spirits in the pineal gland an interaction between mind and body is established. The body causes certain emotions in the soul, and the soul in its turn causes certain movements in the body.[6]

It is as a criticism of these views of Descartes that the Definitions at the beginning of the Third Part of the *Ethics* and the first three propositions are to be understood. Beginning with a criticism of Descartes' use of the terms "actions" and "passions" (Prop. I) and of his conception

[1] *Ibid.*, I, 2.　　　　[2] *Ibid.*, I, 3.　　　　[3] *Ibid.*, I, 5.
[4] *Ibid.*, I, 7.　　　　[5] *Ibid.*, I, 17.　　　　[6] *Ibid.*, I, 34.

of the relation between mind and body (Props. II–III), he then passes on to the discussion of the emotions (Props. IV ff.).

To begin with, Spinoza gives a new meaning to the terms "action" and "passion." Action and passion, he seems to argue, do not refer to one and the same thing, which is termed an action in respect to him who causes it to occur and a passion in respect of the subject to which it occurs; they refer rather to two different things, the difference between which consists in their relation to their respective causes. For causes are of two kinds: an adequate cause (*causa adaequata*), and an inadequate or partial cause (*causa inadaequata, seu partialis*) — a distinction which may be traced to the distinction between *causa totalis* and *causa partialis* in Duns Scotus [1] and Heereboord,[2] or to the distinction between *causa efficiens sola efficit* and *cum aliis* in Petrus Ramus,[3] or to similar distinctions which can be found in the history of logic since Plato.[4] As defined by Spinoza an adequate cause is one "whose effect can be clearly and distinctly perceived by means of the cause." An inadequate or partial cause is one "whose effect cannot be understood by means of the cause alone." [5] It is with reference to these two kinds of causes that effects are called either actions or passions. "I say that we act when anything is done, either within us or without us, of which we are the adequate cause. . . . On the other hand, I say that we suffer when anything is done within us, or when anything follows from our nature, of which

[1] *Quaestiones in Libros Physicorum*, Liber II, Quaest. 8, No. 5 (cf. R. P. M. Fernandez Garcia, *Lexicon Scholasticum*, p. 126, Col. 1).

[2] *Meletemata Philosophica, Disputationes ex Philosophia Selectae*, Vol. II, Disp. XX, IV.

[3] Cf. *Dialecticae libri duo. . . . Cum Commentariis Georgii Dounami Annexis* (London, 1669), Lib. I, Cap. 4.

[4] See Dounamus' commentary, *ad loc.*   [5] *Ethics*, III, Def. 1.

we are not the cause excepting partially." [1] Inasmuch as
in our mind some ideas are adequate and some are mutilated
and confused,[2] "our mind acts at times and at times suffers:
in so far as it has adequate ideas, it necessarily acts; and
in so far as it has inadequate ideas, it necessarily suffers." [3]

Then, in the next place, Spinoza proceeds to criticize
Descartes' conception of the relation between mind and
body. Though Descartes considers mind and body as two
independent substances which cannot act upon one another,
still, in the language of Spinoza himself, "he affirms that the
soul or mind is united specially to a certain part of the brain
called the pineal gland, which the mind by the mere exercise
of the will is able to move in different ways, and by whose
help the mind perceives all the movements which are excited
in the body and external objects." [4] This pineal gland is
characterized by Spinoza as "a certain small portion of extended matter," [5] and consequently, he argues, when Descartes and his followers maintain that the mind is able to
move the pineal gland in different ways, they really maintain
that "solely at the bidding of the mind, the body moves
or rests, and does a number of things which depend upon
the will of the mind alone, and upon the power of thought." [6]

Furthermore, Descartes confidently declares that we shall
not find much difficulty in discovering the peculiar and dis-
tinctive functions of the soul and of the body and their relations to each other "if we realize that all that we experience
as being in us, and that to observation may exist in wholly
inanimate bodies, must be attributed to our body alone." [7]

---

[1] *Ibid.*, III, Def. 2.
[2] *Ibid.*, III, Prop. 1, Demonst., referring to *Ethics*, II, Prop. 40, Schol. [1].
[3] *Ibid.*, III, Prop. 1.　　　　　[4] *Ibid.*, V, Praef.
[5] *Ibid.*: "cuidam quantitatis portiunculae" (*Opera*, II, p. 279, l. 27).
[6] *Ibid.*, III, Prop. 2, Schol. (*Opera*, II, p. 142, ll. 2–4).
[7] *Les Passions de l'Ame*, I, 3.

Against this Spinoza argues as follows: "For what the body can do no one has hitherto determined, that is to say, experience has taught no one hitherto what the body, without being determined by the mind, can do and what it cannot do from the laws of nature alone, in so far as nature is considered merely as corporeal." [1]

Again, "in order to render this more intelligible," says Descartes, "I shall here explain in a few words the whole method in which the bodily machine is composed," [2] and after having explained the structure of the body, Descartes claims to have considered "all the functions which pertain to the body alone." [3] It is evidently in answer to this that Spinoza says: "For no one as yet has understood the structure of the body so accurately as to be able to explain all its functions." [4]

Finally, concludes Spinoza, Descartes has not explained "by what means or by what method the mind moves the body, nor how many degrees of motion it can communicate to the body, nor with what speed it can move the body." [5] The conclusion is that Descartes and his followers "do nothing but confess with pretentious words that they know nothing about the cause of the action, and see nothing in it to wonder at." [6]

Against this denial of the mind's action upon the body Spinoza now quotes three objections in the name of unspecified opponents. First, it is a matter of common observation that the mind does influence the motion of the body. Second, it is also a matter of common observation that the mind

[1] *Ethics*, III, Prop. 2, Schol. (*Opera*, II, p. 142, ll. 4–8).
[2] *Les Passions de l'Ame*, I, 7.
[3] *Ibid.*, I, 17.
[4] *Ethics*, III, Prop. 2, Schol. (*Opera*, II, p. 142, ll. 8–10).
[5] *Ibid.* (l. 14). Cf. *Ethics*, V, Praef.
[6] *Ibid.*, III, Prop. 2, Schol. (ll. 19–20).

does originate certain actions in the body, such, for instance, as speech and silence. This argument is analogous to Saadia's argument for the freedom of man's will from the fact that "man feels that he can speak or remain silent." [1] Third, without the guidance of the mind, by the mere mechanical motions of the body, certain purposive actions, such as generally come under the designation of human art, could not have originated in men. This argument, too, is analogous to Saadia's argument for the belief that man is the crown of creation from the fact that he has been endowed by God with superior intelligence to be able to produce the various arts and sciences. He mentions among them, as does here Spinoza, the art of building. [2]

In answer to the first objection, Spinoza points out, as indeed it was pointed out before him by Aristotle, [3] that just as mind is observed to influence the motions of the body, so also is the body observed to influence the actions of the mind. The conclusion Spinoza evidently wants us to draw from this is that just as the latter fact is not taken by his opponents to prove that the body determines the actions of the mind, so the former fact cannot be taken by them to prove that the mind determines the motions of the body. All that we observe is that there is a certain coincidence between the actions of the mind and those of the body, of which his own explanation is as valid as that of his opponents, and, in fact, more valid, inasmuch as it is consistent in excluding the action of the mind upon the body as well as the action of the body upon the mind. In answer to the second objection, he restates his earlier view that all our conceptions as to the mind's freedom to originate action are a delusion based

[1] *Emunot we-De'ot*, IV, 4. Cf. above, Vol. I, p. 427.
[2] *Ibid.*, IV, 1.
[3] *De Anima*, I, 1, 403a, 3 ff.

upon our ignorance of the infinite causes by which every seemingly free act is determined. In answer to the third objection, he maintains that his opponents are not justified in assuming to have a knowledge of what the body by its own motion could or could not do.

With his new definition of the terms "action" and "passion," and with his rejection of any kind of interaction between mind and body, Spinoza also discards Descartes' statement that the actions of the soul are all "forms of will" [1] and that the passions of the soul are divided into (*a*) those which have the soul itself as a cause and (*b*) those which have the body as a cause.[2] "The actions of the mind," Spinoza argues, are not forms of the will, but "arise from adequate ideas alone." [3] Nor are there any passions of the mind which have the soul itself as a cause, for "the passions [of the mind] depend upon those [ideas] alone which are inadequate," [3] and inadequate ideas are not caused by the mind itself. [4] Furthermore, Descartes is wrong in his statement that "what in the soul is a passion is in the body commonly speaking an action," [5] for "I could show that passions are referred to individual things in the same manner as they are referred to the mind." [6] By individual things (*res singulares*) here he means bodies, just as the term thing (*res*) in Proposition V is explained later in the Demonstration of Proposition X to mean our body (*corpus nostrum*).

Similarly Descartes' definition of the emotions and their identification with the passions of the soul which are caused by the body must likewise be rejected. A new definition of the emotions is now given by Spinoza — one in accord with

[1] *Les Passions de l'Ame*, I, 17; cf. above, p. 186, n. 1.
[2] *Ibid.*, I, 19; cf. above, p. 186, notes 2 and 3.
[3] *Ethics*, III, Prop. 3.   [4] Cf. above, pp. 106 ff.
[5] *Les Passions de l'Ame*, I, 2; cf. above, p. 187, n. 1.
[6] *Ethics*, III, Prop. 3, Schol.

his own use of the terms "action" and "passion" and with his own conception of the relation between body and soul.

In accordance with his own peculiar definition of the terms "action" and "passion," Spinoza dissociates the emotions for which the Latin term used by him is *commotiones* [1] from the term *passiones* and identifies them with the term *affectus*. To understand the significance of this step taken by Spinoza we must explain the use of the terms *passio*, *affectus*, and *affectio* by Spinoza as well as by his predecessors. According to Augustine, the emotions of the soul (*animi motus*) are called by the Greeks πάθη, "while some of our own writers, as Cicero, call them *perturbationes*, some *affectiones* or *affectus*, and some, to render the Greek word more accurately, *passiones*." [2] On the whole, mediaeval authors use these three terms *passio*, *affectus*, and *affectio* synonymously.[3] Descartes, however, uses *affectio* as synonymous with *qualitas*, whereas the term *affectus* is used by him in the sense of *passio*,[4] or, rather, the passions of the soul, i.e., emotions. Again, the term *passio*, as we have seen,[5] in addition to its being used by Descartes in the sense of the emotions of the soul, is also used by him in the general sense of suffering action and as the opposite of action. All these usages of the three terms by Descartes may be traced, I think, to the following three senses of the term πάθος in Aristotle: (1) in the general sense of accident (συμβεβηκός),[6] (2) in the sense of the emotions (κινήσεις) [7] of the soul, which are also called by him

---

[1] *Ibid.*, III, *Affectuum Definitiones*, 27, Expl. (*Opera*, II, p. 197, l. 18); V, Praef.: "Commotiones animae" (*Opera*, II, p. 279, l. 7); V, Prop. 2: "animi commotionem"; cf. V, Prop. 20, Schol.: "affici, sive moveri" (*Opera*, II, p. 293, l. 23).

[2] *De Civitate Dei*, IX, 4.

[3] See L. Schütz, *Thomas-Lexikon* (1895), s.v.

[4] See E. Gilson, *Index Scolastico-Cartésien*, p. 9.   [5] Cf. above, p. 185.

[6] *De Generatione et Corruptione*, I, 4, 320a, 1. Cf. my *Crescas' Critique of Aristotle*, p. 516, n. 9.

[7] *Nicomachean Ethics*, II, 5, 1105b, 20; *De Anima*, I, 4, 408b, 4.

the qualities (ποιότητες)[1] of the soul, and (3) in the general sense of suffering as the opposite of ἔργον.[2] Returning now to Spinoza, we find that the term *affectio* is used by him, as by Descartes, in the sense of accident, mode, or modification,[3] that is to say, the equivalent of πάθος in the sense of συμβεβηκός. The term *passio*, as we have seen, is defined by Spinoza in a sense unlike that in which it is used by Descartes, and for that matter unlike any of the senses in which its Greek equivalent πάθος is used by Aristotle. But the term *affectus* is used by him in the same sense as it is used by Augustine and Descartes, that is to say, as the equivalent of πάθος in the sense of the emotions of the soul. Of course, exceptions to these usages of the terms occur occasionally in Spinoza. Thus *affectus* is sometimes used by him in the sense of *affectio*,[4] *affectio* is used by him in the sense of *affectus*,[5] and *passio* is used by him in the Cartesian sense of emotion.[6]

Again, in opposition to Descartes' view as to the interaction between soul and body, and in accordance with his own view as to the parallelism between the order and connection of ideas and the order and connection of things, Spinoza defines the emotions, or, as he calls them, the affects, as the affections of the body together with the ideas of these affections. But inasmuch as "affections" is a general term designating any kind of mode or accident or modification of the body, whether its power of acting is increased or diminished by it or whether it is neither increased nor diminished, it is only those affections of the body by which the power of act-

---

[1] *Categories*, 8, 9b, 36.   [2] *De Anima*, I, 1, 403b, 12.

[3] *Ethics*, I, Prop. 4. Cf. G. T. Richter, *Spinozas Philosophische Terminologie* (Leipzig, 1913), pp. 82 ff.

[4] *Ethics*, II, Prop. 17.

[5] *Ibid.*, V, Prop. 20, Schol. (*Opera*, II, p. 293, ll. 10–13); cf. editor's note (*Textgestaltung*, p. 390) ad loc., quoting Camerer, *Lehre Spinozas*, p. 280.

[6] *Ibid.* (l. 26): "impotentia autem, seu passio." Cf. *Tractatus Theologico-Politicus*, Ch. 3 (*Opera*, III, p. 46, l. 29).

ing of the body itself is increased, diminished, helped, or hindered, together with the ideas of these affections, that form what are called affects or emotions. Furthermore, inasmuch as we can be either the adequate cause of any of these affections or their inadequate or partial cause, the emotions, again in opposition to Descartes, may be either actions or passions.[1]

II. Conatus and Primary Passive Emotions

But increase and diminution imply a certain standard of measurement. What the standard is by which the affections of the body are measured, to ascertain whether the acting power of the body is increased or diminished by them, is explained by Spinoza in Propositions IV–X. The standard of measurement, he says, is the conatus (effort, impulse) by which each thing endeavors to persevere in its own being. Every affection of the body is said to increase the acting power of the body in so far as it increases that endeavor for self-preservation; it diminishes the acting power of the body in so far as it diminishes that endeavor. This endeavor for self-preservation is the first law of nature and is the basis of all our emotions.

The antiquity of the principle of self-preservation as the first law of nature is well known.[2] The Stoics are generally credited with the view that "an animal's first impulse (ὁρμήν, appetionem) . . . is to self-preservation."[3] According to Cicero this view is nothing but a repetition of the Peripatetic view, which in his restatement reads: "Every natural organism aims at (vult) being its own preserver."[4]

[1] *Ibid.*, III, Def. 3 and Post. 1.

[2] Cf. Pollock, *Spinoza*, p. 117; Eisler, *Wörterbuch der philosophischen Begriffe* (1927), under "Erhaltung."

[3] Diogenes Laertius, *De Vitis, Dogmatibus et Apophthegmatibus Clarorum Philosophorum*, VII, 85.   [4] *De Finibus Bonorum et Malorum*, IV, 7, § 16.

Augustine devotes a chapter in his *De Civitate Dei* to showing how all things in nature wish to exist (*se esse velle*) or to conserve their existence (*suum . . . esse conseruent*).[1] Thomas Aquinas reproduces this principle in the statement that "every natural thing aims at (*appetit*) self-conservation."[2] Duns Scotus similarly says that "every natural being desires (*appetit*) with a natural desire to continue in existence."[3] Dante expresses the same sentiment in his statement that "everything which exists desires (*appetat*) its own existence."[4] Telesius similarly sets forth self-preservation as that at which all things aim (*appetens*),[5] and the same principle is restated by other philosophers of the Renaissance. At the time of Spinoza the principle of self-preservation became a commonplace of popular wisdom, so much so that in the Hebrew collection of sermons by his teacher Rabbi Saul Levi Morteira one of the sermons begins with the statement that "Nature, mother of all created beings, has implanted in them a will and impulse to strive for their self-preservation."[6]

Now, in all these quotations, it will have been noticed, self-preservation is spoken of as a sort of wish or will or desire expressed by such terms as *vult, velle, appetit*. These terms may all be traced to the Greek ὁρμή which is used in the passage quoted above. But ὁρμή, as we shall see, can also be translated by *conatus*. Cicero himself uses *conatus* and *appetitio* as synonymous terms, and considers both of them as Latin equivalents of the Greek ὁρμή.[7] Furthermore, ac-

---

[1] *De Civitate Dei*, XI, 27.

[2] *Quaestiones Disputatae de Potentia*, Quaest. V, Art. I, 13.

[3] *Quaestiones in Libros Physicorum*, Lib. I, Quaest. 22, No. 6: "Quodlibet ens naturale appetit seipsum permanere appetitu naturali." Cf. R. P. M. Fernandez Garcia, *Lexicon Scholasticum*, p. 850, col. 2.

[4] *De Monarchia*, I, 13 (or 15): "Omne quod est appetat suum esse."

[5] *De Rerum Naturae*, IX, 3, beginning.   [6] *Gibe'at Sha'ul*, XVIII.

[7] *De Natura Deorum*, II, 22, § 58; cf. II, 47, § 122.

cording to Hobbes, the term *appetitus* or *cupido*, which he uses as the Latin equivalent of the Greek ὁρμή, is a form of *conatus*,[1] so that subsequently, in the following passage, he uses the verb *conor* in connection with the striving for self-preservation: "And in the way to their end, which is principally their own conservation . . . [they] endeavor (*conatur*) to destroy, or subdue one another."[2] From whatever source, therefore, Spinoza has directly drawn his formulation of the principle of self-preservation, there is a historical connection between the term *conatus* and the term ὁρμή. Besides *conatus* Spinoza sometimes uses simply the term "force" (*vis*)[3] or the expression "natural love" (*natuurlyke Liefde*).[4] The expression "natural love" may be traced to a combination of two sets of sources. In the first place, Augustine describes the universal principle of self-preservation by the term "love" (*amor*).[5] In the second place, as an example of the effort for self-preservation in inanimate bodies, Augustine mentions the fact that they all "either seek the upper air or sink deep."[6] Now, this natural tendency of bodies to move upward or downward is described by Thomas Aquinas and Leo Hebraeus as natural love (*amor naturalis*).[7]

In the formulation of the Stoic principle of self-preservation both by Cicero and by Diogenes Laertius it is to be noticed that in addition to an affirmation of the principle of self-preservation there is also a denial of the existence of a natural desire for self-destruction. Cicero says definitely that "immediately upon birth (for that is the proper point to start from) a living creature feels an attachment for itself,

[1] *Leviathan*, I, 6.   [2] *Ibid.*, I, 13.
[3] *Ethics*, II, Prop. 45, Schol.; *Cogitata Metaphysica*, II, 6.
[4] *Short Treatise*, Appendix II, § 6 (*Opera*, I, p. 118, l. 7).
[5] *De Civitate Dei*, XI, 27–28.   [6] *Ibid.*, XI, 27.
[7] *Summa Theologica*, Prima Secundae, Quaest. 26, Art. 1; *Dialoghi d'Amore*, II, p. 67 (Bari, 1929). Cf. below, p. 201.

and an impulse to preserve itself . . . while on the other hand it recoils from death, and from all that seems to induce death." [1] Similarly Diogenes Laertius denies in the name of Zeno that there is a natural instinct for self-destruction, "for it was not likely that nature should estrange the living thing from itself." [2] Evidently following these or similar sources, Spinoza restates the principle of self-preservation in both these forms. Beginning with a negative formulation of the principle, he denies that there is a natural impulse for self-destruction. If we do observe that men malinger and destroy themselves, he says, it is due to external causes (Props. IV–V). Or, as he says elsewhere, "no one, I say, refuses food or kills himself from a necessity of his nature, but only when forced by external causes." [3] Then, restating the principle in its positive form, he says that "each thing, in so far as it is in itself, endeavors (conatur) to persevere in its being" (Prop. VI). This conatus for self-preservation is not an act of free will; it is rather determined from the necessity of the divine nature by which all things exist and act (Prop. VII). Or, as Spinoza again says elsewhere, "they need the same power to enable them to go on existing as to enable them to begin to exist. From which it follows, that the power, by which natural things exist, and therefore that by which they operate, can be no other than the external power of God itself." [4] The conatus for self-preservation, then, is identical with the existence of a thing which Spinoza calls here the actual essence (essentia actualis) of a thing (Prop. VII) or the given essence (essentia data) of a thing (ibid., Demonst.), as contrasted with the ideal essence (es-

---

[1] De Finibus, III, 5, § 16..

[2] De Vitis, VII, 85.

[3] Ethics, IV, Prop. 20, Schol. Cf. Prop. 18, Schol; Prop. 19; above, p 178; below p. 237.

[4] Tractatus Politicus, Ch. 2, § 2. Cf. Ethics, II, Prop. 45, Schol., end.

sentia idealis).[1] By the ideal essence of a thing he means the conception of a thing in the mind, irrespective of its existence or inexistence outside the mind — a contrast which in a letter to de Vries is formulated by Spinoza as a contrast between one kind of definition which "explains a thing as it exists outside the intellect" and another kind of definition which "explains a thing as it is conceived or can be conceived by us."[2] This identity of the conatus with the existence of a thing itself is stressed by Spinoza in the *Cogitata Metaphysica*, I, 6, in his argument against those who "distinguish between the thing itself and its conatus, by which each object is conserved." And inasmuch as the conatus for self-preservation follows from the necessity of the eternal power of God itself, this conatus does not involve finite but indefinite time (Prop. VIII). If a thing does happen to cease to exist, it is not by its own nature, but rather by an external cause.

So far Spinoza has developed his own conception of the conatus along the lines of the principle of self-preservation as laid down by the Stoics.

There is, however, a difference between the Stoic conception of the conatus for self-preservation and that of Spinoza. To the Stoics the conatus for self-preservation is confined only to animal beings. Both Diogenes and Cicero speak of animals (τὸ ζῷον, *animal*). Diogenes, furthermore, says definitely that although nature regulates the life of plants too, in their case there is no conatus (ὁρμῆς).[3] And so also Cicero, after mentioning the term "animal," remarks parenthetically, "for that is the proper point to start from."[4] To Spinoza, however, to whom all things may be called animate,[5] the conatus for self-preservation is to be found in everything.

---

[1] *Tractatus Politicus*, Ch. 2, § 2.   [2] *Epistola* 9 (*Opera*, IV, p. 43, ll. 11 ff.).
[3] *De Vitis*, VII, 86.   [4] *De Finibus*, III, 5, § 16.
[5] Cf. above, p. 58.

Throughout Propositions IV–VIII, it will have been noticed, he speaks of things, and of "each thing" at that, and not of animals. In the philosophy of Spinoza the distinction between animate and inanimate things plays no part; instead there is in it a distinction between bodies and minds, that is to say, between modes of extension and modes of thought. By the "thing" and the "each thing" of which he has so far spoken in Propositions IV–VIII is meant "body," as becomes evident from the opening statement in the Demonstration of Proposition X. What Spinoza has therefore maintained so far is that there is a conatus for self-preservation in bodies. Now, the main activities of bodies as modes of the attribute of extension are, according to Spinoza, motion and rest, and consequently in this additional non-Stoic element in his theory of the conatus Spinoza may be said to reflect the view of Augustine, who extends the principle of self-preservation not only to plants but also to inanimate objects, and identifies their tendency toward self-preservation with their natural movements upward and downward or with their being balanced in an intermediate position,[1] which means to say, with their motion and rest. In general, it may be said to reflect the view of the philosophers of the Renaissance, such as Telesius and Campanella, who saw an effort of self-preservation even in matter.[2] More specifically do we see in it the influence of Hobbes, who defines the conatus as "these small beginnings of motion, within the body of man, before they appear in walking, speaking, striking, and other visible actions,"[3] and perhaps still more directly may we discern in it the influence of Descartes' first law of nature, that is, the first law of motion, which Spinoza

---

[1] De Civitate Dei, XI, 27.

[2] Cf. R. Eisler, Wörterbuch der philosophischen Begriffe (1927), under "Erhaltung."   [3] Leviathan, I, 6.

has reproduced before.[1] In *Cogitata Metaphysica*, I, 6, Spinoza draws an analogy between Descartes' first law of nature and the conatus of self-preservation, which he also calls there the conatus of self-movement (*conatus se movendi*),[2] though he concedes "that this conatus of self-movement is something more than the laws and nature of motion." This conatus of self-movement seems also to reflect what Augustine indirectly and Thomas Aquinas and Leo Hebraeus directly call natural love (*amor naturalis*), which according to all of them applies to inanimate objects. Augustine illustrates it by the fact that inanimate bodies "either seek the upper air, or sink deep, or are balanced in an intermediate position," [3] Thomas Aquinas illustrates it by the "connaturalness of a heavy body for the centre," [4] and similarly Leo Hebraeus illustrates it by the tendency of "heavy bodies to move downward and of light bodies to move upward."[5] This expression "natural love," as we have pointed out above,[6] is also used by Spinoza in the *Short Treatise* as synonymous with "conatus."

Having first explained the conatus of the body, Spinoza then proceeds to explain the conatus of the mind. If the conatus of the body is to the perseverance in self-movement, the conatus of the mind is to the perseverance in thought, and this irrespective of whether the object of the thought is clear and distinct ideas or only confused ideas. Furthermore, inasmuch as the distinguishing characteristic of the human

---

[1] *Ethics*, II, Corol. to Lemma III after Prop. 13. Cf. above, p. 68, and Pollock, *Spinoza*, p. 218.

[2] Cf. expression "conatus ad motum" in *Principia Philosophiae Cartesianae*, III, Def. 3. For a modern interpretation of this expression, see R. McKeon, *The Philosophy of Spinoza*, p. 121.

[3] *De Civitate Dei*, XI, 27. Cf. also 28.

[4] *Summa Theologica*, Prima Secundae, Quaest. 26, Art. 1.

[5] *Dialoghi d'Amore*, II, p. 67 (Bari, 1929).

[6] Cf. above, p. 197.

mind is consciousness, the mind, unlike the body, is conscious (*conscia*) of its conatus to preserve its own being. Both
these characteristics of the conatus of the mind are stated in
Proposition IX: "The mind, both in so far as it has clear
and distinct ideas and in so far as it has confused ideas, endeavors to persevere in its being for an indefinite time, and
is conscious of this effort." Finally, a third characteristic
of the conatus of the mind is this. Just as the conatus of
the body is only toward self-preservation, and not toward
self-destruction, so the conatus of the mind toward the preservation of its own being implies that the mind only affirms
the existence of the body, but does not exclude it. Hence,
"there is no idea in the mind which excludes the existence of
the body, for such an idea is contrary to the mind" (Prop.
X).[1] Later Spinoza seems to describe this conatus of the
mind to affirm the existence of the body as the "desire by
which each person endeavors from the dictates of reason to
preserve his own being,"[2] or as the demand of "reason"
that "every person should love himself" and "should en
deavor, as far as in him lies, to preserve his own being."[3]
In this Spinoza approaches again the view of the Stoics, who,
having confined the conatus of self-preservation to sentient
beings or animals, maintain that the conatus of animals to
preserve themselves implies a consciousness (συνείδησις,
sensus) of their constitution (σύστασις, *status*) and a feeling
of affection (οἰκειῶσαι, *se diligerent*) for it.[4] By the same
token, since the mind is conscious of the body and of everything that happens in the body, and since also there is a
parallelism between the order and connection of ideas and
the order and connection of things, it follows that "if any-

---

[1] See latter part of Schol. to Prop. 11.
[2] *Ethics*, III, Prop. 59, Schol.   [3] *Ibid.*, IV, Prop. 18, Schol.
[4] Diogenes Laertius, *De Vitis*, VII, 85; Cicero, *De Finibus*, III, 5, § 16.

thing increases, diminishes, helps, or limits our body's power of action, the idea of that thing increases, diminishes, helps, or limits our mind's power of thought" (Prop. XI). These "affections of the body, by which the power of acting of the body itself is increased, diminished, helped, or hindered, together with the ideas of these affections," is what Spinoza calls affect or emotion.¹

The conatus, then, which is the effort of self-preservation in the most general sense, may apply to the body alone (Props. IV–VIII) or to the mind alone (Prop. IX) or to both the mind and the body taken together (Props. X–XI). For the last two cases Spinoza now gives two specific terms. When related to the mind alone, the conatus is called will (*voluntas*), but when it is related at the same time both to the mind and to the body, it is called appetite (*appetitus*).² It will be recalled that in the passages restating the principle of self-preservation quoted above various forms of *voluntas* and *appetitus* are used instead of the *conatus* which is used by Spinoza. Thus Spinoza's substitution here of the terms *voluntas* and *appetitus* for *conatus* is not without a historical justification. In addition to these three terms there is also the term *cupiditas*, which is used by Hobbes as synonymous with *appetitus* and as one of the forms of *conatus*.³ And so Spinoza says here that desire (*cupiditas*), like appetite, is the conatus related at the same time both to the mind and to the body, but it differs from appetite in that it is related to men in so far as they are conscious of their appetites.

¹ *Ethics*, III, Def. 3.

² *Ibid.*, III, Prop. 9, Schol. Logically this Scholium should follow Prop. 10. But so also the latter part of Scholium to Prop. 11, according to Spinoza himself, is an explanation of Prop. 10, and could therefore be an independent Scholium to Prop. 10. Evidently Spinoza was not always careful about placing the Scholia after the propositions to which they belong. Cf. above, Vol. I, pp. 116, 258, n. 3.

³ Cf. above, p. 197.

Later, however, when Spinoza discusses the active emotions and the conatus of the mind to persevere in its own being, he also identifies desire with that kind of conatus, and "therefore desire also is related to us in so far as we think." [1] These two senses of desire are also given by him in his discussion of desire in the Appendix to Part IV. [2]

Thus "conatus," "will," "appetite," and "desire" are all taken by Spinoza as related terms. They all have in common, according to him, the general meaning of a striving for self-preservation and of a pursuance of the means to further the attainment of this self-preservation. This striving is not a free act by which an affirmation or denial is made, but rather an act which follows from the necessity of the eternal nature of God. Desire, then, is not a pursuit of something which has already been adjudged as good, for such a judgment follows rather than precedes this kind of desire. "We neither strive for (*conari*), wish (*velle*), seek (*appetare*) nor desire (*cupere*) anything because we think it to be good, but, on the contrary, we adjudge a thing to be good because we strive for, wish, seek, or desire it." [3] And since to Spinoza any object which affects us with pleasure is called good,[4] what he has said of good applies also to pleasant, that is to say, we do not desire a thing because it is pleasant, but, on the contrary, a thing is pleasant because we desire it. Still, inasmuch as desire is inseparable from pleasure and goodness, Spinoza sometimes speaks of desire as arising from pleasure and pain,[5] from hatred and love,[6] from the recollection of something delightful,[7] and from a true knowledge of good and evil.[8]

---

[1] *Ethics*, III, Prop. 58, Demonst.

[2] Cf. *Ethics*, IV, Appendix, § 2.   [3] *Ethics*, III, Prop. 9, Schol.

[4] *Ibid.*, IV, Prop. 8, Demonst.; cf. Prop. 41.

[5] *Ibid.*, III, Prop. 37; IV, Props. 18 and 60.

[6] *Ibid.*, III, Prop. 37.   [7] *Ibid.*, III, Prop. 36.

[8] *Ibid.*, IV, Props. 15, 16, and 17.

If we are correct in our judgment that to Spinoza not only the good but also the pleasant is the consequent and not the cause of desire, then this view of his can be traced to the Stoics, and perhaps also to Aristotle. Both Cicero and Diogenes Laertius refer to the question whether pleasure (ἡδονή, *voluptas*) is the object to which the first impulse (ὁρμή) of animals is directed.[1] Their conclusion is that pleasure is not the object to which the conatus is directed, but rather something superadded (ἐπιγέννημα) thereto and a result or consequent of it.[2] Similarly Aristotle, in his discussion of the problem whether pleasure is the supreme good, arrives at the conclusion that it is not the supreme good at which all things aim, but that it completes the activity of the senses in the fulfilment of their proper functions. This statement, however, he immediately qualifies by saying that pleasure completes that activity not as a state inherent in it (ἕξις ἐνυπάρχουσα) but rather as a superadded or resultant perfection (ἐπιγινόμενόν τι τέλος).[3] Though Aristotle speaks elsewhere of the pleasant (ἡδύ) as an object of choice,[4] it is probably an intellectual kind of pleasure that is meant there, as may be judged from the context, where pleasure is associated with the noble (καλόν) and the advantageous (συμφέρον). Further proof of the sameness of the Aristotelian and the Stoic view on this point is the fact that Zeno, as reported by Diogenes Laertius, compares the relation of pleasure to the conatus of self-preservation to the relation of cheerfulness to animals and of bloom to plants, just as Aristotle compares the relation of pleasure to the activity of the senses in the fulfilment of their proper functions to the rela-

[1] Diogenes Laertius, *De Vitis*, VII, 85–86; Cicero, *De Finibus*, III, 5, § 17.
[2] Diogenes Laertius, *De Vitis*, VII, 86.
[3] *Nicomachean Ethics*, X, 4, 1174b, 14–33.
[4] *Ibid.*, II, 3, 1104b, 30–31.

tion of the bloom of youth to the young and vigorous.[1] It is therefore clear that both Aristotle and Zeno define pleasure in the same way, except that the former defines it with reference to the activity of the senses in the fulfilment of their proper functions and the latter defines it with reference to the activity of the conatus in animals in the preservation of life. In fact, Aristotle himself has raised the question whether pleasure cannot in a similar way be related to the activity of life, inasmuch as all men aim at life.[2] Now, in his definition of pleasure, Aristotle says that "each of the pleasures is bound up with the activity it perfects" and that "an activity is increased by its proper pleasure."[3] Out of all these, we may assume, have come Spinoza's definitions of desire (*cupiditas*), pleasure (*laetitia*), and pain (*tristitia*). Desire itself is the activity conducive to self-preservation; pleasure is the increase of that activity; pain is the decrease of it.[4] The conception of pleasure as an increase in the activity toward self-preservation may be also detected in Hobbes' definition of pleasure (*voluptas*) as a help to vital motion (*motus vitalis adjutor*).[5]

The terms *laetitia* and *tristitia* used here and elsewhere by Spinoza are taken directly from the Latin translation of Descartes' *Les Passions de l'Ame* (II, 101–102), where the corresponding original French terms are *Ioye* and *Tristesse*. But they reflect the Greek ἡδονή and λύπη respectively, and are one of the many pairs of Latin terms which have been used in translating those two Greek terms. Thus in three Latin translations of Aristotle's *De Anima* printed in the same volume the terms ἡδύ and λυπηρόν are translated by

[1] Diogenes Laertius, *De Vitis*, VII, 86; *Nicomachean Ethics*, X, 4, 1174b, 33.
[2] *Nicomachean Ethics*, X, 4, 1175a, 10 ff.
[3] *Ibid.*, X, 5, 1175a, 29–31.
[4] *Ethics*, III, Prop. 11, Schol.; *Affectuum Definitiones*, 1 and 2.
[5] *Leviathan*, I, 6.

(1) *laetum* and *triste*, (2) *iucundam* and *molestam*, and (3) *delectabile* and *contrista*.[1] Thus also Cicero sometimes expresses a preference for the use of the Latin *laetitia* as the equivalent of the Greek ἡδονή,[2] and sometimes he prefers the use of the Latin *voluptas*.[3] The term *voluptas*, as we have seen, is used by Spinoza as the equivalent of the Greek ἐπιθυμία.[4] Since the terms *laetitia* and *tristitia* represent the Greek ἡδονή and λύπη, they are to be translated according to their primary meanings of "pleasure" and "pain," though in some places they may also mean "joy" and "sorrow."[5] The term *dolor*,[6] which also represents the Greek λύπη, is evidently used by Spinoza in the sense of "grief."

These three emotions are what Spinoza calls "primitive or primary emotions (*affectus primitivos, seu primarios*)";[7] and it is in direct opposition to Descartes, who recognizes six "simple and primitive" passions, namely, wonder (*admiratio*), love, hatred, desire, pleasure, and pain,[8] that Spinoza emphasizes that "besides these three — pleasure, pain, and desire — I know of no other primary emotions."[9] Descartes' sixfold classification of the primary emotions and Spinoza's threefold classification may be compared with the fourfold classification of the Stoics, namely, desire (ἐπιθυμία), pleasure (ἡδονή), pain (λύπη), and fear (φόβος).[10] The three primary emotions of Spinoza are taken directly from Des-

---

[1] *De Anima*, III, 7, 431b, 9. Cf. *Aristotelis De Anima* in *Aristotelis Opera* . . . (Venetiis, apud Iunta), Vol. 6 (1574), fol. 173v, D–E.

[2] *De Finibus*, III, 10, § 35.   [3] *Ibid.*, II, 4, § 12.

[4] Cf. above, p. 166.   [5] As, e.g., *Ethics*, V, Prop. 17.

[6] *Ethics*, III, Prop. 11, Schol. Cf. *dolor* (*douleur*) in *Les Passions de l'Ame*, II, 94.

[7] *Ethics*, III, *Affectuum Definitiones*, 4, Expl.

[8] *Les Passions de l'Ame*, II, 69.

[9] *Ethics*, III, Prop. 11, Schol.; *Affectuum Definitiones*, 4, Expl.

[10] Diogenes Laertius, *De Vitis*, VII, 111; Stobaeus, *Eclogae Physicae et Ethicae*, II, 7 (ed. C. Wachsmuth, Vol. II, p. 88); Cicero, *Tusculanae Disputationes*, IV, 6, § 11; *De Finibus*, III, 10, § 35.

cartes' six, and are designated by the same Latin terms, *cupiditas, laetitia, tristitia*. They reflect on the whole three of the four Stoic primary emotions, though the "desire" in the Stoic list is used in the narrow sense of sensual desire, and though, also, in the history of the transmission of the Stoic in Latin translations other terms are used. Thus, for instance, Cicero uses the terms *libido, laetitia*, and *aegritudo*; [1] the Latin translation of Diogenes Laertius' *De Vitis* uses the terms *concupiscentia, voluptas*, and *dolor*,[2] whereas the Latin translation of Stobaeus' *Eclogae* uses the terms *cupiditas, voluptas*, and *dolor*.[3] Descartes himself opposes his own six-fold classification of the emotions to the scholastic twofold classification into concupiscent (*concupiscibilis*) and irascible (*irascibilis*).[4]

III. Derivative Passive Emotions

From these three primary emotions, says Spinoza here, spring (*oriri*) all the other emotions.[5]   But later he explains that they spring from the primary emotions in two ways — namely, either, like the wavering of the mind (*animi fluctuatio*), they are composed (*componitur*) of them, or, like love, hatred, hope, and fear, they are derived (*derivatur*) from them.[6] This corresponds to Descartes' statement that all the other passions "are composed (*componi*) of some of these six, or are species (*species*) of them."[7] A list of forty-eight emotions, including the three primary ones, is given by Spinoza at the end of Part III under the heading of *Affectuum Definitiones*. Of these forty-eight emotions the first forty-

---

[1] See above, p. 207, n. 10.

[2] See above, p. 207, n. 10, and cf. n. 6.

[3] See above, p. 207, n. 10, and cf. *Joannis Stobaei Eclogarum Libri duo . . . interprete Gulielmo Cantero . . .* (Antverpiae, 1775), p. 175.

[4] *Les Passions de l'Ame*, II, 68. Cf. Thomas Aquinas, *Summa Theologica*, Pars I, Quaest. 81, Art. 2.   [5] *Ethics*, III, Prop. 11, Schol.

[6] *Ibid.*, III, Prop. 56.   [7] *Les Passions de l'Ame*, II, 69.

three are taken from Descartes and with but a few slight exceptions are designated by Spinoza by the same terms that occur in the Latin translation of *Les Passions de l'Ame*.[1]

[1] In this list of terms, which are found both in Spinoza and in Descartes, the number to the right of each term refers to *Ethics*, III, *Affectuum Definitiones*, and the number to the left refers to *Les Passions de l'Ame*. The numbers within parentheses refer to the *Short Treatise*. A comparative list of emotions in *Short Treatise* and *Les Passions de l'Ame* is given also in A. Wolf, *Spinoza's Short Treatise*, p. 207.

1. *Cupiditas*, II, 57 and 86. (II, 7.)
2. *Laetitia*, II, 91. (II, 7.)
3. *Tristitia*, II, 61 and 92. (II, 7.)
4. *Admiratio*, II, 53. (II, 3.)
5. *Contemptus*, II, 54. (II, 8, § 2.)
6–7. *Amor, Odium*, II, 56 and 79. (II, 3, 5, and 6.)
9. *Aversio*, II, 85 and 89. (II, 6, § 4.)
10. *Devotio*, II, 83.
11. *Irrisio*, II, 62; III, 178. (II, 11.)
12–13. *Spes, Metus*, II, 58; III, 165. (II, 9, § 3.)
14–15. *Securitas, Desperatio*, II, 58; III, 166. (II, 9, § 3.)
16. *Gaudium*, II, 61.
17. *Conscientiae Morsus*, II, 60; III, 177. (II, 10.)
18. *Commiseratio*, II, 62; III, 185.
19. *Favor*, II, 64; III, 192. (II, 13.)
20. *Indignatio*, II, 65 and 127; III, 195. (II, 11, § 3.)
21. *Existimatio*, II, 54; III, 149.
22. *Despectus*, II, 55; III, 149.
23. *Invidia* II, 62; III, 82. (II, 11, § 3.)
24. *Misericordia*, III, 186.
25. *Acquiescentia in se ipso*, II, 63; III, 190. (II, 8, § 3: *Edelmoedigheid*.)
26. *Humilitas*, II, 54; III, 155. (II, 8, § 4.)
27. *Poenitentia*, II, 63; III, 191. (II, 10.)
28. *Superbia*, II, 54; III, 157. (II, 8, § 5.)
29. *Abjectio*, II, 54; III, 159 and 164. (II, 8, § 6.)
30. *Gloria*, II, 66 and 88; III, 204. (II, 12: *Eer*.)
31. *Pudor*, II, 66; III, 205. (II, 12.)
32. *Desiderium*, II, 67; III, 209. (II, 14.)
33. *Aemulatio*, II, 59; III, 177. (II, 9, § 5.)
34. *Gratitudo*, II, 64; III, 193. (II, 13.)
35. *Benevolentia*, II, 81 and 83.
36. *Ira*, II, 65; III, 199. (II, 11, § 3.)
37. *Vindicta*, II, 88.
38. *Crudelitas*, III, 207.
39. *Timor*, II, 58.
40. *Audacia*, II, 59; III, 171. (II, 9, § 5.)

Similarly the terms of which Spinoza says in these *Affectuum Definitiones* that he passes them by,[1] as well as most of the terms which he happens to define in Scholia to certain propositions, are also found in Descartes.[2] The forty-eight terms in the *Affectuum Definitiones*, it may be further noted, are arranged according to the following scheme: I. The three primary emotions (1-3). II. Two emotions mentioned by Descartes which Spinoza himself does not regard as emotions (4-5). III. Derivative emotions of pleasure and pain (6-31). Derivative emotions of desire (32-48).

The terms in the last five definitions (Defs. 44-48), namely, *ambitio, luxuria, ebrietas, avaritia*, and *libido*, are not taken from Descartes, and according to Spinoza's own statement they constitute a group by themselves and are distinguished from the other emotions in that they have no contraries.[3] The last three of them occur together in Diogenes Laertius thus: φιλαργυρία (*avaritia*), μέθη (*ebrietas*), ἀκολασία (*intemperantia*).[4] Of these three terms, the first two are rendered in the Latin translation accessible to Spinoza by

---

41. *Pusillanimitas*, II, 59; III, 174. (II, 9, § 5.)
42. *Consternatio*, II, 59; III, 174. (II, 9, § 5.)
43. *Modestia*, III, 205.

The exceptions are the following:

8. *Propensio* for *Complacentia*, II, 85, or *inclinatio*, II, 90.
31. Expl., *Verecundia*, not in Descartes, but cf. *Inverecundia*, III, 207.
38. *Crudelitas, seu Saevitia. Saevitia* not in Descartes.
38. Expl., *Clementia* for *Commiseratio*, III, 207.
43. *Humanitas, seu Modestia. Humanitas* not in Descartes, but cf. *Modestiae aut Humilitatis* in III, 205.

[1] *Ethics*, III, *Affectuum Definitiones*, 5, Expl.: "*Veneratio et Dedignatio.*" Cf. *Les Passions de l'Ame*, III, 162-163.

[2] Prop. 11, Schol., *Dolor*, II, 94; *Hilaritas*, II, 67; III, 210; *Titilatio*, II, 94. Prop. 17, Schol., *Animi Fluctuatio*, II, 59; III, 170. (*Short Treatise*, II, 9, § 5.) Prop. 29, Schol., *Laus et Vituperium*, II, 157; III, 206. Prop. 35, Schol., *Zylotypia*, II, 58; III, 167. (*Short Treatise*, II, 9, § 5.)

[3] *Ethics*, III, Prop. 56, Schol.; *Affectuum Definitiones*, 48, Expl.

[4] *De Vitis*, VII, 111.

avaritia and *ebrietas*, exactly the terms used here by Spinoza, but the third is translated by *intemperantia* as against *libido* used here by Spinoza. In a later revised translation, however, which was published after the death of Spinoza, *libido* is substituted for *intemperantia*.[1] But it would seem that all the five terms are taken from one single source, and some day perhaps some one will stumble upon it.

The emotions enumerated and discussed by Spinoza are those which can be found in any traditional work on ethics that was accessible to him. Still, his definitions of certain individual emotions show some departures from his predecessors. In some instances one can detect in his phraseology certain veiled and indirect criticisms of current definitions. A detailed historical study of each of these definitions, including a minute investigation into the variety of Latin renderings of Greek terms, would yield important results for the student of the history of philosophy. But such a study is too complicated and too important for its own sake to be made a sort of appendage to a study of Spinoza. For our immediate purpose it is sufficient to have indicated in a general way the nature of the problem and to have determined the immediate source of Spinoza's selection of the terms. We shall now add some statement as to what seems to us to be the scheme of the classification of these derivative emotions as given by Spinoza in Propositions XII–LVII, particularly attempting to show the logical order in which Spinoza proceeds in these seemingly disconnected propositions.

As is to be expected, Spinoza begins in Propositions XII–XIII with a general statement as to the essential difference

---

[1] Ed. Amsterdam, 1692. I have not before me the editions of 1602, 1615, 1662, and 1663, to see what term is used there. These three emotions occur together also in Stobaeus' *Eclogae*, II, 7 (ed. Wachsmuth, Vol. II, p. 93), but in Canter's Latin translation (p. 177; see above, p. 208, n. 3) the three Greek terms, φιλογυνία, φιλοινία, φιλαργυρία, are reproduced in their original form without a translation.

between primary and derivative emotions. An emotion is primary, he seems to say, when the pleasure and pain which we experience are caused by an external object which is present and as a result of which we either desire that object, that is to say, "we endeavor absolutely to make it exist," or we do not desire that object, that is to say, "we endeavor to destroy or remove it from us." [1] These are the primary emotions of pleasure, pain, and desire. But sometimes we experience pleasure and pain caused by things which are not present but which are imagined by the mind as being present. Similarly the mind in its imagination desires the preservation of the imaginary presence of things which cause us pleasure and the exclusion of the imaginary presence of those things which cause us pain. These constitute the derivative emotions of pleasure, pain, and desire. (Props. XII, XIII and Corol.) But, Spinoza proceeds to say, when the pleasure or pain is caused not by the actual presence of an external cause but rather by the idea of it, then the pleasure and pain are called respectively love and hatred. Though he does not mention Hobbes here in this connection, it would seem that it is in direct opposition to Hobbes, who distinguishes between desire and aversion on the one hand and love and hatred on the other, in that the former signify the absence of the object whereas the latter signify the presence of the object,[2] that Spinoza defines love and hatred as the pleasure or pain accompanied by the *idea* of an external cause. And so also, though the name of Descartes is not mentioned, it would seem that it was Descartes' conception of love as "the will of the lover to unite himself to the beloved object" [3] that Spinoza meant to repudiate in his contention

---

[1] Cf. *Ethics*, III, Prop. 28, Demonst., where references are given to earlier propositions.   [2] *Leviathan*, I, 6.

[3] *Ethics*, III, *Affectuum Definitiones*, 6. Cf. *Les Passions de l'Ame*, II, 79, and below, pp. 276–277, 279–280.

that love and hatred as distinguished from pleasure and pain do not signify the actual presence of the external cause but only the idea of it. Moreover, maintains Spinoza, like any other experience of pleasure and pain, the experience of love and hatred is inseparable from the endeavor "to keep present and preserve that which one loves" or "to remove and destroy the thing one hates" (Prop. XIII, Schol.).

Now this act of the mind in imagining causes of pleasure and pain and preserving them and destroying them is not an arbitrary act. It follows certain rules and is ultimately determined by actually existing external causes. The rules by which the imagination acts are explained by Spinoza in the subsequent propositions.

First, there is the law of the association of emotions (Props. XIV–XVII). An object which has never caused us pleasure, pain, or desire may become a cause of all these emotions by its being associated in our mind with something which did cause us pleasure and pain and desire. The term "association" is not used here by Spinoza, but what we should call association is described by Spinoza as an accidental (*per accidens*) cause (Prop. XV). Now, the laws of association, as enumerated by Aristotle, are based upon three conditions: (1) similarity, (2) contrast, and (3) contiguity (σύνεγγυς),[1] which, according to Aristotle's use of the term, refers both to contiguity of place and to contiguity of time. Of these three Aristotelian laws of association, two, similarity and temporal contiguity, are described by Spinoza in *Tractatus Theologico-Politicus* as "the law that a man in remembering one thing, straightway remembers another either like it, or which he had perceived simultaneously with it."[2] Above in the Second Part of the *Ethics* Spinoza de-

---

[1] *De Memoria*, 2, 451b, 19–20.
[2] Ch. 4 (*Opera*, III, p. 58, ll. 1–3).

scribed only association by temporal contiguity.[1] Here, again, as in the *Tractatus Theologico-Politicus*, he describes two kinds of association of ideas, or rather of emotions, that of temporal contiguity in Proposition XIV and that of similarity in Proposition XVI.

The discussion of association by similarity in Proposition XVI leads Spinoza to the discussion of what he calls, after the Latin translation of Descartes' *Les Passions de l'Ame*, "*Animi fluctuatio*," [2] i.e., wavering of the mind, for the first kind of this *animi fluctuatio* mentioned by Spinoza, as we shall see, is based upon association by similarity. The original French term used by Descartes for this kind of emotions is "irresolution." Spinoza similarly describes these emotions as inconstant (*non . . . constantes*)[3] and as emotions involving doubt or something like doubt.[4] In Propositions XVII–XVIII and their Scholia, Spinoza enumerates three kinds of such *animi fluctuatio*. The first kind is described by him as a sort of conflict of emotions arising from "causes which bring about one of the emotions essentially (*per se*) and the other accidentally (*per accidens*)," [5] that is to say, by the association of ideas, as, for instance, when an object which causes us pain is similar to another object which causes us pleasure (Prop. XVII). The second kind of *animi fluctuatio* is described by him as arising from "an object which is the efficient cause of both emotions," [6] that is to say, is the essential cause of two opposite emotions. The third kind of *animi fluctuatio* is described by Spinoza as arising from the "image of a past or future thing" (Prop. XVIII), inasmuch

---

[1] *Ethics*, II, Prop. 18. Cf. above, pp. 89–90.

[2] *Ibid.*, III, Prop. 17, Schol. Cf. Descartes, *Les Passions de l'Ame*, II, 59; III, 170.

[3] *Ibid.*, III, Prop. 18, Schol. I (*Opera*, II, p. 155, l. 3).

[4] *Ibid.*, III, Prop. 17, Schol.; Prop. 18, Schol. I.

[5] *Ibid.*, III, Prop. 17, Schol.   [6] *Ibid.*

as "it generally happens that those who possess much experience hesitate when they think of a thing as past or future, and doubt greatly concerning its issue," and "therefore the emotions which spring from such images of things are not so constant, but are generally disturbed by the images of other things" (Schol. I).

Second, there is the law of the imitation of emotions (Props. XIX–XXXII). Though Spinoza uses the expression "imitation of emotions" (*affectuum imitatio*) only with reference to the subject discussed in Proposition XXVII, it may be taken as his explanation of everything discussed in Propositions XIX–XXXII. According to this law, an object which is neither an essential nor an accidental cause of pleasure or pain or desire may become a cause of all these emotions if it happens to cause them to other human beings whose emotions we naturally tend to imitate. In discussing the imitation of emotions Spinoza divides the subject into two parts: First, the imitation of the emotions of those whom we love or hate (Props. XIX–XXVI). Second, the imitation of the emotions of other human beings in general, whom we neither love nor hate (Props. XXVII–XXXII).

The imitation of emotions, however, is used by Spinoza as a very comprehensive principle which manifests itself in various forms of action.

In the first place, we participate in the emotions of those whom we love or hate. The underlying cause for this kind of emotions is that we are pained or pleased at the destruction or preservation of those whom we love (Prop. XIX), and if we are not completely pained at the preservation of those whom we hate, — for even those whom we hate are human beings and we have natural sympathy for them,[1] — we are still partially pleased at their destruction (Prop. XX).

[1] *Ibid.*, III, Prop. 23, Schol.

As a result of this emotion of pleasure and pain we are also affected by the pleasure and pain of those whom we love (Prop. XXI), and we love or hate those who cause pleasure and pain to those whom we love (Prop. XXII). Similarly we are partially pained and pleased respectively at the pleasure and pain of those whom we hate (Prop. XXIII), and we hate or love a person according as he causes pleasure or pain to those whom we hate (Prop. XXIV). All this may be called the Participation of Emotions.

In the second place, we endeavor to affirm concerning those whom we love, as we do concerning ourselves, that which we imagine to produce pleasure, and to deny of them that which we imagine to produce pain (Prop. XXV). Conversely, too, we endeavor to affirm concerning those whom we hate that which we imagine to produce pain, and to deny of them that which we imagine to produce pleasure (Prop. XXVI). This may be called the Affirmation and Denial of Emotions.

These two forms of the imitation of emotions, namely, the Participation of Emotions and the Affirmation and Denial of Emotions, are provoked not only by those whom we love or hate but also by those whom we regard with no emotion whatever, for every human being, by the mere fact that he is like ourselves, will cause us to participate in his emotions and to affirm of him that which we imagine to produce pleasure and to deny of him that which we imagine to produce pain (Prop. XXVII).

Furthermore, there are other forms of the imitation of emotions. In the first place, there is a sort of altruistic emotion, by which we endeavor to do that which we imagine to cause pleasure to others and to desist from doing that which we imagine to cause them pain (Props. XXVIII–XXIX). This altruistic emotion, Spinoza would seem to say, is to be regarded as a form of imitation, for our effort to cause pleasure to others is nothing but an effort on our part to cause others to imitate our own emotions of pleasure. Then, this altruistic emotion reacts upon us and produces in us an imitation of it (Prop. XXX). Moreover, by the imitation of the emotion of others toward an object, our own emotion toward that object, if it is of the same kind, will become intensified, and, if it is of the opposite kind, will come in conflict with it and hence produce a wavering of the mind, *animi fluctuatio* (Prop. XXXI). Finally, emotions which have been produced in us by the imitation of the emotion of others may result in our becoming inimical to the enjoyment by those others of the very same emotions which have originally inspired our own emotions (Prop. XXXII).

This, I believe, is the logical reconstruction of Propositions XIX–XXXII. All of them deal with the theory of the imitation of emotions in its various phases.

The remaining propositions dealing with derivative passive emotions fall into the following groups:

I. Emotions of love and hatred (Props. XXXIII–XLIX).

II. Imaginary hope and fear (Prop. L).

III. Relativity of emotions (Prop. LI).

IV. Wonder (*admiratio*), which, in opposition to Descartes, Spinoza does not consider an emotion,[1] and its derivatives (Prop. LII).

V. Emotions arising from the mind's contemplation of itself (Props. LIII–LV).

VI. The indefiniteness of the number of derivative emotions (Prop. LVI).

VII. Individual and generic differences within each particular emotion (Props. LVII and Schol.).

---

[1] Cf. *ibid.*, III, *Affectuum Definitiones*, 4, Expl.

IV. Active Emotions

These passive emotions which Spinoza also calls the passiveness of the soul (*pathema animi*)[1] or the passion of the soul (*passio animi*)[2] are characterized chiefly by the fact that there is always an external cause which produces them, and that man himself is therefore only their inadequate or partial cause. As against these there are the active emotions, or, as Spinoza describes them, "emotions which are related to the mind in so far as it acts"[3] and of which man is the adequate cause. In contradistinction to the three primary passive emotions there are only two primary active emotions, desire and pleasure, for pain is always a passive emotion. As active emotions, desire is the effort to self-preservation by the dictates of reason, and pleasure is the enjoyment experienced from the mind's contemplation of itself whenever it conceives a true or adequate idea. Truly speaking, these distinctions between the active and passive emotions of desire and pleasure are nothing more than Spinoza's way of reproducing in his own terms the old Aristotelian distinction between rational and irrational desire[4] and between the pleasures of the intellect and the pleasures of the senses.[5] All the actions which follow from these active emotions are ascribed by Spinoza to *fortitudo*, which he divides into *animositas* and *generositas*.

There is a story behind this combination of terms. The term *fortitudo* is generally used as the Latin translation of the Greek ἀνδρεία.[6] According to Thomas Aquinas the term *fortitudo* can be taken in two ways. "First, as simply de-

---

[1] *Ibid.*, III, *Affectuum Generalis Definitio.*
[2] *Ibid.*, Expl.   [3] *Ibid.*, III, Prop. 59.
[4] *De Anima*, III, 9, 432b, 3–6.
[5] *Nicomachean Ethics*, X, 5, 1175a, 26–28.
[6] *Ibid.*, III, 6, 1115a, 6 ff.

noting a certain firmness of mind; and in this sense it is a general virtue, or rather a condition of every virtue, since, as the Philosopher states in *Ethics*, II, it is requisite for every virtue to act firmly and immovably.[1] Secondly, fortitude may be taken to denote firmness only in bearing and withstanding those things wherein it is most difficult to be firm, namely, in certain grave dangers. . . . In this sense fortitude is reckoned a special virtue, because it has a special matter."[2] The term *animositas* is taken by Spinoza from the Latin translation of Descartes' *Les Passions de l'Ame*, where the corresponding French term is *courage*,[3] and consequently it is also a translation of the Greek ἀνδρεία. Similarly the term *generositas* is taken from the same work of Descartes, where it is said to be the equivalent of the scholastic *magnanimitas*[4] and hence a translation of the Greek μεγαλοψυχία.[5] Now, *magnanimitas* is said by Thomas Aquinas to be either identical with *fortitudo*, according to Seneca and Cicero, or a part of *fortitudo*, according to Macrobius.[6] Evidently having all this in the back of his mind, Spinoza says that he ascribes all the actions which follow from the active emotions to *fortitudo*, which he uses as simply denoting what Thomas Aquinas describes as a certain firmness of the mind which is a condition of every virtue. This he then divides into *animositas* and *generositas*, the former of which, as we have seen, is *fortitudo* in the sense of what Thomas Aquinas describes as a special virtue, such as "bearing and withstanding" difficulties in great danger, and the latter of which, being the equivalent of *magnanimitas*, is likewise related to *fortitudo*, being either a kind of *fortitudo* or a part of it.

---

[1] Cf. *Nicomachean Ethics*, II, 4, 1105a, 32–33.
[2] *Summa Theologica*, Secunda Secundae, Quaest. 123, Art. 2.
[3] *Les Passions de l'Ame*, II, 59.   [4] *Ibid.*, III, 161; cf. II, 54.
[5] *Nicomachean Ethics*, IV, 3, 1123a, 34 ff.
[6] *Summa Theologica*, Secunda Secundae, Quaest. 129, Art. 5.

Though the terms *animositas* and *generositas* are both taken by Spinoza from Descartes, it is only the former term that is defined by him as it is defined by Descartes. *Animositas* is defined by Descartes as "a certain heat or agitation which disposes the soul forcibly to bend itself powerfully to the execution of the things which it desires to do." [1] Similarly, Spinoza defines it here with some modifications as "the desire by which each person endeavors from the dictates of reason to preserve his own being." [2] *Generositas* is explained by Descartes in two places. In one place, he simply changes the term *generositas* which appears in the heading of the chapter to the term *magnanimitas* which appears within the text of the chapter, and explains the latter to mean pride (*superbia*),[3] which, of course, is to be taken in the sense of justifiable pride, as its corresponding Greek term μεγαλοψυ-χία is explained by Aristotle.[4] In another place, he similarly explains *generositas* as "that which causes us only to esteem ourselves at a just value." [5] Spinoza, however, uses it in its derivative sense of the good man, which is already given by Aristotle in his discussion of μεγαλοψυχία,[6] and defines it as "the desire by which from the dictates of reason alone each person endeavors to help other people and to join them to him in friendship." [7] Finally, just as Descartes says of *generositas* that it is the "key of all other virtues, and a general remedy for all the disorders of the passions," [8] so Spinoza says of both *generositas* and *animositas* that "nothing can be opposed to these emotions but *generositas* and *animositas*." [9]

[1] *Les Passions de l'Ame*, III, 171.   [2] *Ethics*, III, Prop. 59, Schol.
[3] *Les Passions de l'Ame*, II, 54.
[4] *Nicomachean Ethics*, IV, 3, 1123b, 2 ff.
[5] *Les Passions de l'Ame*, III, 161.
[6] *Nicomachean Ethics*, IV, 3, 1123b, 26 ff.
[7] *Ethics*, III, Prop. 59, Schol.   [8] *Les Passions de l'Ame*, III, 161.
[9] *Ethics*, III, *Affectuum Definitiones*, 48, Expl.

CHAPTER XIX

VIRTUES

IN THE religion upon which Spinoza was brought up the course of human conduct was plotted out for men by a Law which was held to be of divine origin. The expression of an arbitrary will of God, that Law was regarded as an imposition as well as a restraint upon the natural impulses of men. Obedience to it was virtue; disobedience was vice. As man was believed to be free to choose between obedience and disobedience, he was to be rewarded or punished in accordance with his actions. Man was urged, however, not to choose obedience in the hope of receiving the expected reward, nor to eschew disobedience for fear of the threatened punishment. The Law was to be fulfilled for its own sake and not from hope or fear or any other external motive.

As he grew older and began to study the mediaeval theologians, especially Maimonides, Spinoza learned of another conception of the Law. Of divine origin it still was, but not arbitrary and purposeless and contrary to human nature. With the exception of certain precepts for which no obvious reason could be discovered by the human mind — though that by no means precluded the possibility of some reason — the Law as a whole had a double purpose. In the first place, it was to help man to attain the highest moral and intellectual perfection of which as a human being he was capable, and in the second place, it was to bring about the establishment of an ideal social order in which the individual might find the most advantageous conditions for the development of the highest capacities.[1] Such expressions as "rational precepts"[2] and "natural law"[3] as a designation of the divinely revealed precepts and ordinances then came into being. This method of rationalization, Spinoza discovered, was common to both Jewish and Christian theologians, and was continued almost to his own time even by such political thinkers as Grotius [4] and Hobbes.

Upon his becoming acquainted with the works of the ancient pagan philosophers, especially Aristotle, Spinoza recognized in these various attempts to interpret the laws of the Scriptures as laws of nature or of reason merely an application of the ethical speculations of ancient philosophers to the laws of Moses. In the writings of Aristotle and in the works which transmitted the teachings of the Stoics he found the origin of those views which are only faintly reflected in the works of the rationalist Jewish and Christian theologians. To this method of rationalization as a whole he was not averse, and in his own way he has made use of it in his *Tractatus Theologico-Politicus*. In his *Ethics*, however, he chose to follow the method of Aristotle and the other pagan moralists and to present the problems of conduct independently of the Scriptural teachings.

A fault which Spinoza finds alike in the naïve traditional conception of the revealed Law as something arbitrary and in the rationalistic conception of it as something purposive is that they both set up an absolute conception of perfection and goodness. To both of them the revealed Law was an ideal standard for human conduct. The perfect action of man, which by the original use of the term "perfection"

---

[1] *Moreh Nebukim*, III, 27 ff. Cf. below, pp. 326–328.

[2] מצות שכליות, *Emunot we-De'ot*, III, 2.

[3] דת טבעית, *'Ikkarim*, I, 7.

[4] On Grotius, cf. I. Husik, "The Law of Nature, Hugo Grotius, and the Bible," in *Hebrew Union College Annual*, II (1925), pp. 381 ff.

in the sense of "completeness" and of not lacking anything required by one's own nature should mean a maximum attainment of "his power of action, in so far as it is understood by his own nature," [1] has thus come to mean action in conformity with some external code of conduct drawn up either contrary to the nature of man or for a human nature supposed to be ideally conceived in the mind of God and to which man must strive to attain by struggling against his real nature. Similarly goodness, which according to an old philosophic definition adopted by Spinoza means "that which we certainly know is useful to us," [2] has come to mean obedience to the commands of a revealed religion which we are told is useful to us. It is this which has induced men to give "the name good" not only "to everything which leads to health" but also, and very often primarily, to that which leads to "the worship of God." [3]

But even the old pagan philosophers were not completely acceptable to Spinoza. They all speak of virtue and vice as something distinct from emotions. Whatever their metaphysical conception of human freedom is, they all maintain that virtue and vice are voluntary, that our actions originate in ourselves, and that hence we are to be praised for our virtues and blamed for our vices.[4] Spinoza is to disagree with this. Our virtues and vices, he is to argue, are not voluntary, our actions do not originate in ourselves, and hence we are not to be praised for our virtues nor blamed for our vices.

Had Spinoza written his *Ethics* after the manner of the rabbis and scholastics he would have prefaced its Fourth

---

[1] *Ethics*, IV, Praef. (*Opera*, II, p. 208, ll. 28–29). Cf. *Short Treatise*, II, 4, § 5.

[2] *Ethics*, IV, Praef. (*Opera*, II, p. 208, ll. 18–20); Def. 1; *Nicomachean Ethics*, I, 6, 1096b, 14 ff.; Diogenes Laertius, *De Vitis*, VII, 94.

[3] *Ethics*, I, Appendix (*Opera*, II, p. 81, ll. 34–35).

[4] Cf. above, p. 182, and below, pp. 224–225.

Part with a statement which would have read somewhat as follows.

Part IV. Wherein we shall discuss the nature of what is known among the philosophers as virtues and vices, for having discussed in Part III the nature of the emotions, we deem it proper to discuss after that the nature of virtue and vice. We shall divide this Part into two main sections. First, wherein we shall show that the distinction made by the philosophers between emotions and virtues is untenable (Props. I–XVIII). Secondly, wherein we shall outline our own conception of human conduct, based indeed on the writings of the philosophers, but presented in a way which is our own (Scholium to Prop. XVIII–Prop. LXXIII). This second section we shall further subdivide into three topics: (*a*) the relation of happiness to virtue (Scholium to Prop. XVIII–Prop. XXVIII), (*b*) the origin and nature of society (Props. XXIX–XL), and (*c*) the meaning of virtue in general and of certain individual virtues in particular (Props. XLI–LXXIII).

I. Emotions and Virtues

The freedom which to his philosophic predecessors determined the nature of virtue and vice was expressed in two terms, "knowledge" and "will." Sometimes only one of these terms is mentioned, as, for instance, when Socrates says that all virtue is knowledge [1] or when Cicero says that all virtues are dependent on the will,[2] but sometimes the two terms are joined together in one single term, as when, for instance, Aristotle defines virtue as that which is related to choice, and then defines choice as deliberate desire or will, from which he infers that if the choice is to be good both the

---

[1] *Nicomachean Ethics*, VI, 13, 1144b, 17 ff. Cf. Plato, *Laches* 194D.
[2] *De Finibus*, V, 13, § 36.

reasoning must be true and the desire must be right.[1] The fine points of difference between statements that virtue depends upon knowledge and statements that virtue depends upon will do not concern Spinoza for his present purpose. To him, with his own view that intellect and will are identical, there is no difference between these two kinds of statements. What is of interest to him is the general agreement of philosophers that right or wrong conduct for which man is to be praised or blamed is determined by his knowledge or his will, and that man is a free agent to choose his course of action. It is with a criticism of this view that he opens up the Fourth Part of the *Ethics*.

His argument may be outlined as follows. You say that virtue differs from emotion in that the former is dependent upon free will whereas the latter is determined by causes. But I have already shown that there is no free will and that actions, like emotions, are determined by external causes. Now, since in the case of emotions it must be admitted that an emotion which has been determined by an external cause cannot be removed by mere knowledge (Prop. I) or by mere will (Props. II–VII), the same must also be true in the case of actions, namely, that no action which has been determined by an external cause can be changed by mere knowledge or by mere will. There is no difference therefore between virtue and emotion, or, to be more exact, between what is called virtue and vice and the emotions of pleasure and pain (Prop. VIII). The only way in which an emotion can be removed is by another emotion, provided it is stronger than the first on account of its being caused by external causes which are stronger than those which caused the first emotion (Props. IX–XVIII). And so also, I contend, the only way in which an action can be changed is by another action which is

[1] *Nicomachean Ethics*, VI, 2, 1139a, 22 ff. Cf. II, 6, 1106b, 36 ff.

stronger than the first on account of its being caused by external causes which are stronger than those which caused the first action. Now, among the external forces which determine action as well as emotions is the power of reason, or that kind of knowledge which I call the second. It is a power within us, or, if you prefer, I will call it virtue, for the original meaning of the term "virtue" is power, and that power or virtue, when once fully developed within us, acts as do our physiological reflexes, without any intervention of what you call free will. In this sense I admit with you that virtue is dependent upon knowledge, or rather upon reason, and thus, following your example, I too shall make a catalogue of virtues (Scholium to Prop. XVIII–Prop. LXXIII).

But let us now see how this argument which we have put in the mouth of Spinoza unfolds itself in its own propositions.

In the first place, he argues in Proposition I, an emotion cannot be removed by knowledge. Any emotion (*affectus*) which is a passiveness or a passion of the soul (*animi pathema, animi passio*) has already been described as a confused idea (*confusa idea*),[1] and it may therefore be described also as a false idea (*idea falsa*).[2] Now a confused or false idea is like an imagination (*imaginatio*)[3] in that it indicates the present constitution of the human body rather than the nature of the external body which produces the passive emotion.[4] Still, while this kind of knowledge of the external body, being only a confused or false idea of it, is only negative, the emotion itself may be considered as something positive. Thus when we look at the sun and imagine its distance from us to be about two hundred feet, that idea or imagination of its distance, to be sure, is confused and false; still the

---

[1] *Ethics*, III, *Affectuum Generalis Definitio*
[2] *Ibid.*, IV, Prop. 1.   [3] *Ibid.*, Schol.
[4] *Ibid.*, III, *Affectuum Generalis Definitio*, and IV, Prop. I, Schol.

emotion produced by the effect of the sun's heat and light upon us which gives us the impression of nearness is something positive and cannot be removed by a mere knowledge of the sun's true distance. It can be removed only when the sun happens to be shut out by a passing cloud which produces in us a different emotion, based perhaps upon the false imagination that the sun has been swallowed up by some invisible dragon, but still an imagination which is stronger than the first imagination, thus producing upon us a new and stronger impression which removes the first impression of the sun's nearness to us. Consequently, "nothing contained in a false idea is removed by the presence of the true in so far as it is true"; [1] it is removed only when "other imaginations arise which are stronger, and which exclude the present existence of the objects we imagine." [2] Or, as he says later in Proposition XIV, the mere knowledge of the truth of a thing will not remove the present emotion produced by the effect of the thing upon us unless that knowledge itself is transformed into an emotion, and a stronger emotion at that.

In the second place, Spinoza argues in Propositions II–VII, an emotion cannot be removed by will. Will, like appetite and desire, has already been defined by him to mean essentially the conatus to persevere in existence,[3] and consequently in these propositions instead of using the term "will" Spinoza uses the term "conatus" or some form of it. The argument contained in these propositions is closely knit. It may be reproduced as follows: Man is not only a mode or part of God or of the eternal and infinite order of nature, but he is also a part of the common order of nature, an individual thing among many other individual things, all of

---

[1] *Ibid.*, IV, Prop. 1.　　　　　[2] *Ibid.*, Schol.
[3] *Ibid.*, III, Prop. 9, Schol.

which act upon him as external causes, for "it is impossible that a man should not be a part of nature and should not follow her common order; but if he be placed amongst individuals who agree with his nature, his power of action will by that very fact be assisted and supported. But if, on the contrary, he be placed amongst individuals who do not in the least agree with his nature, he will scarcely be able without great change on his part to accommodate himself to them."[1] Consequently, "we suffer in so far as we are a part of [the common order of] nature,[2] which part cannot be conceived by itself nor without the other parts" (Prop. II). Indeed, "the force by which man perseveres in existence" is the actual power of God, that is, of the eternal and infinite order of nature, but not in so far as that power is infinite, but only in so far as it can be manifested by the actual essence of man, that is to say, in so far as it is finite (*ibid.*, Demonst.). That power or conatus is therefore "limited, and infinitely surpassed by the power of external causes" (Prop. III). Since this is so, "it is impossible that a man should not be a part of [the common order of] nature, and that he should suffer no changes but those which can be understood through his own nature alone, and of which he is the adequate cause" (Prop. IV). This consequently leads to the conclusion that "a man is necessarily always subject to passions" (*ibid.*, Corol.). "The force and increase" of any of these passions or emotions are limited only "by the power of an external cause compared with our own power" (Prop. V), and "may so far surpass the rest of the actions or the power of a man that the emotion may obstinately cling to him" (Prop. VI). Once any of these emotions clings to a man

---

[1] *Ibid.*, IV, Appendix, 7.

[2] That the term "nature" in this proposition means the "common order of nature" becomes evident upon comparison with the preceding quotation.

it "cannot be restrained nor removed unless by an opposed and stronger emotion" (Prop. VII).

With the elimination of the difference between emotion and virtue the difference between physical and moral good and evil likewise disappears. In the philosophic writings with which Spinoza was acquainted the good was always discussed in connection with the useful and the pleasant. Socrates maintained that goodness is utility.[1] Aristotle speaks of the "good, or pleasant, or useful," and adds that the "useful may be taken to mean productive of some good or of pleasure."[2] Or he distinguishes between things good in themselves and things useful, and among the former he includes certain pleasures.[3] The Stoics argue that the good cannot be identified with pleasure; still it is identified by them with the advantageous.[4] Spinoza combines all these utilitarian and hedonistic conceptions of the good into his various definitions of the term. He sometimes speaks of the good as consisting of "every kind of pleasure (*laetitiae*),"[5] and sometimes he says that the good is "that which we certainly know is useful to us."[6] In this he is merely following the well-established philosophic tradition, using it, as we have suggested above, in opposition to the traditional religious conception that the good is that which conforms to the precepts of the revealed Law. But while he follows the phraseology of the old philosophic tradition, he in no way accepts its implication. For to his philosophic predecessors the good, however defined, whether as pleasure or as utility, was an object of deliberate desire or choice or will. "There are three objects of choice," says Aristotle, "the noble, the

---

[1] Plato, *Protagoras* 333D.

[2] *Nicomachean Ethics*, VIII, 2, 1155b, 19–20.

[3] *Ibid.*, I, 6, 1096b, 14–18.

[4] Diogenes Laertius, *De Vitis*, VII, 94.

[5] *Ethics*, III, Prop. 39, Schol.   [6] *Ibid.*, IV, Def. 1.

advantageous, the pleasant." [1] But to Spinoza the element
of choice or will is eliminated. Only that of consciousness is
present. "Knowledge of good and evil is nothing but the
emotion of pleasure and pain in so far as we are conscious of
it" (Prop. VIII). Good, whether physical or moral, is a
consciousness of pleasure; evil, again whether physical or
moral, is a consciousness of pain.

Spinoza has thus in the first eight propositions laid down
the general principle that emotions, and for that matter also
actions, are not determined by mere knowledge or will, and
he has also defined the meaning of good and evil. Now in
the next ten propositions (IX–XVIII) he undertakes to
show how in the conflict of emotions, without any knowledge or will on the part of him who suffers the emotions,
weaker emotions are removed by stronger emotions. These
ten propositions fall into two equal groups of five each. Each
of these two groups begins with a proposition which may be
considered as introductory. The subject of the first group
is the conflict between emotions toward objects which differ
either with reference to the future, present, or past time of
their existence, or with reference to the necessity, contingency, or possibility of their existence (Props. X–XIII). This
is introduced by the general statement that an emotion is
stronger if its cause is imagined to be present than if it is not
imagined to be present (Prop. IX). The subject of the second group is the conflict of desires, in which either only one
of the conflicting desires (Prop. XV) or both conflicting desires (Props. XVI–XVII) spring from a true knowledge of
good and evil, i.e., from the consciousness of pleasure and
pain (Props. XV–XVII), or one of the conflicting desires
springs from pleasure and the other from pain (Prop. XVIII).
This is introduced by the general statement that the knowl-

[1] *Nicomachean Ethics*, II, 3, 1104b, 30–31.

edge of good and evil can be a determining factor in the conflict of desires only in so far as it is considered as an emotion,
i.e., as a consciousness of pleasure and pain (Prop. XIV).

Thus an emotion cannot be removed by mere knowledge or
will, but only by another emotion which happens to be
stronger. The emotions, like other physical forces in nature,
follow from the necessity of the eternal order of the universe.
The emotions sometimes cross one another and come into
conflict with one another just as do any other physical
forces of nature. When such a conflict arises, the stronger
emotion will subdue the weaker just as in the conflict of any
other physical forces of nature. And just as in the case of
the conflict of the physical forces of nature man may suffer
evil, so in the case of the conflict of his emotions and the inevitable victory of the stronger emotion over the weaker
man may suffer evil or pain or a diminution of his power of
action toward his self-preservation. This is what Spinoza
describes as "human impotence and want of stability"[1]
or that "impotence of man to govern or restrain the emotions" which constitutes his "servitude," inasmuch as a man
who is at the mercy of his emotions "is not his own master,
but is mastered by fortune, in whose power he is, so that he
is often forced to follow the worse, although he sees the better before him."[2]

Man, however, is not left unprotected against his own
emotions any more than he is left unprotected against the
physical forces of nature. Reason, and the knowledge
which springs from reason, is a means whereby man can not
only master the adverse forces of nature but can also overcome the assaults of his own emotions. In its capacity as an
instrument for self-preservation, reason overcomes the ad-

---

[1] *Ethics*, IV, Prop. 18, Schol.
[2] *Ibid.*, IV, Praef. (*Opera*, II, p. 205, ll. 7–12).

verse forces of nature by setting up against them favorable forces which are stronger. Similarly, in its capacity as an instrument for self-mastery, it overcomes the emotions which are passive by producing against them stronger emotions which are active. In either case reason is the blind tool of nature, and not an instrument wielded by man as a free agent. Reason (*ratio*) is that which Spinoza calls the second kind of knowledge. It is a knowledge of the rules of the game of nature. It is not confused or false knowledge, nor is it even true knowledge of an isolated single fact. It is the knowledge of the common notions and the adequate ideas of the properties of things and of the true deductions from these common notions.[1] To act according to reason, however, does not imply freedom of the will. Reason itself is a part of nature, and it follows from the necessity of the attribute of thought. When Spinoza urges man to act according to reason, then, unlike all his predecessors who had similarly used this phraseology in prescribing human conduct, he does not mean thereby an exhortation to man to exercise his free will; with him it is only an exhortation to man to acquire the proper kind of knowledge upon which reason is nurtured, so that it may grow in strength and assert itself in its full power when called into action. At the challenge of the emotions reason springs into action in the same manner as our eyelids close at the sudden approach of danger to our eyes. In this sense indeed knowledge is virtue, and a life according to virtue will be a life according to reason — a kind of reason which follows by necessity from one's true knowledge. How reason works for the wellbeing of man against the assaults of his own emotions is explained by Spinoza in what he calls the "Dictates of Reason" (Prop. XVIII, Schol. ff.).

[1] Cf. above, pp. 117 ff., 138–140, 149.

II. Happiness and Virtue

In his "Dictates of Reason," the problems which Spinoza has set himself, the answers which he gives, and the methods by which he proceeds all reflect the common tradition of religious and philosophical writings. Like Socrates and Aristotle, he starts out with the question of what happiness is and what virtue is. Taking up again the philosophic commonplace that the primary conatus of every person is towards self-preservation, he arrives at the conclusion that happiness consists in man's ability to preserve his own being. Together with Aristotle, the Stoics, and the masters of his own religion, he repeats that virtue is to be desired for its own sake. Then in the Scholium to Proposition XVIII and in a series of propositions to the end of the Fourth Part he deals with certain stock problems of ethical philosophy in the following order:

I. Happiness and Virtue (Props. XIX–XXVIII).
II. Society and the State (Props. XXIX–XL).
III. Catalogue of Virtues (Props. XLI–LXXIII).

It is, however, Aristotle's *Nicomachean Ethics* which has served Spinoza as the basic and direct source of his succeeding propositions, especially Propositions XIX–XXVIII. He seems to have had in his mind, while drawing up these propositions, a topical outline of that book, and upon it he has modelled his own discussions of goodness, virtue, happiness, and of the life in accordance with reason. He seems to have followed that outline quite closely, agreeing with certain parts of it while disagreeing with others. That outline, we may assume, must have run as follows:

Everything aims at some good. The good is therefore that at which all things aim (ἐφίεται). The good is also pleasant and useful,[1] and it is called the end (τέλος),[2] or that "for the sake of which everything else is done." [3]

In order to know what the good of man consists in, and especially his highest good, it must be first determined whether man has any function, and, if so, what that function is, "for, as with a flute-player, a sculptor, or any artist, and in fact anybody who has a definite function and action, his goodness and efficiency seem to lie in his function, so it would seem to be with man, if indeed he has a definite function." [4] Now, man has a definite function, just as each of the various members of the body manifestly has a certain function of its own. This definite function of man may seem to be the mere act of living, but it is not, for this is shared even by plants, whereas what we are looking for is the function which is peculiar to man. Nor is sentient life the peculiar function of man, for this is shared by animals. The peculiar function of man as man pertains to that which is peculiar to man alone. It is the activity of soul in accordance with reason. This, however, is only the general function of man as a human being. Besides this, there are certain particular functions which belong to individual human beings as individuals, for just as one harpist may play the harp better than another, so there are certain individual human beings who may perform the general function of man better than others. The particular form of goodness or proficiency with which an individual man is capable of performing his general human function is called his virtue (ἀρετή), and a man is therefore said to perform his general human function successfully if he performs it in accordance with his own proper virtue. The good of man as an individual human being is

[1] *Nicomachean Ethics*, I, 1, 1094a, 1–3.
[2] *Ibid.*, I, 2, 1094a, 18 ff.   [3] *Ibid.*, I, 7, 1097a, 10 ff.
[4] *Ibid.*, 1097b, 25–28.

therefore defined as "an activity of soul in accordance with virtue." [1]

Goods are many, and among them there is one which is the highest good. This highest good is spoken of by "both the multitude and persons of refinement" as happiness (εὐδαιμονία), and "they conceive that to live well (εὖ ζῆν, *bene vivere*), or to do well (εὖ πράττειν, *bene agere*), is the same thing as to be happy (εὐδαιμονεῖν, *felicem esse*)." [2]

Happiness, then, is some form of activity. It is an activity according to virtue, which is also according to reason. Being an activity according to virtue, happiness is an activity desirable in itself, since "this is felt to be the nature of actions in conformity with virtue; for to do noble and virtuous deeds is a thing desirable for its own sake." [3]

The definition of goodness as an activity of the soul in accordance with virtue leaves still one question unsolved. Virtues are twofold, moral and intellectual, determined by activities of different parts of the soul. Which of these virtues, then, will characterize the highest good of man? Aristotle's answer is that it is the virtue of the best part of us, that is, of reason. The highest good of man is contemplative activity. In proof of this he shows that contemplation is the highest form of activity, that it is the most continuous, that it is the most pleasant, that it is the most self-sufficient, and, finally, that it is the activity of the divine in man. [4]

This is a topical outline of the *Nicomachean Ethics* as it must have presented itself in the mind of Spinoza. Let us now see how Spinoza reproduces it and modifies it.

Like Aristotle, Spinoza begins with the general statement that "according to the laws of his own nature each person aims (*appetit*) at that which he considers to be good" (Prop.

---

[1] *Ibid.*, 1098a, 16–17.　　　[2] *Ibid.*, I, 4, 1095a, 19–20.
[3] *Ibid.*, X, 6, 1176b, 7–9.　　　[4] *Ibid.*, X, 7.

XIX). The term *appetit* here, which I have translated by "aims at," reflects the Greek ἐφίεται in the corresponding passage of Aristotle, for so also in the Latin version of Averroes' *Middle Commentary* on the *Nicomachean Ethics* is that Greek term translated by *appetunt*. As that which all things aim at is also called by Aristotle the end, Spinoza says that "by end (*finis*, τέλος), for the sake of which we do anything, I understand appetite (*appetitum*),"[1] that is to say, that which is aimed at. That Spinoza is consciously imitating Aristotle in his discussion of the problem of the highest good and happiness may be gathered also from the *Tractatus de Intellectus Emendatione*, where he follows Aristotle still further in enumerating three things, outside contemplation, which are generally considered by men as the highest good, namely, riches, honor, and pleasure.[2] In the course of his discussion here in the *Ethics* he also repeats his own view, for which, as we have seen, there are philosophical precedents,[3] that the good is also pleasant and useful.[4] In all this, he is following Aristotle.

But when he comes to define what the good is, he departs from Aristotle. In opposition to Aristotle, he seems to contend that in order to find out what the good is at which all men by the necessity of their nature aim we must not ascertain what the particular function of man as a rational being is, nor even what his more general functions as a sentient and living being are, but rather what his function as a mere being, as a part of nature, is. Taking up again the old principle of self-preservation which originally was used by the Stoics in connection with animate beings but which Spinoza,

---

[1] *Ethics*, IV, Def. 7.

[2] *Tractatus de Intellectus Emendatione*, § 3 (*Opera*, II, pp. 5–6); cf. *Nicomachean Ethics*, I, 5.

[3] Cf. above, pp. 229, 233–234.

[4] *Ethics*, IV, Prop. 18, Schol.; Prop. 19, Demonst.; Prop. 20.

as we have seen, preceded by others, extended to include
inanimate objects,[1] he now repeats it with special application to man, namely, that the good at which each man aims
is the preservation of his being (Prop. XX). This striving
for self-preservation is described by him again as the love of
each person of himself.[2] Again as before,[3] he restates this
principle also negatively, namely, that each person by the
laws of his own nature necessarily avoids that which is
painful, evil, and leading to self-destruction, and that if we
sometimes notice that a man acts contrary to this natural
conatus, it is due to some physical or psychological compulsion, both of which are to be considered as external (Props.
XIX, XX, and Schol.).

While this natural force of self-preservation runs throughout all individual human beings, some of them are capable
of effecting it with greater proficiency and excellency than
others. The degree of power a man possesses to effect his self-
preservation is called his virtue in the sense in which Aristotle, as we have seen, has used its Greek equivalent, ἀρετή,
and a man is said to act in accordance with virtue if he effects
his self-preservation in accordance with the full powers of his
nature. It is in this sense that Spinoza uses "virtue" (*virtus*)
and "power" (*potentia*) as synonymous terms and defines
virtue, in so far as it is related to man, as "the essence itself
or nature of the man in so far as it has the ability (*potestas*)
of effecting something which can be understood through the
laws of that nature alone,"[4] or, as he paraphrases it afterwards, "virtue means nothing but acting according to the
laws of our own nature."[5] And so he says now: "The more

---

[1] Cf. above, pp. 199–201.
[2] *Ethics*, IV, Prop. 18, Schol. Cf. above, p. 197.
[3] Cf. above, pp. 178, 197–198.
[4] *Ethics*, IV, Def. 8.
[5] *Ibid.*, IV, Prop. 18, Schol.

each person strives and is able to seek what is useful to him, that is to say, to preserve his being, the more virtue does he possess; on the other hand, in so far as each person neglects what is useful to him, that is to say, neglects to preserve his own being, is he impotent" (Prop. XX).

Since self-preservation is the ultimate good at which all men aim, it is to be identified with what, according to Aristotle, is spoken of by both the multitude and persons of refinement as happiness. It follows therefore, says Spinoza, "that happiness (*felicitas*, εὐδαιμονία) consists in this — that a man can preserve his own being."[1] And consequently, "no one can desire to be happy (*beatum esse*), to act well (*bene agere*), and live well (*bene vivere*), who does not at the same time desire to be, to act, and to live, that is to say, actually to exist" (Prop. XXI). Note how these three expressions *beatum esse*, *bene agere*, and *bene vivere* are literal translations of Aristotle's εὐδαιμονεῖν, εὖ πράττειν, and εὖ ζῆν, which we have quoted above. The last two expressions, it will be further noted, are reproduced by Spinoza in exactly the same language in which they occur in the Latin version of the *Nicomachean Ethics* printed by the Juntas. In the first expression the term used there is *felicem* instead of *beatum*. Spinoza may have changed *felicem* to *beatum* in order to give it a theological tinge.[2] Being the ultimate good, this "conatus after self-preservation is the primary and only foundation of virtue" (Prop. XXII, Corol.),[3] and "no virtue can be conceived prior to this" (Prop. XXII). All other virtues or powers of man by which he strives and is able to seek certain benefits for himself are ultimately prompted by the conatus of self-preservation. The ethical truism, then, that man should act in conformity with virtue really means

[1] *Ibid.*   [2] Cf. below, p. 311, n. 3.
[3] Cf. also *Ethics*, IV, Prop. 18, Schol.

that he should act in conformity with this conatus for self-preservation.

Still, for man to act in conformity with virtue means more than this. He must act in conformity with his own virtue, which, by definition, means that his action must follow from the laws of his own nature alone, and hence must be determined by reason. To act in conformity with virtue, then, is to be said only when a man is determined to action because he understands (*intelligit*) (Prop. XXIII). Properly speaking, therefore, such stock phrases as "to act absolutely in conformity with virtue," "to act, to live, and preserve our being in accordance with the dictates of reason," "to seek what is useful to one's self," all mean the same thing (Prop. XXIV). This conatus for self-preservation which is the foundation of virtue is also the ultimate end of virtue. Spinoza applies to it the Aristotelian saying made popular by the Stoics that "virtue is to be desired for its own sake," [1] for "no one endeavors to preserve his own being for the sake of another object" (Prop. XXV).

The life the preservation of which is an end in itself, continues Spinoza, is what Aristotle calls the life of reason, or perhaps more literally the life according to reason (κατὰ τὸν νοῦν βίος).[2] In trying to prove this view in the next three propositions Spinoza follows closely Aristotle's arguments in proof that the contemplative activity (ἐνέργεια θεωρητική) or the life according to reason is the highest good or happiness, and that it is this activity which is said to be in accordance with virtue. One argument given by Aristotle is that "the activity of contemplation may be held to be the only activity that is loved for its own sake: it produces no result

---

[1] *Ibid.* Cf. *Nicomachean Ethics*, X, 6, 1176b, 7–9; Diogenes Laertius, *De Vitis* VII, 127.

[2] *Nicomachean Ethics*, X, 7, 1178a, 6–7.

beyond the actual fact of contemplation." [1] So also here says Spinoza: "All efforts which we make through reason are nothing but efforts to understand, and the mind, in so far as it uses reason, adjudges nothing as useful to itself excepting that which conduces to understanding" (Prop. XXVI). Another argument given by Aristotle is that "the activity of reason is felt . . . to contain a pleasure peculiar to itself," [2] or that "the life according to reason is the best and the pleasantest life for man." [3] So also using the term "good" for Aristotle's "pleasant," Spinoza says here: "We do not know that anything is certainly good . . . excepting that which truly conduces to understanding" (Prop. XXVII). A third argument given by Aristotle for the supremacy of the life of reason is the fact that "man will achieve such a life not in virtue of his humanity but in virtue of some divine element within him, and the superiority of this activity to the activity of any other virtue will be proportionate to the superiority of this divine element in man to his composite nature. If then reason is divine . . . the life according to reason is divine." [4] It is with this passage in view that Spinoza concludes that "the highest good of the mind is the knowledge of God, and the highest virtue of the mind is to know God" (Prop. XXVIII), for it is the knowledge of God which renders the life according to reason divine.

III. Society and the State

Towards the end of his discussion of the superiority of the intellectual virtues and of the life of reason Aristotle says that the means of attaining these virtues and of achieving this life are supplied by the state. And thus he shows how closely the state is related to the individual or politics to

---

[1] *Ibid.*, X, 7, 1177b, 1 2.   [2] *Ibid.*, 19 21.
[3] *Ibid.*, 1178a, 6–7.   [4] *Ibid.*, 1177b, 27–31.

ethics.[1] Still the state and politics are not dealt with by him
in his *Nicomachean Ethics*, but rather in his special work on
Politics. In the *Nicomachean Ethics*, in Books VIII and IX,
which deal with friendship, he confines himself to what may
be called the sociological aspects of the state, or rather to
the social instinct in man which is the foundation of the state.
Similarly Spinoza in the book which he calls by the name of
Aristotle's chief work on ethics, after stating the superiority
of the life of reason, passes on to a discussion of the foundations of social life. The transition from the problem of individual life to that of society is explained by Spinoza in his
statement that the life of reason cannot fully flourish except
in society — a good Aristotelian principle which is made
much of also by Maimonides.[2] "Indeed," says Spinoza, "so
far as the mind is concerned, our intellect would be less perfect if the mind were alone, and understood nothing but itself." [3] The study of society is thus a proper subject to be
included in the *Ethics*. The study of the state, however, as a
special kind of human society is dealt with by him, again as
in Aristotle, in two separate works, in the last five chapters
of the *Tractatus Theologico-Politicus* and in the *Tractatus
Politicus*. The limits of his treatment of society in the *Ethics*
are indicated by him in his *Tractatus Politicus* (Ch. II, § 1),
where he says: "In our *Tractatus Theologico-Politicus* we
have treated of natural and civil right, and in our *Ethics*
have explained the nature of wrong-doing, merit, justice,
injustice."

His theory of society is unfolded in a systematic and
logical manner in Propositions XXIX-XL, and this is preceded by a general outline of the subject in the Scholium to
Proposition XVIII.

[1] *Ibid.*, X, 9.   [2] *Moreh Nebukim*, III, 27 ff.
[3] *Ethics*, IV, Prop. 18, Schol.

He begins in Propositions XXIX–XXXI by stating certain laws of the individual organism.

In nature, which in its common order is a system of interrelated causes and effects, no individual thing can exist or be determined to action unless it be determined to existence and action by another cause.[1] The nature of that cause must be understood by the same attribute as that by means of which the object affected by it is conceived.[2] A body can affect another body, and a mind can affect another mind, but no mind can affect a body, and no body can affect a mind. No object, therefore, can determine the existence and action of another object if their natures are altogether different. But, on the other hand, the contrary is also true, namely, that no object can determine the existence and action of another if they are absolutely the same, for if they are absolutely the same they are one and the same thing and there can be no relation of cause and effect between them, unless in the sense of being *causa sui*. For an object, therefore, to determine the existence and action of another object it must have something in common with the other object, that is, it must be a mode of the same attribute, and it must also differ in something from the other object, that is, it must differ from it in those individual differentia which distinguish one mode from another. This is advanced by Spinoza as a general law of nature which applies equally to man who is a part of nature. For like any other individual thing in nature, man's existence and action are determined by other individual things, food, drink, air, and in general the things which he absorbs and the things which he comes in contact with, for "the human body needs for its preservation many bodies by which it is, as it were, continually regenerated."[3] These

---

[1] *Ibid.*, I, Prop. 28.   [2] *Ibid.*, II, Prop. 6.

[3] *Ibid.*, II, Post. 4 after Prop. 13.

external bodies which our body absorbs or comes in contact with sometimes agree with our body and sometimes are contrary to it. They agree with our body in so far as they have something in common with it; they are contrary to it in so far as they differ from it. In so far as a thing is contrary to our body it is evil; but in so far as it agrees with our body it is necessarily good. This is advanced by Spinoza as a general physiological law of the human body, probably derived from the common observation of the ordinary processes of the assimilation and absorption of food. This is the substance of the argument contained in Propositions XXIX–XXXI.

Now in Propositions XXXII–XXXVII Spinoza applies, by analogy, these general laws of the individual organism to the social organism.

Man needs for his preservation not only food and drink and air and clothes but also the society of other men, for of all the things "outside us which are useful to us . . . none more excellent can be discovered than those which exactly agree with our nature," that is to say, human beings who are like ourselves, and "nothing, therefore, is more useful to man than man." [1] But, still, though all men are alike in so far as they are human beings and modes of the attributes of extension and thought, there is something with respect to which they differ in nature. They differ in nature in so far as they are subject to passion (Prop. XXXII). In this, too, there is an analogy between the social organism and the individual organism, for men who are assailed by passions may become different in nature from one another in the same way as an individual man under similar circumstances may undergo conflicting changes in his own nature, for "men may differ in nature from one another in so far as they are assailed by affects which are passions, and in so far also as

[1] *Ibid.*, IV, Prop. 18, Schol.

one and the same man is assailed by passions is he change-able and inconstant" (Prop. XXXIII). And, consequently, in so far as men differ in nature they can also become contrary to one another (Prop. XXXIV). Men remain, however, like one another, and always agree in their nature, if they live in conformity with the guidance of reason (Prop. XXXV). They cannot then be contrary to one another, for the highest good of those who live in conformity with the guidance of reason and who follow after virtue is the knowledge of God or the life of reason, and this is common to all, and all may equally enjoy it (Prop. XXXVI). Furthermore, it is characteristic of this knowledge of God or the life of reason that he who seeks it for himself will also desire it for other men, and this altruistic desire will be greater in proportion as one has a greater knowledge of God (Prop. XXXVII). This desire on the part of man to have others share in the true knowledge of God and to have them rejoice in the good in which he rejoices,[1] adds Spinoza in the first Scholium, is not to be confused with intolerance and persecution and the attempts by man "to make others love what he himself loves, and to make others live according to his way of thinking (*ex ipsius ingenio*)." The former is based on reason and it endeavors to lead others by reason. Spinoza calls it piety.[2] The latter is based on emotion and it acts from mere impulse (*impetus*). It is called by Spinoza ambition.[2] It is in this activity of reason that Spinoza finds the origin of religion, piety, and honor (*honestas*), the last of which is the basis of friendship (*amicitia*), which in its turn is the foundation of a state (*civitas*).[3]

In Spinoza's explanation of the origin and nature of society three main principles are discernible. First, the exist-

---

[1] *Ibid.*, IV, Prop. 37, Demonst. 2.   [2] *Ibid.*, V, Prop. 4, Schol.
[3] *Ibid.*, IV, Prop. 37, Schol. 1. Cf. below p. 246.

ence of a natural social impulse which gives rise to society. Second, the organic conception of society and the analogy between the individual organism and the social organism. Third, the conception that likeness of kind is the basis of social coherence. All these principles reflect the discussion about the nature of society which are to be found in the works of the ancient philosophers as well as in the works of philosophers who lived immediately before Spinoza.

In declaring that there exists a natural social impulse in man and that man has a natural desire to have others rejoice (*gaudere*) in the good in which he rejoices, Spinoza has aligned himself with Aristotle, the Stoics, and Grotius, as against the Epicureans and Hobbes, for Hobbes, like the Epicureans, maintains that "men have no pleasure (*voluptas*), but on the contrary a great deal of grief (*molestia*), in keeping company, where there is no power able to over-awe them all." [1] Spinoza himself quotes Aristotle's dictum that man is a social animal (*animal sociale*, πολιτικὸν ζῷον).[2] When he illustrates, however, the benefits of society by saying that "if, for example, two individuals of exactly the same nature are joined together, they make up a single individual, doubly stronger than each alone," [3] he seems to reflect the sayings of Seneca in a similar connection that "by concord small things increase," [4] and that man, "who, being alone and separated, was the least and feeblest of all the rest, is become [by union with others] the master of all things." [5] Similarly his qualifying statement that "a proper regard, indeed, to what is useful to us teaches us the necessity of uniting ourselves with men, but not with beasts, nor with things whose nature is

---

[1] *Leviathan*, I, 13.
[2] *Ethics*, IV, Prop. 35, Schol. Cf. Aristotle, *Politics*, I, 2, 1253a, 3.
[3] *Ethics*, IV, Prop. 18, Schol.
[4] *Epistulae Morales*, Epist. 94, § 46.
[5] *De Beneficiis*, IV, 18, § 2.

different from human nature," [1] seems to reflect the Stoic teaching that "there can be no question of right as between man and the other animals, because of their unlikeness." [2]

So also the organic conception of society and the analogy between the social organism and the individual organism were current in literature. Marcus Aurelius declares that "the principle which obtains where limbs and body unite to form one organism, holds good also for rational things with their separate individualities, constituted as they are to work in conjunction," [3] and Hobbes begins the *Leviathan* by calling the state an artificial man, and by comparing it to the human body.

Finally, the principle advanced by Spinoza that likeness of kind is the basis of social coherence reflects Aristotle's discussion as to the nature of friendship whether it is based on likeness or on unlikeness, [4] and his conclusion that the perfect form of friendship is that which is based upon a likeness in virtue, and which exists between good men. [5] Such a kind of friendship, as we have seen, is called by Spinoza a friendship (*amicitia*, Aristotle's φιλία) [6] based on honor (*honestas*, Aristotle's τὸ καλόν), which he considers the foundation of the state (*civitas*, Aristotle's πόλις). And so also Marcus Aurelius, reflecting the Stoic view, explains social coherence on the basis of the universal principle of like flowing to like. [7]

While society in its natural state (*statu naturali*) is based upon the social instinct of man and is a natural form of organization, the special form of society called "state" (*civitas*)

---

[1] *Ethics*, IV, Prop. 37, Schol. 1.
[2] Diogenes Laertius, *De Vitis*, VII, 129. Cf. Cicero, *De Finibus*, III, 20, § 67.
[3] *Meditations*, VII, 13. Cf. II, 1.
[4] *Nicomachean Ethics*, VIII, 1.
[5] *Ibid.*, VIII, 3, 1156b, 7–8.   [6] Cf. below, p. 304 n. 1.
[7] *Meditations*, IX, 9.

or society in its civil state (*statu civili*) is an artificial product, the result of an agreement, or contract, or compact. In this, then, Spinoza follows the ancient doctrine of the Epicureans and what was in his time the recent doctrine of Hobbes. The civil state is not a natural structure. It grows out of a contract which men enter into with each other in order that they may put an end to what Hobbes calls the war of everyone against everyone (*bellum omnium contra omnes*),[1] so that, as Spinoza puts it, "they will do nothing by which one can injure the other." [2] But there is the following difference between Hobbes and Spinoza. According to Hobbes the war of everyone against everyone expresses the original nature of man: the state of peace is due only to "fear of death" and to a "desire of such things as are necessary to commodious living, and a hope by their industry to obtain them"; [3] according to Spinoza it is a vitiation of the original nature of man by emotions which surpass his native power or virtue. To Hobbes, again, the civil state with its laws is to serve as a curb upon the native impulse of man; to Spinoza it is an instrument whereby man is enabled to live according to his native impulses. All this goes back to the more fundamental difference between them. To Hobbes, the self which man's first impulse endeavors to preserve is of a purely egotistic nature and excludes other beings; to Spinoza the self of self-preservation is an expanded self of which the need of the society of others is a constituent part.

Still, the civil state is an artificial organism and the laws by which it is governed are man-made laws, which are to be contrasted with the laws existing in the state of nature. The contrast is expressed by Spinoza as that between the right of

---

[1] *Leviathan*, I, 13.
[2] *Ethics*, IV, Prop. 37, Schol. 2 (*Opera*, II, p. 238, ll. 1–2).
[3] *Leviathan*, I, 13.

nature (*jus naturae*)[1] and the right of the state (*jus civitatis*),[2] or that between the "law of nature" (*lex naturae*)[3] and "law" (*lex*) unqualified.[4] Similarly, corresponding to good and evil in the state of nature there is a good and evil in the civil state, "where it is decided by universal consent what is good and what is evil, and where everyone is bound to obey the state."[5] It is where legislated conceptions of good and evil exist and where obedience to law is enforced that the conceptions of sin (*peccatum*) and merit (*meritum*) are to be found, the former meaning disobedience, the latter meaning obedience. The term *peccatum* is used by Spinoza both in the religious sense of sin and in the civil sense of crime,[6] just as he uses the term *delictum* also in the sense of sin against God.[7] The conception of sin or crime, as Spinoza defines it, exists only "under dominion" (*in imperio*), whether it be a state or a church, where the conceptions of good and evil have been arbitrarily determined and set down in the form of law.[8] Without such legislated conceptions of good and evil, to act contrary to the dictates of reason, to violate the eternal decrees of nature or of God, cannot properly be called sin or crime; the proper designation is "weakness of the mind" or "servitude."[9] If the laws of the state or of the church happen to agree with the dictates of reason and the eternal decrees of nature or of God, then the violation of these dictates of reason and eternal decrees of nature can be called sin or

---

[1] *Ethics*, IV, Prop. 37, Schol. 2 (*Opera*, II, p. 237, ll. 20 and 34).

[2] *Ibid.*, IV, Prop. 37, Schol. 2 (*Opera*, II, p. 238, l. 27); Prop. 73, Demonst. (p. 265, l. 9).

[3] *Ibid.*, III, Praef. (p. 137, l. 9); Prop. 2, Schol. (p. 142, l. 34).

[4] *Ibid.*, IV, Prop. 37, Schol. 2 (p. 238, ll. 10 and 15); Appendix, 24. Evidently Spinoza makes no distinction between the terms *jus* and *lex* such as is made by Hobbes (*Leviathan*, I, 14).   [5] *Ibid.*, IV, Prop. 37, Schol. 2.

[6] See "peccatum" against God in Epistola 19.

[7] Epistola 21 (*Opera*, IV, p. 131, l. 18).

[8] *Tractatus Politicus*, Ch. 2, § 19.   [9] Cf. above, p. 184.

crime in an indirect sense, in the sense that it is a violation of
what happens to be also the conventional law of the state or
the church.[1]

Artificial though the state may be in its form, it is still
essentially based upon a natural social impulse. It may
therefore be considered as something organic and it may be
compared to the individual organism. That is good for the
state which is good for the body. In the case of the human
body we consider that as useful or good for it which enables
the body to be completely adapted to its physical environment and to function properly in all its powers, that is to
say, "to be affected in many ways, and to affect other bodies"
(Prop. XXXVIII); we consider also that as useful or good
for the body which enables it not only to continue its physical
existence but also to maintain the identity of its personality,
that is to say, "to preserve the proportion of motion and
rest which the parts of the human body bear to each other"
(Prop. XXXIX). For death, Spinoza adds in the Scholium,
does not come when the body "is changed into a corpse";
a man may be called dead if he "undergoes such changes
that he cannot very well be said to be the same man," even
though physiologically he is still alive. Anything contrary to
this is evil. So also in the case of the state. Good is that
which makes for complete harmony between the individual
members of the state and for the stability of the state as
an organic unit. "Whatever conduces to the universal fel-
lowship of man, that is to say, whatever causes men to live in
harmony with one another, is useful, and, on the contrary,
whatever brings discord into the state is evil" (Prop. XL).
Spinoza's analogy is somewhat reminiscent of Plato's analogy
between justice in the state and bodily health.[2]

Though Spinoza does not carry out the implied analogy

---

[1] *Ibid.*, §§ 20–22.　　　[2] *Republic*, IV, 444 C–D.

between what he considers the death of an individual, mentioned by him in the Scholium to Proposition XXXIX, and what he would consider the death of the state, we can continue his reasoning for him. The life of the state, like the life of the individual, he would say, does not end only with the physical disappearance of its people. It ends with the disappearance of the institutions by which it has enjoyed historical continuity as an individual entity. It is because of this view, which here in the *Ethics* is only implied, that Spinoza elsewhere explicitly expresses his opinion that "every state should retain its form of government, and, indeed, cannot change it without danger of the utter ruin of the whole state."[1] In this Spinoza seems to reflect Aristotle's view that "since the state is a partnership, and is a partnership of citizens in a constitution, when the form of the government changes, and becomes different, then it may be supposed that the state is no longer the same,"[2] for "the sameness of the state consists chiefly in the sameness of the constitution."[3] And what is true of the state, Spinoza would undoubtedly say, is true of any other form of group life. A people dies and disappears not when it is physically exterminated but when its national culture and institutions are radically changed. Speaking of his own people, Spinoza says that the Jews have maintained their historical continuity as a people because they have preserved the historical continuity of certain institutions, and he refers to the fact that a number of Jews in Spain who have broken away from their past have disappeared as Jews, even though they were not physically exterminated.[4] The national existence of a people, Spinoza would conclude, is preserved in the continuity of its social inheritance and not in its mere biological continuity.

[1] *Tractatus Theologico-Politicus*, Ch. 18 (*Opera*, III, p. 228, ll. 11-13).
[2] *Politics*, III, 3, 1276b, 1-4.   [3] *Ibid.*, 10-11.
[4] *Tractatus Theologico-Politicus*, Ch. 3 (*Opera*, III, p. 56, ll. 20 ff.).

IV. Catalogue of Virtues

If, as we have been trying to show, the group of propositions from XIX to XXVIII in the Fourth Part of Spinoza's *Ethics* correspond to the discussion of the highest good or happiness in the First and Tenth Books of Aristotle's *Nicomachean Ethics*, and the group of propositions from XXIX to XL correspond to Aristotle's discussion of friendship in the Eighth and Ninth Books of his *Nicomachean Ethics*, enlarged to be sure by the discussion of the origin and nature of society and the state by other writers, then the next group of propositions from XLI to LXXIII correspond to Aristotle's catalogue (διαγραφή)[1] of virtues in Books II, 7– VI of the *Nicomachean Ethics*, enlarged and modified, again, by the influence of discussions of the same subject in other works.

The nature of goodness or virtue is, according to Aristotle, determined in two ways. In the first place, it is "the mean rather than the excess (ὑπερβολὴν) or deficiency." In the second place, "the mean is such as right reason prescribes" (ὡς ὁ λόγος ὁ ὀρθὸς λέγει).[2] Of these two ways of determining goodness, the first, namely, that it is not excessive nor deficient, is only indirectly suggested by Spinoza in such statements as "hilarity can never be excessive (*excessum*), but is always good" (Prop. XLII), "titillation may be excessive and evil" (Prop. XLIII), "love and desire (*cupiditas*) may be excessive" (Prop. XLIV), and "a desire (*cupiditas*) which springs from reason can never be in excess" (Prop. LXI). But the second determination of goodness given by Aristotle, namely, that which right reason prescribes, is the one directly adopted by Spinoza. An emotion

---

[1] *Nicomachean Ethics*, II, 7, 1107a, 33.

[2] *Ibid.*, VI, 1, 1138b, 18–20.

is good which is according to the guidance (*ex ductu*) or the dictate (*ex dictamine*) of reason (Propo. XLVI, L, LXII, LXV, LXVI), or agrees (*convenire*) with reason (Prop. LI), or arises (*oriri*) from reason (Props. LI–LIV, LVIII, LXI), or is determined (*determinari*) or led (*ducitur*) by reason (Props. LIX, LXIII). The same definition of virtue is also implied in his statement in the *Short Treatise* (II, 26) that "without virtue or (to express it better) without the guidance of the understanding, all tends to ruin." All these expressions reflect the Aristotelian expression ὡς ὁ λόγος ὁ ὀρθὸς λέγει, quoted above, which in the Latin translation of the *Nicomachean Ethics* is rendered by "sicut ratio recta *praescribit*" and in the Latin translation of Averroes' *Middle Commentary* is paraphrased by "et terminus medij *convenit* cum termino rationis sanae." An exact reproduction of the Latin translation of the Greek occurs in the Scholium to Proposition XVIII: "quod ratio nobis *praescribit*," [1] and the term *convenit* used in the Latin translation of Averroes is reproduced in the term *convenire* used in Proposition LI quoted above. Now, the right reason which prescribes the mean or goodness is said by Aristotle to be the calculative (λογιστικόν) or deliberative (βουλευτικόν) part of the rational (λόγον ἔχον) part of the soul [2] by means of practical wisdom or prudence (φρόνησις). Prudence is one of the five means by which the soul arrives at truth, the other four being art (τέχνη), scientific knowledge (ἐπιστήμη), philosophic wisdom (σοφία), and intelligence (νοῦς), and all these five are contrasted with the following two, conjecture (ὑπόληψις, *existimatio*, *putatio*) and opinion (δόξα), in which, he says, there is the possibility of error. [3] This contrast between the former five and the latter

---

[1] *Opera*, II, p. 222, l. 12.
[2] *Nicomachean Ethics*, VI, 1, 1139a, 3–15
[3] *Ibid.*, VI, 3, 1139b, 15–17. Cf. above, p. 151.

two kinds of knowledge corresponds respectively, as we have already suggested,[1] to Spinoza's second kind of knowledge and his first kind of knowledge. Spinoza is thus following the Aristotelian tradition when he says that goodness is that which is according to the guidance of "reason" (*ratio*), "ratio" being his technical designation for the second kind of knowledge. In the *Short Treatise* (II, 2, § 3) he expresses it more explicitly when he says that "from the first [kind of knowledge] proceed all the passions which are opposed to good reason; from the second, the good desires."

There seems to be no significance in the number of virtues and vices selected by Spinoza for special discussion in these propositions nor in the order in which they are arranged. Similarly the form in which they are couched and the sentiment which they express seem on the whole to be devoid of any individuality. They carry to us a familiar ring of the proverbial wisdom of all the sages who have ever tried to express in pithy sayings the universal morality of the Ten Commandments and the Golden Rule. Had these propositions been written by a pagan in about the first century of the Christian era their author would undoubtedly have been declared to be a Stoic, if he had happened to live in Alexandria or Rome, or a disciple of the rabbis, if he had happened to live in Jerusalem. But having been written in the seventeenth century by a Jew acquainted also with the teachings of Christianity, these propositions as well as the Appendix at the end of Part IV are significant only in so far as they were used by Spinoza to adorn certain points in his own philosophy.

Still it would be of importance to collect a complete catena of parallel sayings from the entire ethical and proverbial literature accessible to Spinoza. Perhaps, then, by a close

[1] Cf. above, p. 146.

comparison of phraseology we could determine the immediate sources of some of his utterances; also one could discover
in some variation of phraseology or in some uncalled-for
emphasis of statement a certain new element of philosophical
or ethical significance. When Spinoza declares, for instance,
that "repentance (*poenitentia*) is not a virtue, that is to say,
it does not spring from reason; on the contrary, the man
who repents of what he has done is doubly wretched or impotent" (Prop. LIV), we may wonder what significance to
attach to this declaration. It may be nothing but a paraphrase of Descartes' contention that repentance is often the
experience of feeble minds (*imbecilliores animi*) and that it
is "an imperfection in them deserving pity." [1] Spinoza's
subsequent statement in the Demonstration that the peni-
tent "allows himself to be overcome first by a depraved desire and then by pain (*tristitia*)" seems, furthermore, to
reflect two sources — first, Descartes' statement that repentance is a "species of pain (*tristitiae*)," [2] and second,
Seneca's statement that repentance (*paenitentia*), fear
(*timor*), and wavering of the mind (*animi iactatio*) come to
men "because they can neither rule nor obey their desires." [3]
That there is a connection between the statements of Seneca
and those of Descartes may be shown by the fact that, just
like Seneca, who groups repentance, fear, and wavering of
the mind (or irresolution) together, Descartes suggests that
the remedies of repentance are "the same as those which
serve to remove wavering of the mind (*irresolution, fluctua-
tioni*)." [4] But it may also be that in this proposition, while
verbally it is a copy of the statements of Seneca and Descartes, Spinoza meant to inveigh against the great emphasis
laid upon repentance in both Judaism and Christianity. His

[1] *Les Passions de l'Ame*, III, 191.   [2] *Ibid*.
[3] *De Tranquilitate Animi*, Ch. 2, § 8.   [4] *Les Passions de l'Ame*, III, 191.

apology in the Scholium for the commendation of repentance by the Prophets would seem to indicate that this was the intention of the proposition. Further still, is it not also possible to discover in this decrial of repentance some biographical element of personal experience? This is merely an indication of what can be done with these propositions if studied in connection with their sources.

The last seven propositions of this Part (Props. LXVII–LXXIII), however, owe some of their external literary form to a source which can be easily identified. These seven propositions are written in the form of an apotheosis of the free man (*homo liber*) corresponding to the Stoic apotheosis of the wise man (τὸ σοφός, *sapiens*). In each one of these seven propositions the expression "free man" occurs, and the propositions were undoubtedly meant to constitute an independent group by themselves and to form a sort of epilogue to Part IV. The use of the adjective "free" as a description of the man who lives according to the guidance of reason is sufficiently explained by Spinoza's use of the term "servitude" as a description of "the impotence of man to govern or restrain the emotions." [1] But it may also be explained as a reminiscence of the Stoic teaching that the wise man is free from all passions or perturbations of the mind ("illum [= sapientem] enim putas omni perturbatione esse liberum"),[2] from vanity, pretense, business care, and the like. Or, perhaps, it may also be a reminiscence of the saying of the rabbis that the sage is the only man who can be called free.[3] While the virtues enumerated in these seven propositions are those with which the ideally good and wise men everywhere are generally accredited, their description con-

---

[1] *Ethics*, IV, Praef., beginning.
[2] Cicero, *Tusculanae Disputationes*, IV, 27, § 58. Cf. IV, 4, §§ 7–9, and Diogenes Laertius, *De Vitis*, VII, 117.   [3] *Abot*, VI, 2.

tains certain terms and phrases which indicate some connection with the writings of Seneca. We shall make brief comment upon these propositions merely in order to show what could be done with Spinoza's lists of emotions and virtues in the Third and Fourth Parts of the *Ethics* if a complete catena of parallel lists were gotten together.

Proposition LXVII attributes to the free man the rule of conduct which has previously been recommended by Spinoza in Proposition LXIII. In that earlier proposition and its Corollary Spinoza inveighs against the pious moralists of all religions, designated by him "the superstitious (*superstitiosi*)," "who know better how to rail at vice than to teach virtue," and he has laid down there as a guiding principle of conduct the rule of reason that "we follow good directly and avoid evil indirectly." Now, in this proposition, he says of the free man who lives according to the dictates of reason that in his actions he "is not led by the fear of death . . . but directly desires the good," so that his "wisdom is not a meditation upon death but upon life." His statement "ejus sapientia non mortis, sed vitae meditatio est" seems to be a direct challenge to Thomas à Kempis' counsel to meditate on death (*De Meditatione Mortis*)[1] and always to remember the end (*memento semper finis*).[2]

Some Christian theological exegesis of the story of the fall of Adam in the Book of Genesis is undoubtedly the direct source of Proposition LXVIII. The Scholium seems to indicate such a source. The allegorical explanation of the fall of Adam as symbolizing man's backsliding from the dictates of reason by succumbing to the lure of sensation, symbolized by Eve, through the influence of pleasure, symbolized by the serpent, goes back to Philo.[3]

---

[1] *De Imitatione Christi*, I, 23, title.   [2] *Ibid.*, I, 25, § 11.
[3] *Sacrarum Legum Allegoriarum post Sex Dierum Opus*, II, xviii, 71 ff.

Aristotle's and Seneca's discussion of courage is the literary background of Proposition LXIX. Courage (ἀνδρεία, *fortitudo*) is according to Aristotle the mean between fear (φόβος, *timor*) and confidence (θάρρη, *fiducia, audacia*). The excess of fear is cowardice (δειλία, *ignavia, timiditas*), and the excess of confidence is rashness or foolhardiness (θράσος, *audacia, procacitas*).[1] The courageous man is defined by Aristotle as "he who fearlessly confronts a noble death, or some sudden peril that threatens death; and the perils of war answer this description most fully. . . . Also courage is shown in dangers where a man can defend himself by valor or die nobly."[2] Seneca, in his discussion of courage, argues that courage does not mean the confronting of danger but rather the avoidance of it. "As it seems to you, says he, a courageous man shall thrust himself into dangers. No, he shall not fear them, but shall avoid (*vitabit*) them. Wariness (*cautio*), not fear (*timor*), becomes him. . . . It [*fortitudo*, courage] is not unadvised rashness (*temeritas*), not love of dangers, nor a desire of fearful things. It is a science that distinguishes good from evil."[3] Evidently drawing upon these discussions of courage, Spinoza says here that the courage (*animi virtus, seu fortitudo = animositas*) "which is required to restrain rashness (*audacia*) must be equally great with that which is required to restrain fear (*metus*)," so that courage is "as great in avoiding (*declinandis*) danger as in overcoming it" (Prop. LXIX and Demonst.). Courage is caution, for "a free man chooses flight by the same courage (*animositas*) or presence of mind as that by which he chooses battle" (Corol.) — which reminds us of the lines:

"For he who fights and runs away
　May live to fight another day."

[1] *Nicomachean Ethics*, II, 7, 1107a, 33 ff.　　　[2] *Ibid.*, III, 6, 1115a, 32 ff.
[3] *Epistulae Morales*, Epist. 85, §§ 26 and 28.

Proposition LXX reflects Seneca's discussion of the question whether favors (*beneficia*) should be received from everybody. His answer is in the negative. Reason, he says, which must be our guide, first of all will advise us this: "That we ought not to receive a favor at every man's hands. From whom then shall we receive? To answer thee in a word: It is from those to whom we should have given," for "it is a grievous torment to be indebted and obliged to him, to whom thou wouldst owe nothing." This does not counsel discrimination against any of "those truly wise and virtuous men," but against "these imperfect men." The reason of it is that the acceptance of favors unites men in friendship, which "friendship must continue and flourish between us," and consequently "the law of friendship admonishes me, that I receive not a kindness from any that is unworthy." [1]   To this general rule an exception is to be made in the case where a present is given by a tyrant who will consider a refusal as "an injury and indignity"; the rule is thus "not intended in a case of great violence and fear, because where these prevail, election perisheth." [2]   The similarity as well as the differences between this proposition and Seneca are obvious. The term "ignorant" (*ignaros*) used by Spinoza in this proposition needs an explanation. The terms used by Seneca in the corresponding passages are "imperfect" (*imperfectis*) [3] and "unworthy" (*indignum*).[4] But among the many terms by which the Stoic wise man and foolish man are respectively designated there are also the terms "learned" (*eruditus, sciens*) and "ignorant" (*nesciens*), which are used by Seneca himself.[5] The contrast between

---

[1] *De Beneficiis*, II, 18, § 6.   [2] *Ibid.*, II, 18, §§ 6–7.
[3] *Ibid.*, II, 18, § 4.   [4] *Ibid.*, II, 18, § 5.
[5] *Epistulae Morales*, Epist. 94, § 11. Cf. Adolf Dyroff, "Die Ethik der Alten Stoa," in *Berliner Studien für classische Philologie und Archaeologie*, N. F. 2 (1897), p. 186, n. 3.

the terms "wise man" (*sapiens*) and "ignorant man" (*ignarus*) is also used by Spinoza later in the Preface to Part V of the *Ethics* [1] and elsewhere.[2]

The next proposition (LXXI), which deals with gratitude, likewise reflects Seneca's discussion of gratitude in the *De Beneficiis*, where it follows immediately upon his discussion of the acceptance of benefits from the unworthy [3] and is continued intermittently throughout the rest of the book.

The virtue of honesty and good faith has been extolled in every copy-book, and it is therefore not surprising to find it one of the characteristics of Spinoza's free man (Prop. LXXII). Nor are we to look for any special significance in Spinoza's metaphysical proof that honesty is the best policy. But the practical question raised by him in the Scholium whether a man is allowed to break faith in order to escape from the danger of instant death seems to reflect some actual discussion of a similar problem in some work on casuistry which some one may accidentally stumble upon some day. Spinoza's negative answer seems to reflect the following sentiment expressed by Seneca: "Fidelity (*fides*) is the holiest good that may be in a man's breast; by no necessity is it constrained to deceive; it is corrupted by no reward. 'Burn,' says she, 'beat, kill, I will not betray; but how the more pain shall seek to discover secret things, by so much will I the more deeply hide them.'" [4]

Participation in the organized life of society is recommended to the philosopher by Aristotle and to the scholar by the rabbis. Among the Stoics, according to Seneca and others, it was considered one of the characteristic virtues of

---

[1] *Opera*, II, p. 277, l. 12.
[2] *Ethics*, V, Prop. 42, Schol
　De Beneficiis, II, 24 ff.
　Epistulae Morales, Epist. 88, § 29.

the wise man.[1] It was therefore logical for Spinoza to put it at the end of his list of virtues which characterize his free man. "A man who is guided by reason is freer in a state where he lives according to the common laws than he is in solitude, where he obeys himself alone" (Prop. LXXIII).

[1] Seneca, *De Otio*, III, 2.   Cf. Zeller, *Die Philosophie der Griechen*, III. 1 (4th ed.), p. 300, n. 4.

CHAPTER XX

LOVE, IMMORTALITY, AND BLESSEDNESS

I. A Metaphysic for Bilious Souls

THE last three parts of the *Ethics* may be considered as a discussion of what Spinoza calls in the *Short Treatise* (II, 2) the "effects" of the three kinds of knowledge. The enumeration of these three kinds of knowledge, it will be recalled, occurs toward the end of the Second Part. Part III and Part IV to Proposition XVIII deal with the effects of the first kind of knowledge, which are described in the *Short Treatise* as "the passions which are opposed to good reason."[1] The remaining propositions in Part IV (Props. XIX–LXXIII) deal with the effects of the second kind of knowledge, which are described in the *Short Treatise* as "the good desires."[2] The first ten propositions of Part V continue to deal with the effects of the second kind of knowledge. But beginning with Proposition XI of Part V, the *Ethics* takes up the discussion of the effects of the third kind of knowledge, which in the *Short Treatise* are described as "true and sincere love with all its offshoots."[3] In an earlier statement in the *Ethics* Spinoza has already prepared us for what we are to find in Part V. It is to speak of the "excellence and value" of the third kind of knowledge,[4] it is to show the "principal advantages" which his system of philosophy, especially his doctrine of necessity,[5] has for man,[6] and finally it is to ex-

---

[1] *Short Treatise*, II, 2, § 3. [2] *Ibid.*
[3] *Ibid.* [4] *Ethics*, II, Prop. 47, Schol.
[5] Cf. *Short Treatise*, II, 18, §§ 1–2.
[6] *Ethics*, II, Prop. 49, Schol. (*Opera*, II, p. 131, ll. 28–29, and p. 135, ll. 32 ff.).

plain in what degree the things which are injurious or useful to the human body may also "injure or profit the mind."[1] From the context, it is clear that this last statement refers to the second kind of knowledge and hence to the first ten propositions of Part V.

Now in the preface of the Fifth Part Spinoza again gives an outline of Part V. Its chief purpose concerns "the method or way which leads to liberty." With this as its general purpose it is to treat of two main topics. First, in opposition to those who believe in will and its freedom, of whom the Stoics and Descartes are mentioned specifically, it is to show how the power (*potentia*) or knowledge (*cognitio*) of the mind (*mentis*) or reason (*rationis*) itself, without any will and the freedom of the will, but as determined by intelligence (*intelligentia*) alone, can to some extent, though not absolutely, restrain and govern the emotions. This evidently refers to the second kind of knowledge the effects of which are dealt with in the first ten propositions. Second, it is to explain what freedom of mind and blessedness (*beatitudo*) is and how everything which relates to the blessedness of the mind is deduced from the mere knowledge of the mind. This evidently refers to the third kind of knowledge the effects of which are dealt with in the rest of Part V. The Fifth Part furthermore falls into three sections, the first two of which are described by Spinoza himself. The first deals with matters "relating to this present life"[2] (Props. I–XX), the second deals "with those matters which appertain to the duration of the mind without relation to the body"[3] (Props. XXI–XL), and the third, which is not described by Spinoza, deals with general observations on the religion of reason (Props. XLI–XLII).

[1] *Ibid.*, IV, Prop. 39, Schol.   [2] *Ibid.*, V, Prop. 20, Schol., end.
[3] *Ibid.*; cf. also *ibid.*, V, Prop. 40, Schol.

The special phase of the second kind of knowledge, or the power of reason which Spinoza is now to deal with in the first ten propositions, is of a practical nature. Having explained in Part IV how by the guidance of reason the emotions of desire and pleasure are no longer passions but are rather actions by which one may attain the preservation of his own being (Props. XIX–XXVIII) as well as the preservation of the being of others and the joining of men in friendship (Props. XXIX–XXXVII), and having also given a list of emotions which are the effects of reason (Props. XXXVIII–LXXIII), he is now to give a few practical hints as to how a man can prevent himself from becoming a victim of his passions. He refers to these practical hints as "remedies (*remedia*) against the emotions," [1] and the irrational emotions themselves are described by him as a sickness of the mind (*animi aegritudo*).[2] In Tschirnhaus' conversation with Leibniz, furthermore, the last part of the *Ethics* is described as "de . . . beatitudine seu perfecti hominis idea, de Medicina mentis, de Medicina corporis." [3] This use of medical terminology reflects the attitude of moralists throughout history that vice is a disease of the soul and like the diseases of the body can be cured as well as prevented. Cicero refers to the Stoics, especially Chrysippus, who "give themselves unnecessary trouble to show the analogy which the diseases of the mind have to those of the body," and though he dismisses "all that they say as of little consequence" [4] and makes use of that analogy "more sparingly than the Stoics," [5] he still tries to find "what remedies (*remedia*) there are

---

[1] *Ibid.*, V, Praef., end.

[2] *Ibid.*, V, Prop. 10, Schol. (*Opera*, II, p. 288, ll. 26–27).

[3] Cf. K. I. Gerhardt, "Leibniz und Spinoza," in *Sitzungsberichte der koniglich preussischen Akademie der Wissenschaften zu Berlin* (1889), p. 1076.

[4] *Tusculanae Disputationes*, IV, 10, § 23.

[5] *Ibid.*, IV, 12, § 27.

which may be applied by philosophy to the diseases of the mind (*morbis animorum*)." [1] Similarly Maimonides, quoting the ancients, whom he does not specify, says that "there is a health and sickness of the soul as there is a health and sickness of the body," [2] and that "the improvement of the virtues is nothing but the therapeutics of the soul and its faculties." [3] Descartes, too, speaks of a remedy (*remedium*) for the disorders of the passions (*Affectuum vitiis, dereglemens des Passions*).[4]

The view that the emotions are remediable has its root in the principle laid down by Aristotle that "moral virtue comes about as a result of habit." [5] Everything therefore that goes into the formation of habit must enter as an ingredient into the specific that is to cure the weaknesses of the soul and to bring out its virtues and powers. Right thinking as is taught in logic and right living as is taught in medicine are both regarded as the foundations of habit and virtue. In fact those theologians who tried to transform the social customs and inherited beliefs of religion into a rational system of a revealed philosophy have found in the ceremonials and dogmas of the religion of the Bible an ideal manual of instruction for the formation of good habits and the development of moral virtues.[6] Spinoza is in agreement with all this. He is even willing to admit that the laws of the Bible and the morality it teaches are in agreement with reason, though he will not admit that the same is true of the purely ceremonial law and of the purely speculative teachings of the Bible.[7] But here in the *Ethics* he is not to deal with these problems. Mentioning specifically logic and

[1] *Ibid.*, IV, 27, § 58.　　　　　[2] *Shemonah Perakim*, Ch. 3.
[3] *Ibid.*, Ch. 1.　　　　　　　　[4] *Les Passions de l'Ame*, III, 161, end.
[5] *Nicomachean Ethics*, II, 1, 1103a, 17.
[6] *Moreh Nebukim*, III, 27 ll.
[7] Cf. *Tractatus Theologico-Politicus*, Ch. 15, *et passim*.

medicine, he says he has nothing to do with them here.[1] We know, however, that logic, in so far as it leads to the improvement of the understanding, is dealt with by him in his unfinished *Tractatus de Intellectus Emendatione*,[2] and that the system of morality of the Bible is also dealt with by him in the *Tractatus Theologico-Politicus*. Here in the Preface, he says, he is to confine himself to remedies which he thinks "every one experiences, but does not accurately observe nor distinctly see."[3] Later in the Scholium to Proposition XX he further says that he has "included all the remedies for the emotions, that is to say, everything which the mind, considered in itself alone, can do against them." The remedies offered by him are indeed such as popular wisdom in the past has reduced to the form of proverbs, which are writ large on the pages of copy-books. In our own time they have been garbed in a technical nomenclature and reduced to a science, and are administered in the form of incantations. Spinoza prescribes them as a metaphysic and dispenses them in geometric propositions.

The metaphysic of the remedy is given in Proposition I. It is the assertion that despite the principle that mind and body do not act upon each other the mind can control the affections of the body. Justification for this assertion is found in the view that there is a parallelism between mind and body, that the mind is the idea or form of the body, and furthermore that the mind has knowledge of its body and through it of other bodies. From all this it follows that "the order and connection of ideas in the mind is according to the

---

[1] *Ethics*, V, Praef. (*Opera*, II, p. 277, ll. 12–16).

[2] In this work, though he confines it to logic, Spinoza refers also to the importance of moral philosophy, the science of the education of children, medicine, and mechanics as aids in the attainment of human perfection. Cf. *Tractatus de Intellectus Emendatione*, § 15 (*Opera*, II, p. 9, ll. 3–10).

[3] *Ethics*, V, Praef. (*Opera*, II, p. 280, ll. 23–24).

order and connection of the affections of the body," and, "*vice versa*, the order and connection of the affections of the body is according to the order and connection in the mind of the thoughts and ideas of things." The result of this is that the mind, which in its own sphere is independent of the body, deriving as it does its power of thinking from the attribute of thought, can harmonize the order and connection of the bodily affection with the order and connection of its own ideas. Reason, then, can guide and control the body and even dictate to it. The remedial value of this metaphysic for the weakness of the mind or the passive emotions is that by the exercise of reason the passions become actions and irrational desires are transformed into desires which are rational.

The remedies are described in Propositions II–XX. An outline of these propositions is given by Spinoza himself in the Scholium to Proposition XX. But this outline, as his other similar outlines of propositions which occasionally occur in the *Ethics*, was not meant by him to be a complete analysis of the propositions or of the arguments contained in them. Logically these propositions fall into two groups: first, Propositions II–X, which enumerate and describe the remedies, and second, Propositions XI–XX, in which the remedies are reduced to one sovereign remedy, namely, the love for God. Altogether, six remedies are enumerated by Spinoza in the first group of propositions, although in his outline in the Scholium to Proposition XX he mentions only five. All these remedies are based upon the principle, laid down by Spinoza himself, that emotions can be destroyed by other emotions which are stronger and more powerful.

By definition a passive emotion is a confused idea.[1] The first way, therefore, of remedying a passive emotion is to remove the confusion of the idea and to transform it into an

---

[1] *Ethics*, III, Def. 3, and *Affectuum Generalis Definitio*.

idea which is clear and distinct. To accomplish this, we must study our emotions and try to get a clear understanding of their nature. By so doing, we shall find that many of our emotions are spurious emotions, perverted forms of emotions which are of an entirely different and opposite nature. It is, in fact, these spurious and perverted emotions which usually run to excess and become ailments of the soul. To desire what we really desire, to love whom we really love, and to hate whom we really hate, does not as a rule cause us serious trouble. We are troubled in our spirit only when we seem to desire what we really spurn or when we seem to love and hate whom we really do not love and do not hate. As an illustration of a spurious emotion Spinoza mentions intolerance, which he himself calls ambition and describes as a form of pride. Intolerance or ambition arises from the fact "that human nature is so constituted that every one desires that other people should live according to his way of thinking" (Prop. IV, Schol.). In its excessive form this desire manifests itself in the persecution of others for the differences in their beliefs and practices, which causes pain both to those who persecute and to those who are persecuted. But this causing of pain to ourselves and to others does not really express the true nature of the emotion, which, on the contrary, consists in a desire on the part of each man to cause others to rejoice in the good in which he rejoices. Were man, therefore, only to realize the true nature of this particular emotion, then ambition, in Spinoza's terminology, would give place to what he calls piety, and he who is now ambitious, instead of forcing others against their own will to live according to his way of thinking, would act with piety and "endeavor to lead others by reason" and to treat them "with humanity and kindness." [1] In the knowledge itself of the

[1] *Ibid.*, IV, Prop. 37, Demonst. 2 and Schol. 1, reference to which is given in V, Prop. 5, Schol.

emotions, then, are the emotions to be remedied (Props. III IV).[1]

A knowledge of the true nature of our emotions, furthermore, would enable us to detach them from the external cause with which, again, by definition,[2] an emotion must be connected. This constitutes the second remedy (Prop. II). The specific set of emotions to which Spinoza applies this remedy is described by him in a general way as "love or hatred towards the external cause, and the fluctuations of the mind which arise from these emotions" (*ibid.*). His use of the expression "love or hatred" rather than "love and hatred" indicates that he means love and hatred which go together, as, for instance, in frustrated love, which is described by him elsewhere as turning into hatred [3] or as engendering hatred.[4] Similarly by the "fluctuations of the mind which arise from these emotions" he means jealousy and envy, which are described by him elsewhere as arising from love and hatred when they are felt together.[5] The remedy prescribed by Spinoza for this special kind of ailment is to detach the emotion of love, and the hatred and the jealousy and envy which arise from it, "from the thought of an external cause and connect it with other thoughts" (Prop. II). Later, for "other thoughts" he uses the expression "true thoughts" (Prop. IV, Schol.). What Spinoza means to say is this: While it is true that by definition love is caused by an "idea of an external cause," [6] the idea of any particular cause which happens to evoke love is not essential to love itself, and the loss of that external cause, therefore, does not change the love into hatred and produce the fluctua-

---

[1] Spinoza himself in his outline in the Scholium to Prop. 20 puts this remedy, described in Props. 3–4, before the next remedy, which is described in Prop. 2.

[2] *Ethics*, III, Def. 3.   [3] *Ibid.*, III, Prop. 35.

[4] *Ibid.*, III, Prop. 36.   [5] *Ibid.*, III, Prop. 35, Schol.

[6] *Ibid.*, III, *Affectuum Definitiones*, 6.

tions of the mind out of the conflict of the two. The particular external cause in any experience of love is only accidental and can be replaced by some other cause, less troublesome.

The evil to which some of our emotions give rise is often due to our erroneous belief that certain single and free causes are solely responsible for whatever happens to us. To eradicate this evil, therefore, we must bring ourselves to realize that no cause can be singled out as being solely responsible for whatever happens and that nothing happens but by the necessity of an infinite series of causes. In connection with this remedy (Props. V–VI) Spinoza especially mentions the emotions of love and hatred and pity, and indirectly refers to the emotion of disappointment. We love and hate a person, he says elsewhere, because we think that he is the sole cause [1] or the free cause [2] of our pleasure or pain. The remedy for this, he adds now, is to be found in the knowledge that those we love or hate are neither the sole nor the free causes of pleasure or pain. Disappointment (*conscientiae morsus*), he says again elsewhere, is a "pain with the accompanying idea of something past, which, unhoped for, has happened." [3] To cure this feeling of disappointment, he says now, we must realize that all things happen by necessity and as the consequence of an uncontrollable concatenation of causes, "for we see that pain caused by the loss of anything good is diminished if the person who has lost it considers that it could not by any possibility have been preserved" (Prop. VI, Schol.). Similarly pity (*commiseratio*), which is defined by Spinoza elsewhere as "pain with the accompanying idea of evil which has happened to some one whom we imagine like ourselves," [4] will disappear

[1] *Ibid.*, III, Prop. 48.   [2] *Ibid.*, III, Prop. 49.
[3] *Ibid.*, III, *Affectuum Definitiones*, 17.
[4] *Ibid.*, 18.

if we consider the evil which has befallen him who is the object of our pity as something as inevitable and universal as the infant's inability to speak, to walk, or to reason (Prop. VI, Schol.). In conclusion Spinoza adds that "many other facts of a similar kind we might observe" (*ibid.*).

Pains and pleasures and desires produced by actual causes which exist before us and stare us in the face are perhaps less numerous and not so disturbing to our peace of mind as are those emotions of which the causes are intangible and absent. Examples of this type of emotion are included by Spinoza in his list of emotions at the end of the Third Part of the *Ethics*. Among these are fear, despair, disappointment, and regret. The common characteristic of all these emotions, as Spinoza says here in Proposition VII, is that they "are related to individual objects which we contemplate as absent." By his own definitions, fear (*metus*) is related to the "idea of something future or past, about the issue of which we sometimes doubt";[1] despair (*desperatio*) is related to the "idea of a past or future object from which cause for doubting is removed";[2] disappointment (*conscientiae morsus*) is related to the "idea of something past, which, unhoped for, has happened";[3] regret (*desiderium*) is related to an object of memory.[4] These ailments of the soul cannot be cured by directly attacking their causes, for their causes are not bodily present; only their ghosts haunt our mind. The cure for these, says Spinoza, is to expel the ghosts by peopling our mind with living beings. The mind's capacity is limited, and can hold so much and no more, and if we fill it with one kind of content there will be no room for another kind. Now the idea of almost anything that is real and present may become the catharsis of our fears and worries; but if in this

[1] *Ibid.*, 13.   [2] *Ibid.*, 15.
[3] *Ibid.*, 17.   [4] *Ibid.*, 32.

embarrassment of riches we are at a loss to know which to choose, there is always the universe of the common properties of things before us. They are real and always present, and, by becoming the object of our contemplation, will cause the disappearance of our fears and worries about things unreal and absent, for "the emotions which spring from reason or which are excited by it are, if time be taken into account, more powerful than those which are related to individual objects which we contemplate as absent" (Prop. VII). While contemplation on the laws that govern the stars may not cure a toothache, it may expel worries and anxieties and the spectres of things inexistent that haunt the vacant spaces of our mind.

But one does not have to go to the common properties of things in order to find a puissant object of contemplation to expel the emotions that assail us. The emotions themselves may become such an object of contemplation. The ailments which the emotions bring in their train are often due to the fact that we brood over them without knowing their causes, or that we misunderstand their nature by attributing them to a single cause which happens to come to our attention. To be sure, "an emotion is stronger in proportion to the number of simultaneous concurrent causes whereby it is aroused" (Prop. VIII); still a knowledge of the multiplicity and unavoidableness of the causes of the emotion together with an understanding of the nature of the emotion itself will remove the sting and pang of the emotion (Prop. IX). Were we only to know the nature of our emotions in all their bearings and in their relation to all their causes, the emotions themselves would become an object of intellectual contemplation and would thereby cease to be passions. The pain they cause us would be forgotten in the pleasure afforded by the very act of our understanding them. We

should cease to be the slaves of our passions and become
their masters, for "if we are affected by an emotion which
is related to many and different causes, which the mind
contemplates at the same time with the emotion itself, we
are less injured, suffer less from it, and are less affected
therefore towards each cause than if we were affected by
another emotion equally great which is related to one cause
only or to fewer causes" (Prop. IX).

Finally, says Spinoza, all these remedies are more effective as preventive measures than as cures. In our moral
economy as in the management of our worldly affairs we
must always plan ahead. We must not allow ourselves to
drift and to be caught unprepared. In fair weather we must
prepare for rainy days, and in time of peace of mind we must
prepare for war on the emotions. Ere we are faced by a problem of conduct, and while the serenity of our mind is still
undisturbed, we must map out a plan of action and a method
of attack. The emotions are treacherous enemies. They lie
in ambush, waiting for our moments of weakness, when we
are off our guard, to spring their fury upon us. We must be
fully armed beforehand, so that when they come down upon
us they will be met by the fire of our reason, for "so long as
we are not agitated by emotions which are contrary to our nature do we possess the power of arranging and connecting
the affections of the body according to the order of the
intellect" (Prop. X).

The therapeutic principle in all these remedies is that they
produce in us an active emotion which is more powerful than
the particular passive emotion to which we happen to be
slaves; the active emotion overwhelms the passive and re-
places it. By one emotion being more powerful than another,
Spinoza seems to say here, two things are meant: first, it
is more constant or presents itself more frequently than the

other, and second, it occupies the mind more than the other, and, furthermore, he seems to say, that which makes an emotion more powerful in both these two meanings is the greater number of objects to which it is related (Prop. XI). These objects, he then says, restating his own previous views, may be either "things which we clearly and distinctly understand" (Prop. XII), that is to say, "the common properties of things or what are deduced from them" (*ibid.*, Demonst.), or any other individual things (Prop. XIII). But since whatever is, is God, he finally in concludes, it is the emotion evoked in us by the idea of God, or what is generally called the love for God, that constitutes the most powerful emotion which can occupy our minds fully, to the exclusion of all other emotions (Props. XIV–XV). The love for God is thus the sovereign remedy for the ailments of the soul.

This sovereign remedy for the ailments of the soul is really nothing but the old consolation held out to its faithful by every religion. Spinoza's advice to men to have all the affections of their body or the images of things related to the idea of God (Prop. XV) reads like the old teachings about faith and trust in God. "Cast thy burden upon the Lord, and He will sustain thee." [1] God is the great provider, the great comforter, the rock of our salvation, the refuge in the day of evil. Or, to quote the following characteristic description of the benefits of the old-fashioned trust in God: "As for the benefits which accrue to one in the present life as a result of trust in God, there is to begin with the peace of the heart as it rests from worldly cares and the relief from the fluctuations of the mind and its anxiety over its disappointments in its bodily desires and the feeling of ease and comfort and rest in the life allotted to one." [2] Spinoza's

---

[1] Psalms 55, 23.   [2] *Ḥobot ha-Lebabot*, IV, Introduction.

sovereign remedy, that of having all the affections of the body or the images of things related to the idea of God, does not seem to promise to men in the present life more than this trust in the old-fashioned God, and it would seem rather strange that after all his skirmishes with rabbis and school-men, after all his searches for a new philosophy, he should land in the same old mystic circle, the refuge in God. But perhaps Spinoza did not mean to promise more than that, for he did not set out to prove that the consolation of his own philosophy is greater than the consolation of the old religion. His contest with the theologians was not an old-fashioned contest between the followers of Dagon and the followers of Jehovah to see which god was the mightier and more bountiful. What he did set out to do was to establish certain truths about the nature of God, to deny of Him certain elements of personality with which He has been invested even by the most speculative of theologians, and to show that such a God, depersonalized as He is, does not cease to be a force and a power for goodness in man's life. He has already shown how his God can be like the God of tradition, a rock of our salvation and a refuge in the day of evil. He now proceeds to show still further how great the power of his de-personalized God may be in human life.

II. Love and Impersonality of God

One can see distinctly the clear and sharp outlines of the syllogisms as they unroll themselves in the remaining propositions of this group. Spinoza seems to say to his opponents: What do you mean when you speak of the personality of God? "Although we are not ignorant of the term [personality, *personalitas*], we are ignorant of its significance, and unable to form any clear concept of its content."[1] If it

---

[1] *Cogitata Metaphysica*, II, 8.

means anything at all, you may mean by it two things. In the first place, you may mean that you behave yourselves towards God as if He were a person like yourselves. In the second place, you may mean that God behaves himself towards you as if He were a person like yourselves. Now I am going to show that it is only the first sense of personality that has any meaning at all, and in that sense even my God may be said to have personality. The second sense in which you say God has personality, I am going to show, has no meaning at all, and is a mere empty phrase even when you use it with reference to your own God.

In the Hebrew Bible and throughout post-Biblical Hebrew literature the religious attitude of man towards God is described by two terms, fear and love. Whatever the relative position of these two elements of the religious attitude may have been in the early history of the Jewish religion, in the course of its subsequent development fear was gradually relegated to the background and love emerged as the highest motive in religious worship. The rabbis of the Talmud speak of those who worship out of fear and those who worship out of love and proclaim the superiority of the latter over the former.[1] The mediaeval speculative theologians try to define the nature of these two religious elements and their relation to each other. According to Bahya, the fear of God is a necessary preliminary stage in man's spiritual development, for it is impossible for man to attain the love of God without having first purged his heart of passions through the fear of God.[2] According to Maimonides, the prescribed practices of the Law, which to him are of lesser importance than the right knowledge of God, inculcate into man's heart the fear of God, whereas the true knowledge of God's nature creates

[1] *Sotah* 31a. Cf. *Sifre* on Deuteronomy (ed. Friedmann), § 32.
[2] *Ḥobot ha-Lebabot*, X, Introduction.

in him the love of God.[1] Crescas, who unlike Maimonides does not place a higher value upon right knowledge than upon right action, also makes the love of God, from which he seems not to differentiate the true fear of God, the final goal of the religious life.[2] In Christianity, where the love of God as a religious principle was introduced after it had already gained complete ascendancy in Judaism, it has subsequently developed, under the influence of philosophy, along the same lines as in Judaism. A parallel development of the principle of the love of God is to be found also in Islam.[3]

From the widespread discussions of the love of God throughout the religious literatures in the languages accessible to Spinoza, and especially in Hebrew, we may gather four distinct characteristics of the nature of love in general and of the love of God in particular which, as we shall see anon, stand out as the main assumptions of Spinoza's treatment of the subject.

In the first place, love means a union with the object of love. Says Crescas: "From the nature of love in general it is clear that the love for God results in a union with God, for even in the case of physical objects it is evident that love and concord among them are the causes of their perfection and unity. In fact, one of the ancients was of the opinion that the origin of generation is love and union, whereas the origin of decay is hatred and separation. If this is so in the case of physical objects, how much more must it be so in the case of spiritual beings, namely, that union and unity result from love and concord between them."[4] Meir ibn Gabbai similarly says: "Love means true unity, and true unity is that which is called love. . . . And it is incumbent upon

---

[1] *Moreh Nebukim*, III, 52, end.   [2] *Or Adonai*, II, vi, 1 (p. 53b).

[3] Cf. I. Goldziher, "Die Gottesliebe in der islamischen Theologie," in *Islam*, IX (1919), pp. 144 ff.; J. Obermann, *Der philosophische und religiöse Subjektivismus Ghazalis*, pp. 272 ff.   [4] *Or Adonai*, II, vi, 1 (p. 55a).

man to love God and become united with Him, for the desired end of all created nature is to bring all things into union. This is what is meant by love. There must be no sign of division and separation in nature, and still less in man himself, whose purpose is to become united with his Creator and to show no sign of division in himself." [1] This conception of love as union which Crescas in the passage quoted from him ascribes to one of the ancients, meaning Empedocles,[2] is ascribed by Aristotle also to the Symposium and Aristophanes.[3] It is discussed by Thomas Aquinas,[4] by Leo Hebraeus,[5] and by Descartes.[6]

In the second place, love may be divided into different kinds, in accordance with the variation in the perfection of the object loved. Says Crescas again: "In proportion to the perfection of the object desired is the love and the pleasure of the desire. . . . For according to the degree of goodness of the object loved is the degree of the love." [7] The origin and the history of the classification of love will be discussed later in connection with the intellectual love of God.[8]

[1] *'Abodat ha-Kodesh*, I, 27.

[2] Crescas may have got his knowledge of Empedocles from Aristotle's references to him, such as in *De Anima*, III, 6, 430a, 28 ff.

[3] *Politics*, II, 4, 1262b, 10 ff.

[4] *Summa Theologica*, Prima Secundae, Quaest. 28, Art. 1.

[5] *Dialoghi d'Amore*, I, p. 45 (Bari, 1929). On Leo Hebraeus and his relation to Spinoza, see B. Zimmels, *Leo Hebräus, etc.* (Breslau, 1886), p. 74, n. 3; Edmondo Solmi, *Benedetto Spinoza e Leone Ebreo* (Modena, 1903); Carl Gebhardt, "Spinoza und der Platonismus," in *Chronicon Spinozanum*, I (1921), pp. 178 ff.; Giovanni Gentile, "Leone Ebreo e Spinoza," in *Studii sul Rinascimento* (Firenze, 1923), pp. 96 ff.; Heinz Pflaum, *Die Idee der Liebe: Leone Ebreo* (Tübingen, 1926); Joseph Klausner, "Don Jehudah Abarbanel u-Filosofiat ha-Ahabah Shelo," in *Tarbiz*, III (Jerusalem, 1932), pp. 67 ff.

On the whole, Leo Hebraeus' influence upon Spinoza has been unduly exaggerated. The passages from the *Dialoghi d'Amore* examined by us in connection with Spinoza have all proved to be philosophic commonplaces. Nor has it been possible to establish any direct literary relationship between these passages and Spinoza.

[6] *Les Passions de l'Ame*, II, 79.   [7] *Or Adonai*, II, vi, 1 (p. 54b).

[8] Cf. below, pp. 302 ff.

In the third place, this love of God is said to spring from the knowledge of God. We have already quoted one statement from Maimonides in which the knowledge of God's existence and unity, that is to say, His nature as far as it can be known, leads to the love of God. A still more explicit statement by Maimonides is the following: "One cannot love God except through the knowledge with which one knows Him, and the love is in proportion with the knowledge; the less of the latter the less of the former, and the more of the latter the more of the former." [1] Again, "we have already shown in the *Mishneh Torah* [2] that this love is only possible when we comprehend the real nature of things and understand the divine wisdom displayed therein." [3] The question whether knowledge is the cause of love is discussed with reference to love in general by Thomas Aquinas, who quotes earlier authorities, and the answer given is in the affirmative. [4] In Crescas, however, there is a denial that love is connected with intelligence, and he lays down the principle that "love and pleasure are in the will without any act of intelligence." [5] This statement, however, is not to be taken as a denial of the principle that love is based on knowledge. It only means to say that love is independent of the act of intelligence, that is, of reason and of knowledge based upon reason, which Spinoza calls the second kind of knowledge. It seems to me also that it is with reference to this contention of Crescas that Leo Hebraeus argues that "even though in corporeal objects love differs from intelli-

---

[1] *Mishneh Torah, Teshubah*, X, 6.

[2] *Ibid., Yesode ha-Torah*, II, 2.

[3] *Moreh Nebukim*, III, 28.

[4] *Summa Theologica*, Prima Secundae, Quaest. 27, Art. 2.

[5] *Or Adonai*, II, vi, 1 (p. 54b). In connection with the relation of Maimonides' and Crescas' discussion of love to that of Spinoza, cf. Joël, *Spinoza's Theologisch-Politischer Traktat*, p. ix and pp. 44 ff.

gence . . . in intellectual and immaterial essences they exist together." [1]

In the fourth place, this love for God ought to occupy one's entire mind so that no room is left for any other desires. Thus describes Baḥya Ibn Pakuda the state of the human soul after she has attained love for God. "She devotes herself exclusively to God; her heart is wholly given to Him, to love Him, to trust in Him, to long for Him. She has no other occupation than that of serving Him, she has no thought of anybody but Him. . . . If He deals kindly with her, she is thankful, and if He afflicts her, she endures with patience, and despite everything that happens to her, her love for Him and her trust in Him increase." [2] So also Maimonides: "It is well known and quite evident that the love for God cannot strike deep root in the heart of man unless it occupies his mind constantly so that nothing in the world matters to him but this love for God." [3]

These four characteristics of love are all found in Spinoza.

In the first place, he discusses the problem whether love implies a will to union with the object of love. In the formal definition of love as given by him in the *Short Treatise* love is said to be nothing else "than the enjoyment of a thing and union therewith." [4] This definition is directly taken from Descartes. [5] In the *Ethics*, however, where the first part of the definition is given as "pleasure with the accompanying idea of an external cause," the second part, which is given as "the will of the lover to unite himself to

---

[1] *Dialoghi d'Amore*, III, p. 373 (Bari, 1929): "Giá sai che, se bene ne le cose corporee l'amore è diverso da l'intellezione . . . che ne l'essenzie intellettuali e immateriali stanno insieme."

[2] *Ḥobot ha-Lebabot*, X, 1.   [3] *Mishneh Torah*, *Teshubah*, X, 6.

[4] *Short Treatise*, II, 5, § 1.

[5] *Les Passions de l'Ame*, II, 79. Cf. Sigwart, *Benedict de Spinoza's Kurze Tractat*, etc., *ad loc.*

the beloved object" and is attributed to some authors (*auctorum, auctoribus*), is said to express "not the essence (*essentia*) of love but a property (*proprietas*) thereof." [1] This, on the whole, agrees with Thomas Aquinas, who treats of union under the effects (*effectus*) of love as contrasted with the cause (*causa*) of love,[2] though Spinoza's contrast here between the "essence" and the "property" of love would seem to be based upon Descartes' statement that the distinction between the love of benevolence and the love of concupiscence "concerns the effects of love alone, and not its essence." [3] Still the phraseology of Crescas is discernible even in this discussion of the *Ethics* which is entirely based upon Descartes. In his comment upon the statement with which he agrees that "it is a property in a lover to will a union with the beloved object" he says that he does not understand by will (*voluntas*) "a consent or deliberation, that is to say, a free decree of the mind." This is directly aimed at Descartes' statement that "by the word will I do not here intend to talk of desire . . . but of the consent, etc." [4] But when Spinoza goes on to say that "by will I understand the satisfaction (*acquiescentia*) that the beloved object produces in the lover by its presence, by virtue of which the pleasure of the lover is strengthened, or at any rate supported," he seems to reflect Crescas' statement that love is a pleasure or satisfaction in the will. The formal definition of love as given by Crescas is expressed in the phrase "agreeableness of will." [5] It would seem that it is in this sense that Spinoza uses the term "will" here.

[1] *Ethics*, III, *Affectuum Definitiones*, 6.
[2] *Summa Theologica*, Prima Secundae, Quaest. 28, and cf. Quaest. 27.
[3] *Les Passions de l'Ame*, II, 81.
[4] *Ibid.*, II, 80.
[5] ערבות הרצון, *Or Adonai*, I, III, 5 (p. 27a), or ערבות הרצון, *ibid.*, II, vi, 1 (p. 54b).

In the second place, Spinoza also speaks of love as being divided according to the qualities or perfections of its objects. The objects of love are classified by him into three kinds, eternal, transient, and those which are transient by their own nature but eternal by virtue of their cause.[1] The origin of this classification has already been discussed above.[2] Of the various kinds of love the highest is that of God who is eternal, and whom he designates also as Truth — a divine appellation which is common in Arabic and Hebrew [3] as well as in scholastic [4] literature. As synonymous with the "love of God," Spinoza repeatedly uses the expression "union with God." [5]

All this, however, occurs only in the *Short Treatise*. In the *Ethics* there is no definite statement either as to the division of love in accordance with its object or as to the union with God. But even in the *Ethics* there is an indirect allusion to both these views in the statement that the love for God is a love "towards an immutable and eternal object (see Prop. XV, Part V) of which we are really partakers (see Prop. XLV, Part II)." [6] To say that the love towards God is a love "towards an immutable and eternal object" undoubtedly reflects his division of love into the love of something eternal, of something transient, and of something which is eternal only by virtue of its cause. Then also to say that "we are really partakers" of the immutable and eternal

---

[1] *Short Treatise*, II, 5, §§ 1 ff.

[2] Cf. above, Vol. I, pp. 252–253.

[3] *Al-Najat*, III: *Metaphysics*, II (p.63); *Shahrastani*, p. 375; *'Olam Ḳaṭan*, III (p. 58); *Emunah Ramah*, II, iii (p. 54); *Mishneh Torah*, *Yesode ha-Torah*, I, 4; *'Iḳḳarim*, II, 27. Cf. D. Kaufmann, *Geschichte de Attributenlehre*, p. 333, n. 204.

[4] Cf. Augustine, *De Cognitione Verae Vitae*, Ch. 7 (Migne, *Patrologia Latina*, Vol. 40, Col. 1011); Thomas Aquinas, *Summa Theologica*, Pars I, Quaest. 16, Art. 5.

[5] *Short Treatise*, II, 4, § 10, 19, § 14, and 22, §§ 2 ff.

[6] *Ethics*, V, Prop. 20, Schol.

objects which we love necessarily implies that the love of God is a union with God.

In the third place, following the common philosophic tradition, Spinoza makes the general statement that man loves God "solely because he has a knowledge of God," [1] or that the love for God springs (*oritur*)[2] or flows forth (*pro-fluit*)[3] or flows (*fluit*)[4] from the knowledge of God. But as knowledge according to Spinoza is a general term, including three different kinds, it is only the third kind of knowledge which leads directly to the love of God, as he makes quite clear subsequently in Propositions XXVII–XXXIII. It is the intuitive and immediate kind of knowledge and not reason (*ratio*) that is the source of the love of God, though, of course, the second kind of knowlege may lead to the third and hence to the love of God. Spinoza thus reflects Crescas' statement quoted above that love is without intelligence, which we have explained to mean that it is without any kind of knowledge which arises from reason. An indirect allusion to this view that it is only the third or the immediate kind of knowledge that leads to love for God may be found in the *Short Treatise* in the statement that we come to love God and to be united with Him "if once we get to know God, at least with a knowledge as clear as that with which we also know the body," [5] that is to say, with an immediate kind of knowledge. It is in the light of this discussion that we can see the logical sequence between Proposition XIV and Proposition XV. Stating first that "the mind can cause all the affections of the body or the images of things to be related to the idea of God" (Prop. XIV), that is to say, to know

[1] *Tractatus Theologico-Politicus*, Ch. 4 (*Opera*, III, p. 60, l. 33).

[2] *Ibid.* (p. 61, l. 30).

[3] Epistola 19 (*Opera*, IV, p. 94, l. 15).

[4] Epistola 21 (*Opera*, IV, p. 128, l. 1).

[5] *Short Treatise*, II, 19, § 14 (*Opera*, I, p. 93, ll. 20–22).

them by the third kind of knowledge, he proceeds to say that
" he who clearly and distinctly understands himself and his
emotions loves God, and loves Him better the better he understands himself and his emotions " (Prop. XV), which view
he later restates by saying that this kind of knowledge "be-
gets a love towards an immutable and eternal object (see
Prop. XV)." [1]

In the fourth place, again following tradition, Spinoza says
that this love for God, which rises out of man's having a
clear and distinct knowledge of himself and his emotions, or,
as he has put it in Proposition XIV, of his relating them to
the idea of God, becomes better the better man understands
himself and his emotions (Prop. XV), and, furthermore, that
"this love to God above everything else ought to occupy the
mind" (Prop. XVI).

So far Spinoza has been merely applying the common
utterances of traditional theology about the God of tradition
to his own God. His own God, he was arguing in effect, has
as much personality as the God of tradition, if by personality
is meant a personal relation on the part of man toward God
as it expresses itself in the attitude of love. But now he
wants to show wherein his God differs from the God of tradition. He differs from the latter, he is going to say, in that
He cannot be conceived, as the traditional God is generally
conceived, as acting like a person in His relation to man,
that is to say, in having personality in the sense that He
behaves himself toward man as if He were a person.

In traditional philosophy, just as the personal attitude of
man towards God is described by the phrase "love for God,"
so the personal attitude of God towards man is described by
applying to Him the terms "pleasure" or "joy," "pain" or
"sorrow," and "love." The attempt to find the first trace of

[1] *Ethics*, V, Prop. 20, Schol.

personality in God in the fact that He has the experience of
pleasure has already been made by Aristotle, in his statement
that the incessant actual contemplation of God is an activity
which is pleasure ($\dot{\eta}\delta o\nu\dot{\eta}$) and is the most pleasant ($\ddot{\eta}\delta\iota\sigma\tau o\nu$)
activity.[1] In Jewish philosophy, especially in Crescas,[2] it is
argued that even though no other "passion"[3] can be attributed to God, the attribution of pleasure or joy [4] is permissible, inasmuch as the term is applied to God throughout the
Prophetic and the Talmudic writings. As for the term
"pain" or "sorrow," [5] Crescas refers to the "ancients," evidently including Maimonides, who allowed its application
to God only in a figurative sense, on the principle that
Scripture speaketh in accordance with the language of man.[6]
But even the attribution of pleasure or joy to God, argues
Crescas, is permissible only in a figurative sense, for there is
no analogy at all between our pleasure or joy and the pleasure
or joy attributed to God. Our pleasure or joy consists in the
passing from a lesser perfection to a greater perfection, as,
e.g., from ignorance to knowledge, whereas in the case of
God, in whom no change or transition of any kind is possible, pleasure or joy is only that feeling which is associated
with His love — a love which is but an exercise of goodness
and a desire to allow His goodness to overflow. This view
is reflected also in the Hymn of Unity: "Joy and sorrow
occur not in Thee." [7] Love then alone can be attributed to
God, and just as man ought to love God, God loves man, so
that in the Scriptures the patriarchs are said to have loved
God and God is said to have loved the patriarchs.[8] The

---

[1] *Metaphysics*, XII, 7, 1072b, 16 and 24.
[2] *Or Adonai*, I, iii, 5. Cf. also *'Ikkarim*, II, 15.
[3] הפעלות, $\pi\acute{a}\theta$os.   [4] שמחה.   [5] עצבון.
[6] *Moreh Nebukim*, I, 29.
[7] *Shir ha-Yihud*, III.
[8] *Or Adonai*, II, vi, 1 (p. 54b).

reciprocal love between man and God is explained also by Meir ibn Gabbai as follows: "We have already stated that love for the one God consists in man's complete unity with Him . . . and so as a result of his love for the one God man is loved by God in return . . . for he who conceives of God's unity in this way causes pleasure to his Creator, so that the latter loves him after the manner of those who are pleased with one another, in which case each one is pleased with the other and each one loves the other. In this way it is possible that there should be reciprocal love between God and Israel. In another way, too, is it possible that there should be recip-rocal love between God and Israel, namely, after the manner of the love of a father for his son, for Israel is a part of God and is in close relationship to Him." [1] But here again these two loves are of a different nature, for the love of God for man is nothing but the love of the perfect Good to exercise His goodness, and is identical with the essence of God itself.[2]

The upshot of all this is that God may be spoken of as being affected by the emotions of pleasure and pain and love, but all these are to be taken in a sense in which the terms in question are not ordinarily understood. We can readily see the objections that Spinoza raised in his mind against such a view — objections of the kind he has raised on several oc-casions before against the homonymous use of terms in their application to God. If pleasure and pain and love and all other similar emotions are to be applied to God in a sense entirely divorced from their original meaning, why not say that God is not pleased and is not pained and does not love? And so Spinoza, with such reasoning in his mind, says, "God is free from passions, nor is He affected with any emotion of pleasure or pain" (Prop. XVII), for "God can

[1] *'Abodat ha-Kodesh*, I, 28.
[2] *Or Adonai*, I, iii, 5 (p. 27a), and II, vi, 1 (p. 54b).

neither pass to a greater nor to a less perfection" (Demonst.), and so also, "properly speaking, God loves no one and hates no one" (Corol.). In the *Short Treatise* Spinoza summarizes his objections to God's love for man in two arguments: "In the first place, we have said that to God no modes of thought can be ascribed except those which are in creatures; therefore, it cannot be said that God loves mankind, much less [can it be said] that He should love them because they love Him, or hate them because they hate Him. . . . Besides, this would necessarily involve nothing less than a great mutability on the part of God, who, though neither loved nor hated before, would now have to begin to love and to hate, and would be induced or made to do so by something supposed to be outside Him; but this is absurdity itself." [1] Now, it will be observed that these arguments were not unknown to the mediaevals and that they anticipated them by declaring that God's love for man is unlike the love which we find in the creatures. But here, as on many other occasions, Spinoza dismisses the distinctions of the mediaevals as mere quibbling and revives against them their own arguments.

The denial of God's love for man and in general the denial of any personal reciprocal relations between God and man will eliminate certain difficulties which are bound to come up if one affirms such a relation between God and man. Spinoza enumerates three such difficulties which are now eliminated by him.

In the first place, says Spinoza, the affirmation that God is pleased or is sorry or that He loves, however attenuated these terms may become by the explanations they undergo, must inevitably imply that His pleasure and sorrow and love are called forth by the manner in which men behave them-

[1] *Short Treatise*, II, 24, § 2.

selves towards Him. The entire conception of obedience and disobedience and of reward and punishment in every revealed religion is based upon the fundamental belief that God is variously affected by the conduct of man and that there is a certain relation between desert and retribution. But the facts are against this, and God seems to be angry at those with whom He should be pleased and to hate those whom He should love. The problem of evil and of divine injustice must thus inevitably come up as a result of this fundamental belief of all religions. Of course, theology tries to answer such difficulties and to free God from all charges of injustice by arguing that He is not directly responsible for evil.[1] But there is no escaping from the conclusion that if God is affected by human conduct, and if He is capable of pain and grief and anger as well as of pleasure and love, He must be directly the author of evil as well as of good. Man who suffers unjustly is bound to rebel against God and to hate Him. All those qualities which religion tries to inculcate in man — acquiescence, resignation, contentment, and peace of mind — by its preaching the doctrine that man must love God thus disappear as a result of its preaching also the doctrine that God loves man. But if you deny outright that God is affected by human conduct or that He is pleased or pained at man's action or that He loves man, then "no one can hate God" (Prop. XVIII), and "love to God cannot be turned into hatred" (Corol.), and we do not hold God responsible for pain and sorrow (Schol.). In the *Short Treatise*, the existence of a causal relation between God's love for man and man's love for God is rejected on the ground that it would imply freedom of the will on the part of man, "for in that case we should have to suppose that people do so [love God] of their own free will, and that they do not de-

---

[1] Cf. *Moreh Nebukim*, III, 10; *Emunot we-De'ot*, I, 3, Fifth Theory, end.

pend on a first cause; which we have already before proved
to be false." [1]

In the second place, the assertion that God loves man must
inevitably lead man to love God in expectation of being
loved by Him in return. Of course, religion preaches that
the love for God must be a disinterested love, and that nothing is to be expected in return, for then and then only will
the love for God be the ultimate and highest happiness. But
this, Spinoza seems to argue, is humanly impossible. If God
can love man, then man will love God in expectation that
God will love him in return. The love for God thus ceases
to be the highest good; it becomes a commodity in trade.
But if you deny outright that God can love man, then "he
who loves God cannot strive that God should love him in
return" (Prop. XIX).

Finally, Spinoza seems to repeat his previous contention
that the conception of an impersonal God "contributes to
the welfare of our social existence, since it teaches us to hate
no one, to despise no one, to mock no one, to be angry with
no one, and to envy no one." [2] All these purposes are de-
feated by the conception of a God who loves mankind, for
if He loves them, He must necessarily reveal His law to
them,[3] and He must reveal it to them in different ways and
in different places. Man's love for God, which according to
the teachings of all religions should lead to men's love for one
another, thus leads to dissension among men, and all because the God whom they are bidden to love is conceived to
love mankind in return. But if you deny outright that God
can love man, then "this love to God cannot be defiled by
the emotion either of envy or of jealousy, but is the more
fostered the more people we imagine to be connected with
God by the same bond of love" (Prop. XX).

[1] *Short Treatise*, II, 24, § 2.   [2] *Ethics*, II, Prop. 49, Schol.
[3] *Short Treatise*, II, 24, § 4. Cf. below, pp. 225–226.

III. Immortality and Intellectual Love of God

The transition from the subject-matter discussed in the preceding propositions and the subject-matter discussed in the propositions which are to follow is explained by Spinoza himself. "I have now concluded all that I had to say relating to this present life. . . . It is time, therefore, that I should now pass to those matters which appertain to the duration of the mind without relation to the body." [1] But Spinoza also had before him a literary model in which the immortality of the soul was connected with the love of God. Crescas, whose discussion of the love of God, as we have seen, must have been one of the many possible sources on which Spinoza could have drawn for his own treatment of the subject, similarly proceeds from the discussion of the love of God to the discussion of the immortality of the soul, stating his conclusion that "philosophic speculation is in agreement with what has been shown to be the view according to the teachings of Scripture and tradition, namely, that true love is that which is conducive to the final end of the eternal remaining-in-existence of the soul which is an accepted belief of our people, upon which we have been brought up, concerning which Scripture has enlightened our eyes, and with which, in addition, philosophic speculation is in agreement, being opposed to nothing in it." [2]

The belief in the immortality of the soul is naturally dependent upon a belief that the soul is something different from and independent of the body. If the soul, for instance, were conceived of as what Aristotle describes as a kind of harmony (ἁρμονία τις),[3] that is to say, a physiological process

---

[1] *Ethics*, V, Prop. 20, Schol., end.
[2] *Or Adonai*, II, vi, 1 (p. 55a).
[3] *De Anima*, I, 4, 407b, 30 ff.

of the body, there could be no belief in its immortality. Assuming, then, that the soul in order to be immortal must be
something distinct from body, it was considered by some
as a self-subsisting spiritual substance contrasted with body
which is a self-subsisting material substance, and by others
as a sort of inseparable form of the body of which only a
certain part, called the hylic intellect, may acquire self-
subsisting substantiality and become what is known as the
acquired intellect. This is a broad statement of two contrasting views under each of which all other views may be subsumed. Immortality is possible according to the proponents
of both of these views, but the immortality is differently conceived by them. To those who consider the soul to be a self-
subsisting spiritual substance which happens to exist for a
certain tract of time in the body but is never part of it, the
soul in its entirety is said to be immortal. But to those who
consider the soul to be an inseparable form of the body, the
soul as a whole is destroyed with body and only that part of
it which becomes a self-subsisting spiritual substance, namely,
the acquired intellect, remains immortal. This latter view
is clearly expressed by Ibn Ezra in the following passage:
"For the spirit of man by which he lives and experiences
sensation is the same as that of beasts; as the one dies, so
dies the other, except for that supernal part wherein a man
has a pre-eminence above a beast." [1] Even in the rational
part of the soul Maimonides denies immortality to the hylic
intellect and confines it only to the acquired intellect. He
says: "The form of the soul [i.e., the acquired intellect] is
not composed of the elements, and consequently it does not
have to resolve into them. Nor is it a faculty of the soul
which stands in need of the soul as the soul in its turn stands
in need of the body. It is rather something which comes

[1] Commentary on Genesis 3, 6. Cf. *Cuzari*, V, 12.

from God above. Therefore, when the body, which is composed of the elements, dissolves, and the soul, on account of its having existence only together with the body and on account also of its standing in need of the body in all its functions, likewise perishes, the form of the soul [i.e., the acquired intellect] is not destroyed, inasmuch as it does not stand in need of the soul in any of its functions, but of its own nature knows and comprehends ideas apart from bodies and knows the Creator of the universe. It thus continues in its existence eternally." [1] Similarly Gersonides, after enumerating different opinions as to whether the hylic intellect is immortal,[2] concludes, like Avicenna and Maimonides, that only the acquired intellect is immortal.[3] Spinoza's own teacher, Manasseh ben Israel, in a special treatise on the immortality of the soul, reproduces Maimonides' view with approval.[4] The view that immortality is to be attributed only to the rational part of the soul and not to its other functions may be traced throughout the history of philosophy back to Plato, though, it has been pointed out, Plato himself is inconsistent in his statements on this question.[5]

Spinoza's view as to the nature of the soul or mind, as we have already seen, is more like the second of the two views we have stated. The mind is inseparable from the body; and consequently some of its functions, like imagination and memory, which are dependent upon sensation, must disappear with the disappearance of the body. Still the mind, according to Spinoza, is not merely a physiological function of the body which is born with the body and which must

---

[1] *Mishneh Torah, Yesode ha-Torah,* IV, 9. The terms used in this passage are: נשמה = שכל נקנה ; הדעה שהשיגה מהבורא והשיגה הדעות הנפרדות = צורת הנפש = הנשמה הצריכה לגוף. Cf. *Mishneh Torah, Teshubah,* VIII, 3, and below, p. 314, n. 2.   [2] *Milḥamot Adonai,* I, 8.
[3] *Ibid.,* I, 10.   [4] *Nishmat Ḥayyim,* II, 1.
[5] Cf. Grote, *Plato* (1867), II, p. 160.

completely disappear with it. This is only true of some of its functions. But in its thinking essence it comes from above, like the acquired intellect in the passage we have quoted from Maimonides; it is a mode of the eternal and infinite attribute of thought. That part of mind existed from eternity prior to the existence of its particular body, and it remains to eternity even after the death of the body.

This is the substance of Spinoza's argument in Propositions XXI–XXIII, which we shall now try to unfold.

Mind and body, begins Spinoza, are indeed inseparable, and consequently as long as one of them is said to exist the other also must be said to exist. But existence is of two kinds. One kind of existence is said of things which are conceived of as actual in so far as they are conceived to exist in relation to a fixed time and place. The other kind of existence is said of things which are conceived of as actual in so far as they are conceived to be contained in God and to follow from the necessity of the divine nature.[1] Spinoza variously describes these two kinds of existence by calling the former existence (*existentia*),[2] formal being (*esse formalis*),[3] actual essence (*essentia actualis*),[4] or given essence (*essentia data*),[5] and the latter essence (*essentia*),[6] ideas of nonexistent things (*ideae rerum non existentium*),[7] ideal essence (*essentia idealis*),[8] or formal essence (*essentia formalis*).[9] In both these cases of existence the mind is inseparable from the body, and both the mind and the body are said to exist with the same kind of existence. The mind of an actually existent body has actual existence which is characterized by its posses-

---

[1] Cf. *Ethics*, II, Prop. 8, Corol., and V, Prop. 29, Schol.

[2] *Ibid.*, I, Prop. 24; V, Prop. 22, Demonst.; *Cogitata Metaphysica*, I, 2.

[3] *Ethics*, II, Prop. 5.   [4] *Tractatus Politicus*, Ch. 2, § 2. Cf. above, p. 198.

[5] *Ibid.*   [6] Cf. above, n. 2.

[7] *Ethics*, II, Prop. 8. Cf. above, p. 29.   [8] Cf. above, n. 4.

[9] *Ethics*, I, Prop. 17, Schol.; II, Prop. 8. Cf. above, p. 29.

sion of the powers of imagination and memory, both of which are based upon sensation. With the cessation of the actual existence of the body, these powers of the mind also cease to exist, for "the mind can imagine nothing, nor can it recollect anything that is past, except while the body endures" (Prop. XXI). But even after the body has actually ceased to exist, it still has ideal existence, for "in God, nevertheless, there is necessarily granted an idea which expresses the essence of this or that human body under the form of eternity" (Prop. XXII). This idea or conception in God which expresses the essence of the human body is something which pertains to the essence of the human mind, for the human body is the object of the idea constituting the human mind.[1] He thus concludes that "the human mind cannot be absolutely destroyed with the body, but something of it remains which is eternal" (Prop. XXIII). That something is the thinking essence of the mind which after the death of the body returns to unite itself with the attribute of thought whence it came,[2] even as the acquired intellect, according to mediaeval philosophers, returns after the death of the body to unite itself with the Active Intellect, or with God.

The existence, then, which is attributed to that part of the mind which remains eternal after the destruction of the body is not the same kind of existence that is attributed to it during the existence of the body. For one thing, it does not know its own body. For another thing, it does not know other bodies. And without its knowledge of bodies, it does not experience all the pleasures that arise from such knowledge. It is only the element of thought in the mind that continues to exist after death as a part of the attribute of thought — a thought stripped of sensation, memory, imagination, and everything that goes with them. Now, it could be argued

---

[1] *Ethics*, II, Prop. 13.   [2] Cf. *Short Treatise*, II, 23.

that an eternal existence of that kind could also be attributed to the body. Death brings destruction only to the particular shape and form of the human body, the frame in which it is encased and the earthly qualities with which it is endowed, but its essence, which is extension, remains as a part of the attribute of extension and continues to exist with a kind of existence which is related to the existence of the body prior to death as the existence of human thought after death is related to the existence of the human mind before death. Both mind and body, Spinoza will admit, come from God, and unto God shall they return. This being the case, it may be asked, why should not Spinoza speak of the immortality of the body as well as of the immortality of the soul? [1] It is well for those who believe that God is immaterial and hence pure thought to speak only of the immortality of the soul, for to them it is only the soul that comes directly from God; body does not come directly from God; and consequently to them it is only the soul that returns unto God. If they do sometimes say that the body is to live again, it is only in the sense that in some miraculous way it will be resurrected to a new life. But as for Spinoza, to whom both soul and body are modes of God's attributes of thought and extension and to whom the essential extension of the body is not more destructible than the essential thought of the mind, why should he speak of the immortality of the soul rather than of the immortality of the body?

We can reason out how Spinoza would answer this question if it were actually raised against him.

In the first place, he would say, by immortality is not meant the mere conservation of thought or extension in the universe. In that general sense of immortality, both thought and extension, to be sure, may be said to be equally con-

___

[1] Cf. Pollock, *Spinoza*, p. 295.

served, for the death of the individual does not diminish the total amount of extension in the universe any more than it diminishes the total amount of thought. Nothing is lost in nature; there is only a change in form. But immortality means more than that. It means the eternal preservation of something that was peculiar to a particular human being during his lifetime. In this respect, Spinoza would say, there is a difference between mind and body. The thought element of the mind that survives death bears the particular characteristics of the individual during his lifetime, for, as we shall see, the immortality of the soul, according to Spinoza, is personal and individual.[1] There are, however, no such particular characteristics of the individual in the extension element of the body that remains after death. Consequently, while it is proper to retain the traditional vocabulary and speak of the immortality of the soul, there is no ground for speaking in the same sense of the immortality of the body.

In the second place, Spinoza would say, what is that ideal existence which both the thought element of the human mind and the extension element of the human body have after the death of the individual? Is it not the conception or the idea which necessarily exists in God and expresses the essence of this or that human body?[2] Now this conception or idea which God has of the extension of the human body is different from the conception or idea which He has of the thought of the human mind. Of the latter it is direct, but of the former it is indirect, for the conception or idea which God has of extension is something which directly pertains to the essence of the human mind.[3] The inference to be drawn from this is that the body is said to have an eternal

[1] Cf. below, pp. 318 ff. [2] *Ethics*, V, Prop. 22.
[3] *Ibid.*, V, Prop. 23, Demonst., referring to *Ethics*, II, Prop. 13.

essence not because of the eternity of the extension of which
it is a mode but rather because of the eternity of its mind
from which it is inseparable and which is a conception or
idea in God. Extension itself, in fact, is said to have such an
ideal existence only because in God there exists an idea of
it, for "in God there necessarily exists an idea of His essence." [1] Consequently, if we were to say that there is an
immortality of the body in the same sense as there is an immortality of the mind, the immortality of the former would
be due to the immortality of the latter, for "this idea which
expresses the essence of the body under the form of eternity
is, as we have said, a certain mode of thought which pertains
to the essence of the mind." [2]

In Judaism the immortality of the soul was quite independent of its pre-existence. If the soul of each human being was not necessarily created with each individual body,
it was created at the creation of the world. Immortality
merely meant the eternity of the soul *a parte post* but not
a parte ante. Spinoza's conception of immortality, however,
included its pre-existence. A similarity to the Platonic conception of the soul thus suggests itself. That Spinoza was
conscious of this similarity is evident from the fact that he
tries to disclaim the assumption that from his belief in the
eternity of the soul, or rather in its pre-existence, one may
infer the doctrine of recollection. It is quite evident that it
is against Plato that he argues that "it is impossible, however, that we should recollect that we existed before the body,
because there are no traces of any such existence in the body"
(Prop. XXIII, Schol.). But, continues he, although "we do
not recollect that we existed before the body, we feel that
our mind . . . is eternal." This statement, we shall now

[1] *Ibid.*, II, Prop. 7.
[2] *Ibid*, V, Prop. 23, Schol.

try to show, is Spinoza's own introduction to the next group of propositions, which are to deal, as we shall see, with the question to what extent immortality is personal and individual.

The mediaeval conception of immortality as a sort of union of the acquired intellect with God gives rise to a series of questions. The first question is whether such immortality is personal or not, that is to say, whether that sort of immortality is affected by the individual's character during his lifetime. If it is affected, the next question is whether these individual differences continue to exist among the immortal souls. Again, if it is affected by the individual's character during his lifetime, the question is whether it is affected only by his intellectual attainments or also by his moral conduct. Then also the question may be raised whether the soul after the death of the body can acquire new knowledge or not. If not, the question is, How can its existence be described as eternal bliss, when any kind of pleasure or satisfaction is possible only when there is a transition from a less perfect state to a more perfect?

All these questions, the discussion of which is to be found in mediaeval authors, Spinoza now tries to answer in connection with his own conception of immortality. He seems to say as follows: It is idle to speculate about the actual state of the human mind after the dissolution of the body. Still, we can have some inkling of it, for even during our lifetime we can experience that state of immortality which I sometimes describe as the union with God, and sometimes, especially in the *Ethics*, as the love for God, and which is a state of mind in which one experiences the highest possible peace. Now this experience of immortality during our lifetime is personal and individual, as is everything else we experience during our lifetime. It is attained by knowledge, of the kind which I call the third (Props. XXIV ff.). It means a union with God, or, as I prefer to call it in the *Ethics*, a love for God (Prop. XXXII, Corol. ff.). Though it is a static sort of perfection and there is in it no transition from the less perfect to the more perfect, still I call it blessedness, by which I mean an eternal state of pleasure (Prop. XXXIII, Schol.). Finally, though it is attained principally by knowledge, still right conduct, as I understand it, is essential to it (Props. XXXIX–XL).

But let us work out the details of the propositions in which these views of Spinoza are developed.

Though Spinoza believes that we have a direct, intuitive knowledge of the existence of God, he still admits with Maimonides, who was in fact expressing a common attitude, that "a man must devote himself to the knowledge and understanding of the sciences dealing with things so that he may understand God in so far as it is in the power of man to know and comprehend Him." [1] Spinoza expresses the same sentiment in the *Tractatus Theologico-Politicus* when he says that "we have greater and more perfect knowledge of God in proportion to our knowledge of natural phenomena;" and "the greater our knowledge of natural phenomena, the more perfect is our knowledge of the essence of God." [2] And so also here in the *Ethics* he says: "The more we understand individual objects, the more we understand God" (Prop. XXIV). Still, this kind of knowledge is only preliminary to the highest kind of knowledge which he has designated knowledge of the third kind, that is, the direct and intuitive knowledge of God. For that kind of knowledge the mind has a natural impulse, a conatus like that which all things have for the preservation of their self (Prop. XXV). The certainty

[1] *Mishneh Torah, Teshubah*, X, 6.
[2] *Tractatus Theologico-Politicus*, Ch. 4 (*Opera*, III, p. 60, ll. 6–11).

with which Spinoza makes this statement seems to have its basis in Aristotle's view that "all men by nature desire to know," [1] which means, as Cicero puts it, "the mind possesses an innate love of knowledge." [2] Descartes identifies this love of knowledge with curiosity (*curiositas*), and he considers it a species of desire (*cupiditas*).[3] Reflecting these views, Spinoza says here that this conatus of the mind to know things by the third kind of knowledge is a conscious effort or a desire (*cupiditas*), that is to say, it is a determination to understand things by the third kind of knowledge, and the more apt the mind becomes for that kind of knowledge by the development of its powers through a greater understanding of individual objects, the more it desires to understand things by the third kind of knowledge (Prop. XXVI). The mind is thus always in a restless state of endeavor for the fulfilment of a certain desire, for the attainment of the longed-for third kind of knowledge. Once this kind of knowledge is attained, man thereby attains his greatest peace and satisfaction of the mind, for "from this third kind of knowledge arises the highest possible peace of the mind — *summa, quae dari potest, Mentis acquiescentia*" [4] (Prop. XXVII). This peace of mind, which the third kind of knowledge brings to us during our lifetime, Spinoza seems to say, is a foretaste of the eternal blessedness which awaits us after death. Here, again, Spinoza reflects certain ideas which had been current throughout the history of philosophy. That the state of immortality is a state of eternal peace and satisfaction, and that even during our lifetime the possession of knowledge is a satisfaction to the soul, were commonly expressed views, as will be shown in the course of our subse-

---

[1] *Metaphysics*, I, 1, 980a, 21.   [2] *De Finibus*, IV, 7, § 18.
[3] *Les Passions de l'Ame*, II, 88.
[4] Cf. "*Gerustheid des gemoeds*" in *Short Treatise*, II, 24, § 1.

quent discussion. But a few statements from Ibn Gabirol may prove illuminating in this connection. The blessedness which awaits the righteous during their immortal state is described by Ibn Gabirol as an "eternal delight"[1] or "infinite pleasure,"[2] and the Throne of Glory in which the immortal souls abide is described by him as a place where "those who failed of strength may here find repose"[3] and as a place of "rest."[4] Furthermore, even during our lifetime, says Ibn Gabirol, "the understanding of the simple substances and the apprehension as much as is possible for us of the knowledge of those substances constitute the greatest peace (*requies*)[5] and the maximum pleasure (*suavitas*)[6] of the rational soul, and in proportion to the strength of the soul in the knowledge of these simple substances, its diffusion through them, its comprehension of their forms and properties, and its understanding of their actions and passions, will be its strength in the knowledge of God and its union with Him."[7]

But what is that third kind of knowledge? Though Spinoza has already discussed this kind of knowledge toward the end of the Second Part, he restates here his explanation briefly and with a few additional points and a new emphasis. Previously (Prop. XXIV) he has stated that the understanding of individual things will be helpful toward the attainment

---

[1] תענוג עולם. *Keter Malkut*, l. 50, in *Selected Religious Poems by Solomon Ibn Gabirol*, translated into English verse by Israel Zangwill from a critical text edited by Israel Davidson, 1923. (L. 32, in *Shire Shelomoh Ben Yehudah Ibn Gabirol*, III, edited by Ḥ. N. Bialik and J. Ḥ. Rawnitzki, *Tel-Aviv*, 1928.)

[2] נעם בלי תכלית וקצבה. *Ibid.*, l. 330. (L. 223, *ibid.*)

[3] ושם ינוחו יגיעי כח. *Ibid.*, l. 329. (Ll. 222–223, *ibid.*)

[4] זאת המנוחה. *Ibid.*, l. 336. (L. 227, *ibid.*)

[5] מנוחה.   [6] תענוג.

[7] *Fons Vitae*, III, 49 (p. 189, l. 24–p. 190, l. 7); *Liḳḳutim min Sefer Meḳor Ḥayyim*, III, 31. Cf. I. Heinemann, *Die Lehre von der Zweckbestimmung des Menschen im griechisch-römisch Altertum un im jüdischen Mittelalter*, p. 52, n. 5.

of the third kind of knowledge. The emphasis in that statement is upon the term "understanding," or, rather, in the form in which the term is used in that proposition, "we understand (*intelligimus*)." It is only when we have adequate ideas of individual things, as when we know their common properties or when we know them in their mutual relations, that we understand them, and it is only such an understanding that will lead to the highest kind of knowledge. To have only mutilated and confused ideas of individual things is of no help in the attainment of that highest kind of knowledge. And so when Spinoza says that the mind has a conatus (Prop. XXV) or a desire (Prop. XXVI) to know things by the third kind of knowledge, that conatus or desire "cannot arise from the first, but from the second kind of knowledge" (Prop. XXVIII).

Now it is the nature of the mind in its second kind of knowledge, or, as it is called by Spinoza, reason (*ratio*), to see things under the form of eternity.[1] Furthermore, the mind cannot know external bodies except through the knowledge of its own body.[2] Consequently, if the mind knows external things under the form of eternity, it must know them only through its knowledge of its own body under the form of eternity, for "everything which the mind understands under the form of eternity, it understands not because it conceives the present actual existence of the body, but because it conceives the essence of the body under the form of eternity" (Prop. XXIX). And so also, of course, must the mind know itself under the form of eternity. Knowing, then, itself and the body under the form of eternity, the mind "necessarily has a knowledge of God, and knows that it is in God and is conceived through Him" (Prop. XXX). This knowledge of

[1] Cf. above, Vol. I, pp. 160–161.
[2] Cf. above, p. 78.

God and of one's being in God and of one's being conceived through God is the subject-matter of the third kind of knowledge.[1] Consequently the third kind of knowledge, which depends upon the mind as its formal cause, implies that the mind itself is eternal (Prop. XXXI). But inasmuch as Spinoza has shown before (Prop. XXVI) that the third kind of knowledge is the object of the conscious effort and desire of the mind during its existence in the human body, he has thereby also shown that during our lifetime we are conscious of the eternity of our mind. This possibility of experiencing the pleasure of the union with God during our lifetime is also suggested in the passages quoted later from Abraham Ibn Ezra[2] and Maimonides.[3]

Spinoza now returns to his previous statement that from the third kind of knowledge there arises the highest possible satisfaction of the mind (Prop. XXXII), and elaborates it more fully. In the Corollary of this thirty-second proposition he introduces the phrase "the intellectual love of God" (*amor Dei intellectualis*). Probably no phrase in Spinoza's philosophy is so well known as this one, and no phrase of his lends itself to so many homiletical interpretations. But the meaning of the phrase as well as its form may be best explained by a reconstruction of the idea which it tries to convey.

Ever since the time of Aristotle it has been an accepted principle in philosophy that the acquisition of any kind of knowledge, from the lowest form of sensation to the highest form of intelligence, is associated with a feeling of pleasure. "There is a pleasure," says Aristotle, "in respect of all sensation, and similarly in respect of thought and contemplation."[4] As proof of our natural desire for knowledge Aristotle

---

[1] Cf. above, pp. 140 ff   [2] Cf. below, pp. 313–315. Cf. above, p. 300.
[3] Cf. below, p. 310, n. 1.   [4] *Nicomachean Ethics*, X, 4, 1174b, 20–21.

refers to the delight (ἀγάπησις, *dilectio*) we take in our senses.[1] Similarly Gersonides speaks of the joy and agreeableness that accompany the acquisition of knowledge,[2] and Crescas says succinctly that "comprehension is agreeable to those who comprehend."[3] But this pleasure which is associated with the experience of knowledge, it is generally agreed, varies in accordance with the object of knowledge. Here again Aristotle advances the view that "pleasures differ in kind," for "the activities of thought differ from those of the senses, and both differ among themselves, in kind; so, therefore, do the pleasures that complete them."[4] Similarly Crescas, among many others, repeats that "the nobler the comprehension of things is, the greater is the agreeableness and joy which accompany the comprehension."[5]

There is thus a pleasure of the senses and a pleasure of the intellect, and Aristotle speaks definitely of the contrast between bodily pleasures and pleasures of the soul,[6] the latter undoubtedly referring to all the faculties of the soul, including the intellectual. Thus Descartes, evidently on the basis of those Aristotelian distinctions, uses the expression "intellectual joy" (*gaudium intellectuale*).[7] Now, since love cannot be dissociated from pleasure, and it is defined by Spinoza either, after Descartes, as the "enjoyment of a thing and union therewith,"[8] or, against Descartes, as "pleasure with the accompanying idea of an external cause,"[9] one would naturally expect a classification of love similar to that

---

[1] *Metaphysics*, I, 1, 980a, 21–22.
[2] *Milḥamot Adonai*, I, 4 (p. 26).
[3] *Or Adonai*, I, iii, 5 (p. 26b, end).
[4] *Nicomachean Ethics*, X, 5, 1175a, 21–28.
[5] *Or Adonai*, I, iii, 5 (pp. 26–27).
[6] *Nicomachean Ethics*, III, 10, 1117b, 28–29.
[7] *Principia Philosophiae*, IV, 190.
[8] *Short Treatise*, II, 5, § 1. Cf. above, p. 279.
[9] *Ethics*, III, *Affectuum Definitiones*, 6. Cf. above, pp. 279–280.

of pleasure. In fact, Aristotle's classification of φιλία, friendship, which may also mean love, into that of utility, that of pleasure, and that of virtue,[1] reflects a classification similar to his own classification of pleasure quoted above, and thus his friendship of virtue refers both to moral and to intellectual virtue, with the implication that there is a friendship as well as a love which may be called intellectual. Leo Hebraeus, in a classification of love which seems to be an elaboration of Aristotle's classification of friendship, describes that which Aristotle would call friendship of virtue as love based upon both moral and intellectual virtue (*virtù morali e intellettuali*) and as proceeding from right reason (*retta ragione*).[2] Similarly Jehiel of Pisa, who was a younger contemporary of Leo Hebraeus, classifies love,[3] in direct imitation of Aristotle's classification of friendship, into love of pleasure,[4] love of utility,[5] and true love,[6] by the last of which he evidently means what Aristotle calls friendship of virtue, describing it, partly as Leo Hebraeus, in terms of intellectual virtue, to wit, a love "which is caused by and is associated with the principles of spiritual ideas of the mind" and "is dependent upon the eternal things which proceed from the transparency of the knowledge of the true intellectual concepts." [7] A model classification of love in which intellectual love is included is given by Thomas Aquinas. He distinguishes be-

---

[1] *Nicomachean Ethics*, VIII, 3. In Hillel of Verona's Hebrew version of this classification of friendship, the term φιλία is rendered by "love" (אהבה). Cf. Miscellany in the printed edition of *Tagmule ha-Nefesh*, p. 42b. Similarly in the Hebrew translation of the *Nicomachean Ethics*, the term used is "love." Cf. *Sefer ha-Middot le-Aristoteles*, VIII, 3. In the Latin translations of the *Nicomachean Ethics* with Averroes' Middle Commentary, the terms "love" (*dilectio*) and "friendship" (*amicitia*) are used indiscriminately. Cf. *Aristotelis Omnia Quae Extant Opera . . .* (Venetiis, apud Iuntas), Vol. III (1574), fols. 112 ff. Cf. above, p. 246, n. 6.

[2] *Dialoghi d'Amore*, II, pp. 66–67 (Bari, 1929).

[3] האהבה. [4] אהבת הערב.

[5] אהבת המועיל. [6] האהבה האמתית.

[7] *Minḥat Ḳena'ot*, p. 1. Cf. N. Sokolow, *Baruch Spinoza u-Zemano*, p. 49, n. 28.

tween (*a*) natural love (*amor naturalis*) which exists even in inanimate objects, (*b*) sensitive or animal love (*amor sensitivus, animalis*), and (*c*) intellectual, rational, or spiritual love (*amor intellectivus, intellectualis, rationalis, spiritualis*).[1] It is this classification of Thomas Aquinas which seems to be the origin of Leo Hebraeus' threefold classification of love into natural, sensitive, and rational and voluntary (*naturale, sensitivo, et rationale volontario*).[2] The last kind of love is also called by him mental love (*l'amore mentale*),[3] or, as in Thomas Aquinas, intellectual love (*l'amore intellettivo, intellettuale*).[4] Thus the expression "intellectual love" has been generally used as a description of that kind of love which could not properly be described as sensitive or animal love. Inasmuch as the love for God which has been recommended in every religious book since the Bible as the highest goal in the religious life of man could not be taken in the sense of sensitive or animal love, it naturally had to be understood in the sense of intellectual love.

We return now to Spinoza. The highest pleasure, according to him, consists in that acquiescence of the mind which he has shown previously in Proposition XXVII to arise in the third kind of knowledge. Drawing therefore upon Aristotle's statement that we take delight (ἀγάπησις, *dilectio*) in every form of knowledge, Spinoza says here with special reference to the third kind of knowledge that "we delight (*delectamur*) in whatever we understand by the third kind of

[1] *Summa Theologica*, Prima Secundae, Quaest. 26, Art. 1; Quaest. 27, Art. 2; Secunda Secundae, Quaest. 26, Art. 3. For other references, see L. Schütz, *Thomas-Lexikon* (1895), under "Amor" a) 4.

A somewhat similar classification of love is to be found in Augustine, *De Civitate Dei*, XI, 27-28.

[2] *Dialoghi d'Amore*, II, p. 67 (Bari, 1929).

[3] *Ibid.*, I, p. 45 (Bari, 1929).

[4] *Ibid.*, III, p. 373 and p. 378 (Bari, 1929). Cf. B. Zimmels, *Leo Hebräus*, p. 76, note.

knowledge" (Prop. XXXII). But this delight "is accompanied with the idea of God as its cause" (*ibid.*). It may therefore be called love, for by definition "love is pleasure with the accompanying idea of an external cause."[1] As the object of the love is God, it is called the love of God. Furthermore, as the love of God is not an animal love or a sensitive love, it is to be called, according to the conventional phraseology of the time, the intellectual love of God (*amor Dei intellectualis*) (*ibid.*, Corol.). This is the origin and history and meaning of this phrase. It is useless to speculate from whom Spinoza took it; it was as common a property of philosophy as the term "substance." He could have taken it from various sources, and had he had no sources to guide him he could have coined it himself to describe what was generally meant by the love of God.

That by the expression "intellectual love of God" Spinoza means nothing but a love which cannot be called animal love or sensitive love may be further inferred from his kindred expression "intellectual knowledge of God" (*intellectualis Dei cognitio*)[2] which is hardly ever referred to. By the "intellectual knowledge of God" he means, as he himself explains, a knowledge which is not based upon imagination, still less upon the external senses. It is the accurate[3] and true[4] knowledge attained only by philosophers of the absolute essence of God[5] or of any attribute of God which expresses His absolute essence,[6] in contrast to the knowledge of God's divine justice and charity,[7] that is, the knowledge of His relation to created things,[8] or in contrast to the knowl-

---

[1] *Ethics*, III, *Affectuum Definitiones*, 6.

[2] *Tractatus Theologico-Politicus*, Ch. 13 (*Opera*, III, p. 168, l. 28, and p. 171, l. 25).

[3] *Ibid.* (p. 168, l. 28).

[4] *Ibid.* (p. 172, l. 25).

[5] *Ibid.* (p. 169, l. 0).

[6] *Ibid.* (p. 169, ll. 22-23).

[7] *Ibid.* (p. 168, l. 32).

[8] *Ibid.*, (p. 169, l. 9).

edge of God's "deeds and promises, that is, the knowledge of His power, as manifested in visible things,"[1] which was attained by the prophets, who were "gifted with extraordinary powers of imagination, but not of understanding (*intelligendi*)."[2]

The intellectual love of God, Spinoza proceeds to say, is eternal (Prop. XXXIII). It is eternal in two of the senses which the term "eternity," as we have shown before, had in the history of philosophy.[3] In the first place, it "has no beginning" (*ibid.*, Schol.), and, for that matter, no end, for it is not born with the body, nor does it end with the body. In the second place, during its beginningless and endless existence it is in a uniform state of being within which there is no change or motion or transition from the less perfect to the more perfect. The delight which is inseparably associated with the intellectual love of God and the third kind of knowledge, out of which both the delight and the love arise,[4] are likewise in the same permanent state of being without undergoing any change or transition, for "the mind has eternally possessed these same perfections which we imagined as now accruing to it" (*ibid.*, Schol.).

But here Spinoza becomes conscious of a difficulty. Pleasure has always been understood, as he himself has defined it, to consist in the transition to a greater perfection.[5] So also Crescas, re-echoing a common opinion, maintains that "the delight we take in comprehension is to be experienced only in the act of causing it to pass from potentiality to actuality," and he proves it by the fact that "we experience no pleasure in the possession of the primary notions."[6] How then can

[1] *Ibid.* (p. 169, ll. 23–24).   [2] *Ibid.* (p. 167, l. 7).
[3] Cf. above, Vol. I, pp. 358 ff.
[4] *Ethics*, V, Prop. 32, and Demonst. and Corol.
[5] *Ibid.*, III, Prop. 11, Schol.
[6] *Or Adonai*, I, iii, 5 (p. 27a).

any pleasure be associated with the intellectual love of God, which love is immutable and arises in the third kind of knowledge which is perfection itself and in which there is not any transition?

The answer given by Crescas and others in connection with a similar question is that there is a certain kind of pleasure which is *sui generis* and consists in the permanency of its state of being, in the constancy of its perfection, and in the freedom from any change and transition. Of this nature, for instance, says Crescas, is the pleasure of God, if pleasure is attributed to Him.[1] Thus also those who conceive immortality to accrue to the acquired intellect by reason of its being in possession of knowledge explain eternal bliss to consist in the pleasure experienced by the immortal souls in their continuous possession of perfect knowledge.[2] This kind of pleasure is also that which Aristotle attributes to God, a pleasure which consists in being forever in a state of actuality and in the actual possession of the object of thought.[3] The same kind of answer is also given here by Spinoza. He has already explained that pleasure which is related to the mind in so far as we act does not consist in a transition to a greater perfection but rather in the mind's contemplation of itself and of its own power of acting.[4] Of the same nature, he now says, is the pleasure associated with the intellectual love of God. It is *sui generis;* and he calls it by the traditional name of Blessedness (*beatitudo*). Unlike ordinary pleasure, there is no transition to a greater perfection in it, for "if pleasure consists in a transition to a greater perfection, blessedness must indeed consist in this, that the mind is endowed with perfection itself" (*ibid.*, Schol.).

---

[1] *Ibid.*   [2] *Ibid.*, II, vi, 1 (p. 52b).
[3] *Metaphysics*, XII, 7, 1072b, 14 ff.
[4] *Ethics*, III, Prop. 58.

The pre-existence of the mind and its immortality make the short tract of time during which it is encased in a body only an episode in its history. During that episode, indeed, "the mind is subject to emotions which are related to passions" (Prop. XXXIV), but these passive emotions, among which there are all kinds of bodily and sensitive loves, are not of the nature of the mind itself; they appear with the body and disappear with it. Only one kind of love belongs to the mind itself and is co-eternal with the mind, and that is the love which is called intellectual (*ibid.*, Corol.). Sometime even during the lifetime of our body we experience that kind of intellectual love, as when, for instance, by philosophic contemplation we understand things by the third kind of knowledge, and then, rising above all the passive emotions of the body, we attain "the highest possible peace of mind."[1] This is one way in which Spinoza proves that we are conscious of the eternity of our mind. Another way in which he proves it is from the "common opinion of men," whose beliefs in immortality, crude as they are, indicate that "they are conscious of the eternity of their mind," though in their usual manner they confuse the true blessedness of the eternal mind with the temporary emotions arising from imagination and memory which are experienced by us during the lifetime of our body. As a result of this confusion, the common mass of people conceive of immortality as merely a continuation of our present experience. "If we look at the common opinion of men, we shall see that they are indeed conscious of the eternity of their minds, but they confound it with duration, and attribute it to imagination or memory, which they believe remain after death."[2] This view, of course, is condemned by Spinoza as a specimen of the confused thinking

---

[1] Cf. *Ethics*, V, Prop. 27.
[2] *Ibid.*, V, Prop. 34, Schol.

which characterizes the common opinion of men. So did also Maimonides enumerate and condemn the various crude beliefs of the common people as to the nature of the life of the soul in the hereafter, which he explains as being due to the fact that during our lifetime we cannot comprehend the nature of spiritual pleasures, at least not "immediately, but only after a long process of reasoning."[1] Maimonides' conclusion, like that of Spinoza's here, is that the bliss and happiness of the immortal souls consist in the delight they take in the knowledge of the essence of God, and in proof of this he quotes rabbinic passages.

Such a conception of immortality, Spinoza is now anxious to show, is nothing supernatural. It is the logical consequence of his own natural philosophy. Given a God who through His attribute of thought is self-conscious of His infinite perfection and of the fact that He is the cause of himself, such a God must love himself with an infinite intellectual love (Prop. XXXV). Then, given again a mind which is only a part of God's attribute of thought, such a mind will love God, and its love will be "part of the infinite love with which God loves himself" (Prop. XXXVI). In this sense, Spinoza now tries to reverse or at least to qualify his previous position and to maintain that in a certain sense God can be said to love men. While "properly speaking," as he has said before, "God loves no one,"[2] that is to say, if you mean by love a passive affection, still, he says now, "in so far as He loves himself, He loves men" (*ibid.*, Corol.). Indeed, some mediaevals have said the same thing, for Crescas, in an attempt to show that God's love for men is the greatest love possible, maintains that the object of that love is God's own esssence and that He loves men through His

[1] Introduction to *Perek Ḥelek* (ed. J. Holzer), p. 19
[2] *Ethics*, V, Prop. 17, Corol.

love of His own essence.[1] But still, Spinoza would argue, the love which the mediaevals attribute to God, though explained by them as part of God's own love for himself, is after all a love which is affected by man's attitude towards God, and it gives rise to revelation and retribution.

Thus Spinoza has arrived at the conclusion that the state of immortality, by whatever name it is called, salvation (*salus*, σωτηρία), blessedness (*beatitudo*, μακαρισμός), liberty (*libertas*, ἐλευθερία),[2] or regeneration (*Wedergeboorte*, παλιν-γενεσία),[3] consists in the reciprocal love of God and man. This, Spinoza was quite aware, was nothing new; theologians before him had said it. But, as we have pointed out before, it was not Spinoza's intention to lead men to a new way of salvation. To show that he was merely reaffirming an old traditional belief, Spinoza adds that "this love or blessedness is called Glory in the sacred writings, and not without reason." [4]

Now, to what particular passage in the Bible does Spinoza have reference here when he says that "glory" means this blessedness or love or union or peace of mind?

The verse "the whole earth is full of His glory" (Isaiah 6, 3) is generally taken to be the reference.[5] But there is

[1] *Or Adonai*, II, vi, 1 (p. 54b).   [2] *Ethics*, V, Prop. 36, Schol.

[3] *Short Treatise*, II, 22, § 7. These four terms, three in Latin and one in Dutch, are traceable to the New Testament, from which I have taken the Greek equivalents reproduced in the text. The Latin terms agree with those used in the Vulgate. Cf. Luke 19, 9; Romans 4, 6; James 1, 25; Matthew 19, 28. It is interesting to note that Maimonides, too, gives a list of terms by which the state of immortality is designated in The Old Testament: "This future blessedness is referred to by many names, as, for instance, 'the mountain of the Lord,' 'His holy place,' 'the way of holiness,' 'the courts of the Lord,' 'the graciousness of the Lord,' 'the tabernacle of the Lord,' 'the temple of the Lord,' 'the house of the Lord,' and 'the gate of the Lord.' Among the rabbis this blessedness which is in store for the righteous is referred to metaphorically as a 'feast'; but more frequently they refer to it as 'the world to come'" (*Mishneh Torah*, *Teshubah*, VIII, 4).

[4] *Ethics*, V, Prop. 36, Schol.

[5] Baensch's note *ad loc.* in his German translation of the *Ethics*; Gebhardt, "Spinoza und der Platonism," in *Chronicon Spinozanum*, I (1921), p. 220.

nothing in the context of that verse to make it more applicable to Spinoza's particular purpose here than any of the other
one hundred and ninety-odd passages in the Old Testament
in which the word *kabod*[1] occurs, or the one hundred and
fifty-odd passages in the New Testament in which the word
δόξα occurs. Furthermore, an alleged source of Spinoza's
statement here has been identified in Leo Hebraeus' *Dialoghi
d'Amore*, I, where the author is supposed to describe the
"atto coppulativo de l'intima cognizione divina" by the
Biblical expression "eterna gloria."[2] This is wrong. Leo
Hebraeus does not describe the union with God by any such
Biblical expression as "eterna gloria." Quite the contrary,
what Leo Hebraeus says is that Scripture, speaking of the
final end, "says: 'But cleave unto the Lord your God'
[Joshua 23, 8], and in another place, promising the final
happiness, it only says: 'and unto Him shall ye cleave'
[Deut. 13, 5], without promising any other thing, such as
life, eternal glory, highest pleasure, infinite joy and light,
and other similar things."[3]

Now, in order to identify the exact Biblical passage which
Spinoza had in mind, it is not sufficient to pick out in the
Bible the first Hebrew word for "glory" that happens to
strike our eye. We must look for a passage in which glory
is associated with love and joy and eternal bliss, and if there
is no such passage, we must find a passage which might have
been taken by Spinoza to suggest such an association. The
most likely passage that might have carried to Spinoza such
a suggestion is to be found in Psalms 16, 8–11:

[1] כבוד.   [2] Gebhardt, *loc. cit.*

[3] *Dialoghi d'Amore*, I, p. 46 (Bari, 1929): "E per questo la sacra scrittura
. . . dice, per ultimo fine: *Pertanto con esso Dio vi coppulate;* e in un' altra parte,
promettendo l'ultima felicitá, solamente dice: *Et con esso Dio vi coppularete;* senza
promettere nlcouna altra cooa, oomo vita, otorna gloria, oomma dilottamone, alle-
grezza e luce infinita, e altre simili."

"8. I have set the Lord always before me;
    Surely He is at my right hand, I shall not be moved.
"9. Therefore my heart is glad, and my *glory* rejoiceth;
    My flesh also dwelleth in safety;
"10. For Thou wilt not abandon my soul to the netherworld;
    Neither wilt Thou suffer Thy godly one to see the pit.
"11. Thou makest me know the path of life;
    In Thy presence is fulness of joy,
    In Thy right hand bliss for evermore." [1]

The context of this passage is quite appropriate for our purpose. It speaks of the fulness of joy and the eternal bliss in the presence of God, and may therefore be taken to refer to immortality. Furthermore, in connection with these it mentions the term "glory."

Still we feel that this is not quite sufficient for our purpose. What we need is a passage where the term "glory" itself means, or could have been taken by Spinoza to mean, love or blessedness, which, as he says, "may be properly called acquiescence of spirit." Let us then consult the Hebrew commentators to see if they have interpreted these verses for Spinoza so as to enable him to find in the term "glory" love and blessedness and acquiescence of spirit. It happens that Abraham Ibn Ezra in his commentary gives us the answer to this question. Says he in interpretation of these verses:

"8. *I have set the Lord always before me.* The counsel and instruction [referred to previously in verse 7] have caused him to set the Lord before him day and night, with the result that his rational soul has become united with its Creator even before its separation from the body, and since *I have set the Lord . . . before me . . . at my right hand, I shall not be*

[1] Jewish Publication Society version.

moved — that is to say, he will not go astray from the path of righteousness.

"9. *Therefore my heart is glad. Heart* means the common sense (*sensus communis*).[1]

"*My glory rejoiceth. Glory* means the rational soul.[2]

"*My flesh also. Flesh* means the body.

"The meaning of the entire verse is as follows: Inasmuch as he is united with the Supernal Power, his soul[3] rejoiceth. Similarly his union with the Supernal Power will guard him against sicknesses in the change of seasons. Consequently his body also dwelleth in safety in the present world.

"10. *For.* He now states the reason for his rational soul's [glory's] rejoicing: it is because it will not perish and come to nought.

"11. *Thou makest me know, etc.* The meaning of the entire verse is as follows: When the body dies, then *Thou makest me know the path of life*, that is to say, the path whereby I ascend to heaven to be there with the celestial angels.

"*Thou makest me know.* That is to say, it is then that Thou dost wean away the soul from the affairs of the world, and it sees the truth eye to eye.

---

[1] The Hebrew term used here is שכל הדעת, literally, *knowing intelligence*. But I take it to have been used here by Ibn Ezra in the technical sense of *sensus communis*, and this is my reason. In his commentary on Ecclesiastes 7, 3, after enumerating the three souls in man, Ibn Ezra says: "And God has implanted in man an intelligence (שכל), called heart (לב), which is to bring to fulfilment the purpose of each soul in its time." From his description of *intelligence* in this passage it is clear that he means by it the *sensus communis*. The reason why Ibn Ezra calls the *sensus communis* "heart" may be explained by the fact that according to Aristotle the heart is the seat of the *sensus communis* (cf. *De Juventute*, 3, 469a, 11–12).

[2] נשמה. By this Hebrew term Ibn Ezra designates the rational soul in his commentary on Ecclesiastes 7, 3, and elsewhere. Cf. also *Emunot we-De'ot*, VI, 3; *Hegyon ha-Nefesh*, II, p. 11a; *Emunah Ramah*, I, 6 (p. 33). Maimonides, however, uses this term to include the lower faculties of the soul (cf. above, p. 291, n. 1).

[3] נפש, which is used here as a general term for soul.

"*In Thy presence is fulness of joy.* That is to say, he will partake in the enjoyment of the splendor of the divine Shekinah.

"*In Thy right hand bliss.* That is to say, the soul will enjoy itself in God.

"*In Thy right hand bliss.* That is to say, as if the Lord will be distributing with His right hand blissful gifts to those who love Him.

"*For evermore.* That is to say, His gifts will never stop.

"Thus the reward of the righteous is fully described in this Psalm."

Ibn Ezra's interpretation makes it quite clear that the expression "my glory rejoiceth" means that the soul rejoices in its eternal union with God which takes place during the lifetime of the body and continues forever after the death of the body. Similar interpretations of the term "glory" occur also in other Hebrew works. Thus in Ibn Yaḥya's commentary on the Psalms the terms "my heart," "my glory," and "my flesh" in this verse are taken to refer respectively to the rational, sensitive, and vegetative souls. According to Abraham Shalom these three terms refer respectively to the appetitive, the rational, and the sensitive faculties of the soul.[1]

Another Scriptural verse, again according to Ibn Ezra's commentary, similarly uses the term "glory" in the sense of immortality and blessedness. The verse is Psalms 73, 24. Ibn Ezra suggests two possible interpretations of the verse, the second of which is followed by the English Authorized Version, which, incidentally, explains its departure from the rendering of the Vulgate. It reads as follows: "Thou shalt guide me with Thy counsel, and afterward receive me to glory." In commenting upon this verse, Ibn Ezra says:

[1] *Neweh Shalom*, VIII, 5 (p. 132a).

"The word 'receive' (literally: 'take'), when it does not refer to death by plague,[1] refers to the union of the soul of the righteous with the supernal beings who are incorporeal and immortal. Thus the verse concerning Enoch, which reads: 'And Enoch walked with God, and he was not; for God took him' (Genesis 5, 24), means that he had accustomed himself to walk with the angels, with the result that God took him (i.e., transformed him into an angel)." The verse under consideration is thus interpreted by him as follows: "And afterward Thou shalt take me and I shall be 'glory' like one of the angels."

One more question, however, still remains in connection with this statement of Spinoza. After having said that "this love or blessedness is called Glory in the sacred writings," he continues to say that "whether this love be referred to God or to the mind, it may properly be called acquiescence of spirit, which (Defs. XXV and XXX of the Emotions) is, in truth, not distinguished from glory." What he wants to say is quite clear. He wants to say that whether we take "love" in the sense of God's love for men or whether we take it in the sense of men's love for God, that love, which is an acquiescence of spirit, is not distinguished from "glory," by which name it is called in the sacred writings. But why should Spinoza want to say this? It would seem that unless there was some doubt as to which of these two kinds of love the term "glory" in the Biblical passage in question applied to, there was no need for this statement of his.

But this, too, it seems to me, can be explained by a discussion which occurs in the philosophic and Cabalistic Hebrew literature as to the meaning of the term "glory," es-

[1] Literally: "taking away without a plague." לקיחה בלא דבר. Ibn Ezra alludes here to Ezekiel 24, 16: "I take away from thee the desire of thine eyes with a stroke." Cf. Ibn Ezra on Genesis 5, 24.

pecially in the expression "the glory of the Lord" (Exodus 24, 16). According to some, "glory" refers to the essence of God, and it is thus used as a surrogate to God. According to others, it refers to something emanated from God's essence. I have elsewhere traced the history of this discussion from Philo to Crescas.[1] With the possibility of these two meanings of the term "glory" before him, Spinoza could readily see that the expression "my glory rejoiceth" in Psalms 16, 9, which Ibn Ezra and others interpreted as "my soul rejoiceth," might also mean "my God rejoiceth." Drawing then upon these two possible explanations of "glory," Spinoza says here that "whether this love be referred to God or to the mind, it may properly be called acquiescence of spirit, which (Defs. XXV and XXX of the Emotions) is, in truth, not distinguished from glory," for the Biblical expression "my glory rejoiceth" may mean either "my God rejoiceth" or "my mind rejoiceth."

On the whole, then, Spinoza's conception of immortality is that which was commonly held by mediaeval philosophers. It is a union with God which in the *Ethics* he calls the love of God. But still the mediaeval philosophers, who insist upon the traditional beliefs of reward and punishment and who consequently look upon this union as a sort of reward, consider it also possible for the soul to be punished by its not becoming united with God, so that in course of time it would be utterly destroyed and come to nought. Thus Crescas, representing this view, says: "The soul of the transgressor, the disobedient, after its departure from the body, suffers keen anguish in that it remains in darkness contrary to its nature. Traditional utterances have compared it to the agony of being burned and have named it hell-fire." To the question how such punishment can be explained by

---

[1] Cf. my *Crescas' Critique of Aristotle*, pp. 459–462.

reason, Crescas makes the following answer: "Inasmuch as the soul is a spiritual substance, it is quite evident that it attains the highest possible joy and pleasure when it becomes united with something spiritual for which by its very nature it has had a longing. . . . But, on the other hand, when it does not attain that for which by its very nature it has had a longing, it suffers thereby such keen anguish that in course of time there may result to it therefrom utter destruction." [1] It is against this view that Spinoza comes out now. He aligns himself with those who since Plato have held that the soul, or at least part of it, is by its very nature eternal and hence indestructible. "This intellectual love necessarily follows from the nature of the mind, in so far as it is considered, through the nature of God, as an eternal truth" (Prop. XXXVII, Demonst.), and consequently, "there is nothing in nature which is contrary to this intellectual love, or which can destroy it" (Prop. XXXVII).

Still, though all souls are immortal and all of them are united with God, there exist certain differences between the individual souls which remain after death. They do not all merge in one universal soul. Immortality is in a certain sense personal and individual. In the Middle Ages, among those who conceived immortality as a union with God, the individual differences of the immortal souls were explained as resulting from the differences in the nature and degree of the intellectual attainments of the individual persons during their lifetime. Says Gersonides: "The cause of this difference is to be found in the difference between men in the acquisition of conceptions both qualitatively and quantitatively. When a person has acquired many conceptions of a certain science, the unity which these conceptions form in his acquired intellect after death will differ from the unity

[1] *Or Adonai*, III, iii, 1 (p. 73a).

formed in the acquired intellect of another person who has acquired fewer conceptions of the same science. Similarly, in the case of him who has acquired conceptions of a certain science which differs from the science of which another person has acquired conceptions, his acquired intellect will thereby be different from the acquired intellect of the other person. In this way there is a vast variety of differences between the various degrees of those who have attained blessedness." [1] In Crescas, this view is summed up in the following words: "Some of them believe that this blessedness will be greater the greater the numbers of things conceived by the mind, be they corporeal or incorporeal things . . . others believe that only that which the human intellect conceives in a true manner of the existence of God and His angels will remain immortal." [2] Re-echoing these statements, Spinoza says that "the essence of the mind consists of knowledge . . .; therefore, the more things the mind knows by the second and third kinds of knowledge, the greater is that part of it which remains" (Prop. XXXVIII, Demonst.).

These individual differences which exist between the disembodied souls after death exist between them also while they are in bodies during the lifetime of men. As Spinoza has already said before, we get a foretaste of the bliss of immortality even during our lifetime in the peace of mind which comes to us from the third kind of knowledge, and in part also from the second kind, which leads to the third. This peace of mind renders us impassive to evil emotions and frees us from the fear of death. This foretaste of immortality, too, differs in different individuals in accordance with their intellectual attainments, for "the more objects the mind understands by the second and third kinds of knowl-

[1] *Milḥamot Adonai*, I, 13 (p. 90).
[2] *Or Adonai*, II, vi, 1 (p. 52b).

edge, the less it suffers from those emotions which are evil, and the less it fears death" (Prop. XXXVIII)

So far Spinoza has been speaking of knowledge as the only condition of immortality. He now revives the old question, common to the speculative theology of all religions, as to how much action counts among the factors which make for immortality. In Jewish philosophy the problem assumes the form of an investigation as to the relative importance of right opinions about the nature of God and the world and right conduct in matters pertaining to the observance of the Law. Maimonides deals with the question after the manner of Aristotle's treatment of the relation between moral and intellectual virtues, and like Aristotle he makes the moral virtues subordinate to the intellectual. "The general object of the Law," he says, "is twofold: the well-being of the soul and the well-being of the body. Of these two objects, the one, the well-being of the soul . . . comes absolutely first in rank. . . . For it has already been found that man has a double perfection: the first perfection is that of the body, and the second perfection is that of the soul. The first consists in his being healthy and in the best possible bodily condition. . . . The second perfection of man consists in his becoming an actually intelligent being; i.e., he knows about things in existence all that a person most perfectly developed is capable of knowing. It is evident that this second perfection does not include any actions and moral virtues, but only intellectual conceptions, which are arrived at by speculation and are the result of reasoning. It is also evident that the second and superior kind of perfection can only be attained when the first perfection has been acquired. . . . But when a person is in possession of the first perfection, then he may possibly acquire the second perfection, which is undoubtedly of a superior kind, and is alone the source of

eternal life." [1] Crescas, rightly or wrongly, finds this view
"destructive of the principles of both Scripture and tradition," for "it is one of the principles of Scripture and tradition," he says, "that it is by the performance of the commands of the Law that man attains life everlasting." [2] Leo
Hebraeus re-echoes the opinion of Aristotle and Maimonides
when he says that "moral virtue is the necessary road to happiness, but the appropriate subject of it is wisdom, which,
however, cannot be attained without moral virtue." [3]

Spinoza strips the problem of its theological aspect and
treats it simply as a question of whether the perfection of
the body contributes anything to the perfection and hence the
eternity of the mind. His answer, like that which would have
been given by Aristotle or Maimonides, is in the affirmative.
"He who possesses a body fit for many things possesses a
mind of which the greater part is eternal" (Prop. XXXIX).
Not only does such a body contribute to the eternity of our
mind that remains after death, but it also helps our mind to
experience during our lifetime that peace and satisfaction
which frees us from the fear of death and renders us unaf-
fected by those emotions which are related to memory or
imagination (ibid., Schol.). This potential fitness of the body
for many things becomes an actual perfection by acts that
the body performs, for, as he could have quoted from what
Aristotle says of virtues, "we are adapted by nature to receive them, and are made perfect by habit." [4] But there is a
reciprocal relation, adds Spinoza, between perfection and
the activity which forms habit. "The more perfection a thing

---

[1] *Moreh Nebukim*, III, 27.

[2] *Or Adonai*, II, vi, 1 (p. 52b).

[3] *Dialoghi d'Amore*, I, p. 36 (Bari, 1929): "Le virtú morali son vie necessarie
per la felicitá; ma il proprio suggetto di quelle è la sapienzia, la quale non saria
possibile averla senza le virtú morali."

[4] *Nicomachean Ethics*, II, 1, 1103a, 25–26.

possesses, the more it acts and the less it suffers, and conversely the more it acts the more perfect it is" (Prop. XL). From this it follows that that part of our mind through which alone we are said to act is the most perfect part in us (*ibid.*, Corol.), and that part is the intellect as distinguished from the imagination and the other functions of the mind. Consequently, while action may lead to the perfection of the intellect, it is in the activity of the intellect, as said Aristotle and Maimonides, that the highest happiness is to be found.[1]

We have thus seen that Spinoza's conception of the immortality of the soul, in its main outline, does not go beyond that of any rationalist theology, and like that of any rationalist theology it may be regarded with respect to other conceptions of the hereafter as either an affirmation of immortality or a denial of it. In so far as it denies that the soul continues to exist after death in its entirety and as an individual entity, it is a denial of immortality; in so far, however, as it denies the utter destructibility of the soul, it is an affirmation of immortality. Now whenever we meet with such a bilarious doctrine in the work of any author, we must find out what the opposite doctrine was against which the author in question aimed his own doctrine in order to be able to determine which of its two possible aspects he meant to emphasize. In the case of Maimonides, for instance, we know definitely against what kind of opposition his own doctrine of immortality was aimed. It was aimed against all the crude forms of commonly held popular beliefs about the hereafter which he enumerates, describes, and criticizes.[2] So emphatic was he in his rejection of all such popular beliefs that he was accused of denying the traditional doctrine of resurrection, against which accusation he felt called upon

[1] Cf. *ibid.*, X, 7.
[2] Cf. Introduction to *Pereḳ Ḥeleḳ*. Cf. above, p. 310.

to defend himself.[1] But in the case of Spinoza it is not clear what particular view of the hereafter he meant to counteract by his own theory of immortality. There can be no denying the fact that in some respect he aimed it against popular conceptions of eschatology.[2] But this, I believe, was only incidental to the main object of his theory of immortality. Its main object was to affirm the immortality of the soul against those of his own time who denied it. The principal target of the implied criticism of his statements, as I shall try to show, was Uriel Acosta, whose arguments against immortality have come down to us in the *Tratado da Immortalidade da Alma* (Amsterdam, 1623) of his opponent Samuel da Silva.[3] We shall thus find Spinoza in the unblemished company of Samuel da Silva and Manasseh ben Israel [4] battling on the side of tradition in defence of immortality against the heretical onslaughts of Uriel Acosta.

In his arguments against immortality Acosta identifies the human soul with the vital spirit situated in the blood, and maintains that the only difference between the human soul and the animal soul is that the former is endowed with reason.[5] This soul, he further maintains, is inseparable from the body,[6] and it dies with the body, for "it cannot be proven from the Law that the human soul is immortal." [7]

Spinoza's recorded utterances on the subject of the immortality of the soul will be found upon examination to have

---

[1] Cf. *Ma'amar Teḥiyyat ha-Metim*, in *Ḳobeẓ Teshubot ha-Rambam we-Iggerotaw* (Leipzig, 1859).   [2] Cf. above, p. 309.

[3] Reprinted with German translation in Carl Gebhardt, *Die Schriften des Uriel da Costa* (1922), pp. 35–101. References to Acosta given below are to this work.

[4] *De Resurrectione Mortuorum* (Amsterdam, 1636). Sections of this work which contain answers to Acosta are reproduced with German translation in Carl Gebhardt, *op. cit.*, pp. 188–195. But also his Hebrew work *Nishmat Ḥayyim* (Amsterdam, 1651), which is a defence of immortality, contains in its Introduction an allusion to Acosta.   [5] Pp. 35 and 65.

[6] P. 36, ll. 19 ff.; p. 66, ll. 26 ff.   [7] P. 37, ll. 10–11; p. 67, ll. 22–23.

literary relationship to those of Acosta. In his youth he shocked the Jewish community in Amsterdam by declaring: "With regard to the soul, wherever Scripture speaks of it the word soul is used simply to express life, or anything that is living. It would be useless to search for any passage in support of its immortality."[1] This, as can be readily recognized, is nothing but an echo of what Acosta has said. He similarly re-echoes Acosta when he declares in the *Ethics* that the soul is inseparable from the body, or, as he expresses himself in positive terms, "the human mind is united to the body."[2] But then he seems to turn against Acosta. Whereas Acosta denies the immortality of the soul in any sense whatsoever, maintaining that man "is not the image of God in immortality, for this is a property of God and not of man,"[3] Spinoza argues that "the human mind cannot be absolutely destroyed with the body, but something of it remains which is eternal,"[4] and, furthermore, that that something which remains is eternal because, again in opposition to Acosta, "the human mind is a part of the infinite intellect of God,"[5] or that it "follows from the divine nature."[6] The direct opposition to Acosta is still further evident in the following statements: Acosta declares that the soul has no immortality whatsoever, even in the sense of another kind of life which is "blessed (*bem aventurada*), eternal, and reposeful (*descansada*),"[7] and, furthermore, that "it cannot be proven from the Law . . . that another life, pain, or glory (*gloria*) is reserved for it."[8] Spinoza, in opposition to this, identifies immortality with "salvation, or blessed-

---

[1] Lucas, *La Vie de feu Monsieur de Spinoza* in A. Wolf, *The Oldest Biography of Spinoza*, pp. 46 and 98.

[2] *Ethics*, II, Prop. 13, Schol. Cf. above, p. 55.

[3] P. 44, ll. 14–15; p. 76, ll. 12–14.   [4] *Ethics*, V, Prop. 23.

[5] *Ibid.*, II, Prop. 11, Corol.; V, Prop. 40, Schol.   [6] *Ibid.*, V, Prop. 36, Schol.

[7] P. 40, ll. 32–33; p. 72, ll. 6–9.   [8] P. 37, ll. 10–12; p. 67, ll. 22–24.

ness (*beatitudo*), or liberty," which "may properly be called repose (*acquiescentia*) of spirit"[1] and may be regarded as consisting "in a constant and eternal love towards God, or in God's love towards men," which "love or blessedness is called glory (*gloria*) in the sacred writings."[2] That Spinoza's statements are directed against Acosta is quite evident from his enumeration of those conditions of the eternal life which Acosta explicitly denies, namely, that it is "blessed" and "reposeful" and is called "glory," and, furthermore, that "glory" as a description of eternal life is to be found in the "sacred writings" or, as Acosta would say, in the "Law."[3]

IV. THE RELIGION OF REASON

Historically the problems of the love of God, of immortality, and of revelation are interwoven. They are especially so in Crescas. The love of God is that which leads to immortality, and it is through His love for men that God has caused His Law to be revealed to them, the purpose of which Law is to guide men in the attainment of the love for God. The three problems are dealt with by him in the same group of chapters.[4] We have seen how in this part of the *Ethics* Spinoza likewise proceeds from the discussion of the love of God to that of immortality. In the *Short Treatise* (II, 24) he similarly combines the love of man for God with immortality, and then, as if he meant directly to contradict Crescas,

[1] Spinoza's indiscriminate use of *mens* (*Ethics*, V, Prop. 27) and *animus* (here) with *acquiescentia* reflects Acosta's use of *alma* and *espirito* with *descansada*.

[2] *Ethics*, V, Prop. 36, Schol.

[3] Acosta's use of the term "Law" in his statement, "It cannot be proven from the Law that the human soul is immortal," refers to the rabbinic contention that there is evidence for resurrection in the "Law (*Torah*)," as, for instance, in such expressions as "He who says that the resurrection of the dead is not intimated in the Law" (*Mishnah, Sanhedrin*, X, 1) and "Whence is it proven that the resurrection of the dead is intimated in the Law?" (*Sanhedrin* 90b.)

[4] *Or Adonai*, II, vi, 1–5.

he concludes from his own denial of God's love for man "that God gives no laws to men so as to reward them when they fulfil them and to punish them when they transgress them." [1] But instead of divine laws which are revealed through prophets he discusses there his own conception of divine laws which are stamped by God on nature. It is in accordance with these literary models of Crescas and with his own treatment of the subject in the *Short Treatise* that at the conclusion of his discussion of love and immortality he proceeds to explain in the last two propositions of the *Ethics* his own conception of divine law as contrasted with that of revealed religion.

Now, revealed religion is always of two types, that of the multitude and that of philosophers. Spinoza sketches before us in the Scholium to Proposition XLI, rather grotesquely, the salient features of what he describes as the general creed of the multitude (*communis vulgi persuasio*). According to this general creed of the multitude, by which he especially means the creed of the average Jew, the natural impulse of man is to do evil or to follow the inclination of his heart, for, as he could have quoted Scripture, "every imagination of the thoughts of his heart is only evil continually" (Genesis 6, 5), which is interpreted by the rabbis as referring to the evil impulse (*yezer ha-ra'*) in man. [2] Spinoza infers from this that "most persons seem to believe that they are free in so far as it is allowed to them to obey their lusts." The purpose of the revealed Law was therefore to curb these natural inclinations of man, and consequently men think "that they give up a portion of their rights, in so far as they are bound to live according to the commands of divine Law." The Law is therefore called by them a "burden

---

[1] *Short Treatise*, II, 24, § 4.
[2] On the "Evil Impulse" (יֵצֶר הָרָע), see S. Schechter, *Some Aspects of Rabbinic Theology*, pp. 242 ff.; G. F. Moore, *Judaism*, I, pp. 478 ff.

(*onus*)." This is a reference to the Hebrew term "yoke"[1] which is sometimes applied in rabbinic literature to the Law, though not in a derogatory sense.[2] It is because of this conception of the Law as a burden or a yoke, Spinoza continues, that men "hope to be able to lay [it] aside after death." This is again a reference to the rabbinic interpretation of the Biblical expression "free among the dead" (Psalms 88, 6) as meaning that "as soon as a man dies he becomes free of the Law and the commands."[3] Furthermore, concludes Spinoza, the common believer does good in the hope of receiving some reward in the hereafter, and eschews evil for fear of punishment.

The philosophic conception of the divine Law, to which Spinoza makes no allusion here, is, however, different. The Law is not a burden, but rather a joy.[4] The Law is not imposed upon man arbitrarily from above as something which is contrary to his nature, but it is a Law based upon reason, and all its commands, according to Maimonides, can be explained to have a twofold purpose which may be subdivided into three. "It aims *first* at the establishment of good mutual relations among men by removing injustice, and by the acquisition of excellent moral virtues so that [*a*] the orderly life of the people of a country may continue uninterruptedly and [*b*] every individual may acquire his first perfection [i.e., the well-being of the body]. *Secondly*, it seeks to train us in

---

[1] עֹל, *Abot*, III, 5. Cf. the term ζυγός (*jugum*) as applied to the ordinances of the Law in Acts 15, 10 and Galatians 5, 1. Spinoza's use here of *onus* instead of *jugum* may be accounted for by the fact that in Matthew 11, 30 *jugum* and *onus* (φορτίον) are used as equivalent terms and, furthermore, that the term *onus* is used as a description of the legal ordinances in Matthew 23, 4 and Luke 11, 46.

[2] On the meaning of the "Yoke of the Law," see S. Schechter, *Some Aspects of Rabbinic Theology*, pp. 70 ff.; G. F. Moore, *Judaism*, I, p. 465; II, pp. 86, 166, 173.

[3] *Shabbat* 30a.

[4] Cf. S. Schechter, *Some Aspects of Rabbinic Theology*, Ch. XI: "The Joy of the Law," pp. 148 ff.

correct beliefs and to impart to us true opinions whereby we may attain the last perfection [i.e., the well-being of the soul]." [1] Furthermore, the hope of reward and the fear of punishment are not to be the motives for obedience of the Law. The classic utterance on this point is: "Be not like servants that serve their master with the view of receiving reward." [2] The love of God, a disinterested love, is to be the motive for the obedience of the Law.

Now, the religion of reason which Spinoza briefly outlines for us here is nothing but a modified form of the philosophic conception of Judaism as described by Maimonides. The chief points of difference between them are two. In the first place, Spinoza eliminates the element of revelation. In the second place, he narrows down the scope of religion to what Maimonides considers to be the first object of the Law, namely, right living, and eliminates from it right thinking, which according to Maimonides is a second object of the Law. In the *Tractatus Theologico-Politicus*, aiming his remarks explicitly against Maimonides, he maintains that the purpose of Scripture is to teach only moral virtue, and not philosophic truth.[3] But within its limited sphere of practical wisdom the religion of Spinoza, which here in the *Ethics* is presented as independent of Scripture, contains the two elements which Maimonides finds in the ethical part of the religion of Scripture. These two elements are called by Spinoza strength of mind (*animositas*) and generosity (*generositas*).[4] The former consists of individual virtue, and is defined by Spinoza "as the desire by which each person endeavors from the dictates of reason alone to preserve his own being." [5] The latter consists in social virtue, and is de-

---

[1] *Moreh Nebukim*, III, 27. [2] *Abot*, I, 3.
[3] *Tractatus Theologico-Politicus*, Chs. 7, 13, 15, *et passim*.
[4] On the meaning of these terms, see above, pp. 218-220.
[5] *Ethics*, III, Prop. 59, Schol.

fined by Spinoza as "the desire by which from the dictates of reason alone each person endeavors to help other people and to join them to him in friendship."[1] The two of them correspond on the whole to the two aspects of the perfection of the body mentioned by Maimonides, namely, individual well-being and social well-being, and also to the two ways mentioned, again, by Maimonides, of preserving the social well-being, namely, the highly moral character of each individual and the maintenance of good relations between the different individuals.[2] Such a religion of personal and social virtue and of everything which is related to "strength of mind and generosity," says Spinoza, is a religion of reason and is not the work of revelation. Furthermore, such a religion of reason and virtue would be regarded by us as of primary importance even if we did not know that our mind is eternal (Prop. XLI), for the eternity of our mind and the blessedness that goes with it is not a reward of virtue, but is virtue itself (Prop. XLII). Nor is the practice of virtue to be considered as an exercise of our freedom of will in restraining our lusts (*libidines*), for there is no freedom of the will, and our lusts can be conquered only, as has been said above,[3] by the force of some other emotion which is greater and more powerful. But our lusts as well as all our other emotions will be subdued and will disappear of themselves once we experience the joy of the virtuous life, and this because the joy of the virtuous life constitutes one of the greatest of all emotions (*ibid.*).

With this the *Ethics* ends. But the philosophy of Spinoza does not end here. The religion of reason based upon individual and social virtue to which almost the entire *Ethics* is a sort of philosophic preamble would have been an effective

[1] *Ibid.*   [2] *Moreh Nebukim*, III, 27.
[3] Cf. above, pp. 230 ff., 272-273.

instrument of education only for a new-born race of men
placed under the tutelage of philosophers like Spinoza. But
the world in which Spinoza wanted to make the practical
lesson of his philosophy effective was an old world in which
rooted institutions and beliefs held sway and truths were
embodied in writings which were regarded as sacred. Made
of sterner stuff and living a few centuries later, Spinoza
would have perhaps demanded the overthrow of the old order
with its effete institutions so as to build upon its ruins a new
society of a new generation raised on his new philosophy.
He would then perhaps have become one of the first apostles
of rebellion. But being what he was and living at a time when
belief in the potency of reformation had not yet been shaken
by doubt, he chose to follow in the footsteps of rationalizers
throughout history. The story of his rationalization is the
story of his *Tractatus Theologico-Politicus*, but that is another book and another story.

CHAPTER XXI

WHAT IS NEW IN SPINOZA?

NOVELTY in philosophy is often a matter of daring rather than of invention. In thought, as in nature, there is no creation from absolute nothing, nor are there any leaps. Often what appears to be new and original is nothing but the establishment of a long-envisaged truth by the intrepidity of some one who dared to face the consequences of his reasoning. Now the long-envisaged truth which was established by the intrepidity and daring of Spinoza was the principle of the unity of nature, which in its double aspect meant the homogeneity of the material of which it is constituted and the uniformity of the laws by which it is dominated. But his predecessors, who formulated that principle and openly avowed it or rhapsodized about it, as a rule failed to adhere to it. To all of them there was a break somewhere in that unity. Man was believed by them to be, as Spinoza aptly puts it, an empire within an empire,[1] and God, as he could have put it quite as aptly, a super-empire. The difficulty of maintaining this logical anomaly of asserting the uniformity of the laws of nature, on the one hand, while, on the other hand, asserting the autonomy of man within nature and the suzerainty of God over nature was keenly felt by them, but all they did toward overcoming this difficulty was to try to patch it up somehow, never daring to cross the boundaries set up by tradition. It was Spinoza who first dared to cross these boundaries, and by the skilful use of weapons accumulated in the arsenals of philosophy itself he succeeded in

[1] *Ethics*, II, Praef. (*Opera*, II, p. 137, ll. 11-12).

bringing both God and man under the universal rule of nature and thus establishing its unity.[1] In attempting, therefore, to sum up what is new in Spinoza, we shall describe his contributions as acts of daring.

The search of the early Greek philosophers for a single element to serve as a substratum of which all the other bodies were modifications may be regarded as the first recorded step in the history of European philosophy toward the establishment of the principle of the homogeneity of the constituent materials of nature. The next step may be found in the introduction of an underlying formless and potential matter which, with the adoption of four simple elements, came to be considered the ultimate substratum of these four simple elements as well as of all the bodies which were composed of them. From that time on and to the very time of Spinoza, matter was looked upon as the principle which formed the homogeneity of nature. Indeed, in certain quarters, a distinction was drawn between the matter of the terrestrial bodies and the matter of the celestial bodies. But that distinction was abolished by Crescas' contention that the same matter, not in the Aristotelian sense of pure potentiality but as something actual, underlies the terrestrial as well as the celestial bodies.[2] In a similar vein Bruno argued for an identical matter throughout the universe, below the moon as well as above the moon.[3] By the time of Descartes, it would seem, this principle of the homogeneity of matter was already fully established, so that he could declare with positiveness and without any argument that "the matter of the heavens and of the earth is one and the same."[4] Still, to all these philosophers the homogeneity of

[1] Cf. above, Vol. I, pp. 33–34.
[2] Cf. my *Crescas' Critique of Aristotle*, pp. 103–104, 119, 120, 261, 594–598.
[3] *De Immenso et Innumerabilibus*, IV, 1–2.
[4] *Principia Philosophiae*, II, 22.

matter did not establish the homogeneity of the nature of the entire universe, for material bodies, according to them, constituted only one part of the universe. Besides bodies, their universe contained beings which were without bodies and which had nothing in common with bodies, not having matter as their substratum. To some of them the soul of man was such an independent and immaterial being. To others, who followed Aristotle in considering soul as something inseparable from body, there were immaterial beings outside the body, called angels or Intelligences. To still others, who like Ibn Gabirol denied the immateriality of angels or Intelligences,[1] there was at least one being who was immaterial, and that was God, and while God was spoken of metaphorically as outside and beyond the universe, He was really a part of it in so far as He was considered its ruler and governor, if not also its creator. Thus, however much the principle of materiality was extended to the various parts of the universe, the universe as a whole was still divided into two distinct realms, a material world and an immaterial God.

By declaring that God has the attribute of extension as well as of thought, Spinoza has thus removed the break in the principle of the homogeneity of nature. This is his first act of daring.

So also with the principle of the uniformity of the laws of nature, which, though long recognized as prevailing in the physical universe, Spinoza has extended to include God.

When Aristotle reduced all the changes that come under our observation to four kinds of motion, and further reduced these four kinds of motion to locomotion, and then traced this locomotion to the prime mover which was itself immovable, he established systematically the principle of the uniformity of the laws of nature. Later, with the identification

[1] Cf. above, Vol. I, p. 223.

of the God of Scriptural tradition with this prime mover, God became a cognomen of the universal laws of nature and the source of their uniformity. Indeed, God still continued to be spoken of as governor and ruler, and still continued to be described as most powerful, but He was shorn of that arbitrariness which was His characteristic as a primitive deity. He became now a constitutional monarch, whose powers were limited by the laws of His own nature, unable to change the nature and behavior of things which He himself had laid down from eternity. Theologians were vying with each other to declare that God cannot make a square whose diagonal shall be equal to one of its sides, or that He cannot cause one substance to have at the same time two opposite properties.[1] But the constitution by which according to the rationalist theologians God had limited His own power was only partly written and known to us. A great part of it was unwritten and unknown to us, and therefore by certain prerogatives retained by Him God could do many things which according to our way of thinking would seem to be arbitrary and a subversion of what we consider the laws of nature. Thus to them it was conceivable that God could create the world *ex nihilo*, that He could know individual things, that He could have a foreknowledge of what man would do without depriving him of freedom of choice, that He could change His will while remaining immutable, and that He could perform all kinds of miracles. The inconsistencies of these beliefs with the conception of God as a constitutional monarch limited by eternal and immutable laws were generally recognized, widely discussed, and somehow reconciled, but all the attempts at their reconciliation were really nothing more than a declaration that a part of the divine constitution was never communicated to man and that we are ignorant of

[1] *Moreh Nebukim*, I, 75; II, 13. Cf. above, Vol. I, p. 312.

the laws by which God operates in the universe. This was the general attitude of all the theologians, even of those who went to the farthest extremes in their rational explanation of religion. It was left for Spinoza to do away with the unwritten and unknown part of the constitutional privileges of God's rule. God to him is law without any loophole and without any escape to ignorance. The laws of nature which are operative in the universe from eternity, he declares, can never be upset by a power above them for a purpose unknown to us.

By denying design and purpose in God Spinoza has thus removed the break in the principle of the uniformity of the laws of nature. This is his second act of daring.

With his denial of the immateriality of God, Spinoza also denies the separability of soul from body in man. For the separability of soul from body, either of soul as a whole or of a certain part of the soul, may be considered a corollary of the immateriality of God. Soul, either in whole or in part, was generally spoken of as of divine origin and as having been joined to the body only for the brief period of its existence. Now, as long as God was assumed to be immaterial and to exist apart from bodies, the soul, or at least that part of it which was held to be of divine origin, could not be considered a part of the body and inseparable from it even during the period of their conjoint existence. It had to be something separable from body, and as separable from it as God was considered to be from the world, thus breaking up the continuity of nature within the physical world itself. But when Spinoza assumed God to be both extension and thought, either one of which was inseparable from the other, and when he further assumed man to be a mode of God, his body being a mode of God's attribute of extension and his soul being a mode of God's attribute of thought, then in man soul had to be inseparable from body just as in God thought was inseparable from extension.[1]

Spinoza's insistence upon the complete inseparability of soul from body has thus removed another break in the homogeneity of nature. This is his third act of daring.

But what is soul?

In the philosophy against which Spinoza took the field, soul was generally described as consisting of a certain number of functions which it performed and by which its existence was known. These functions were nutrition, growth, sensation, imagination, memory, consciousness, will, and intellect or, rather, understanding. Now, as Spinoza's purpose was to discuss those functions of the soul which are peculiar to man, epitomized by him in the term "human mind," he did not bother about the functions of nutrition and growth, which are also common to plants and animals. Confining himself, then, to the functions of sensation, imagination, memory, consciousness, will, and intellect, he defined mind or the human soul, in departure from most of his predecessors, as one's consciousness of one's own body,[2] and then he reduced sensation, imagination, and memory to the mind's consciousness of its body and intellect to the mind's consciousness of itself,[3] and, following out the reasoning of his predecessors, he identified will with intellect.[4] But at the same time, having always in view his main purpose, namely, the establishment of the principle of the unity of nature, he endeavored to show that consciousness, which we know to exist in man, must also exist in God,[5] and that will as something independent of intellect exists neither in God nor in man.[6] This is how we are to understand the main drift of

---

[1] Cf. above, p. 52, but see pp. 76 ff.　　[2] Cf. above, Chapter XIII.
[3] Cf above, Chapter XIV.　　[4] Cf. above, Chapter XVII.
[5] Cf. above, pp. 166, 169 ff.　　[6] Cf. above, Chapters XII and XVII.

Spinoza's discussion of mind in its bearing upon the main thesis of his philosophy.

Now, to define mind as one's consciousness of one's own body, all that Spinoza had to do was to state that one's consciousness of one's own body is prior to one's consciousness of other bodies, and that that consciousness of one's own body, which constitutes the being of mind, is associated with the mind's consciousness of itself. To reduce sensation, imagination, and memory to consciousness of one's own body, again, all he had to do was to explain them physiologically as consequences of such consciousness and as accidental facts in the history of the mind, and not of its essence. Intellect or understanding and all the other functions of thought are similarly explained by him as arising from the mind's consciousness of itself. But consciousness, which is an observed fact in man, must also be assumed to exist in God, for on the principle of the unity of nature God must contain in His essence everything that is found in particular things, and consequently, just as Spinoza was forced to assume extension in God because of the existence of matter in the world of our observation, so was he also forced to assume consciousness in God because of the existence of mind in man. This principle, however, does not demand that everything that is found in God should be found in every particular thing, and consequently Spinoza does not assume that every particular thing within the universe has consciousness, and this despite his repetition of the assertion common among certain philosophers that all things are animate.[1]

To make will identical with intellect, again, all that Spinoza had to do was to eliminate a distinction made by Aristotle and the mediaevals between the practical and the theoretical intellects and between the human and divine

[1] Cf. above, pp. 56 ff.

intellects. The practical intellect, according to Aristotle, acts toward an external end, and because of that it must be conjoined with the appetitive faculty or will in order to produce action, for intellect by itself is only a cognitive faculty and cannot of itself produce action. The theoretical intellect, on the other hand, finds its end in its own activity, and therefore does not involve will. This distinction between practical and theoretical intellect Aristotle finds only in man and not in God, and accordingly, while the uniformity in human actions is ascribed by him to the purposive actions of the will, the uniformity in the motions of the universe as a whole is ascribed by him to the eternal necessity of God's purposeless activity. As against this, the mediaevals, reasoning from the analogy of the Aristotelian explanation of the uniform actions of man, explain the uniform and orderly laws of nature as determined by a divine will, though, unlike the human will, which is distinct from intellect, they identify the divine will with the divine intellect. Now Spinoza reverses the mediaeval reasoning [1] and, proceeding from the Aristotelian explanation of the orderly processes of nature as a whole, explains the orderly and seemingly purposive actions of man as determined by an eternal law of necessity. He calls that law the conatus for self-preservation. In its universality this law applies to every individual thing within the universe, man as well as beast, and in a certain sense also to inanimate objects.[2] Each particular thing within the universe, by the eternal necessity of the nature of the universe as a whole of which it is a part, strives to maintain its existence, which is life in the case of living beings and motion in the case of non-living beings. It is this eternal necessity, and not will and its free exercise, that makes man's actions,

[1] Cf. above, Vol. I, p. 404.
[2] Cf. above, pp. 199–201.

and the actions of non-living beings too, assume a tendency toward a certain end as if guided by an intellect and carried out by a will.

Spinoza's insistence upon the elimination of freedom of the will from human actions has thus removed another break in the uniformity of the laws of nature. This is his fourth act of daring.

Genetically, it may be said, the first philosophic conception of nature as an organic whole began with an analogy between the universe and man, the macrocosm and the microcosm, and historically, it may be further said, there is no conception of nature which cannot be presented in the form of such an analogy. Spinoza himself makes an attempt at such an analogy, covertly and indirectly, to be sure, in one place of his *Ethics*,[1] but had he wished it he could have epitomized his entire philosophy by drawing, like Maimonides,[2] a parallel between man and the universe. He would probably have proceeded somewhat as follows: Know that this universe, in its entirety, is nothing but one individual being, like Tom, Dick, or Harry. All the particular things within the universe are like the organs and members of the human body intricately connected with one another to form a united whole. Man is composed of body and mind, and all his modes of behavior are either forms of motion, which constitutes the action of his body, or forms of knowing, which constitutes the action of his mind. So also the universe consists of extension and thought, and all the modes of the behavior of things within the universe are either forms of motion, which constitutes the action of extension, or forms of intellect or understanding, which constitutes the action of thought. And in this manner he could have spun out his analogy to cover the minutest detail of his philosophy.

[1] Cf. above, pp. 7 ff.   [2] *Moreh Nebukim*, I, 72.

But Spinoza labored under the disadvantages of tradition. His philosophy is not written in the form of direct philosophic observations on nature, but in the form of animadversions on books about the philosophy of nature. In presenting his case he had to follow an order which had already been prepared for him by his predecessors; he had to discuss their views, meet their arguments, and use their terminology. Using, therefore, the terminology of the time, he describes the universe in which we live and which we know and which consists of the things of which we ourselves are parts as "the face of the whole universe" [1] — an inadequate expression, indeed, since the universe to Spinoza, as to all his contemporaries, was infinite in extent. The two forms of activity which we observe in this "face of the whole universe" he describes quite appropriately as "motion" and "intellect," for the latter using also such terms as "absolutely infinite Intellect," "an infinite power of thought," and "idea of God." [2] But these two observable forms of activity, he maintains, are only two aspects of something transcending the universe of our experience, which something in its entire and true nature is unknown to us. That unknown transcendent something is given by Spinoza the familiar name of "substance" or "God" or "nature," contrasted with which all other things, the universe of our experience as a whole, its observed forms of activity, and the particular things of which it consists, are called "modes." In contradistinction to modes, which need causes for their existence, substance is the cause of itself. That such a substance exists and is not a figment of our imagination is asserted by Spinoza to be a fact of our immediate knowledge, which assertion he presents in the traditional form of proofs of the existence of

---

[1] Cf. above, Vol. I, pp. 244 ff.
[2] Cf. above, Vol. I, pp. 238–242.

God. The aspects under which substance appears to us are given by him the conventional name of "attribute," and since substance appears to us under the aspect of two forms of activity, motion and intellect, he calls these respectively the attributes of extension and thought. These two attributes, however, according to Spinoza, do not exhaust the entire nature of substance. It has other attributes, infinite in number, which are unknown to us and perhaps also unknowable, though in one place he seems to suggest that more than the two now known attributes may become known to us.[1] The relation of substance to modes is conceived by Spinoza after the manner of the relation of a cause to its effects, and he speaks of modes as "following" from God or as being "produced" by God.[2] He thus describes "motion" and "intellect" (or the equivalent terms of the latter) as "immediate infinite modes," the "face of the whole universe" as a "mediate infinite mode," and the particular things as "finite modes."

If we examine closely the concept of substance used by Spinoza in his philosophy, we shall find that it contains four characteristics. In the first place, it is a transcendent whole which serves to hold together as within a logical shell the individual parts which make up the universe of our observation. In the second place, unlike the individual things within the universe, which require causes for their existence, substance is causeless. In the third place, the relation of substance to the universe of our observation is conceived after the manner of cause and effect. In the fourth place, substance is infinite, in the sense that the entirety of its nature is unknown to us and that only two of its infinite attributes manifest themselves to us in the universe of our observation.

[1] Cf. *Short Treatise*, I, 1, § 8, note 3 (*Opera*, I, p. 17, ll. 36–38): "We have *so far* not been able to discover more than two attributes which belong to this all-perfect being."   [2] Cf. above, Vol. I, p. 373.

Now, of these four characteristics of substance, Spinoza was logically quite justified in assuming the first, second, and third. His very conception of the eternity of the universe necessarily compelled him to conceive of substance as a whole which transcended the mere aggregate of parts that made up the universe, and to conceive of it also as being *causa sui*. For to explain the universe as eternal, he had to resort to one of three possibilities. He had to assume, with Aristotle, the existence of an immaterial cause, or he had to assume, with Epicurean atomism, that the universe is an automaton and its eternity is due to the action of its constituent parts, or, else, he had to assume that eternity, while it could not be explained by anything in the nature of the parts, could be explained by something in the nature of the whole. But since Spinoza rejected the Aristotelian conception of an immaterial cause,[1] and since he also rejected Epicureanism on the ground that it was a denial of causality and an affirmation that things happened by chance,[2] he necessarily had to resort to the third possibility and declare substance to be a transcendent and causeless whole. That this was his reasoning can be gathered from his arguments in his Dialogues for the distinction of the whole from the sum of its parts,[3] and from his approval in one of his letters to Meyer of Crescas' argument that an infinite series of causes and effects was possible provided we assumed that the totality of the series forms a whole which is causeless.[4] By the same token, he was also logically justified in characterizing his substance as cause in the conventional sense in which a transcendent whole had been spoken of by philosophers as cause, namely, an immanent cause. But there would seem

---

[1] Cf. above, Vol. I, p. 222.   [2] Cf. above, Vol. I, p. 318.
[3] Cf. above, Vol. I, pp. 323–328.
[4] Epistola 12. Cf. above, Vol. I, p. 196.

to be no logical justification at all for his fourth characteristic of substance. For if it is assumed that the universe must have a logical shell within which to be enclosed, why not assume also that that shell is known to us in its entirety through its manifestation in the universe? Why not assume that the two attributes through which it is known to us exhaust its entire nature, and it has no other attributes? Beyond his statement in his definition of God that he understands by the term "God" a "Being absolutely infinite, that is to say, substance consisting of infinite attributes," [1] and similar statements elsewhere, Spinoza does not try to prove the infinity of God's attributes. Even his proofs for the existence of God which are supposed to establish the existence of "God, or substance consisting of infinite attributes" [2] assume only an immediate knowledge on our part of God as a being whose essence involves existence (First Proof), or as a being whose existence is necessary *per se* (Second Proof), or as a being who is most powerful (Fourth Proof). They do not assume that our immediate knowledge of God conceives Him as a being who has an infinite number of attributes, though, of course, Spinoza could have started with such an assumption and given us a fourth form of the ontological proof in which the term "infinity" would have been substituted for the terms "essence involving existence," "necessary existence *per se*," and "most powerful." [3] In fact, in the *Short Treatise* Spinoza seems to state that the conception of infinite attributes is involved in our immediate knowledge of God as a perfect being. [4] "Perfection," as will be recalled, is one of the three terms round which Descartes builds his ontological proofs. [5]

---

[1] *Ethics*, I, Def. 6.   [2] *Ibid.*, I, Prop. 11.

[3] Cf. above, Vol. I, pp. 177 ff., 213.

[4] *Short Treatise*, I, 1, § 8, note 3 (*Opera*, I, p. 17, ll. 36–47).

[5] Cf. above, pp. 180, 207.

The fact is, however, that it is not logical reasons but rather psychological ones that we must look for in trying to explain Spinoza's characterizations of substance. Two motives seem to have been at play in Spinoza's philosophy — one that of criticism, and another that of interpretation. On the one hand, he was trying to show that God was material, that He worked for no external purpose, that the soul was inseparable from the body, and that man was not endowed with freedom — the four points which are to be regarded as cardinal in his philosophy. But, on the other hand, he was also trying to show that these were by no means contrary to what was true and essential in past beliefs of man about God and his own self. Like all rationalists, Spinoza felt that the idea of God which was intuitive in man and which existed as a universal belief under various forms must contain a germ of truth which the philosopher had only to disentangle from the crudities in which it had become enmeshed. Now, God was conceived by the primitive mind as a body like any other body within the universe. Of course, God is not a body, said Spinoza; but still there is truth in that primitive conception of God as something which is not totally unlike the things which constitute the universe — in fact, more truth than in the sophisticated theological conception of God as something totally different from the universe. Why not restate this truth by the assertion that God has the attributes of both extension and thought? God has always been considered as a cause. Why not continue to speak of Him as cause — a cause, indeed, not in the sense of creator, maker, and governor, but in that attenuated sense known as immanent cause? God has been spoken of by theologians as infinite and unknowable. Why not retain the infinity of God and His unknowability? For do we really know the universe as it is, in all its powers and possibilities? Is not our knowledge of it commensurate with our knowledge of natural phenomena, and thus capable of growth?[1] God has always been called a living God, living in the sense of having consciousness and of acting for a purpose. Of course, God cannot act for a purpose, but still He can be conscious. In fact, the assumption of God's consciousness is required on independent ground, in order to maintain the principle of the unity of nature. Finally, God has always been spoken of as the last refuge of man in time of trouble. His own God, Spinoza concludes, is no less powerful to answer to this human need.[2]

Still, attempting though he did to accommodate his philosophy to the traditional conceptions and vocabulary of religion, Spinoza marked a radical departure from the traditional theologies of the three revealed religions — Judaism, Christianity, and Mohammedanism. In the traditional conceptions of God of these three religions, however variedly stated, there was one common element which was considered essential. It was the element of the personality of God, by which was meant the existence of a certain reciprocal relation between the conduct of man toward God and the conduct of God toward man, commonly expressed in terms of mutual love. Theologians may have openly rejected primitive anthropomorphism, they may have vehemently affirmed their belief in the immateriality of God, His immutability, His unlikeness to man, His independence of the world, His indifference to human conduct, but despite all this God is conceived after the manner of human personality — He is a creator, a governor, a lawgiver; He acts by will and design; He is responsive to human needs; He rewards and punishes; He loves men and expects to be loved by them. Spinoza denies all this. His substance with which he identifies the

---

[1] Cf. above, pp. 128, 298.   [2] Cf. above, pp. 273 ff.

traditional God is nothing but a logical shell holding the particular things of the universe together, conceived as acting by the necessity of its own nature, an eternal machine incapable of changing the course of its own action, still less the action of others.

In its most essential feature, the theology of Spinoza may be regarded as a return to the theology of Aristotle, with its conception of an impersonal deity devoid of will and acting by necessity, against which the mediaevals constantly argued. Now when Aristotle began to apply the term "God" to his impersonal prime mover, and ere he endowed it with thought, he felt a certain impropriety in his identifying it with the god of Greek popular religion, and he asked himself: "If it thinks nothing, what is there here of dignity? It is just like one who sleeps." [1] He eased his intellectual conscience, however, by endowing his prime mover with thought of itself, and, having done so, he was quite pleased with his performance and believed that he had thereby succeeded in transforming it into a "living being, eternal, most good." [2] Perhaps Spinoza, too, felt some qualms of intellectual conscience when he identified the God of Scriptural tradition with his substance, and perhaps, like Aristotle, he justified himself by endowing his substance with consciousness and believed that thereby his substance was transformed into a "living being, eternal, most good." But still, the life which characterizes the Scriptural conception of God and which theologians, Jewish, Christian, and Mohammedan, who wished to remain true to Scriptural tradition tried to preserve, often in violation of their logic, was not the life of an eternal paralytic, who is conscious and sees all and hears all and knows all, but is helpless to do anything at will; it was the life which, after the analogy of our own life, meant a capacity for

---

[1] *Metaphysics*, XII, 9, 1074b, 17–18.   [2] *Ibid.*, XII, 7, 1072b, 29.

change and a consciousness of freedom of action. It is the anthropomorphisms and anthropopathisms of the Scriptures, which theologians tried to explain away, just as much as the monotheism, which they were so eager to justify, that constitute, historically, the essential character of the Scriptural God, and it was for this reason that theologians throughout the ages tried to save as much of these anthropomorphisms and anthropopathisms as possible, even though sometimes what they succeeded in saving was only the empty sounds of words. By depriving God of this kind of life, by exploding even the fiction that such a kind of life was attributed to Him when words to that effect were used, by openly disclaiming the need of maintaining such a fiction, Spinoza broke away from the traditional theology and started a new kind of theology and a new kind of rationalization.

Had this breaking away from tradition been deliberately intended as such by Spinoza it could have been regarded as a fifth act of daring on his part. But Spinoza seems to have been under the delusion that he was merely spinning on the traditions of religion and that he was only seeing in a truer light that which others before him had seen, to use his own expression, "as if through a mist." [1] The true nature of his new theology, however, was more accurately understood by others than by himself. The contemporaries of Spinoza, those theologians who openly attacked him in their writings, instinctively felt this departure, and hence they condemned him, despite his use of the term "God," as a denier of God, for, imbued as they were with the spirit of theological traditions, they knew that Scripture, which contrasts its own God, as a "living God" (Joshua 3, 10), "a saviour" (Isaiah 45, 21), and "our help and our shield" (Psalms 33,

[1] *Ethics*, I, Prop. 7, Schol.

20), with gods that are "dead" (Psalms 106, 28), that "cannot save" (Isaiah 45, 20), and that "do not profit" (Jeremiah 2, 8), would place Spinoza's substance among gods which it calls "no-gods" (Jeremiah 2, 11). That Spinoza himself was not fully conscious of his own radical departure, that he speaks of the opposition to his views as due to "the prejudices of the theologians" [1] and of the "atheism" with which the common people accused him as an untrue accusation,[2] that he continues to consider himself a successor of the religious thinkers of the past who tried to discover the truth that lay hidden in the pages of Scripture, and that he occasionally speaks of his God in the pious phrases of tradition — all this is due to the inherent tendency of men to rationalize and to accommodate old beliefs to their own thought. His reputed God-intoxication was really nothing but a hang-over of an earlier religious jag.

This tendency toward rationalization with its resulting attempt to show that his new philosophy can be put to work in this fixed and established world of ours without disturbing its order is evidenced also in Spinoza's treatment of the dictates of reason. Tradition has always considered man to be master of his own fate. Man is pictured in Scripture as standing at the parting of the ways, on the one side the way of life and on the other the way of death. Being free, he is assumed to be able to choose which way to follow. To guide him, he has a Law revealed to him by God. Now, Spinoza has deprived man of freedom of choice and of a God who could reveal to him His word. But still he is anxious to show that he has not deprived him of the guidance which revelation is supposed to furnish him with and of the power which freedom of choice is supposed to confer upon him. Spinoza offers substitutes for both revelation and the freedom of

---

[1] Epistola 30 (*Opera*, IV, p. 166, l. 22). [2] *Ibid.* (ll. 25–26).

the will, and these are what he calls the Dictates of Reason. There are tens of commandments and golden rules, he argues, which are not any the less effective as guides to man for their being the revelation of the human mind and not of God. Guided by the principle of self-preservation and helped by the power of reason, man can work out those very same laws of conduct which have been hitherto attributed to a divine revelation. Indeed, reason has no messengers, like the God of old, to enforce its dictates, and man, though not free, can be tempted away from them by the new Satan, ignorance, without even having his old power of saying, "Get thee behind me." Still, though not free, man can condition himself by knowledge against this new Tempter. Not that knowledge itself is power, but it is the fuel on which the light of reason feeds.[1]

A similar mode of rationalization may also be discerned in Spinoza's treatment of immortality.

The indestructibility of the mind could have been treated by Spinoza purely as a philosophic principle. He could have spoken of it with the same unconcerned objectivity that a scientist speaks of the conservation of matter and energy. But in his treatment of the subject Spinoza goes beyond that and uses his own principle of the indestructibility of the soul as an interpretation of the traditional religious belief in the immortality of the soul. Now as a religious principle of belief the immortality of the soul did not consist in the mere fact of its indestructibility; it consisted primarily in the fact that its survival was conditioned upon the conduct of the individual man during his lifetime. Whether conduct only was necessary, or also intellectual attainments, was a debatable point, but the essential point was that immortality was considered a matter of reward for

[1] Cf. above, pp. 226, 231-232.

the obedient, and the withholding of immortality, which was held to be possible, was considered a matter of punishment for the disobedient. And for this reason, when Plato wanted to give to his purely philosophic notion of the indestructibility of the soul a religious tinge, he had to borrow from popular religion the theories of reward and punishment and the transmigration of souls, though these were hardly warranted by his own philosophy. Similarly Spinoza, merely out of the desire to accommodate his philosophy to tradition, adopts certain phases of popular conceptions of immortality. He speaks of conduct and intellectual attainments as conditions of immortality. But at the same time, on the mere grounds of his philosophy, he is bound to affirm the indestructibility of any soul irrespective of the conduct and the intellectual attainments of the individual. Nor does he make it clear how the individual souls after death will differ as a result of the differences in their life during their mundane existence. Spinoza also uses religious terms in describing the eternal happiness enjoyed by the soul after death, and he even speaks of our foretaste of it during our lifetime. Philosophically, however, all he can assume is that the indestructible mind on becoming reunited with God after the death of the individual will have consciousness, since God has consciousness, but that that consciousness is not a continuation of the consciousness of the individual during his lifetime. As I have shown above,[1] some of the most significant expressions in Spinoza's discussion of immortality bear the unmistakable evidence of having been meant as a direct criticism of Uriel Acosta's open denial of that traditional doctrine.

Spinoza is represented by those who knew him as having lived a life of retirement, though one not devoid of friendship.

[1] Cf. above, pp. 323 ff.

We should like to agree with his biographers that he was guided into this mode of life by his philosophy, but unfortunately recluses are not made by philosophies, not even by philosophies which, unlike the philosophy of Spinoza, preach retirement from life as an ideal virtue; they are made, rather, by the inhospitableness of the social environment and by the ineptitude of their own individual selves. But for the circumstances, environmental and personal, which had cut his normal contacts with society, Spinoza, who defined man, after Aristotle, as a social animal,[1] would undoubtedly have guided himself by the same dictate of reason that he had prescribed for others — by his maxim that man is freer when he participates in the life of society than when he lives in solitude.[2] In conformity with this maxim of his, then, he would undoubtedly have joined in the active life of the communities in which he lived after his departure from his native Amsterdam — Rijnsburg, Voorburg, and The Hague; he would have become a substantial, respectable, and public-spirited burgher and a pillar of society. Perhaps, also, despite differences in theology, he would have joined the Lutheran church of his friend Doctor Cordes in The Hague. And I can picture him, once of a Sunday, at the invitation of the good old Doctor, taking the services in the church. He preaches a sermon which is an invective against what he styles "the prejudices of the theologians of our time."[3] In it he inveighs against prevailing credulous beliefs in the spirituality of God, His personal relation to men, His direct guidance of human affairs, the divine origin of the Scriptures, human freedom of the will, the separability of soul from body, and the survival of the soul after death as an

---

[1] Cf. above, p. 245.   [2] *Ethics*, IV, Prop. 73.

[3] Cf. Epistola 30 (*Opera*, IV, p. 166, l. 22): "præjudicia theologorum"; Epistola 6 (p. 36, l. 16): "theologi nostri temporis."

individual entity. The sermon over, he pauses and says, "Now let us pray." And in his prayer he thanks God, "the creator of the universe," for His bountiful goodness; he begs for the forgiveness of "our sins," asks for divine enlightenment in the true understanding of "Thy revealed Word," and petitions for divine grace in "guiding us" in the paths of righteousness, to the end that "we may inherit" life everlasting and enjoy eternal bliss in the presence of "Thy glory." As he is about to close his prayer, he catches a glimpse of the congregation and suddenly realizes that he is in a Christian church. Immediately he adds: "In the name of Christ, the mouth of God,[1] whose spirit is the idea of God,[2] which alone leads us unto liberty, salvation, blessedness, and regeneration.[3] Amen."

These observations on what is new in Spinoza may be finally clinched by a formal summary, complete though brief, of the philosophy of Spinoza as it unfolds itself in the pages of this work. Beginning with the traditional definition of "substance," Spinoza applies that term only to God, designating all the other so-called substances as well as all the so-called accidents by the term "mode," under which he includes the physical world as a whole and the variety of individual things of which it consists (Chapter III). This in itself would seem to be merely a verbal difference. But a real difference appears when he afterwards contends that God must be material, or extended, as he calls it, on the ground that the theory of an immaterial God would inevitably lead to all the insurmountable difficulties to which any conceivable attempt at the explanation of the origin of the material world would necessarily give rise (Chapter IV).

---

[1] *Tractatus Theologico-Politicus*, Ch. 4 (*Opera*, III, p. 64, l. 19): "os Dei."

[2] *Ethics*, IV, Prop. 68, Schol.: "Spiritu Christi, hoc est, Dei idea, a qua sola pendet, ut homo liber sit."   [3] Cf. above, p. 311.

This material God, however, continues to be described by Spinoza by all the terms by which the traditional immaterial God has been described: He is necessary existence or *causa sui* in whom there is no distinction of essence and existence; He is infinite in the sense that He is unknowable in His essence; He is known only through His attributes, that is to say, by the manner in which He manifests himself to our mind in the physical universe as it is perceived by us (Chapter V). But while His essence is unknown, the fact of His existence, that He is a real being and not a mere figment of our imagination, is known to us — and it is known to us by a direct and immediate kind of knowledge which of all the kinds of knowledge is the most valid (Chapter VI).

Of the infinite number of attributes which God in the traditional conception of Him is supposed to possess there are only two through which He manifests himself to us in the world, and these two are the two conventional constituent elements of the world, matter and form, or, as Spinoza prefers to call them, extension and thought (Chapter VII). The attribution of extension to God, to which Spinoza has been driven by the difficulties of the old problem of creation, becomes all the easier for him because, in departure from the older tradition of philosophy, though not altogether without a precedent, he considered extension to be infinite (Chapter VIII). Since Spinoza's God, unlike the traditional conception of Him, is material, the old conventional saying that all things are in God ceases to be a mere pious expression of praise and glorification and assumes a meaning which corresponds exactly to the literal meaning of its words. Again, following tradition, Spinoza continues to speak of God as cause, but with his attribution of extension to God he is enabled to use with greater accuracy and with more logical consistency all the conventional terms by which the causality of God has always been described, such as "universal," "efficient," "first," "principal," and "free"; and, moreover, he is led to reject the description of God as transeunt cause, which term in the restricted sense of separate or immaterial cause has been explicitly stated to be applicable to God, and to make Him exclusively an immanent cause in the special sense in which he uses the term "immanent" (Chapter IX). Similarly, in the manner of tradition, He describes God also by the term "eternal" in all the three senses in which the term "eternal" has been generally used in its application to God, though "eternal" in the sense of immutable is not, according to him, an exclusive property of God (Chapter X). Admitting with tradition that God is a conscious cause, he contends, without precedent since Aristotle, that God has no will and acts without design, so that the modes, which to him are not outside of God but within God (Chapter XI), are produced by the necessity of God's nature and without any purpose (Chapter XII).

Man, of course, is a part of nature, a mode like any other mode, consisting of what is commonly known as body and mind; and, following the traditional phraseology, Spinoza speaks of mind as being of divine origin, but, inasmuch as according to his own view body can be equally spoken of as being of divine origin, he declares, in opposition to tradition, that mind is inseparable from body (Chapter XIII). He continues to follow tradition in his description of the various functions of the mind: sensation, imagination, memory, consciousness, and reason (Chapter XIV), all of which constitute the sources of the greater part of our knowledge — knowledge as a whole being divided, as it has always been, into three kinds, of which one kind, he declares in common with others, may be false and two kinds are true (Chapter XVI), using as his criteria of truth two definitions of the term which have come down from Aristotle (Chapter XV). No less traditional is his description of the human will, but he opposes tradition by eliminating from it any kind of freedom (Chapter XVII). With this denial of the freedom of the will in man, the old traditional distinction between emotions and virtues disappears; but still Spinoza's treatment of emotions and virtues is only a variation of the traditional manner of treatment; what is commonly considered as good and evil continue to be with him good and evil, though their definitions are somewhat modified; man, though unable to choose, will still by the guidance of reason continue to act in pursuit of what is good and in avoidance of what is evil; and instruction in the ways of good and evil will still continue to be profitable to man (Chapters XVIII–XIX). God, though no longer endowed with will and design, can still continue to play His old traditional part of the supreme object of satisfaction to the human mind and the supreme power for goodness in human conduct; the soul, though no longer separable from the body, can still be immortal after the manner in which immortality was conceived by religious philosophers; and, finally, though the revelation of a law by God is no longer thinkable, still a religion of reason can be built up which in all essential respects would be like the rational religion of theologians (Chapter XX).

LIST OF EDITIONS OF TEXTS USED

LIST OF EDITIONS OF TEXTS USED

Spinoza Opera. Im Auftrag der Heidelberger Akademie der Wissenschaften, herausgegeben von Carl Gebhardt, Heidelberg, 1925, 4 volumes. Section numbers in *Tractatus de Intellectus Emendatione* are from ed. C. H. Bruder, Lipsiae, 1843–1846. English translations quoted are from the following: *Ethic,* by W. Hale White, revised by A. H. Stirling, 4th ed., London: Milford, 1929; *Tractatus de Intellectus Emendatione,* by W. Hale White, revised by A. H. Stirling, New York: Macmillan, 1895; *Spinoza's Short Treatise on God, Man, and His Well-Being,* by A. Wolf, London: Black, 1910; *The Correspondence of Spinoza,* by A. Wolf, London: Allen and Unwin [1928]; *The Principles of Descartes' Philosophy by Benedictus de Spinoza* (including *Cogitata Metaphysica*), by H. H. Britan, Chicago: Open Court, 1905; *Tractatus Theologico-Politicus* and *Tractatus Politicus* in *The Chief Works of Benedict de Spinoza,* by R. H. M. Elwes, London: Bell, 1917

Abraham ibn Daud, *Emunah Ramah,* ed. S. Weil, Frankfurt a. M., 1852

Abraham bar Ḥiyya, *Hegyon ha-Nefesh,* ed. E. Freimann, Leipzig, 1860

Abraham Shalom, *Neweh Shalom,* Venice, 1575

Alanus de Insulis (or Nicolaus of Amiens), *De Arte seu Articulis Catholicae Fidei* in Migne, *Patrologia Latina,* Vol. 210

pseudo-Alanus, *De Trinitate* in *Philosophisches Jahrbuch,* VI (1893)

Albertus Magnus, *Opera Omnia,* Paris, 1890–1899

Albo, Joseph, *Sefer ha-'Iḳḳarim,* critically edited . . . and provided with a translation and notes, by Isaac Husik, Philadelphia, 1929–1930

Alfarabi, *Sefer ha-Hathalot* in Ẓ. Filipowsky's *Sefer ha-Asif,* Leipzig, 1849

Algazali, *Maḳaṣid al-Falasifah,* Cairo, no date

—— *Tahafut al-Falasifah,* ed. M. Bouyges, Beyrouth, 1927

—— *Mizan al-'Amal,* Cairo, A. H., 1328; Hebrew translation under the title of *Mozene Ẓedeḳ* by Abraham bar Ḥasdai, ed. J. Goldenthal, Leipzig and Paris, 1839

Altabrizi, Commentary on Maimonides' Twenty-five Propositions, Hebrew translation by Isaac ben Nathan in *She'elot Sha'ul* by Saul ha-Kohen and Isaac Abrabanel, Venice, 1574

Anatolio, Jacob (*or* Judah Ibn Tibbon), *Ruaḥ Ḥen,* ed. D. Slucki, Warsaw, 1865

Anselm, *Opera*, Paris, 1721

Aristotle, *Opera*, ed. I. Bekker, Berlin, 1831–1870. Latin translations quoted are from *Aristotelis omnia quae extant opera . . . Averrois in ea opera . . . commentarii . . .* Venetiis, apud Iuntas, 1573–1576, 11 volumes. English translations: *Analytica Posteriora* by G. R. G. Mure, Oxford, 1928; *Physics* by Thomas Taylor, London, 1812, and by R. P. Hardie and R. K. Gaye, Oxford, 1930; *De Anima* by W. A. Hammond, London, 1902, by R. D. Hicks, Cambridge, 1907, and by J. A. Smith, Oxford, 1931; *Parva Naturalia* by W. A. Hammond, London, 1902, and by J. I. Beare and G. R. T. Ross, Oxford, 1931; *Nicomachean Ethics* by J. E. C. Welldon, London, 1897, and by W. D. Ross, Oxford, 1925

Augustine, *Opera Omnia*, Paris, 1836–1839

Averroes, Latin translations of the Long Commentary on *Analytica Posteriora*, of the Middle Commentaries on *Physics* and *Nicomachean Ethics*, and of the Epitomes of *De Memoria et Reminiscentia* and of *Metaphysics* in *Aristotelis omnia quae extant opera . . .* apud Iuntas, 1573–1576. Hebrew translations of the Epitome of Porphyry's *Isagoge*, in *Kol Meleket Higgayon le-Aristoteles mi-Kizzure Ibn Roshd (Mabo)*, Riva di Trento, 1559, of the Epitome of *Physics*, in *Kizzure Ibn Roshd 'al Shema' Tibe'i le-Aristoteles*, Riva di Trento, 1560, of the Epitome of *De Memoria et Reminiscentia*, MS. New York, Jewish Theological Seminary, of the Middle Commentary on *Metaphysics*, MS. Paris, Bibliothèque Nationale, Cod. 954

—— *Kitab Faṣl al-Maḳal*, ed. M. J. Müller, in *Philosophie und Theologie von Averroes*, München, 1875

—— *Tahafut al-Tahafut*, ed. M. Bouyges, Beyrouth, 1930. Hebrew translation (*Happalat ha-Happalah*), MS. Bodleian 1354. Latin translation from the Hebrew (*Destructio Destructionum Philosophiae Algazelis*), in *Aristotelis omnia quae extant opera . . .* apud Iuntas, 1573–1576, Vol. IX

Avicenna, *Risalah fi al-Nafs*, ed. S. Landauer (*Die Psychologie des Ibn Sînâ*) in *Zeitschrift der Deutschen Morgenländischen Gesellschaft*, 29 (1875)

—— *Al-Najat*, published together with *Kitab al-Kanon*, Rome, 1593

—— *Al Shifa'*, published in part in German translation (*Die Metaphysik Avicennas*) by M. Horten, Halle a. S., 1907

Azariah dei Rossi, *Me'or 'Enayim*, ed. D. Cassel, Wilna, 1866

Bacon, F., *Works*, London, 1857–1874

Baḥya ibn Paḳuda, *Ḥobot ha-Lebabot*, Wilna, no date. Arabic: *Al-Hidāja 'Ilā Farā'iḍ Al-qulūb*, ed. A. S. Yahuda, Leyden, 1912

Boethius, *De Trinitate, Liber de Hebdomadibus (Quomodo Substantiae Bonae Sint)*, and *De Consolatione Philosophiae* in *The Theological Tractates and The Consolation of Philosophy* by H. F. Stewart and E. K. Rand,

London and New York, 1918; *Euclidis Geometriae Interpretatio* in Migne, *Patrologia Latina*, Vol. 63

Bonaventura, *Opera Omnia*, Ad Claras Aquas prope Florentiam, 1882–1902

Bruno, Giordano, *De la Causa, Principio, et Uno* and *De Immenso et Innumerabilibus* in *Opera Latina Conscripta*, I, 1–2, ed. F. Fiorentino, Neapoli, 1879–1884; *De l'Infinito Universo et Mondi* in *Opere Italiane*, ed. P. de Lagarde, Gottinga, 1888

Burgersdijck, Franco, *Institutiones Logicae*, Cantabrigiae, 1680

—— *Institutiones Metaphysicae*, Lugduni Batavorum, 1642

Cassiodorus, *De Artibus et Disciplinis Liberalium Litterarum* in Migne, *Patrologia Latina*, Vol. 70

Cicero, *Scripta quae manserunt omnia*, ed. C. F. W. Mueller, Leipzig, 1878–1898. English translations: *The Academic Questions, Treatise De Finibus, and Tusculan Disputations of M. T. Cicero*, by C. D. Yonge, London, 1853; *De Finibus*, by H. Rackham, London and New York, 1914

Comtino, Mordecai, Commentary on Maimonides' *Millot ha-Higgayon*. *See* Maimonides

Crescas, Asher, Commentary on Maimonides' *Moreh Nebukim*. *See* Maimonides

Crescas, Ḥasdai, *Or Adonai*, Vienna, 1859. Book I, Part I, Chs. 1–25, and Part II, Chs. 1–14, critically edited and with an English translation, in *Crescas' Critique of Aristotle*, by H. A. Wolfson, Cambridge, 1929

Descartes, *Oeuvres de Descartes*, ed. Adam et Tannery, Paris, 1897–1910. Latin translation of *Les Passions de l'Ame* in *Renati Des-Cartes Opera Philosophica* [Part IV], Amsterdam, 1685. English translation: *The Philosophical Works of Descartes*, by E. S. Haldane and G. R. T. Ross, Cambridge, 1911–1912. 2 volumes

Diogenes Laertius, *De Vitis, Dogmatibus et Apophthegmatibus Clarorum Philosophorum*. Greek with Latin translation and notes, Amsterdam, 1692. Greek with English translation: *Lives of Eminent Philosophers*, by R. D. Hicks, London and New York, 1925

Dounamus, Georgius. *See* Ramus, Petrus

Duns Scotus, *Opera Omnia*, Paris, 1891–1895

Erigena, Joannes Scotus, *De Divisione Naturae*, Monasterii Guestphalorum, 1838

Eusebius, *Praeparatio Evangelica*, Oxford, 1843

Eustachius a Sancto Paulo, *Summa Philosophiae Quadripartita, De rebus Dialecticis, Ethicis, Physicis, et Metaphysicis*, Cantabrigiae, 1648

Galileo, *Le Opere di Galileo Galilei*, Firenze, 1890–1909

Galitius, M. A., *Summa Totius Philosophiae Aristotelicae ad mentem S. Bonaventurae*, Rome, 1635

Gershon ben Solomon, *Sha'ar ha-Shamayim*, Rödelheim, 1801

Gerson, Joannes, *Opera Omnia*, Antwerpiae, 1706

Gersonides, Commentary on the Bible in the Rabbinic Bible *Ḳehillot Mosheh*, Amsterdam, 1724–1728

—— *Milḥamot Adonai*, Leipzig, 1866

Ḥayyim Vital, *Sha'are Ḳedushshah*, Zolkiev, 1780

Heereboord, A., *Meletemata Philosophica*, Amsterdam, 1665

—— *Hermeneia Logica*, Cantabrigiae, 1680

Herrera, Abraham de, *Sha'ar ha-Shamayim*, Hebrew translation of his *La Puerta del Cielo*, Warsaw, 1864; MS. of Spanish original in the Library of the Portugeesch Israëlietisch Seminarium ETS HAIM in Amsterdam; Latin abridged translation from the Hebrew under the title of *Porta Cœlorum*, Solisbaci, 1678

Hillel of Verona, Commentary on Maimonides' Twenty-five Propositions, together with *Tagmule ha-Nefesh*, ed. S. J. Halberstam, Lyck, 1874

—— Miscellany, *ibid.*

Hobbes, *Works*, London, 1839–1845

Ibn Ezra, Abraham, Commentary on the Bible in various editions of Rabbinic Bibles

—— *Yesod Mora*, ed. M. Creizenach, Frankfurt a. M., 1840

Ibn Gabirol, Solomon, *Fons Vitae*, ed. C. Baeumker, Münster, 1895. *Liḳḳuṭim min Sefer Meḳor Ḥayyim* (Hebrew abridged version of the Arabic original of the *Fons Vitae*) in S. Munk's *Mélanges de Philosophie Juive et Arabe*, Paris, 1859

—— *Keter Malkut* in *Selected Religious Poems by Solomon Ibn Gabirol* by I. Davidson and I. Zangwill, Philadelphia, 1923, and *Shire Shelomoh Ben Yehudah Ibn Gabirol* by Ḥ. N. Bialik and J. Ḥ. Rawnitzki, Tel-Aviv, 1924–1928

Ibn Yaḥya, Joseph, Commentary on Psalms in the Rabbinic Bible *Ḳehillot Mosheh*, Amsterdam, 1724–1728

Isaac Israeli, *Sefer ha-Yesodot*, ed. S. Fried (German title: *Das Buch über die Elemente*), Drohobycz, 1900

Jehiel of Pisa, *Minḥat Kena'ot*, ed. D. Kaufmann, Berlin, 1898

John of Damascus, *Opera Omnia Quae Extant*, Paris, 1712

John of Salisbury, *Policraticus*, ed. C. C. I. Webb, Oxford, 1909

Joseph Ibn Ẓaddiḳ, *'Olam Ḳaṭan*, ed. S. Horovitz (German title: *Der Mikrokosmos des Josef Ibn Ṣaddiḳ*), Breslau, 1903

Judah ben Barzillai, *Perush Sefer Yeẓirah le-Rabbi Judah bar Barzillai*, ed. S. J. Halberstam, Berlin, 1885

Judah ha-Levi, *Cuzari*, Arabic and Hebrew texts, ed. H. Hirschfeld (German title: *Das Buch Al-Chazari*), Leipzig, 1887; Hebrew with commentaries *Ḳol Yehudah* and *Oẓar Neḥmad*, Wilna, 1904; English translation: *Judah Hallevi's Kitab Al Khazari* by H. Hirschfeld, new revised edition, London, 1931

Leibniz, *Nouveaux Essais sur l'Entendement Humain* in *Oeuvres Philosophiques de Leibniz*, Vol. I, Paris, 1900

Leo Hebraeus, *Dialoghi d'Amore*, ed. S. Caramella, Bari, 1929

Locke, *An Essay Concerning Human Understanding* in *The Philosophical Works of John Locke*, London, 1892

Maimonides, *Introduction to Perek Ḥelek*, Hebrew and Arabic texts in *Zur Geschichte der Dogmatenlehre in der jüdischen Religionsphilosophie des Mittelalters*, by J. Holzer, Berlin, 1901

—— *Shemonah Perakim*, ed. D. Slucki, Warsaw, 1863

—— *Ma'amar Teḥiyyat ha-Metim* in *Kobez Teshubot ha-Rambam we-Iggerotaw*, Leipzig, 1859

—— *Millot ha-Higgayon*, with commentaries by Mordecai Comtino and Moses Mendelssohn, ed. D. Slucki, Warsaw, 1865

—— *Mishneh Torah*, Berlin, 1880

—— *Moreh Nebukim*, Hebrew translation of Samuel Ibn Tibbon with the commentaries of Profiat Duran (Efodi), Shem-Ṭob, Asher Crescas, and Isaac Abarbanel, Wilna, 1914; Arabic and French by S. Munk: *Le Guide des Égarés*, Paris, 1856–1861; English by M. Friedländer: *The Guide of the Perplexed*, London, 1881–1885. Whenever possible the phraseology of Friedländer's translation has been preserved in passages quoted in this work

Manasseh ben Israel, *Nishmat Ḥayyim*, Stettin, 1861

—— *De Resurrectione Mortuorum* in *Die Schriften des Uriel da Costa* by Carl Gebhardt, Heidelberg, 1922

Marcus Aurelius, *The Communings with Himself of Marcus Aurelius Antoninus*, ed. C. R. Haines, London and New York, 1916

Meir ibn Gabbai, *'Abodat ha-Kodesh*, Slavuta, 1827

Morteira, Saul, *Gib'at Sha'ul*, Warsaw, 1912

Moscato, Judah Aryeh. *See* Judah ha-Levi

Moses Cordovero, *Elimah Rabbati*, Brody, 1881

—— *Pardes Rimmonim*, Koretz, 1786

Moses ha-Lavi, *Ma'amar Elohi*, MS. Bodleian 1324.5

Narboni, Moses, Commentary on Maimonides' *Moreh Nebukim*, ed. J. Goldenthal, Vienna, 1852

Philo, *Opera quae supersunt*, ed. L. Cohn et P. Wendland, Berlin, 1896–1930

Plotinus, *Enneades*, ed. Fr. Creuzer et G. H. Moser, Paris, 1855; R. Volkmann, Leipzig, 1883–1884

Porphyry, *Isagoge et in Aristotelis Cagorias Commentarium*, ed. A. Busse, Berlin, 1887

Porphyry, *Sententiae ad Intelligibilia Ducentes* in *Plotini Enneades*, ed. Fr. Creuzer et G. H. Moser, Paris, 1855

Proclus, *Institutio Theologica* in *Plotini Enneades*, ed. Fr. Creuzer et G. H. Moser, Paris, 1855

Profiat Duran, *Ma'aseh Efod*, ed. J. Friedländer et J. Kohn, Vienna, 1865

Ramus, Petrus, *Dialecticae libri duo. . . . Cum Commentariis Georgii Dounami Annexis*, London, 1669

Rashi, Commentary on the Bible, in any edition of Rabbinic Bibles

Saadia, *Emunot we-De'ot*, Hebrew, Yosefov, 1885. Arabic: *Kitâb al-Amânât wa'l-I'tiqâdât*, ed. S. Landauer, Leyden, 1880

Samuel bar Kalonymus (?), *Shir ha-Yihud*, in *Mahzor: Service of the Synagogue. A New Edition of the Festival Prayers with an English Translation in Prose and Verse. New Year*. London, 1908. pp. 40–60

Seneca, *Opera quae super sunt*, ed. Hermes, Hosius, Hense, *et al.*, Leipzig, 1898–1907. English translation: *The Works of Lucius Annaeus Seneca* by Thomas Lodge, 1620

Shabbethai Sheftel Horvitz, *Shefa' Tal*, Hanau, 1612

Shahrastani, *Kitab al-Milal wal-Nihal*, ed. W. Cureton (English title: *Book of Religious and Philosophical Sects*), London, 1846

Shem-Tob ben Joseph Falaquera, *Sefer ha-Nefesh*, Warsaw, 1881

Shem-Tob ben Joseph Ibn Shem-Tob, Commentary on Maimonides' *Moreh Nebukim*. See Maimonides

Silva, Samuel da, *Tratado da Immortalidade da Alma* in *Die Schriften des Uriel da Costa* by Carl Gebhardt, Heidelberg, 1922

Stobaeus, Joannes, *Joannis Stobei Anthologium* recensurunt Curtius Wachsmuth et Otto Hense, Berlin, 1884–1912. Latin: *Joannis Stobaei Eclogarum Libri duo . . . interprete* Gulielmo Cantero, Antverpiae, 1575

Suarez, *Disputationes Metaphysicae*, Genevae, 1614

Talmud, Mishnah, Midrash: *The Mishnat ha Middot*, the first Hebrew Geometry of about 150 C. E. . . . a new edition . . . with introduction, translation and notes, by Solomon Gandz. Berlin, 1932

Telesius, B., *De Rerum Natura*, ed. V. Spampanato, Modena, 1910–1923

Thomas Aquinas, *Opera Omnia*, Parmae, 1852–1873. *Summa Theologica* . . . Literally translated by Fathers of the English Dominican Province. London, 1911–1922

Zanchius, H., *De Operibus Dei intra Spacium Sex Dierum Opus*, Neustadii in Palatinatu, 1602

INDEXES

INDEX OF REFERENCES

* The section numbers are from ed. C. H. Bruder, Lipsiae, 1843–1846.

DIOGENES LAERTIUS

*De Vitis, Dogmatibus et Apophthegmatibus
    Clarorum Philosophorum*

ḤAYYIM VITAL

Shaʿare Kedushshah

HEEREBOORD, ADRIANUS

Hermeneia Logica

Meletemata Philosophica, Disputationes ex Philosophia Selectae

HERRERA, ABRAHAM

Porta Cælorum

Puerta del Cielo

Shaʿar ha-Shamayim

HILARY

De Trinitate

HILLEL OF VERONA

Commentary on Maimonides' Twenty-five Propositions

Miscellany

HOBBES

Elementa Philosophiae

Leviathan

MANASSEH BEN ISRAEL

Nishmat Ḥayyim

MARCUS AURELIUS

Meditations

MEIR IBN GABBAI

'Abodat ha-Kodesh (or *Mar'ot Elohim*)

MORTEIRA, SAUL

Gib'at Sha'ul

MOSCATO, JUDAH ARYEH

Ḳol Yehudah on *Cuzari*

MOSES CORDOVERO

Elimah Rabbati

Pardes Rimmonim

MOSES HA-LAVI

MOSES NARBONI

Commentary on Moreh Nebukim

ZANCHIUS, HIERONYMUS

De Operibus Dei intra Spacium Sex Dierum Opus

INDEX OF TERMS

A. LATIN

(Including some Dutch, French, Italian, and Portuguese terms, which are printed in italics and designated by initials)

B. GREEK

C. HEBREW

D. ARABIC

INDEX OF SUBJECTS AND NAMES

classification of causes, i, 307, 308, 390; ii, 188; creation in time, i, 414; good, i, 417; final causes, i, 105, 431, 433, good and evil, i, 436. *See also* Index of References

Hegel, i, 298

Heinemann, I., ii, 300

Helias Hebraeus Cretensis, i, 11–12

Hell-fire, ii, 317

Helmont, J. B. van, ii, 57

Herrera, Abraham — influence on Spinoza, i, 17; argument against finite emanations, i, 102; *parzupim*, i, 245; why not more *sefirot*, i, 314–315; eternity, i, 366, 367; impossibility of infinite effects, i, 377; *zimzum*, i, 394–395; God's freedom of will, i, 408. *See also* Index of References

Hicks, R. D., ii, 91, 146

Hilary — truth, ii, 99

Hillel of Verona — whether substance has a definition, i, 160. *See also* Index of References

Hobbes — time, i, 356; names as signs of conceptions, ii, 137; self-preservation, ii, 197; conatus, ii, 200; pleasure, ii, 206; love and hatred, ii, 212; rational interpretation of the Bible, ii, 222; society, ii, 245; organic conception of the state, ii, 246; contract theory of the state, ii, 247. *See also* Index of References

Höffding, H., i, 330

Honor, ii, 244

Horovitz, S., i, 190; ii, 82

Horten, M., i, 186

Hugo of St. Victor — threefold classification of knowledge, ii, 133

Husik, I., ii, 222, 359

Ibn Ezra, Abraham — psychology under metaphysics, i, 37; immortality, ii, 290, 302; the common sense, ii, 314. *See also* Index of References

Ibn Gabirol, Solomon — his *Tikkun Middot ha-Nefesh* and the title of *Trac-*

tatus de Intellectus Emendatione, i, 35; dialogical and poetical forms in philosophy, i, 39; materiality of the Intelligences, i, 94, 223; no materiality of God, i, 222–223; microcosm and macrocosm, ii, 7; the immediacy of the knowledge of the mind, ii, 149, 156; immortality, ii, 300. *See also* Index of References

Ibn Tibbon, Judah, i, 341. *See also* Anatolio

Ibn Tibbon, Samuel, i, 341

Ibn Yahya, Joseph — the meaning of "glory," ii, 315. *See also* Index of References

Idea — association of ideas, ii, 98–99, 213–215; definition and use of the term, ii, 18, 46–47; distinguished from images and words, ii, 174; fictitious, false, and doubtful, ii, 113; idea of God, i, 238–241, 248, 378, 380; ii, 20–21, 340, 352; idea of an idea, ii, 90–91, 93–95; inadequate ideas, ii, 106–109; infinite idea, i, 241; innate ideas, i, 164, 369; ii, 71, 155–156; mind idea of body, ii, 42–48; not positively false, ii, 110–112; simple ideas, ii, 112 113; true and adequate ideas, ii, 105, 109–113, 117 ff.

Ihwan al-Safa — psychology under metaphysics, i, 37; ethics under theology, i, 38; time and duration, i, 335–336, 341, 353; microcosm and macrocosm, ii, 7. *See also* Index of References

Imagination — general discussion of the subject, ii, 80–90; retentive and compositive, ii, 82; relation to memory, ii, 84–87; contrasted with reason and intellect, ii, 160; together with desire produces concupiscence, ii, 165; used by Hobbes and Spinoza also in the sense of thought and reason, i, 356, 438

Imitation of emotions, ii, 215–217

Immanent. *See* Cause

Immediate infinite modes. *See* Mode

Immortality — general discussion of the subject, ii, 289–325; evaluation of